LEGAL WRITING AND OTHER LAWYERING SKILLS

Third Edition

Nancy L. Schultz
Associate Professor, Chapman University School of Law
Louis J. Sirico, Jr.
Professor, Villanova Law School

1998

D0063759

MATTHEW BENDER

QUESTIONS ABOUT THIS PUBLICATION?

For questions about the **Editorial Content** or reprint permission,please call:

Lori Wood, J.D., at .... 1-800-252-9257 (ext. 2636)
Cheryl Goodwine-Pittman, J.D., at .... 1-800-252-9257 (ext. 2019)

For assistance with shipments, billing or other customer service matters, please call:
Customer Services Department at .... (800) 533-1646
Outside the United States and Canada, please call   .... (518) 487-3000
Fax number .... (518) 487-3584

Library of Congress Cataloging-in-Publication Data

Legal Writing and Other Lawyering Skills/Nancy L. Schultz
    [Louis J. Sirico.] — 3rd ed.
      534 p.   cm.—
    Rev. ed. of: Introduction to Legal Writing and Oral Advocacy/Nancy L. Schultz
    [et. al.] . 2nd ed. c 1993
    ISBN 0-8205-3120-0 (softcover)
    1. Legal composition.   2. Oral pleading—United States.
I. Sirico, Louis J.   II. Introduction to legal writing and oral advocacy.   III. Title.
    KF250.S38   1998
    808'.06634—dc21   CIP-98-10240
                                              93-3196

MATTHEW◆BENDER

MATTHEW BENDER & CO., INC.
Editorial Offices
2 Park Avenue, New York, NY 10016-5675 (212) 448-2000
201 Mission St., San Francisco, CA 94105-1831 (415) 908-3200

Acknowledgements

We have used the materials in this book to teach legal writing and analysis to students at Villanova Law School, George Washington University National Law Center, and Chapman University School of Law. We wish to thank them for all they have taught us about teaching the subject. Most of the sample documents in this book are the products of our students. The names of the authors of documents reproduced in the appendices appear with their documents. Nancy Schultz also thanks Barbara Babcock for secretarial assistance, Al Fuller for his thoughtful contributions to the writing on client counseling and negotiations, Katie Harrington-McBride for providing sample documents, and Thomas Robichaux for his nearly boundless energy and enthusiasm throughout the process of putting this book together.

TABLE OF CONTENTS

Part I: INTRODUCTION

Chapter 1

Overview

Chapter 2

Learning About the Legal System

Chapter 3

How to Brief a Case

Chapter 4

Introduction to Legal Logic

Chapter   5

Legal Analysis

Chapter   6

Research Strategy

Part II: STYLE AND SUBSTANCE: WRITING THE LEGAL ANALYSIS

Chapter 7

Purpose, Context, and Structure

Chapter 8

Make Your Themes Stand Out

Chapter 9

Help the Reader To Understand You

Part III: PRE-LITIGATION LAWYERING

Chapter 10

Meeting the Client

Chapter 11

Writing the Client Opinion Letter

Chapter 12

Introduction to the Memo

Chapter 13

The Memo: Heading, Issue, and Conclusion

Chapter 14

The Memo: Facts and Discussion

Chapter 15

Advising the Client

Chapter   16

Negotiating

Chapter   17

Drafting Settlement Agreements

(Matthew Bender & Co., Inc.)

Part IV: PRE-TRIAL LITIGATION

Chapter 18

Drafting Pleadings

Chapter 19

Discovery

Chapter 20

Writing Persuasively

Chapter 21

Writing Pre-Trial Motions

Part V: TRIAL AND APPEAL

Chapter 22

Drafting Jury Instructions

Chapter 23

Introduction to Writing Briefs

Chapter 24

Appellate Process and Standard of Review

Chapter 25

The Appellate Brief:
The Introductory Parts

Chapter 26

The Appellate Brief:
Statement of Facts; Summary of Argument

Chapter 27

The Appellate Brief:
Argument and Conclusion

PART VI: THE ORAL ARGUMENT

Chapter 28

Basic Principles of Oral Communication

Chapter 29

The Appellate Argument

APPENDICES

INDEX

PART I

INTRODUCTION

CHAPTER 1

OVERVIEW

§ 1.01 Introduction

To be a successful lawyer, you must write and speak effectively. In your profession, you will spend much of your time crafting legal documents and speaking with clients, courts, and other lawyers. In this book, we help you learn some of the skills you will need to be a lawyer. You will learn how to draft memoranda, opinion letters, pleadings, briefs, and other legal documents. You also will learn about client counseling, negotiations, and how to make oral arguments in court. You will master an approach that emphasizes precision, good organization, and plain English. By learning to communicate clearly, you will increase your effectiveness as a lawyer.

Our educational philosophy is to teach you how to write and argue in a traditionally accepted style. As you gain experience, you will develop a style that reflects your personality and particular strengths. At this stage, however, you should learn the standard method as a foundation for later growth.

This chapter gives you an overview of the book. It briefly discusses the legal system and legal analysis and then describes the major types of legal writing. It also explains our approach to writing style, discusses citation form, and introduces the lawyering skills you need to learn.

§ 1.02 The Legal System and Legal Analysis

Before you can make legal arguments or draft legal documents, you need to learn about the American legal system and about accepted methods of legal analysis. You need to learn more than television and the movies have taught you. You also need to unlearn some of what they have taught you.

Television and the movies offer a simplified view of the law. Though they frequently portray trials, they rarely show lawyers engaging in legal research and drafting documents. The media spend little time on pretrial proceedings and on courts that hear appeals from trial decisions. The media almost never tell us that this country has many court systems: every state has its own courts, and the federal government has not only the United States Supreme Court, but also trial courts, appeals courts, and various specialized courts.

The media also fail to offer even a glimpse of how lawyers construct legal arguments. Though television and the movies frequently present arguments based on common sense, they do not show how these arguments must be stylized to become legal arguments that lawyers will find persuasive. Legal analysis is not particularly difficult or different than other methods of reasoning. Nonetheless, you must expend considerable effort to become good at it. In this book, we teach you about the legal system and legal reasoning. Over the next several years, these subjects will occupy much of your time. Our introduction will aid you in your other courses.

§ 1.03 Types of Legal Writing

[1] The Case Brief

A case brief is a summary of a court opinion. As a student, you undoubtedly are writing case briefs in most of your courses. Writing the brief helps you prepare for class. During class, the brief serves as an accessible set of notes on the case. Chapter 3 offers help in reading and briefing cases.

The word "brief" has another meaning. It also refers to the written argument that a lawyer presents to a court deciding a case. See Section 1.03[9].

[2] The Memorandum

By "memorandum" or "memo" we mean the interoffice memorandum. It discusses the law concerning a client's legal problem and predicts how a court or other body would decide the issue presented. The memo, then, is essential in determining how to proceed. The writer of the memo first must research the law thoroughly and then explain how it supports his or her conclusion.

The word "memorandum" sometimes is used to describe the written argument that a lawyer presents to a court or administrative agency. The lawyer may write this type of memo to support or oppose a pretrial motion, to summarize the argument in a trial or administrative hearing, or to support the client's argument before an appellate court. In the latter case, most courts would call the document a brief. In all cases, the document is similar to a brief. See Section 1.03[9].

[3] The Client Opinion Letter

The client opinion letter advises the client how the law applies to a particular problem and suggests a course of action. The lawyer should explain any legal concepts in lay language.

[4] The Settlement Agreement

Settlement agreements are documents that reflect the terms upon which parties have agreed to settle a dispute. They are contracts between the parties and will frequently not be presented to a court, although if a matter is already in litigation when it is settled, there are times when the agreement will become part of the court file. Sometimes courts will approve or disapprove settlements. Settlement agreements should be drafted precisely and should anticipate contingencies.

[5] Pleadings

Pleadings are the written papers that a lawyer serves on the opposing side and files with the court to begin litigation. In a noncriminal case, for example, the plaintiff's lawyer files a complaint asserting that the client has suffered a legal wrong and that the defendant is liable. The defendant's lawyer files an answer and may file a counterclaim asserting claims against the plaintiff. Other pleadings may also be filed.

Complaints are the first opportunity the lawyer has to state the case in writing. They must be drafted clearly and precisely, and establish sufficient facts to support the alleged cause of action or the court may refuse to hear the case and dismiss the complaint.

[6] Motions

Before trial, a lawyer may file a motion asking the court to deal with a particular issue. For example, the defendant's lawyer might move to dismiss the plaintiff's claim and argue that even if all the plaintiff's assertions are true, the defendant still would not be liable. Motions are persuasive documents and should follow the principles of advocacy writing. There are very few formal rules that govern the format of motions, so you will need to learn the procedures that are followed in your jurisdiction and in the law office where you work.

[7] Discovery

Discovery includes written and oral requests for information from parties and potential witnesses about a matter. These requests are made before the case goes to court. The primary forms of written discovery are interrogatories, requests for production of documents, and requests for admissions. Oral discovery takes place at depositions, where the lawyers pose and potential witnesses answer questions about the facts of the case in front of a court reporter. We will not discuss depositions in this book. Written discovery must be drafted precisely and must anticipate interpretations that would allow a party to avoid directly answering the question posed.

[8] Jury Instructions

Jury instructions are drafted by the lawyers and submitted to the judge for approval when a case is ready to go to trial. The final jury instructions will be read to the jury, and must outline the applicable law in a clear, logical, easily comprehensible fashion.

[9] The Brief

By "brief," we mean the appellate brief. It is the written document that the lawyer submits to the court when the client's case is on appeal. It includes a factual explanation of the case and an argument based on detailed legal analysis of relevant cases and other authorities as well as fairness and social policy concerns. Some courts call the brief a memorandum. See Section 1.03[2]. "Brief" also refers to the written argument that the attorney presents at the pretrial or trial level.

Different courts have different rules for the format of the brief. In this book, you will learn a standard form that you can easily adjust to meet the requirements of a particular court.

§ 1.04 Writing Style

This book is about writing and speaking like a lawyer. A lawyer should write and speak clearly, concisely, and forcefully. So should other professionals. Our profession faces a particular problem, because it has inherited a tradition of poor writing. Many of the court opinions in your casebooks offer sad examples of this tradition. If the judges had written the opinions clearly, you would understand the decisions better and spend less time reading and briefing them.

Lawyers frequently justify lapses in comprehensibility by emphasizing the need to convey highly technical information and complex ideas. We reject such excuses. As a lawyer, you can write and speak clearly. Lawyers and scholars concerned with this matter agree. Current books and articles make clear that short sentences and plain English are the trend. Rambling sentences and legalese are out. You may recognize this philosophy if you have read *The Elements of Style* by Strunk and White,[1] and *On Writing Well* by William Zinsser.[2]

Some first-year students are shocked when they receive their writing assignments back from the writing instructor. They find their papers covered with red-penned criticisms. Often the real shock comes to students who always believed they were excellent writers. In undergraduate school, they received praise and good grades and gained confidence in their ability. For them, legal writing seems to be a totally new form of writing.

Throughout this book, we use the written work of our students to provide good and bad examples of legal writing. The bad examples were written by intelligent, capable students. Most of the students came to law school confident about their writing abilities. They discovered they had more lessons to learn if they were to be good legal writers. They mastered those lessons and improved their legal writing style.

Your pre-law writing experience may not be a valid predictor of your initial performance in legal writing. Legal writing can be equally difficult for students of all backgrounds.

---

[1] William Strunk & E.B. White, The Elements of Style (3d ed. Macmillan 1979).

[2] William Zinsser, On Writing Well (3d ed. Harper & Row 1985). A number of books urge lawyers to write in plain English. They include Irwin Alterman, Plain and Accurate Style in Court Papers (ALI-ABA 1987); Gertrude Block, Effective Legal Writing (4th ed. Foundation Press 1992); Ronald Goldfarb & James Raymond, Clear Understandings: A Guide to Legal Writing (Random House 1982); David Mellinkoff, Legal Writing: Sense and Nonsense (West 1982); Louis J. Sirico, Jr. and Nancy L. Schultz, Persuasive Writing for Lawyers and the Legal Profession (Matthew Bender 1995); Henry Weihofen, Legal Writing Style (2d ed. West 1980); Richard Wydick, Plain English for Lawyers (3d ed. Carolina Academic Press 1994).

You may have been an English major who wrote brilliant essays or poetry for years. You may experience strong feelings of hurt and discouragement if you receive a paper that the writing instructor has torn apart. The instructor then gently tries to lessen the pain by explaining that you now are learning a new and very different method of writing. It is best for you to accept this fact now, before you hand in your first assignment.

On the other hand, you may have been an Accounting or Science major in undergraduate school with little writing experience and with many fears about legal writing. You may be delighted to discover that you can write very well in the legal setting.

We do not claim that the writing style we teach is superior to all other writing styles. Many great works of literature conform to other styles. Much good journalism lacks the precision that we demand. We make only one claim: The writing style that we teach is the best style for legal writing.

Many lawyers cling to the old ways. Some of your future employers may be among them, and you may have to compromise if you cannot persuade them to give you a free hand. But the tide is turning. Your efforts at communicating clearly will pay off. Judges, clients, and other lawyers will be more likely to understand you. They will also find you more persuasive. Lawyers who refuse to abandon verbosity and jargon may find themselves viewed as dinosaurs in a modern world.

§ 1.05 Citation Form

As a lawyer, you will rely heavily on constitutions, statutes, prior cases, and other authorities. To cite authority means to refer to specific statutes, cases, and the like when you prepare an analysis of a legal point or make a legal argument. You may cite authority to provide important information, to support your argument, or to acknowledge adverse authority that you must distinguish or contest.

When you cite authority in a written document, you must include enough information so that the reader can make an initial decision about the authority's importance. For example, the reader may find it important to know how old a case is, whether the court is a local one, and whether the court is prestigious. You also must include enough information to enable the reader to find the authority in the library. For a case, a successful library search requires knowing the case's name, the set of books in which it appears, the volume, and the page number.

A standard set of rules dictates the information you must include in a citation and the format you must use. The rules appear in *The Bluebook: A Uniform System of Citation* (16th ed. 1996), published by a group of law reviews spearheaded by the *Harvard Law Review*. The manual, commonly known as "the Bluebook," is highly technical and difficult for the novice to use. To assist you, we have included an appendix that gives you step-by-step instruction in citation form for virtually all authorities that you might use at this stage in your legal career.

Critics have attacked the Bluebook as arbitrary in its rules, unnecessarily elaborate, and too time consuming to use.[3] The *University of Chicago Law Review* has challenged its dominance by proposing a far simpler system of citation, *The University of Chicago Manual of Legal Citation*.[4] We agree with the Chicago critics wholeheartedly and hope they prevail. There are other efforts currently underway to revise the way legal authority is cited. Some of these efforts are a reflection of the fact that much legal authority is now available on the Internet, and so the traditional citations to legal publishers are not always necessary. In the meantime, we feel obliged to teach you the Bluebook rules. Most courts, law reviews, and legal publishers still conform to the Bluebook. For many highly-placed aficionados of the Bluebook, deviations from its rules mark the writer as an inept lawyer. To preserve your credibility, you should adhere to the Bluebook until you gain enough prestige to challenge it.

§ 1.06 Communications Skills

[1] Client Interviewing and Counseling

Lawyers have occasion to generate written documents only if they have clients to represent. You must be able to convince a potential client that you are the right person to handle the important and delicate matter that he or she proposes to hand over to your keeping. You will be able to do this if you plan your interviews to maximize the likelihood that you will get all necessary information and be able to accurately assess the client's problem and develop appropriate options for resolving it. You will have satisfied clients and lots of work if you can help clients to resolve their legal dilemmas in ways that meet their needs and take their goals and priorities into account. To be able to do this consistently requires skill and practice. We will introduce you to some of the fundamental skills and concepts that underlie this vital work.

[2] Negotiation

The vast majority of legal problems are resolved outside of court. Negotiation is a critical lawyering skill. In this book, we introduce you to some issues of fundamental importance to effective negotiation--preparation, information exchange, keeping track of concessions, and the tone and style of the negotiation. We discuss both adversarial and problem-solving "win/win" strategies for negotiating. You will discover that negotiating is a very human process, with few rules and lots of psychology.

[3] Oral Argument

Lawyers make oral arguments before legislatures and administrative bodies and in courts. In this book, you will learn specifically how to make an oral argument

---

[3] See Richard Posner, *Goodbye to the Bluebook*, 53 U. Chi. L. Rev. 1343 (1986); Louis J. Sirico, Jr., *Fiddling with Footnotes*, 60 U. Cin. L. Rev. 1273 (1992) (book review).

[4] University of Chicago Law Review & University of Chicago Legal Forum ed. (1989).

when a court is hearing your client's case on appeal. In an appellate court, you submit your written argument in a brief, and you also may get the opportunity to address the court in oral argument.

Appellate argument differs in style from college debate and other apeaking occasions. A formal etiquette governs what you say and how you say it. By using this book, you will learn when to sit, when to stand, how to begin your argument, and the like. You also will learn how to structure your argument, what to emphasize, and how to answer questions. In addition, you will learn how to be persuasive.

Learning effective legal writing and oral advocacy is a demanding and exciting task. We wish you well.

CHAPTER **2**

LEARNING ABOUT THE LEGAL SYSTEM

§ 2.01   The Legal System and Legal Writing

Much of the legal writing you will do in your career will involve analyzing legal problems. To analyze a legal problem, you must understand the sources of our law and their relationships to each other. You must also understand the workings of our legal system. This chapter provides a broad introduction to our court system, the common law, and statutory law and interpretation. Once you understand these aspects of the legal process, you will be able to evaluate a legal problem properly and prepare an accurate and well-reasoned legal analysis.

§ 2.02   Sources of Law and Their Hierarchy

There are three primary categories of law: constitutions, statutes and common law. The Constitution of the United States and the 50 state constitutions set out the structure and powers of government, protect individual liberties, and define the reach of statutory authority. Statutes are passed by legislatures and govern a host of areas ranging from crime to social security benefit levels. The common law is the law judges make when they rule on cases. When a case is decided, it becomes a precedent for future, similar, legal conflicts in the same jurisdiction.

An applicable constitutional provision, statute or common law rule always governs the outcome of a legal problem. The existing case law will assist you in interpreting the statute or constitutional provision in the context of your particular case. When there is no relevant constitutional provision or statute, as there often is not, the existing body of case law, called the common law, is the sole source of authority for evaluating and resolving your case.

§ 2.03   The Court System

Two court systems operate simultaneously in the United States: the state court system and the federal court system. In both the state and federal court systems there are two types of courts: trial courts and appellate courts. The following is an overview of each system.

[1] The State Courts

Each of the 50 states has a court system. Although the structure of that system differs from state to state, it is always hierarchical. There are trial courts, often an intermediate appellate court, and a court of last resort--the tribunal at the top tier of the court system. In addition, there also may be numerous other courts that perform specialized roles, such as small claims courts, juvenile courts and housing courts.

A trial court is presided over by one judge, and may or may not include a jury. The function of a trial court is to determine the facts by evaluating the evidence in a case and to arrive at a decision by applying the law to the facts. Trial courts at the state level may be divided into courts of limited jurisdiction and courts of general jurisdiction. Pursuant to the provisions of the state constitution and state laws, courts of limited jurisdiction rule on certain specific matters such as violations of criminal law. Courts of general jurisdiction are empowered to hear a broader range of civil and criminal matters and often also review appeals from courts of limited jurisdiction.

From the decision of a trial court, the losing party may appeal to the next level, the appellate court. The appeal is heard by a panel of three to five judges, of whom a majority must agree on a particular result. That result forms the basis of the court's opinion deciding the case. The appellate court evaluates the lower court's decision and determines whether it committed any legal error that would warrant reversing or modifying the decision or ordering a new trial. The decision of the appellate court may be appealed to the state's highest court, which has discretion to choose most cases it will hear. The decisions of the courts of last resort are final, and there is no further appeal of state law issues.

This diagram of the California courts illustrates a typical state court system.

CALIFORNIA COURT STRUCTURE*

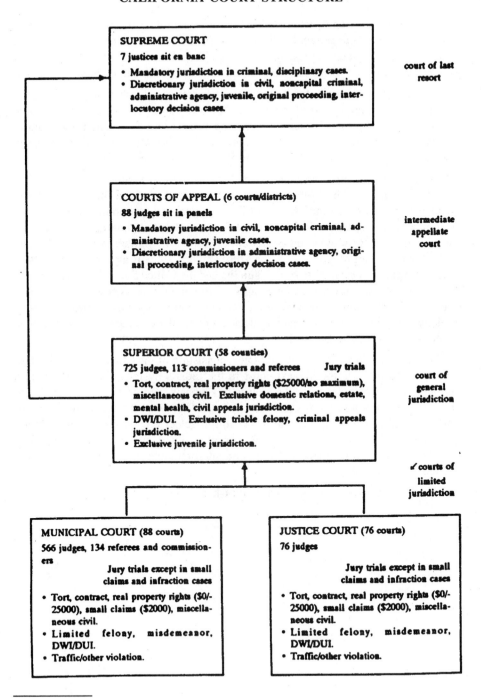

SUPREME COURT

7 justices sit en banc
- Mandatory jurisdiction in criminal, disciplinary cases.
- Discretionary jurisdiction in civil, noncapital criminal, administrative agency, juvenile, original proceeding, interlocutory decision cases.

court of last resort

COURTS OF APPEAL (6 courts/districts)

88 judges sit in panels
- Mandatory jurisdiction in civil, noncapital criminal, administrative agency, juvenile cases.
- Discretionary jurisdiction in administrative agency, original proceeding, interlocutory decision cases.

intermediate appellate court

SUPERIOR COURT (58 counties)

725 judges, 113 commissioners and referees   Jury trials
- Tort, contract, real property rights ($25000/no maximum), miscellaneous civil. Exclusive domestic relations, estate, mental health, civil appeals jurisdiction.
- DWI/DUI. Exclusive triable felony, criminal appeals jurisdiction.
- Exclusive juvenile jurisdiction.

court of general jurisdiction

courts of limited jurisdiction

MUNICIPAL COURT (88 courts)

566 judges, 134 referees and commissioners

Jury trials except in small claims and infraction cases
- Tort, contract, real property rights ($0/-25000), small claims ($2000), miscellaneous civil.
- Limited felony, misdemeanor, DWI/DUI.
- Traffic/other violation.

JUSTICE COURT (76 courts)

76 judges

Jury trials except in small claims and infraction cases
- Tort, contract, real property rights ($0/-25000), small claims ($2000), miscellaneous civil.
- Limited felony, misdemeanor, DWI/DUI.
- Traffic/other violation.

---

* This diagram is adapted from that contained in *State Court Caseload Statistics: Annual Report 1988,* published by the National Center for State Courts.

[2] The Federal Courts

The Constitution and certain federal statutes establish the federal courts and empower them to hear certain kinds of cases. Federal courts hear all cases that arise under federal law, such as those involving the United States Constitution or federal statutes, disputes between two states, or cases in which the United States is a party.

Like the state systems, the federal court system is divided into trial courts, appellate courts and a court of last resort. The trial courts are called district courts. Each state has at least one district court, and that court's jurisdiction is limited to the territory of its district. In a district court case, a judge sits with or without a jury, depending on the nature of the case and the wishes of the parties.

The intermediate appellate courts in the federal system are called the United States Courts of Appeals. The Courts of Appeals hear appeals from the district courts located in the same circuit. A circuit is a designated geographical area usually encompassing several states. The United States is divided geographically into 13 circuits. Eleven of these circuit courts are identified by number, for example, The United States Court of Appeals for the Third Circuit. There is also the United States Court of Appeals for the District of Columbia and the United States Court of Appeals for the Federal Circuit, which hears appeals in patent cases, certain international trade cases and some cases involving damage claims against the United States. Usually, three judges sit on a panel to decide a particular case, and at least two must agree for a decision to be reached.

The Supreme Court of the United States, consisting of the Chief Justice and eight Associate Justices, is the highest court in the federal system. The Court hears a limited number of cases from the Courts of Appeals, and on certain issues, from the district courts and the highest state courts. The Court must accept review of certain types of cases but has the discretion to select others. Cases heard by the Supreme Court generally involve new or unresolved questions of federal law affecting people throughout the country and interpretations of federal statutes or the United States Constitution.

This diagram illustrates the federal court hierarchy:

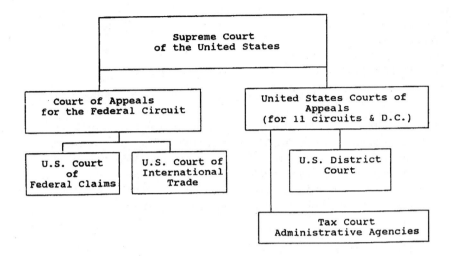

§ 2.04   The Common Law

The phrase common law refers to legal principles created and developed by the courts independent of legislative enactments. It is the body of law which judges create when they decide cases. The doctrine of *stare decisis* mandates that a court follow these common law precedents. Under our system of precedent, however, courts must follow only those precedents that are mandatory or have binding authority. Case law that is not binding is often referred to as persuasive authority.

[1]   Mandatory Authority

When you are presented with a legal problem, you research the statutory and case law of the controlling jurisdiction to resolve that problem. If there is an applicable statute, the court is bound to follow that statute as previously interpreted by the courts. If there is no statute, you will look for case law that is binding on the court where the case is pending.

A precedent becomes binding on a court if the case was decided by that court or a higher court in that same jurisdiction, and the material facts of the pending case and the decided case, as well as the legal reasoning applicable to the two cases, are indistinguishable. For example, a state trial court is bound by the decisions of that state's intermediate appellate courts and its highest court. A federal district court is bound by the decisions of the court of appeals of the circuit in which the district court is situated and the decisions of the Supreme Court. District courts are not bound by the decisions of other district courts, or by those of the courts of appeals of other circuits. The courts of appeals are bound by their own decisions and those of the Supreme Court. They are not bound by the decisions of other courts of appeals.

Suppose you are arguing a case in a jurisdiction and your research discloses a case from a higher court in the same jurisdiction with similar material facts and applicable reasoning. The material facts are those relied upon in reaching the decision. The court you are before is bound by the holding of the previous case. The holding is the court's decision on the issue before it. All other discussion of tangential issues is called dicta and is not binding.

[2] Persuasive Authority

Sometimes your research will show that your jurisdiction has neither a statute nor legal precedent to govern your case. You must then rely on persuasive authority to help analyze the issue. As its name indicates, persuasive authority provides guidance, but is not binding. Precedents from other states that have decided your issue are persuasive authority. In the federal system, precedents from other district courts and other courts of appeals are persuasive authority. Other types of persuasive authority are discussed in Chapter 4 and throughout this book. The court before which you are arguing will take such authority into account and may, in fact, be persuaded by it.

[3] The Weight of Authority

When you draft your legal papers for the court, you must decide which cases to include in your discussion to present the most compelling argument. Certain cases will be more persuasive than others. How persuasive a case is, that is, what weight it carries, depends on a number of factors, including:

(a) the level of the court. The decision of a higher court is more authoritative than that of a lower court.

(b) factual similarity. When the cases you cite have facts similar to your case, their value as precedent increases.

(c) the year of the decision. A more recent opinion is more useful than one that is dated.

(d) the judge. Look for an opinion written by the judge presiding over your case or by a judge with a good reputation.

(e) majority decisions. Language from a majority decision carries more weight than that from a concurring or dissenting opinion.

(f) the state in which the court deciding the case sits.

(i) geographic proximity. A case from a state that is relatively close geographically is often more helpful than one from a state that is far away.

(ii) certain states, like New Jersey, are often at the forefront of emerging case law.

§ 2.05 Statutes and Their Interpretation

[1] The Supremacy of the Legislature and the Legislative Process

Under our system of government, the United States Congress and the state legislatures are the supreme lawmakers, subject only to the limitations of the federal and state constitutions. Therefore, statutes provide the binding rules of decision that courts must follow. Statutes prevail over common law if there is a conflict between the two. Here is a brief discussion of how statutes come into being.

A member of Congress introduces a bill in either the House or the Senate.[1] It is then referred to the appropriate committee, which conducts hearings and issues a report. There is discussion of the bill on the floor, and a vote is taken. If it passes, it goes to the other chamber, where it goes through a similar process. If different versions of the bill are passed by the House and Senate, the bill may be sent to a conference committee for resolution of the differences. Finally, it goes to the President for signature or veto.

In finished form, state and federal statutes usually have certain parts: a preamble, which may include a statement of policy or purpose; a definition section, which attempts to define the significant words used in the statute; the substantive provisions; and any procedural provisions. Consider the following Maryland statute:

§ 81. Definition of flag.

The word "flag" as used in this subtitle, shall include any flag, standard, color, ensign or shield made of any substance or represented or produced thereon, and of any size, evidently purporting to be such flag, standard, color, ensign or shield of the United States or of this State.

§ 82. Exhibition or display.

No person shall, in any manner, for exhibition or display;

(a) Place or cause to be placed any word, figure, mark, picture, design, drawing or advertisement of any nature upon any flag, standard, color, ensign or shield of the United States or of this State, or authorized by any law of the United States or of this State; or

(b) Expose to public view any such flag, standard, color, ensign or shield, upon which shall have been printed, painted or otherwise produced, or to which shall have been attached, appended, affixed or annexed any such word, figure, mark, picture, design, drawing or advertisement; or

(c) Expose to public view for sale, manufacture, or otherwise, or to sell, give or have in possession for sale, for gift or for use for any purpose, any substance, being an article of merchandise, or receptacle, or thing for holding or carrying merchandise, upon or to which shall have been produced or attached any such flag, standard, color, ensign or shield, in order to advertise, call attention to, decorate, mark or distinguish such article or substance.

§ 83. Mutilation, defacing, etc.

A person may not intentionally mutilate, deface, destroy, burn, trample upon, or otherwise use a flag:

---

[1] For our purposes, we simply note that the processes in the federal and state systems are similar.

(1) In a manner intended to incite or produce an imminent breach of the peace; and

(2) Under circumstances likely to incite or produce an imminent breach of the peace.

§ 84. Exceptions.

This statute shall not apply to any act permitted by the statutes of the United States (or of this State), or by the United States Army and Navy regulations, nor shall it apply to any printed or written document or production, stationery, ornament, picture, apparel or jewelry whereon shall be depicted said flag, standard, color, ensign, or shield with no design or words thereon and disconnected with any advertisement.

§ 85. Penalty.

Any violation of § 82 shall be a misdemeanor and punishable by a fine of not more than five hundred dollars. Any violation of § 83 shall be punishable by a fine of not more than one thousand dollars, or by imprisonment for not more than one year, or by both fine and imprisonment, in the discretion of the court.

§ 86. Construction.

This subtitle shall be so construed as to effectuate its general purpose to make uniform the laws of the states which enact it.

§ 87. Short title.

This subtitle consisting of §§ 81 to 87 of this article, both inclusive, may be cited as the Uniform Flag Law.

Md. Crimes and Punishments Code Ann. §§ 81-87 (1992)

As you see, while the Maryland statute has no preamble, it does have a definition section and substantive and procedural sections, including penalty and construction provisions.

[2]   The Relationship between Statutory Law and Common Law

After the applicable constitutional provisions, enacted statutes are the highest authority in a jurisdiction. The courts are bound by them. A legislature may enact a statute that overrules or modifies existing common law. It may enact a common law rule into a statute. Courts, however, rule on whether statutes are constitutional.

When deciding a case governed by a statute, the court must decide how to apply and enforce that statute. Courts rely on certain aids in interpreting the meaning of a statute. You will rely on those same aids in urging the court to adopt a particular construction.

Most statutes are deliberately drafted in broad language because they are written to establish a principle rather than to solve a specific problem. The general language serves as the basis for common law development of the statute by the courts. It is the court's application of a statute to particular cases that gives meaning to the statute's language and provides guidance for future cases.

To interpret broad and ambiguous statutory language, courts look to the following for guidance:

1. The actual language of the statute, the words chosen by the legislature.

2. The context within the statute. What is the subject or purpose of other headings or sections in the same statute? What language do complimentary statutes contain? Is there a statutory statement of legislative purpose? Legislatures sometimes attempt to avoid ambiguity problems by including statements of legislative purpose as a preamble to the statute itself.

3. The legislative history of the statute. A statute's legislative history provides information to the court about the legislature's intent in adopting the statute. It consists of the "official comments," the floor debate, the committee reports, and the committee hearings. Unfortunately, on a state level, the legislative history is often nearly non-existent and on every level it may be very difficult to obtain.

4. Administrative interpretations by the agency charged with administering the statute. They occasionally provide a more specific indication of the statute's meaning.

5. The interpretation of other courts. Consider how courts at a higher level, the same level or even a lower level have applied the statute.

6. The broader context of the statute. What kinds of events were taking place that caused the legislation to be created? What goals were to be furthered by enacting the statute? If a statute overrules common law or tries to fill in a gap in the common law, understanding the problems that led to the enactment can help define the scope of the statute.

7. The common law. When a statute codifies existing common law, the body of cases that developed the common law rule provides highly useful guidance.

8. A comparison with similar statutes of other jurisdictions.

9. Scholarly interpretations, if available.

Courts sometimes also look to canons of statutory construction. These are maxims intended to provide guidance. However, courts are free to disregard them. Here are the most commonly used canons:

1. The "plain meaning rule." In construing a statute, the court shall not deviate from its literal meaning except as required by internal context or the need to avoid absurd results.

2. The rule of "negative implication." When the legislature has covered a certain subject in a statute, it must have intended to exclude everything not mentioned.

3. The principle of construing penal statutes narrowly.

(Matthew Bender & Co., Inc.)   (Pub. 676)

4. The principle of construing statutes in derogation of the common law narrowly.

Although some canons of interpretation have themselves been adopted by statute,[2] as a rule they reflect common sense and do not provide technical help in construing a statute. As between the available aids in interpretation, courts will more likely be persuaded by intrinsic factors such as the statute's language and "plain meaning," than by extrinsic factors such as legislative history.

[3] The Roles of the Court and the Legislature--An Illustration

The question of whether flag burning is permissible has been addressed by the legislature and courts in turn. It provides an excellent illustration of the interaction between the two in the context of statutory interpretation.

The Texas Penal Code stated:

Desecration of Venerated Object.

(a) A person commits an offense if he intentionally or knowingly desecrates:

(1) a public monument;

(2) a place of worship or burial;

(3) a state or national flag.

(b) For purposes of this section, "desecrate" means deface, damage or otherwise physically mistreat in a way that the actor knows will seriously offend one or more persons likely to observe or discover his action.

Tex. Penal Code Ann. § 42.09 (West 1989).

While the Republican National Convention was taking place in Dallas in 1984, Gregory Lee Johnson participated in a political demonstration that included the

---

[2] A Pennsylvania statute states:

RULES OF STRICT AND LIBERAL CONSTRUCTION

The rule that laws in derogation of the common law are to be strictly construed, shall have no application to the laws of this Commonwealth hereafter enacted.

All provisions of a law of the classes hereafter enumerated shall be strictly construed:

(1) Penal provisions;

(2) Retroactive provisions;

(3) Provisions imposing taxes;

(4) Provisions conferring the power of eminent domain;

(5) Provisions exempting persons and property from taxation;

(6) Provisions exempting property from the power of eminent domain;

(7) Provisions decreasing the jurisdiction of a court of record;

(8) Provisions enacted prior to the effective date of this law which are in derogation of the common law.

All other provisions of a law shall be liberally construed to effect their objects and to promote justice.

1 Pa. Cons. Stat. § 1928 (1975).

(Matthew Bender & Co., Inc.)

public burning of an American flag. He was convicted of desecrating a flag in violation of Texas law. This conviction was affirmed by a Texas district Court of Appeals, but was subsequently reversed by the Texas Court of Criminal Appeals. The United States Supreme Court granted certiorari.

Texas claimed its interest in preventing breaches of the peace justified Johnson's conviction under the statute. In fact, however, there was no breach of the peace. The Supreme Court heard the case on appeal and observed that Texas was essentially making the argument that an "audience that takes serious offense at a particular expression is necessarily likely to disturb the peace and that the expression may be prohibited on this basis." *Texas v. Johnson*, 491 U.S. 397 (1989). The Court also found that the asserted state interest in "preserving the flag as a symbol of nationhood and national unity" could not survive the scrutiny imposed on state actions that attempt to regulate speech content protected by the First Amendment.

The federal flag burning statute in effect at the time of the *Texas v. Johnson* ruling stated:

Desecration of the flag of the United States; penalties

(a) Whoever knowingly casts contempt upon any flag of the United States by publicly mutilating, defacing, defiling, burning, or trampling upon it shall be fined not more than $1,000 or imprisoned for not more than one year, or both.

(b) The term "flag of the United States" as used in this section, shall include any flag, standard, colors, ensign, or any picture or representation of either, or of any part or parts of either, and of any substance or represented on any substance, of any size evidently purporting to be either of said flag, standard, colors, or ensign of the United States of America, or a picture or a representation of either, upon which shall be shown the colors, the stars and the stripes, in any number of either thereof, or of any part or parts of either, by which the average person seeing the same without deliberation may believe the same to represent the flag, standards, colors, or ensign of the United States of America.

(c) Nothing in this section shall be construed as indicating an intent on the part of Congress to deprive any State, territory, possession, or the Commonwealth of Puerto Rico of jurisdiction over any offense over which it would have jurisdiction in the absence of this section.

18 U.S.C. § 700 (1989).

Congress responded to the *Texas v. Johnson* case by removing the "casts contempt" language from subsection (a) of the statute, reasoning that now the flag burning prohibition was not content-based. The revised statute read, in relevant part:

An Act

To amend section 700 of title 18, United States Code, to protect the physical integrity of the flag.

Be it enacted by the Senate and House of Representatives of the United States of America in Congress assembled,

This Act may be cited as the "Flag Protection Act of 1989".

SEC. 2. CRIMINAL PENALTIES WITH RESPECT TO THE PHYSICAL INTEG-
RITY OF THE UNITED STATES FLAG.

(a) In General -- Subsection (a) of section 700 of title 18, United States Code, is amended to read as follows:

(a)(1) Whoever knowingly mutilates, defaces, physically defiles, burns, maintains on the floor or ground, or tramples upon any flag of the United States shall be fined under this title or imprisoned for not more than one year, or both.

(2) This subsection does not prohibit any conduct consisting of the disposal of a flag when it has become worn or soiled.

(b) Definition. -- Section 700(b) of title 18, United States Code, is amended to read as follows:

(b) As used in this section, the term 'flag of the United States' means any flag of the United States, or any part thereof, made of any substance, of any size, in a form that is commonly displayed.

18 U.S.C. § 700 (Supp. II 1990).

Shortly after the passage of the revised Flag Protection Act, Shawn Eichman and two friends set several United States flags on fire on the steps of the United States Capitol during a political demonstration. Their protest was, in part, intended to demonstrate their objection to the newly enacted statute. In *United States v. Eichman*, 496 U.S. 310 (1990), the Supreme Court found that the revised language failed to make the statute constitutional.

Although the Flag Protection Act contained no explicit content-based limitation on prohibited conduct, it was nevertheless clear that the Government's asserted interest was related to the suppression of free expression, and concerned with the content of such expression. The Government's interest in protecting the physical integrity of a privately owned flag rests upon a perceived need to preserve the flag's status as a symbol of our Nation and certain national ideals. But the mere disfigurement of a particular manifestation of the symbol, without more, does not diminish or otherwise affect the symbol itself in any way. For example, the secret destruction of a flag in one's own basement would not threaten the flag's recognized meaning. Rather, the Government's desire to preserve the flag as a symbol of certain national ideals is implicated only when a person's treatment of the flag communicates a message to others that is inconsistent with those ideals.

Moreover, the precise language of the Act's prohibitions confirmed Congress' interest in the communicative impact of flag destruction. The Act criminalized the conduct of anyone who knowingly mutilated, defaced, physically defiled, burned, maintained on the floor or ground, or trampled upon any flag. Each of the specified terms -- with the possible exception of "burns" -- unmistakably connotes disrespectful treatment of the flag and suggests a focus on those acts likely to damage the flag's symbolic value. And the explicit exemption for disposal of worn or soiled flags protected certain acts traditionally associated with patriotic respect for the flag.

Although Congress cast the Flag Protection Act in somewhat broader terms than the Texas statute at issue in *Johnson*, the Act still suffered from the same fundamental flaw: it suppressed expression out of concern for its likely communicative impact. *United States v. Eichman*, 496 U.S. 310, 312-326 (1990).

It is clear that Congress wanted to enact a law that prohibited flag burning. However, it seems equally clear that regardless of the form of such a statute, it most likely would not survive a constitutional challenge. Re-read the Maryland flag burning statute at the beginning of this section. Is it possible that the Maryland legislature has drafted a statute that would survive constitutional scrutiny? The statutory language suggests that the statute will be enforced only when the circumstances surrounding the flag burning are likely to create a breach of the peace.

As you see, enacted statutes have no meaning or effect until they are interpreted by the courts and applied in context. Statutory analysis is an important function of our court system.

CHAPTER **3**

HOW TO BRIEF A CASE

§ 3.01 What Is a Brief?

[1] Briefing Is Taking Notes

In your first year of law school, your professors will expect you to brief the cases that they assign. The word "brief" has two meanings in law. A brief is a written argument that an attorney submits to a court deciding a case. A brief also is a summary of a court opinion. In your initial law school classes and in this chapter, your concern is with this second type of brief.

Because briefing is new to you and because law school is also new, you may think that briefing is very different from anything you have done before. If you examine the task closely, however, you will discover that it is a very familiar one.

Briefing a case is taking notes on the case. By this time, you are a veteran at taking notes on what you read. You probably started taking notes in high school or college. Briefing a case seems different, because it is a highly structured method of taking notes. It requires you to identify various parts of a case and summarize them.

[2] The Purposes of Briefing

Briefing has two purposes. First, it helps you to focus on the important aspects of the case. A court opinion may ramble on page after page. Your brief, however, will be no longer than one or two pages. Because briefing forces you to get to the heart of the case, it forces you to grapple with the essentials.

Second, briefing helps you prepare for class and serves as a source of reference during class. You cannot brief a case properly unless you understand it. Briefing insures that you understand the case before you discuss it in class. During class, you will find yourself referring to your brief. The discussion in a law school class goes far beyond what the brief contains. Your professor uses a court opinion only as a springboard to a sophisticated treatment of legal doctrine and legal process. Without the sort of understanding of basic aspects of a case that briefing demands, you will not get off the springboard and will fail to gain what the class has to offer.

Your case briefs are your personal notes. Your professors are not going to grade them. They probably never will read them unless you ask for assistance. Few students refer to their briefs when preparing for exams. View your briefs as your private study tools for class preparation.

Because you will not be handing in your briefs to your professors and will not use them at semester's end, you may be tempted not to brief cases. Briefing can be time consuming, and your time is limited. We strongly encourage you to stay with briefing at least for the first few months of law school.

At the initial stage of your legal education, you should brief all assigned cases. As your grasp of the law grows, you will switch to writing short summaries or even writing notes in the margins of your case books. For now, however, brief your cases diligently. Briefing serves an important educational purpose, and briefs will help you understand what is going on in class, not always an easy task.

§ 3.02 How to Brief

[1] The Format

The typical brief includes: the name of the case, its citation, the important facts in the case, the case's procedural status, the issue in the case, the court's holding, and the court's reasoning.

Different professors may ask you to brief cases in different ways. We offer you a typical format for a case brief. If a professor asks for a slightly different format, be sure to oblige him or her. You will find that despite deviations in format, all professors want you to abstract essentially the same information.

[2] Parts of the Brief

[a] An Exercise

Here is an exercise to help you learn about briefing cases. Please read the trial court's opinion in *Conti v. ASPCA*. You may read it again in your Property course. After you read it, go back and take notes on it. You need not follow any particular format. Just take notes as if you were taking notes on a college reading assignment. Following the case is a brief of the case. Please do not read it until after you have completed taking notes.

As you read the opinion, note its format, the typical format for this sort of opinion. It begins with the name of the case, with the plaintiff's name coming first. It then lists citations, which tell you what library books contain the opinion. Next is the name of the judge who wrote the opinion. Finally comes the text of the opinion. It contains the facts of the case, the court's reasoning, and the court's decision.

CONTI v. ASPCA

77 Misc. 2d 61, 353 N.Y.S.2d 288 (Civ. Ct. 1974)

MARTIN RODELL, JUDGE.

Chester is a parrot. He is fourteen inches tall, with a green coat, yellow head and an orange streak on his wings. Red splashes cover his left shoulder. Chester is a show parrot, used by the defendant ASPCA in various educational exhibitions presented to groups of children.

On June 28, 1973, during an exhibition in Kings Point, New York, Chester flew the coop and found refuge in the tallest tree he could find. For several hours the defendant sought to retrieve Chester. Ladders proved to be too short. Offers of food were steadfastly ignored. With the approach of darkness, search efforts were discontinued. A return to the area on the next morning revealed that Chester was gone.

On July 5th, 1973 the plaintiff, who resides in Belle Harbor, Queens County, had occasion to see a green-hued parrot with a yellow head and red splashes seated in his backyard. His offer of food was eagerly accepted by the bird. This was repeated on three occasions each day for a period of two weeks. This display of human kindness was rewarded by the parrot's finally entering the plaintiff's home, where he was placed in a cage.

The next day, the plaintiff phoned the defendant ASPCA and requested advice as to the care of the parrot he had found. Thereupon the defendant sent two representatives to the plaintiff's home. Upon examination, they claimed that it was the missing parrot, Chester, and removed it from the plaintiff's home.

Upon refusal of the defendant ASPCA to return the bird, the plaintiff now brings this action in replevin.

The issues presented to the Court are twofold: One, is the parrot in question truly Chester, the missing bird? Two, if it is in fact Chester, who is entitled to its ownership?

The plaintiff presented witnesses who testified that a parrot similar to the one in question was seen in the neighborhood prior to July 5, 1973. He further contended that a parrot could not fly the distance between Kings Point and Belle Harbor in so short a period of time, and therefore the bird in question was not in fact Chester.

The representatives of the ASPCA were categorical in their testimony that the parrot was indeed Chester, that he was unique because of his size, color and habits. They claimed that Chester said "hello" and could dangle by his legs. During the entire trial the Court had the parrot under close scrutiny, but at no time did it exhibit any of these characteristics. The Court called upon the parrot to indicate by name or other mannerisms an affinity to either of the claimed owners. Alas, the parrot stood mute.

Upon all the credible evidence the Court does find as a fact that the parrot in question is indeed Chester and is the same parrot which escaped from the possession of the ASPCA on June 28, 1973.

The Court must now deal with the plaintiff's position that the ownership of the defendant was a qualified one and upon the parrot's escape, ownership passed to the first individual who captured it and placed it under his control.

The law is well settled that the true owner of lost property is entitled to the return thereof as against any person finding same. (*In re Wright's Estate*, 15 Misc. 2d 225, 177 N.Y.S.2d 410) (36A C.J.S. Finding Lost Goods § 3).

This general rule is not applicable when the property lost is an animal. In such cases the Court must inquire as to whether the animal was domesticated or ferae naturae (wild).

Where an animal is wild, the owner can only acquire a qualified right of property which is wholly lost when it escapes from its captor with no intention of returning.

Thus in *Mullett v. Bradley*, 24 Misc. 695, 53 N.Y.S. 781, an untrained and undomesticated sea lion escaped after being shipped from the West to the East Coast. The sea lion escaped and was again captured in a fish pond off the New Jersey Coast. The original owner sued the finder for its return. The court held that the sea lion was a wild animal (ferae naturae), and when it returned to its wild state, the original owner's property rights were extinguished.

In *Amory v. Flyn*, 10 Johns. (N.Y.) 102, plaintiff sought to recover geese of the wild variety which had strayed from the owner. In granting judgment to the plaintiff, the court pointed out that the geese had been tamed by the plaintiff and therefore were unable to regain their natural liberty.

This important distinction was also demonstrated in *Manning v. Mitcherson*, 69 Ga. 447, 450-451, 52 A.L.R. 1063, where the plaintiff sought the return of a pet canary. In holding for the plaintiff the court stated, "To say that if one has a canary bird, mocking bird, parrot, or any other bird so kept, and it should accidentally escape from its cage to the street, or to a neighboring house, that the first person who caught it would be its owner is wholly at variance with all our views of right and justice."

The Court finds that Chester was a domesticated animal, subject to training and discipline. Thus the rule of ferae naturae does not prevail and the defendant as true owner is entitled to regain possession.

The Court wishes to commend the plaintiff for his acts of kindness and compassion to the parrot during the period that it was lost and was gratified to receive the defendant's assurance that the first parrot available would be offered to the plaintiff for adoption.

Judgment for defendant dismissing the complaint without costs.

Now that you have completed reading the case and taking notes on it, compare your notes with a typical brief of the case.

CONTI (pl.) v. ASPCA (def.)

77 Misc. 2d 61, 353 N.Y.S.2d 288 (Civ. Ct. 1974)

FACTS: ASPCA owned Chester, a show parrot. On June 28, he escaped to a tree and def. could not retrieve him. The next day, he disappeared. On July 5, pl. found Chester and enticed him to his home. ASPCA learned about this and took Chester back. Pl. brought replevin action. (There was a question whether the parrot really was Chester, but the court decided he was, based on the evidence.)

PROCEDURE: Action for replevin. Court dismissed the complaint, in def.'s favor. (Note: This is a trial court decision.)

ISSUE: Whether, when a domesticated animal escapes, ownership passes to the person who next captures it.

HELD: The parrot here is a domesticated animal (no discussion). When a domesticated animal escapes, ownership remains with original owner.

ANALYSIS: The owner of a wild animal (*fera naturae*) loses ownership when it escapes with no intention of returning. This rule does not apply to domesticated animals (animals that have been trained and disciplined). They are treated as lost property, and ownership remains with the original owner. The court fails to state a rationale explicitly, but cites the *Manning* case: a contrary holding would contradict "all our views of right and justice." The court relies on three cases:

> *Mullett:* A sea lion is treated as fera naturae. Upon escape, the new captor gains ownership.

> *Amory:* Court treats wild geese as tamed and therefore unable to gain their natural liberty.

> *Manning:* Escaped pet canary is treated as a domesticated animal and as belonging to the original owner.

Your notes probably contain most of the information that the sample brief contains. The organization, however, may be quite different. You can see how the briefing format forces you to focus on essential information and state it concisely in a logical order. Now let us use the *Conti* case and the sample brief to examine the parts of a brief.

[b]   Name of the Case

Copy the name of the case. When you determine which party is the plaintiff and which is the defendant and, on appeal, which is the appellant or petitioner, and which is the appellee or respondent, write down this information as well. Some opinions are written in a way that makes these vital facts difficult to discover. In *Conti*, the plaintiff's name comes first, but in some cases it comes second. If you fail to write down which litigant is which, you may forget this information at a crucial moment in class.

[c]   Citation

The citation contains the information that you need to find the case in the library. If you do not know how to use a cite to find a case, you will learn very shortly. Most casebooks offer abridged versions of cases. Your curiosity sometimes will lead you to search for the complete case in the library. If you have the cite in your brief, you will not have to return to your casebook to find it when you head for the library.

[d]   Facts of the Case

Write down the facts that you think were important to the court in deciding the case as well as any additional facts that are important to you. Court opinions often contain pages of facts. You would be wasting time and paper if you were to copy them. You want only the essential facts. If you read the entire case before you begin to brief it, you will have a much better sense of which facts are the essential ones. If you fail to read the case first, you run the risk of getting mired in a complex set of facts and writing pages of useless information.

The *Conti* case has relatively few essential facts. These facts are that Chester, a domesticated parrot, flew away from its owner, the ASPCA, and ultimately landed in the home of Conti, who now claims ownership. Chester's height and coloring are not significant. These characteristics would be significant if the opinion focused on whether Conti's parrot really was Chester. Therefore you need not write down Chester's description. The details of Chester's escape and ultimate welcome at the Conti household also are not essential. We know we can disregard this information, because we have read the rest of the case.

[e] Procedure

Answer three questions:

(1) *Who is suing whom for what?* In *Conti*, the answer is clear.

(2) *What is the legal claim?* Here, the plaintiff is suing in replevin. In some other case, a plaintiff might sue for breach of contract, false imprisonment, negligence, relief granted by a statute, or on one of many other grounds. If you come across a word like "replevin" and do not know its meaning, look it up in a dictionary. "Replevin" tells us that Conti was asking the court to order the ASPCA to return the bird to him. If you did not know the meaning of replevin, you might have thought that Conti might have been satisfied to receive the dollar value of the bird.

(3) *How did the lower court rule in the case?* It heard the arguments, considered the evidence, and rendered the decision. The trial court wrote the *Conti* opinion. Therefore we have no decision by an even lower court. Suppose Conti was dissatisfied with the court's decision and appealed to a higher court, which decided the case and issued a written opinion. If we were briefing that opinion, we would note in our brief that the court below had dismissed Conti's complaint.

[f] Issue

The issue is the legal question that the court must decide in order to reach its conclusion. In *Conti*, the issue is whether the owner of a domesticated animal loses ownership when it escapes and someone else captures it. Sometimes a court opinion will state the issue explicitly. Sometimes it will state the issue only implicitly and leave you the task of articulating it explicitly.

The *Conti* court states the issue in a very shorthanded way: "If it is in fact Chester, who is entitled to its ownership?" We are ignoring the court's first issue -- whether the parrot is Chester -- because the court finds the issue uncontroversial and quickly decides it without analysis. You must flesh out the issue in order to state it in more general terms. The issue deals not just with a parrot named Chester, but with any domesticated animal who escapes and undergoes capture under similar circumstances. Ultimately the court must decide the case on the basis of a general rule applicable to individuals and animals who are similarly situated.

How narrowly or broadly you phrase the issue is, in part, a matter of taste. In the sample brief, we phrase the issue broadly:

> Whether, when a domesticated animal escapes, ownership passes to the person who next captures it?

Another lawyer might phrase it more narrowly -- that is, more tailored to the facts of the specific case:

> Whether, when a domesticated parrot escapes, ownership passes to the person who next captures it?

Still another lawyer might phrase it even more narrowly:

> Whether the finder of Chester, an escaped parrot, owns it when the parrot was a domesticated animal that the ASPCA trained and disciplined and used in educational exhibitions?

In our experience, beginning law students frame issues too narrowly or too broadly. When they frame an issue too narrowly, they focus too much on the facts of the case and fail to understand that it applies to a broad range of cases. When they frame an issue too broadly, they fail to appreciate how important the specific facts of a case are to the court deciding it.

Learning to frame an issue is an art that takes time to learn. Your professors will give you guidance in mastering the art. They also will let you know how narrowly or broadly they want you to frame issues in their respective courses.

[g] Holding

The holding is the court's decision and thus its resolution of the issue in the case. It usually requires rephrasing the issue from a question to a declarative sentence. In *Conti*, the holding is:

> When a domesticated animal escapes, ownership remains with the original owner.

As with framing issues, different professors will have individual preferences on how broadly or narrowly they want you to state the holding.

[h] Analysis

Explain the court's reasoning in reaching its decision. Again, reading the case before you brief it will save you an enormous amount of time. Understanding the court's reasoning is not always easy. Sometimes the reasoning will be unclear or contain gaps in its logic or require the reader to discern what the court is saying only implicitly. These defects and similar ones often will be the subject of class discussion.

A court frequently explains that its decision furthers important social policy. In your brief, identify these policy considerations. In *Conti*, the court quotes an earlier decision to the effect that a contrary holding would contradict "all our views of right and justice." If the *Conti* court had written a more expansive opinion, it might have stated that its holding protected the right of property ownership, because it forbids an individual to casually seize and keep the property of another.

Court decisions often include dicta. Dicta are discussions of law that are not necessary to the court's decision in the case before it. The singular of "dicta" is "dictum." The discussion of the *Conti* court about the rule to follow when an undomesticated animal escapes is dictum. The court's discussion of that situation is not essential to deciding the case of a domesticated parrot that escapes. It is a wise practice to note dicta in your brief.

Be sure to read any footnotes. Most cases appearing in law school case books are edited versions. The editor has omitted most footnotes. If the editor has retained a footnote, he or she believes that it is important to the student's understanding of the case. A footnote sometimes contains the key to the case.

Do not ignore dissenting and concurring opinions. Again, if an editor retains a dissent or concurrence, he or she has done so for a reason. Do not be surprised if your professor asks you if you agree with the majority or the dissent. If you fail to brief the dissent, you probably will be unable to answer the question.

[i]   More Sample Briefs

Here are two additional briefs of the *Conti* case. Each differs slightly from the sample brief we have studied. Our purpose is to show you that there is not just one way to brief a case. Just as different people take notes in different ways, different people brief cases in different ways. In each, however, the essential information is the same.

FIRST SAMPLE BRIEF

CONTI v. ASPCA

77 Misc. 2d 61, 353 N.Y.S.2d 288 (Civ. Ct. 1974)

FACTS: on June 28, 1973, the ASPCA's parrot, Chester, flew away. On July 5, Conti (Pl.) found a bird the court determined was Chester in his backyard. Conti caged the parrot and called the ASPCA for information on parrot care. The ASPCA (Def.) suspecting the parrot was Chester went and took the parrot from Conti. Def. refused to return the parrot to Pl.

PROCEDURE: Trial court decision on a replevin action. Replevin is an action where a person seeks to recover possession of particular goods.

ISSUE: Who has rightful possession of an escaped parrot originally owned by one party and recaptured by another?

HELD: Ownership of a domesticated parrot does not terminate upon escape, but continues as against the one who recaptures the escaped animal.

ANALYSIS: The true owner of lost property is entitled to its return. Ownership of a wild animal (fera naturae) ends when it escapes and returns to its natural liberty. A domesticated animal (one that has been trained and disciplined) is treated as lost property and is subject to return upon recapture.

In determining whether the parrot was domesticated or wild, the court considered three cases and three guidelines. *Mullet* found an untrained sea lion to be fera naturae. *Amory* held geese that had been trained were domesticated. *Manning* determined extinguishing ownership of a pet canary was "wholly at variance with all our views of right and justice." Chester had been trained, disciplined and was like a canary. Ownership continued to be held by the ASPCA because Chester was domesticated.

SECOND SAMPLE BRIEF

CONTI v. ASPCA

77 Misc. 2d 61, 353 N.Y.S.2d 288 (Civ. Ct. 1974)

FACTS: Defendant ASPCA conducted a demonstration with a parrot named Chester during which the bird escaped. A week later, a parrot with markings and colorings similar to Chester's appeared in plaintiff's yard and remained with the plaintiff for two weeks before being caged. The ASPCA removed the bird after plaintiff called for advice about its care. ASPCA claimed the bird was Chester and belonged to the organization.

PROCEDURE: Action for replevin -- plaintiff wants the bird back.

ISSUE: Court identified two issues: 1. Whether the bird is actually Chester; and 2. Who gets him?

HELD: ASPCA gets the bird because: 1. The court found that the bird was Chester; and 2. As a domesticated animal, Chester does have a true owner, whose rights are not lost when the bird escapes.

ANALYSIS: The key issue in determining ownership was whether the rule of ferae naturae applied. This rule states that an owner acquires only qualified rights in a wild animal that are extinguished if the animal escapes. The court found that Chester was subject to training and discipline and therefore was not wild.

[3] Problem

Here is another case that many of you will read during your first year in law school. Please brief it. Following the opinion are three sample briefs of the case. Compare your brief to them. Please do not read these briefs until you have written your own. If you ignore this instruction, you will learn far less.

As you read the opinion, note that it is an appellate opinion. The trial court decided in favor of the defendant, and the plaintiff has appealed to the appropriate appeals court, here, the Massachusetts Supreme Judicial Court.

Note also the format of the opinion. It begins with the name of the case. Here, the first name is McAvoy, the name of the plaintiff, who is now the appellant. Though some courts put the name of the appellant first, others do not necessarily do so. In each case, you need to check. Next is the citation you need to find the case in the library. Then come the facts of the case and, then, the name of the justice who wrote the opinion. Most of the time, the name of the judge appears before the statement of the facts. In virtually all appellate cases, several judges decide the case, and one judge writes the opinion. Here, Justice Dewey had that task. After the opinion discusses the case, it gives the court's ruling. In this case, the court overruled the plaintiff's exceptions and upheld the decision of the trial court. Exceptions are the grounds on which the plaintiff sought the appeal.

McAVOY v. MEDINA

93 Mass. (11 Allen) 548 (1866)

[Tort action to recover sum of money found by plaintiff in defendant's shop.]

At the trial in the superior court, before Morton, J., it appeared that the defendant was a barber, and the plaintiff, being a customer in the defendant's shop, saw and took up a pocket-book which was lying upon a table there, and said, "See what I have found." The defendant came to the table and asked where he found it. The plaintiff laid it back in the same place and said, "I found it right there." The defendant then took it and counted the money, and the plaintiff told him to keep it, and if the owner should come to give it to him; and otherwise to advertise it; which the defendant promised to do. Subsequently the plaintiff made three demands for the money, and the defendant never claimed to hold the same till the last demand. It was agreed that the pocket-book was placed upon the table by a transient customer of the defendant and accidentally left there, and was first seen and taken up by the plaintiff, and that the owner had not been found.

The judge ruled that the plaintiff could not maintain his action, and a verdict was accordingly returned for the defendant; and the plaintiff alleged exceptions. (citations omitted.)

DEWEY, J. It seems to be the settled law that the finder of lost property has a valid claim to the same against all the world except the true owner, and generally that the place in which it is found creates no exception to this rule. 2 Parsons on Con. 97. *Bridges v. Hawkesworth*, 7 Eng. Law 7 Eq. R. 424.

But this property is not, under the circumstances, to be treated as lost property in the sense in which a finder has a valid claim to hold the same until called for by the true owner. This property was voluntarily placed upon a table in the defendant's shop by a customer of his who accidentally left the same there and has never called for it. The plaintiff also came there as a customer, and first saw the same and took it up from the table. The plaintiff did not by this acquire the right to take the property from the shop, but it was rather the duty of the defendant, when the fact became thus known to him, to use reasonable care for the safe keeping of the same until the owner should call for it. In the case of *Bridges v. Hawkesworth* the property, although found in a shop, was found on the floor of the same, and had not been placed there voluntarily by the owner, and the court held that the finder was entitled to the possession of the same, except as to the owner. But the present case more resembles that of *Lawrence v. the State*, 1 Humph (Tenn.) 228, and is indeed very similar in its facts. The court there makes a distinction between the case of property thus placed by the owner and neglected to be removed, and property lost. It was there held that "to place a pocket-book upon a table and to forget to take it away is not to lose it, in the sense in which the authorities referred to speak of lost property."

We accept this as the better rule, and especially as one better adapted to secure the rights of the true owner.

In view of the facts of this case, the plaintiff acquired no original right to the property, and the defendant's subsequent acts in receiving and holding the property in the manner he did, does not create any. Exceptions overruled.

FIRST SAMPLE BRIEF

McAVOY (pl.) v. MEDINA (def.)

93 Mass. (11 Allen) 548 (1866)

FACTS: Pl. customer found a pocketbook lying on a table in def.'s barbershop. Def. agreed to hold it in case the owner returned. The owner never showed up and apparently was a transient customer. Def. refused to give pocketbook to pl.

PROCEDURE: Pl. brought tort action to recover money in the pocketbook. T.C.: Pl. could not maintain the action; verdict for def. Pl. appeals. Ct. here affirms (exceptions overruled).

ISSUE: Does the finder have a valid claim to property that the owner voluntarily placed in a given location and forgot to retrieve (*i.e.* property that the owner mislaid)?

HELD: No.

ANALYSIS: The finder of lost property has a valid claim to it as against all but the true owner. But property that is voluntarily placed somewhere, like the table in the barbershop, and accidentally left behind is not lost property. The finder has no right to it. The owner of the location has the duty to take reasonable care of the property until the owner calls for it. This rule is better adapted to secure the rights of the true owner.

SECOND SAMPLE BRIEF

McAVOY v. MEDINA

93 Mass. (11 Allen) 548 (1866)

FACTS: McAvoy (P) was a customer in Medina's (D's) barbershop. P found a pocketbook containing money on a table in the shop. P & D agreed (at least at the time of trial) that it was placed on the table and accidentally left by a transient customer. P left the pocketbook with D who promised to advertise it. No one claimed it, and D refused to give P the money found in it.

PROCEDURE: P appeals from the trial court, which found he could not maintain a tort action for the value of the money.

ISSUE: Whether the finder of property determined to be accidentally left has the same property right as the finder of lost property?

HOLDING: The finder of mislaid or forgotten property acquires no right to the property found against the shopowner where the article was left.

ANALYSIS: Property voluntarily placed and accidentally left in a shop does not give the finder a valid claim against all but the true owner. A shopowner has the responsibility to use due care for the property until the true owner returns. Creating a property interest in the shop owner supports its return to its proper owner.

The court uses *Bridges* and *Lawrence* to show that finding the property in the shop is not the determinative factor. The distinction is between deciding if it is lost (*Bridges* -- found on the floor), in which case the finder gets it and finding if it is mislaid or forgotten (*Lawrence* -- found on a table).

THIRD SAMPLE BRIEF

McAVOY v. MEDINA

93 Mass. (11 Allen) 548 (1866)

FACTS: Plaintiff McAvoy saw a purse on a table in def.'s barbershop and asked def. to give it to the owner or to advertise it. When the owner did not show up to claim the purse, pl. demanded it.

PROCEDURE: Action in tort to recover money. Pl. appeals from lower court verdict for def.

ISSUE: If the purse is not treated as lost, but as accidentally left behind, would the finder be entitled to keep it if the true owner does not show up?

HELD: Pl.'s appeal was denied (exceptions overruled). The court held that the purse would not be treated as lost under the circumstances and thus pl. acquired no right to the property.

ANALYSIS: The court relied on *Lawrence v. State* in which the court distinguished between property "placed by the owner and neglected to be removed" and property lost. The court felt that treating the mislaid property differently and giving it to the owner of the location created a rule that was "better adapted to secure the rights of the true owner."

§ 3.03 Beyond Briefing

Briefing is just the beginning of preparing for class. Once you brief a case, you need to think about the opinion critically. You will spend most of your time in class evaluating the opinion rather than merely restating what the court said. By the time class is over, you may decide that you disagree with the court. After a class on the *Conti* case, you still may agree with the outcome, but you may question at least some of the court's reasoning. In a class on the *McAvoy* case, you may learn that the trend among courts is to reject its holding. Here are three questions to help you think about the cases you have briefed.

(1) *Do you agree with the court's holding and reasoning?* Does the logic flow? Does the court rely on assumptions -- explicit or implicit -- with which you would disagree? Do you agree with the social policies that the court purports to further?

(2) *Would you use the court's holding to decide a case with similar, but not identical, facts?* In *Conti*, suppose Chester was an untamed wolf instead of a tamed parrot? Suppose he was a tiger who escaped from the zoo? Would the court still find for the ASPCA, even though the animal was undomesticated? Would you?

(3) *Why did my professor or the casebook's editor select this case?* What larger lessons are they trying to teach? Why are *Conti* and *McAvoy* usually near the beginning of Property casebooks, as opposed to the middle or end? If you think about each case as part of a series of cases that you are studying, do you see a big picture in addition to a series of narrow rules?

EXERCISE

Pick a case that you have briefed for one of your classes. Ask your professor to read it and suggest ways to improve it. You will discover that most professors will be very willing to spend the time with you.

CHAPTER **4**

INTRODUCTION TO LEGAL LOGIC

§ 4.01 Introduction

Largely because of the adversary system, American legal logic has at its core the common law doctrine of stare decisis, which means "to stand with things decided." In other words, earlier cases are precedents whose holdings determine the outcome of later cases. Constitutions, statutes, and other sources of law are frequently the bases of court decisions. Courts must determine the meaning of these law sources as they apply to specific situations. Thus, analysis of case precedent forms the core of legal logic, and legal logic is primarily applying court-made law to the facts of the current case. In every case, lawyers on opposite sides will be using the same facts and law, but hoping to persuade the court to reach diametrically opposed conclusions.

There are three steps for developing a legal argument:

1. Determine all legal authority, or general rules, applicable to your case.

2. Apply this legal authority to the facts of your particular case.

3. Draw a conclusion based on the legal authority that you have applied to your case.

For example:

STEP ONE—
GENERAL RULE: A lawyer may not knowingly make a false state-
                        ment of material fact or law to a tribunal.

STEP TWO—
PARTICULAR CASE: Sandra North is a lawyer and she knows that an
                        important case she wanted to rely on in her brief
                        has just been overruled.

STEP THREE—
CONCLUSION: Sandra North must not rely on the overruled
                        case in her brief, because that would be a false
                        statement of material law.

The next two sections discuss legal authority and how to use deductive reasoning to apply authority to your case.

§ 4.02   Legal Authority

Legal authority is whatever a lawyer relies on to support a conclusion. It may be cases, statutes, or any other form of law. Lawyers rely on two types of legal authority to make their arguments:

1. Mandatory authority

2. Persuasive authority

[1]   Mandatory Authority

Mandatory authority is authority that you must rely on because it binds the court in your jurisdiction. It is unethical to omit from a legal argument mandatory authority that is adverse to your client's interests.

Mandatory authority is controlling law, including constitutions, statutes, regulations, and court decisions. As you may recall from Chapter 2, binding authority is primary authority that is "on point," which means that it specifically addresses the issues and facts that your case raises and determines the outcome.

For example, if you are appearing in a state trial court, you must recognize that a decision by the state's highest court is binding on your court. If the facts of your case are identical in all material respects to the case that the highest court decided, that case determines the outcome of your case. However, you will rarely, if ever, find such identity of precedent in your legal research.

[2]   Persuasive Authority

Persuasive authority is non-mandatory legal authority. It is authority that may persuade a court to decide a certain way but does not require a particular decision. Persuasive authority includes:

1.   Primary authority that does not control your case because the rules are not directly applicable or the relevant facts are distinguishable. For example, assume that in a particular case a court finds that the defendant was liable for assault for brandishing a real gun at plaintiff. This holding may not apply to a subsequent case in which a defendant brandishes what is obviously a toy gun at a plaintiff.

2.   Secondary authority, such as treatises, hornbooks, or law review articles, which present only authors' viewpoints about law but are not themselves the law.

3.   Dicta in court opinions, which are discussions that are explanatory, but not necessary, to the decisions. For example, the court in the gun assault case may suggest that brandishing a knife also can constitute an assault. An actual case involving brandishing of a knife, however, may not involve an assault unless all the circumstances create that offense. The victim, for example, may have felt no real threat from the defendant's brandishing the knife, and therefore no assault occurred. The court deciding the knife case will not be constrained by the suggestion in the earlier case that brandishing a knife may be an assault.

There are several ways to use relevant legal authority when you write a legal argument. This chapter will introduce you to deductive reasoning. In Chapter 5 you will learn how to apply the law to the facts of your case and to use policy and equity analyses in your argument.

§ 4.03 Arguing Deductively

Legal logic relies on deductive reasoning. When you argue deductively, you take three steps:

1. Apply a general rule (of law), which usually derives from a particular statute or case but also may be derived from a variety of different sources,

2. To a particular case, and

3. Draw a conclusion.

For example:

GENERAL RULE: All teachers are cruel and heartless.

PARTICULAR CASE: John Doe is a teacher.

CONCLUSION: John Doe is cruel and heartless.

In a legal argument, the general rule is the relevant legal authority; the particular case is the facts of your case; and the conclusion is the result reached by applying the legal authority to the facts.

For example:

The general rule is a court decision stating that all golfers have a legal duty to avoid injuring other golfers, and a golfer fulfills this duty by yelling "fore" when hitting a golf ball. In this particular case John Doe is a golfer. Therefore, the conclusion is that John Doe has a duty to avoid injuring other golfers, and he can fulfill this duty by yelling "fore" when he hits a golf ball.

When broken into its components, the deductive reasoning applied here looks like this:

GENERAL RULE: All golfers have a legal duty to avoid injuring
                         other golfers and can fulfill this duty by yelling
                         "fore" when hitting golf balls.

PARTICULAR CASE: John Doe is a golfer.

CONCLUSION: John Doe has a legal duty to avoid injuring
                         other golfers and can fulfill this duty by yelling
                         "fore" when hitting golf balls.

[1] Limitations

Deductive reasoning, however, is only a framework or a starting point for formulating a legal argument. It does not always dictate the outcome of a case with great precision and may only give you a "ballpark" prediction of what the outcome of your case should be. Remember that the party on the other side of the case also will apply deductive reasoning, using the same facts and law, to arrive at a very different conclusion about the case. Deductive reasoning is only as valid as your interpretation of the general rule and your application of that rule to the particular case.

For example, with regard to the case above, suppose you found the general rule in a California case, but New York law governs your case and does not follow the California rule. If New York law is settled, it controls; that is, if New York law specifically holds that yelling "fore" is not required, the California case has no precedential value. If it is unsettled, then the California rule is, at best, persuasive authority. Thus, if New York courts have said only that golfers must take "reasonable steps" to avoid injuring other golfers, you might want to argue that the California rule is more specific and should be adopted.

With regard to the same case, suppose John Doe the golfer is a child. Or suppose he was incapable of yelling "fore," either because he could not speak or he speaks a foreign language. These differences in the facts might make your authority nonmandatory and maybe not even persuasive.

If the general rule is very broad or very narrow, or if your understanding of how the rule applies to the particular case is in some way not totally accurate, your conclusion may not be persuasive to a court. Reasoning deductively is not always as easy as it appears, but it is still a useful framework for legal logic.

[2] Maximizing Use of Deductive Reasoning

To use deductive reasoning for legal argument, you must:

1. Be sure that your general statement, or rule of law, is correct by analyzing all relevant law and predicting accurately the rule you think the court will apply to your case.

2. Be sure that your statement of the facts in the particular case is accurate and does not ignore anything that might alter application of the general rule.

3. Be sure that your final conclusion follows logically from the rule and facts.

If there are several issues in your case, you should apply deductive reasoning to each issue separately, again taking great care as to your interpretation of what the law is and its application to your own situation. One issue may contain many sub-issues, each of which requires a separate application of deductive reasoning.

[3] Application

When writing your argument with deductive analysis, always state your conclusion first, because readers of legal writing do not want to be left waiting in suspense for the conclusion. After you state the conclusion, identify the key issue and the applicable rule, and present the relevant legal authority. Next apply the legal authority to the facts of your case. Finally, restate the conclusion you have drawn from your analysis.

(Matthew Bender & Co., Inc.)

Here is an example of this form of analysis:

CONCLUSION: The defendant here had a duty to shout "fore"
                         to the plaintiff.

ISSUE: The key issue is when a golfer has a duty to yell
                         "fore" when hitting a golf ball in the direction
                         of another golfer on an adjacent fairway.

MAJOR PREMISE: In *Allen v. Pinewood Country Club, Inc.*, 292
(Relevant legal   So.2d 786, 789 (La. App. 1974), the court held
Authority)   that golfers have a duty to yell "fore" if they hit
                         a golf ball and another golfer on a different fair-
                         way is standing in the ball's line of flight. The
                         court found that all golfers have a duty of rea-
                         sonable care and must avoid injuring other golf-
                         ers. *Id.* To fulfill this duty, a golfer must give
                         timely and adequate warning to other golfers in
                         the golf ball's line of flight. *Id.* Therefore, a
                         golfer has a duty to yell "fore" when hitting a
                         golf ball that veers toward another fairway and
                         a golfer on the other fairway is standing in the
                         ball's line of flight. *Id.*

PARTICULAR CASE: Under *Allen*, the defendant in the present case
(Applying the   had a duty to yell "fore" to the plaintiff. The de-
relevant legal   fendant hit a golf ball from the fairway of the
authority to   sixth hole. The ball hooked towards the fairway
the facts)   of the fifth hole. The plaintiff was standing on
                         the fairway of the fifth hole and was in the di-
                         rect line of flight of the golf ball hit by the de-
                         fendant. Therefore, the facts of the present case
                         fall squarely within the holding in *Allen*.

CONCLUSION: Since the defendant hit a golf ball that hooked to-
                         ward the plaintiff who was on an adjacent fairway
                         and was in the direct line of flight of the golf ball,
                         the defendant had a duty to shout "fore" to the
                         plaintiff.

The conclusion at the end is not just a simple paraphrase of the conclusion at the
beginning. It should be developed more fully and should include the relevant, concrete facts of the case.

§ 4.04 Applying the Law to the Facts

A legal argument is meaningless unless you apply the relevant legal authority
directly to the facts of your case. The most important aspect of legal argument is
taking the general rule of law and applying it to the particular situation. Applying

the law to the facts makes your argument concrete and tells the court how you think it should resolve your case. Chapter 5 gives you a step-by-step approach to constructing legal arguments by synthesizing legal rules and particular fact situations.

EXERCISES

1. Your instructor will assign a memo in Appendix IV. Identify all uses of deductive reasoning in that memo and label the general rule, particular case, and conclusion for each use of deductive reasoning.

2. Find and explain a use of deductive reasoning in a case you have read for another course.

CHAPTER 5

LEGAL ANALYSIS

§ 5.01 Introduction

Teachers and practitioners of legal writing often disagree about whether legal writing is really a different kind of writing, or just "normal" writing about a different kind of subject matter. Simple, clear sentence structure and concrete language will work well in virtually any context. There are, however, very definite, fixed expectations about the structure and content of legal analysis that are foreign to most non-legal writers.

The focus of this chapter will be on introducing you to those expectations and on teaching you, in a very functional way, how to meet them. After a brief overview of the process, you will see a legal analysis of an issue arising out of a case similar to the *McAvoy v. Medina* case presented in Chapter 3. We will then proceed step-by-step through two examples of legal analysis, one relying solely on cases, and one adding statutory construction to the mix. As we go along, you will be asked to write out the analysis that follows from the discussion.

§ 5.02 The Basic Approach

The single most important thing to remember about legal analysis is that completeness is everything. The goal is not to arrive at an answer as quickly as possible, but to lay out, in what often seems like excruciating detail, how you got from the question to the answer. In most cases, if a thought goes through your head that helps you arrive at a conclusion, it should appear on the paper. Readers of legal analysis, generally busy practitioners and judges, do not want to work at analyzing the problem while they read. They want to pick up the document you have submitted, read through it quickly, and understand instantly how you reached every conclusion you present.

How does this process work? Assume you have been asked to predict the outcome of a particular client's situation. You have identified the relevant case law, and are preparing to write out an analysis that explains how the case law applies to your client's situation. Until you become comfortable with this analytical process and develop your own personal style, you should go through the following steps *in writing*. First, brief the cases you will be analyzing. Summarize the facts, holding, and rationale of each decision. Find and identify the rule of law applied by the court in each case. Add the procedural history, if it is relevant to the discussion.

Once you have the building blocks, try to formulate a general principle, or principles, that explain the decisions reached by the courts. Are they applying the same rules? If the courts seem to be arriving at the same end by different routes, compare and evaluate the various approaches. If the courts arrive at different results, try to figure out what distinguishes the cases. Are the facts different? Are the courts trying to implement different policies?

When you have figured out why the courts reached the decisions they did, look for analogies between the decided cases and the case you have been asked to analyze. Compare the facts. Identify the policy or policies behind the decisions, and try to decide what outcome that policy would mandate in your case. By policy, we mean the societal interest or goal that is served by the decision. Look at the equities -- did the courts seek out the "fair" result, and what would that be in your case? How do these policy and equity arguments relate to the legal rules announced or applied by the courts?

After you have gone through these steps, it is time to begin writing out your analysis. When you do, *integrate* your analysis of your case with your discussion of the decided cases. Integration means you do not present all of the relevant law and then discuss its application to your case. An effective legal analysis will make comparisons between the decided cases and the case being discussed wherever appropriate, whether those comparisons are of facts, applicable policies, or equities. You want to synthesize the existing law and your client's situation by demonstrating how they fit together, and by explaining how what has happened in the past will or should inform the decisions of those faced with the current situation.

§ 5.03 An Example of Legal Analysis

This section will present a sample legal analysis of a question regarding whether a piece of property was "lost" or "mislaid," and thus who can claim ownership of it. First, reread the *McAvoy v. Medina* case from Chapter 3. Assume that the only other relevant authority is the following case:

DURFEE v. JONES

11 R.I. 588

July 21, 1877. DURFEE, C.J. The facts in this case are briefly these: In April, 1874, the plaintiff bought an old safe and soon afterwards instructed his agent to sell it again. The agent offered to sell it to the defendant for ten dollars, but the defendant refused to buy it. The agent then left it with the defendant, who was a blacksmith, at his shop for sale for ten dollars, authorizing him to keep his books in it until it was sold or reclaimed. The safe was old-fashioned, of sheet iron, about three feet square, having a few pigeon-holes and a place for books, and in back of the place for books a large crack in the lining. The defendant shortly after the safe was left, upon examining it, found secreted between the sheet-iron exterior and the wooden lining a roll of bills amounting to $165, of the denomination of the national bank bills which have been current for the last ten or twelve years. Neither the plaintiff nor the defendant knew the money was there before it was found. The owner of the money is still unknown. The defendant informed the plaintiff's agent that he had found it, and offered it to him for the plaintiff; but the agent declined it, stating that it did not belong to either himself or the plaintiff, and advised the defendant to deposit it where it would be drawing interest until the rightful owner appeared. The plaintiff was then out of the city. Upon his return, being informed of the finding, he immediately called on the defendant and asked for the money, but the defendant refused to give it to him. He then, after taking advice, demanded the return of the safe and its contents, precisely as they existed when placed in the defendant's hands. The defendant promptly gave up the safe, but retained the money. The plaintiff brings this action to recover it or its equivalent.

The plaintiff does not claim that he acquired, by purchasing the safe, any right to the money in the safe as against the owner; for he bought the safe alone, not the safe and its contents. See *Merry v. Green*, 7 M. & W. 623. But he claims that as between himself and the defendant his is the better right. The defendant, however, has the possession, and therefore it is for the plaintiff, in order to succeed in his action, to prove his better right.

The plaintiff claims that he is entitled to have the money by the right of prior possession. But the plaintiff never had any possession of the money, except, unwittingly, by having possession of the safe which contained it. Such possession, if possession it can be called, does not of itself confer a right. The case at bar is in this view like *Bridges v. Hawkesworth*, 15 Jur.1079; 21 L.J.Q.B. 75 A.D. 1851; 7 Eng. L. & Eq. 424. In that case, the plaintiff, while in the defendant's shop on business, picked up from the floor a parcel containing bank notes. He gave them to the defendant for the owner if he could be found. The owner could not be found, and it was held that the plaintiff as finder was entitled to them, as against the defendant as owner of the shop in which they were found. "The notes," said the court, "never were in the custody of the defendant nor within the protection of his house, before they were found, as they would have been if they had been intentionally deposited there." The same in effect may be said of the notes in the case at bar; for though they were originally deposited in the safe by design, they were not so deposited in the safe, after it became the plaintiff's safe, so as to be in the protection of the safe as *his* safe, or so as to affect him with any responsibility for them. The case at bar is also in this respect like *Tatum v. Sharpless*, 6 Phila. 18. There it was held, that a conductor who had found money which had been lost in a railroad car was entitled to it as against the railroad company.

The plaintiff also claims that the money was not lost but designedly left where it was found, and that therefore as owner of the safe he is entitled to its custody. He refers to cases in which it has been held, that money or other property voluntarily laid down and forgotten is not in legal contemplation lost, and that of such money or property the owner of the shop or place where it is left is the proper custodian rather than the person who happens to discover it first. *State v. McCann*, 19 Mo. 249; *Lawrence v. The State*, 1 Humph. 228; *McAvoy v. Medina*, 11 Allen, 549. It may be questioned whether this distinction has not been pushed to an extreme. See *Kincaid v. Eaton*, 98 Mass 139. But, however that may be, we think the money here, though designedly left in the safe, was probably not designedly put in the crevice or interspace where it was found, but that, being left in the safe, it probably slipped or was accidentally shoved into the place where it was found without the knowledge of the owner, and so was lost, in the stricter sense of the word. The money was not simply deposited and forgotten, but deposited and lost by reason of a defect or insecurity in the place of deposit.

The plaintiff claims that the finding was a wrongful act on the part of the defendant, and that therefore he is entitled to recover the money or to have it replaced. We do not so regard it. The safe was left with the defendant for sale. As seller he would properly examine it under an implied permission to do so, to qualify him the better to act as seller. Also under the permission to use it for his books, he would have the right to inspect it to see if it was a fit depository. And finally, as a possible purchaser he might examine it, for though he had once declined to examine it, the defendant, having found in the safe something which did not belong there, might we think, properly remove it. He certainly would not be expected either to sell the safe to another, or to buy it himself without first removing it. It is not pretended that he used any violence or did any harm to the safe. And it is evident that the idea that any trespass or tort had been committed did not even occur to the plaintiff's agent when he was first informed of the finding.

The general rule undoubtedly is, that the finder of lost property is entitled to it as against all the world except the real owner, and that ordinarily the place where it is found does not make any difference. We cannot find anything in the circumstances of the case at bar to take it out of this rule.

Here are the facts of the case to be analyzed.

Fact Pattern: Lost or Mislaid?

While collecting books for reshelving, P., an employee at a law library, discovered a black valise lying on its side on the floor between two bookshelves. He picked up the valise and brought it to the circulation desk, where he searched the contents for some identification of the owner.

A few days later D., a student at the law school, came to the circulation desk to find a black valise she had lost. P. showed D. the found valise. D. said that it looked like her case but wished to check the contents to be sure. P. agreed and opened the valise for D.

While examining the contents, D. discovered a secret compartment that contained a diamond engagement ring. D. pocketed the ring, leaving her name with P. in case the original owner should turn up, and left the library. P. followed, requesting that D. return the ring to the valise. D. refused. P. now sues for return of the ring.

D. claims that the ring was lost, so D., as finder, is entitled to it unless the real owner claims it. P. claims that the ring was intentionally left in the secret compartment and, as a result, was not "lost" in a legal sense. P. insists that he is a custodian of the mislaid property and is entitled to keep the ring unless the real owner claims it.

Analysis

The principal issues to be addressed in this case are whether either the ring or the valise fits the legal definition of "lost," and thus whether D. could legally have "found" the ring. Although the valise was "lost," and the ring was not, D. does not have a legal claim to custody of either one.

The rule that "the finder of lost property is entitled to it as against all the world except the real owner," *Durfee v. Jones*, 11 R.I. 588 (1877), applies to the valise. P. found the valise lying on its side, in a manner and in a place suggesting it was not left there intentionally. Consequently, P. acquired a legal interest in the valise analogous to the interest acquired by the plaintiff in the *Durfee* case when he purchased a safe containing money that had slipped into a crevice inside the safe. Durfee did not find the money while the safe was in his possession. The defendant legally acquired custody of the safe from Durfee, found the money, removed it and then returned the safe. Durfee sought the return of the money as well, but the court held that the money had not been intentionally placed into the crevice and was thus "lost." Therefore the defendant had title to the money, subject only to the title of the true owner. The only difference between the interests of Durfee and P. is that Durfee was entitled to the safe against all others whereas P. is only entitled to the valise if the original owner does not turn up.

Conversely, if the original owner places property in a particular location, intending to retrieve it, the finder is not entitled to the property but is expected to "use reasonable care for the safe keeping of [the property] until the owner should call for it." *McAvoy v. Medina*, 93 Mass. (11 Allen) 548 (1866). In that case the owner of a shop was held to have the obligation to keep a pocketbook left on a table by a customer. The plaintiff "found" the pocketbook and later attempted to obtain custody of the money inside it from the defendant shopkeeper, but the court rejected the plaintiff's claim.

These cases lead to the conclusion that an individual who acquires possession of a piece of personal property assumes only a custodial interest over any property intentionally hidden inside it. In the present case, D. cannot argue that the position of the ring within the valise was the product of some accident, as was the location of the money in *Durfee*. The ring had been deliberately placed in a secret compartment in order that it be protected. Since P., as finder, was entitled to the valise, D. could not lay claim to anything intentionally hidden within it, even if P. did not know of its existence.

Even if D. could legally "find" the ring, P. gave D. leave to look inside the valise solely to determine the identity of its owner. D. did not have to search for secret compartments to see if it was her case. The court in *Durfee* indicates that a finder must have at least implied permission to examine the property. In the present case, P. opened the case so that D. could check to see if it belonged to her. P. did not give D. permission to conduct an exhaustive search of the lining, and there was nothing inherent in the determination of whether it was D.'s valise that would have implied permission to do so.

Thus, P. may claim the valise against all but the true owner, but has only a custodial interest in the ring. D. has no claim whatsoever to either the valise or the ring.

§ 5.04   Case Analysis

Now that you have seen what the final product looks like, we will break the process into its component parts so you can learn how to produce a good legal analysis when you are assigned to do so. Assume that you are an associate in a law firm and a partner has presented you with the following situation:

> A few days ago, a business client of ours came to us with a personal problem. Paul Trune, an auditor for the Internal Revenue Service, was making a pilgrimage to Baraboo, Wisconsin to visit the birthplace of the Ringling Bros. & Barnum & Bailey Circus. Unfortunately, while on the way to Baraboo, Paul became quite lost and ended up driving down some unknown Wisconsin back road with an overheating radiator. Paul was forced to pull off the road next to a stretch of woods. He grabbed an empty bottle that he kept in the car for such emergencies, and began walking in search of water. After a mile or so, the woods gave way to a clearing in which there was a well. Paul looked around for a farmhouse or any other building, but he didn't see any. Seeing no fences or signs either, Paul walked up to the well to take some water.
>
> Just as Paul was raising the bucket from the bottom of the well, he heard a voice ring out behind him. Paul turned to see a farmer gesticulating wildly and yelling at him about "trespassing." As the farmer got closer, Paul saw he had a dead, bloody rabbit in his left hand and a rifle slung around his back. The farmer then bellowed at Paul that he "knew how to take care of trespassers", and ordered him to start walking in the direction of a small hill. Seeing that the farmer had a gun and the ability to use it, and given the man's irate state, Paul decided that it was best not to say anything and just obey.
>
> Once at the crest of the hill, Paul saw a small farmhouse and barn below. The farmer marched Paul into the barn and told him to wait until he called the sheriff. The farmer closed the door to the barn, but didn't lock it. Paul feared for his safety so he stayed put. After about two hours in the barn, with no sign of the farmer or a sheriff, Paul peeked outside. Not seeing the farmer anywhere in sight, he took off.

Paul now wishes to know if he has a cause of action against the farmer for the intentional tort of false imprisonment.

Next, assume that there are only two cases in Wisconsin that address the tort of false imprisonment. Here they are, in relevant part:

DUPLER v. SEUBERT

Supreme Court of Wisconsin
69 Wis. 2d 373; 230 N.W.2d 626 (1975)

OPINION: WILKIE, C.J. This is a false imprisonment action. On April 23, 1971, plaintiff-appellant Ethel M. Dupler was fired from her job with the defendant-respondent Wisconsin Telephone Company. She was informed of her discharge during an hour-and-a-half session with her two superiors, defendants-respondents Keith Peterson and Helen Seubert, who, Dupler claims, falsely imprisoned her during a portion of this time period. A jury found that Peterson and Seubert did falsely imprison Dupler and fixed damages at $7,500. The trial court gave Dupler the option of accepting a lower amount -- $500 -- or a new trial on the issue of damages. The option was not exercised, judgment for $500 was entered, and Mrs. Dupler appeals. We reverse and remand for a new trial on the issue of damages, but give plaintiff-appellant an option to accept $1,000 damages in lieu of a new trial.

Dupler had worked for the telephone company as a customer service representative since 1960. At approximately 4:30 on April 23rd, Seubert asked Dupler to come to Peterson's office. When all three were inside, sitting down, with the door closed, Seubert told Dupler the telephone company would no longer employ her and that she could choose either to resign or be fired. Dupler testified that she refused to resign and that in the conversation that followed, Peterson discussed several alternatives short of dismissal, all of which had been considered but rejected.

At approximately 5 o'clock, Dupler testified, she began to feel sick to her stomach and said "You have already fired me. Why don't you just let me go." She made a motion to get up but Peterson told her to sit down in "a very loud harsh voice." Then, Dupler testified, she began to feel violently ill and stated "I got to go. I can't take this any more. I'm sick to my stomach. I know I'm going to throw up." She got up and started for the door but Seubert also arose and stood in front of the door. After Dupler repeated that she was sick, Seubert allowed her to exit, but followed her to the ladies' washroom, where Dupler did throw up. Following this, at approximately 5:25, Seubert asked Dupler to return to Peterson's office where she had left her purse to discuss the situation further. Dupler testified that she went back to the office and reached for her purse; Seubert again closed the door and Peterson said [in] a loud voice, "Sit down. I'm still your boss. I'm not through with you." At approximately 5:40 Dupler told Peterson her husband was waiting for her outside in a car and Peterson told her to go outside and ask her husband to come inside. Dupler then went outside and explained the situation to her husband who said, "You get back in there and get your coat and if you aren't right out I'll call the police." Dupler returned to Peterson's office and was again told in a loud tone of voice to sit down. She said Seubert and Peterson were trying to convince her to resign rather than be fired and again reviewed the alternatives that had been considered. Dupler then said: "What's the sense of all this. Why keep torturing me. Let me go. Let me go." She stated that Peterson replied, "No, we still aren't finished. We have a lot of things to discuss, your retirement pay, your vacation, other things." Finally, at approximately 6 o'clock Peterson told Dupler they could talk further on the phone or at her house, and Dupler left. When asked why she had stayed in Peterson's office for such a long time, Dupler replied:

> Well, for one thing, Helen, Mrs. Seubert, had blocked the door, and tempers had been raised with all the shouting and screaming, I was just plain scared to make an effort. There were two against one.

Peterson and Seubert did not dispute that Dupler had been fired on April 23rd, or that the conference lasted from 4:30 to 6 p.m., or that Dupler became very upset and sick to her stomach and had to leave to throw up. Peterson admitted that Dupler had asked to leave and that he requested that she stay and continue talking so she could indicate whether she wished to resign or be fired. Seubert said Dupler did not so indicate until "within three minutes of her leaving." Both denied that any loud or threatening language had been used, or that Dupler was detained against her will. Peterson said neither he nor Seubert even raised their voices. He said the session was so lengthy because Dupler continued to plead for another chance, and to request reasons for the dismissal.

The jury found that both Peterson and Seubert falsely imprisoned Dupler and fixed her damages at $7,500. At the same time, the jury found that Dupler's co-plaintiff husband was not entitled to any damages. It found that Peterson and Seubert had not acted maliciously and thus did not award any punitive damages.

The issue raised by a motion for review filed by defendants-respondents is: Is the jury's verdict, finding that Dupler was falsely imprisoned, supported by the evidence?

The essence of false imprisonment is the intentional, unlawful, and unconsented restraint by one person of the physical liberty of another. In *Maniaci v. Marquette University*, the court adopted the definition of false imprisonment contained in sec. 35 of the Restatement of Torts 2d, which provides in part:

> False Imprisonment
>
> (1) An actor is subject to liability to another for false imprisonment if
>
> (a) he acts intending to confine the other or a third person within boundaries fixed by the actor, and
>
> (b) his act directly or indirectly results in such a confinement of the other, and
>
> (c) the other is conscious of the confinement or is harmed by it.

Secs. 39 and 40 provide that the confinement may be caused by physical force or the threat of physical force, and the comment to sec. 40 indicates the threat may either be express, or inferred from the person's conduct. As Prosser comments:

> Character of Defendant's Act
>
> The restraint may be by means of physical barriers, or by threats of force which intimidate the plaintiff into compliance with orders. It is sufficient that he submits to an apprehension of force reasonably to be understood from the conduct of the defendant, although no force is used or even expressly threatened. . . . This gives rise, in borderline cases, to questions of fact, turning upon the details of the testimony, as to what was reasonably to be

understood and implied from the defendant's conduct, tone of voice and the like, which seldom can be reflected accurately in an appellate record, and normally are for the jury.

This is precisely such a case and we conclude that the record contains sufficient evidence from which the jury could have concluded that Mrs. Dupler was intentionally confined, against her will, by an implied threat of actual physical restraint. She testified that defendant Peterson ordered her in a loud voice to remain seated several times, after she expressed the desire to leave. She reported being "berated, screamed and hollered at," and said the reason she did not just walk out of the room was that "Mrs. Seubert had blocked the door, and tempers had been raised with all the shouting and screaming, I was just plain scared to make an effort. There were two against one." The jury obviously believed Mrs. Dupler's rather than the defendants' account of what transpired, as it had the right to do, and we conclude her testimony was sufficient to support the jury's verdict.

HERBST v. WUENNENBERG

Supreme Court of Wisconsin
83 Wis. 2d 768, 266 N.W.2d 390 (1978)

OPINION: ABRAHAMSON, J. Carol Wuennenberg appeals from a judgment entered by the trial court on a jury's special verdict finding that she falsely imprisoned Jason A. Herbst, Ronald B. Nadel, and Robert A. Ritholz ("plaintiffs"). Because there is no credible evidence to sustain a finding of false imprisonment, we reverse the judgment and order the cause remanded so that plaintiffs' complaint can be dismissed and judgment entered in favor of Wuennenberg.

I.

In April 1975, plaintiffs initiated a civil action charging Wuennenberg with false imprisonment, malicious prosecution, and abuse of process. Plaintiffs' cause of action for false imprisonment arose from an incident which took place on September 19, 1974 in the vestibule of a three-unit apartment building owned and lived in by Wuennenberg and located within the district which Wuennenberg represented as alderperson in the city of Madison. Plaintiffs' causes of action for malicious prosecution and abuse of process arose from trespass actions brought against the plaintiffs by the city of Madison after Wuennenberg had registered a complaint about the September 19, 1974 incident.

On September 19, 1974, the plaintiffs were comparing the voter registration list for the City of Madison with names on the mailboxes in multi-unit residential dwellings in Wuennenberg's aldermanic district. Plaintiffs' ultimate purpose was to "purge the voter lists" by challenging the registrations of people whose names were not on mailboxes at the addresses from which they were registered to vote.

The plaintiffs and Wuennenberg gave somewhat differing accounts of the incident which gave rise to the action for false imprisonment, but the dispositive facts are not in dispute.

According to Ritholz, whose version of the incident was corroborated by Herbst and Nadel, when the plaintiffs reached Wuennenberg's house at approximately 4:30 p.m. they entered unannounced through the outer door into a vestibule area which lies between the inner and outer doors to Wuennenberg's building. The plaintiffs stood in the vestibule near the mailboxes, which were on a wall in the vestibule approximately two feet inside the front door to the building. Neither he nor the other plaintiffs touched the mailboxes, stated Ritholz; he simply read the names listed for Wuennenberg's address from a computer printout of the registered voters in Wuennenberg's district, and the others checked to see if those names appeared on the mailboxes.

When they were half way through checking, testified Ritholz, Wuennenberg entered the vestibule from an inner door and asked plaintiffs what they were doing. Ritholz replied that they were working for the Republican party, purging voter lists. According to Ritholz, Wuennenberg became very agitated and told the plaintiffs that she did not want them in her district. "At first she told us to leave," testified Ritholz, "and we agreed to leave, but she very quickly changed her mind and wanted to know who we were. Since we already agreed to leave, we didn't think this was necessary."

After the plaintiffs had refused to identify themselves to her, Wuennenberg asked them whether they would be willing to identify themselves to the police. Ritholz replied that they would be willing to do so. Nonetheless, testified Ritholz, he would have preferred to leave, and several times he offered to leave. Both Nadel and Herbst, who agreed that Ritholz was acting as spokesman for the group, testified to Ritholz's statement to Wuennenberg that the plaintiffs were willing to identify themselves to the police.

Subsequently, Wuennenberg's husband came to the vestibule to see what was going on, and Wuennenberg asked him to call the police. About this time Wuennenberg moved from the inner door to a position in front of the outer door. According to Nadel, Wuennenberg blocked the outer door by "standing there with her arms on the pillars to the door to block our exit." The plaintiffs agreed that Wuennenberg had not threatened or intimidated them and that they neither asked her permission to leave nor made any attempt to get her to move away from the doorway. When asked why he had not attempted to leave the vestibule, each of the plaintiffs answered, in effect, that he assumed he would have had to push Wuennenberg out of the way in order to do so.

The plaintiffs waited in the vestibule, stated Ritholz, until the police came some five minutes later. They gave their names and explained their errand to a police officer who told them that they were not doing anything wrong and that they could continue checking the mailboxes in the district.

Wuennenberg testified that she and her husband were in their living room watching television and reading the paper when she heard the plaintiffs enter her vestibule. She came to the inner door, noted Herbst with his hands on the mailboxes, and asked the plaintiffs if she could be of any assistance to them. Ritholz answered "No." She next asked if they were looking for someone in the building. Ritholz again answered "No." . . . Ritholz . . . stated that the plaintiffs were election officials, volunteering their services. At this point, stated Wuennenberg, she told the plaintiffs that it did not seem proper for citizen volunteers to be interfering with mailboxes and that she considered the plaintiffs to be trespassing on her property. Ritholz, speaking in "an authoritative tone," replied that the vestibule to Wuennenberg's building was "just like a public street" and that he had a right to be there.

After Ritholz told Wuennenberg that the plaintiffs would not identify themselves to her, but that they would identify themselves to the police, Wuennenberg's husband came out to see what was happening. She explained and then told him, "It looks like you'll have to call the police." Her husband looked at the plaintiffs, and they "nodded their approval to this."

After her husband left to call the police, testified Wuennenberg, she positioned herself in front of the outer doorway because she could watch for the arrival of the police from that vantage and because "I didn't want someone trying to run away at that point." She stated she did not brace her arms against the door frame. She would not have made any effort to stop the plaintiffs had they attempted to leave, stated Wuennenberg, because, "I'm not physically capable of stopping anybody."

Plaintiffs' causes of action for false imprisonment, abuse of process, and malicious prosecution were tried before a jury. At the close of the evidence, the trial court granted Wuennenberg's motion for a directed verdict on the causes of action for malicious prosecution and abuse of process but denied Wuennenberg's motion for a directed verdict on the cause of action for false imprisonment.

The jury returned a special verdict finding that Wuennenberg had falsely imprisoned the plaintiffs and awarded Herbst, Nadel and Ritholz a total of $1,500 in actual damages. The jury found that Wuennenberg's acts had not been malicious and thus declined to award punitive damages.

II.

We reiterate the rule which this court must follow in reviewing the record to determine if the jury verdict is supported by the evidence: A jury verdict will not be upset if there is any credible evidence which under any reasonable view fairly admits of an inference supporting the findings. The evidence is to be viewed in the light most favorable to the verdict. A jury cannot base its findings on conjecture and speculation. We hold that the evidence adduced in the case before us does not support a finding that the plaintiffs were falsely imprisoned, and accordingly we reverse the judgment of the trial court.

The action for the tort of false imprisonment protects the personal interest in freedom from restraint of movement. The essence of false imprisonment is the intentional, unlawful, and unconsented restraint by one person of the physical liberty of another. *Dupler v. Seubert*, 69 Wis.2d 373, 381, 230 N.W.2d 626 (1975). There is no cause of action unless the confinement is contrary to the will of the "prisoner." It is a contradiction to say that the captor imprisoned the "prisoner" with the "prisoner's" consent. Harper & James, The Law of Torts sec. 3.7, p. 227 (1956).

In *Maniaci v. Marquette University*, 50 Wis.2d 287, 295, 184 N.W.2d 168 (1971) and in *Dupler v. Seubert, supra,* 69 Wis.2d at 381, we adopted the definition of false imprisonment given by the Restatement of Torts, Second, sec. 35:

(1) An actor is subject to liability to another for false imprisonment if

(a) he acts intending to confine the other or a third person within boundaries fixed by the actor, and

(b) his act directly or indirectly results in such a confinement of the other, and

(c) the other is conscious of the confinement or is harmed by it."

After review of the record we conclude that the evidence is not sufficient to support the conclusion that Wuennenberg's acts "directly or indirectly [resulted] in . . . a confinement of the [plaintiffs]," a required element of the cause of action.

The Restatement lists the ways in which an actor may bring about a "confinement": "by actual or apparent physical barriers" [Sec. 38, Comment *a*]; "by overpowering physical force, or by submission to physical force" [Sec. 39]; "by submission to a threat to apply physical force to the other's person immediately upon the other's going or attempting to go beyond the area in which the actor intends to confine him" [Sec. 40]; "by submission to duress other than threats of physical force, where such duress is sufficient to make the consent given ineffective to bar the action" (as by a threat to inflict harm upon a member of the other's immediate family, or his property) [Sec. 40A]; "by taking a person into custody under an asserted legal authority" [Sec. 41].

The plaintiffs do not contend that confinement was brought about by an actual or apparent physical barrier, or by overpowering physical force, or by submission to duress, or by taking a person into custody under an asserted legal authority. The parties agree that the central issue is whether there was confinement by threat of physical force and thus argue only as to the applicability of section 40 of the Restatement, which we cited and applied in *Dupler v. Seubert*, 69 Wis.2d at 382. Section 40 provides:

§ 40. Confinement by Threats of Physical Force

The confinement may be by submission to a threat to apply physical force to the other's person immediately upon the other's going or attempting to go beyond the area in which the actor intends to confine him.

The comments to section 40 provide that a person has not been confined by "threats of physical force" unless by words or other acts the actor "threatens to apply" and "has the apparent intention and ability to apply" force to his person.[2]

---

[2] Restatement of Torts, Second, Section 40, Comments:

a. Under the rule stated in sec. 35, the actor's threat may be by words as well as by other acts. It is not necessary that he do any act actually or apparently effectual in carrying a threat into immediate execution. It is enough that he threatens to apply and has the apparent intention and ability to apply force to the other's person immediately upon the other's attempting to escape from the area within which it is the actor's intention to confine him.

b. The submission must be made to a threat to apply the physical force immediately upon the other's going or attempting to go beyond the area within which the threat is intended to confine him. Submission to the threat to apply physical force at a time appreciably later than that at which the other attempts to go beyond the given area is not confinement.

It is not a sufficient basis for an action for false imprisonment that the "prisoner" remained within the limits set by the actor. Remaining within such limits is not a submission to the threat unless the "prisoner" believed that the actor had the ability to carry his threat into effect.[3]

Dean Prosser comments on the elements of false imprisonment as follows:

Character of Defendant's Act

The restraint may be by means of physical barriers, or by threats of force which intimidate the plaintiff into compliance with orders. It is sufficient that he submits to an apprehension of force reasonably to be understood from the conduct of the defendant, although no force is used or even expressly threatened. The plaintiff is not required to incur the risk of personal violence by resisting until it actually is used. It is essential, however, that the restraint be against the plaintiff's will; and if he agrees of his own free choice to surrender his freedom of motion, as by remaining in a room or accompanying the defendant voluntarily, to clear himself of suspicion or to accommodate the desires of another, rather than yielding to the constraint of a threat, then there is no imprisonment. This gives rise, in borderline cases, to questions of fact, turning upon the details of the testimony, as to what was reasonably to be understood and implied from the defendant's conduct, tone of voice and the like, which seldom can be reflected accurately in an appellate record, and normally are for the jury.

As plaintiffs state in their brief, the question before this court is whether there is any credible evidence which supports a conclusion that the plaintiffs did not consent to the confinement and that they remained in the vestibule only because Wuennenberg indicated by standing in the doorway that she had "the apparent

---

c. Submission to threats. The other must submit to the threat by remaining within the limits fixed by the actor in order to avoid or avert force threatened to the other. The other's remaining within such limits is not a submission to the threat unless the other believes that the actor has the ability to carry his threat into effect unless prevented by the other's self-defensive action or otherwise, and that it is, therefore, necessary to remain within these limits in order to escape or avert the violence threatened.

d. It is not necessary that the force threatened be such that a reasonable man would submit to confinement rather than sustain the harm threatened; it is sufficient that the actor threatens physical force with the intention of confining the other and that the other submits to the threat.

[3] Other commentators have agreed that submission must be to an apprehension of force and that a voluntary submission to a request does not constitute an imprisonment. For example, Harper and James have stated that:

. . .In ordinary practice, words are sufficient to constitute an imprisonment, if they impose a restraint upon the person and the party is accordingly restrained; for he is not obligated to incur the risk of personal violence and insult by resisting until actual violence is used.. . . . *If the plaintiff voluntarily submits there is no confinement, as where one accused of crime voluntarily accompanies his accusers for the purpose of proving his innocence.* And where no force is used, submission must be by reason of an apprehension of force or other unlawful means, *mere moral persuasion not being sufficient.* 1 Harper & James, *Torts* sec. 3.8 (1956).

intention and ability to apply" force to their persons should they attempt to leave. We have reviewed the record, and we find that it does not support this conclusion. Ritholz testified that Wuennenberg had not verbally threatened the plaintiffs, and since none of the plaintiffs asked Wuennenberg to step aside, it could be no more than speculation to conclude that Wuennenberg would not only have refused this request but also would have physically resisted had the plaintiffs attempted to leave. At best, the evidence supports an inference that plaintiffs remained in the vestibule because they assumed they would have to push Wuennenberg out of the way in order to leave. This assumption is not sufficient to support a claim for false imprisonment.

We do not intend to suggest that false imprisonment will not lie unless a "prisoner" attempts to assault his captor or unless he fails to make such attempt only because he fears harm. The plaintiffs in the case at bar were not required to obtain their freedom by taking steps dangerous to themselves or offensive to their reasonable sense of decency or personal dignity. See Restatement of Torts, Second, sec. 36. At a minimum, however, plaintiffs should have attempted to ascertain whether there was any basis to their assumption that their freedom of movement had been curtailed. False imprisonment may not be predicated upon a person's unfounded belief that he was restrained. *White v. Levy Brothers*, 306 S.W.2d 829, 830 (Ky. 1957). *Cf. Riggs National Bank v. Price*, 359 A.2d 25 (D.C. App. 1976).

. . . Plaintiffs were not "berated, screamed, and hollered at"; they outnumbered Wuennenberg three-to-one; and they gave no testimony to the effect that they were frightened of Wuennenberg or that they feared she would harm them.

Viewed in the light most favorable to plaintiffs, the evidence shows that the plaintiffs were willing to identify themselves to the police, but that they would have preferred to leave Wuennenberg's premises. It is not a sufficient basis for an action for false imprisonment that the plaintiffs remained on the premises although they would have preferred not to do so. Because plaintiffs did not submit to an apprehension of force, they were not imprisoned.

Judgment reversed, and cause remanded with directions to the trial court to enter judgment in favor of Wuennenberg dismissing plaintiffs' complaint.

You are now faced with something of a dilemma. You have only two cases, and they reach opposite conclusions. You must decide which case is more like Mr. Trune's situation, and why. If you feel strongly that Mr. Trune's case is more like either *Herbst* or *Dupler*, try to figure out why. Identify the key facts, and the rule that makes those facts relevant.

Alternatively, you may have noted similarities (and differences) to both cases, and may be thinking that Mr. Trune's case could go either way. If so, welcome to the reality of law practice! In our adversary system, there will always be lawyers on both sides of a case, using the same facts and law to argue for opposite results. Your job is to make your argument more persuasive than the other side's.

EXERCISE

1. Identify the issue in *Herbst* and *Dupler.*

2. State the rule each court applies.

3. Write down the relevant facts from each case.

4. Write down the holdings of both cases.

5. Write out the rationales for both decisions.

6. Identify the policy or policies served by the decisions.

7. Decide whether the results are fair, in a purely equitable sense. Why or why not?

8. Identify the similarities and differences between *Herbst* and *Dupler* and Mr. Trune's case.

Now you must make a prediction. Will Mr. Trune be able to make out a case of false imprisonment? Why or why not? One of the most difficult ideas to get used to is that it almost does not matter which way you answer these questions. There is no right or wrong answer, only strong or weak analysis. Even so, you should still try to reach a conclusion about the most likely result. It is almost never enough merely to describe the applicable precedents; your reader will want you to predict the most likely result when those precedents are compared to the case under consideration.

Once you choose a position, you should be prepared to explain it. Identify factual analogies, previous applications of legal rules, and policy and equity considerations that make your predicted result seem likely. You should start with a statement of the applicable legal rule as presented by the courts, explain how that rule has been applied in the past and why, and then explain how it applies to your case.

The structure of your analysis will depend on the type of question you are discussing. In our case, dealing with the tort of false imprisonment, the courts tend to break the tort down into specific elements that must be satisfied. *See Dupler* and *Herbst* excerpts. Where the decisions give you this kind of structure, use it. The format of your analysis should generally track the format of the analysis presented by the courts. It is always easier for a reader to process a message if it is structured in a familiar manner.

If you structure your analysis by elements, instead of case by case, you will probably find that you discuss each case more than once. You can avoid redundancy by presenting the facts and any other relevant aspects of the case in detail the first time you cite the case, and then referring to the case subsequently using a shorthand form, offering detail only on the portion(s) of the case on which you are relying at that point in the discussion.

You should discuss the application of each element to your case at the same time you discuss the application of that element to previously decided cases. Do not wait until you have discussed all the elements to go back and try to explain all at once how the elements apply to your case. If you save all of your application for the end, you force the reader to remember too much at once. It is much easier to deal with one element at a time, and to thoroughly understand the application of that one element, both to the decided cases and to the case being discussed.

In a truly good legal analysis, you will not stop at supporting the result you think is most likely. You will also identify, explain, and respond to the arguments likely to be made by the other side. You do not want to make better or more persuasive opposing arguments than are likely to be made by opposing counsel, but you must deal with any arguments you *know* must be made on behalf of the other party. A good lawyer understands that there are two sides to almost every argument and acknowledges the legitimacy of the other side, while at the same time explaining why the preferred result is more likely. Consider: Are the factual differences between the adverse authority and your case more significant than the factual similarities? Are the policy goals behind the rule better served by a decision along the lines you advocate? Is fairness better served by the result you have predicted? These are the questions you must answer if your legal analysis is to be considered complete and persuasive.

EXERCISE

Write out a full analysis of Mr. Trune's case in essay form. Can he make out a case for false imprisonment? Why or why not? What is the applicable rule? What do the decided cases hold? What are the reasons for those decisions? What policies are served by the decisions? How are the facts of those cases similar or dissimilar to Mr. Trune's case? How do those factual similarities or dissimilarities affect the rationales for the decisions and the policy goals being served? Why is the result you predict equitable? What are the arguments on the other side? Why are they less persuasive than the arguments in support of the result you advocate? (Remember, you should reach a conclusion regarding the most likely result in Mr. Trune's case.) If you answer all of these questions, you will be well on your way to writing good legal analysis.

§ 5.05 Statutory Analysis

Here is another example, this time adding the variable of a statute that must be interpreted and applied to the client's situation. These are your facts:

> I was visited today by the son of an old client who found himself in a bit of trouble over the weekend. Apparently there was a gathering of Vietnam veterans at the Vietnam Veterans' Memorial on the Mall [in Washington, D.C.] on Saturday. This young man, R. Abel Rowser, chose this occasion to protest what he sees as continuous U.S. aggression against weaker powers around the world. Wearing a sign on his back that said "Vietnam, the Persian Gulf, Bosnia, -- NO MORE!!!," he climbed to the top of the wall, pulled out an American flag, poured kerosene on it, and ignited it.
>
> Mr. Rowser says that he truly believed that most Vietnam Veterans would agree with him that U.S. military involvement in places such as Bosnia and the

Persian Gulf is a mistake. He believes that the Vietnam experience should have taught us to keep our noses out of other people's business. He used the flag burning to get their attention and then fully expected to lead a rally and perhaps even a march on the White House in support of his position. We may, perhaps, question his grip on reality, but I honestly believe that his description of his intent is sincere.

Mr. Rowser's recollection of what happened after he burned the flag is a bit fuzzy, perhaps because he was running for his life at the time, but he recalls a great deal of yelling and shouting. Several of the gathered veterans apparently started running in his direction in a manner that led him to believe he may have made an error in judgment, and he took off. He escaped, so there were no face-to-face confrontations with any of the veterans.

Mr. Rowser is also not entirely clear about what was happening when he arrived, but he thinks it may have been some sort of religious service. There was a man standing at the front of the crowd wearing a clerical collar, and the group was singing something.

Please read the D.C. disorderly conduct statute and the applicable cases and let me know whether you think the statute applies to Mr. Rowser's conduct under these circumstances.

This is the relevant statute:

§ 22-1121. Disorderly conduct.

Whoever, with intent to provoke a breach of the peace, or under circumstances such that a breach of the peace may be occasioned thereby: (1) Acts in such a manner as to annoy, disturb, interfere with, obstruct, or be offensive to others; (2) congregates with others on a public street and refuses to move on when ordered by the police; (3) shouts or makes a noise either outside or inside a building during the nighttime to the annoyance or disturbance of any considerable number of persons; (4) interferes with any person in any place by jostling against such person or unnecessarily crowding him or by placing a hand in the proximity of such person's pocketbook, or handbook, or handbag; or (5) causes a disturbance in any streetcar, railroad car, omnibus, or other public conveyance, by running through it, climbing through windows or upon the seats or otherwise annoying passengers or employees, shall be fined not more than $250 or imprisoned not more than 90 days, or both.

Assume that the only relevant cases are these two (edited here to include only those parts of the discussion useful for our purposes).

RODGERS v. UNITED STATES AND DISTRICT OF COLUMBIA

District of Columbia Court of Appeals
290 A.2d 395 (1972)

OPINION: HOOD, Chief Judge: In a concurrent trial before a judge and jury, the judge found appellant guilty of disorderly conduct, and the jury found him guilty of destruction of property but acquitted him of assault. Appellant makes a feeble attack on the destruction of property conviction, but we find no merit in it. His attack on the disorderly conviction requires more consideration.

Appellant was arrested following a series of incidents which occurred in and around the Crampton Auditorium on the Howard University campus. On that night a blues concert was being held in the auditorium outside of which a large crowd had gathered.

Appellant, who had no ticket, made numerous attempts to gain entry to the concert. He first presented an invalid press pass which was not accepted. He then repeatedly attempted to enter the auditorium by carrying instruments for band members. This ploy also failed. Appellant then attempted to enter through the basement accompanied by a large group of people. He finally kicked the glass out of a portion of one of the doors in the main entrance. In the course of attempting to gain entry appellant sought the assistance of the crowd outside by shouting obscenities at the campus policemen inside the auditorium and by threatening to kick down one of the doors if the crowd would follow. These activities continued for approximately 2 hours until three members of the University Special Police Force approached appellant, placed him under arrest after a scuffle and turned him over to the Metropolitan Police Department.

Appellant attacks his disorderly conduct conviction on four grounds. He first claims the information was insufficient. The information, filed under D.C. Code 1967, § 22-1121, the pertinent part of which is set out below, charged that appellant did:

> . . . under circumstances such that a breach of the peace might be occasioned thereby act in a manner as to annoy, disturb, interfere with, obstruct and be offensive to others by *loud boisterous [conduct] and fighting* in violation of Section 22-1121(1) of the District of Columbia Code.

It is appellant's contention that the information is insufficient in that it fails to charge that he engaged in any activity with an intent to provoke a breach of the peace or under circumstances which threaten a breach of the peace. We disagree. This court has held that an intent to provoke a breach of the peace is not an essential element in the proof of disorderly conduct. *Sams v. District of Columbia*, D.C. App., 244 A.2d 479 (1968); *Rockwell v. District of Columbia*, D.C. Mun. App., 172 A.2d 549 (1961). It has likewise been held that proof of an actual breach of the peace is not required under § 22-1121. *Stovall v. District of Columbia*, D.C. App., 202 A.2d 390 (1964); *Scott v. District of Columbia*, D.C. Mun. App., 184 A.2d 849 (1942). It is sufficient that the alleged conduct be under circumstances such that a breach of the peace might be occasioned thereby.

Appellant further contends that the evidence presented at trial was not sufficient to support his conviction. It is argued that the conviction should be reversed because appellant's "conviction is unsupported by any evidence to show . . . that anyone other than the police were annoyed or disturbed." We disagree. Appellant was not convicted merely for conduct which was annoying or disturbing to the policemen present, but rather, he was convicted for disorderly conduct carried out under circumstances whereby a breach of the peace might have been occasioned.

The Supreme Court in *Cantwell v. Connecticut*, 310 U.S. 296 (1940), concluded that not only violent acts but acts and words likely to produce violence on the part of others were included within the purview of breach of the peace. Here we have evidence of a course of action including both acts and words which can be said to be likely to produce violence among some or all of a crowd estimated at between 300 and 400 persons. Appellant's conduct over the 2-hour period with which we are concerned included several instances falling within the purview of § 22-1121 which may be deemed disorderly conduct. In examining his conduct as to interfering with others, it is readily apparent that appellant's conduct interfered with the orderly progression of events related to attendance at a concert where such attendance was limited to those persons holding valid tickets, a requirement which appellant did not meet at any time during the course of the evening. The record plainly reveals numerous attempts by appellant to gain entry into the auditorium. Each attempt invoked counterefforts by the special police whose task it was to maintain order during the concert. These actions on the part of the appellant were obstructive to persons holding valid tickets.

By their very nature appellant's actions would tend to slow down and even halt orderly ingress to the auditorium. The holders of valid tickets, seeking orderly admission, have a right to peaceful enjoyment of the concert without unwarranted disturbances by trespassers. It is these same ticket holders to whom appellant's actions would be patently offensive, as well as annoying and disturbing. *Heard v. Rizzo*, 281 F. Supp. 720, 741 (E.D. Pa. 1968), *aff'd*, 392 U.S. 646 (1968).

ROCKWELL v. DISTRICT OF COLUMBIA

District of Columbia Court of Appeals
172 A.2d 549 (1961)

HOOD, Associate Judge. Appellant, the leader of the American Nazi Party, was arrested for disorderly conduct on July 3, 1960, after rioting and fighting broke out at a rally he and his followers were holding in the park area at Ninth Street and Constitution Avenue, N. W. While awaiting trial on that charge he was again arrested for disorderly conduct on July 24, 1960, this time at Judiciary Square during the course of another outdoor gathering which he was attempting to address.

The two informations were consolidated for trial without a jury, and appellant was found guilty on both charges. He appeals the two convictions claiming that his freedom of speech, as guaranteed by the First Amendment, was obstructed by the arrests for disorderly conduct; that he was unable to obtain service of process on key defense witnesses; and that a certain letter he offered in evidence was wrongfully excluded by the trial court.

At trial the evidence revealed the following circumstances leading to the arrests. On July 3, 1960, appellant and his followers held a rally at Ninth Street and Constitution Avenue, N. W. At about 2:00 p. m. appellant began to speak from a platform within a roped-off area. Standing inside the enclosure were appellant's followers, some of whom wore red swastika armbands. Numbering 100 to 300 people, the audience outside the enclosure included many opponents of appellant's theories and party. Fourteen members of the U. S. Park Police were also in the audience, though only eight of them were in uniform. The spectators greeted appellant's opening words with hissing, booing and derisive chanting, the noise at times growing so loud that appellant could not be heard. This turmoil continued for about an hour and a half until suddenly an unknown number of spectators breached the enclosure and attacked appellant and his followers. As the fighting began the police moved in and arrested appellant, all of his followers and apparently some of the spectators who had participated in the attack.

During the trial there was a great deal of prosecution testimony concerning appellant's reaction to the crowd noises interrupting his speech. Witnesses testified that at different times they heard appellant shouting [various negative and offensive comments regarding Jews]. . . .

One Government witness also stated that at one point appellant started shouting, "Jews, Jews, sick -- dirty Jews, filthy Jews * * *," and shortly thereafter the spectators broke through the ropes and attacked appellant and his followers. Another prosecution witness testified that in the course of his speech appellant referred "to the Jewish race as traitors; or labeled the race as traitorous to our country."

Conceding he impatiently shouted, "Dirty Jews. Rotten Jews. Miserable Jews. Shut up, Jews. Go on and yell, Jews," appellant denied he made the other statements attributed to him. He stated he had been forewarned of possible disorder by Government officials and had done all in his power to prevent trouble, short of refusing to exercise his constitutional right of free speech. Even during the course of his speech he sent several of his men to warn the police that the crowd was getting dangerously unruly. According to appellant, the police replied to his warning by informing his men that the way to restore order was for appellant to stop talking.

On the second occasion that appellant was arrested he was conducting another rally in Judiciary Square. This time appellant -- his followers in two ranks directly behind him -- began to address an audience of about fifty people. As soon as appellant began his speech the spectators started to heckle him. Appellant responded by calling them "Jews" and "cowards," thereby increasing the intensity of the badgering from the audience. According to one prosecution witness, appellant "sort of lost his temper, and he turned around, and he says, 'Go get 'em, boys.' " At the command appellant's followers with their arms folded in front of them moved into the audience. One spectator was struck under the chin, and as a result appellant and his men were arrested for disorderly conduct.

Denying that anyone in the audience had been assaulted, appellant explained his actions on July 24 by referring to the near riot on July 3. Conscious that more trouble was to be expected if he spoke again, he had trained his men to move out into the audience at the first sign of possible disorder. Apparently these men were to surround hecklers and shout back at them, all the time under strict orders to keep their arms folded in front to avoid any suggestion of an invitation to combat. As to the command he gave on July 24, appellant testified he merely said, "First and second squads move out," which was the signal for his men to go into the audience in the manner described above.

The conviction that grew out of the July 24 charge of disorderly conduct does not even raise a constitutional question. It is clear from the record that appellant ordered his followers into a hostile audience to stop the heckling that was interrupting his speech. Under the circumstances we cannot conceive of a better way to cause disorder than that adopted by appellant. Whether appellant intended that result is not controlling. An assault on one of the spectators did occur as a direct result of appellant's command to his followers to move into the audience and the trial court could without error convict appellant of disorderly conduct.

Appellant was charged and convicted under a statute which reads in part as follows: "Whoever, with intent to provoke a breach of the peace, or under circumstances such that a breach of the peace may be occasioned thereby * * *." Code 1951, § 22-1121, Supp. VIII. It is clear that the language quoted is to be read disjunctively, and that one lacking an intent to be disorderly may nevertheless be guilty of the charge if his conduct is "under circumstances such that a breach of the peace may be occasioned thereby * * *." The only question the trial court had to decide was did appellant's statements constitute disorderly conduct under the circumstances of July 3. As we have indicated, we believe there was sufficient evidence for the trial court to answer as it did.

Affirmed.

While both *Rockwell* and Mr. Rowser's case have fairly obvious free speech implications, confine your analysis to the question of whether Mr. Rowser's actions amount to disorderly conduct. Any time you are analyzing a legal question involving a statute, you should begin with an analysis of the language of the statute itself. The relevant language of the D.C. disorderly conduct statute seems to be the following:

> Whoever, with intent to provoke a breach of the peace, or under circumstances such that a breach of the peace may be occasioned thereby: (1) Acts in such a manner as to annoy, disturb, interfere with, obstruct, or be offensive to others. . . .

Look at the statute and be sure you understand why we have chosen this language.

Did Mr. Rowser intend to provoke a breach of the peace? Does that matter? Why or why not? What do the cases say on this point?

Did Mr. Rowser act under circumstances likely to occasion a breach of the peace? How do you know? Can you answer this question without reference to the decided cases?

EXERCISE

1. Identify the issue(s) in the *Rodgers* and *Rockwell* cases.

2. Identify the statutory language applied by the court in each case.

3. Identify the relevant facts of each case

4. State the holdings of those cases.

5. Describe the rationales of those cases.

6. Identify the policy or policies served by the decisions.

7. Decide whether the results are equitable. Why or why not?

8. Identify the similarities and differences among the *Rodgers* case, the *Rockwell* case and Mr. Rowser's situation. Consider facts, issues, policies, and equitable issues.

Now go through the same process you went through with Mr. Trune's case. What is the most likely outcome? Why? Have you identified the arguments on both sides? (Be careful here -- since both of the decided cases find disorderly conduct, many people have a tendency to find it automatically in Mr. Rowser's case as well.) How will you structure your discussion? Since there are no elements here, you may find it useful to deal briefly with the intent question first, then analyze the decided cases in detail in the context of whether they took place under circumstances likely to cause a breach of the peace, comparing Mr. Rowser's situation to each case as you go along.

If another approach seems more logical to you, try it -- you will find that your written product is better and more persuasive if you structure it in a way that makes sense to you. Many students make the mistake of trying to copy examples or to write the way they think their instructor is telling them to write. Follow your own instincts, while observing the general guidelines discussed here.

EXERCISE

Write out, in essay form, your analysis of Mr. Rowser's case. Predict whether he will be convicted of disorderly conduct and justify your prediction, using both the language of the statute and the decided cases. Focus on important facts, and use policy and equity arguments where appropriate. Don't forget to discuss and analyze the arguments on the other side, explaining why you find them less persuasive.

§ 5.06 Legal Analysis Checklist

Until you have performed enough legal analyses that the process becomes second nature to you, you might want to refer to this checklist to be sure you have not left out any important steps that your reader will be expecting to see in your written product. There is no magic format that will work in every context, or for every style, so you will have to experiment until you find the right structure for you, the case you are addressing, and the particular audience for the document. Nevertheless, any good legal analysis must contain the following information, presented in some logical order.

_____ Make your prediction. Your written analysis should begin with a statement of your ultimate conclusion.

_____ Identify the rule that governs your case, and cite to its source, whether statutory or common law.

_____ Identify the structure of your argument, using elements of a tort, statutory requirements, or any other method that will help the reader understand how your ideas relate to each other.

_____ Identify the key facts of your case.

_____ Discuss the facts, holdings, and rationales of all important relevant cases.

_____ Compare the facts of those cases with the facts of your case, and explain why the courts' rationales apply or do not apply. Do not forget to argue the equities of the case or the policies behind the courts' decisions, if such arguments are helpful to your position.

_____ Identify any persuasive adverse authority or arguments likely to be presented by the other side. Explain why your predicted result is the better outcome. Be careful here; remember not to make arguments that are better than opposing counsel is likely to make.

_____ Summarize the key points in your argument. Persuade the reader of the overall strength of your position by reminding him or her of the highlights of what you have presented.

CHAPTER 6

RESEARCH STRATEGY

§ 6.01 Introduction

For purposes of this discussion of research strategy, we assume that you have already learned or are learning how to use specific materials in the library. The goal of this chapter is to teach you how to integrate your knowledge of the materials in the library with what we are trying to teach you about legal writing and analysis.

In other words, once you have your writing assignment in hand, how do you approach the research process? Where do you start? How many places do you look? When do you stop? How do you keep track of your research so that you don't end up covering the same ground repeatedly? We will take up each question in turn, using the Paul Trune problem we analyzed in Chapter 5. As you may recall, the issue was whether Mr. Trune could bring a civil action for false imprisonment.

As we go through this discussion, do not be concerned if you see angles you would like to try that are not discussed here. This is an attempt to show you how one person might effectively research this particular problem. If there are other approaches you would try, go ahead; you may find that they work for you, or you may find that they were not included because they were unproductive.

§ 6.02 Where do you start?

As you begin the research process, identify the key legal terminology that will help you access the appropriate research sources. If you are unfamiliar with the area of law presented by the research problem, you need to begin your research with a secondary resource that discusses the broad legal principles and rules that govern the area. Examples of such sources include hornbooks, treatises, and legal encyclopedias. If you do have some knowledge of the field, you can go directly to sources of primary authority such as digests and annotated statutes. We will discuss the use of each of these resources in Mr. Trune's case.

[1] Statutes

Many law students reflexively think of statutes when beginning research tasks. If you are researching a problem in an area that is likely to have been addressed by a legislature, that is not a bad reflex to have. When you are unfamiliar with the law in your jurisdiction, begin by determining whether there is a relevant statute.

Is there a false imprisonment statute in Wisconsin? Section 940.30 of the Wisconsin statutes, governing false imprisonment, provides that "[w]hoever intentionally confines or restrains another without the person's consent and with knowledge that he or she has no lawful authority to do so is guilty of a Class E felony."

Before you start searching the annotations under Section 940.30 for helpful cases, read the statute carefully. The question you have been asked is whether Paul Trune can bring a *civil* action for false imprisonment. You are researching false imprisonment as a tort, not a crime. Thus, the statute's characterization of false imprisonment as a felony should tip you off that the statute does not apply to your client's situation, and you should ignore it.

[2] Treatises

If you are researching an area, such as tort law, that tends to be governed almost exclusively by common law decisions, how do you begin your research? The answer to this question will depend in large part on how familiar you are with the subject matter of your research project. If you know the elements of false imprisonment, and are familiar with the key terminology, you will probably begin with the relevant digests. For purposes of this discussion, however, we will assume that you need some background information about the topic first, and that you would therefore start with a secondary source such as a treatise. In a treatise, you can read generally about the applicable legal principles as well as begin to identify specific cases. *Prosser and Keeton on the Law of Torts* (5th ed.) is one of the primary treatises in the area of tort law. Here is a sample page from the false imprisonment section of the treatise:*

---

* Copyright © 1984 by West Publishing Company. Reprinted with permission.

unusual consequential damages as the theft of the plaintiff's automobile when the arrest compels the plaintiff to leave it unguarded.[25] Because of the malevolent intentions which usually accompany false imprisonment, or at least the reckless disregard of the plaintiff's interests, it is usually a proper case for the award of punitive damages;[26] but where any such element of bad intent or wanton misconduct is lacking, and the imprisonment is the result of a mere mistake, either as to identity of the party or as to the propriety of arrest or imprisonment, punitive damages are denied.[27]

Character of Defendant's Act

The restraint may be by means of physical barriers,[28] or by threats of force which intimidate the plaintiff into compliance with orders.[29] It is sufficient that the plaintiff submits to an apprehension of force reasonably

to be understood from the conduct of the defendant, although no force is used or even expressly threatened.[30] The plaintiff is not required to incur the risk of personal violence by resisting until it actually is used.[31] It is essential, however, that the restraint be against the plaintiff's will; and if one agrees of one's own free choice to surrender freedom of motion, as by remaining in a room or accompanying another voluntarily, to clear oneself of suspicion or to accommodate the desires of the other,[32] rather than yielding to the constraint of a threat, then there is no imprisonment.[33] This gives rise, in borderline cases, to questions of fact, turning upon the details of the testimony, as to what was reasonably to be understood and implied from the defendant's conduct, tone of voice and the like, which seldom can be reflected fully in an appellate record, and normally are for the jury.[34]

Bolton v. Vellines, 1897, 94 Va. 393, 26 S.E. 847; Schiller v. Strangis, D.Mass.1982, 540 F.Supp. 605.

25. Whitehead v. Stringer, 1919, 106 Wash. 501, 180 P. 486.

26. Atkinson v. Dixie Greyhound Lines, 5th Cir. 1944, 143 F.2d 477, certiorari denied 323 U.S. 758, 65 S.Ct. 92, 89 L.Ed. 607; Lindquist v. Friedman's, 1937, 366 Ill. 232, 8 N.E.2d 625; Sternberg v. Hogg, 1934, 254 Ky. 761, 72 S.W.2d 421; Parrott v. Bank of America National Trust & Savings Association, 1950, 97 Cal.App.2d 14, 217 P.2d 89; McAleer v. Good, 1907, 216 Pa. 473, 65 A. 934. See supra, § 2.

27. Kroger Grocery & Baking Co. v. Waller. 1945. 208 Ark. 1063, 189 S.W.2d 361; Walker v. Tucker, 1955, 131 Colo. 198, 280 P.2d 649; S. H. Kress & Co. v. Powell, 1938, 132 Fla. 471, 180 So. 757; Shelton v. Barry, 1946, 328 Ill.App. 497, 66 N.E.2d 697; Heinze v. Murphy, 1942, 180 Md. 423, 24 A.2d 917.

28. Salisbury v. Poulson, 1918, 51 Utah 552, 172 P. 315; cf. Cieplinski v. Severn, 1929, 269 Mass. 261, 168 N.E. 722 (refusal to stop moving automobile).

29. Meints v. Huntington, 8th Cir. 1921, 276 F. 245; Mahan v. Adam, 1924, 144 Md. 355, 124 A. 901; Garnier v. Squires, 1900, 62 Kan. 321, 62 P. 1005; Second Restatement of Torts, § 40.

30. Stevens v. O'Neill, 1900, 51 App.Div. 364, 64 N.Y.S. 663, affirmed 1902, 169 N.Y. 375, 62 N.E. 424; Hales v. McCrory-McLellan Corp., 1963, 260 N.C. 568, 133 S.E.2d 225; W. T. Grant Co. v. Owens. 1928, 149 Va. 906, 141 S.E. 860; Sinclair Refining Co. v. Meek, 1940, 62 Ga.App. 850, 10 S.E.2d 76; Panisko v. Dreihelbis, 1942, 113 Mont. 310, 124 P.2d 997.

One's belief that one is being restrained by another is not sufficient unless there is reasonable ground to

apprehend force upon an attempt to assert liberty. Hoffman v. Clinic Hospital, 1938, 213 N.C. 669, 197 S.E. 161.

31. Brushaber v. Stegemann, 1871, 22 Mich. 266; Meints v. Huntington, 8th Cir. 1921, 276 F. 245; Halliburton-Abbott Co. v. Hodge, 1935, 172 Okl. 175, 44 P.2d 122; and see cases cited in the preceding note.

32. State for Use of Powell v. Moore, 1965, 252 Miss. 471, 174 So.2d 352; Meinecke v. Skaggs, 1950, 123 Mont. 308, 213 P.2d 237; Hunter v. Laurent, 1925, 158 La. 874, 104 So. 747; James v. MacDougall & Southwick Co., 1925, 134 Wash. 314, 235 P. 812. Cf. Great Atlantic & Pacific Tea Co. v. Billups, 1934, 253 Ky. 126, 69 S.W.2d 5.

33. Payson v. Macomber, 1861, 85 Mass. (3 Allen) 69; Sweeney v. F. W. Woolworth Co., 1924, 247 Mass. 277, 142 N.E. 50; Knowlton v. Ross, 1915, 114 Me. 18, 95 A. 281; see Powell v. Champion Fiber Co., 1908, 150 N.C. 12, 63 S.E. 159.

34. Compare Durgin v. Cohen, 1926, 168 Minn. 77, 209 N.W. 532; Lester v. Albers Super Markets, Inc., 1952, 94 Ohio App. 313, 114 N.E.2d 529; and Swetnam v. F. W. Woolworth Co., 1957, 83 Ariz. 189, 318 P.2d 364, where it was held that no implied threat of force was to be found, with Garner v. Mears, 1958, 97 Ga. App. 506, 103 S.E.2d 610, and Jacques v. Childs Dining Hall Co., 1923, 244 Mass. 438, 138 N.E. 843, where the jury were permitted to find it. Also compare, upon almost identical facts, the opposite conclusions in Weiler v. Herzfeld-Phillipson Co., 1926, 189 Wis. 554, 208 N.W. 599 (also Safeway Stores, Inc. v. Amburn, Tex.Civ.App. 1965, 388 S.W.2d 443), and Dillon v. Sears-Roebuck, Inc., 1934, 126 Neb. 357, 253 N.W. 331.

If you look closely, you will see one Wisconsin case in footnote 34: *Weiler v. Herzfeld–Phillipson Co.*, 189 Wis. 554, 208 N.W. 599 (1926).

[3] The Restatement of Torts

Another good source of general rules, at least in areas of the law for which they exist, are the Restatements. While the Restatements are not the law, unless the courts in your jurisdiction have adopted the relevant provisions, they are often persuasive. In any event, the Restatements provide a good discussion of basic principles, with examples of how those principles can be applied, and the Appendix volumes contain relevant cases, so you can determine whether the Restatement has been cited in your jurisdiction. If a Restatement provision applies to your case, you should not overlook this resource as you search for applicable law.

You should first consult the general index at the end of the pertinent Restatement (*i.e.*, Torts, Contracts, *etc.*). The general index will direct you to the appropriate volume, which will include a more detailed index. Here is the relevant portion of the index for Volume 1 of the Restatement (Second) of Torts:*

---

* Copyright © 1965 by The American Law Institute. Reprinted with the permission of the American Law Institute.

F

FALSE ARREST
See False Imprisonment.

FALSE IMPRISONMENT
Generally, §§ 35–45.
Accompanying actor by compulsion as, § 36 c.
Aid in escape from confinement, refusal of, § 45.
Area of confinement, materiality of, § 36 b.
Arrest,
    As constituting false imprisonment, § 41 a–h.

       [1 Restatement of Torts 2d]

FALSE IMPRISONMENT—Cont'd
Arrest—Cont'd
    False arrest as false imprisonment, § 118 b.
    Instigating or participating in, liability for, § 45 A.
    Misconduct subsequent to, § 136.
    Touching as, § 41 h.
Barriers, confinement by, § 38.
Blocking highway as, § 36 d.
Boundaries fixed by actor, necessity of confinement within, § 35 (1) (a).
Cause of confinement, materiality of, § 37.
Completeness of confinement within boundaries fixed by actor, § 36 (1) (2).
Confinement,
    Asserted legal authority, § 41.
    Completeness of, § 36 (1) (2).
    How caused, § 37.
    Knowledge of, necessity of, § 42.
    Physical barrier, § 38.
    Physical force, § 39.
    Threats of physical force, § 40.
    What constitutes, § 36.
Consciousness of confinement, see Knowledge, infra, this title.
Consent,
    Arrest, effect of consent to release after, § 136 f.
    What constitutes consent to confinement, §§ 49, 892–892 D.
Constant motion, effect of place of confinement being in, § 36 c.
Custody under asserted legal authority, confinement based upon, § 41.
Desire to offend, confinement as requiring, § 44.
Direct or indirect causation of confinement, §§ 35 (1) (b), 37 a.
Duress other than threat of force, as confinement, § 40 A.
Duty to release another from confinement, refusal to perform, § 45.

Escape,
    Aid in, refusal to give, § 45.
    Completeness of confinement as affected by reasonable means of, § 36 (2).
    Knowledge of plaintiff of, as affecting confinement, § 36 a.
    Means of, as affecting confinement, § 36 a.
    Physical barriers, prevention of means of escape as confinement by, § 38 b.
    Refusal of plaintiff to utilize means of, § 36 a.
Exclusion from area as confinement, § 36 b.
Extent of protection of interest in freedom from confinement, § 35 (2) b.

FALSE IMPRISONMENT—Cont'd

False arrest, see Arrest, supra, this title.

Family members, threat to inflict harm upon, § 40 A a.

Force, see Physical Force, infra, this title.

Harm as essential to liability, § 35 (2) h.

Harm from confinement as factor, § 35 (1) (c).

Harmless confinement, sufficiency of, § 35 (2).

Identity of actor, necessity of knowledge of, § 42 c.

Instigating, liability for, § 45 A.

Intention to confine, necessity of, §§ 35, 37.
   Third persons, act intended to affect, § 43.

Knowledge,
   Actor's knowledge that act would result in confinement, § 35 (1) (a).
   Harm without knowledge of confinement, effect of, § 42 b.
   Identity of actor, necessity of knowledge of, § 42 c.
   Lack of knowledge of confinement, effect of, § 42 a.
   Means of escape, plaintiff's knowledge of, § 36 a.
   Necessity of knowledge of confinement, § 42.

Legal authority, confinement under assertion of, § 41.

Legal cause of confinement, actor's act as, § 37.

Malice, necessity of, § 44.

Mistake of law or fact, submission to asserted authority under, § 41 d.

Negligence, sufficiency of confinement as a result of, § 35 (2) h.

Notice, see Knowledge, supra, this title.

Participating in, liability for, § 45 A.

Personal hostility, confinement as requiring, § 44.

Physical barriers, confinement by, § 38.

Physical force, confinement by, § 39.
   Accompanying actor as a result of, § 36 c.
   Asserted legal authority without, submission to, § 41 b, c.
   Threats of, § 40.
   Use of, § 117.

Place of confinement, § 36 b, c.

Presence of actor required in submission to asserted legal authority, § 41 f.

Prevention of another from going in particular direction as confinement, § 36 (3).

The applicable language of many of these sections is quoted in the decisions discussed in Chapter 5, so we have not reproduced it again here. Here is a sample annotation of a familiar case from an Appendix volume:*

* Appendix Volume through June 1984, § 1-309. Copyright © 1986 by The American Law Institute. Reprinted with the permission of the American Law Institute.

Wis.1978. Quot. and fol. Appeal by defendant from the trial court's judgment entered on a jury's special verdict finding that defendant had falsely imprisoned plaintiffs. Defendant was the owner of, and a resident at, a three-unit apartment building where the incident occurred. She also represented her district as alderperson in her city. Plaintiffs were comparing the voter registration list for the city with names on the mailboxes in defendant's aldermanic district. Plaintiffs' ultimate purpose was to purge the voter lists. Plaintiffs had walked into the vestibule of defendant's building when defendant heard them and questioned them about what they were doing. Plaintiffs reportedly told defendant that they were working for the Republican Party, purging voter lists. When plaintiffs refused to identify themselves, defendant asked if they would be willing to identify themselves to the police. Plaintiffs said that they would be willing to do so, and defendant's husband called the police while defendant stood blocking the doorway. There was no evidence that defendant threatened or intimidated plaintiffs, that plaintiffs asked defendant's permission to leave, or that they made any attempt to get her to move from the doorway. The court reversed and remanded, holding, inter alia, that plaintiffs' beliefs that they were being restrained were unfounded. Herbst v. Wuennenberg, 83 Wis.2d 768, 266 N.W.2d 391, 395.

As noted, the Restatement is cited extensively in both *Herbst* and *Dupler*, so you should not be surprised to find the *Herbst* case here. If you check earlier volumes of the Appendix, you will also find *Dupler*. Remember that you must check several volumes to be sure you have discovered all of the relevant authority.

[4] Legal Encyclopedias

Finally, legal encyclopedias are another good source of general rules and a good starting point for finding primary authority. If you have found a good treatise, you may not need to check an encyclopedia as well. Looking in an encyclopedia may also be unnecessary if there is an applicable Restatement, at least if the Restatement has been adopted in your jurisdiction. If, however, you have not located any other resources that can help you learn the basic rules and terminology of your field of inquiry, encyclopedias should do the job. Until you become comfortable with legal research and the resources available to you, you may want to check more than one source anyway, to be sure you genuinely understand the legal issues involved, and to see if the different sources contain different types of useful information.

Many states have their own legal encyclopedias, and you should start there if you can find one. In this discussion, we will take on the slightly more difficult task of trying to find Wisconsin precedent in the general encyclopedias, *Corpus Juris Secundum* and *American Jurisprudence*. You would follow the same procedure in a state encyclopedia as we do here. If you look in Volume 32 of *American Jurisprudence 2d*, at the start of the chapter on false imprisonment you will find the following information: *

---

* Reprint permission has been granted by the copyright holder, Lawyers Cooperative Publishing, a division of Thomson Legal Publishing Inc.

FALSE IMPRISONMENT

by

Leonard I. Reiser, J.D.

Scope of Topic: The discussion herein concerns false arrest or imprisonment as a tort, primarily, treating such matters as the nature and elements of the wrong, liability therefor, circumstances constituting a justification thereof, the proceedings for its redress by one aggrieved thereby, and the damages recoverable therefor. Some consideration is given also to false imprisonment as a crime.

---

b. Asserting Legal Authority

(1) In General [§§ 20–24]

§ 20. Generally
§ 21. Arrest at unlawful or unreasonable time
§ 22. Arrest outside territorial jurisdiction of arresting officer
§ 23. Failure to declare authority and intention to arrest
§ 24. Use of excessive force

(2) Conduct Following Arrest [§§ 25–32]

§ 25. Delay in presentment before magistrate
§ 26. —As trespass ab initio
§ 27. —Factors affecting liability
§ 28. —Liability of one other than arresting person or his superior or employer
§ 29. —Waiver of delay in presentment before magistrate
§ 30. Denial of opportunity to give bail
§ 31. —Waiver of opportunity to give bail
§ 32. Delay in releasing prisoner

c. Commitment of Mentally Ill Person

§ 33. Generally; commitment pursuant to valid legal proceeding
§ 34. Immunity of judges
§ 35. Immunity or privilege of examining physician
§ 36. Reliance on advice of counsel as defense
§ 37. Liability for particular acts or omissions

As you scan the outline, section II, "Elements," should look like a good place to start. More specifically, sections 8–11 and 14–18, dealing with the basic elements of unlawfulness and confinement, should look particularly interesting. Those sections will give you a general discussion of when confinement is unlawful and what constitutes sufficient restraint. The next step is to look for cases in your jurisdiction demonstrating how the courts have applied those concepts.

When you look under sections 8–11, however, you will find that only the footnotes to section 8 contain any citations to Wisconsin cases. Moreover, the footnotes cite only two Wisconsin cases. The first is *Weiler v. Herzfeld-Phillipson Co.*, 208 N.W. 599 (Wis. 1926) (n. 65), which, you may recall, was also cited in *Prosser and Keeton* (holding that there is no false imprisonment where a supervisor interrogates an employee suspected of dishonesty in the supervisor's office for a lengthy period; the court pointed out that the employee was being compensated for the time, and was under the direction of the employer so long as she remained an employee). The second is *Bergeron v. Peyton*, 82 N.W. 291 (Wis. 1900) (n. 67) (holding that there was false imprisonment where the police arrested an individual suspected of larceny for the purpose of inducing the individual to repay the money rather than for the purpose of beginning criminal proceedings). Here is a sample of what you would find in the *American Jurisprudence* volume: *

----

* Reprint permission has been granted by the copyright holder, Lawyers Cooperative Publishing, a division of Thomson Legal Publishing Inc.

32 Am Jur 2d   FALSE IMPRISONMENT   **§ 8**

B. Imprisonment, Confinement, or Restraint [§§ 8–37]

1. In General [§§ 8–12]

§ 8. Generally; unlawfulness.

Mere loss of freedom cannot constitute false imprisonment even though it is unjust;[64] the imprisonment, confinement, or restraint must be unlawful.[65] No system of jurisprudence has yet been invented that is infallible. Mistake and injustice to the individual will occur under any judicial system, in the application of either civil or criminal jurisprudence. One may be acquitted upon the merits of the case, or discharged upon some question of law, but that fact does not in and of itself make the restraint placed upon his liberty false imprisonment.[66] But any intentional restraint by one person of the personal liberty of another is unlawful unless justified by some valid authority or right.[67] Generally, restraint or detention, reasonable under the circumstances and in time and manner, imposed for the purpose of preventing another from inflicting personal injuries or interfering with or damaging real or personal property in one's lawful possession or custody, is not unlawful.[68]

One who is detained for no fault of his own, but merely as a witness to the

---

64. McMechen ex rel. Willey v Fidelity & Casualty Co., 145 W Va 660, 116 SE2d 388.

65. Martin v Lincoln Park West Corp. (CA7 Ill) 219 F2d 622; Page v Citizens' Banking Co., 111 Ga 73, 36 SE 418; Meyers v Dunn, 126 Ky 548, 104 SW 352; New York, P. & N. R. Co. v Waldron, 116 Md 441, 82 A 709; Durgin v Cohen, 168 Minn 77, 209 NW 532; Levin v Burlington, 129 NC 184, 39 SE 822; Finney v Zingale, 82 W Va 422, 95 SE 1046; Weiler v Herzfeld-Phillipson Co., 189 Wis 554, 208 NW 599.

The gist of any complaint for false arrest or false imprisonment is an unlawful detention. Marshall v District of Columbia (Dist Col App) 391 A2d 1374.

66. Coverstone v Davies, 38 Cal 2d 315, 239 P2d 876, cert den 344 US 840, 97 L Ed 653, 73 S Ct 50; Brinkman v Drolesbaugh, 97 Ohio St 171, 119 NE 451.

An acquittal is not a bar to an adjudication that an arrest based upon an offense committed in the presence of the officer is lawful. People v Edge, 406 Ill 490, 94 NE2d 359 (pointing out that judgment of not guilty is only determination that evidence presented did not approve offense charged); Ryan v Conover, 59 Ohio App 361, 11 Ohio Ops 565, 26 Ohio L Abs 593, 18 NE2d 277.

If the information laid before a justice of the peace is sufficient to give him jurisdiction and to call upon him for a decision as to whether a warrant should issue, a warrant issued on that information is not void, and the arrest is not unlawful, even though the complainant is unable at the trial to sustain his charges, or though the accused is able to meet them fully. Vittorio v St. Regis Paper Co., 239 NY 148, 145 NE 913.

An arrest is not necessarily unlawful so as to afford ground for an action of false imprisonment, merely because the person arrested was innocent of the offense for which the arrest was made, if the forms of law were observed, as where the warrant was issued upon proper complaint by an official clothed with authority to issue it, and the arrest was made by a proper officer in a lawful manner. Finney v Zingale, 82 W Va 422, 95 SE 1046.

67. Meints v Huntington (CA8 Minn) 276 F 245; Floyd v State, 12 Ark 43; Maxwell v Maxwell, 189 Iowa 7, 177 NW 541; Palmer v Maine C. R. Co., 92 Me 399, 42 A 800; McAleer v Good, 216 Pa 473, 65 A 934; Smith v Clark, 37 Utah 116, 106 P 653; Goodell v Tower, 77 Vt 61, 58 A 790; Bergeron v Peyton, 106 Wis 377, 82 NW 291.

As to justification, see §§ 80 et seq., infra.

68. Sindle v New York City Transit Authority, 33 NY2d 293, 352 NYS2d 183, 307 NE2d 245 (school bus driver acting to protect bus from damage by student-passengers).

As to protection of personal or property rights, generally, see §§ 88, 91, infra.

65

In sections 14-18, you will find the *Weiler* case again, under section 15, n. 32, but no new cases. An examination of the pocket part discloses no additional Wisconsin cases. The cases you have found will get you started on the question of what constitutes false imprisonment in Wisconsin, but given their age, you should try to find something a little more recent.

An examination of Volume 35 of *Corpus Juris Secundum* will yield a similar outline:*

---

* Copyright © 1960 by The American Law Book Co. Reprinted with permission of West Publishing Company, now the copyright owner.

35 C. J. S.

FALSE IMPRISONMENT

This Title includes restraint of the person of another, without sufficient authority, not merely incident to a malicious prosecution; justification or excuse for such restraint; and liabilities and remedies therefor, civil or criminal.

Matters not in this Title, treated elsewhere in this work, see Descriptive-Word Index

Analysis

See also descriptive word index in the back of this Volume

(Matthew Bender & Co., Inc.) (Pub.676)

FALSE IMPRISONMENT

 (Pub.676)

"Nature and Elements," sections 9, 11, 14, and 23, again dealing with basic requirements of restraint and unlawfulness, should look like good places to start. In the main volume, you will find no Wisconsin cases under any of these notes, but if you look in the pocket part, you will find three: *Drabek v. Sabley*, 142 N.W.2d 798 (Wis. 1966) (finding unreasonable restraint and therefore false imprisonment where defendant caught a boy throwing snowballs at his car, and then took him downtown to turn him over to police instead of contacting his parents, who lived across the street) (Sec. 9, n. 82); *Herbst v. Wuennenberg* (discussed in Chapter 5) (Sec. 9, n. 90); and *Maniaci v. Marquette University*, 184 N.W.2d 168 (Wis. 1971) (holding that there is no false imprisonment where there is a police arrest that follows the formal requirements of the applicable law) (Sec. 14, n. 52). Here is a sample of the relevant text from the main volume and the footnotes from the 1997 Cumulative Annual Pocket Part for *Corpus Juris Secundum*:*

---

* Main volume copyright © 1960 by The American Law Book Co.; 1997 Pocket Part copyright © 1997 by West Publishing Company. Both reprinted with permission of West Publishing Company.

35 C.J.S.

FALSE IMPRISONMENT § 9

§ 9. Sufficiency

Any intentional conduct chargeable to defendant that results in the placing of a person in a position where he cannot exercise his will in going where he may lawfully go may constitute false imprisonment.

The imprisonment, detention, or restraint on which an action for false imprisonment may be based may have been effectuated by the employment of actual force, by threats, or by the causing of plain-tiff to submit to reasonably apprehended force or to apparent legal authority[81] as discussed infra §§ 10–12. Any intentional conduct chargeable to defendant that results in the placing of a person in a position where he cannot exercise his will in going where he may lawfully go may constitute false imprisonment.[82] Although there is authority to the contrary,[82.5] generally, it is not essential that there shall have been an actual arrest of plaintiff,[83] or

---

§§ 9–10 FALSE IMPRISONMENT

35 C.J.S.

a formal declaration of arrest,[84] or that the person detaining plaintiff should have any real or pretended authority for taking him into custody.[85] It is sufficient if one is restrained unlawfully in any manner of his right of freedom of locomotion;[86] and shadowing a person so as to show that, if necessary, force will be used to detain him,[87] or using improper means to decoy him into the jurisdiction,[88] may constitute false imprisonment. Where plaintiff is detained for a refusal to comply with a condition, which defendant had no right to impose, defendant is liable.[89]

The detention must have been against the will of the person detained,[90] who must have been conscious of confinement.[90.5] A mere voluntary remaining in custody on the part of plaintiff is not sufficient,[91] as, for example, where he submits to avoid the payment of a small license fee,[92] nor is a voluntary yielding to misrepresentations and threats inducing plaintiff to go to another place and remain in concealment for a time.[93]

Detention in or of automobile. The driver of a car in which plaintiff is unlawfully made an unwilling passenger falsely imprisons him,[94] as where the driver so operates the automobile that plaintiff may not leave it with safety,[95] and a plaintiff may be falsely imprisoned by a combination of orders to remain and disabling of his car which in concert prevent his departure.[96] Where defendant unlawfully controls and moves plaintiff's car against plaintiff's will and while plaintiff lawfully remains therein, defendant is guilty of a false imprisonment, even though plaintiff was at liberty to step from the car and depart as a pedestrian.[97]

§ 9. Sufficiency

Library References

False Imprisonment ⊕6.

page 633

81. U.S.—Clark v. Kroger Co., C.A.Ind., 382 F.2d 562.

Ky.—Grayson Variety Store, Inc. v. Shaffer, 402 S.W.2d 424.

La.—Clark v. I. H. Rubenstein, Inc., 326 So.2d 497, on remand 335 So.2d 545.

Or.—Roberts v. Coleman, 365 P.2d 79, 228 Or. 286—Lukas v. J. C. Penney Co., 378 P.2d 717, 233 Or. 345 Gaffney v. Payless Drug Stores, 492 P.2d 474, 261 Or. 148.

Wash.—Kilcup v. McManus, 394 P.2d 375, 64 Wash.2d 771.

    Moore v. Pay'N Save Corp., 581 P.2d 159, 20 Wash.App. 482.

82. Ga.—Lowe v. Turner, 154 S.E.2d 792, 115 Ga. App. 503.

Ill.—Karow v. Student Inns, Inc., 357 N.E.2d 682, 2 Ill.Dec. 515, 43 Ill.App.3d 878, 98 A.L.R.3d 531.

Minn.—Blaz v. Molin Concrete Products Co., 244 N.W.2d 277, 309 Minn. 382.

Neb.—Herbrick v. Samardick & Co., 101 N.W.2d 488, 169 Neb. 833—Schmidt v. Richman Gordman, Inc., 215 N.W.2d 105, 191 Neb. 345.

N.M.—Martinez v. Sears, Roebuck & Co., App., 467 P.2d 37, 81 N.M. 371.

Tex.—Kroger Co. v. Warren, Civ.App., 420 S.W.2d 218.

Vt.—State v. May, 367 A.2d 672, 134 Vt. 556.

Wis.—Drabek v. Sabley, 142 N.W.2d 798, 31 Wis.2d 184, 20 A.L.R.3d 1435.

Wyo.—Waters v. Brand, 497 P.2d 875.

Incarceration in office

Mo.—Schwane v. Kroger Co., App., 480 S.W.2d 113.

Objection standard

Alaska—City of Nome v. Ailak, 570 P.2d 162.

Momentary pause in progress

    Momentary pause in progress of grocery store patron through check out line was not too inconsequential to constitute "detention" or "imprisonment" for purposes of patron's false imprisonment claim.

Ga.—Williams v. Food Lion, Inc., 446 S.E.2d 221, 213 Ga.App. 865.

83. Fla.—Washington County Kennel Club, Inc. v. Edge, App., 216 So.2d 512.

N.Y.—Pearson v. Pearson, 212 N.Y.S.2d 281, 29 Misc.2d 677.

page 634

85. Va.—Zayre of Va., Inc. v. Gowdy, 147 S.E.2d 710, 207 Va. 47.

86. U.S.—Trahan v. Bellsouth Telecommunications, Inc., W.D.La., 881 F.Supp. 1080, affd. 71 F.3d 876.

N.M.—Diaz v. Lockheed Electronics, App., 618 P.2d 372, 95 N.M. 28.

Wash.—Kilcup v. McManus, 394 P.2d 375, 64 Wash.2d 771.

90. Miss.—State for Use of Powell v. Moore, 174 So.2d 352, 252 Miss. 471.

N.C.—Black v. Clark's Greensboro, Inc., 139 S.E.2d 199, 263 N.C. 226.

    Shaw v. Rose's Stores, Inc., 205 S.E.2d 789, 22 N.C.App. 140.

Tex.—Browning v. Pay-Less Self Service Shoes, Inc., Civ.App., 373 S.W.2d 71.

Wis.—Herbst v. Wuennenberg, 266 N.W.2d 391, 83 Wis.2d 768.

Hospital patient

Ohio—Bailie v. Miami Valley Hospital, 221 N.E.2d 217, 8 Ohio Misc. 193.

90.5 N.Y.—Sager v. Rochester General Hosp., 647 N.Y.S.2d 408—Mubarez v. State, 453 N.Y.S.2d 549, 115 Misc.2d 57.

Contemporaneous awareness of unlawful restraint or confinement is not an essential element of the tort of false imprisonment, instead, the relevant factor is whether the unlawful restraint or confinement resulted in harm.[90.10]

90.10 Cal.—Scofield v. Critical Air Medicine, Inc., 2 Dist., 52 Cal.Rptr.2d 915, 45 C.A.4th 990, mod. on denial of reh., review den.

91. U.S.—Reicheneder v. Skaggs Drug Center, C.A.Tex., 421 F.2d 307—Leonhard v. U.S., C.A.N.Y., 633 F.2d 599, cert. den. 101 S.Ct. 1975, 451 U.S. 908, 68 L.Ed.2d 295.

    Trahan v. Bellsouth Telecommunications, Inc., W.D.La., 881 F.Supp. 1080, affd. 71 F.3d 876.

Ark.—Pounders v. Trinity Court Nursing Home, Inc., 576 S.W.2d 934, 265 Ark. 1, 4 A.L.R.4th 442.

Fla.—Gatto v. Publix Supermarket, Inc., App., 387 So.2d 377.

Ga.—Abner v. W. T. Grant Co., 139 S.E.2d 408, 110 Ga.App. 592.

La.—Eason v. J. Weingarten, Inc., App., 219 So.2d 516—Rougeau v. Firestone Tire & Rubber Co., App., 274 So.2d 454.

Md.—Fine v. Kolodny, 284 A.2d 409, 263 Md. 647, cert. den. 92 S.Ct. 1803, 406 U.S. 928, 32 L.Ed.2d 129.

Minn.—Peterson v. Sorlien, 299 N.W.2d 123, 11 A.L.R.4th 208, cert. den. 101 S.Ct. 1742, 450 U.S. 1031, 68 L.Ed.2d 227.

N.J.—Cooke v. J. J. Newberry & Co., 232 A.2d 425, 96 N.J.Super. 9.

Negotiating discharge terms

Ala.—Uphaus v. Charter Hosp. of Mobile, Civ.App., 582 So.2d 1140.

Remaining on premises or within limits

Wis.—Herbst v. Wuennenberg, 266 N.W.2d 391, 83 Wis.2d 768.

Financial or economic restraint is not sufficient to constitute false imprisonment.[93.5]

93.5 U.S.—Trahan v. Bellsouth Telecommunications, Inc., W.D.La., 881 F.Supp. 1080, affd. 71 F.3d 876.

94. Ark.—Pettijohn v. Smith, 502 S.W.2d 618, 255 Ark. 780.

D.C.—Faniel v. Chesapeake and Potomac Tel. Co. of Maryland, App., 404 A.2d 147.

95. Hawaii—Noguchi v. Nakamura, 638 P.2d 1383, 2 Haw.App. 655.

§ 6.03   How Many Places Do You Look?

[1]   Digests

Now that you have a greater familiarity with the elements of false imprisonment and have identified a few cases to read, you can move on to the digests, which will not give you general descriptions of the law, but will probably give you more cases. Again, many states have their own digests, and you should use them if they exist, but you can also look in the regional digests published by West. In the *Northwestern Digest 2d*, you will find the following outline for false imprisonment: *

---

* Copyright © by West Publishing Company. Reprinted with permission.

FALSE IMPRISONMENT

SUBJECTS INCLUDED

Restraint of the person of another, without sufficient authority, not merely incident to a malicious prosecution

Justification or excuse for such restraint

Liabilities and remedies therefor, civil or criminal

SUBJECTS EXCLUDED AND COVERED BY OTHER TOPICS

Arrest, right to make, see ARREST

Governmental units' liability for false imprisonment or wrongful conviction, see MUNICIPAL CORPORATIONS, STATES

Habeas corpus for release from improper imprisonment, see HABEAS CORPUS

For detailed references to other topics, see Descriptive-Word Index

---

Analysis

I. CIVIL LIABILITY, ⟜1–42.
    (A) ACTS CONSTITUTING FALSE IMPRISONMENT AND LIABILITY THEREFOR, ⟜1–15(3).
    (B) ACTIONS, ⟜16–42.

II. CRIMINAL RESPONSIBILITY, ⟜43, 44.

I. CIVIL LIABILITY.

(A) ACTS CONSTITUTING FALSE IMPRISONMENT AND LIABILITY THERE-FOR.
    ⟜1. Nature and elements of false imprisonment.
      2. —— In general.
      3. —— False imprisonment and malicious prosecution distinguished.
      4. —— Intent and malice.
      5. —— Act or means of arrest or detention.
      6. —— Extent of restraint.
      7. —— Illegality of arrest.
        (1). In general.
        (2). Liability of judicial officers.
        (3). Liability of officer or other person making arrest and persons assisting officer.
        (4). Liability of person instigating arrest.
        (5). Effect of subsequent adjudications.
        (6). Waiver of defects or objections.
      8. —— Illegality of detention after arrest.
      9. Defenses.
      10. —— In general.
      11. —— Exercise of authority or duty.

I. CIVIL LIABILITY.—Continued.
  (A) ACTS CONSTITUTING FALSE IMPRISONMENT AND LIABILITY THERE-
     FOR.—Continued.
      12. —— Judicial process.
      13. —— Probable cause.
      14. —— Advice of counsel.
      15. Persons liable.
         (1). In general.
         (2). Persons procuring or instigating arrest.
         (3). Liability of principal for acts of agent.

Assuming that your primary goal is to determine what the cases have to say about
the sufficiency of restraint as an element of false imprisonment, you should find
notes 1-6 relevant. As you look at the annotations under those key numbers, these
are the Wisconsin cases you will find:*

---

* Copyright © by West Publishing Company. Reprinted with permission.

⊷2. —— **In general.**

Wis. 1978. Action for tort of false imprisonment protects personal interest in freedom from restraint of movement; essence of false imprisonment is intentional, unlawful, and unconsented restraint by one person of the physical liberty of another.—Herbst v. Wuennenberg, 266 N.W.2d 391, 83 Wis.2d 768.

There is no cause of action for false imprisonment unless confinement is contrary to the will of the "prisoner"; it is a contradiction to say that captor imprisoned "prisoner" with prisoner's consent.—Id.

It is not a sufficient basis for action for false imprisonment that plaintiffs remained on premises although they would have preferred not to do so.—Id.

Wis. 1975. False imprisonment involves the unlawful restraint by one person of the physical liberty of another.—Laska v. Steinpreis, 231 N.W.2d 196, 69 Wis.2d 307.

Wis. 1975. "False imprisonment" is intentional, unlawful and unconsented restraint by one person of physical liberty of another.—Dupler v. Seubert, 230 N.W.2d 626, 69 Wis.2d 373.

Wis. 1968. The tort of "false imprisonment" is the unlawful restraint by one person of the physical liberty of another.—Strong v. City of Milwaukee, 157 N.W.2d 619, 38 Wis.2d 564.

To constitute "false imprisonment" the act of the defendant in confining the plaintiff must be done with intention of causing a confinement, and if confinement is due to defendant's negligence, defendant may be liable as for negligence, but action is then governed by rules and principles of tort of negligence, according to which plaintiff is required to show actual damages, and, in other words, there can be no such tort as negligent false imprisonment.—Id.

False imprisonment or false arrest is generally considered to be within framework of intentional torts.—Id.

Wis. 1965. "False imprisonment" is the unlawful restraint of a person's physical liberty.—Lane v. Collins, 138 N.W.2d 264, 29 Wis.2d 66.

Wis. 1947. The essence of tort of false imprisonment is deprivation of liberty without lawful justification.—Weber v. Young, 26 N.W.2d 543, 250 Wis. 307.

Wis. 1944. "False imprisonment" is unlawful restraint of the physical liberty of another.—Hadler v. Rhyner, 12 N.W.2d 693, 244 Wis. 448.

⊷4. —— **Intent and malice.**

Wis. 1975. A required element of a cause of action based on a claim of false imprisonment is intent to cause confinement.—Laska v. Steinpreis, 231 N.W.2d 196, 69 Wis.2d 307.

Wis. 1968. Intent with which tort liability for false imprisonment is concerned is not necessarily a hostile intent or a desire to do any harm.—Strong v. City of Milwaukee, 157 N.W.2d 619, 38 Wis.2d 564.

If imprisonment is result of pure accident, and defendant did not intend to imprison plaintiff and was not guilty of any negligence, there is no liability on part of defendant.—Id.

Intent to cause confinement is an essential element in tort of false imprisonment.—Id.

Wis. 1948. A peace officer's mistake in arresting the wrong person, although he strongly resembles person desired, while not a justification, may reduce damages and show want of malice, but officer is liable if he fails to take proper precaution to ascertain right person, or if he refuses information offered that would have disclosed his mistake, or if he detains the person an undue length of time without taking proper steps to establish his identity.—Wallner v. Fidelity & Deposit Co. of Md., 33 N.W.2d 215, 253 Wis. 66, 10 A.L.R.2d 745.

⊷5. —— **Act or means of arrest or detention.**

Wis. 1981. One who has police authority to maintain peace has the privilege to use force, and question then becomes whether force was excessive for the accomplishment of the purpose; reasonableness of the force depends upon the facts of each case, and is a question to be resolved by the jury.—Johnson v. Ray, 299 N.W.2d 849, 99 Wis.2d 777.

Wis. 1966. Motorist who pursued 10-year-old boy who had been throwing snowballs at automobile, caught him, and, holding him by the arm, took him to automobile and directed him to enter it, and then drove into village and turned boy over to police officer, was guilty of actionable "false imprisonment" and at least a nominal "battery" except for possible justification. W.S.A. 48.28.—Drabek v. Sabley, 142 N.W.2d 798, 31 Wis.2d 184, 20 A.L.R.3d 1435.

Reasonableness of motorist's conduct in catching and holding one of boys who had thrown snowballs at automobile, and holding him while he obtained his name and admonished him, was for jury in action for battery and false imprisonment, but putting boy in automobile a few yards from his home and driving him into village to turn him over to police officer was unreasonable as matter of law.—Id.

As you can see, there are several Wisconsin cases. Some of them should look familiar, but there are also approximately a half dozen new ones. The advantage of the digests over the treatises and encyclopedias is that the digests provide very brief descriptions of the cases, which you can use to decide whether you want to read any particular case in full. In making this decision, always remember that such a short description of the case cannot possibly alert you to every aspect of the decision that might be useful, and that these "squibs" are occasionally inaccurate.

Even so, you can often use the annotations to eliminate cases that have no relevance to the situation you are researching. For example, if you look at the description of *Wallner v. Fidelity & Deposit Co. of Md.*, you should conclude that you are not likely to find anything helpful in that case, because the facts are so different as to make it difficult to compare the cases. Given that you have several other cases that outline the general requirements for making out a claim of false imprisonment, you do not need this case for any general language it might contain.

An examination of the pocket part to the digest will reveal no new Wisconsin cases, so you should start to feel fairly confident that you have now identified the most relevant and up-to-date precedent on your issue. Also note that you are starting to see some of the same cases repeatedly, which is a good sign — it means that you are finding the limits of the legal universe in which you are operating.

[2]   Computer Research Services

If you have access to them, consider the computer services. LEXIS and WESTLAW can be used most efficiently when you have enough of an understanding of the legal terminology that you can frame a search that will retrieve only relevant cases. For example, if you go into a database of Wisconsin state cases with the search "false imprisonment," you will retrieve 331 cases on LEXIS and 332 cases on WESTLAW.

When a client is paying for your time on the computer, you simply cannot read through more than three hundred cases on-line. Even if a client is not paying, it makes no sense to go screen by screen through all those cases, when a glance through an encyclopedia or a digest will let you know much faster whether you need to read the cases in their entirety or not. In all likelihood, the vast majority of those three hundred plus cases do not deal substantively with false imprisonment, or they may involve criminal charges or aspects of the tort that are not at issue in your case.

Do not attempt to use the specific facts of your case to narrow your search. It is highly unlikely that you will find other cases involving fact patterns just like yours, and your real concern is to find cases dealing with the same issues that your case raises. For example, you could narrow your search by adding the concept "farmer" to your search request, which will get you 11 cases on LEXIS and 12 cases on WESTLAW. You could even add "farmer* w/2 craz!", which will get you one irrelevant case on LEXIS and the same irrelevant case on WESTLAW. You should know by now that it does not really matter that the defendant is a farmer, and such a search will only exclude helpful cases from your review.

As you attempt to narrow your search, focus on terminology that will call up cases dealing with the elements of the tort with which you are concerned. Your primary concern in Mr. Trune's case is whether there was sufficient restraint to make out that element of the tort. Thus, you might try a search along the lines of "false imprisonment and restrain! w/20 suffic!", which will yield eight helpful cases on WESTLAW, and eleven on LEXIS. If you perform the search, you will note that at least some of these cases look very familiar.

[3] Shepard's

Always update your case research by Shepardizing, either in the books or on-line. Once you have identified your key cases, Shepardize them. Do this not only to make sure they are good law, but also to see whether there are any subsequent cases that might be even more helpful. Remember that Shepard's can be just as useful as a casefinder as it is as a citator. Assuming that we have decided that the *Dupler* and *Herbst* cases are the ones we are most interested in, a check of Shepard's reveals the following, beginning with the main volume and moving forward to the current advance sheet pamphlet: *

---

* From Shepard's Northwestern Reporter citations, 1993 Bound Volume; Shepard's Citations for Annotations, 1989 Bound Volume; May 1997 Annual Cumulative Supplement Vol. 94, No. 5; November 1997 Advance Sheet Edition. Reproduced by permission of Shepard's/McGraw-Hill, Inc. Further reproduction is strictly prohibited.

NORTHWESTERN REPORTER, 2d SERIES

Vol. 230

—626—

Dupler v
Seubert
1975

(69Wis2d373)
260NW^{3}793
266NW^{7}394
d 266NW^{8}395
297NW^{7}77
f 312NW^{6}817
342NW^{9}791
405NW364
409NW^{3}136
409NW^{9}442
d 468NW6
　Mo
734SW867
35A2273s
48A4177n
48A4214n

Vol. 230

Vol. 230

Vol. 266

—391—

Herbst v
Wuennenberg
1978

(83Wis2d768)
343NW134
f 450NW467
467NW^{3}149
　Cir. 3
551FS^{7}541
　Cir. 7
643FS^{5}1104
　D C
404A2d151

Vol. 266

—391—
WIDk ^{3}
　[93-3452
WIDk ^{p}
　[96-0645

Vol. 266

—391—
563NW^{5}561
563NW^{6}561

Notice that, while all reported cases appear in the main volume, not all cases appear in the Citations for Annotations or the pocket part updates. You have no way of knowing whether or not a case will appear in either of these. It is therefore extremely important that you always check the most current updates available from the publisher. If your library does not have the most recent release, or if you are not certain if it does, you can use electronic Shepard's on Lexis-Nexis to complete your search.

While you can confirm the continued validity of *Herbst* and *Dupler* as authority, you should also notice that the listed citations do not look familiar. Thus you would need to review these cases, at least briefly, to determine whether they add anything to the analysis offered by *Herbst* and *Dupler*.

In addition to Shepard's, on-line sevices such as WESTLAW's KeyCite and LEXIS/NEXIS' AutoCite can serve as research and citation reference tools. West's KeyCite is the newest of these services, and claims to be the most accurate and comprehensive, but the jury is still out. This service is simply not old enough to have gained the full and complete confidence of the legal community, and it will be a long time before KeyCite replaces Shepard's Citations.

[4] ALR and Legal Periodicals

If you wish to be especially thorough, and to find out what others have written on your topic, you might want to consult other sources, such as the *American Law Reports* (ALR), the *Current Law Index*, or one of the indexes to legal periodicals. For a topic as straightforward as this one, involving an intentional tort that has been reasonably well-defined by the courts, such additional research will probably not be necessary. If you were doing this research in a firm, at a client's expense, you would almost certainly not go to such lengths. While you are in law school, however, and are still learning the law with the luxury of enough time to fully investigate all potentially helpful options, you might want to at least take a quick look at these kinds of supportive resources. If you happen to come across an annotation or law review article specifically on your topic, you might even *save* time on your research.

If you did look at the A.L.R. index, this is what you would find: *

---

* From E-H *ALR Index* (1992). Reprint permission has been granted by the copyright holder, Lawyers Cooperative Publishing, a division of Thomson Legal Publishing Inc.

ALR INDEX

(Matthew Bender & Co., Inc.)   (Pub.676)

And, if you searched the *Current Law Index* for False Imprisonment, this is representative of what you would find.*

F

* * *

FALSE imprisonment
  Mandated affidavit required in false imprisonment case
against hospital. (Missouri) (Case Note)
  -Religious aspects
  He who controls the mind controls the body: false
imprisonment, religious cults, and the destruction of
volitional capacity. by Laura B. Brown
        25 Valparaiso University Law Review
              407-454 Spring '91

The vast majority of articles reported here deal with criminal False Arrest and Imprisonment; only two seem to have any civil or tortious implications and they do not appear to be relevant. Notice that this Index covers all common law jurisdictions, including the United States, Great Britain, Australia, New Zealand and parts of Canada. While these articles are not very useful or relevant to our false imprisonment tort claim, you might find useful information in this index for another, more novel claim where you must persuade the court to rule in a way that would bring local law in line with the law of other jurisdictions.

You can use your own judgment as to whether you would read any of these annotations or articles, but again, if you were doing this research at a client's expense, you should consider whether the expenditure of the time required would be cost-effective, given the likely benefits of the research.

§ 6.04   When Do You Stop?

Perhaps the single most frustrating element of legal research for those who are learning it is knowing when to stop. In their zeal to leave no stone unturned, fledgling lawyers tend to explore every conceivable alternative, to look in every resource book the library has to offer, and to read every case that even mentions the type of cause of action at issue in the case they are researching. Telling you that you will develop instincts that will help you avoid wasting time in the library or on-line (which you will) may offer some long-term comfort, but it will not get you through those frustrating early efforts. Thus, we offer a few guidelines that should help streamline your first research efforts.

---

[1] Look for the Most On-Point Cases First

Students sometimes have a tendency to try to identify the entire universe of available case law before beginning to read the decisions, and then to read all the decisions in no particular order. You will save yourself time and effort, and conclude your research sooner, if you try to identify the most useful cases right from the start, and then read them before you go on. Identify these cases by looking for factual similarities or statements of holdings that sound like they could easily apply to your case.

By Shepardizing these close cases and also reading cases cited in the decisions that support propositions important to you, you should be able to narrow the scope of your subsequent research. You should find that using these cases as a jumping off point will eliminate the need to read cases that do no more than outline general principles without offering useful applications to your situation.

[2] Stop When You Come Full Circle

One of the surest signs that you should stop looking for new cases is repeatedly coming across citations to the same cases in different sources. Thus, if you find the same cases in the digest and the encyclopedia, even when you are researching different key words, you can be confident that you have identified the most relevant case law, and you should focus any additional research on leads provided by those key cases.

[3] Do Not Follow Every Lead

One of the most common problems encountered by students is the frustration that comes from realizing that you have wasted valuable time reading cases that have only the most tangential relevance to your situation. Often, this is the result of deciding to read a case of possible but questionable relevance, then discovering a citation to an even more tenuously related decision, following up on that one too, and perhaps going on to follow the chain even farther afield. While you do not want to miss any genuinely useful authority, you must constantly remind yourself what your case is really about.

To avoid these trips down blind alleys, draft a one-page outline of your tentative analysis and keep it with you at all times. By regularly referring to the outline, you will keep focused on the real issue in your case. If you are not ready to draft an outline, find another way to stay focused, for example, keeping with you any written information that you have about your assignment.[1] Creative analysis of problems is to be encouraged, but if you

---

[1] If you do end up reading irrelevant cases, avoid the temptation to find a way to work them into your written product anyway, just to show your instructor (or your supervisor) how much work you did. You will only frustrate the reader by

are finding it difficult to connect the product of your research to your main issue, imagine how difficult it will be for your reader!

If you stay focused, sometimes you will not find cases on point, but only cases tenuously related to the topic of your research. In this predicament, your only recourse is to read many cases in search of the few that contain some useful language or fact patterns. All you can do is try to analogize these cases to yours, either factually, or by looking at the underlying legal or policy issues.

Finally, if you feel that you are spending an inordinate amount of time in the library, ask yourself if you might be continuing your research as a way of avoiding the need to start writing. Students are often afraid to begin writing, or are simply not looking forward to the struggle of putting their ideas and research findings into some logical order, and then into sentences, paragraphs, and pages. Spending time on research can be justified as working on the assignment, but once you pass the point where it is really productive, move on. Writing can actually be fun, if you give it a chance!

§ 6.05 How Do You Keep Track?

In order to avoid wasting time later, spend time early on creating a research path. When you consult a digest or encyclopedia and find a relevant case, copy down the case's full name and citation. This way, you will not spend valuable time tracking down missing parts of citations or pulling cases off the shelves only to discover that you have already read and rejected them.

When you read the case, make a note next to the citation that indicates whether it was helpful or not, and whether you plan to return to it, or to cite it in your written analysis. Most of us find that making copies of useful cases is a good way to keep track of them, and to make sure that we have all the necessary information for citation purposes. The problems tend to arise in losing track of the cases we decide not to use, and it is worth a few extra minutes of your time to make a complete record of your research process.

Whenever your notes get disorganized, it is worth stopping to make a clean list of useful cases and rejected cases. This way, you will not have to wonder whether you have already read a case.

§ 6.06 Research Checklist

Here is a checklist designed to provide a simple reference to remind you of basic sources and approaches as you work your way through the library on a research project. You will not need to follow each step for every

---

overwhelming him or her with useless information, and you may make him or her wonder whether you really understood the issue at all.

(Matthew Bender & Co., Inc.)

assignment, but the checklist should enable you to consciously reject a step or resource rather than forgetting its existence.

I. Process

_____ Start with secondary sources such as treatises and encyclopedias if you need to learn the fundamental rules that govern your area of the law.

_____ Look for an applicable statute if you think there might be one, but be sure the statute actually applies before reading any annotated cases.

_____ Go to the digests when you know the key words that will help you identify relevant cases.

_____ Update your research, and check the validity of the sources you intend to rely on.

_____ Read on-point cases first, Shepardize them, and read cited decisions on important points

_____ Don't follow tenuous leads

_____ Stop when you see the same cases repeatedly

_____ Keep a research path

II. Sources

_____ Statutes

_____ Treatises and Hornbooks

_____ Restatements

_____ Encyclopedias

_____ Digests

_____ Computer-Assisted Legal Research (if it is cost-effective and you know the key words)

_____ Shepard's (use as a casefinder, not just to check whether a case is good law)

_____ A.L.R.

_____ Periodicals

_____ Other sources, such as looseleaf services, that might apply to different types of problems.

PART II

STYLE AND SUBSTANCE: WRITING THE LEGAL ANALYSIS

(Matthew Bender & Co., Inc.)

CHAPTER **7**

PURPOSE, CONTEXT, AND STRUCTURE

§ 7.01 Introduction

In their eagerness to get on with the writing process, many writers forget to think about the "big picture" aspects of what they are writing about. If you consciously address the elements of purpose, context, and structure *before* you start constructing sentences and paragraphs, your finished product will be much more polished and comprehensible. This chapter will discuss each in turn and offer strategies for incorporating this kind of thinking into your writing process.

§ 7.02 Purpose

It seems fairly obvious to say that you should understand why you are writing a document before you begin putting words on paper. Surprisingly, many writers are so anxious to get their ideas into concrete form that they do not stop to think about what the document must accomplish and what the intended reader needs from the document. Here are two key questions to ask yourself before you begin writing (or, for that matter, before you begin researching):

    * For whom am I writing this?

    _____   client (consider education, level of sophistication about legal matters, anxiety level, stage of case, nature and length of relationship between you and client)

    _____   supervising attorney (consider what you know about expectations based on your and others' previous experiences)

    _____   judge (consider what you know about judge, level of court, stage of proceeding)

    * What am I trying to accomplish?

    _____   answer a specific question (keep that question in mind at all times and be sure you actually answer it)

    _____   advise reader generally on the state of the law in a particular area (consider why reader needs information and tailor presentation to what you know about that need)

_____   persuade reader to adopt a particular course of action (Do you want
your client to do something? Do you want the trial court to grant or
deny a motion? Do you want the appellate court to affirm or
reverse the trial court? Do you want opposing counsel to respond to
a settlement offer?)

Your answers to these two questions should go a long way toward dictating the
structure and tone of the final document. For example, a letter to a client who wants
to know if she has a malpractice claim will have very little in common with a motion
for summary judgment to the trial judge on that same claim. If you keep the intended
audience and goal in mind at all times, you should be able to avoid the trap of going
on at great length about issues the reader does not care about, or simply has no need
to think about. Likewise, you will be sure that you actually do address the issue or
issues that are of primary importance to the reader.

§ 7.03 Context

Context is closely related to purpose, but it encompasses a few additional elements. In addition to remembering for whom you are writing and what you need
to accomplish, you need to consider the forum in which you are writing. Is this a
memo in a law office? A brief to a court (trial or appellate)? A letter to a client?
Each type of document involves different expectations regarding format, tone,
amount and type of information, and writing style. A brief to a court will be presented in a very formal tone, and must conform to fixed and specific rules regarding
format, while the tone and format of a letter to a client are more flexible. An office
memorandum should be presented in a tone and format that is consistent with the
expectations of the particular office in which it is written.

We will discuss several different types of documents in this book, but any time
you are faced with the need to draft a document of a type with which you are
unfamiliar, you should find similar documents intended for the same or a similar
audience, and learn whatever you can about the contextual expectations. Read the
samples, ask questions (preferably of the intended reader, if possible), and look at
any written guidelines, such as court rules, that may govern the final product.

§ 7.04 Structure

The structure of a document is much like the foundation and framework of a
building. Both need to be carefully constructed, and, if done well, both will
strengthen and define the finished product. There are many aspects to the structure
of a piece of written discourse, and all of them require conscious thought and
strategic planning. We will discuss structural issues such as outlining and the
placement of arguments, and signalling tools such as road map paragraphs, thesis
sentences, and transitions. We will also briefly touch on the placement of authorities
and different types of argument within an argument or discussion. Because we do
discuss the specifics of particular types of documents in later chapters, the approach

here will be to present more general rules that should guide your preparation every time you write.

[1] Outlining

For most people, the really important thing to know about an outline is that you should do one.[1] There is no formula for outlining that will work for everyone. What is crucial is that you sit down before you begin to write and plan the flow of your discussion. Here are some considerations you should take into account in that planning process:

* What are the key points to be analyzed?

* How many points do you need to make?

* What is the most logical order in which to make those points?

* How do the different parts of your discussion relate to each other?

* Which are your strongest and weakest points?

* How does the legal authority you intend to rely on fit into your arguments? Are there different cases or statutes on each point, or do you need to use the same authority to support several arguments?

Once you have done enough research to get a preliminary idea of the types of arguments you need to make, you should make a sketchy outline. There is no need to write out full sentences in the outline at this point; you will most likely be identifying only the major points to be made. You should keep this preliminary outline with you as you continue your research and analysis. It will help to keep you focused as you sort through the available authority.

You may find that the initial outline is incomplete, or that it does not present the parts of the discussion in the most logical order. You should be flexible enough to recognize this, and to adjust your outline in any way and as many times as seems appropriate. Even in the midst of writing, you may need to rethink your outline and restructure your presentation.

When you have collected all the authority you intend to rely upon, go back to your outline and "plug in" the authorities. Decide which cases or statutes are most helpful on particular points, and add them to the outline in the appropriate places. Then organize the authorities into the proper order.

---

[1] We say "for most people," because there are those who can construct a perfectly coherent, logical discussion every time they sit down to write. If you are one of those rare people, the extra step of creating an outline may not be a terribly useful or efficient way to spend time. For most of us, however, whether we are writing memos, briefs, or law school exams, making the effort to outline the structure of our argument before we flesh it out in full paragraph form is the only way to ensure that the final product is a sensible, focused communication to the intended reader. This is true even though outlining is a more natural process for some than for others. There may be writers for whom it is a sufficiently foreign way of thinking as to be almost counterproductive, but in the context of legal writing it is usually a necessary if difficult endeavor, because it is the only way to ensure that our ideas will be communicated in a way that is useful to our busy readers.

As you finalize the outline, you may want to flesh out your major points. You can do this by writing them out in full sentences and by adding subpoints. Some writers need to, and should, construct very detailed outlines, while others can write just as efficiently with less thorough guidance. Regardless of your approach, do not forget to identify the purpose, audience, and context of your document before constructing your final outline. *Now* you are ready to begin writing.

Keep your outline in front of you at all times during the writing process. This will keep you from trying to make all of your points at once or in the order they occur to you as you are writing, which may or may not be the order that makes the most sense. Also, referring to the outline when you are struggling to develop a point may help you understand how that point relates to the rest of the document, which may sometimes be enough to get the writing process back on track.

If the outlining approach discussed here does not work for you, there are alternatives. You can create a very general heading-only outline, write up the discussion, and then rearrange sections of the discussion as necessary. You can write the sections in a different order than set forth in the outline if one or two points are giving you particular trouble. Starting with the easier section or sections will at least get the writing process started, and you may then discover that the difficult sections become more manageable. You also can write without an outline to get the ideas down on paper, then superimpose an outline on the discussion after you have written it, to be certain your final structure makes sense.

Let's go back to the lost ring case discussed in Chapter 5, and outline the analysis in § 5.03. Remember that there are many ways to outline any discussion, but here is one approach.

    I.   Was the valise lost?

        A.   *Durfee* -- definition and rule for lost property

        B.   *McAvoy* -- definition and rule for mislaid property

    II.   Was the ring lost?

[Note that you will only apply the rules here, since you have already defined them in Section I, and it would be unnecessary in such a short document to repeat your discussion of the cases]

    III.   Who gets the ring?

        Durfee -- finder must have permission to examine property

This is obviously a very simple discussion, and the outline is likewise simple. You can apply the same process and principles to a much more complex discussion, and it will give you a clearer picture of where the document is going and what it will accomplish when you are finished.

EXERCISE

Select a memorandum from Appendix IV in the back of the book and outline the discussion.

(Matthew Bender & Co., Inc.)

[2]   Deciding on a Structural Strategy

One of the decisions about structure you need to make as you begin writing is the order in which you will present the arguments. Sometimes there will be an inherently logical approach to ordering the arguments; for example, if you are discussing a tort or statute that sets forth specific elements that must be, or always are, discussed in a particular order, you should order your discussion accordingly.

The false imprisonment problem discussed in Chapter 5 presents just such a situation. Both cases rely on the Restatement (Second) of Torts, which presents the elements in a specific order: 1) intent to confine, 2) actual confinement, and 3) consciousness of confinement. In this situation, it is easier and more likely to meet the expectations of your reader to follow this structure. However, do not feel that you must devote equal time to each element. If there is a genuine issue as to whether one or two elements are present in your case, while the other element or elements are clearly satisfied, you can allude only briefly to the elements not at issue, and devote the bulk of your analysis to the elements in dispute. If you are writing an advocacy document, most experts will advise you to start with your strongest argument. This is good strategic advice, as long as it does not create a conflict with the type of inherent order discussed above, and so long as it does not cause you to make the argument in an order that does not make logical sense.

Some people will also advise you to end your discussion on a strong note, so that you leave a favorable impression with the reader. Again, if you can do so logically, this is sound advice. If you have not already guessed, this strategic approach to ordering your arguments will leave your weaker points in the middle of the discussion, where they are most likely to be forgotten.

For a concrete example of strategic structuring of an argument, look at the first two briefs in Appendix V. The issue addressed by both briefs is whether a decedent's estate can bring a tort action against the hospital that employed the decedent. The decedent was murdered while working at the hospital on the late shift. The hospital sought to bar the claim by arguing that the only available remedy lay in the applicable workers' compensation statute. The crux of the argument was whether a statutory exception to the exclusivity of the workers' compensation remedy applied. Note the placement of the discussion of the exception in the two briefs.

In the hospital's brief, the statutory argument is outlined as follows in the Table of Contents:

I.   WORKMEN'S COMPENSATION SHOULD BE THE EXCLUSIVE REMEDY FOR INJURIES SUSTAINED BY AN EMPLOYEE IN THE COURSE OF HER EMPLOYMENT FROM AN ATTACK BY A THIRD PERSON WHEN NO RELATIONSHIP BETWEEN THE THIRD PERSON AND EMPLOYEE EXISTED PRIOR TO THE ATTACK.

   A.   *Workmen's Compensation Is Intended To Be the Sole Remedy for Injuries Sustained in the Course of One's Employment.*

   B.   *The Attack upon Charla Louis Was Not for Reasons Personal within the Meaning of the Workmen's Compensation Act and Is Only Compensable Through Workmen's Compensation.*

Here is the outline of the statutory argument from the estate's perspective:

I.   THE ESTATE OF A HOSPITAL EMPLOYEE WHO WAS ATTACKED AND MURDERED WHILE WORKING, BY AN ASSAILANT WITH PERSONAL MOTIVATION TO COMMIT SEXUAL ASSAULT, IS NOT LIMITED BY THE REMEDIES OF THE WORKMEN'S COMPENSATION ACT.

   A.   *An Exception Provided by the Act Disallows Compensation for All Personally Motivated Assaults by Third Parties.*

   B.   *The Fact that the Victim Was Present on the Premises of the Employer as Required by Her Job Does Not Limit Recovery to that Provided by the Act when the Third Party Attack is Personally Motivated.*

      1.   Preexisting personal animosity is not dispositive or even highly indicative of the assailant's motivation since his motivation at the time of attack is at issue.

      2.   The nature of sexual assault indicates personal motivation in the form of anticipated sexual gratification; rape is not usually motivated by work-related activity.

   C.   *An Employee Who Is Not Required by Her Job to Have Personal Contact with the Public Does Not Assume the Risk of Personal Assault so as to Bring Sexual Assault by a Third Party Under the Provisions of the Act.*

If you read the arguments in the two briefs, you will gain a fuller understanding of how argument placement can affect persuasiveness.

In addition to thinking strategically about the order in which you present your arguments, you should consider how much space you will devote to each argument. A reader is likely to assume that an argument that occupies a substantial amount of room is important. Why would a writer spend a lot of time and effort developing a point that is of only passing significance? No writer would, unless that writer got so caught up in developing a tangential or tenuous analogy that the writer lost sight of the need to do a cost-benefit analysis during the writing process. Ask yourself whether the amount of time and space you spend on an argument is proportional to the persuasive impact the argument will have in the context of your overall presentation. If not, consider whether the argument can be edited substantially, or perhaps cut altogether.

[3]   Road Maps, Topic Sentences, and Transitions

It is not enough to have a structure for your document. You must let the reader know what that structure is. If the reader knows up front where the document is going, and gets messages along the way that help to orient him or her, the document will be easier to read and the analysis will seem more logical and possibly even more persuasive.

The simplest way to orient the reader early on is to provide a "road map" paragraph. This introductory paragraph highlights the most significant parts of your analysis, as well as stating your ultimate conclusion. At the risk of abusing our analogy, by identifying the destination and the major landmarks at the beginning of the journey, you make the trip easier and more comfortable for the traveler.

A road map paragraph can be very explicit, as is the paragraph introducing the negligence argument in the first appellate brief in Appendix V:

> The Estate's action is premised on a negligence theory of liability. However, as the court emphasized in *Murphy v. Penn Fruit Co.*, 274 Pa. Super. 427, 418 A.2d 480 (1980), negligence is not established by the mere happening of an attack on the decedent. *Id.* at 432, 418 A.2d at 483. The estate must plead and prove each element of the tort to establish liability. The necessary elements to maintain a negligence action are: a duty or obligation recognized by the law, requiring the actor to conform to the standard required; a failure to conform to the standard required; a causal connection between the conduct and the resulting injury; and actual loss or damage resulting to the interests of another. *Morena v. South Hills Health System*, 501 Pa. 634, 642, 462 A.2d 680, 684 (1983) quoting Prosser, *Law of Torts*, § 30 at 143 (4th ed. 1971). Each of these elements will be examined in turn as they apply to the facts of this case.

You can also take a slightly less detailed approach, as the writer of this memo does:

> Ms. Holmes was falsely imprisoned by Dean James. Dean James had probable cause to question Ms. Holmes about the materials found in her locker, but he acted unreasonably in confining Ms. Holmes and causing her to miss her exam. Dean James' conduct was without legal justification, and the confinement was therefore unlawful.

Both examples inform the reader of the writer's ultimate conclusion, as well as providing information about how the argument will progress. That is all a road map paragraph needs to do.

Topic sentences and transitions are the landmarks that let readers know where in the discussion they are at any given point. The first sentence of any paragraph should give the reader a clue as to what the rest of the paragraph will be about. As a general rule, a single paragraph should not develop more than one idea, and the purpose of that first, or topic, sentence is to identify that idea. We discuss paragraph construction in greater detail in Chapter 8.

As you shift between the major points you identified in the road map paragraph, make a conscious effort to put distinct transitions between them. Sometimes the transitions will be as simple as an introductory sentence that identifies the element you are about to discuss, as you will see if you look at the first about false imprisonment in Appendix IV.

EXERCISE

Choose one of the remaining memos in Appendix IV, and identify all thesis sentences and transitions. Are there any paragraphs that do not begin with topic sentences signaling what the paragraph is about? If so, does this cause confusion or frustration as you try to pull the central idea from each paragraph? If not, it may be that the topic has been implicitly signaled in some other way. Do the transitions act as landmarks that relate back to the road map? Does this help you, as a reader, understand the progression of the discussion and where you are in the analysis at any particular point?

[4] Organizing Within Arguments

Thus far, we have explored ways of structuring your document at the "macro" level -- outlining the progression of the discussion, choosing the order in which to present your points, and making your organizational scheme apparent to the reader. In this section, we will discuss organization at a more "micro" level. How do you decide where to present authorities within an argument or part of a discussion, and how much space do you devote to each? How do you integrate law, policy, and equity arguments? The answer is that you apply the same principles we discussed earlier, *i.e.*, you start with the stronger authorities and arguments, and devote proportionally more space to them as well.

How do you know which authorities are strongest? We discussed the different types and weight of authority in Chapter 2. Here is a summary that should help:

1. On-point decisions by higher courts in your jurisdiction are binding, and should be featured conspicuously. If such decisions go against you, first look for a relevant way to distinguish them, pointing out differences between the facts or policies at issue in those cases and your case. If they cannot be distinguished, you need to deal with them in other ways, perhaps by arguing that they were wrongly decided or that times have changed sufficiently that a new rule is called for. Unless such adverse decisions are truly dispositive of your case, you can still place them strategically in the middle of your argument, using the more prominent beginning and ending positions for authority that is more helpful to you.

2. Decisions by lower courts in your jurisdiction are very persuasive, and should also be given appropriate space and position. The same rules about distinguishing or otherwise dealing with adverse authority apply.

3. Recent decisions are generally more persuasive than older decisions, all other things being equal (i.e., if the facts in the older decision are significantly more analogous to your case, you might want to spend more time on the older decision).

4. Federal decisions interpreting state law are persuasive, and should be given some attention if they fill in gaps in the state decisions, or articulate the rationale for the state decisions particularly clearly. Unless you have no better authority, you do not want to use disproportionate amounts of space on such decisions.

5. Decisions from other jurisdictions and secondary authorities are only as persuasive as you make them. This almost inevitably means that you will have to devote considerable space to making analogies or articulating policy justifications for adopting rules from such sources. If you have no other authority, perhaps because the question you are addressing is a novel one in your jurisdiction, it may be worth your effort to do so. You may be able to discover and argue a developing trend in the law that supports adoption of the rule you advocate. If, however, you have other authority that the reader is likely to find more useful, you should think twice about using valuable space and reader energy on such subordinate points. Remember that the reader is likely to equate the time needed to develop and understand an argument with the importance of that argument, so make your decisions accordingly.

[5] Placement of Policy and Equity Arguments

Keep your strategic sense working on the question of integrating law, policy, and equity arguments as well. As you learned in Chapter 5, policy arguments are based on societal goals that would be served by the result you seek, and equity arguments are based on notions of general fairness as applied to the particular facts of your case. Remember that courts of law are essentially conservative institutions, bound to a large extent by precedent and notions of *stare decisis*. This means that you should feature your legal arguments in the prominent positions, and devote more time to them. Policy and equity arguments are supportive, and will seem more persuasive if they are closely tied to your legal arguments. Therefore, on any given point, you should start with your legal arguments and authorities, and then follow immediately with related and reinforcing policy and equity arguments.

If you do not have on-point authority to support your position, you may be able to find authority to support pure policy arguments. Think about other areas of the law that have important similarities to yours and that serve the same policy goals. Look for cases in those areas that have similar facts and the result you want. Policy arguments should generally be given more prominence than purely equitable, fact-based arguments. While equitable arguments are useful, and judges generally like to feel that they are being fair in rendering their decisions, you do not want to devote a lot of time to such arguments, or lead off with them, unless you have nothing else.

§ 7.05 Context and Structure Checklist

_____ Identify and articulate the goal of your document.

_____ Identify your audience and any expectations you know or suspect that audience has for your document.

_____ Outline the major points you need to make in the document to accomplish your goal.

———   Fill in details such as legal authorities, and revise the outline as necessary as you go along.

———   Make sure you start and end with a strong point, to the extent logic permits.

———   Organize your legal authorities according to the appropriate hierarchy, giving more space to more persuasive authorities.

———   Organize your legal, policy, and equity arguments so that the more persuasive arguments receive greater prominence in terms of both position and space.

———   Write your road map paragraph, and check your document for transitions and thesis sentences that will let the reader know where in the analysis you are and where the analysis is going.

CHAPTER **8**

MAKE YOUR MAIN THEMES STAND OUT

§ 8.01 Introduction

Sometimes we read a court opinion, a memo, or an appellate brief and do not understand its message until we reach the end. After we finish reading the document, we think about the conclusion and try to synthesize all the information and analysis that we have read. As we synthesize, we may find ourselves returning to earlier paragraphs in the document and puzzling over them. If we think about this process of digesting information, we probably will conclude that it is inefficient and creates the risk that the reader will misunderstand the message that the writer seeks to convey. When it comes to writing, we may conclude, there must be a better way.

There is a better way. From the very beginning of the document, let the reader know what your message is. Instead of waiting until the end to pull the rabbit out of the hat, make your main themes stand out throughout the document. Let the reader know where you are going.

To accomplish this task, apply three principles: make the outline of your argument or discussion stand out; put your conclusions first; and write well-organized paragraphs.

First, as suggested in Chapter 7, make an outline of your writing. An outline will clarify your organization for you, and your reader will benefit because of it. Because your first draft is never your best work, you should revise your outline and your writing several times.

Second, in any legal document, put your conclusions at the beginning of your writing. At the outset, the reader wants to know your conclusions about the law as applied to the facts of your case. Although you may well decide to recapitulate your conclusion at the end, the end is not the place to state your conclusion for the first time.

Third, write well-organized paragraphs. Within your document, paragraphs are major units of discourse. If the reader easily grasps the idea of each paragraph, follows the discussion of that idea, and can make a smooth transition to the idea in the next paragraph, he or she will understand your message.

§ 8.02 Make the Outline of Your Argument or Discussion Stand Out

As we discussed in Chapter 7, In order to make the outline of your argument or discussion* stand out, you should begin with an outline. Many students are not accustomed to making outlines of their writing in advance. They write first and outline later. For most people, this approach just does not work. Make an outline.

Your initial outline is a simple listing of the major points in your discussion or argument. As your research and analysis progress, you can develop a more comprehensive outline using full sentences.

Here is part of a sample sentence outline in an appellate brief concerning an adverse possession case. The case takes place in Pennsylvania. The plaintiff in the case is attempting to take ownership of a property from the owner who has a deed to that property. Under Pennsylvania law a trespasser can gain ownership of property by possessing it for twenty-one years and performing certain acts of ownership.

Sample Sentence Outline:

    I. SMITH HAS ACQUIRED SUFFICIENT INTEREST IN THE DISPUTED TRACT OF LAND TO ENTITLE HIM TO OWN THE LAND BY ADVERSE POSSESSION.

        A. *Smith's Possession of the Disputed Tract of Land Has Been Actual, Continuous, Visible, Notorious, Exclusive, Distinct, and Hostile for the Statutory Period of Twenty-One Years as Required to Satisfy the Elements of Adverse Possession.*

          1. Because Smith intends to hold this land for himself and has manifested his intention by many acts of possession, his decision to discontinue one act, grazing sheep, during the requisite period does not break the continuity of his possession.

Here is another example. In this case, two workers had a verbal dispute that was work-related. Six months later, they engaged in a personal fight during working hours. One of the workers was injured and now seeks recovery under the Pennsylvania Workers' Compensation Act. An outline for part of a memorandum on the case might look like this:

Sample Sentence Outline:

    I. BECAUSE THE FIGHT WAS PURELY PERSONAL, THE INJURED WORKER CANNOT RECOVER UNDER THE ACT.

        A. As interpreted by case law, the Act excludes injuries arising when the attacker acts for purely personal reasons.

---

* The word "argument" here means arguing your client's case in a brief that goes to the court. You will learn how to write an argument in Part V on "The Brief." The word "discussion" here means an objective discussion of the law, without argument, in legal memoranda and client letters. You will learn how to write discussions in Part III on "The Memorandum".

    B.   As interpreted by case law, the Act is remedial and should be liberally construed in favor of the injured worker.

    C.   Nonetheless, all similar cases permitting recovery were over work-related issues with no mention of personal matters.

    D.   In light of the case law, the earlier dispute is too remote to permit describing the fight as work related. Therefore the injured worker probably will lose.

To complete this outline, you would fill it out by including throughout some information about the cases that you plan to discuss.

In order to make the outline of the argument stand out, you should follow that outline in your writing. With the outline in hand, you should find that you will write more easily. If you run into difficulties, you may decide that your outline is faulty and that you need to revise it.

After you turn your outline into a draft, do not let the first draft be your final writing. First-year students face many time pressures and often want to save time by not revising their writing. Many students who receive lower grades in legal writing than they expected readily admit, "Well, I didn't revise my writing. I only wrote one draft.'

The usual reason the student gives is lack of time. Lawyers face just as many time pressures. Bear in mind that you will be working for clients when you become a lawyer, and your best writing is never the first draft. Your rule of thumb should be to go through at least three drafts, if not more. Make the time to go through as many revisions as necessary to make your final product the best it can be.

Once you have written a first draft, go back over it and make sure it follows your outline perfectly. If you find that the outline is forcing you to organize your discussion in an awkward way, revise your outline.

Structure your discussion so that your organization is clear to the first-time reader. In this book you will learn and re-learn many rules that will help you achieve this goal. As you go through your revisions, make sure you apply each rule.

§ 8.03   Put Your Conclusion First

A conclusion is usually at the end of a writing. In order to make your theme stand out, however, put it at the beginning. Depending on what you are writing, you may find it desirable to also recapitulate it at the end.

The basic rule of expository writing is:

    Tell your readers what you are going to say.
    Say it.
    Tell them what you just said.

Tell your reader your conclusion at the outset. Then discuss the rationale for your conclusion. Then remind the reader of the conclusion you have justified in your discussion.

The reader wants to know, right up front, what the law is as applied to the given situation and does not want to be "held in suspense" until the end of the memorandum, brief, or letter. You are not writing a mystery novel!

Do not make the reader wait until the end to see where you are going. If you think your writing will become repetitive, you are right. Some repetition is necessary to make your point.

The following is an edited excerpt from a student's legal memorandum. In this sample, the student stated the conclusion at the beginning of the discussion and provided an emphatic recapitulation at the end.

> In this case, a court should hold the minor operator of a rider mower to an adult standard of care, because the fourteen-year-old's operation of the mower was a dangerous activity that adults normally perform. Courts generally require a minor to exercise the same standard of care that would be exercised under similar circumstances by a reasonably careful minor of the same age, intelligence, and experience. Nonetheless, they make an exception in the case of motor vehicles.
>
> In two cases involving the operation of motor vehicles by minors, the Supreme Court of Arkansas decided to hold minor operators to an adult standard of care. In one decision the court required an adult standard of care from a fifteen-year-old boy who was riding a motorcycle on a public street. *Harrelson v. Whitehead*, 365 S.W.2d 868 (Ark. 1963). In a second decision the court held that a fourteen-year-old boy operating a farm tractor in a cotton field should adhere to the same standard of care as a reasonably careful adult. *Jackson v. McCuiston*, 448 S.W.2d 33 (Ark. 1969). In *Jackson*, the court recognized that applying an adult standard of care to a minor who operates a motor vehicle is "an exception to our general rule that a minor owes that degree of care which a reasonably careful minor of his age and intelligence would exercise under similar circumstances.'
>
> . . . .
>
> The court should impose an adult standard of care on a minor operator of a rider mower. This activity requires an adult standard of care for the safety of the operator as well as for the safety of anyone else in the vicinity. The exception to the general rule is justified, because rider mowers are inherently dangerous, and adults normally operate them. A minor who undertakes the operation of a dangerous adult activity in the business world of adults cannot avoid the standard of care of a reasonably careful adult.

Some lawyers would call the first paragraph of this excerpt a "thesis paragraph,' because it states the conclusion and indicates how the writer reaches it. More specifically, in stating the conclusion, it presents the issue in concrete terms by using the facts of the case and justifies the conclusion by identifying the applicable rule, statute, or case precedent and briefly explaining how it applies.

Putting the conclusion first creates a "road map" in the reader's mind. Because the reader knows where the writer is going, the reader finds the discussion more meaningful from the outset. As readers, we find nothing more frustrating than plodding through a legal memorandum or brief that does not give us this road map. Without it, we find ourselves silently asking, "Now where is this writer taking me?'

Even though the student stated the conclusion at both the beginning and end of the discussion, the discussion is not too repetitive. The writer tells you what the conclusion is, explains the rationale for the conclusion, then restates the conclusion at the end as justified by the discussion. You do not have to guess at the outset where the writer is taking you -- there is no mystery here.

Note that the writer's conclusion at the end does not simply repeat the conclusion at the beginning. Instead, it makes clear the justification for the court decisions. Often the conclusion at the end will be more concrete or more emphatic than the conclusion at the beginning. Frequently, it will contain new information or a new insight.

Sometimes you will decide not to place a conclusion at the end, because you find it superfluous. In such instances, the conclusion is so dominant throughout the discussion that you see no need to repeat it. Still, do not let your ending trail off. End with some emphasis, perhaps by using a pithy sentence, a compelling example that justifies your conclusion, or a suggestion on what to do next.

Compare the following edited excerpt from another memorandum on the same subject with the one above:

> Courts have tended for the past twenty years to create exceptions to the general rule governing minors' responsibility for their negligent actions. In this society with rapid technological change, courts have faced the necessity of changing many rules to keep up with the use of sophisticated equipment in the form of farm machinery, automobiles, and the like. Public policy has compelled these changes in the interest of safety in a changing world.
>
> Although minors have had to adhere to a minor's standard of care, exceptions have evolved. Today's minors operate very sophisticated equipment, and public policy requires a higher standard of care from them. Minors do have accidents as a result of their handling sophisticated equipment, and safety requires that they be responsible to a greater extent than they were in the past.

The writer gives you no idea at the outset what the memorandum will conclude. After reading two paragraphs, you have no idea what this memorandum will say about the case involved. The main theme does not stand out. In comparison, the first sample memorandum excerpt requires only a quick glance for the reader to know what the writer's conclusion is.

At the outset, always let the reader know what your conclusion is. Then explain that conclusion within the context of the discussion. Finally, if desirable, present a recapitulation at the end.

§ 8.04   Write Effective Paragraphs

In making your main theme stand out, you must pay attention to how you present and develop ideas. You present and develop them within your primary units of discourse: sentences and paragraphs. In this section, we discuss writing effective paragraphs. You will learn how to present the idea in a paragraph, how to develop that idea, how to give the paragraph unity and direction, and how to connect sentences and paragraphs so that your analysis flows smoothly.

[1] Use Topic Sentences

Every paragraph should present one major idea. In most paragraphs, you will first present that idea in one sentence or in a group of sentences called topic sentences. (Most of the time, you will use one topic sentence.) These sentences provide the topic for the discussion that goes on in the rest of the paragraph.

Here is an example of a paragraph with a topic sentence in its most typical location, the very beginning. The writer is arguing against a court decision that upholds a statute as constitutional.

> The majority defines the right at stake too narrowly and treats the developmentally challenged as second class citizens with second class rights. No legislature would even consider drafting a provision like § 4693(c) and applying it to legally competent adults. Just as with the legally competent, individuals like D.T. must enjoy their fundamental liberty and privacy rights if they are to develop to their maximum economic, intellectual, and social levels.

In this paragraph, the topic sentence clearly states the point. The rest of the paragraph develops the point by explaining why the writer disagrees with the majority.

Here is the same paragraph with the sentences arranged in a different order:

> No legislature would even consider drafting a provision like § 4693(c) and applying it to legally competent adults. The majority defines the right at stake too narrowly and treats the developmentally challenged as second class citizens with second class rights. Just as with the legally competent, individuals like D.T. must enjoy their fundamental liberty and privacy rights if they are to develop to their maximum economic, intellectual, and social levels.

This paragraph is unsatisfactory, because the topic sentence is in the wrong place. A paragraph works well when the topic sentence states the idea, and the remaining sentences develop that idea. Here, the paragraph begins with the development, then states the topic, and then continues the development. In its original form, the paragraph succeeds because it begins with the conclusion and then develops it.

Instead of being at the beginning of the paragraph, the topic sentence can be at the end. In this instance, the paragraph builds to a conclusion. Here is an example:

> Just as with the legally competent, individuals like D.T. must enjoy their fundamental liberty and privacy rights if they are to develop to their maximum economic, intellectual, and social levels. Their development, however, is frustrated by § 4693(c). No legislature would even consider drafting a similar provision and applying it to legally competent adults. By upholding this statute, the majority defines the right at stake too narrowly and treats the developmentally challenged as second class citizens with second class rights.

You often will write this type of a paragraph as an introductory or concluding paragraph to a document or to a large section of a document. In these locations, readers frequently prefer a paragraph that builds to a conclusion. However, in other locations, be cautious about putting the topic sentence at the end. As you know, readers normally like conclusions to come first and therefore like topic sentences at the beginning.

Consider this paragraph:

> The State and the independent counsel for D.T. filed identical motions requesting the Probate Court to dismiss the parents' petition. They argued that § 4693(c) bars the relief requested and that it is constitutional. The court granted the motions and dismissed the petition. On appeal, the Superior Court issued a brief per curiam opinion affirming the Probate Court's opinion.

This paragraph lacks an explicit topic sentence. Nonetheless, we know the theme of the paragraph: the procedural history of the case. As the paragraph illustrates, sometimes a paragraph has no topic sentence.

You can omit a topic sentence when the general idea of the paragraph is clear to the reader. In a sense, the idea is present by implication. Narrative paragraphs are the most typical example.

Although you sometimes can forgo a topic sentence, do not be too quick to do so. Readers like topic sentences, because they make a paragraph's theme unambiguous. Err on the side of including topic sentences.

[2] Write Cohesive Paragraphs

Although writing a good topic sentence will go a long way toward making your theme stand out, you also must make certain that the discussion part of your paragraph supports and develops the topic sentence. When the topic sentence and the discussion work together, your paragraph will have unity and direction.

[a] Write Focused Discussion Sections

In different paragraphs, the discussion sections serve different purposes. For example, the discussion section may offer an example to illustrate the point of the topic sentence, elaborate on the topic sentence, furnish a logical argument supporting the point of the topic sentence, or provide a narrative that the topic sentence introduces. In each case, the discussion section discusses the idea in the topic sentence and focuses the reader's attention on it.

In the next paragraph, the discussion section offers an example. The topic sentence tells us that a court has declined to apply strict liability when the plaintiff is an expert in dealing with a potentially dangerous product. The discussion section discusses one case in which the court refused to find strict liability for this reason.

> The Washington Supreme Court has refused to extend strict liability to cases in which expert handlers suffer injury while working with a potentially dangerous product. For example, in *Spellmeyer v. Weyerhauser*, 544 P.2d 107 (1975), a longshoreman was injured when a bale of wood pulp fell on him.

According to the court, strict liability was inappropriate, because only expert loaders and carriers were required to deal with the bale. The court found that because of the plaintiff's status as such an expert, the policy considerations favoring strict liability were too diluted to be persuasive. *Id.* at 110.

Here is a paragraph in which the discussion section elaborates on the topic sentence:

> In *Seary v. Chrysler Corp.*, 609 P.2d 1382 (1980), the Washington Supreme Court refined the *Spellmeyer* holding to permit some expert handlers to successfully invoke strict liability. In *Seary*, a worker, an expert handler, was injured while loading a truck chassis onto a convoy trailer. He was operating a temporary device that was placed on the chassis specifically for the purpose of moving and unloading. The court imposed strict liability on the manufacturer of the temporary device, but only because the expert handler was the device's intended ultimate user. *Id.* at 1385. Although the court extended strict liability to an expert handler, it still limited the doctrine to situations in which a finished product is not safe for its intended use.

In this paragraph, the topic sentence tells us that a court used a case to refine its holding in an earlier case. The rest of the paragraph tells us about the new case and how the court used it to clarify its position on strict liability.

In the next paragraph, the discussion section presents a logical argument in support of the proposition in the topic sentence.

> When the user of a product is an expert in the care and handling of such products, the product is not unreasonably dangerous if the manufacturer fails to furnish instructions on its care and handling. By definition, an expert handler knows how to handle and move a wide variety of products. The handler possesses the experience, knowledge, and judgment necessary to protect himself or herself. Although, presumably, a significant percentage of products do not come to the docks equipped with loading instructions, it would be absurd to term all these products unreasonably dangerous to their handlers.

Note that the sentences in the discussion section appear in a carefully arranged sequence. The writer thought out the argument and made it one step at a time. If we were to rearrange the sentences in the discussion group, we would upset the logical order and seriously weaken the argument.

In the next paragraph, the discussion section provides a narrative that the topic sentence introduces.

> The injury occurred when the longshoremen attempted to load two steel drafts onto a barge. After both drafts arrived at the dock, the loaders safely loaded them onto the barge by using a sling of chain steel suspended from a shoreside crane. The loaders then determined that the drafts would fit better if loaded in the opposite direction. Therefore, they directed the crane operator to rehoist the drafts above the barge. Despite the availability of a nearby forklift and the obvious danger posed by the weight of the drafts, the loaders swung the drafts around in midair. The drafts collided with the forklift, slipped free from the sling, and crushed Mr. Smyth under their combined weight.

In this paragraph, the topic sentence tells you that the rest of the paragraph is going to describe the circumstances of the accident. When you read the paragraph, you may have thought that the topic sentence provided you with some help, but that it was not essential to your understanding. As discussed in § 8.04[1], in narratives, topic sentences are not always necessary. The reader usually knows the idea of the paragraph--to tell the story. The theme of the paragraph is implicit.

[b]   Avoid Extraneous Sentences

In writing the discussion section, make sure that all the material in the discussion relates to the topic sentence.

Consider this paragraph:

> Because the plaintiff failed to employ a sheriff to serve the garnishment writ on the defendant, the service was ineffective. Rule 402(a) permits a plaintiff to make service without a sheriff only when the plaintiff makes service within the Commonwealth. Because the plaintiff chose to make service at the defendant's Illinois office, Rule 402(a) cannot be successfully invoked. The plaintiff requests the court to overlook any error in service, because plaintiff could have served the writ at the defendant's office in the Commonwealth.

In this paragraph, the first sentence is the topic sentence. It states that the plaintiff's service of process was ineffective, because the plaintiff failed to employ a sheriff. The discussion section provides the supporting argument. It gives us the rule for when a plaintiff can make service without a sheriff and explains why that rule does not apply here. However, the last sentence of the paragraph is not part of that discussion. Instead of supporting the argument in the topic sentence, it puts forth the plaintiff's argument why the court should accept the service as valid. Although this sentence is about service of process, it does not directly relate to the topic sentence and is not part of the argument in the discussion section. As a result, it detracts from the unity and direction of the paragraph. It belongs in another paragraph.

Consider this paragraph:

> The discovery rule would not excuse the Johnsons from failing to satisfy the two-year statute of limitations. Under the rule, the statute would have begun running when the Johnsons should have known all the relevant facts. Although they had this knowledge shortly after their child's birth, they did not bring their action for another four years. However, the Johnsons could prevail under another exception to the two-year statute of limitations: the concealment exception. This exception tolls the statute of limitations when the defendant's fraud or concealment causes the plaintiff to relax his or her vigilance or fail to inquire further. In the present case, fraud and concealment were present and lulled the Johnsons into a false sense of security. Therefore the exception should apply.

The point of the topic sentence is that the discovery rule will not assist the Johnsons. We would expect the discussion section to explain why the discovery rule does not apply here. The first part of the discussion section satisfies our expectations. However, in the middle of the paragraph, the discussion shifts to the concealment rule. The rest of the paragraph fails to support the point of the topic sentence. Therefore, it belongs in a separate paragraph. In fact, the last four sentences of the paragraph should stand by themselves as a separate paragraph.

As the last two examples demonstrate, each paragraph can present only one central idea. Every sentence in the paragraph should deal directly with that idea. The focus on a single idea is what gives the paragraph unity and direction. Sentences that focus on some other idea are extraneous and must be omitted or placed in a different paragraph.

[3]   When Necessary, Use Transitions and Repeat Words

If the reader does not find a connection between the ideas within paragraphs and among paragraphs, he or she will not follow your analysis or argument. You create continuity by arranging your ideas in a logical or chronological order and by using transitional words -- for example, however, therefore, in addition, consequently, in contrast, and moreover -- and repeating words and ideas that you have used in earlier sentences and paragraphs. Here, we focus on transitions and repetition.

This paragraph illustrates how to use transitions and repetition:

> *The Supreme Court of Puerto Rico* has adopted the principle that rights and liabilities in tort must be determined according to the law of the jurisdiction having dominant contacts with the parties and the occurrence. *By adopting this approach, the court* has accepted the approach of the Restatement (Second) of Torts, which calls for applying the law of the state with the most significant relationship to the parties and the event. *The court thus* appears to conform to the Restatement's assertion that, in a personal injury case, a court should choose the law of the state where the injury occurred, unless another state's relationship to the injury is more significant.

The italicized words provide continuity between the sentences. The first sentence introduces the court. The remaining sentences make repeated references to the court and force the reader to remember that the paragraph is focusing on the Puerto Rico Supreme Court's resolution of a legal issue. The first four words of the second sentence refer back to the idea in the first sentence and let the reader know that the second sentence builds on the first. The third sentence contains the transitional word "thus"and tells the reader that the third sentence reaches a conclusion based on the preceding sentences. Repetition and transition thus give this paragraph cohesiveness.

The sample paragraph contains only one transitional word, "thus." As you work on your writing, you will discover that when you place your sentences in the proper sequence and repeat words and ideas that you introduced earlier, you will not need to clutter up your sentences with a large number of transitional words.

You also may have been concerned that the subject of every sentence in the paragraph is the same. You may have been taught that if you begin sentences with the same subject, you will bore the reader. Yet, you probably did not realize the repetition the first time you read the paragraph, and you probably did not become bored. Concern over excessive repetition is greatly exaggerated. Using the same subject for a series of sentences usually gives legal writing great continuity.

We will use the next paragraph to learn about transitions between paragraphs.

Ms. Joseph should be able to make out a prima facie case for disparate treatment. To make out her case, she must persuade the court that there is sufficient evidence to prove four elements: (1) that she belongs to a protected class; (2) that she applied for an available position for which she was qualified; (3) that she was rejected; and (4) that after the rejection, the employer continued to seek applicants. She should be able to provide sufficient evidence to establish these elements. First, as a woman, she is a member of a protected class. Second, she applied for a position as a firefighter for which she was fully qualified. Third, she was rejected under circumstances that give rise to an inference of discrimination. Fourth, after she was rejected, the city continued to seek applicants.

Suppose the writer believes that it is necessary to elaborate on Ms. Joseph's evidentiary proof for each of the elements. The writer then might follow this paragraph with four paragraphs, one for each element. The first of these paragraphs might begin: "As for the first element. . . ." The second might begin: "As for the second element. . . ." In each case, the new paragraph begins with a repetition of relevant words from the first paragraph.

Suppose the writer does not believe that these four paragraphs are needed and wishes to move directly to the defendant's response. The writer might begin the second paragraph with this sentence: "If Ms. Joseph establishes her prima facie case, the defendant has the opportunity to rebut the presumption of discrimination." The first clause in the sentence repeats the idea in the preceding paragraph. It thus connects the paragraphs. Alternatively, the writer might begin the second paragraph with this sentence: "However, the defendant should not necessarily admit defeat." By using "however,"a transitional word, the writer connects the paragraphs. As you can see, repetition and transitional words also are tools for connecting paragraphs.

EXERCISE

Here is a sequence of three paragraphs. Please rearrange the sentences to make the paragraphs more effective. You may move sentences from one paragraph to another and, if necessary, revise the sentences slightly.

Since two years have passed since the last permissible filing date, the statute of limitations, strictly read, would bar the action. Although this state's law normally imposes a two year statute of limitations for personal injuries, the Johnsons still may be able to bring an action for wrongful birth. In medical malpractice cases, the courts have recognized an exception called the "discovery rule." The rule does not require the plaintiff to know that the physician was negligent. This exception may apply to the Johnsons' action.

In applying the rule, the courts use a three-pronged test. The discovery rule applies to plaintiffs in medical malpractice actions. Under the rule, when the plaintiff cannot reasonably ascertain the existence of an injury, the statute of limitations does not begin to run until the injury's existence is known or discovered or becomes knowable or discoverable through the exercise of due diligence.

The statute begins to run when the plaintiff knows or, through reasonable diligence, should know of: (1) his or her injury; (2) the operative cause of the injury; and (3) the causal relationship between the injury and the operative.

CHAPTER **9**

HELP THE READER TO UNDERSTAND YOU

§ 9.01 Introduction

In this book you will learn to write documents such as legal memoranda for internal use in a law office, briefs for the courts' use in deciding your cases, and opinion letters for distribution to your clients.

Each form of legal writing has only one goal: to inform the reader in a clear and concise way. Help the reader out in every way you can. You should not try to impress your reader with your lawyering skills and language, but tell your reader your interpretation of the law in clear language.

Always assume that:

(1) the senior attorney who reads your internal legal memorandum may know little or nothing about the law as applied to the current case;

(2) the judge who reads your brief may know little or nothing about the law as applied to the current case; and

(3) the client who reads your opinion letter probably knows little or nothing about the law as applied to the current case.

Chapter 8 explained how to make your theme stand out. It thus explained one method of helping your reader to understand your writing. In this chapter you will learn other, often more subtle, methods for expressing your points clearly in writing.

Writing clearly, briefly, and precisely requires attention to detail. Many law students and young lawyers learn this lesson the hard way. A poor choice of words or a badly constructed sentence here and there really makes a difference.

We have organized this chapter into three topics: general advice, sentence structure, and sentence content. We also have included exercises to help you apply what you have learned.

§ 9.02 General Advice

[1] Get to the Point

If you do not get to the point immediately, you will lose your reader at the outset. The reader is most often a very busy person who does not have the time or patience to ferret out what you are trying to say.

In Chapter 8 you learned one of the best ways of getting to the point: State your conclusions first. Suppose a senior attorney asks you to write a memo to address how the courts in your state would resolve a particular dispute. In the course of your research, you may learn a historical lesson on how the relevant law developed. In the relevant cases, you also may come across dozens of pithy quotations. You also may summarize dozens of cases. You may be tempted to begin your memo with a historical essay, fill the remainder with quotations, and include a series of paragraphs each furnishing a mini-brief of each case you read. However, before you fall into these traps, remember your assignment. The senior attorney asked you to answer a specific question. Instead of loading your memo with irrelevant information, include only information that answers the question.

First, state your conclusion. Then, state the controlling rule or holding in your jurisdiction and explain how the courts have applied the rule to cases with facts similar to yours. Distinguish adverse cases with different facts. Include your historical information, your quotations, and your cases only to the extent that they help you answer the question that you were asked. In other words, get to the point. Use information only to help you explain your point.

[2] Use Concrete Language

Your writing should paint a picture in the reader's mind. You will not paint this picture unless you use concrete language and avoid abstractions. Do not try to achieve a lofty tone in legal writing. Your goal should be just the opposite. Follow these rules:

(1) Use the simplest language possible, as if you are telling a story orally.

(2) Use language the reader is least likely to have to look up in a dictionary.

(3) Use words that describe things in concrete terms.

Test your writing for concrete language and simplicity by reading it aloud. Does it sound interesting? Better still, read your writing to a non-lawyer, or a non-law student. Does that person understand it completely?

These examples illustrate how to change abstract to concrete language:

Bad: On the day the defendant's automobile collided with the minor, the precipitation level was very high, and the automobile hydroplaned.

Better: On the day Ms. Smith's car hit Sally Jones, it was raining hard and the car skidded off the road.

———————

Bad: The landlord had an obligation to secure the premises by preventing the entry of the criminal element into the domicile.

Better: The landlord should have provided adequate locks and windows on the doors to the apartment.

Bad: Mr. Jones committed his signature to writing on the document conveying the real estate to the new record title holder.

Better: Mr. Jones signed the deed to the land, transferring it to Ms. Smith.

Bad: The assailant brandished the weapon in the air at the victim, inflicting severe emotional distress and injuries to his person.

Better: The robber waved a gun at Mr. Jones, frightening him and severely gashing his forehead.

In each of the examples, abstract language became concrete language, and complex concepts became clear pictures.

Look at each sentence you write, and check to see whether you have used the simplest, most direct language possible. This instruction may appear contrary to what you think you should be learning at the professional school level. The poor writing you often see in case opinions reinforces the assumption that you should use complicated words and phrases and write abstractly. But this sort of writing is the opposite of what you should strive for. Only by writing simply and clearly can you communicate your ideas effectively.

[3]   Use the Active Voice

This rule is one of the hardest for writers to follow. Read the following examples:

Passive Voice: Mary was hit by Sarah.

Active Voice: Sarah hit Mary.

Passive Voice: The ball was thrown by Jeff.

Active Voice: Jeff threw the ball.

In the passive voice examples, the sentences focus on the objects of the action (Mary and the ball). The subject or actor in each sentence (Sarah and Jeff) that does something to the object takes a secondary role. In the active voice, the subject appears before the verb. It may be helpful to diagram the first example:

	(object)	(verb)	(preposition)	(subject)
(Passive)	Mary	was hit	by	Sarah

	(subject)	(verb)		(object)
(Active)	Sarah	hit		Mary

The more powerful, compelling way to express ideas in English is to use the active voice. There will be times when the passive voice is necessary, and there is no better way to express what you have said. But most of the time you can eliminate it with a little time and effort.

(Matthew Bender & Co., Inc.)   (Pub. 676)

A few examples from legal writing may illustrate the effectiveness of the active voice. Suppose you are a district attorney prosecuting a criminal case. Which of the following would sound more persuasive in your brief for the case?

> *Passive Voice:* The victim was hit by the defendant. Then she was raped by the defendant and shoved into the trunk of his car.

> *Active Voice:* The defendant hit the victim, raped her, and shoved her into the trunk of his car.

The sentence in the active voice is more forceful. It makes a declarative statement, emphasizes the defendant's actions, and implies knowledge and purpose on the defendant's part.

Suppose you represent Mr. Smith in a case in which he claims a parcel of land. Which of the following would sound more persuasive in your brief for the case?

> *Passive Voice:* Mr. Smith's intentions were evidenced by the facts that the land was occupied by him, the land was used by his sheep for grazing, and the land was used by him for planting crops.

> *Active Voice:* Mr. Smith showed his intentions by occupying the land, using it for sheep grazing, and farming it.

Use of the active voice connotes concrete actions by Mr. Smith. The active voice also helps eliminate some unnecessary words to streamline the sentence.

> *Passive Voice:* It was found by the court that the defendant was guilty, and he was sentenced to three years in prison.

> *Active Voice:* The court found the defendant guilty and sentenced him to three years in prison.

> *Passive Voice:* Title was quieted in Mr. Smith by the court, and Mr. Jones was found to no longer own the land.

> *Active Voice:* The court quieted title in Mr. Smith and found that Mr. Jones no longer owned the land.

> *Passive Voice:* The defendant was frisked by the detective, and this frisk turned up a loaded semi-automatic pistol, which was forcibly taken from his person.

> *Active Voice:* The detective frisked the defendant, and this frisk turned up a loaded semi-automatic pistol, which the detective forcibly took from the defendant.

It is often difficult to eliminate the passive voice from writing. The best method is to go over your last draft, sentence by sentence, and read each sentence again for only one purpose--to eliminate the use of passive voice. As you find each use of passive voice, ask yourself, "How can I convert this to the active voice, and will the sentence be better if I do convert it?'

Once you have learned how to eliminate passive voice, then you will begin to learn when you can use it effectively in certain situations. For example, the following passage by the famous lawyer Clarence Darrow depends on the passive voice (italicized) for dramatic effect:

> I don't believe in man's tinkering with the work of God. I don't believe that you and I can say in the light of heaven that, if we *had been born* as he *was born*, if our brains *had been molded* as his *was molded*, if we *had been surrounded* as he *has been surrounded*, we might not have been like him.**1**

In this example, Darrow is using the passive voice to put emphasis on the verbs. One way to emphasize a word or phrase is to place it at the end of a sentence or clause. Here, Darrow places the verbs in these positions. If he used the active voice, he would have been unable to place the verbs in these positions. The desire to emphasize the verbs prevailed over any disadvantages of using the passive voice.

[4] Avoid Legalese

Lawyers and judges too often use the jargon of the law, "legalese," in their writing. The frequent use of legalese is unnecessary and can result in unclear writing. You should avoid legalese not only because it results in ambiguity, but also because you may not yet fully understand the meanings of legal terms. Legal dictionaries do not always explain the full meanings of those terms. You will have opportunities to use the new language you are learning, but try to suppress the urge to over-use it in your writing.

A true story might be helpful here. Many first-year students love to use the word "dicta." They use "dicta" proudly and profusely in writing assignments. One student had been using the word in writing assignments throughout his first year of law school. At the end of the year, he told his professor that it was only then that he realized the full meaning of the word.

This student had used a dictionary definition of the term but, because of his limited experience, he did not understand precisely what that word meant. The word "dicta" refers to language in a court opinion that is unnecessary to the holding of a case. However, the student had been using the term to refer to actual holdings on issues other than those he had researched for his own research projects. He had not understood the term and had applied it too broadly.

Aside from this practical reason for not using legalese, the most important reason to avoid it is that you must write clearly, and use of legalese defeats this purpose. Legalese has developed over many centuries and stems from several languages -- notably, Latin, French, and Old and Middle English. Very little legalese is plain, simple, modern English that everyone can understand.

However, do not avoid using necessary terms of art, which you cannot replace with everyday words. The term "assault," for example, is a term of art; and you

---

1 Clarence Darrow, in defense of William D. Haywood for the murder of ex-governor Frank Steunenberg of Idaho, on the night of December 30, 1905. From G. J. Clark, *Great Sayings by Great Lawyers*, (Vernon Law Book Co., 1926).

cannot use another term such as "hit" to replace it. "Proximate cause" is a term you will learn, and you should not attempt to find a substitute for it. "Exigent circumstances" is a term in criminal procedure which has its own special meaning, and you should not attempt to simplify it. Aside from certain terms of art such as these, you can eliminate most legalese from your writing.

Do not strive to impress your reader with your newly learned legalese. Strive to impress your reader with your ability to communicate effectively.

Examples

Legalese: The parties agree only to the terms and conditions set forth *herein..*

Plain Language: The parties agree only to the terms and conditions *in this agreement.*

Legalese: The plaintiff *instituted legal proceedings* against the defendant.

Plain Language: The plaintiff *sued* the defendant.

Legalese: In the event that the defendant defaults on her obligation, she will *forfeit* her rights.

Plain Language: If the defendant defaults on her obligation, she will *lose* her rights.

Legalese: Subsequent to his decision, the judge changed his mind.

Plain Language: After his decision, the judge changed his mind.

Legalese: She is to pay him $10,000 *per annum.*

Plain Language: She is to pay him $10,000 *a year.*

The examples show that you can substitute simple words and phrases for most of the terms and phrases that are peculiar to the law. Always read over your final draft of a legal document to purge it of all legalese.

[5] Define Technical Terms

In the last subsection, you learned that you should avoid legalese. However, at times you cannot escape the use of technical terms. If you must use a technical term, define it immediately so you are sure the reader understands it. Of course, always consider your audience. Use your judgment when you decide whether the reader will understand the terms you use. A lawyer or judge may understand certain terms which a client would not understand. If you decide that it is necessary to define a term for your readers, either you can follow the term with a parenthesized definition, or you can define the term with a phrase or a sentence.

The following are examples of how to define technical terms in your writing:

(1) Mr. Barnes filed suit against Mr. Ewing to quiet title in the land. To "quiet title" means to ask the court to decide who owns the land.

(2) Mr. Barnes filed a suit against Mr. Ewing claiming adverse possession of the land. By invoking adverse possession, Mr. Barnes claimed he had gained ownership of Mr. Ewing's land by conducting certain acts with regard to the land for a certain time period.

(3) The defendant argued that a parent-child testimonial privilege should apply in this case. She argued that the court should not allow her son to testify against her in court because of the family relationship.

(4) Mr. Kramden argued that the insurance company's employee had apparent authority to bind the company. "Apparent authority" means that the insurance company represented to the public that the employee could make promises that the company must keep.

(5) The court ruled that the child should adhere to an adult standard of care (that is, that the child should have acted as a reasonable adult under the circumstances).

Never assume that your reader, whether another attorney or a judge, knows the meaning of every technical term you use. You do not want to insult your reader's intelligence, but you do not want to confuse your reader either.

[6] Write in the Appropriate Tone

Much of what you have learned thus far may appear to work against using any formality in legal writing. Nevertheless, legal writing is formal writing. Although you must strive for simplicity, clarity, and brevity, you still must achieve the appropriate tone.

Setting the appropriate tone in your writing is where you can be "lawyerly" and sound "like a lawyer." Later in this chapter, you will learn the mechanics of tone at the word and phrase level -- you will learn to avoid colloquialisms and contractions and not to personalize your writing with first ("I,' "we') and second ("you') person pronouns. Learning those mechanics will help you write in the appropriate tone.

The tone in legal writing is similar to that in good business writing. Some helpful hints:

(1) Do not use colloquialisms or slang.

(2) Do not use contractions.

(3) Do not personalize your writing.

(4)   Do not sound "preachy" or take the "soapbox" approach (*see* Chapter 12, § 14.03[4]).

(5)   Do be serious. Legal documents are serious matters, and your clients have serious concerns. Legal documents are generally not the place for humor or lightness.

Although the cases you read in your casebooks may not always be the best examples of good legal writing, they usually illustrate the tone you should set in your writing. They are usually good examples for you to study.

EXERCISES FOR § 9.02

The following exercises give you an opportunity to put into practice some of the rules that we have just covered. Identify the errors and, to the extent possible, rewrite the sentences to eliminate those errors. You may have some difficulty rewriting some of the sentences as the original author would have, because they are taken out of context. Do the best you can. For these exercises, you may assume facts not given if they are necessary.

(1) Although Pennsylvania does not provide for depositions in these circumstances, other state and the federal courts call for depositions. In *United States v. Linton*, 502 F. Supp. 878 (D. Or. 1980), the court stressed that where testimony can be adequately secured by deposition, an incarcerated witness should not be further detained. In *Linton* the witness had been in jail for two months. At that time the trial was postponed. The court held that this was an "exceptional circumstance," and that it was "in the interest of justice that his testimony be taken by deposition." *Id.* at 879. The court delineated a comprehensive method of deposition-taking which includes videotaped examinations and cross-examinations.

Therefore, considering that Pennsylvania statute and case law strongly indicate material witnesses may not be held indefinitely, that the brothers were not afforded counsel to challenge their incarceration, and that deposition is a viable alternative to incarceration, the Fernandez brothers should be released from jail.

(2) The said canine caught the minor child's (Sally's) hand in his mouth, inflicting an injury which required ten sutures.

(3) The patient listed his unhealthy habits as the consumption of tobacco and alcoholic beverages and a lack of physical activity.

(4) The Texaco signs were put up by Bi-Rite Oil Company, which is Butterbaugh's distributor out of Monroeville and is independent of Texaco; the signs were provided by Bi-Rite free of charge.

(5) A criminal complaint was filed against defendant by the district attorney on November 5, 1995, charging the defendant with indecent assault. A preliminary hearing was scheduled by the district magistrate on November 14, 1995, but the hearing was not held because the defendant was not ready. Another hearing was

scheduled for November 21, 1995, but was continued by the magistrate because a government witness was unavailable. The preliminary hearing was rescheduled for November 26, 1995, but was continued by the magistrate because defendant's attorney was unavailable. Finally, on December 10, 1995, a preliminary hearing was held by a district magistrate, and a prima facie case was established by the district attorney at that time. On December 12, 1995, the magisterial transcript was sent to the court by the clerk and was received by the district attorney on December 19, 1995. The information was filed on January 14, 1996, and the date for arraignment was set for January 22, 1996, on which date arraignment occurred.

(6) FINDINGS OF FACT

(1) The aforesaid respondent, [　], Esq., is an attorney admitted to practice law in the Commonwealth of Pennsylvania, and his last place of business was located at [　].

(2) Subsequent to February 1995, respondent's wife died suddenly, leaving him with two minors to care for.

(3) The sudden demise of respondent's spouse resulted in extreme mental trauma and shock to respondent thereafter.

(4) Respondent entered a period of severe depression and began heavy consumption of alcohol at or about the time of his wife's demise.

(5) Subsequent to March 1996, respondent attempted suicide and was in a state of severe psychotic depression.

(6) The suicide attempt closely paralleled the first anniversary of his wife's demise.

(7) During the period following his wife's death, and at all times material herein, respondent suffered an impairment of judgment and a diminished mental capacity.

(8) During the period of impaired judgment and diminished mental capacity, respondent committed the wrongful acts hereinafter set forth.

(9) All conditions precedent and contained in the aforesaid Agreement of Sale have been met, have been waived by defendant's aforesaid conduct or have been prevented by the defendant's aforesaid conduct.

(10) The court requested further investigation as to whether decedent was ever married or had issue. Mr. Lochner questioned, *inter alia*, whether decedent's father, Robert F. Atkinson, was in fact the uncle of Franklin A. Allen, and mentioned other possible discrepancies in the family tree. Mr. Lochner's correspondence was referred to the trustee ad litem. Franklin A. Allen died testate on March 19, 1997.

(11) In that case, where plaintiff sued a bank for conversion of checks payable to plaintiff which were paid over alleged forged endorsements to plaintiff's bookkeeper, the bank's joinder of plaintiff's accounting firm alleging negligence in permitting the embezzlement may be properly dismissed since the theory of such joinder was distinct and unrelated to the theory of plaintiff's

original complaint. Moreover, the defendant and additional defendant are not joint tortfeasors.

(12) This court should not allow the lower court's decision to stand. You have a duty to protect kids from dangerous people like the defendant. You also have a duty to support the cops, who work hard to catch people like the defendant. If you don't overturn the lower court's decision in this case, you'll negate everything we prosecutors work for. The defendant didn't even provide an excuse for her actions. Our case against her should be the winner here.

§ 9.03 Structure

When you put sentences together, the most important guideline is to limit each sentence to one thought. Plan your sentences before you commit them to paper. After several weeks of intensive research and thought about a problem, you may find yourself trying to say too much too quickly. The result can be long, rambling, almost "stream of consciousness" strings of words that obscure the central idea. Here are some ways to avoid this result.

[1] Write Short Sentences

The easiest way to keep your writing clear and readable is to write short sentences. The basic sentence includes a subject, a verb, and usually an object. In most cases those elements are all you need to express a single idea. Choose your words with care and work to communicate rather than impress. You then should have no trouble writing short, precise sentences, and your reader will understand you quickly and easily.

Bad: In this case, there was no public controversy involving the concert, because the concert affected only its small number of participants, and even if there was plaintiff did not thrust himself to the forefront of the controversy -- he was involuntarily drawn into it either by virtue of his position as promoter of the concert or by the defendant's cablecast.

Better: In this case no public controversy involving the concert existed. The concert affected only its small number of participants. If a public controversy existed, plaintiff did not thrust himself into it. He was involuntarily drawn into it, either because of his position as the concert's promoter or because of the defendant's cablecast.

Bad: The court in its opinion, however, found that the record indicated that hospital security was "more lax than it could have been," sufficiently so that the court decided to hold the hospital liable based solely on the issues of law presented in the pleadings, and on the facts as revealed in the deposed testimony of the hospital's own employees.

Better: However, the court found that, according to the record, hospital security was "more lax than it could have been." Therefore, it held the hospital liable solely on the pleadings and on the facts revealed in the depositions of the hospital's employees.

Bad: Appellant's failure to respond to the motion, however, goes to the heart of the suit, and, if he is allowed to ignore proper procedure, the judicial process will be threatened with paralysis as the court will be unable to determine when it is appropriate to assume no response will be forthcoming from appellant.

Better: Appellant did not respond to the motion. This failure goes to the heart of the suit, because it paralyzes the judicial process. When a court does not know whether a litigant plans to respond to a pleading, it is unable to proceed.

The repairs to these sentences took several forms: dividing the long sentence into several smaller sentences, removing unnecessary phrases, and rewording sentences to make them more direct. Correcting one long sentence occasionally results in a longer discussion. It is an acceptable result to have more words and sentences if the final product is clearer.

Not all the revised sentences are short, one clause sentences. Legal writing does not look like the text of a book for grade school children. If you need to use a complex sentence, use it. First, however, try to reduce your ideas to short sentences that flow.

[2] Put the Parts of Your Sentence in a Logical Order

One of the most common errors writers make is failing to put sentences together in a logical sequence.

Bad: First, this court properly dismissed plaintiff's claim for fraud since plaintiff's injury, the job loss, was due to the use of information by the employer supplied by the defendant and not due to the defendant's alleged misrepresentation.

Better: First, this court properly dismissed plaintiff's claim for fraud, since plaintiff's job loss was not due to the defendant's alleged misrepresentation, but rather to the employer's use of information that the defendant supplied.

Comment: Rewriting this sentence as at least two shorter sentences would be an even greater improvement.

The problem stems from "stream of consciousness" writing. Sometimes thoughts make perfect sense in a certain order in your mind, but become confusing when you write them. The problem generally results from not planning sentences and trying to put too many ideas into too few words.

Avoid confusing sentences by taking the time to read what you have just written. Put yourself in the reader's shoes. Will the reader understand the sentence easily? Will the reader understand it more easily if you place the ideas in a different sequence, perhaps a sequence more chronological or logical?

The best way to catch logical errors is to put the writing aside for a while and read it later when you have greater objectivity. Then, be willing to revise it. One of the writer's hardest tasks is to proofread with a willingness to make substantial changes. It also is one of the most profitable.

Here is another example.

Bad: Any disposition of property to a third person who had notice of the pendency of the matrimonial action or who paid wholly inadequate consideration for such property may be deemed fraudulent and declared void.

Better: A court can declare fraudulent and void any disposition of property to a third person when the third person knew that a matrimonial action was pending or when that person paid wholly inadequate consideration for the property.

[3] Avoid Intrusive Phrases and Clauses

Writers sometimes burden their sentences with clauses and phrases that are not needed to convey the main idea. These inserts break the sentence flow and create difficulty for the reader. Intrusive phrases appear when writers rush onto paper the many thoughts cluttering their minds.

Bad: While the Third Circuit test is on its face similar, it can lead to results such as the issue at bar, that are inconsistent with the limited public figure status determination by this Court in *Gertz.*

Better: While the Third Circuit test is facially similar to this Court's, it can lead to results that are inconsistent with this Court's definition of limited purpose public figure in *Gertz.*

Comment: The rewrite eliminates the intrusive phrase "such as the issue at bar." Awkward phrases "on its face" and "status determination" become the simpler words, "facially" and "definition." To clarify the comparison between the tests of the two courts, the writer inserted "this Court's" in two appropriate locations.

Bad: The Third Circuit erred in determining plaintiff was a limited purpose public figure, because in reality, under the approach taken by the United States Supreme Court, plaintiff at best would be classified as an involuntary public figure at the extreme.

Better: The Third Circuit erred in determining that plaintiff was a limited purpose public figure. Under the Supreme Court's approach, plaintiff is an involuntary public figure at best.

Comment: The rewrite eliminated the intrusive phrase "in reality." The passive "could be classified as" became "is". For further clarification, the long sentence became two shorter sentences.

Bad: With keeping the above in mind, the court of appeals notes that plaintiff thrust himself into the public eye by actively seeking publicity for the event.

Better: As the court of appeals noted, plaintiff thrust himself into the public eye by actively seeking publicity for the event.

Comment: The phrase eliminated, "with keeping the above in mind," could almost be described as "throat clearing" before getting to the point.

Writers occasionally use intrusive phrases as a substitute for more detailed analysis. Avoid phrases like "such as the issue at bar" in the first example. Instead, make the comparison in a clear and concrete way. Other phrases, such as those removed from the second and third examples, serve no useful purpose and may create confusion.

[4]   Use Full Sentences

The occasional result of convoluted phrasing and writing too fast is a sentence that is not a sentence at all. Here are some examples:

    (1)   The estate failed to meet its evidentiary burden because sufficient evidence from which the trial court could have reasonably concluded that the decedent's death was the result of pre-existing animosity between the assailant and the decedent.

    (2)   A position which this Court soundly rejected in *Gertz.*

    (3)   The way in which the average person viewing the statement in its intended circumstances is of critical import.

[5]   Use Parallel Structure

Maintain a consistent structure when joining phrases or clauses. Writers sometimes change verb tenses or use different introductory words for clauses that require the same word.

Bad: The hospital owes its invitees reasonable protection or to warn its invitees to the potential acts of third parties.

Better: The hospital owes its invitees reasonable protection or a warning about the potential acts of third parties.

Comment: The writer shifted from the noun "protection" to the verb "to warn" when discussing what the hospital owed its invitees. Using two nouns makes the sentence correct and comprehensible.

Bad: The plaintiff did not allege that the defendant acted specifically for the plaintiff to lose his job, but rather acted to induce the plaintiff's cooperation.

Better: The plaintiff did not allege that the defendant acted with the specific intent to have the plaintiff lose his job. He alleged only that the defendant acted to induce plaintiff's cooperation.

Comment: The failure to include some form of the verb "allege" in both parts of the sentence made the original sentence difficult to understand. Dividing the sentence into two shorter sentences clarifies it further. However, the final version still takes some effort for the reader to understand. Although revising complicated sentences makes them easier to understand, it does not remove the inherent complexity of the underlying idea. We can improve comprehensibility, but the reader still may have to do some work.

Bad: The security guard had no recollection of checking the laundry room doors before the murder and he also did not check the doors to the medical records office to see if they were locked.

Better: The security guard did not recollect checking the laundry room doors or the doors to the medical records office before the murder to see if they were locked.

Comment: In the first version, the combination of "had no recollection of checking" and "he also did not check' makes the sentence more complicated than it needs to be.

Bad: The definition established three criteria: there must exist a public controversy, into which an individual has become voluntarily or involuntarily involved for the purpose of assuming special prominence in the resolution of that issue within the controversy.

Better: The definition established three criteria: 1) A public controversy must exist; 2) The individual must become involved in that controversy voluntarily or involuntarily; and 3) The individual must intend to assume special prominence in the resolution of the controversy.

Comment: When providing a list, make sure the elements of the list are immediately apparent to the reader.

As you can see, mistakes involving parallel structure often center around verbs. Writers either use too many verbs in different forms or do not repeat the necessary verbs when they should.

§ 9.04 Content

This section focuses on choosing the right words. Make sure that you choose the words that express your idea most precisely. Your words also must be appropriate for your medium of communication and your audience. They should be more formal and technical for briefs and memoranda and less formal for letters to clients. Writers sometimes choose words that obscure meaning, that are inappropriate for their intended audience and, occasionally, that do not mean what the writers intended. Careful attention to your own writing will help you avoid these problems.

[1] Use Positives Rather Than Negatives

If you emphasize the positive and avoid qualifiers, the reader probably will understand you better. Your writing also will set a tone that encourages the reader to agree with you. If you sound as if you believe what you are saying, the reader will be more likely to believe you.

Sometimes a negative word or phrase is necessary to express an idea precisely or to emphasize a point. However, use care to prevent a negative from making your message unclear or incorrect. Some writers use negatives when they are unnecessary or inappropriate. Occasionally, a writer will commit that unpardonable sin that our first grammar teachers warned us against -- the double negative.

Here is an example of an awkward use of negatives:

> The district court exercised its discretion in allowing seventeen days to pass before treating our opponent's non-response as not contesting the motion.

The sentence conveys the same idea but is easier to understand if phrased as follows:

> When our opponent failed to respond, the district court exercised its discretion in allowing seventeen days to pass before treating the motion as uncontested.

Another aspect of using positive rather than negative language is the avoidance of qualifying words. Students and lawyers are sometimes less than totally confident in their positions. They reflect their insecurity in their choice of words. Avoid phrases like "it would seem," "it would appear," and "we would argue." These phrases are rarely necessary. They may even highlight areas of your argument that are particularly vulnerable.

[2] Avoid Ambiguous Words and Phrases

Students and young lawyers have a natural desire to "sound like lawyers." They sometimes use ambiguous words or phrases that obscure the intended meaning but sound more "professional." Sometimes you will want to obscure the exact meaning of your message, such as when you make an argument that is less than airtight, but normally you should strive for clarity and ease of understanding. In the following examples, the writers failed to convey their meaning clearly. It is therefore not possible to rewrite the sentences in "better" form.

Bad: In such cases as *Hutchinson* and *Wolston*, this Court stressed that it is not the quantity of the relationship of the individual to the media but also the quality to which the individual subjects himself to the public.

Comment: Although there are several problems with this sentence, one of the most glaring is that the words "quantity" and "quality" are virtually meaningless. Although, in this context, these words may have a particular meaning for the writer, they do not have the same meaning for the reader. In trying to set up a stylistic contrast, the writer leaves the reader at a loss in trying to determine what the writer means.

Bad: However, as stated earlier in reference to access to the media, this would be inconsistent with this Court in the position taken in *Time* for much of the same rationale.

Comment: The writer is trying to reinforce a point made earlier without actually making the point again. The result is an almost indecipherable sentence that requires the reader to do far too much work. If you need to repeat yourself or to refer to an earlier point and explain it briefly, do so.

Bad: Plaintiff for the most part, pleaded only conclusions which, while they may indicate that the end result of defendant's actions was outrageous conduct, do not indicate facts which show that his actions were outrageous conduct in themselves.

Comment: The writer repeats the phrase "outrageous conduct" but gives the reader no clue to what it means. The writer must provide more information.

Bad: Defendant's interview with plaintiff did not constitute the severity of an ultimatum found in *Richette.*

Bad: The defendant did not constitute an employee.

Comment: The misuse of the word "constitute" in the examples above represents the affinity some writers have for words they do not quite understand. When in doubt, use a dictionary or use simpler words that express the same idea. For example, the writer could re-word the second sentence above to say "[t]he defendant was not an employee.'

[3] Avoid Colloquialism

Although we often hear that we should write the way we speak, certain words and phrases should rarely find their way onto paper. You can rely on common sense to identify language that is inappropriate for a written document. For example, you should not say that a court has "come up with" a particular definition. You also should avoid contractions such as "can't," "don't," and "won't." They are too conversational for the vast majority of written documents you will prepare. Here is an example from a student brief that demonstrates language you should avoid:

> While these matters might be interesting to some people, the events of a small loosely run beauty pageant would hardly make a dent in the priority list of the public at large. Most people don't know when the pageant is held and a great number don't really care.

[4] Do Not Personalize

Some writers cannot resist the temptation to refer either to themselves or to their readers with pronouns such as "I," "we," "our," or "you." These words may be appropriate for this book, but they are not appropriate in formal legal writing. Phrases such as "we submit," "I believe," or "our position is" only weaken your argument by reminding the reader that you are making arguments. When writing a brief or memorandum, make your arguments sound like statements of law rather than statements of personal opinion. A judge or a senior attorney may not care about your personal opinion. That judge or attorney wants to know what the law is and how it applies to your case.

When referring to the court to which a brief is addressed, use "this court." In a memorandum, you may refer to a senior attorney as "you," but many attorneys consider the pronoun too informal even for inter-office memoranda. It is safer to avoid its use. You also should avoid the more formal and often awkward "one."

[5] Avoid Excessive Variation

Many students learn to use a different word every time they refer to the same person or thing. Using different words and phrases to refer to the same thing serves the laudable goal of preventing the reader from getting bored by repetition. Excessive variation, however, backfires. It is unaesthetic and sometimes comical. It also creates confusion when the writer uses inaccurate words rather than repeating accurate ones.

Legal terms of art offer an example. In Torts, "standard of care" has a precise meaning that many court decisions have developed. If you use the phrase "standard of negligence" rather than repeat the term of art, the educated legal reader will not understand what you are saying. Excessive variation creates ambiguity.

In the following example, confusion results because the writer uses different words to refer to the same litigants.

> According to the record, Sam Spade had never before met the plaintiff. Although the plaintiff alleges that Mr. Spade already possessed some information about the plaintiff, there is no indication of any reason why this information might lead our client to maliciously intend to injure the appellant or to inflict losses upon him.

You might think that this excerpt mentions four people. It actually mentions two. "Sam Spade" and "our client" are the same person, as are "plaintiff" and "appellant."

In summary, the lessons are twofold. First, avoid boring the reader with repetition. Be creative, but do not overdo it. Second, be repetitive rather than imprecise or confusing.

EXERCISES FOR §§ 9.03 AND 9.04

The following exercises are sentences taken from student briefs and memos. They give you an opportunity to put into practice some of the principles discussed above. Identify the errors and, to the extent possible, rewrite the sentences to eliminate those errors. You may have some difficulty rewriting some of the sentences as the author would have, since they are taken out of context. Do the best you can.

(1) However, since the issue has been raised it has become necessary to demonstrate that even though a second motion to dismiss was not required, by submitting a letter of request to the judge and providing opposing counsel with a copy of the letter, the judge correctly found that the letter was sufficient to comply with all applicable rules of procedure regarding motions.

(2) The fundamental principle of the fourth amendment is ensuring "one's privacy against arbitrary intrusions by the police," *Wolf v. Colorado*, 338 U.S. 25, 27 (1949) and "intended as a restraint upon the activities of sovereign authority, and was not intended to be a limitation upon other than governmental agencies . . . ." *Burdeau v. McDowell*, 256 U.S. 465, 475 (1921).

(3) Taking into consideration the Pennsylvania Rules of Civil Procedure, which limit the amount of time in which an affirmative request for a jury trial must be made and the rulings of the courts in these cases concerning the implications of failing to file for a jury trial at all, it would be difficult, after not requesting a jury trial within the past 30 days and the trial date approaching so soon, to convince the court to allow Olive Holmes' case to be heard by a jury.

(4) The question thus is whether our client's promise that she would return to talk to the police signified voluntary willingness to be confined, or whether the Dean's refusal to allow her to leave is a detaining force sufficient from which she has no legal obligation to resist in order to prove lack of consent.

(5) In *Medico*, the court held that a press defendant could relieve itself of liability without establishing the truth of the substance of the statement reported by claiming the fair report privilege when its publication contains matters of public concern and is based on acts of the executive or administrative officials or governmental reports.

(6) Ms. Holmes can establish the tort of false imprisonment against The Law School due to the fact that Ms. Holmes's nonconsensual confinement by the school dean can be predicated as false imprisonment since Ms. Holmes was exonerated of the charge establishing the basis for the school dean's confinement of Ms. Holmes.

(7) The security guard deposed that the assailant entered the hospital through the emergency room when he confronted him about an hour before the murder and that there was no other security guard on duty who was monitoring the emergency entrance.

(8) Insofar as the court moved for a summary judgment in the Estate's favor based on the evidence in the depositions, it decided that a negligent breach of duty was shown as a matter of law and that the only reasonable inference was that its negligence, and not the criminal act of the assailant, was the proximate, legal cause of plaintiff's death.

(9) The state's patient-physician privilege imputes such information as being highly confidential and personal.

(10) The key issue to be determined is whether The Law School's answer to the complaint for false imprisonment is the last pleading directed to such issue or

whether the dean's answer to the Law School's third party complaint for indemnification is not the last pleading directed to that issue, but only to the issue of indemnity.

(11) Nor is there liability if the plaintiff fails to show that the private matter of the alleged publicity is not of legitimate public concern.

PART III

PRE-LITIGATION LAWYERING

(Matthew Bender & Co., Inc.)

CHAPTER 10

MEETING THE CLIENT

§ 10.01 Purpose of the Initial Interview

As you plan for the initial interview with a client, ask yourself what you need to accomplish in that interview. Remember that the client is not a walking, talking legal problem, but a living, breathing human being with feelings, goals, and priorities, who happens to have a current problem that may have some legal dimensions. Of course you do need to ascertain the scope of the problem that brings the client to you, but you need to find out more than the legally relevant facts. You need to understand the client. What kind of person is the client? What does he or she hope to accomplish by coming to see a lawyer?

You also need to lay the groundwork for a working relationship. Clients need to feel comfortable with you. They need to be able to trust that you will handle the problem appropriately and with sensitivity. Since the only way you will be able to make a living as a lawyer is if clients retain you, you must sell yourself. For most clients, you do not sell yourself best by overselling yourself. You sell yourself best by creating trust, by opening the channels of communication in both directions, and by conveying confidence and competence.

Remember that this is also a business relationship. It is sometimes difficult to bring up the subject of money when a client is presenting you with what may be the most pressing and difficult situation in his or her life at that moment. If you do not address the business aspects of the relationship early on, however, you open yourself up to the very real possibility of misunderstandings and unnecessary problems later. Although this may sound obvious, you need to get a clear commitment from the client to hire you before you begin working on the client's behalf.

The client will also likely want an initial assessment of the legal situation. Clients frequently ask questions such as "What are my rights?" "Can he do that?" "How can I get my money back?" "Will I have to go to jail?" Because you are a lawyer, clients expect you to have the answers to those questions. As you go through law school, you learn that there are far more questions than answers, and that you have to do research before you can answer most questions. One of the most delicate tasks to accomplish with a new client is to let the client know that you need more information, both factual and legal, before you can give an accurate answer to the problem. At the same time, you should try to give the client some idea of what might happen. What are some available dispute resolution options? How does the legal system treat these kinds of problems? Can you provide a preliminary assessment of the client's problem based on your existing legal knowledge?

§ 10.02 Planning the Initial Interview

Here are some goals for an initial interview with a client:

* Get the facts
* Get to know the client
* Understand the client's feelings, goals and priorities
* Begin building trust
* Explain your fees
* Get hired
* Offer a preliminary assessment of the problem

You cannot accomplish these tasks without a plan. This is not the type of conversation where you can just sit back and see where it goes. As you gain more experience, you will develop a pattern for approaching interviews that allows you to accomplish your goals, but at first you must consciously structure your approach to the conversation. Plan a strategy for building trust, getting information, getting the client to retain you, and beginning to address the client's problem. It is probably a good idea to have a written form of some kind in front of you that reminds you of the various components of the initial interview. The rest of this chapter offers advice on how to structure the initial interview so you do not forget any critical steps.

§ 10.03 Greeting the Client

It may sound artificial to suggest that you plan your greeting to the client. However, as we all know, first impressions are frequently lasting impressions, and you should consider whether you want the client's first impression of you to be that you are cold, calculating, and money-hungry, or that you are a considerate, caring human being. You will be easier to confide in if you spend a bit of time in casual conversation about non-threatening topics such as the weather or traffic or similar "elevator" conversation. It may seem awkward and forced, particularly at first, but it does allow the client to settle down, assess the surroundings, and prepare to discuss more difficult topics. If you can seem comfortable and genuinely interested in a relaxed approach to the conversation, hopefully the client will follow your lead. You will find it easier to get information if the tension level in your office is low.

Be careful about accomplishing your atmospheric goal by commenting on any aspect of the client's appearance. Besides being a bit personal, you never know what might be a sensitive subject. For example, if the client is coming to you about a divorce, you may start the interview off on exactly the wrong note by commenting on what a beautiful diamond ring she is wearing.

§ 10.04   Preparatory Explanation

It is generally a good idea to offer a roadmap of the interview before you start questioning the client. You might ask whether the client has ever seen a lawyer before, as a means of gauging what the client's expectations are likely to be. If the client has never seen a lawyer before, it is a good idea to outline the procedure you intend to follow during the interview. For example, explain how long the interview is likely to last, what your goals are, that you will be asking questions and taking notes, that the client will have a chance to ask questions, that you will try to begin developing options for resolving the client's problem, and that you will discuss the likely cost of handling the problem. You may also want to remind the client of your ethical obligations relating to confidentiality.

If the client has seen a lawyer before, it is a good idea to get a feel for whether that was a positive or negative experience. If the client comes in skeptical or suspicious about lawyers because of a previous bad experience, it is helpful for you to know that sooner rather than later. If the client has had prior negative experience with attorneys, your goal is to persuade the client that you are a valuable ally, not a necessary evil. You can best do this by taking the time to show the client that you care about him or her as a whole person, not just a legal problem or a source of money.

§ 10.05   Getting the Client's Perspective

As lawyers, we frequently are in a hurry to find out what the legal problem is. We are trained in law school to spot issues, to sift through the facts presented until we find the ones that matter, and then offer an analysis of how the law applies to those facts. That is only a small part of what you must accomplish with a client. Avoid the temptation to become impatient when the client seems to ramble, or starts talking about feelings. You cannot adequately represent a client without knowing how the client feels about the problem, what the client hopes to accomplish in coming to see you, and what the client's priorities are.

You will be tempted to substitute your own value system for the client's, to think about how you would handle the problem if it were yours. It is not your problem, and you must never lose sight of that fact, even if the client tries to hand you the problem. Clients frequently come to you and ask "What should I do?" The only good answer to that question is the one the client arrives at after being given a full understanding of the likely consequences of different approaches. Your job is to inform the client so that he or she can make a decision based on his or her own value system. You will do this better if you understand the client's perspective on the problem.

[1]   Getting Started

The easiest way to begin the interview is to ask a simple, open question such as, "What brings you here today?" Or "How can I help you?" Let the client know that you want to hear the story in his or her own words, then let the client tell it. Resist the temptation to break in with constant questions. If you are afraid you will forget to ask about a needed detail, jot it down. If you derail the client's story with questions, you may end up missing key facts or elements in the story. Do not try to put legal labels on the client's problem too soon: "Oh, this is a contracts problem." If you do that you will start focusing on questions you were trained to ask about contracts, and you may never find out that the client has also brought you a tax problem and a criminal problem, or you may find out at a time and in a manner that is awkward and difficult.

If the client has difficulty knowing where to start, you might suggest a time frame. "Start at the beginning." "What event made you decide to come see a lawyer?" If the client offers unhelpful generalizations such as "I have a problem with my partner," then you want to try a few direct questions to get the story going. "Do you mean a business partner?" "What kind of business do you have?" "Does the problem relate to the business?" Once the client gets into the story, stop the questions and let the client talk.

[2] Keeping Track

It is difficult to balance your need to keep track of information the client is giving you with the client's need to feel that you are listening. You will probably want to take some notes, but try not to spend the entire session staring at your legal pad as you write. Eye contact is a very important part of the conversation, not only for the client but for you. You may gain valuable clues to the client's personality and sensitive aspects of the problem by watching the nonverbal channels of communication. If you can, listen for a while, then write down only the most important aspects of the story. Jot down details such as names and dates, but don't try to record every word the client says. If you do not feel that you will be able to accurately remember the client's message if you wait too long, you may want to ask the client if you may record the conversation. Having a tape recording will free you to really concentrate on the client's message and the way it is being communicated.

[3] Getting the Details

You do need some details. You need detailed information about the client, including addresses and phone numbers so that you will be able to contact him or her throughout your handling of the matter. You may also need names, addresses, and phone numbers of other individuals who are involved in the matter or who may be potential witnesses. You need dates, times, places, and relevant documents. Thus you will need to ask focused, closed questions at some point in the interview. Try not to interrogate the client. If the client becomes defensive, you will likely not get information you need. It is a good idea to explain to the client why you need so much information. You may also want to have a written questionnaire for the client to take home, at least for cases such as divorce or bakruptcy, where you need a great deal of detail about personal and financial matters.

Try to get a chronological version of events. Ask for the sequence of events, and ask for dates. Find out who else is involved, and who else knows what is going on. Find out if there are any documents you need to look at and if the client can get them for you. It is a good idea to recap the client's story, perhaps several times, depending on the complexity of the story and the organization (or lack of organization) of the information provided. Telling the client what you have understood lets the client know that you were listening, and often provides an opportunity to get additional information. You may discover that you got some aspect of the story wrong, or your recap may prompt the client to fill in gaps in the story.

You will also need information the client may not think to give you, because the client does not know it is important. Clients do not know the law or may have incorrect ideas about what the law says. Therefore they may have a different idea of what information is relevant than you do. They may also have personal reactions or priorities that give them a different sense of what is relevant or important. For example, it may be very important to the client that you understand that he was treated disrespectfully, while that fact may have no legal significance. Do not dismiss facts that the client thinks are important, but stay focused enough to get the facts you need.

The client may be embarrassed about certain facts; the client wants you to think that he or she is a good person and has a good case, so there may be a temptation not to tell you about things that reflect negatively on the client's character or the case. Remind the client that what is said to you will be kept in confidence (subject to certain exceptions such as information relating to imminent harm to another, which you may disclose), and that you can only provide the best possible representation if you have the full story. It is frequently a good idea to ask the client what the other party is likely to say about the situation. This allows the client to give you necessary and possibly damaging information without having to acknowledge its accuracy or validity.

[4] Goals and Priorities

We have emphasized the need to get the client's perspective on the problem and potential solutions. How do you accomplish this? The simplest way is to ask: "What would you like to see happen?" If you had to choose between X and Y, which would you choose?" The client may not have thought about the answers to these questions, assuming that you would tell him or her what to do or what would happen next. Do not succumb to the temptation to do that; explain the importance of understanding the client's wants and needs to your representation. If you do not accomplish this important step, you may very well present the client with what you think is a very good settlement offer, only to have the client reject it because it does not meet some fundamental need you were unaware of. For example, in a defamation case, if you think the client wants as much money as possible but it turns out the primary concern is the client's reputation, you may get a good monetary settlement but not push for an apology or retraction or some other measure that might rehabilitate the client's damaged reputation. These are the kinds of misunderstandings that lead to malpractice actions.

§ 10.06 Preliminary Assessment of the Client's Problem

You should try to offer a preliminary assessment of the client's problem, at least to the extent of determining whether it is an appropriate situation for legal intervention of some kind. Some problems simply do not lend themselves to legal solutions (some neighborhood or family disputes come to mind), or you may find that the client presents a problem you are not qualified or do not wish to handle. If so, you should tell the client that. If you think the client presents a problem with potential, you need to be honest about your expertise in the area. There is no shame in needing to do research or further investigation before deciding how to proceed with a matter, and you need to develop the confidence to present this need for further inquiry as part of your competence rather than something you need to apologize for. You should, however, share with the client any judgments you are able to make about likely actions or events that might resolve the client's problem, and you should offer some assessment of the likelihood that the client's goals can be met. You should also be very clear that these assessments are preliminary and may very well change as additional facts and law are discovered.

§ 10.07 Developing Options

Once you have preliminarily assessed the client's problem, you may begin a discussion of options to be pursued. For example, you can try to get a sense of whether the client is interested in litigating the matter, or prefers a more amicable and informal resolution such as negotiation or mediation. You should take any nonlegal concerns of the client (such as a desire for an apology or to redeem his reputation) into account in developing the options, and you should encourage the client to participate in this process with you. Has the client thought about desirable outcomes, and possibly even ways to accomplish them? As you begin to develop options, you should explore the likely consequences of pursuing each option. What are the advantages and disadvantages? How likely is it that the option will actually workout? For example, if the dispute involves a lot of anger or other negative emotions on both sides, a quick and amicable negotiated resolution is unlikely.

§ 10.08 Fees

As we said previously, you must deal with the subject of money. There are several ways to structure fee agreements. You may bill your time at an hourly rate or charge a flat fee. In an appropriate case, where you are hoping to recover a sum of money for the client, you may take your fee out of the recovery. This is called a contingent fee, because you will not get paid if the client does not recover. Many jurisdictions require that you present the client with a written statement of your fees at the outset of the relationship, at least in matters where you intend to charge a contingent fee.

You should put in writing your entire agreement with the client about the scope of your representation, including fees. This is called a retainer agreement. Even if it is not required, it demonstrates good business sense to agree in writing with the client what you will and will not do. In addition, signing the agreement will bring home to the client the necessity of paying the fee.

Most clients understand that this is a business relationship, and they will be relieved to get that part of the transaction out of the way. All you have to sell is your time and expertise, and you should not be embarrassed about that fact. If a client genuinely cannot pay, or wants to work out a contingency arrangement, you will have to decide whether this is an appropriate case to handle on a reduced-fee or pro bono basis, or whether any possible recovery justifies the contingency fee. Regardless of the fee arrangement you work out, you should present it to the client in writing and get it signed, so that it is clear from the outset what you will be charging and what the client has agreed to pay.

When do you bring up the subject of money? It is not advisable to start the interview by talking about fees. This is partly because you will only reinforce negative stereotypes of "moneygrubbing" lawyers by doing so, and partly because you cannot possibly assess the most appropriate fee structure or the likely ultimate cost to the client without having some sense of what the problem is. We advise you to get the client's story and begin the assessment process before you get to the subject of fees. The beginning of the discussion regarding your client's legal and nonlegal options is a very logical point at which to bring up the subject of cost.

Remember that the client's ultimate cost concern will be the total amount of money needed to resolve the problem, so do not simply quote your hourly rate, if that is how you propose to charge the client. Try to estimate the likely total cost of the case, always remembering (and telling the client) that the final cost will depend on many factors that you may not be able to anticipate right now, such as the stubbornness of the other side, whether the other party hires a lawyer who likes to generate lots of paper and drag things out, the difficulty of finding necessary witnesses and evidence, and the like. At a minimum provide an estimate of the cost of handling the initial stage(s) of the matter. For example, tell the client how long it will take you to conduct preliminary research and generate a letter explaining the situation to the client or to other involved parties.

§ 10.09 Closing the Interview

At the end of the interview, it can be very easy to simply end the conversation and say good-bye. This may be the most important point in the interview for the client's long-term confidence in you, if you handle it right. Clients' most frequent complaint about their lawyers is that lawyers do not keep them informed about the process. Clients who are insecure about the status of their case and who do not understand the steps in the process may make frequent phone calls to get answers. Nervous clients may make phone calls anyway, but well-informed clients should be less likely to contact their attorneys when there is nothing happening in the case that justifies contact.

Do not let the client leave without carefully explaining what happens next, when it will happen, and whose responsibility it is. If you are going to contact the attorney for the other side, tell the client when you will do so, and when you will let the client know about any response you receive. Give the client some "homework." This may sound odd, but if there is a way the client can help with the case, perhaps by retrieving documents or phone numbers, you give the client some measure of control over a difficult problem, which is usually reassuring. Handling the end of the interview in a concrete way gives the client confidence in you and gives you specific and immediate goals to achieve on behalf of the client.

Remember that you must also formalize the attorney-client relationship and confirm that the client wants you to handle the matter. If the client has not decided to hire you, do not agree to do any work for the client, unless the terms and conditions under which you will do some work are clearly specified, preferably in writing. Set a time frame within which the client must decide to hire you or you will close the file. This should help to reduce the possibility of misunderstandings about whether you were hired, the scope of your representation, and any deadlines involved. The best possible scenario is that you give the client a written retainer agreement that includes fees, and it is signed on the spot, or the client agrees to return it to you within a few days.

EXERCISE

Here is a draft intake form for an interview with a client who is coming to see you about a personal injury case. The only thing you know before the interview is that the injury is the result of an automobile accident. What would you add to this form? Is there another approach to structuring the interview that makes more sense to you? How will you begin the interview? What kinds of questions will you start with? What kinds of details will you need? What do you need to know about the law of your jurisdiction? E.g., is yours a comparative or contributory negligence jurisdiction? What sorts of documents might be available that will help you prepare the case? What sorts of fee agreements might be appropriate? Write out your answers to these questions and redraft the form so you could actually use it effectively during the interview.

Client Intake Form

Name:
Address:
Phone Number:
Client's Description of Events:

Date of Accident:

Other Parties:

Potential Witnesses:

Client's Stated Goal(s):

Fee structure discussed and agreed to:

Client Interview Checklist

_____ Planning the initial interview: How will you get necessary information? What topics do you need to cover? Do you have fee agreements ready to be executed?

_____ Greeting the client: How might you best put the client at ease? Does the client seem nervous, or eager to get down to business?

_____ Preparatory explanation: Roadmap the interview, talk about process and confidentiality.

_____ Getting the client's perspective: Ask about the client's goals and priorities. Let the client tell the story his or her own way! Ask what the client would like to see happen.

_____ Preliminary Assessment: Is this problem appropriate for legal action? Is it a problem you are qualified or prepared to handle? How much additional legal or factual research do you need to do?

_____ Developing Options: Is this matter headed for litigation or can it be resolved amicably? What ideas does the client have for resolving the problem? What are the advantages and disadvantages of pursuing various options? ·

_____ Fees: What fee structure is appropriate for handling this case? Did you get a written fee agreement signed? Did you give the client an estimate of the likely total cost of the matter?

_____ Closing the interview: Was it clear what will happen next, when it will happen, and whose responsibility it is? Did you ask the client to provide you with any information or documents? Does the client understand the immediate plan of action?

CHAPTER 11

WRITING THE CLIENT OPINION LETTER

§ 11.01   Introduction

Writing and speaking to your client is perhaps the most important communicating you will do in your career as a lawyer. Attorneys sometimes become so involved in their cases that they forget the human element. Learn to communicate well with clients and you will have more work than you know what to do with. Clients like to be told what is happening in a case, why it is happening, and what is going to happen next.

One important way to keep the client informed is the opinion letter. An opinion letter advises a client how the law applies to a particular case and suggests action to be taken based on that law. The letter serves as a record of the progress of a case for the attorney and the client. This chapter gives you some simple rules to follow in preparing these important documents.

§ 11.02   Write in an Appropriate Style

[1]   Focus On Your Audience

Remember to write for your reader. In the case of an opinion letter, your reader will usually be either an individual who does not have a great deal of legal knowledge or another lawyer, perhaps your client's general counsel, who is legally sophisticated. Such sophisticated clients often request "formal" opinion letters that involve analysis of, and citation to, relevant legal authority, much like the office memorandum. Each client is different. Your goal must be to write a letter that will help the individual client in a particular case. The better you know your client, the more likely it is that you will be able to achieve that goal.

[2]   Be Concrete

Your clients want to know what is likely to happen in their cases. A lengthy, abstract discussion of the law without applying it to the client's case will have very little meaning for the client. Explain the applicable rules to the client, but do it in the context of the case at issue.

In this chapter we use examples from student assignments. All of the examples in this chapter are taken from student opinion letters discussing a single case. The case involved a criminal attack on two guests at a hotel. The issue is whether the guests can sue the hotel for negligence. Under tort law, to find negligence in such a case:

> (1) the hotel must have a duty to protect its guests from criminal attacks,
>
> (2) it must unreasonably fail to perform that duty,
>
> (3) the failure must have caused the attack at least in part, and
>
> (4) damage must result.

Read this passage as if you were the clients to whom it is addressed. In this case, the clients are the hotel guests who were attacked.

> Although Florida law has no statutes for a tort action for the criminal acts of third parties committed on a hotel's premises and no security standards have been adopted by the hotel industry, we think that you can bring a successful negligence action against Palm Court Hotel. Our opinion is based on past cases tried in Florida that are similar to your case and that set precedent for the courts to follow. In these past cases both motels/hotels and landlords were held liable for assaults committed by third parties on their premises when plaintiffs could prove that the hotel/motel or landlord had acted negligently in protecting its guests. These rulings are supported by Florida statutes for landlords and innkeepers.

As the clients, what have you learned? Do you understand how previous cases will help the court decide your case? Do you understand the significance of the presence or absence of statutes or industry standards? These are the kinds of questions to which clients should be able to answer "yes" after reading a letter from you. The clients who read this letter would answer "no."

Compare the next two examples and decide which you would prefer to receive if you were the same clients.

First Example

> A hotel has a duty to protect its guests from harm based on the nature of the business and the social policies involved. In general, a hotel's duty is to exercise reasonable care in protecting its guests. The test for "reasonableness" is whether a reasonable person knew or should have known that there was potential danger based on the circumstances (for example, area crime rate, occurrence of similar crimes on the premises, design of the hotel, etc.) and whether appropriate precautions were taken to prevent or deter such danger. This determination is made on a case-by-case basis.

Second Example

> Generally, in cases like yours two things are required to find the hotel liable. First, the hotel must have had cause to believe that such an attack might occur. Second, a court must find that the hotel did not take reasonable steps to prevent such an attack.

The second example is much more concrete. The sentences are shorter and the language is simpler. Obviously, the analysis must be fleshed out and the law applied to the case, but at least you have a better understanding of the legal test. The concrete examples provided in parentheses in the First Example would fit nicely in this paragraph. What else would you add?

[3] Avoid Sounding Colloquial

Even when you are writing for lay clients and want to use language they can understand, maintain a formal tone. The rules for opinion letters are the same as for other legal documents. Avoid contractions, slang, and other colloquialisms. You do not want to sound stuffy or cold, but you do want to sound professional. Avoid sentences like:

> I don't see any problem with this.

> We have several things going in our favor.

[4] Avoid Jargon and Stilted Language

You should avoid using unnecessary legal jargon and stilted construction. Again, remember your audience. If you are writing to a lay person, avoid legal terminology altogether if possible. But where you are writing to another attorney, use of appropriate legal terminology is expected. For example, you might include this passage in a letter to the general counsel for the Palm Court Hotel:

> Palm Court Hotel had a legal duty to exercise "reasonable care" for the safety of its guests. The hotel was obligated to use whatever security devices the average reasonable person would have used in the same circumstances. In view of the hotel design and location, and the criminal activity in the area, there should have been some control over access to the building.

> By failing to control or even monitor access to the guest building, Palm Court negligently breached its duty of reasonable care for the Smiths' safety.

Conversely, if you were writing to the Smiths, you would use simpler language, and explain legal concepts rather than using terms of art.

> Palm Court failed to provide chain locks on the guest room doors. While no hotel industry standard requires a chain lock, providing a lock in your case would have enabled Mr. Smith to keep the door locked when checking to see who was at the door.

> The extent of a hotel's liability depends in large part on the crime rate in the area surrounding the hotel and the occurrence of similar crimes on or near the premises. If Palm Court was not aware of the sharp increase in the crime rate in the area surrounding the hotel, it should have been. Palm Court was also aware of several similar crimes which had taken place at the Seaside Inn, a sister resort located directly across the street.

> A hotel's response to foreseeable danger and its attempts to exercise reasonable care can be measured most easily by the security measures and personnel it provides. Palm Court provided only one guard to patrol the entire resort, including the main buildings, four outlying guest buildings, and the grounds. The hotel also kept the access doors to the guest buildings unlocked

at all times. Our security expert will testify that such security measures are clearly inadequate to protect a facility as large as Palm Court.

[5] Use Correct Spelling and Grammar

It is just as important to spell correctly when you write to a client as it is when you write to the courts or to other lawyers. Avoid the grammatical errors we discuss in this book. Failure to write proper English will destroy your credibility as a professional. A client quite rightly will wonder about the impression you will make on judges and other attorneys if it appears that you cannot write grammatically or spell accurately. A few extra minutes will help you avoid this problem.

§ 11.03   Answer the Question

Usually a client's specific question prompts you to write the letter. Make certain that your letter gives the client all of the information necessary to make an educated decision. Here are five rules that will help you provide this information effectively.

[1] Include Important Facts Provided By The Client

Before you analyze the problem presented by your client, you should restate the important facts the client previously provided. The client knows what happened, but your job is to connect those events to the law and give your professional opinion on the probable outcome of the case. It is important to be certain that you and the client have the same understanding of the facts. Recording the known facts in a letter to the client may jog the client's memory about something else important that happened. If other, less helpful, facts surface later, you will be able to remind your client that your more optimistic assessment of the case was based on the facts that came from the client, as outlined in the letter. Your presentation of the facts in our case might look something like this:

> I understand the basic facts of your case to be as follows: Palm Court is a Florida resort complex with 200 rooms and extensive grounds. It is illuminated mainly by pathway lights, and none of the five buildings have exterior lights. The access doors of the building in which you were staying were never locked. Although the steel door of your suite was spring-locked and had a doorknob with an anti-picking device, there was no safety chain on the door. The door's observation port did not permit you to see to the sides of the door. No trained security guard was on duty at the time of the attack, though there had recently been a dramatic increase in the crime rate in the area, including several thefts at Palm Court and several assaults on persons at the Seaside Inn across the street. On the evening of the attack, you heard a knock on your door. You did not see anyone when you looked out the port, so you opened the door. The attack then took place.

[2] Be Accurate

You should have legal authority to support any argument you make. Although you do not cite that authority in a letter to a lay client, you should be prepared to cite appropriate authority in a formal opinion letter. In either case, you must be confident that the relevant authority supports the conclusions you state. The client will make decisions about future actions based on your advice. Provide the best guidance you can.

In our sample case, one writer declared:

> One of the areas of law that pertains to your case involves the responsibility of Palm Court for the acts of your assailants. Palm Court is responsible for the crimes you suffered while you were their guests. A hotel is in the business not only of providing lodging but also of providing its guests with reasonable care for their safety.

The last sentence in the paragraph states the law fairly accurately, but the middle sentence creates a misleading impression. It is up to a court, not the lawyer, to decide whether the hotel is legally responsible for an attack on its guests.

[3] Explain Your Answer

It is not enough to tell a client that you advise a certain course of action. Explain the reasons for your recommendation. The reasons may be legal or practical. In either case, make sure you explain the reasons clearly in the letter. In explaining the legal basis for an opinion, be sure you apply the law to your client's case. You learned to integrate your discussion of the law and the facts in Chapter 5. Apply the same rules here.

First Example

We must prove that the hotel failed to exercise reasonable care. Though the hotel exercised some degree of care in the safety measures and procedures adopted, we believe this security was inadequate. We believe that there was a need for not one, but two, patrolling security guards whose shifts would start at 7:00 p.m., not 10:00 p.m. This proposed level of security would have been sufficient to deter the type of crimes which occurred. In addition, Palm Court was or should have been aware of the increasing crime rate in the area and the recent assaults in the vicinity that make this type of crime foreseeable. Palm Court will probably say that the security provided was adequate under the circumstances and, therefore, that it exercised the reasonable care required.

Second Example

The security provisions of the hotel, both guards and physical security devices, were found to be inadequate. The number of guards was insufficient for a hotel of that size, and the hours patrolled were too few. The physical security devices were also insufficient, since Mr. Smith had to open the door to see who was there when he heard the knock.

As far as the clients could tell from either of these examples, all the writers have presented are their personal opinions. In the first example, the writer even said "we believe" in two separate places. In the second example, the writer says the security measures "were found to be inadequate." By whom? In both cases, the writer should have given the client some legal basis for the conclusions reached.

The idea is not necessarily to cite cases or other authority, but to explain the legal standards by which a court will judge the actions of the parties. Here is a revision of the second example.

> A hotel has a legal obligation to take reasonable steps to insure the safety of its guests. What is reasonable depends on the circumstances. In this case, the increase in crime in the area and the attacks at the Seaside Inn made the attack on you more likely and therefore legally foreseeable. Our security expert will testify that these facts made the security provisions of the hotel inadequate. The number of guards was insufficient for a hotel of that size, and the hours patrolled were too few. The physical security devices were also insufficient, since Mr. Smith had to open the door to see who was there when he heard the knock.

[4] Do Not Promise What You Cannot Deliver

In addition to making sure that your conclusions are accurate, be certain that your advice is honest. One student wrote:

> In regard to your claim against Palm Court Hotel for the attack which occurred on May 31, 1986, I have concluded that if you decide to proceed, you will probably recover a large sum of money in damages because the hotel was negligent in failing to prevent the crime.

This is a dangerous approach. You may create expectations that you will not be able to fulfill. Even though the law may appear to be in your favor, there are many other factors that can affect the outcome of a legal proceeding. You do not have control over some of these factors, such as the judge or jury who ultimately decides the case, so you should not make promises you may not be able to keep.

Do not interpret this rule to mean that you should take a negative approach when you advise your client. As explained by one writer:

> Not only should advice be affirmative, but the giving of it, as of all things, should be cheerful. Even as with the physicians, while clients come to us for advice, it is usually more for comfort and assurance that they seek us and this is so whether the client be a poor widow or the president of a wealthy corporation. While we must not close our eyes to the bad or disadvantageous or dangerous aspects of the client's problem or situation, we should endeavor to find its most favorable aspect and, from that vantage point, advise him cheerfully and affirmatively what to do. One who has a problem which seems dark and hopeless is not helped by a lawyer who sheds only new darkness upon it. We should remember that the leaders of lost causes were never men of dismal minds. No opinion letter should import fear into the client's mind, unless the writer of it at once eradicates that fear by strong affirmative advice.[1]

---

[1] Arthur Littleton, Writing an Opinion Letter to a Client (1959) (unpublished).

As with most legal tasks, you must strive to find the proper balance when you give honest advice to your client.

[5]   Address Your Client's Concerns

If you are aware of any special concerns of your client, address them in your letter. If your client is a cost-conscious business person, you might want to stress the cost effectiveness of a particular course of action. If your client has never had any contact with the legal system and is somewhat afraid of it, be especially reassuring. Tell the client that you are available to answer questions and that you will be there every step of the way.

Clients like to feel that their lawyers think of them as human beings and not just as files or cases. It does not take much effort to add the little touch that lets a client know you have paid attention to what the client has told you. Listen carefully, be considerate, and communicate effectively.

§ 11.04   Tell the Client Where You Are Going

As you conclude the letter to your client, continue to think concretely. What is the next step? Who should take that step and when will it happen? Use the final paragraph of your letter in a productive manner. It is not necessary to summarize what you have said previously in the letter. The document is not that long. You should not offer general predictions about what might or might not happen in the case. Avoid writing something like this:

> For all of these reasons our case against the hotel is strong. Because of previous attacks at the Seaside Inn and the size and expanse of Palm Court we should be able to prove the hotel should have realized the possibility of an attack on its patrons. Whether the judge or jury believes our security expert will be crucial to our case; however, established law does support our expert. The lack of TV monitoring equipment and security access doors also supports our case. Although I cannot assure a decision in our favor, I feel confident that the hotel will be found liable if we bring this action.

The writer could have concluded more effectively by offering to begin legal action upon instructions from the client. In some situations you might suggest a meeting with the client. Sometimes the next step is to wait for action from the court or the opposing party. If so, tell the client that you advise doing nothing and why. Tell the client what will happen next as precisely as possible. The client then will feel more comfortable with the progress of the case and with your representation.

EXERCISES

Rewrite the following letters using the rules you have just studied. The first letter discusses the same case you have read about throughout this chapter. The second letter discusses a similar case involving an attack at an apartment complex. If you do not feel like you have enough information to completely rewrite the second letter, write out the suggestions for improvement you would make to the author of the letter. Be as specific and detailed as you can.

Letter 1

Dear Mr. & Mrs. Smith:

This letter pertains to the suit we are bringing against the Palm Court Hotel where you both were assaulted in May of 1986. We are asserting that the hotel was negligent of its required duties to the two of you as guests. To establish negligence we must first prove that the hotel was negligent of its required duties to the two of you as guests. To establish negligence we must first prove that the crime committed against you was foreseeable. Secondly, we must show that the hotel responded inadequately to that foreseeable crime. In establishing foreseeability of the crime, we will try to show that criminal activity within the community and within the immediate vicinity should have alerted the management that a similar crime may occur on their premises. After establishing that the crime was indeed foreseeable, we must then assert that the Palm Court Hotel took insufficient security measures to deter or prevent the occurrence of the crime. An analysis of the security precautions taken by the hotel and testimony from an expert witness will be instrumental in deciding whether the hotel instituted the necessary security system to deter or prevent the foreseeable crime.

We expect the outcome of the suit to be in your favor. There is ample evidence of similar crime within the immediate area of the Palm Court Hotel. We feel that the court will find that the hotel neglected its duties to secure the grounds in light of the foreseeability of the crime. We have evidence that the security staff was insufficient and that the premises were vulnerable to crime. With a judgment in your favor, we can request compensatory and punitive damages. Compensatory damages are damages to compensate you for some of the injuries you sustained and some of the grief you have suffered, however inadequate this may be in reality. Punitive damages are a form of punishment levied upon the hotel for negligence.

Sincerely,

Letter 2

Ms. Esther Summerson

Holborn Arms Apartments

Lincolnshire, PA 19105

RE: Summerson v. Holborn Arms Apartments, Inc. and Lawrence Boythorn
Dear Ms. Summerson:

This letter is a follow-up to our recent meeting and should answer your questions regarding a possible lawsuit against your landlord.

In Pennsylvania, a landlord does not have a general duty to protect tenants from criminal attack. However, if the landlord has instituted a security program and runs the program negligently, the landlord can be held responsible for injuries that an adequate program might have prevented.

A security program exists when personnel are hired to patrol or protect the property. The guard assigned to your garage shows that the landlord set up a security program. Although more facts are needed to establish the guard's exact duties and responsibilities, it is safe to say that the Holborn Arms Apartments does have a security program.

It is also necessary to prove that the program was run negligently. We must prove that the guard neglected his duties and his neglect was directly responsible for your injuries. Again, more facts are needed about the exact duties of the guard, but his duties almost certainly included patrolling the garage and preventing the entry of unauthorized people. The guard's failure to detect Mr. Carstone's entry and the assault definitely point to neglect by the guard.

In addition to proving the guard's neglect of duty, we must show that his neglect caused your injuries. Put another way, we must show that if the guard had done his job, the attack would not have occurred. The presence of Mr. Carstone in the garage shows the guard's failure to prevent entry by unauthorized people. If the guard had acted correctly, he would have stopped Mr. Carstone's entry, either through the main entrance or through the broken window. The guard also should have discovered the assault in the garage by routine surveillance. Since the guard neither prevented Mr. Carstone from entering nor prevented the assault by proper surveillance, we can prove that your injuries were caused by the guard's neglect.

Based on the facts you have presented, the chances of a successful suit against the Holborn Arms Apartments and Lawrence Boythorn appear good. If you wish to pursue this matter and bring a suit against them please make an appointment with my secretary and we will discuss the matter further. If you have any questions please feel free to contact me.

Sincerely,

CHAPTER 12

INTRODUCTION TO THE MEMO

§ 12.01 What Is a Memo?

The memorandum of law, or memo, is an internal office document. It is a research tool that analyzes the law as it applies to the facts of a client's case and offers an unbiased evaluation.[1] A memo includes both helpful and damaging information. It suggests solutions to a legal problem or predicts the outcome of a dispute. It is the precursor to informed decision-making about a case.

The memo is the most basic of legal documents and is essential to the practice of law. During the course of your legal career, you likely will write a multitude of memos for more senior attorneys. They will vary in length and in topic. They will also serve as a gauge of your ability to analyze and present a legal problem. Once you master this type of writing, you will draft other kinds of legal documents with greater skill and ease.

This chapter introduces you to the memo. It describes the purposes of a memo, the parts of a memo, and the hallmarks of a well written memo. Chapters 13 and 14 focus on the parts of a memo in more detail, and demonstrate how to draft each section effectively.

§ 12.02 The Purposes of a Memo

The purpose of a memo is to provide a realistic analysis of the law as it applies to the facts of the client's case. That analysis will be the basis for giving advice or making decisions about the case.

A memo can serve many purposes. Its purpose determines how extensive the research should be, what the nature of the analysis should be, and how it should be written. The memo should be written to serve the specific purpose for which it was requested. By way of example, an attorney may use a memo to:

    (1)   evaluate the merits of a case,

    (2)   decide whether to settle or try a case,

---

[1] This chapter concerns interoffice memos only. There also are memoranda of law that are submitted to the court. They are more akin to briefs and should not be confused with the office memo.

(3)   decide whether to accept a case,

(4)   inform the reader of the status of the law,

(5)   present recommendations as to how to proceed with a case,

(6)   conclude that more information is needed to properly evaluate the case,

(7)   identify the legal theories applicable to the case,

(8)   decide whether to file any motions,

(9)   prepare for trial,

(10)   form the legal foundation of motions, pleadings, and briefs,

(11)   prepare a contract, will, settlement agreement, or corporate papers,

(12)   prepare for negotiations, or

(13)   prepare for an appeal.

The memos you prepare during the course of a case will provide a convenient summary of the facts, issues, legal theories, and arguments involved in the case. You and any other attorneys on the case will refer to them to refresh your memories as the case progresses.[2]

§ 12.03   The Parts of a Memo

The memo is a structured document that is divided into distinct but related sections. Each section is labeled and performs a particular function. There is no universal memo format, and no mandatory order in which to present the parts of a memo. Many law firms, corporate legal departments, and government offices prescribe a standard form. You should find out whether there is a standard format in your office, or if not, whether the attorney for whom you are preparing the memo prefers a certain format. Although there are many variations in the structure of a memo, the following format is widely used:

(1)   a heading,

(2)   a brief statement of the issue to be discussed,

(3)   a conclusion,

(4)   a brief statement of the facts, and

(5)   a discussion of the pertinent authorities.

Appendix IV contains sample memoranda. Please review those memoranda in conjunction with this chapter.

---

[2] Many law firms index and file the memoranda of law prepared by their attorneys. These memos are a valuable asset. A question may arise in a pending case that a previous memo already addresses. The attorney need only update the research in the memo. This procedure saves the attorney time and the client money.

[1] The Heading

The Heading indicates that the document is a memorandum, the person to whom the memorandum is addressed, the person who wrote it, its date, and its subject matter, in the following form:

MEMORANDUM

TO:
FROM:
DATE:
SUBJECT: (or RE:)

[2] The Issue

The Issue, sometimes called the Question Presented, frames the legal question to be resolved by the memo. If there is more than one issue or several subparts to an issue, number each issue and subpart separately. The Issue section of the memo informs the reader of the scope of the memo. A memo should not go beyond the scope of the Issue.

[3] The Conclusion

The Conclusion, sometimes called the short answer, provides a complete, but brief, answer to the Issue. At times an attorney will refer only to the Conclusion, at least initially. The Conclusion includes a concise statement of the reasons for your conclusion. It also orients the reader to the general thrust of the discussion. The Conclusion does not contain a detailed discussion of how you reached the conclusion. Citations to authority and cross-references to the body of the memo are inappropriate. In a memo that discusses more than one issue, number the conclusions to reflect the issues to which they refer.

[4] The Facts

This section requires a clear and concise statement of the facts relevant to the legal analysis presented by the memo. The facts let the reader know what happened. The purpose of the memo is to evaluate the soundness of a particular legal position given certain facts. Therefore, present the facts objectively and include both favorable and unfavorable information. Include all the facts that you will raise in the Discussion section.

[5] The Discussion

The Discussion section is the heart of the memo. In it you analyze the pertinent legal authorities and apply them to the facts of the problem. If there is more than one issue, address each issue separately. The Discussion, like the Facts, should be objective, not argumentative. Evaluate both helpful and damaging authorities. At the end of the Discussion, summarize the findings presented by the memo.

§ 12.04   The Hallmarks of a Well-Written Memo

The purpose of a memo is to inform and explain. If your memo bears the hallmarks enumerated below, it will achieve this dual purpose.

[1]   Thorough Research

Thoroughly research the question you are assigned. Evaluate the law you find within the context of the facts of your case. Find and analyze all of the pertinent legal authorities, those that are helpful to your case and those that are damaging to it. Do not cite or rely on any authority without critically reading it yourself. Treatises and encyclopedias state the law only in general terms. Look up the cases on which they rely. Never rely on headnotes to cases. Remember that major decisions about the case will be made based on your memorandum, and that incomplete or inaccurate research will have far-reaching implications.

[2]   Good Judgment

Be certain that the memorandum you prepare is what the assigning attorney wants. When you are given the assignment, be sure you understand what purpose the memo is to serve, when it is to be submitted, and how detailed it should be. Also be certain that you understand the question that you are to research. Even if the initial instructions are clear, problems may arise later. As your research progresses, the issue may take on a different focus, unanticipated questions may arise, or additional facts may become important. Return to the assigning attorney and resolve these problems. But use good judgment. Do not trouble the attorney with questions you should be able to resolve yourself or with the help of one of your peers.

[3]   Objective Analysis

A memo must be objective. This is as crucial as it is simple. Your analysis of the legal authorities must be realistic and comprehensive. Examine your own arguments. Evaluate those you anticipate from opposing counsel. Consider the issues from every perspective. Honestly and thoroughly assess the strengths and weaknesses of your position. A memo is not the forum for persuasion, or for advocacy. Major choices and decisions will be made on the basis of the memo you write. Those choices and decisions can be made intelligently only on the basis of an objective memo. Indeed, the client's interests would not be served if the appraisal of his position were anything less than scrupulously realistic and objective.

[4]   Clear Writing Style

A memo is a complete and independent document. Another attorney who reads it should be able to fully understand the matter and make a decision. The memo memorializes, for all future readers of the file, the reasons those handling the case chose a particular course of action. By now you have read enough cases in your classes to appreciate the importance of writing style. Any poorly written legal document leads to confusion and uncertainty. A memo should be precise, accurate and well-organized in order to explain a legal question effectively.

[a]   Good Organization

The foundation of a good memo is careful, detailed organization. The memo must be organized and written so that your thoughts are clearly presented and precisely stated. Skillful writing, thoughtful analysis, and clear presentation will be wasted unless your work is organized intelligently. The reader should not have to work at comprehending your discussion. No one reads memos for entertainment. Your legal analysis and your approach to the problem should be apparent from your organization. Make the reader's task as easy as possible.

As with other types of legal writing, memo writing requires a particular organizational framework. State your conclusions first. Follow them with your reasoning. Use mechanical aids such as headings and sub-headings to help you organize the memo.

As we discussed in Chapter 7, outlining is a necessary organizational technique and one that will save you time. Outlining forces you to develop your analysis one step at a time and will expose the gaps in your discussion. Chapters 13 and 14 will instruct you in the principles of organization as they apply to each section of the memo.

[b]   Write for the Reader

Analyze and consider the problem and your memo in detail. Remember that your primary audience is the attorney who requested it. You are not writing for yourself.

Include all of the facts that you were given when you were assigned the problem. Do not assume that, because the assigning attorney is familiar with the matter, he or she will remember exactly what you were told. You must include every fact you rely on in your analysis.

Explain the significance of the legal authorities in the context of the facts of the problem. Be certain that your conclusions do not appear without the benefit of the analysis that preceded them. Your discussion must progress logically. Carefully and clearly guide the reader through the memo. One way to do this, as you will learn in Chapter 14, is to provide the reader with a "road map," a guide to the discussion contained in the memo.

The memo is the end product of your exploration of the problem and its implications. Put yourself in the position of the person for whom you are writing the memo. Ask yourself whether your memo provides that person with a thoughtful analysis of the problem. Only when you are satisfied that the memo is complete, that it fully answers the question put to you, and that it is your best work, should you submit it.

[c]   Precision and Clarity

To communicate your thoughts effectively, you must be precise and clear. You have been asked to resolve a concrete problem. Make certain that you provide a concrete answer and specific reasons for it. Be precise about the facts and the law, but do not miss the forest for the trees. Make it clear why the authorities you rely on are relevant. Do not just tell the reader that they are pertinent. Show how those authorities apply to your case. Draw the conclusions yourself. When reading your memo, the reader should fully understand it and should be satisfied with your resolution of the problem.

[5] Creativity

Your memo should present a comprehensive and organized analysis of the law in the context of the facts of your client's problem. On occasion, it might also display some legal creativity in regard to your recommendation for further action. When you are researching and writing the memo, be alert for alternative theories or creative approaches to the problem. Because you are the one who is most immersed in the issue and who is most aware of its permutations, you are the ideal person to provide a fresh perspective. Manifesting such creativity will demonstrate your initiative, even where your theory may ultimately not be workable.

[6] Correct Citation Format

Your memo must include citations to the authorities on which you rely. Moreover, the cites must be complete, accurate, and in proper Bluebook form. Correct citation form is important for at least two reasons. First, sloppy and incomplete citations give the reader cause to suspect that the substance of your analysis is equally weak. Second, if you include an inaccurate citation in the memo, you probably will copy that citation in subsequent documents that rely on the memo's research. Simply put, bad citations can haunt you and create an extremely negative impression of your work.

CHAPTER 13

THE MEMO: HEADING, ISSUE, AND CONCLUSION

As you learned in Chapter 12, the memo is a structured document that is divided into distinct sections. Each section has a label and performs a particular function. In Chapters 13 and 14, you will learn how to write each of these sections.

§ 13.01   The Heading

The Heading uses the following format to set out the most basic information about the memo.

MEMORANDUM

TO: Leslie O'Brien-Wallace

FROM: Michael R. North

DATE: August 7, 1993

RE: *Dane v. Lapp*; file no. 56432-007; Recovery for
                          negligent infliction of emotional distress under
                          Pennsylvania law.

The centered heading indicates that the document is a memorandum. "TO" indicates the person to whom the memorandum is addressed. "FROM" indicates who wrote the memorandum. Although practices vary from one office to the next, the recipient and the sender of the memo are usually referred to by their full names. Occasionally the tone is more formal and titles are used, for example, Ms./Miss/Mrs. O'Brien-Wallace and Mr. North. Do not include job titles such as senior partner or associate after the name of the recipient or sender.

"DATE" indicates the date you submitted the memo. Including the date is important. Any reader of the memo must be able to assume that the research and analysis contained in the memo are accurate and complete as of the date of the memo. The law, however, may have changed by the time you or another attorney next refer to the memo. The date will advise the reader whether the research requires updating.

"RE" indicates the subject matter of the memo. You may also see "SUBJECT" used instead of "RE'. Include the case name, or the client name if no case is pending, and the office file number. Describe briefly and broadly the legal question the memo addresses. Because most case files contain a large number of documents, including numerous memoranda, this information will make it easy to locate a particular memorandum in the future. In addition, the explanation of the subject matter facilitates indexing and filing of the memorandum for general research purposes so that it may be used for future reference in other cases.

Suppose for purposes of illustration that you have just been called into the office of a more senior attorney and given the following facts.

> William Dane has retained the firm to file suit for injuries he sustained in an automobile accident. Mr. Dane also would like the firm to file suit on behalf of his fourteen-year-old niece, Edna. Edna witnessed the automobile accident. The accident occurred on June 10, 1997. Mr. Dane had volunteered to help his recently divorced sister by taking Edna to school. At 8:00 a.m. Mr. Dane dropped Edna off at school and drove away, intending to go to the grocery store. Edna waved good-bye to her uncle and turned to talk to some friends. As she was walking through the schoolyard with her friends, Edna heard a loud crash, followed by an explosion. When she turned to see what had happened, Edna saw that a car had collided with her uncle's car at an intersection one block away from the school. Her uncle's car was on fire. Edna ran to the scene of the accident. By the time she arrived, her uncle had been pulled from his car. Edna saw that her uncle had been severely burned and that he had a large gash on his forehead. Ever since the accident, Edna has suffered from recurring nightmares, a debilitating fear of automobiles, and chronic stomach problems. These conditions did not exist prior to the accident. An investigation of the accident disclosed that Mrs. Donna Lapp, the driver of the other car, had run a red light while intoxicated.

You have been asked to research whether, under these facts, Edna can make out a cause of action for negligent infliction of emotional distress under Pennsylvania law. The sample heading at the beginning of this section incorporates the information that would be required in the Heading of the memo concerning this case.

Before writing the Heading for your memo, review a few recent memos prepared by other attorneys in your office to determine the preferred style. You may find that there are minor variations from the format we describe.

§ 13.02   The Issue

The memo begins with the Issue section, also called the Question Presented. The Issue section of the memo states the legal question presented in your case. Here is an example of an issue concerning the *Dane* case:

> Whether, under Pennsylvania law, a niece who witnesses the aftermath of an automobile accident involving her uncle from a block away can recover for negligent infliction of emotional distress when she arrives at the scene and observes his severe injuries.

Here is another equally acceptable way to frame the issue:

> Under Pennsylvania law, can a niece recover for negligent infliction of emotional distress if she is one block away when an automobile accident involving her uncle occurs and, immediately after the accident, arrives at the scene and observes her uncle's severe injuries?

The Issue section informs the reader of the scope of the memo. The scope of the memo should never exceed the scope of the Issue. Frame the question precisely. Failure to do so will mislead the reader about the limits of your discussion and analysis.

Identifying the issue is the foundation of effective analysis. On some occasions, the attorney who requests the memo will identify the issue clearly for you. More often, you will be able to identify the precise issue only after you have thoroughly researched and thoughtfully analyzed the problem. For this reason, finalize your draft of the Issue only after you have written the Discussion section of the memo.

To frame an issue, you must do two things. First, identify the precise rule of law. Second, identify the key facts. Key facts are legally significant facts. Key facts are those facts that determine whether and how a particular rule of law applies to your situation. These facts are of crucial importance to the outcome of the case. Once you have fully researched the law within the context of your facts, you can determine which facts are key. Finally, after identifying the precise rule of law and the key facts, draft the Issue to ask whether the rule of law applies under the particular facts of your case.

Consider the following examples of poorly phrased Issues, and ask yourself what the writers have done incorrectly:

> Whether a bystander to an accident can recover for negligent infliction of emotional distress under Pennsylvania law.

> Whether a bystander at an automobile accident will be able to bring a tort action to recover for negligent infliction of emotional distress.

> Whether, under current Pennsylvania law, a bystander at an automobile accident can successfully bring a tort action for negligent infliction of emotional distress.

Comment: Although the writers properly identified the ultimate legal question, they failed to include the key facts. The reader is left to wonder about the circumstances that prompted the question. The reader should understand the question without having to refer to the facts section. If you fail to include key facts, you will draft an abstract question, a question without context. The writers of two of the Issues include a reference to Pennsylvania law. When possible, state the jurisdiction since the law may vary dramatically from one state to the next.

> Whether a niece who witnesses the aftermath of an accident involving her uncle will be able to state a cause of action for negligent infliction of emotional distress.

Comment: The writer of this Issue omitted one very significant fact: the niece's distance from the accident. The writer should also have included a reference to Pennsylvania law as the controlling jurisdiction.

Whether Edna can recover damages for negligent infliction of emotional distress as a result of witnessing an accident involving Mr. Dane.

Comment: When including the key facts in your Issue, avoid identifying any of the people, places, or things in your case by proper name. Names may have no meaning to your reader because the facts section of your memo does not come until later. Even if you, the author of the memo, return to the file after the case has been dormant, you may not recall who all the players are. Instead of using proper names, use general categories to describe the people, places, or things in the Issue.

The Issue should consist of a concise, one-sentence question. The Issue usually starts with "whether" and should call for a yes or no in response. The Issue also may begin with an interrogative such as "is' or "can." Be certain that your Issue is precise and complete. Do not, however, draft a question that is so complex, lengthy, and awkward that your reader cannot follow it. Ask yourself whether the rule of law is stated clearly and succinctly. Examine your facts and critically evaluate which are essential to the Issue. Do not generalize because you will risk distorting the Issue.

A memo can address several questions. The questions might be distinct or related and can consist of several individual questions or a question with subparts. Writing and rewriting the questions and their subparts often promotes a more thorough understanding of the problem. Generally, the more specifically the question is phrased, the more precisely it will be understood. Do not, however, divide the Issue into so many questions and subquestions that the reader will become confused. Do not use a single subquestion. If the question is divided into subparts, there must be at least two subparts.

Do not forget that the memo is an informative document that realistically evaluates your client's position. Adopt an objective, non-partisan tone. Even if a key fact is unfavorable to your client's position, you must include it. Do not draft a question to suggest a certain answer. Avoid advocacy in issue writing.

Here are two good examples of Issues. They come from different cases:

Under the Pennsylvania Workers' Compensation Act, can an employee recover for injuries that he sustained in a personal fight with a co-worker during working hours when, six months earlier, he had a work-related dispute with the same co-worker?

Under New Jersey law, can the parents of a child born with Down's Syndrome rely on the "discovery rule" or the "concealment exception" to bring an action for wrongful birth two years after the statute of limitations has run when:

A. before the birth, their physician stated that amniocentesis would detect any genetic defects in the fetus;

B. the mother underwent amniocentesis; and

C. after the birth, the physician stated that the amniocentesis had not detected Down's Syndrome, even though he knew that the technician had made errors in performing the test and had arrived at an incorrect result?

These Issues are well written. Both include the legal question and the facts that are key, according to the case law. The questions are precise and objective. They advise the reader of the scope and focus of the memo. As the samples demonstrate, there is no one correct way to draft an Issue. Simply be certain that your Issue contains all of the necessary elements, that you have framed it succinctly and accurately, and that you have made it comprehensible.

§ 13.03   The Conclusion

The Conclusion, sometimes called the Brief Answer or Short Answer, provides a short answer to each question that the Issue section poses. In addition to answering the question, this section includes a concise statement of the reasoning that supports the conclusion. The Conclusion section provides immediate answers to the questions that the memo raises.

The Conclusion section immediately follows the Issue section. For that reason, some attorneys begin with a direct response to each of the questions, such as "yes," "no," "probably," "probably not," and "maybe." Because few things in the law are ever absolutely clear, and because a non-committal answer adds little to a well written conclusion, we prefer memoranda without this type of response. Nevertheless, opinions and practices vary; therefore, be alert to the preferences of those for whom you are working.

In writing the Conclusion section, accommodate the reader. In a memo discussing more than one issue, identify each conclusion with a number corresponding to the issue to which it refers. Be certain that each answer is self-contained. While each answer should contain a succinct explanation of the reasoning that supports your conclusion, do not discuss the details of your analysis. Do not include citations to cases, statutes, regulations, or other types of authority on which you rely. Only on the rare occasion when an authority is dispositive of the question, should you note it in the Conclusion. Relegate all suppositions and hypotheses to the Discussion section.

You may find it helpful to draft the Conclusion after you have drafted the Issue and written the Discussion. Drafting these sections will force you to understand fully the reasons for your conclusion. Writing the Conclusion is a two step process. First, begin the Conclusion by restating your Issue as a declarative sentence. Second, add a brief explanation of the reasoning supporting your conclusion. The Conclusion should be ten to fifteen lines.

Consider again the facts of the Dane matter, the illustrative case for this chapter. Then, please review the following sample Conclusions from student memoranda.

Under Pennsylvania law, a niece will be able to recover damages for negligent infliction of emotional distress if the emotional distress was foreseeable to the defendant. The factors determining foreseeability include: (1) whether the plaintiff was near the scene of the accident, (2) whether the shock resulted from the direct emotional impact upon the plaintiff from the sensory and contemporaneous observance of the accident, and (3) whether the plaintiff and the victim were closely related.

Comment: The writer has done only part of the job. This Conclusion sets out the elements of the test that a plaintiff must meet to recover. The recitation of the law is correct. The Conclusion, however, fails to answer the question.

A Pennsylvania court would hold that the bystander at the automobile accident could recover for negligent infliction of emotional distress because such emotional distress was reasonably foreseeable.

Comment: Strictly speaking, the writer has answered the question and provided a succinct explanation of the reason for the answer. The Conclusion, however, lacks key facts. When the issue is devoid of key facts, the Conclusion is often similarly defective. Key facts are as critical to a Conclusion as they are to an Issue. While you need not reiterate every key fact in your Conclusion, include enough facts to give the Conclusion context and meaning. Legal conclusions are based on interpretations of facts in the context of the applicable law.

Edna will be allowed to recover for her emotional distress because of her close proximity to the accident, her shock as a result of the perception of the accident, and her relationship with Mr. Dane.

Comment: The writer has answered the question and summarized the reasons for it. The writer's use of proper names, however, deprives the reader of the ability to identify the players and their roles.

A niece/bystander can recover for negligent infliction of emotional distress because the emotional distress was reasonably foreseeable to the defendant. Pennsylvania, in *Sinn v. Burd*, 486 Pa. 146, 404 A.2d 672 (1979), adopted a three-step test to evaluate whether the emotional distress was foreseeable: (1) whether the plaintiff stood near the scene of the accident, (2) whether the emotional impact and distress followed sensory observance of the accident, and (3) whether the plaintiff and the victim were closely related. The niece stood only one block from the accident. The niece saw her uncle immediately before the event, heard the event, and saw the scene and her uncle immediately after the event. The niece/uncle relationship is a close relationship. All elements of the test are therefore satisfied and a claim for negligent infliction of emotional distress is made out.

Comment: In the Conclusion, do not set out the governing standard, or the applicable law, in such detail. Do not apply the law to your facts. Application in the Conclusion section is usually ineffective because it is too general. It can be misleading because it is usually incomplete. If the attorney reading the Conclusion develops a misimpression, you are responsible. Do not condense your analysis. The Discussion section should be the sole source of analysis. Provide only the answer and a brief statement of your reasoning. This Conclusion is too long given the nature of the question. Moreover, citations to authority are improper in the Conclusion.

Here are two good Conclusions:

(1)   A Pennsylvania court would allow a niece who witnessed an automobile accident involving her uncle from one block away to recover for negligent infliction of emotional distress because: (1) she was near the location of the accident, (2) her shock was a result of her direct sensory perception of the accident, and (3) she is closely related to the victim.

(2)   A Pennsylvania court would permit a niece who heard a car accident involving her uncle from a block away and who then immediately witnessed his severe injuries to recover for negligent infliction of emotional distress.

As with the Issue, there is no one correct way to write a Conclusion. Be certain that you answer the question and that you provide a brief statement of the reasoning that supports that answer, as the writers of the above two samples have done.

Writing good Conclusions and Issues is difficult. If you follow the principles that have been discussed, review the sample memoranda in Appendix IV, and practice by writing and rewriting your Conclusions and Issues, you will soon master the task.

EXERCISES

Suppose a more senior attorney, Dewey D. Delaney, has called you into his office and told you the following:

The Firm has recently been retained by Jack Montagne to file suit against Asten Lift Company, Ltd. ("Asten'), a manufacturer of double and triple chair ski lifts based in Colorado. The file number is 98876-001. The basis of the suit he seeks to bring is an accident which occurred on Devil's Mountain, located in Pennsylvania. The accident involved his stepsister, Monica Gordon, who was thrown out of a triple chair lift and killed when a cable broke. Due to the circumstances of the accident, I think we might be able to state a cause of action for negligent infliction of emotional distress.

The facts of the case as I understand them are as follows. Jack, who is apparently an avid skier, took a ski vacation last winter with his stepsister, Monica. The two went to Devil's Mountain, as I said, where they rented a chalet for two weeks. Every morning they would have a quick breakfast, step outside, snap on their skis and ski the one hundred yards to the base of the mountain and the Diamond Triple Chair Lift, which would take them to the midpoint of the mountain. From there they would ride the Devil Triple Chair Lift (the "Devil Chair') to the peak. Once at the peak, they would separate, Jack to ski the wide open "bowls" on the back of the mountain and Monica to ski the trails on the face of the mountain. However, they had a standing agreement to meet for lunch at one o'clock at Tipler's, the restaurant at the top of the Devil Chair. They had consistently followed this schedule for seven days, and would not have deviated from it on the eighth day but for the accident.

On the day of the accident, Jack was standing near the top of the Devil Chair waiting for Monica and enjoying the sunshine. It was 12:50 p.m. Waiting for her there had become his habit. Ever since their first day on the mountain she had timed her skiing so that her last run before lunch was down Go Devil, the trail which wound back and forth under the Devil Chair, and ended at the midpoint. A run down Go Devil would take approximately half an hour. Then she would take the Devil Chair back to the top and Tipler's, a ride that took approximately twenty-five minutes. Jack had met her at the top of the chairlift every day, and she had consistently arrived within five minutes of the appointed time. Jack had been scanning the skiers as they came into view for about five minutes when he heard a loud noise that sounded like a large branch breaking off of a tree. The lift slowed to a stop and the chairs rolled back approximately 25 feet. Then, as Jack and those around him watched in horror, a wave raced up the cable, abruptly pulling the chairs ten or twelve feet up into the air and dropping them again just as suddenly. The chairs had no safety bar and Jack, who could see approximately ten percent of the chairs from his vantage point, saw people hurled out of their chairs and to the ground, which he knew was at times a 35 foot drop. Some skiers were miraculously able to hold on and remain in the chairs.

Jack could think only of Monica, who he knew had been riding the lift but who might now be lying injured or dead on the mountain. Jack started down the mountain, frantically seeking Monica in her polka-dotted ski jacket. Other skiers and the ski patrol were rushing to help those who had been thrown to the ground. Screams and moans filled the air and while some skiers writhed in pain, others seemed not to move at all. Dark blotches of blood stained the snow.

When he had gone approximately one hundred yards down the mountain, Jack still had not seen his stepsister and the trail wound away from the lift. He was almost frantic with fear and worry. Abandoning the trail to continue his search, Jack skied down directly under the chair. As he made his way through the crunchy snow and around the rocks, Jack reassured the skiers lying on the ground and those clinging to the chairs that help was en route, but he did not stop. Then he saw her. She lay on the ground, perfectly still, near a large rock. Jack took off his skis and made his way to her side. She made no sound. As he held her, he saw the gash and the blood caked to the back of her head. Her pulse was weak and irregular. Jack covered her with his jacket. Within ten minutes help arrived, and Monica was taken down to the base of the mountain in a stretcher. Jack never left her side. Within minutes of reaching the makeshift emergency center she died of head injuries sustained in the fall. She had never regained consciousness. Less than four minutes had passed from the moment Jack witnessed the skiers being thrown from their chairs and the moment he reached Monica.

Since the accident, Jack has had recurring nightmares, has suffered severe depression, and has experienced significant weight loss. He has been under continuing medical supervision for these conditions, none of which afflicted him prior to the accident.

Jack and Monica had been close since his mother and her father were married when he was 16 and she was 15. Both were only children who had longed for a sibling. At the time of the accident, both were in graduate school in Philadelphia. They talked often and met regularly for meals. Ever since Monica's father had died three years ago, and Jack's mother six months later, the two had taken a skiing vacation around Christmas and New Years so that they could spend the holidays together.

Suppose you are to prepare a memo on whether Jack Montagne could successfully state a cause of action for negligent infliction of emotional distress.

    (1)   Write the Heading of the memo.

    (2)   Review the material in this chapter on the Dane case, the illustrative case in this chapter, and:

        (a)   identify the key facts in the Montagne case;

        (b)   write the Issue as it would appear in the memo;

        (c)   write the Conclusion as it would appear in the memo.

CHAPTER **14**

THE MEMO: FACTS AND DISCUSSION

§ 14.01   Facts

When you receive an assignment to write a memo, either the attorney tells you the facts of the case or you go through the case file to get the facts. Once you know the facts, you must determine which of those facts belong in the memo's Facts section. Include only those facts that affect the outcome of your analysis, and enough background facts to allow the reader to understand the analytically significant facts.

To determine which facts are analytically significant, research the relevant legal authority. As you read the cases, identify the facts upon which the courts rely in reaching their holdings. After you complete your research, determine which facts in your case are analogous to the important facts in the decided cases. Also determine which of your facts are distinguishable from important facts in adverse holdings. Include those facts in the Facts section. Include the facts even if you think the reader knows them.

The Facts section must be objective. Include facts that are both favorable and unfavorable to your case. Just as you analyze adverse case law in the discussion section, you must include unfavorable facts in the Facts section.

Organize the Facts section logically so that the reader understands what happened. The most logical organization is a chronological organization. A chronological organization is also an objective organization, because it emphasizes no one fact or set of facts.

Make the Facts section clear, concise, and complete. After you write the Facts section, read it again and streamline it by eliminating all unnecessary facts. Do not make your reader hunt through the Facts section to find the relevant facts. At the same time, make certain you have included all relevant facts. If you discuss a fact in the Discussion section of your memo, it should also appear in the Facts section.

Here is an example of how to write a Facts section. In order to write a Facts section, you must get the facts from the client and analyze those facts in light of the relevant legal authority.

Here are all of the facts provided by the client:

> On June 10, 1997, Edna Smith witnessed an automobile accident in which her uncle, Wilbur Smith, was injured. Edna suffered and has continued to suffer emotional distress as a result of witnessing that accident.

On the day of the accident, Mr. Smith drove Edna to school. Edna's mother usually drove her to school, but her mother was sick. Edna attended Central High School and was a ninth grader.

Mr. Smith drove a 1991 Honda Civic. He was a good driver and had never received any speeding tickets.

Mr. Smith dropped Edna off at school at 8:00 a.m. and drove away to get some groceries for Edna's mother. Edna waved goodbye and turned to talk to her friends, Gertrude Jones and Florence Kramer.

Shortly thereafter, Edna heard a loud crash. She turned around and saw that a car had crashed into her uncle's car in an intersection located one block from the school. Her uncle's car was on fire.

By the time she arrived at the accident, her uncle had been pulled from the burning car. She saw that he was severely burned and had a large gash on his forehead.

Mrs. Polly Palmer was the driver of the car that hit Mr. Smith. She was intoxicated at the time of the accident and ran a red light.

Edna now suffers from recurring nightmares, a debilitating fear of automobiles and chronic stomach problems. None of these conditions existed prior to the accident.

Here is a synopsis of the governing case law:

1. *Sinn v. Burd*, 486 Pa. 146, 404 A.2d 672 (1979).

In *Sinn*, the court held that a bystander at an automobile accident has a valid cause of action for negligent infliction of emotional distress if the injury to the bystander is reasonably foreseeable to the defendant. The court formulated a three-part foreseeability test to determine whether the bystander's injury was reasonably foreseeable:

   1)   whether the bystander was located near the scene of the accident,

   2)   whether the shock resulted from a direct emotional impact upon the bystander from sensory and contemporaneous observance of the accident, as contrasted with learning of the accident from others after its occurrence, and

   3)   whether the bystander and the victim were closely related.

2. *Anfuso v. Smith*, 15 Pa. D. & C. 389 (Northampton Cnty. 1980).

In *Anfuso*, the court held that a mother, who was inside her home when she heard a car accident occur outside and rushed out to see her daughter injured in the accident, could recover for negligent infliction of emotional distress. The court applied the *Sinn v. Burd* three-part test to determine whether the mother's injury was foreseeable. The court found that the first part of the test was satisfied because the mother was sufficiently near the scene of the accident even though she was inside her house and the accident occurred on the street. The court further found that the second part of the test was satisfied because the mother heard the accident happen and then ran out and witnessed her daughter's injuries. The mother, therefore, had a sensory and contemporaneous observance of the event rather than learning about it from others. Finally, the court found that the third part of the test was satisfied because a mother-daughter relationship is a sufficiently close relationship.

　3.　*Yandrich v. Radic*, 495 Pa. 243, 433 A.2d 459 (1981).

In *Yandrich*, the court held that a father did not have a valid cause of action for negligent infliction of emotional distress because he did not witness the car accident in which his son was injured, nor did he hear the accident. Instead, he merely saw his injured son lying on the ground after the accident occurred.

MODEL FACTS SECTION

On June 10, 1997, Edna Smith's uncle, Wilbur Smith, drove her to school. He dropped her off at the school at 8:00 a.m. and then drove away. Edna turned to talk to some friends.

At an intersection located one block from the school, Polly Palmer, the defendant, ran a red light and crashed into Mr. Smith's car. Edna did not see the accident occur, but she heard it. Edna turned around and saw the accident scene. She could see that her uncle's car was on fire.

By the time she arrived at the accident, her uncle had been pulled from the burning car. She saw that he was severely burned and had a large gash on his forehead.

Edna now suffers from recurring nightmares, a debilitating fear of automobiles, and chronic stomach problems. None of these conditions existed prior to the accident.

In the above example, the writer included only the facts that are relevant under the applicable case law and enough background facts so that the reader can understand what happened to Edna. For example, since distance from the accident is an important factor under *Sinn v. Burd*, the writer described Edna's distance from the accident. The writer eliminated extraneous facts, such as the year of the car Mr. Smith was driving and the names of Edna's friends. The writer included all of the unfavorable facts, such as the fact that Edna did not see the accident. Finally, the writer organized the facts clearly and logically by stating them in chronological order.

Here is an example of a bad Facts section. Compare it with the Model Facts section.

Edna Smith suffers from severe emotional distress as a result of witnessing an automobile accident. The accident was the fault of Polly Palmer. In the accident, Edna's uncle, Wilber Smith, was horribly injured and he almost died.

The accident occurred on June 10, 1997. Edna's Uncle drove her to school. He dropped her off at school at 8:00 a.m. and drove away.

Polly Palmer, the defendant, ran a red light and slammed into Mr. Smith's car. His car exploded and Edna heard the explosion. Edna saw his car enveloped in flames. Edna also saw his severely burned body and the large gash on his forehead that was spurting blood.

Edna now suffers from horrible, recurring nightmares, she is terrified of cars, and she has excruciating stomach pain. Polly Palmer negligently caused Edna's injuries.

The above example of a Facts section is poorly written because it is not objective. The writer left out adverse facts, such as Edna's distance from the accident. In addition, the writer used value-laden words, such as "horrible" and "excruciating" to describe Edna's and her uncle's injuries.

The writer also made legal conclusions, instead of just stating facts. For example, the writer stated that the defendant negligently caused Edna's injuries. Moreover, the writer did not organize the facts clearly and logically.

§ 14.02   Discussion

The Discussion section is composed of legal arguments resolving the issues and subissues. Use the methods for writing legal arguments you learned in Chapters 4 and 5:

1) use deductive reasoning,

2) apply the law to the facts,

3) make analogies, and

4) make policy and equity arguments.

Ideally, you want to use all of these types of arguments in the Discussion section. Circumstances may limit the types of arguments available to you or may dictate that you emphasize one form of argument over another.

Divide the Discussion into sections that correspond to the issues and subissues. In each section, discuss the law applicable to the issue or subissue, and apply it to the facts that are relevant to the issue or subissue. Remember that all the facts to which you refer in the Discussion should be in the Facts section of your memo.

Write the Discussion clearly and logically. As we suggested in Chapter 7, give your reader a road map paragraph at the beginning of the Discussion, including a statement of your ultimate conclusion. As noted previously, readers of legal prose are not looking for suspense, they are looking for explanations. Explain the organization of the Discussion so the reader can follow it easily.

The Discussion section must be objective. Include both favorable and unfavorable facts and legal authority. Discuss arguments in favor of your client first, and then potential counterarguments. If you can, distinguish cases that are unfavorable to your client's position.

Be objective, but think strategically. If any argument supports your client's position, discuss that argument. The senior attorney who assigned the memo wants you to find a way for your client to win. Do not, however, misrepresent the strength of your client's position. The reader relies on your research and analysis. If your client is going to lose, do not assert that the client will win. You do not want a senior attorney to take the wrong action for a client. It will come back to haunt you.

Remember to come to conclusions and make recommendations. Do not simply present the information and force the reader to reproduce your analysis. At the end of the Discussion section, summarize all the conclusions you reached and recommend actions the reader can take. The conclusion at the end of the Discussion should be brief but may offer more detail than the Conclusion section of your memo.

Here is an example of how to write a discussion. The example is drawn from the case discussed in Chapter 13 and in the first section of this chapter.

> Edna Smith has a valid cause of action for negligent infliction of emotional distress. In *Sinn v. Burd*, the court held that a bystander at an automobile accident has a valid cause of action for negligent infliction of emotional distress if the injury to the bystander is reasonably foreseeable to the defendant. 486 Pa. 146, 173, 404 A.2d 672, 686 (1979). The court formulated a three-part test to determine whether the bystander's injury was reasonably foreseeable:
>
> > 1) whether the bystander was located near the scene of the accident,
> >
> > 2) whether the injury resulted from a direct emotional impact upon the bystander from sensory and contemporaneous observance of the accident, as contrasted with learning of the accident from others after its occurrence, and
> >
> > 3) whether the bystander and the victim were closely related.
>
> *Id.* at 170-71, 404 A.2d at 685. The present case meets all three parts of the *Sinn v. Burd* test. Each part of the test is discussed separately below.

> A. *Distance From the Scene of the Accident*

> The issue in Edna's case is whether someone standing one block from the scene of the accident is located near the scene of the accident. The decided cases suggest that one block is close enough to meet the test.

> In *Sinn*, the court held that a mother who witnessed an accident on the street from the front door of her house was located near the scene of the accident. *Id.* at 173, 404 A.2d at 686. Similarly, in *Anfuso v. Smith*, the court held that a mother who was inside her home when she heard an accident occur on the street was located near the scene of the accident. 15 Pa. D. & C. 3d 389, 393 (Northampton Cnty. 1980). In *Bliss v. Allentown Public Library*, the court held that a mother who was twenty-five feet away from her child when she heard a metal sculpture fall on him was located near the scene of the accident. 497 F. Supp. 487, 489 (E.D. Pa. 1980).

> In *Sinn*, *Anfuso*, and *Bliss*, the bystanders were close enough to the accident to see it happen or to see its aftermath. None of the cases required the bystander to be standing at the accident site in order to be located near the scene of the accident. In the present case, Edna was close enough to the scene of the accident that she could see its aftermath. Accordingly, Edna was located near the scene of the accident, and the first part of the test has been met.

B. Direct Emotional Impact

The issue here is whether someone who heard an accident rather than saw it had a sensory and contemporaneous observance of the accident. Edna's emotional distress was a direct result of hearing the accident as it occurred and, therefore, the relevant case law supports the conclusion that the second part of the *Sinn v. Burd* test has been met.

In *Bliss*, the court held that a mother who heard a metal sculpture fall on her child but did not see it fall had a sensory and contemporaneous observance of the event. *Id.* at 489. The court stated that it would not deny a suit simply because of the position of the plaintiff's eyes at the split second the accident occurred. *Id.* The court found that the entire incident produced the emotional distress the plaintiff suffered. *Id.* Similarly, the *Anfuso* court held that a mother who heard a car accident while inside her home and rushed out to see her daughter injured in the accident had a sensory and contemporaneous observance of the event. 15 Pa. D. & C. 3d at 393.

The facts of the present case are similar to the facts of *Bliss* and *Anfuso*. Edna heard the accident and then turned and saw its aftermath. Her emotional distress resulted from a direct emotional impact upon her from both hearing the accident and seeing its aftermath. Her observance of the accident was both sensory (hearing and sight) and contemporaneous (she heard it as it happened and then turned and saw its aftermath). Therefore, the second part of the *Sinn* test has been met.

The present case is distinguishable from *Yandrich v. Radic*, 495 Pa. 243, 433 A.2d 459 (1981). There, the court held that a father did not have a valid cause of action for negligent infliction of emotional distress. *Id.* at 245, 433 A.2d at 462. In *Yandrich*, the father did not hear or see the car accident in which his son was injured. Instead, he saw an ambulance race past him with its lights flashing and its sirens on. When he arrived at home, he saw the ambulance and saw his injured son lying on the ground. *Id.* The court found that he did not have a valid cause of action because he did not hear or see the accident as it occurred. *Id.*

In the present case, however, Edna heard the accident occur. She did not learn that an accident had occurred by seeing an ambulance. Therefore, the holding in *Yandrich* is inapplicable to the present case.

C. Close Relationship

The final issue is whether an uncle-niece relationship is a sufficiently close relationship to satisfy the third part of the test. Relevant decisions suggest that Edna and her uncle are closely enough related to meet the third part of the *Sinn v. Burd* test, although none of the cases involved a directly analogous relationship.

In *Sinn*, the court held that a mother-child relationship was a sufficiently close relationship to satisfy the third part of the test. 486 Pa. at 173, 404 A.2d at 686. In *Anfuso*, the court held that a mother-child relationship and a sibling relationship were sufficiently close relationships to satisfy the third part of the test. 15 Pa. D. & C. 3d at 391.

In *Sinn* and *Anfuso*, the courts held that two types of blood relatives satisfied the third part of the test. Edna and her uncle are blood relatives, although Edna's uncle is not a member of her immediate family. Parents, children and siblings are immediate family members. However, since none of the courts state that only immediate family members can satisfy the third part of the test, we should argue that an uncle-niece relationship is sufficiently close.

Edna Smith has a valid cause of action for negligent infliction of emotional distress. Edna was located near the scene of the accident, her injury was a result of a direct emotional impact from sensory and contemporaneous observance of her uncle's accident, and Edna and her uncle are closely related. Since all three parts of the *Sinn* test have been met, the firm should file suit on Edna's behalf.

In the above example, the writer divided the Discussion into sub-issues that correspond to the three parts of the *Sinn* test. In each section, the writer discussed the law applicable to the specific part of the test and applied that law to the facts relevant to that part of the test. All of the facts referred to in the Discussion came from the Facts section example in the first part of this Chapter.

At the beginning of the Discussion, the writer provided a road map for the sections discussing the individual parts of the test. The writer gave conclusions at the beginning of each section and summarized those conclusions at the end of the discussion. The writer also recommended an action for the reader to take -- to file suit.

Finally, the writer discussed unfavorable facts and cases. For example, the writer stated that Edna and her uncle are not immediate family members. In addition, the writer distinguished an unfavorable case, *Yandrich v. Radic*.

Now that you have seen an example of a well-constructed Discussion section, the next segment of this chapter offers some tips on how to avoid mistakes that students and young lawyers commonly make when writing legal memoranda.

§ 14.03   Make Your Reasoning Readily Apparent

"Ambiguous" is a word that writing instructors often write on first-year law students' papers. The student will often respond by pointing out the intended meaning, perhaps not even seeing the alternate meaning that made the expression ambiguous to the reader.

Always put yourself in your reader's shoes. Assume your reader knows nothing about the subject, and strive for a self-contained document that treats your subject thoroughly. Your reader should have no trouble understanding your reasoning in applying the law to the case at hand.

[1] Avoid the "Digest" Approach

A writer who uses the digest approach recites a series of mini-briefs of cases and fails to integrate the law and the facts.

In the following example of the "Digest" Approach, the writer "recites" the law but does not apply it.

> Article 2 § 8 of New York State's Bill of Rights (McKinney 1986) reiterates the "right of the people . . . against unreasonable searches and seizures" provided by the fourth amendment to the United States Constitution. "Searches conducted outside the judicial process, without prior approval by judge or magistrate, are per se unreasonable under the fourth amendment . . . subject only to a few specifically established and well-delineated exceptions." *Katz v. United States*, 389 U.S. 347 (1967).
>
> The application of the "plain view doctrine" is contingent upon a showing by the state that the officer's vantage point is a place in which it is lawful for that officer to be. *Ker v. State of California*, 374 U.S. 23 (1963).
>
> The court sets forth the guidelines which govern the application of the "emergency" exception to the warrant requirement in *People v. Mitchell*, 39 N.Y.2d 173, 347 N.E.2d 607, *cert. denied*, 426 U.S. 953 (1976), as follows:
>
> > (1) The police must have reasonable grounds to believe that there is an emergency at hand and an immediate need for their assistance for the protection of life or property.
> >
> > (2) The search must not be motivated primarily by intent to arrest and seize evidence.
> >
> > (3) There must be some reasonable basis approximating probable cause to associate the emergency with the area or place to be searched.
>
> *Id.* at 176, 347 N.E.2d 248.
>
> In *People v. Gallmon*, 19 N.Y. 389, 280 N.Y.S.2d 356 (1967), the police officer's entry without obtaining a warrant was justified by his obligation to assist people in distress.
>
> Under the "fruit of the poisonous tree doctrine" the government cannot use information obtained during an illegal search. *Wong Sun v. United States*, 371 U.S. 471 (1963). *Silverthrone Lumber Co. v. United States*, 251 U.S. 385 (1920).

In this example, the writer has included several paragraphs about the law, but the reader still knows nothing about the case at hand. Each time a rule is articulated, the rule should be applied to the facts of the case being discussed, using the previously decided cases to explain the application.

[2] Avoid the "Historical Development of the Law" Approach

The "historical development of the law" approach, as it implies, goes through the history of the law, often needlessly. Sometimes it is necessary to give some history of the development of a rule -- but not often. This approach is often appropriate in a law review article but has limited usefulness in a legal memorandum or brief. The reader -- whether a lawyer, a judge, or a client -- usually will care little about where the law came from or what led to its development, but will want to see what the law is and how it applies to the current situation.

Here is an example of the "Historical Development of the Law" Approach:

> At common law, an action for wrongful death did not exist. Nevertheless, the Ohio General Assembly recognized such an action in title 21, section 25.01 of the Ohio Rev. Code Ann. § 2125.01 (Anderson Supp. 1985). *Werling v. Sandy*, 17 Ohio St. 2d 45, 46, 476 N.E.2d 1053, 1054 (1985).

> Section 2125.01 provides as follows:

> When the death of a person is caused by wrongful act, neglect, or default which would have entitled the party injured to maintain an action and recover damages if death had not ensued, the person who would have been liable if death had not ensued . . . shall be liable to an action for damages, notwithstanding the death of the person injured. . . .

> Ohio Rev. Code Ann. § 2125.01 (Anderson Supp. 1985).

> Since § 2125.01 refers only to a "person," a key question is whether a viable, unborn child is a "person" within the meaning of § 2125.01. *Werling*, 17 Ohio St. 3d at 46, 476 N.E.2d at 1054.

> The most recent case involving an action for wrongful death under § 2125.01 where the decedent is a stillborn fetus is *Werling v. Sandy*, 17 Ohio St. 3d 476 N.E.2d 1053 (1985). In *Werling*, the Supreme Court of Ohio reaffirmed the position of the Court of Appeals for Madison County in *Stidam v. Ashmore*, 109 Ohio App. 431, 167 N.E.2d 106 (1959). The Supreme Court held in *Werling* that a viable fetus which is negligently injured in its mother's womb and subsequently stillborn may be the basis for a wrongful death action pursuant to § 2125.01. *Werling*, 17 Ohio St. 3d at 49, 476 N.E.2d at 1054.

Notice that you have read several paragraphs and still know nothing about the case the writer is discussing. You cannot even be sure of the specific issue being discussed. Unless it is actually relevant to your discussion to explain how the rule got to its present form, simply state the rule and begin your discussion at that point.

[3] Avoid the Use of Too Many Quotations From Legal Authorities

Many court opinions contain numerous quotations from other cases, legal periodicals, and treatises. It is easier and faster to quote from authorities than to paraphrase them, so some writers tend to use many quotations.

Too many quotations distract the reader, and often the quotations themselves are not clear. A frequent flaw in legal writing is overuse of the "block quote," the indented, single-spaced quote. Many judges, attorneys, and students tend to skip over them. Avoid overuse of block quotes in particular, and avoid overuse of all quotations. Here is an example from a student memo:

> Mr. Walker has a valid cause of action for false imprisonment. In *Barletta v. Golden Nugget Hotel Casino*, 580 F. Supp. 614, 617 (D.N.J. 1984), the court

found that "in order to support a claim for false arrest, the plaintiffs must allege two elements: First, that there was an arrest, and second, that the arrest was without proper legal authority, which has been interpreted to mean without legal justification." In New Jersey, false imprisonment and false arrest are merely separate names for the same tort. *Roth v. Golden Nugget Casino/Hotel,* 576 F. Supp. 262, 265 (D.N.J. 1983).

The court held in *Barletta v. Golden Nugget Hotel Casino,* 580 F. Supp. at 617-18, that:

> A taking into custody need not be done violently to constitute an arrest. . . . The inquiry goes to whether there was any unlawful restraint upon a person's freedom of movement. . . . Further, the assertion of legal authority to take a person into custody, even where such authority does not in fact exist, may be sufficient to create a reasonable apprehension that a person is under restraint.

> Therefore, applying the law to the facts of the present case, we can conclude that an arrest was made.

The student should have used his own words instead of quoting the court. When you read the excerpt, you probably read the first quote hastily and wondered if you could avoid reading the block quote. Most people tend to skip over long quotes. The student also used quotations in place of analysis. He wanted to argue that Mr. Walker has a valid cause of action for false imprisonment. The student should have applied the rule of law to the facts in his case and compared his client's circumstances with those of the plaintiff in *Barletta.* Instead, he quoted generalities from the *Barletta* opinion.

[4] Avoid the "Abstract Writing" Approach

The "abstract writing" approach reads like an essay. This form of writing is easy for students who have written essays in undergraduate school that earned "A's" in English or social sciences. Writers who use this form often discuss their viewpoints on what the law should be, but never get to what the law actually is. The following is an example of the "Abstract Writing" Approach:

> The Court should uphold defendant's conviction for selling cocaine as a matter of public policy. This society is permeated by drugs, and courts should not allow drug dealers to go free.

> The President has recently declared a war on drugs. The use of drugs is so prevalent that recently many celebrities in the entertainment and sports worlds have either died or admitted drug abuse, setting a bad example for young people.

> Defendant's conviction should stand because she is a mother who is a bad example for her children. The evidence against her was overwhelming, and her guilt is indisputable. To let her go free to protect her constitutional rights would be an injustice not only to her drug customers but also to her family.

> That defendant's having to go to prison may split up her family should not be the court's major consideration. Her children will be better off in a drug-free

environment. The defense argues that the police deprived defendant of her constitutional rights but ignores the fact that she is taking others' lives by selling dangerous drugs.

For all these reasons, defendant's conviction must stand.

The memorandum above could also be called the "soapbox" approach to legal writing. The student quite rightly addresses public policy issues, but fails to back up any ideas with constitutional provisions, statutes, or judicial rulings. There is no legal analysis.

[5]   Avoid the "Law Discussion Only" Approach

The next rule concerns the opposite of the "abstract" or "soapbox" approach -- the "law discussion only" approach with no factual, policy, or equity considerations. This approach often gives a very accurate recitation of the law but fails to discuss policies and equities underlying the law or the case on which the writer is working. Here is an example:

> Ohio Rule of Evidence 501 allows Ohio courts to use their discretion in deciding what privileges they will allow. The rule states that "[t]he privilege of a witness, person, state or political subdivision thereof shall be governed by statute enacted by the General Assembly or by principles of common law as interpreted by the courts of this state in the light of reason and experience." Ohio R. Evid. 501.

> The Ohio courts have been consistent in their refusal to extend the privileges beyond those which are specifically listed in the statute. Section 2317.02 recognizes as privileged, communications between attorney and client, physician and patient, clergyman and parishioner, husband and wife, and professional counselor and client.

> In *Belichick v. Belichick*, 37 Ohio App. 2d 95, 307 N.E.2d 270 (1973), the court refused to extend the privilege of physician-patient to include dentists or dental surgeons.

The student tells us about an evidentiary rule that gives Ohio courts discretion in making certain decisions. The student tells us that the courts have not exercised that discretion liberally. We also learn about the holding in one case. The student, however, omits vital information. We need to know what policy considerations guide the court in deciding how to exercise its discretion. We also need to know why the court decided the *Belichick* case as it did. The "law discussion only" approach fails to give us the information we need to engage in legal analysis.

[6]   A Good Example

The following is an edited excerpt from a good discussion of the law, accompanied by appropriate discussion of policies and equities, but avoiding abstraction or "soapboxing':

> Ohio Rule of Evidence 501 allows Ohio courts to use their discretion in deciding what privileges they will allow. The rule states that "[t]he privilege

of a witness, person, state or political subdivision thereof shall be governed by statute enacted by the General Assembly or by principles of common law as interpreted by the courts of this state in the light of reason and experience." Ohio R. Evid. 501.

Because the statutory privileges of § 2317.02 controvert the general policy that disclosure of all information in the possession of witnesses in trials is necessary to insure the disclosure of the truth, the Ohio courts have been consistent in their refusal to extend the privileges beyond those which are specifically listed in the statute. Section 2317.02 recognizes as privileged, communications between attorney and client, physician and patient, clergyman and parishioner, husband and wife, and professional counselor and client.

In *Belichick v. Belichick*, 37 Ohio App. 2d 95, 307 N.E.2d 270 (1973), the court refused to extend the privilege of physician-patient to include dentists or dental surgeons. The court stressed the importance of the disclosure of all information necessary to discover the truth. "The granting of privileges against disclosure constitutes an exception to the general rule, and the tendency of the courts is to construe such privileges strictly and to narrow their scope since they obstruct the discovery of the truth." *Id.* at 96-97, 307 N.E.2d at 271. Further, the court said, "R.C. 2317.02 is in derogation of the common law and must be strictly construed and consequently, the aforementioned section affords protection only to those relationships which are specifically mentioned there-in." *Id.* at 97, 307 N.E.2d at 271. Several other Ohio decisions have refused to extend the privileges of § 2317.02. See *State v. Hallech*, 24 Ohio App. 2d 74, 81, 963 N.E.2d 916, 922 (1970) (no parole officer-parolee privilege); *Arnovitzs v. Wozar*, 9 Ohio App. 2d 16, 21, 222 N.E.2d 660, 665 (1964) (no attorney-witness privilege when witness was not client); *Weis v. Weis*, 147 Ohio St. 416, 423, 72 N.E.2d 245, 252 (1947) (no physician-nurse privilege).

The Ohio courts' refusal to recognize privileges outside those authorized by statute is based on the policy that justice cannot be served if vital information is kept out of the record. The court so firmly believes this that it will refuse to recognize even those privileges authorized by statute where such recognition would protect criminal conduct. In *State v. Tu*, 17 Ohio App. 3d 159, 478 N.E.2d 830 (1984), a defendant who was being criminally prosecuted for vehicular homicide claimed the physician-patient privilege to prevent the introduction of a blood-alcohol test result into evidence at his trial. The court held that the privilege was not absolute and that "statutory privileges, unless they expressly provided otherwise, were simply not designed or intended to shield criminal conduct.'

Id. at 163, 478 N.E.2d at 833.

It follows that even if Ohio did recognize a parent-child privilege, it would never uphold the privilege in a case such as this one, where a defendant seeks to use the privilege to exclude vital evidence in a criminal prosecution for possession and sale of cocaine.

If you apply the lessons of this chapter, and the approach to legal analysis discussed in Chapter 5, to all legal memoranda you write, you should find that your writing will be well-received by those who use it to guide their decisions in practice. You will write clear, concrete, and concise yet thorough documents that will earn you a reputation as a knowledgeable and thoughtful lawyer.

EXERCISE

Below is a poorly written example of part of the Discussion of Edna Smith's case. Identify what is wrong with it.

In *Sinn*, the court held that a mother who witnessed an accident on the street from the front door of her house was located near the scene of the accident. *Id.* at 173, 404 A.2d at 686. Similarly, in *Anfuso v. Smith*, the court held that a mother who heard a car accident while inside her home and rushed out to see that her daughter had been injured in the accident was located near the scene of the accident. 15 Pa. D. & C. 3d 389, 393 (Northampton Cnty. 1980). The *Anfuso* court further held that the mother had a sensory and contemporaneous observance of the event. *Id.* In *Bliss v. Allentown Public Library*, the court held that a mother who was twenty-five feet away from her son when she heard a metal sculpture fall on him was located near the scene of the accident. 497 F. Supp. 487, 489 (E.D. Pa. 1980). The *Bliss* court also held that the mother had a sensory and contemporaneous observance of the event. *Id.*

In *Yandrich v. Radic*, the court held that a father did not have a valid cause of action for negligent infliction of emotional distress. 495 Pa. 243, 245, 433 A.2d 459, 462 (1981). In *Yandrich*, the father did not hear or see the car accident in which his son was injured. Instead he saw an ambulance race past him with its lights flashing and its sirens on. When he arrived at home, he saw the ambulance and saw his injured son lying on the ground. *Id.* The court found that the father did not have a valid cause of action because he did not hear or see the accident as it occurred. *Id.*

Edna was located near the scene of the accident, and the first part of the *Sinn* test has been met. Edna had a sensory and contemporaneous observance of the accident, and the second part of the *Sinn* test has been met. Therefore, Edna will win her case.

CHAPTER 15

ADVISING THE CLIENT

§ 15.01 Purpose of the Consultation

Once you have researched the client's problem and given the client some preliminary feedback in the form of a letter, you are ready to meet with the client again. This is the time to decide how to proceed with the client's matter. The process of decision making in a client-centered approach to counseling requires patience and thoroughness. Remember that the decision is not yours to make, but the client's [Model Rule of Professional Conduct 1.2]. Your purpose at this point in the process is to help the client arrive at a decision that will meet as many of the client's articulated goals as possible. Your purpose is not to tell the client what you would do or to substitute your judgment or priorities for those of the client. Your job is to provide the client with all relevant information so that he or she can make as informed a decision as possible. This includes discussing the most likely consequences of pursuing various options, and the advantages and disadvantages of those options. Your plan for a follow-up meeting with the client should take all these considerations into account.

§ 15.02 The Scenario

As we work through the planning process for a follow-up consultation, assume that you have already interviewed a client and gathered this information:

Susan Starkey is a member of a video dating service. On about December 20, she chose John Partlow from the video dating service. After speaking for hours on the telephone, the two agreed to meet at a dating service party on December 28. At the party, Partlow told Susan she was gorgeous and she reported that she felt sparks, too. They exchanged computer code names and sent more than a dozen computer messages back and forth.

After five days, Susan told Partlow to "get lost," feeling that he was trying to get too close too fast. He was already starting to talk about marriage and kids. On January 6, Partlow left a message on Susan's answering machine telling her he had secretly watched her leave work. She became worried and filed a police report on January 7. Police told Partlow to have no more communication with Susan, computer or otherwise, but no official restraining order was issued.

On January 15, Partlow sent Susan another computer message. "I've been trying to court you, not stalk you. If you let me, I would be the best man, friend, lover you could ever have. I just want to show you how well we go together. You've turned my innocent and somewhat foolish love for you into something bad in your own mind."

When Susan received the message, she replied via e-mail. She sent Partlow a message stating that if he did not leave her alone, he would be sorry.

On January 24, Partlow sent Susan an e-mail, threatening to e-mail the story to all her computer friends, and mail it to her family and old boyfriends. He informed her that "this is the least of the many things I could do to annoy you." He said he knew she must be seeing someone else, and that he had figured out her password and was monitoring her e-mail messages to find out who the other guy was.

This last message frightened Susan, but she is afraid that police action might not deter Partlow, or that it might make things even worse. Since the incident, she canceled her membership with the video dating service. She is afraid to use her computer for any online services and gave a friend her computer code, asking that the friend delete any messages from Partlow before she logs on. She also changed the hard drive on her computer and completely rebuilt her system. She is having trouble sleeping and is considering contacting a counselor to help her deal with the situation.

Susan wants to know whether there is any way she can sue Partlow, to make him pay for all the disruption he has caused in her life. She would like compensation for her distress. She feels that Partlow has diminished the quality of her life with his threats. She told you that she wants her life back.

Susan also expressed interest in finding out if she has any claim against the dating service, since it certainly seems to her that they could screen their clients better. When she called the service to complain about Partlow, the person she talked to said "Oh yeah, him. You know, this is the second or third complaint we've had about him. We may just have to cut him off." The person she talked to was the receptionist, Sandy Adams. Ms. Adams said she would relay Susan's complaint to Tony Benton, the head of the dating service, but she never heard anything from him. Susan made the original call three or four weeks before she came to see you. Assume that the last e-mail from Partlow arrived about two weeks before Susan came to see you.

§ 15.03 Planning the Consultation

As you plan the consultation, start with your understanding of the client's goals and priorities as they have been articulated to you thus far. Susan has told you that she wants compensation, both from Partlow and from the dating service, and that she wants her life back. Compare these goals and priorities with the results of your research as you have set them out in your memo and letter. Assume that your research and analysis have led you to the conclusion that you might be able to bring successful civil suits, against Partlow for intentional infliction of emotional distress and against the dating service for negligence in screening customers.[1] It is also possible to contact the police and pursue criminal charges.

Try to estimate the likelihood of various events with some degree of precision, and think through the consequences, positive and negative, of making each decision. Then, outline the topics you and the client need to discuss. Assume that you believe the suit against Partlow has about an even chance of succeeding, and that the odds of a successful suit against the dating service are slightly better. One distinct disadvantage of either suing Partlow or trying to have criminal charges brought is that Susan will likely have to face him in court at some point. You should also evaluate the likelihood that Partlow will be able to pay a substantial judgment. What other likely consequences can you think of? Advantages and disadvantages?

It is a good idea to find some way to keep track of all this complexity. You may want to make a chart before you begin the consultation. The chart should list the options you have considered in your planning process, and perhaps leave room for other options that might be developed during the consultation. You should identify any advantages and disadvantages that occur to you before the consultation, and leave space for others that might be identified by the client. You might want to include the client's goals and concerns in the chart, so that you will have a ready reference to check as the option development process proceeds. Here is one way you might prepare such a chart:

options	adv.	disav.	goals/concerns
civ. suit--iied			
civ. suit--negligence			
crim. charges			

[1] Depending on your jurisdiction, you might identify other possible causes of action as well. For example, in California it is possible to bring a civil action for stalking.

(Matthew Bender & Co., Inc.)   (Pub.676)

§ 15.04 Beginning the Consultation

You should begin this meeting, as with the initial interview, with a friendly greeting and a little casual conversation. Again, you want the client to relax and feel comfortable. You should also offer a brief preparatory explanation, so the client knows what to expect of this meeting. Share your outline of the meeting with the client, and ask if the client has any topics in mind that you have not included. For example, your consultation with Susan might begin like this:

Q: You: Hi, Susan. How are you today?

A: Susan: Ok, I guess.

Q: You: Are you feeling any better?

A: Susan: I'm hoping you can give me some good news today, and then maybe I will.

Q: You: I hope so too. Can I get you something to drink?

A: Susan: No thanks.

Q: You: Did you get the letter I sent?

A: Susan: Yes.

Q: You: Do you have any questions about the letter?

A: Susan: I don't think so; not right now anyway.

Q: You: What I am hoping we can do today is discuss the options I mentioned in the letter, and any other options or concerns that may have occurred to you. I would like us to review the advantages and disadvantages of all the options, and then try to make a decision about how you wish to proceed. I prepared a little chart that we can use to keep track of our discussion. Do you have any questions, or is there anything you want to add before we get started?

§ 15.05 Reaffirming the Client's Goals and Priorities

Early in the consultation, you should check to make sure that your understanding of the client's goals and priorities is correct, and that they have not changed since you and the client last discussed the matter. If any material facts have changed, or if the client has reassessed the desirable outcomes, you want to know that before you get too deeply into the discussion you have already prepared based on your earlier understanding. Ask if the client has had a chance to review the letter you sent, and if she has any questions about the letter.

To determine Susan's priorities, you may want to ask some questions about choices she would make. For example, ask her whether it is more important that she never have to face Partlow again, or that he be forced to compensate her. Can you think of other questions that might help you prioritize her goals?

§ 15.06   Developing Options

We have identified three preliminary courses of action:

(1)   A civil suit against Partlow for intentional infliction of emotional distress;

(2)   A civil suit against the dating service for negligence;

(3)   Contacting the police in the hope of criminal charges being filed.

[1]   Likely Consequences

In order to help Susan make a decision, you need to share with her your estimation of the likely outcome of these options. You should identify the most likely and least likely outcomes, and perhaps the "best case" and "worst case" scenarios. Clients would obviously like you to predict the likelihood of a particular outcome as precisely as possible, perhaps using percentages— *e.g.*, "we have a 50/50 chance of prevailing in the intentional infliction of emotional distress suit, and a 70% chance of prevailing in the negligence suit against the dating service." Many lawyers are uncomfortable with the idea of attaching numbers to their estimates, fearing that there are simply too many variables to allow such precision. The law is fundamentally a human process, and trying to predict what parties, witnesses, judges, and juries are likely to do is often little more than an educated guessing game.

If you are uncomfortable with the idea of assigning numbers to your estimated chances of success, you must come up with some other way of communicating your perceptions to the client in a way that will be understood. Remember that the client will interpret whatever you say in a way that makes it meaningful for the client. Thus, if you say "we have a pretty good chance of succeeding on this claim," what is that likely to mean to the client? You may mean 50/50 or 60/40, but the client may hear 70/30 or 80/20. You may try to offer a range of numbers, or you may try to be very conservative and guess low. Remember, however, that the client is entitled to your honest assessment of the likelihood of success of the options you discuss.

If you have previous experience in the area, or if you have researched jury verdicts in similar cases, you can share that information with the client. You can discuss the variables that make perfect prediction impossible. If the client understands the complexity of the process, the client may also understand why you can't offer guarantees, or even odds, with any degree of certainty. We do not have the perfect solution to the dilemma; you will have to experiment to find a way of communicating the likelihood of success that you are comfortable with and which gives the client a reasonable opportunity to understand the situation.

[2] Advantages and Disadvantages

You also need to discuss the advantages and disadvantages of each option, and of the various ways of approaching each option. For example, as you discuss the possibility of civil suits, you should always advise the client about the time and costs involved, and of the various alternative dispute resolution mechanisms available. You should discuss the advantages and disadvantages of filing a complaint before attempting to negotiate, and vice versa. You should explain the process of mediation, along with its advantages and disadvantages. Can you think of other consequences, advantages or disadvantages that should be discussed in this case?

You should also explore nonlegal considerations that create advantages and disadvantages, and ask the client to help you think these through. For example, in this case, Susan has obviously suffered a great deal of emotional distress, to the point where she has taken the extreme and possibly irrational action of rebuilding her computer. She needs to think about how it would feel to have this matter occupy another several months, if not years, of her life. Can you think of other questions you might want to ask Susan that would help you understand the implications of the nonlegal concerns that would affect the decision-making process in this case?

It should be clear by now that this option-development process can get quite complicated. It gets even more so as you actually discuss the details of each option. You will find that the discussion of one option leads you into a discussion of another, as you compare and contrast likely consequences. You will move back and forth between the options and the client's goals to check whether proposed options are meeting the client's needs. You will shift back and forth between options, and you may discover that discussing consequences leads you to other options you had not considered.

§ 15.07 Choosing a Course of Action

Once you have gone through this process of option development, it is time to make a decision. You and the client must sift through all the information you have produced as you discussed the options and choose a course of action. If your option development process has produced a clear choice in the form of a single option that has many more advantages and fewer disadvantages than other options, the choice will be easy. Unfortunately, this is frequently not the case. All of the options are likely to have advantages and disadvantages. You may find yourself with too many good choices, too many bad choices, or something in between. You should go back to the client's goals and priorities and try to make a choice that way. Is there one option that meets more goals, or does less damage to the client's goals, than other options? If not, ultimately the client will simply have to make a decision, and make the best of it. Here is one way part of your decision making dialog with Susan might go:

Q: You: Ok, Susan, we have discussed the advantages and disadvantages of our three options. What do you think?

A: Susan: I don't know. It all seems so complicated.

Q: You: I can certainly understand that. Let's try going back to what brought you to see me in the first place. You wanted compensation, and you wanted your normal life back. Do I have that about right?

A: Susan: Yeah, that's about it.

Q: You: Now, we have discussed the likelihood that you will have to face Partlow at some point if you sue him, or if you contact the police about criminal charges. We have also discussed the possibility that Partlow may not be able to afford a lot of money, and that it may be difficult to collect any judgment we do get. You also know how long a lawsuit might take to get resolved. Can you help me balance those concerns against what you were hoping to accomplish?

A: Susan: Well, that all makes suing Partlow seem like it might be more trouble than it's worth. And I don't know if I want him to go to jail. I just want him to leave me alone. What about suing the dating service?

Q: You: I'm glad you asked that; I was going to mention that next. You would probably not have to deal with Partlow in that suit, but it could still take a lot of time to resolve. Like I said, I am hopeful that the dating service might be willing to negotiate a settlement, but you never know. Would you like me to contact them, and see how they respond?

A: Susan: Sure, let's see what they say. I would hope they would understand they made a mistake on this one.

Q: You: So would I. Now, let's get back to the question of how we get Partlow to leave you alone.

* * *

If the client seems stymied, remind her that no decision is also a decision. In other words, discuss the advantages and disadvantages of doing nothing, and compare them to the other choices on the table. If the client asks you what you would do, there are two ways to present your choice. You can articulate the client's values as you understand them, and tell her what choice you would make based on those values, or you can tell her what your values are, and tell her what choice you would make based on those values. Either way, you should not tell her what you would do without articulating the values that guide you to that choice. For example, how risk averse are you, and how much are you guided by emotional as opposed to rational factors in making choices? You may also refuse to tell the client what you would do, and insist that she make the choice.

What if you disagree with her choice? If you are satisfied that she has made an informed choice, and her decision does not pose any ethical or moral dilemmas for you, you should do whatever is necessary and appropriate to implement her decision. If you think she has made a mistake, perhaps because she does not understand some aspect of the likely consequences of her decision, you can try again to educate her by running through the advantages and disadvantages. Always remember, however, that the decision is hers and not yours, and that you owe the client an obligation of competent and diligent representation. Therefore, if you deeply disagree with what the client wants done, to the point that your representation is likely to be compromised, you should say so and offer the client the option of seeking other counsel. If the disagreement is extreme, you may seek to withdraw from the case.

§ 15.08   Getting Settlement Authority

Once the decision is made, you should get explicit instructions from the client about the limits within which you must operate. For example, if you have decided to negotiate with the dating service on the negligence claim, you should discuss with Susan the elements of a settlement agreement that would satisfy her. How much money should you ask for, and what is she willing to settle for? If the dating service wants confidentiality of any settlement terms, does she have a problem with that? Can you think of other elements that might come up in these negotiations? If you do not have this conversation at this point, you may find yourself in a negotiation with no authority to settle. This may frustrate you, your client, and the other party. You will have to come back to her with simple questions that could easily have been answered at this stage if only you had thought to address them.

It should be obvious that we have only touched on the issues that go into helping the client to reach an informed decision. The process is much more complex, and the possibilities more numerous, than we can convey in a few pages. However, if you keep the basic principles in mind that we have discussed here, and come up with organizing strategies that help you and the client keep track of important factors, you should be able to help your clients reach informed decisions that offer as much satisfaction in the long run as is possible given the difficult circumstances that brought the client to you in the first place.

EXERCISE

Make up a chart for your consultation with Susan Starkey that incorporates the issues we have already touched on, and any others that occurred to you as you were reading and answering the questions posed throughout this chapter. There is no particular format that is appropriate for such a chart; play with it until you come up with one that you think will work for you.

§ 15.09 Consultation Checklist

_____ Plan for the consultation by identifying options based on your understanding of the client's goals and priorities and the applicable law you have found. Think about likely consequences, advantages and disadvantages of those options.

_____ Prepare a chart outlining those options, consequences, advantages, and disadvantages. Leave room on the chart for contributions in all these areas that may come up during the consultation.

_____ Remember to greet your client warmly, and have a bit of casual conversation if the client seems to need an opportunity to settle down and relax.

_____ Check with the client to see if anything has changed, if your understanding of the facts is correct, and if you understand the client's goals and priorities. Give the client a chance to react to your letter and to ask any questions.

_____ Go through the options you have developed, including likely consequences, advantages and disadvantages, and give the client ample opportunity to react and contribute. Give the client the best assessment of the likelihood of success that you can.

_____ Get a decision from the client, and discuss how you will act on it. If you are going to negotiate, make sure you understand the limits of your settlement authority.

CHAPTER 16

NEGOTIATING

Negotiating skills are important in many aspects of life. We begin negotiating with our parents at a very young age. We negotiate with employers, with friends and colleagues. We negotiate major purchases such as cars and houses. Lawyers negotiate constantly—plea bargains, settlements, contracts, and many other types of transactions. Along with client counseling, negotiation is the most frequently performed and critical lawyering function. Nevertheless, most of us have never had any formal training or organized learning on the subject. We frequently do not even give much thought to the process. We don't plan our negotiating strategy or analyze how and why the process works the way it does. Nor do we reflect on our negotiations after the fact to figure out how we might have done better.

This chapter gives you an introduction to concepts that will allow you to plan for and learn from your negotiations in an organized way. We help you to begin to understand the inner workings of the negotiations process so that you can control both the process and results to a greater extent, and serve your clients better along the way.

§ 16.01 Purposes of Negotiation

The purpose of any negotiation is to reach an agreement. If that is not your purpose, you might as well save your energy and go to court. The essence of negotiation is compromise and problem-solving. Whether you are trying to decide custody and visitation or how much money an injured victim is entitled to, you must assess the needs and interests of the parties and try to reach a resolution that meets as many of those needs as possible. Obviously some needs and interests will be in conflict, and there must be some balancing and decision-making. The likelihood that you will be able to meet everyone's needs is very small, as is the likelihood that one party will walk away with all the marbles. Therefore, you must plan on giving as well as getting.

§ 16.02 Theories of Negotiation

There are many approaches to negotiating, but we will focus on two approaches here: the adversarial and problem-solving modes of negotiating.[1] Most lawyers, and probably most individuals, at least begin with an adversarial approach to negotiating—that is, the idea that someone must win while the other will lose. The problem-solving approach, which requires a great deal of trust, is less common, particularly among negotiators who have no history with each other. As you gain experience, you will develop a flexible approach to negotiating. You will adapt various methods of negotiating to suit your own personality and the many contextual variables that determine which negotiating approach is most appropriate in any particular situation.

[1] Adversarial Models

We will briefly discuss three models for adversarial negotiating: game theory, economic, and social-psychological. We present the outlines of the theories so that you can gain a preliminary understanding of how theorists look at the negotiating process, and perhaps identify some frameworks that will help you in your negotiation planning. Understanding how and why the other party may be approaching the negotiation may help you plan your own strategy. Our belief is that models have some utility for conceptualizing the process, but that ultimately the process is sufficiently human and therefore unpredictable that you cannot rely too heavily on artificial constructions.

[a] Game Theory

The game theory approach to negotiation views the negotiation as being composed of the usual components of a game: players and rules. If you know the rules, you can predict what the players will do. You can plot out the possible avenues of progress for the negotiation in advance because the players have limited options based on the rules. The chief problem with this approach to negotiation is that it can only really work in a world of perfect information, where you know exactly what everyone else knows and how that information will affect the decisions of all the players. Fortunately or unfortunately, negotiation players do not all play by the same rules, they tend not to share all their information, and they don't behave predictably. Nevertheless, constructing a model for negotiating that uses some of the elements of game theory can be a useful organizing tool.

There are some "rules" of negotiation: for example, most negotiators don't start negotiating at the bottom line—they leave themselves some room to bargain. Also, it is frequently the case that concessions get smaller as

---

[1] For a more in-depth discussion of the theories touched on here, see Bastress and Harbaugh, *Interviewing, Counseling, and Negotiating* (Little, Brown 1990).

bargainers approach their bottom lines. It is at least a convention of negotiating that it is poor form to revoke a concession once firmly made. You may learn or discover some other "rules" that offer some predictability for the process. Let us see how the first two "rules" might help you to predict the "moves" in a negotiation:

Assume that Party A, the plaintiff in a personal injury suit, demands $5,000,000 to start. Because Party B, the defendant, knows that most negotiators set their opening demands to leave bargaining room, B knows that the next "move" is to make a counteroffer rather than simply offer to write a check. If subsequent concessions by A follow this pattern: $4,000,000; $3,500,000; $3,250,000; $3,125,000, B can apply the "rule" of diminishing concessions to infer that A's bottom line is somewhere around $3,000,000. Of course, A can make strategic use of this assumption to suggest a false bottom line. Negotiation is nothing if not a complex strategy game!

You will rarely if ever negotiate in an environment of perfect information. Negotiations frequently take place before discovery is completed, perhaps even before it is begun. Even if discovery has been completed, the likelihood that you know everything there is to know is very small. People simply don't provide complete information in response to discovery requests—the requests may not seek the right information, the respondents may not remember everything, or there may be reasons, such as privilege, for not providing full information.

Finally, negotiators are human beings. They make decisions and choose courses of action for all sorts of reasons. Individuals have different priorities, different levels of risk aversion, and different personal styles. All of these can make it difficult to predict what a negotiator will do. This difficulty becomes compounded by the fact that a negotiator is representing a client, who also has idiosyncratic goals and preferences that may influence the negotiation.

[b] Economic

The economic model of negotiation envisions a continuum along which the negotiation progresses. Each party begins at one end of the continuum, and the parties move together toward the middle until they reach their stopping point, or bottom line. If there is overlap between the stopping points, there is a "zone of settlement" within which the negotiation should settle:

(Assume that Party A starts negotiating at W and sets her bottom line at X)

W>>**X**
($500,000)   **($250,000)**

(Assume that Party B starts negotiating at Y and sets his bottom line at Z)

Z<<<<<<<<<<<<<<<<<<<<<<<<<<<<<<<<<<<<<<<<<Y
($350,000) **($100,000)**

Here the zone of settlement is between Z and X, or between $250,000 and $350,000.

(Party A) W>>>>>>>>>>ZoooooX<<<<<<<<<<<Y (Party B)

If the stopping points fall short of each other, there can be no settlement:

(Party A) W>>>>>>>>>>XoooooZ<<<<<<<<<<<Y (Party B)

This model of negotiation works reasonably well if the subject of the negotiation is an easily measured or relatively fungible item such as money, and the parties can take successive positions along the continuum. It does not work as well where the negotiation involves multiple items, at least some of which cannot be quantified or broken into pieces that can be given up. For example, if the negotiation involves custody of a child, there is no continuum to move along—one parent or the other will get custody, or they will share joint custody. There are no other options.

[c] Social-Psychological Bargaining

We refer to this approach to bargaining somewhat cynically as the "head-game" theory of negotiation, because it involves negotiation by manipulation of perceptions. "Head-game" bargainers don't bargain on the merits of the facts or law; they try to make you uncomfortable in one way or another, or to affect your perceptions in a way that causes you to want to give in. They may try to make you feel intimidated ("I went to an Ivy League law school and have been practicing for twenty years"), or guilty ("How can you represent a client who did such reprehensible things?"), or physically uncomfortable or off-balance (turning up the heat, or providing uncomfortable furniture), with the idea that you may give up just to get away.

There is virtually no limit to the aspects of negotiation process that can be manipulated by a bargainer determined to approach negotiation from this extremely adversarial position. The best defense against a "head-game" bargainer is to recognize the game and ignore it. If you insist on bargaining on the merits, you may be able to neutralize the tactics of your negotiating opponent.

[2]] Problem-solving Negotiation

The problem-solving approach to negotiating requires a paradigm shift. The problem-solving negotiator does not think in terms of concessions, compromise, and positions, but rather analyzes needs and interests, and looks for solutions to the mutual problem facing the negotiators. The problem-solving negotiator looks for ways to make the pie bigger, rather than simply carving it up. A problem-solving negotiation involves more free-flowing information, and brainstorming of possible solutions. The problem-solving negotiation is not constrained by the game board or the economic continuum, but moves outside the lines to address as many needs and interests as possible.

Since this mode of negotiating focuses on your client's needs and interests rather than bargaining positions, using it should enhance the probability of success. The challenge is to determine whether both the personalities and the subject matter involved in the negotiation lend themselves to this approach. If you determine that the subject matter is appropriate, which is particularly likely in a multiple item, non-monetary negotiation, and that you are comfortable with your negotiating counterpart, you might ask about the needs and interests of the other party. Of course, you must be prepared to honestly share your client's goals as well. Then the negotiators can work together to devise options that take into account as many of the needs and interests on the table as possible.

§ 16.03 Styles of Negotiation

The basic personal approaches to negotiation are competitive and cooperative.[2] This is not to say that these are polar opposites; most of us could place ourselves somewhere on a continuum from highly competitive to highly cooperative. Most of us also tend to believe that other people essentially behave the same way we do. Therefore, cooperative bargainers may be vulnerable to exploitation when faced with competitive opponents, because the cooperative bargainer will tend to make concessions in an effort to induce reciprocal behavior. The cooperative bargainer tends to assume that sufficient cooperative behavior must induce reciprocity from an opponent, while the competitive opponent, believing that all people are essentially competitive, will take whatever is given and push for more. This individual does not believe that cooperative bargainers exist, and therefore assumes that the concessions made by the cooperative bargainer are not real concessions—no rational person would give things away unless they did not matter!

There are more effective cooperative negotiators than there are effective competitive negotiators, at least in part because more people tend to be cooperative. In addition, competitive negotiators can sometimes be so abrasive that they cause breakdowns in the process, and so they are less effective.

Cooperative negotiators can protect themselves by making contingent concessions. In other words, do not actually give anything away until you

---

[2] See Charles B. Craver, *Effective Legal Negotiation and Settlement* (3d, ed., Michie 1997). Nancy Schultz is grateful to Charlie Craver for many of the insights that guide her thinking and teaching about negotiations.

have gotten something in return. Make it clear that all proposals on the table are contingent on the final agreement being satisfactory. For example, in a collective bargaining negotiation over compensation, management's counsel might say, "My client might be willing to contribute more to the pension plan, but we would need your client to relax the demand for a large raise in salary. What is your client willing to give up?"

Negotiation models and personal styles can intersect in interesting ways. Cooperative bargainers can adopt adversarial strategies, and competitive negotiators can be problem-solvers. The cooperative negotiator using an adversarial model will offer concessions and compromise, while the competitive negotiator trying to function as a problem-solver will focus only on his or her own client's needs and interests, and will push solutions that meet those needs and interests.

§ 16.04 Planning for Negotiation

You should plan all aspects of the negotiation: the information exchange, your opening position, and subsequent concessions. You should establish an opening offer or demand, a target point at which you would like to end up, and a bottom line below which you will not or may not go. We will discuss each of these stages in turn.

[1] Evaluating the Case

The first step in your planning process is to evaluate the case as objectively as possible. In order to do this effectively, you need to have a thorough understanding of the law and the facts, and how they intersect. The beauty of negotiation is that you are not limited by what a court is likely to do with your case, but assessing the likely result in court is a good starting point for evaluating acceptable settlements. Therefore, you need to research relevant law, and if possible find jury verdicts in similar cases. The general rule of thumb for establishing an acceptable settlement point is the likely verdict multiplied by the likelihood of prevailing. For example, if you think you could get a jury award of $800,000, but you think you only have about a 70% chance of winning, you should settle for $560,000.

How do you figure out the likelihood of prevailing? In addition to the strength of your legal support, look at factors such as the novelty of the claim, the credibility of likely witnesses, the availability of admissible evidence, and the track record of other players in the game, including opposing counsel, judges, and juries. You should also evaluate opportunity costs associated with litigating or not litigating. This is obviously not a science, and it is impossible to calculate the value of the case with mathematical precision, especially given that different people have widely divergent value systems, but you must start somewhere.

[2]   Planning to Exchange Information

Inexperienced negotiators frequently underestimate the importance of information exchange to an effective negotiation. You will feel much more confident in your negotiated result if you have sufficient information about the underlying events, needs, and interests. You will be more successful at obtaining useful information if you plan for the process beforehand. It may help to think about information as belonging to one of three categories: information you want, information you don't want to divulge, and information you want your opponents to have.

You have control over the latter two categories, and it should be relatively simple to categorize the information in your possession. You should, however, think strategically about the dissemination of information. People generally give more weight to information they have to work to get, while ascribing lesser significance to information that is easily obtained. This means that you may be able to get your opponent to devalue damaging information by simply stating it up front. This may seem counterintuitive initially, but if you think about it, it should make sense. Before fighting information requests, you should be sure that information that seems dangerous at first blush is really all that damaging. Frequently there are perfectly logical explanations for facts that seem harmful, and sometimes you may even be able to turn an apparently damaging fact into a useful tool. You will find it easier to evaluate information objectively during your preparation than you will in the heat of the negotiation.

Plan your questioning of your opponent. Identify categories of information you want, and ask questions that are precisely designed to get that information.

[3]   Establishing an Opening, Target, and Bottom Line

Much strategizing is done on the subject of where to begin a negotiation. Some negotiators hesitate to begin negotiating at all for fear of appearing weak. There is little evidence that either party to a negotiation gains an advantage by starting or refusing to start the process. It is possible that the party that makes the first concession will do less well in the final result. Some experienced negotiators prefer to make the first offer or demand, because doing so allows them to set the stage for the negotiation, and begin to limit the playing field. Other negotiators prefer to draw an opening offer or demand to respond to, on the theory that they can set the midpoint of the opening positions (where many results tend to cluster) with their response. You should probably do whatever feels most comfortable to you, or whatever is appropriate in the context of a particular negotiation. For example, plaintiffs in personal injury actions frequently make the first demand.

The trick in establishing an opening offer is to set the starting point at a place that is credible, but that also gives you some bargaining room. Starting too close to your bottom line in an effort to be fair or to make the negotiation more efficient may cause frustration all around. Most negotiators simply will not believe that your opening position is designed to be fair, and there will be quite a struggle to keep the final result in the range you had in mind. Conversely, an outrageous opening offer or demand may cause the other party to refuse to negotiate at all until you have come down to a reasonable point. Outrageous starting positions are difficult to defend, and frequently require huge initial concessions just to get the bargaining started. Try to find a starting point that you can justify with a straight face, and that leaves some room for bargaining and even for the possibility that you may have miscalculated the value of the case. Remember that your opponent knows things you don't know, and this may affect the reasonable settlement point in ways you cannot anticipate.

You should also set a target point, a point at which you would like to settle and that you believe is reasonable based on the information you have. You should try to head toward this target point during the negotiation, and you should make a serious effort not to go below it unless you are persuaded that there can be no settlement in this range. Finally, you should set a bottom line before you go into the negotiation. This should be the point below which you absolutely do not intend to go, and you should hold firm at that point if you get there during the negotiation, unless you are satisfied that you have seriously misanalyzed the problem. Negotiators who do not preset bottom lines frequently find themselves "giving up the farm" during the negotiation. Once you start giving, and begin to feel a commitment to settlement, it can be difficult to refuse that final concession in the interest of finalizing a deal.[3]

You should also think about a concession pattern in advance. How do you plan to get from your opening to your target, and then ultimately to your bottom line if you have to go there? Obviously the actual concession pattern will to some extent be dictated by the events of the negotiation, but you will feel more confident if you have thought about where you want to go after the opponent rejects your opening offer or demand, as is virtually inevitable. If the opening offer or demand is accepted, you have almost certainly badly underestimated the value of the case!

---

[3] Remember that all of this takes place in the context of your instructions from your client. You should know what your settlement authority is before you begin to negotiate, and you may not agree to anything outside of that authority. At best, you can offer to take a proposal to your client that does not satisfy the goals set by you and the client before the negotiation.

[4] Analyzing Needs and Interests

You should make an effort to identify the needs and interests of the parties as accurately as possible before the negotiation. You may want to classify the anticipated needs as essential, important, or desirable, and then try to figure out whether those needs are likely to be shared, independent, or conflicting.[4] The idea of shared needs may seem odd, but it is possible. For example, both parties may want to keep the agreement confidential, or both parties to a custody dispute may want the best for the children—they simply disagree about how to achieve it. Independent needs are those that can be met without creating an adverse impact on the other party. For example, if one party to a negotiation needs the terms of the settlement to be confidential, and the other party has no desire to talk about the deal, the need for confidentiality is an independent need.

This approach is particularly appropriate for a problem-solving negotiation, but it can be useful in virtually any situation. Thinking of a negotiation in terms of needs and interests rather than positions frequently makes the bargaining more flexible and the conversation less strained. It may also open up possibilities for resolution that would not have occurred to you otherwise.

If you can identify independent or shared needs, you should try to start the negotiation there. It is easier to get the process started if you can get an agreement on bargaining items that are not likely to create conflict. Beginning the negotiation with difficult or contentious items can lead to early breakdown. The most likely area of difficulty in the formulation we suggest is the area where essential needs of the parties are in conflict. If you arrive at this point in a negotiation, bring your creativity or prepare to go to trial!

[5] Planning for Personalities

Try to find out what you can about your negotiating partners or opponents. Negotiating style and personality can have a huge impact on the progress of a negotiation. Some people have so much trouble communicating that they simply cannot have lengthy face-to-face meetings. If you find yourself in a negotiating situation with someone who makes you so angry you cannot think straight, get out! You are likely to make mistakes if you are angry or in some other emotional state that clouds your thinking sufficiently that it becomes difficult to make rational decisions. Conversely, if you are negotiating with someone who is fair and reasonable, the process can be a pleasure. Remember that everyone's job is to represent their client, and try not to take it personally if you don't get everything you want.

---

[4] This formulation appears in a very useful chart in Bastress and Harbaugh, supra at 483.

§ 16.05   Beginning the Negotiation

If you have prepared adequately, the beginning of the negotiation should be easy. Try to establish a comfortable, constructive atmosphere for negotiating. If the negotiators don't know each other, a little small talk to allow everyone to relax may be helpful. It may be a good idea to set an agenda for the negotiation. For example, you may agree on an order of topics to be addressed; you may agree in advance that all options put on the table are contingent on an acceptable final settlement. The latter approach is a good way to avoid deadlock later on if the only item left to be discussed is a particularly difficult one, and you find yourself wishing that you had something else left to ask for or to give away. A lot of negotiators try to gain some sort of tactical advantage by playing "head games" in the early stages of a negotiation; this may be effective for some in the short run, but you will generally find that the process works better if everyone just gets down to business and concentrates on trying to deal with the joint problem to be solved that brought you to the table in the first place.

§ 16.06   Information Exchange

As we mentioned earlier, this is obviously a critical phase of the negotiation. How can you reach the optimal resolution of a problem if you don't really understand what the problem is? Again, if you have prepared adequately, this phase of the negotiation should be productive. You want to find out as much as you can about the other side's needs, interests, and priorities. You want to obtain any facts that will help you understand the situation and that might be relevant if the case does go to trial. If you have filed a complaint, you may be able to get some of this information through discovery, but negotiations frequently take place before discovery is completed, and perhaps before it is even begun.

Open-ended questions, such as "What was your client doing right before the accident?", may get you more information, but they also allow more opportunities for evasion if a party is determined to evade the question. Listen very carefully to the answers you get. If the responder is hedging, or seems to be choosing words very carefully, think about the precise words you used in your question, and rephrase the question in a way that leaves less wiggle room, or that is more precisely designed to get the information you seek. For example, if you are negotiating a settlement of the Smiths' claim against the Palm Court Hotel, and you want to establish the Hotel's knowledge of criminal activity in the area, you might ask if hotel personnel were aware of any similar incidents in the area. This question allows the responder to define "similar incidents." If the negotiator chooses to interpret that phrase in a very limited way, he or she might decide that since there were no identical incidents, the answer is "no." You should ask instead whether the Hotel is aware of any criminal activity within a specified radius of the Hotel.

If you get questions you prefer not to answer, there are many blocking techniques available. You can answer with a question, you can "misunderstand" and answer a different question, you can hide your answer in a lot of irrelevant verbiage, you can refuse to answer, you can declare the question irrelevant or out of bounds, or you can answer part of the question. You should consider the likely effect of using too many blocking techniques on your own ability to obtain information. Why should the other party answer your questions if you refuse to answer theirs? You should also be aware of the likelihood that these techniques may be used against you, and watch out for them. If you sense that information requests are being blocked, don't give up—rephrase your questions until you are satisfied that the information does not exist or will not be forthcoming. It is frequently disappointing or worse for negotiators to realize that critical information was available if only they had asked for it in the right way.

All in all, the negotiation will be much more productive if there is a constructive and thorough information exchange. If you want to obtain the best result for your client, you want to provide the information that supports the result you seek. The parties are much more likely to reach a mutually satisfactory resolution of the problem if there is genuine understanding of the issues on all sides. The exchange of information will frequently suggest possibilities for resolution that may not have occurred to anyone during preparation.

§ 16.07 Trading

This is the point of the negotiation where the actual exchanges take place. The key here is to keep track of the concessions and to explain them in terms that are relevant and understandable. Do not make multiple unreciprocated concessions. Do not make concessions that are disproportionately large when compared to your opponent's concessions. Make sure that you explain the rationale for every concession, and every refusal to make a concession. Concessions that are not justified in terms of the applicable law and facts are merely numbers or positions that come from nowhere and have little credibility or persuasive effect. There is nothing to distinguish one number from another if you cannot connect it to something concrete.

For example, if you are seeking damages for the Smiths, explain how you arrived at the number you request using factors such as lost wages and medical expenses, and if you agree to accept a smaller number, explain the concession in terms if something that has happened during the negotiation—a fact of which you were unaware, or a trade-off for something else that will benefit your clients. Negotiations will frequently get to a point where everyone is simply "horse-trading" to arrive at a resolution, and finally perhaps "splitting the difference" to finalize the deal. This should be the natural evolution of the negotiation—not the starting point.

§ 16.08 Closing the Negotiation

Once you believe you have achieved a negotiated resolution, take a few moments to find out if it is possible to adjust the agreement in some way that benefits both parties, or that allows one party to benefit without damaging the other party. These few moments at the end of a negotiation can make a large difference in the parties' commitment to the agreement and willingness to carry it out. They can also go a long way toward preserving or rehabilitating the relationship between the negotiators. You will discover that the importance of reputation cannot be overemphasized in the legal community, and a reputation as a competent, fair negotiator will take you far.

You should also use this final stage of the negotiation to make sure that you have actually reached an agreement. Go back over the terms in detail, and make sure that both parties have the same understanding of the agreement. Proper handling of this crucial step will save you much grief later on. Misunderstandings can cause serious problems and may end up unraveling the whole deal if it turns out that the parties had very different feelings about the meaning of a critical term. One good approach is to send a confirming letter to the other negotiator outlining your understanding of the agreement as you will take it to your client. If both sides are not "on the same wavelength," it should become clear very quickly, indicating a need for further negotiation, or recognition of an impossible situation.

§ 16.09 Negotiation Ethics

There are very few written rules that govern negotiations. There will be no one there looking over your shoulder to see if you behave or not. One rule that does apply is that you may not make a false statement of material fact or law [Model Rule of Professional Conduct 4.1(a)]. This is obviously a simple statement of a complex range of possibilities. For example, when does an omission rise to the level of a misrepresentation? If you know that the opposing party is relying on a misconception about what the facts are, and you do nothing to correct it, are you misrepresenting the facts? Negotiators frequently try to skate this line very closely; you will have to make your own decisions about what kind of negotiator you want to be, and what kind of behavior will allow you to sleep at night. Do remember that your reputation will not only precede you, but will affect how and whether people interact with you.

It is a convention of negotiating that the client's value system is not considered a material fact. Thus you may "lie" about what your client is willing to accept, and even about your bottom line. You do not have to respond honestly to direct questions about what your client wants, as you do to factual questions in other areas. You should know, however, that you may do damage to the negotiating process and to your reputation by lying about such things to the extreme. A certain amount of puffery is expected, but if people learn that you will look someone in the eye with a wounded expression and plead that you are being taken to the cleaners while you are in fact cleaning out your opponents, you will find future negotiations difficult.

Another type of behavior that causes damage to the process is lying about what kind of negotiator you are. Many competitive "sharks" can adopt the language of the cooperative problem-solver while they are taking advantage of genuinely cooperative negotiators. If discovered, however, they may find later negotiations uncomfortable. Again, however trite it may sound, you must let your conscience be your guide in negotiations.

We have obviously only skimmed the surface of the complex set of interactions that is negotiation. However, we believe that we have given you sound advice that will serve you well as you develop your own negotiating style and ideas. You will learn a lot about the process through experience, and there are plenty of books on the market if you wish to do further reading.[5]

§ 16.10   Negotiation Checklist

_____ Prepare, prepare, prepare. Research the law. Know the facts. Plan your information gathering and exchange. Analyze needs and interests. Write down your opening, target, and bottom line, and think about likely and acceptable concession patterns. Find out whatever you can about your negotiating partners and opponents.

_____ Exchange information until you are satisfied that real bargaining can take place in an informed environment.

_____ Keep track of concessions. Justify all requests and concessions with thoughtful explanations of relevant facts and law.

_____ Close the negotiation by checking to see if you can adjust the agreement to benefit one or more parties without damaging others. Make sure all parties have the same understanding of the agreement.

_____ Think about what kind of negotiator you want to be and what kind of reputation you want to have in your negotiating community.

---

[5] For example, you might want to take a look at the classic "Getting to Yes," by Fisher and Ury (Houghton Mifflin 1981), or, for some very practical advice, "Negotiating Your Salary: How to Make $1000 A Minute," by Jack Chapman (Ten Speed Press 1996)

EXERCISE

Here is the general information for a negotiation exercise. Your instructor will distribute confidential information for each party and give you further guidance regarding how to conduct the negotiation.

LANDLORD/TENANT PROBLEM

GENERAL INFORMATION

Millie Graves is 79 years old. For the past fifteen years, she has lived in a second floor apartment in Garden Grove. About a month ago, Millie was mugged outside the front door of her building. Her attacker had apparently followed her from the street, waiting until just before she entered the building, when she was in the shadow of the large bushes growing in the front yard. There is a light over the front door, but it was not on that evening. The attack took place sometime between 9:00 and 9:30 P.M. Millie was not seriously injured, but she suffered bruises and scrapes when her assailant knocked her to the ground after he grabbed her purse. She lost all her identification, credit cards, and approximately $80 in cash. There is normally a doorman stationed at the desk just inside the front door, but he was not at his desk at the time of the attack.

Millie has never been a problem tenant. She doesn't complain and she pays her rent on time. For the past three months, however, she has withheld $100 per month from her monthly rent of $500 in an effort to get the landlord, Sam Simolean, to make several repairs to her apartment. There is a leak in her shower, water damage to her kitchen ceiling from a leak in the apartment above hers, and two of her windows are broken. Her apartment has not been painted in two years, and it shows. There are also quite a number of insects running around the building, particularly in the common areas. Millie has three cats, which was perfectly fine with her previous landlord, but Simolean has instituted a "No Pets" policy for new tenants. Based on Millie's failure to pay her full rent for the past three months, he recently served her with an eviction notice, giving her 60 days to vacate the premises. The lease requires 30 days notice of termination for failure to pay rent. Millie still has 15 months to go on a two-year lease.

CHAPTER **17**

DRAFTING SETTLEMENT AGREEMENTS

§ 17.01　Introduction

Lawyers do a lot of writing that is not directed at a court and, in fact, that has nothing whatsoever to do with a case in litigation. They draft wills, contracts, leases and other property agreements, financial documents, and many other types of written instruments. In Chapter 11, we discussed client opinion letters, which are another type of non-litigation document. In this chapter, we give you a brief introduction to the basic principles that should guide your drafting of almost any type of legal document: precision, clarity, shorter sentences in the active voice, simple and concrete language, and logical structure. We will use the drafting of agreements to settle a dispute as our example of the drafting process.[1] We will discuss the preparation of a settlement agreement and release between the Palm Court Hotel and Mr. and Mrs. Smith. As you may recall from Chapter 11, the Smiths were seeking compensation from the hotel as a result of an attack on them in their hotel room. The Smiths felt that the hotel provided inadequate security to protect its guests.

§ 17.02　The Framework of an Agreement

There are four parts of our settlement agreement: the title, the introduction, the substance of the agreement, and the closing. Agreements often include definitions of terms that may be the subject of dispute or that are used repeatedly throughout the document. Many agreements also include specific references to the background of the agreement. You may have seen agreements containing paragraphs beginning with the anachronistic word "whereas" that generally explain why the parties have decided to reach an agreement. In these types of agreements, the agreement itself usually consists of paragraphs beginning with the words "now, therefore." Because

---

[1] If you wish to explore the principles of drafting in greater detail, as indeed you should if you are required to undertake a drafting project, there are many fine sources available to you. Three of these, which we consulted in our preparation of this chapter, are: Brody, Rutherford, Vietzen and Dernbach, *Legal Drafting* (Little, Brown 1994); Barbara Child, *Drafting Legal Documents: Principles and Practices* (West, 2d ed. 1992); and Scott Burnham, *Drafting Contracts*, 2nd Ed. (Michie 1993). There are also more specialized resources for particular types of documents, such as Robert Martineau, *Drafting Legislation and Rules in Plain English* (West 1991).

our agreement between the Palm Court Hotel and the Smiths will be straightforward, we will not include any definitions or background information.

[1]   The Title

This part of the document is exactly what it sounds like: a descriptive heading at the top of the document that lets the reader know at a glance what type of document he or she is looking at. In our case, we will simply call our document a "Settlement Agreement."

[2]   The Introduction

The very first sentence of a document should identify the parties who will be signing the document and should include some words indicating an agreement, to signify what the parties are trying to accomplish by executing the document. It is common to include the date of the agreement in the introduction. You also may want to devise shorthand references to the parties that you can use throughout the rest of the document. Thus, in our case, the first sentence of our settlement agreement might read:

> On the 19th day of January, 1998, the Palm Court Hotel (the "Hotel"), and John and Mary Smith ("the Smiths"), agree to these terms:

[3]   The Substance of the Agreement

An agreement generally consists of a set of promises. Your goal as drafter of the agreement must be to make sure that it is absolutely clear *who* has promised to do *what*. It is also wise to provide some mechanism for resolving disputes regarding the meaning or the performance of the agreement, such as allowing the parties to designate a third party or parties to decide such matters. You also should provide specifically for the possibility that one or both parties might breach the agreement by spelling out the consequences of a breach. Many agreements also include a provision specifying which jurisdiction's law governs the agreement.

In our case, assume that the Hotel and the Smiths have agreed to these items:

1) A payment of $50,000 from the Hotel to the Smiths;

2) Additional security measures to be provided by the Hotel to its guests, including at least: two security guards on duty at all times, chain locks on the inside of all guest rooms, exterior lights on all guest buildings, and locked access doors to all guest buildings;

3) Confidentiality — both parties have agreed not to disclose the terms of the settlement to anyone; and

4) The Hotel does not have to admit liability for the attack on the Smiths.

We will not draft these provisions yet, because we have not yet discussed the appropriate language for the agreement.

[4]   The Closing

The final requirement of the agreement is that both parties sign it. There is no magic language that must accompany the signatures. Thus, although you may have seen agreements that close with language such as "the parties have hereunto set their hands and seals," there is no need to include anything of the kind. It is a good idea to include a date with the signatures, and the addresses of the parties, if they do not appear anywhere else in the agreement.

§ 17.03   Drafting Clear Language

The rules we have given you for drafting other types of legal documents apply here. Draft agreements in the active voice, so there is no question which party must take the described action. When an agreement says "the seller shall be paid," it is implicit that the buyer is expected to pay. Nevertheless, it is less risky and clearer to say "the buyer shall pay the seller."

Prefer shorter sentences to longer ones and use the simplest, most concrete language that will convey the idea you are expressing. There are a few words that experts on drafting will tell you to use to make your sentences precise. For example, to create an obligation, use "shall," and to create a duty not to act, use "shall not." To indicate permissive authority, use "may," and to negate discretion, use "may not." To create a right, use "is entitled to," and if you wish to negate a right, use "is not entitled to."

Avoid the kinds of legalisms and jargon that have appeared in legal documents for years without adding appreciably to the clarity or precision of such documents. For example, few if any compound prepositions need to appear in any legal document: you do not need words such as "hereunder," "heretobefore," "thereto," "therein," "whereas," and "wherein." "Said" was never intended to be an adjective, and "witnesseth" should be relegated to the history books. Some words commonly appear together that perform perfectly well on their own: "by and between," "as and for," and "on or about" (use "on" unless you really are not sure of the date). Is "in the event that" really any more precise than the simple "if?"

Of course, sometimes legal terms of art must be used if the agreement is to be interpreted correctly, and you should use these terms when necessary. In all other instances, however, choose simple, precise language, avoid unnecessary wordiness, and read your finished product to catch any possibilities of misinterpretation.

If the document is long, consider using headings and subheadings as a helpful way to organize the document for the reader. Make sure that the sequence of provisions in the document is logical and that all important points are easily accessible by even a quick reference to the document.

Now that we have introduced you to the type of language that should appear in a modern legal document, let us go back to the Settlement Agreement between the Palm Court Hotel and the Smiths. Here is one way to draft the provision specifying the additional security measures to which the Hotel has agreed:

The Hotel shall provide, for the security of its guests:

(1) Two security guards on duty twenty-four hours per day;

(2) Chain locks inside the doors of all guest rooms;

(3) Exterior lights on all guest buildings; and

(4) Locks on the access doors of all guest buildings, that will unlock with the guests' room keys.

Compare the above provision with this one:

The Hotel agrees that guests of the Hotel will be better protected by the provision of additional security measures, including the provision of more security personnel on duty for more hours, and security devices such as chain locks, exterior lights, and locked access doors to guest buildings.

Although this language is fairly concrete, there are several problems with it, at least from the Smiths' perspective. Because the sentence is constructed in the passive voice, the Hotel has not actually promised to *do* anything. There is a lack of specificity regarding the "security personnel" — who are they, what does "on duty" mean, and how many hours are we talking about? It is not clear whether some or all, or none, of the listed "security devices" will be provided, or whether they will be added to all rooms and all buildings.

EXERCISE

Draft the remaining provisions of the Settlement Agreement, as outlined in § 17.02[3]. You may include any provisions you think advisable to ensure that the agreement is clear and enforceable.

§ 17.04 The Release

Every time parties settle a claim or lawsuit, the party against whom the claim was brought seeks a written release of the claim by the person who brought it. The release ensures that the claimant will not accept the settlement, then suddenly decide that the settlement was not quite good enough and return to press the claim at a later date. Perhaps no other instrument in legal writing has taken on the degree of arcane linguistic excess that one sees in many form releases. For example:[2]

Know All Men by These Presents, that I, _____ (hereinafter called the Claimant), for and in consideration of the sum of $ _____ lawful money paid by the _____ Railroad Company (hereinafter called the Company) at the time of the sealing and delivery hereof, the receipt whereof is hereby acknowledged, have remised, released and forever quitclaimed and discharged, and by these presents do remise, release and forever quitclaim and discharge the Company and its successors from all claims and demands which the Claimant, or any

---

[2] Both form releases in this section were taken from Edmund O. Belsheim, *Modern Legal Forms*, Ch. 57 (5th Ed. 1969).

person or persons claiming by, through or under the Claimant, may have, or may at any time hereafter have, against the Company or its successors, for, by reason of, or in any manner based upon or growing out of any matter, cause or thing whatsoever, now existing or heretofore occurring, and particularly by reason of personal injury received at or near _____ , on or about the _____ day of _____ , 19 ____. And the Claimant does hereby declare any and all such claims or demands to be, by the payment aforesaid, wholly and forever satisfied and extinguished; it being expressly understood and agreed, however, that the Company in paying the said sum of money does so by way of compromise of the claims and demands aforesaid, and without prejudice or admitting any liability therefor by itself or its successors.

Witness the following signature and seal this ____ day of _____ , 19—.

_____[Seal]

When reading a document such as this, we might wonder whether the poor Claimant had any idea what he or she was agreeing to.

At almost the other end of the spectrum is this release, which presumably is designed to ensure that the party giving the release understands *precisely* what he or she is doing:

SEAMAN'S RELEASE (Red Release) (This form of release was commonly used by insurance companies. It was called a "red release" because of the abundance of red ink used for emphasis.)

READ CAREFULLY—By signing this you give up EVERY right you have.

```
I, _____ Age _____ _____
      (Write your own name and age)    (Write here whether you
                                        are married or single)
Address _____ in exchange for
        (Street and number, city or town, and state)
_____ dollars ($ _____) which I have received, do
hereby _____ and forever discharge
        (Write the word "release" to show
         that you know what you are doing)
```

_____

(Here insert full name of persons, corporations or partnerships
to be released and their heirs, executors, administrators,
successors and assigns, and their several vessels and in
particular the ss. _____ and the owners, agents, operators,
charters, masters, officers, and crews, of said vessels from each
and every right and claim which I now have, or may hereafter have
on account of injuries and illnesses suffered by me as follows:

_____

```
and, in addition to that, I _____ them
                            (Write the word "release" to show
                             that you know what you are doing)
```

from each and every right and claim which I now have or may
hereafter have because of any matter or thing which happened
before the signing of this paper, it being my intention by
signing of this paper to wipe the slate clean as between myself
and the parties released, even as respects injuries, illnesses
rights and claims not mentioned herein or not known to me.

READ THE FOLLOWING SIX NUMBERED STATEMENTS CAREFULLY:

(1) I know that this paper is much more than a receipt. **IT IS A RELEASE. I AM GIVING UP EVERY RIGHT I HAVE.**

(2) I know that in signing this release I am, among other things, now settling in full for all injuries, illnesses and disabilities which I have had already, which I have now, and which I may have in the future, either because of the particular occurrence mentioned above or because of any other occurrence in the past, or because of both, even though I do not know that I have had already, have now or may have in the future such injuries, illnesses and disabilities, and even though they are not mentioned particularly in this release; and I do all this regardless of what anyone may have told me about my injuries, illnesses and disabilities or about anything else.

(3) **I know that doctors and other persons make mistakes, and I am taking the risk that what they may have told me is wrong. If that should be the case, it is my loss, and I cannot back out of the settlement.**

(4) I realize that the payment of the money mentioned above is not an admission that anyone is liable to me for anything.

(5) I am signing this release because I am getting the money. I have not been promised anything else.

(6) I am satisfied.

(Matthew Bender & Co., Inc.)   (Pub. 676)

THE FOLLOWING IS TO BE FILLED IN BY THE
CLAIMANT HIMSELF IN HIS OWN
HANDWRITING.

A.   Have you read this paper from beginning to end? A. _____

B.   Do you know what this paper is that you are signing?
A. _____

C.   What is this paper which you are signing? A._____
_____   (Write here
"release
of everything"

D.   Do you make the six numbered statements printed above
and do you intend that the parties whom you are releasing shall
rely on the statements as the truth? A. _____

E.   Do you know that signing this paper settles and ends
EVERY right or claim you have for DAMAGES as well as for past and
future maintenance, cure, and wages? A. _____

F.   In order to show that you know what you are doing
please copy in your own handwriting, in the space immediately
following, the third numbered statement above which is printed in
red ink...
....
....
....

    Therefore, I am signing my name upon the words this is a
release and alongside the seal, which is printed below and which
is adopted by me as my own, to show that I mean everything that
is said on this paper.
                          Dated _____, 19__

    SIGN
    HERE

                    THIS IS A RELEASE
    +++++++++............................... [Seal]

Claimant, if he wishes to sign and seal this paper, should write his name upon the words "THIS IS A RELEASE" immediately above and alongside the printed seal.

While clarity is an admirable goal, and we want people to understand the contents of legal documents when they sign them, this form is excessive. It is unnecessarily repetitive, and insulting to the intelligence. The goal of comprehensibility could have been achieved much more efficiently.

EXERCISE

Draft a release that will satisfy the Palm Court Hotel that the Smiths are accepting the Settlement Agreement and will not return to press their claim further. Use the principles discussed in this chapter and draw upon any aspects of the two releases presented above that you find helpful.

Use critical judgment when you use a form book to draft a document. Although the forms in form books provide general guidance on the contents of particular documents, they often have not been revised in many years. As a result, the language may be archaic and contain excessive jargon. The forms tend to contain sentences that are poorly structured, too long, and unnecessarily confusing. Always feel free to alter the language and structure of forms to suit your client's needs.

§ 17.05 Drafting Checklist

Here is a summary, in checklist form, of the principles that should guide your document drafting.

_____ Define terms when necessary.

_____ Be precise, especially regarding who is promising to do what.

_____ In general, use the active voice.

_____ Prefer shorter sentences to longer ones.

_____ Use words that are simple and concrete.

_____ Avoid legalese and unnecessary jargon, but use legal terms of art when necessary.

_____ When helpful, use headings and subheadings.

_____ Avoid linguistic excess, both in choice and number of words.

_____ When consulting form books, use critical judgment in deciding which provisions to use and how to tailor them to your client's needs.

PART IV

PRE-TRIAL LITIGATION

(Matthew Bender & Co., Inc.)

CHAPTER **18**

DRAFTING PLEADINGS

§ 18.01 Introduction

The parties in a case use written *pleadings* to present their cases to the court in which the lawsuit begins. This chapter shows you how to write these pleadings. The pleadings determine the issues the court must decide. A court will not decide any issue the pleadings do not raise. Pleadings also notify the parties of the allegations that each side intends to make at trial.

The two basic pleadings are the plaintiff's *complaint* and the defendant's *answer*. The litigants also may file other pretrial pleadings. For example, the plaintiff may file a *reply* to the defendant's answer; the defendant may file a counterclaim against an additional defendant. Defendants may file cross-claims against each other.

§ 18.02 The Purpose and Language of Pleadings

In practice, pleadings are often composed of substantial legalese. Court rules and decisions may require such archaic jargon as "complaint in Assumpsit" instead of "complaint in Contract" or "complaint in Trespass" instead of "complaint in Tort." Custom and practice have embedded in pleadings awkward sentences and confusing words. When local rules and precedents require you to use obscure language, you have no choice but to comply. Even when you are required to use some jargon, however, you still have considerable latitude to write short simple sentences in comprehensible English. In drafting a pleading, use a writing style that furthers your purposes by speaking to your different audiences. For example, when you are drafting a complaint, one audience is the defendant. Although the defendant probably knows the facts, it also needs to know what causes of action you are pursuing. The other audience is the court. The court needs to know both the facts and the causes of action.

To satisfy both audiences you need to tell the factual story and identify the causes of action. You will tell the story by arranging the facts in chronological order and presenting the sequence of events from your client's perspective. You do not editorialize, or use unnecessary modifiers, but the reader of a well-drafted complaint should feel that a wrong has been committed, and that something should be done about it. This feeling should be created even before the specific causes of action are presented.

The causes of action should be identified clearly and precisely. This is often accomplished by using separate counts to identify separate causes of action. To insure clarity, you also should follow the principles of writing set forth in this book: use plain English to the extent possible, write short plain sentences, and use concrete words.

§ 18.03 Following Rules

Pleadings must conform to the rules of procedure of the jurisdiction in which the action begins. Therefore, you must look at the rules in your jurisdiction before drafting a pleading. Our goal here is to give you a general understanding of how to draft a pleading.

In most jurisdictions, the party must make allegations in a pleading in consecutively numbered paragraphs so that the opposing party can answer each allegation using the same numbers. Each paragraph of the pleading must contain only a single allegation so that the opposing party can specifically deny or admit it.

You can find examples of how to draft pleadings in form books. Most jurisdictions have form books containing examples of pleadings. You can find additional examples of pleadings in books in your law library. Law offices also develop forms over a period of time for use in many different situations.

§ 18.04 Captions

All pleadings begin with a caption that identifies the court, the number the court has assigned to the case, the month and year in which the action commenced, the parties, and the type of pleading. Here is an example of a caption for a complaint:

Marilyn Smith	)	Court of Common
12 Main Street		Pleas
Anywhere, PA 19009	)	Bucmont County
Plaintiff,	)	December Term, 1985
	)	
	)	
v.		Civil Action No.
		44,009
Samantha Jones	)	
14 Main Street	)	
Anywhere, PA 19009	)	
Defendant	)	

COMPLAINT

EXERCISE

Using the following information, draft a caption for a pleading.

Bob Dob has sued Joe Doe for assault and battery. You are drafting pleadings for this case in the District Court for Lincoln County. The court has assigned the case number as 98-502, and Bob filed the case in the April Term of 1998. Joe lives at 92 High Street, Hometown. Bob lives at 110 High Street, Hometown. Write a caption to use over a complaint, an answer, or any other pleading.

Save this caption for use in the next sections.

§ 18.05   The Complaint

Following the caption is the body of the pleading, which contains the substance of the pleading, whether it is a complaint, an answer, a reply, or a motion.

Suppose, for example, that your client, Marilyn Smith, wants you to file suit on her behalf so that she can recover damages for injuries she received from a dog bite. Before you draft the complaint, you might write out a summary of the facts provided by the client in paragraph, narrative form. The facts alleged in a Complaint must show that the plaintiff has a cause of action. The Complaint also must give the defendant notice of the plaintiff's claims and an opportunity to defend against them. To show that the plaintiff has a cause of action, the Complaint must allege sufficient facts to demonstrate that the plaintiff has a right to relief under the applicable law. Therefore, you must research the law before you write the Complaint to determine what facts to allege in it. Suppose that the law in your jurisdiction states that the victim of a dog bite can recover under either negligence or strict liability under the following circumstances:

An individual is liable in negligence to another party if:

1) that individual owns or harbors a dog;

2) that individual knew that the dog had previously attacked at least one other person;

3) that individual knew that the dog was likely to harm other persons unless properly confined or otherwise controlled;

4) that individual fails to exercise reasonable care to confine or otherwise control the dog; and

5) the dog attacks and injures the other party.

An individual is strictly liable in tort to another party if:

1) the individual knowingly owns or harbors a dog that is of a vicious nature that is accustomed to attacking and biting other persons;

2) the individual had personal knowledge of the vicious nature of the dog and knew that the dog was accustomed to attacking and biting other persons; and

3) the dog attacks and injures the other party.

The complaint that you would file on behalf of your client might look like this:

COMPLAINT

1. Plaintiff, Marilyn Smith, is an individual and citizen of the Commonwealth of Pennsylvania, residing at 12 Main Street, Anywhere, Pennsylvania 19009.

2. Defendant, Samantha Jones, is an individual and citizen of the Commonwealth of Pennsylvania, residing at 14 Main Street, Anywhere, Pennsylvania 19009.

3. On June 4, 1998, at about 8:00 a.m., the defendant was the owner of or harbored a dog.

4. On June 4. 1998, at about 8:00 a.m., plaintiff was walking in a common driveway at her residence when the dog attacked and bit her without provocation.

5. The dog had attacked at least one other person before attacking the plaintiff.

COUNT I

STRICT LIABILITY IN TORT

6. Plaintiff incorporates by reference paragraphs 1 through 5 of this Complaint.

7. On June 4, 1998, at about 8:00 a.m., defendant knowingly owned or harbored a dog that was of a ferocious nature and that was used and accustomed to attacking and biting other persons.

8. Defendant had personal knowledge of the ferocious nature of the dog and knew that the dog was used and accustomed to attacking and biting other persons.

9. The dog attacked and bit plaintiff, causing her to suffer various physical and mental injuries, including but not limited to lacerations of her left hand and wrist, contusions of her left thumb, and a puncture wound in her left foot. The injuries led to scarring, infection, lameness, and present and future pain, suffering, and mental anguish.

WHEREFORE, plaintiff demands that this court enter judgment in her favor and against defendant in an amount in excess of $10,000, exclusive of interest and costs.

COUNT II

NEGLIGENCE

10. Plaintiff incorporates by reference paragraphs 1 through 5 of this Complaint.

11. Defendant knew that the dog was likely to harm individuals unless properly confined or otherwise controlled.

12. Defendant failed to exercise reasonable care to confine or otherwise control the dog.

13. The dog attacked and bit plaintiff, causing her to suffer various physical and mental injuries, including but not limited to lacerations of her left hand and wrist, contusions of her left thumb, and a puncture wound in her left foot. The injuries

led to scarring, infection, lameness, and present and future pain, suffering, and mental anguish.

WHEREFORE, Plaintiff demands that this Court enter judgment in her favor and against defendant in an amount in excess of $10,000, exclusive of interest and costs.

Attorney for Plaintiff

As you can see from this example, the introductory paragraphs of a Complaint identify the names and addresses of the parties. Here the plaintiff is suing on two separate counts, or causes of action: strict liability in tort and negligence. The next paragraphs (3-5) set out any facts that are common to more than one count of the Complaint. You incorporate those facts by reference in each count of the Complaint. See, for example, paragraphs 6 and 10 of the sample Complaint. This may appear unnecessarily repetitious, but it relates the information in the introductory paragraphs directly to each count and lets the court know that the basic information is the same with regard to each count.

The Complaint shown above is written in plain English, following the principles of clear writing. You see no "hereins" or other stilted language. The writer used every-day language throughout the complaint and no legalese. The final paragraph does use "wherefore," which is the common way to end a Complaint. Otherwise, however, there is no eccentric language.

Most sentences are in simple subject-verb-object structure, such as "The dog had attacked at least one other person," "Defendant had personal knowledge," and "The dog attacked and bit plaintiff." Just as you can present more than one cause of action in a Complaint, you also can present alternative causes of action. Here, the two alternative causes of action are strict liability and negligence. Some jurisdictions require a demand for relief at the end of each Count. Other jurisdictions require a demand for relief at the end of the Complaint instead of at the end of each Count. A demand for relief appears at the end of each Count of the sample Complaint.

The remaining paragraphs of the Complaint present a concise summary of the facts that serve as a basis for the specific causes of action. Complaints do not set out case law or evidentiary matters. In the sample Complaint, the writer did not discuss the elements of the strict liability or negligence causes of action. Instead, the writer set out the facts that establish the required elements of those causes of action.

EXERCISE

Please return to the case we started in the Exercise in Section 18.04 in which Bob Dob is suing Joe Doe. Prepare a complaint based on the following facts, as well as those presented in the "Caption" section. Be sure to put the caption at the beginning of the Complaint.

Bob alleges that, on December 12, 1992, at 6:30 p.m., Joe came to his house to demand payment for a personal loan of $500 Joe had made to him previously.

Bob did not have the money and told Joe that he would have to repay him in January. Bob says that Joe was furious and pulled a knife out of his pocket as they talked in Bob's living room. According to Bob, Joe stood over him while Bob was sitting on the sofa and yelled, "Give me my money back now, or I'll be seein' your liver on the floor!" Bob says he pleaded with him to put the knife away, but that Joe kept yelling and grabbed Bob by the collar, putting the knife point to his neck.

Joe did not know that Alice, Bob's wife, had called her neighbor, a policeman, when she overheard the argument while she was cooking in the kitchen. The policeman, Arnie Force, came in at the moment Joe put the knife point to Bob's neck and stopped the fight. Bob did not file criminal charges but filed a civil suit on two counts, assault and battery, asking for $3,000 in damages.

In your jurisdiction, assault is the intentional making of a threatening gesture that causes another person to become reasonably apprehensive of an anticipated immediate bodily contact. No actual physical contact is required, but the other person must be aware of the anticipated contact. A battery is the intentional and unpermitted or unprivileged touching of another person's body. There must be some bodily contact, no matter how slight.

§ 18.06 The Answer

In an Answer, the defendant admits or denies each factual allegation that the plaintiff makes in the Complaint and raises any defenses to the causes of action presented in the Complaint. The defendant answers each allegation by numbered paragraphs that correspond to numbered paragraphs in the Complaint. The defendant's Answer to the *Smith v. Jones* Complaint set out in § 18.05 might look like this:

ANSWER

1. Admitted.

2. Admitted.

3. Denied. Defendant denies that on June 4, 1998, at about 8:00 a.m., the defendant was the owner of or harbored a dog. The dog in question was owned by Frank Smith, who had brought the dog with him while visiting defendant.

4. After reasonable investigation defendant is without knowledge or information sufficient to form a belief as to the truth of plaintiff's allegation that plaintiff was walking in a common driveway at her residence on June 4, 1998, at about 8:00 a.m., and therefore, denies that allegation and demands strict proof thereof. Defendant denies that the dog in question attacked and bit plaintiff without provocation.

5. Denied. Defendant denies that the dog in question ever attacked anyone, including the plaintiff.

COUNT I

STRICT LIABILITY IN TORT

6. Defendant incorporates by reference her answers to paragraphs 1 through 5 of Plaintiff's Complaint.

7. Denied. Defendant denies that she owned or harbored a dog on June 4, 1998, at around 8:00 a.m. Defendant further denies that the dog in question was of a ferocious nature or was used and accustomed to attacking and biting other persons.

8. Denied. Defendant denies that she knew that the dog in question was ferocious. Defendant further denies that she knew that the dog in question was used and accustomed to attacking and biting other persons.

9. Denied. Defendant denies that the dog in question attacked and bit Plaintiff. Defendant further denies that Plaintiff suffered any illness or injury as a result of any action or inaction on Defendant's part.

WHEREFORE, Defendant demands judgment in her favor and against Plaintiff.

COUNT II

NEGLIGENCE

10. Defendant incorporates by reference her answers to paragraphs 1 through 5 of Plaintiff's Complaint.

11. Denied. Defendant denies that she knew that the dog in question was likely to harm individuals unless properly confined or otherwise controlled.

12. Denied. Defendant denies that she failed to exercise reasonable care to confine or otherwise control the dog in question. Defendant did not have a duty to confine or otherwise control the dog in question. Defendant acted with all due care required of her under the circumstances.

13. Denied. Defendant denies that the dog in question attacked and bit plaintiff. Defendant further denies that Plaintiff suffered any illness or injury as a result of any action or inaction on Defendant's part.

WHEREFORE, Defendant demands judgment in her favor and against Plaintiff.

NEW MATTER

14. The Plaintiff's Complaint and each Count therein fails to state a cause of action, therefor, this action should be dismissed.

15. The Plaintiff failed to join as defendants parties that are indispensable and necessary to a full adjudication of this action and, therefore, this action should be dismissed.

16. Upon information and belief, any injuries, losses or damages sustained by Plaintiff were caused by her own contributory negligence.

_____
Attorney for Defendant

Compare the paragraphs of the above Answer with the paragraphs of the Complaint in Section 18.05.

Unless you deny a factual allegation the plaintiff made in the Complaint, the court will conclude that you have admitted it. Sometimes you do not have sufficient information to know if an allegation made in a Complaint is true or not. In this case, the rules of procedure of many jurisdictions permit you to state that "after reasonable investigation [your client] is without knowledge or information sufficient to form a belief as to the truth of an allegation." In those jurisdictions, this statement has the same effect as a denial. See, for example, paragraph 4 of the sample Answer.

After answering the plaintiff's allegations, set out any affirmative defenses that the defendant intends to raise at trial. Typical affirmative defenses in a tort case include assumption of risk, consent, contributory negligence, fraud, and the statute of limitations. Affirmative defenses are those defenses that the court will conclude are waived unless the defendant raises them. In some jurisdictions, the defendant can plead inconsistent defenses. Put the affirmative defenses in a separate section of the Answer. See, for example, the New Matter section of the sample Answer.

In some jurisdictions you also can raise counterclaims or demurrers in an Answer. In a counterclaim, you allege that the defendant also has a claim against the plaintiff. Counterclaims are governed by the same rules that govern a plaintiff's Complaint. In a demurrer, you allege that the plaintiff has failed to make out a cause of action that can properly be decided by the court. In some jurisdictions, you will file a separate motion to dismiss the Complaint, rather than demurring in the answer. We discuss motions to dismiss in Chapter 21.

EXERCISE

Return to our case of *Dob v. Doe*. Draft an answer to the Complaint by Joe Doe, starting with the caption you wrote in Section 18.04. Joe admits that he went to Bob's house at the designated time on the designated date. However, he denies any wrongdoing. He says that he asked Bob politely for the $500 and told him that his rent was overdue and that he needed the money right away. He says that Bob was upset about Joe's asking for repayment then because Bob thought he had another month in which to raise the money. Joe says that "We horsed around awhile, and I played like I was mad—but I really wasn't, and he knew that." He says he had a knife in his pocket, but he never pulled it out. And, he says, he certainly never threatened Bob or touched him in any way. He denies everything else and says he left Bob in good spirits at 7:00 p.m.

§ 18.07 Verifications

Attorneys must sign all pleadings. In addition, in many jurisdictions, the party signs a verification that is attached to the pleading. In it the party states that the allegations are true. Here is an example of a verification:

I, (name of party), hereby state that I am the (plaintiff/defendant) in this action and verify that the statements made in the foregoing (type of pleading) are true and correct to the best of my knowledge, information, and belief.

_____   _____

Date   Party

EXERCISE

Draft verifications for the Complaint and Answer you wrote for *Dob v. Doe.*

CHAPTER 19

DISCOVERY

§ 19.01 Introduction

As you may be aware, discovery is the process by which lawyers find out the information they need to know in order to pursue a legal claim. Once a complaint is filed, the lawyers may begin requesting information from the parties, and from other individuals who have information about the case. In this chapter, we will briefly discuss the methods available to lawyers to obtain written information from the other parties to an action. Then we will focus on how to write requests for information that effectively fulfill their intended function without disclosing more of your strategy than is necessary.

§ 19.02 Available Forms of Discovery

There are three forms of written discovery commonly used in practice: interrogatories, requests to produce documents, and requests for admission.

Interrogatories are written questions designed to obtain basic facts from the parties to an action, and to ascertain the scope of the knowledge possessed by those parties. Rule 33(b) of the Federal Rules of Civil Procedure defines the scope and use of interrogatories this way:

> Interrogatories may relate to any matters which can be inquired into under Rule 26(b)(1),[1] and the answers may be used to the extent permitted by the rules of evidence.
>
> An interrogatory otherwise proper is not necessarily objectionable merely because an answer to the interrogatory involves an opinion or contention that relates to fact or the application of law to fact, but the court may order that such an interrogatory need not be answered until after designated discovery has been completed or until a pretrial conference or other later time.

With respect to the production of documents, Rule 34(a) provides that the requesting party may seek to "inspect and copy, test, or sample any tangible things

---

[1] Rule 26(b)(1) of the Federal Rules of Civil Procedure identifies the scope of permissible discovery as follows: "Parties may obtain discovery regarding any matter, not privileged, which is relevant to the subject matter involved in the pending action. . . . The information sought need not be admissible at the trial if the information sought appears reasonably calculated to lead to the discovery of admissible evidence."

which constitute or contain matters within the scope of Rule 26(b)." Under subsection (b) of Rule 34, "[t]he request shall set forth the items to be inspected either by individual item or by category, and describe each item and category with reasonable particularity. The request shall specify a reasonable time, place and manner of making the inspection and performing the related acts." For example, a request for production might specify that the requester intends to appear at the offices of the respondent at 9:00 a.m. on January 20 to examine all balance sheets for the years 1993-1998.

Requests for admission seek a party's admission, "for purposes of the pending action only, of the truth of any matters within the scope of Rule 26(b) set forth in the request that relate to statements or opinions of fact or of the application of law to fact, including the genuineness of any documents described in the request." Fed. R. Civ. P. 36(a). For example, with respect to the request to examine balance sheets, the requester could seek an admission that the balance sheets produced on January 20 were all of the balance sheets for the specified period, and that they were accurate in every respect. The stakes in responding to a request for admission are high, because "[a]ny matter admitted under this rule is conclusively established," subject to certain exceptions provided in the rule. Fed. R. Civ. P. 36(b).

§ 19.03 Formulating Discovery Requests

As with any other type of writing, when making discovery requests you must consider the context, purpose, and audience. Context in the case of discovery is quite formal and involves very specific expectations about format. The purpose of a discovery request, of course, is to obtain information, even when the audience is hostile to the request. These factors should guide your preparation of written discovery requests. In the rest of this chapter, we will discuss discovery in the context of the Palm Court Hotel case that was presented in Chapter 13. In that case, the Smiths wished to bring an action against the hotel as a result of an attack on them while they were guests at the hotel. The Smiths alleged that the security at the hotel was inadequate.

Assume that you are counsel for the Smiths, and have filed an action against the Palm Court Hotel. Now you are preparing to conduct discovery. Here are the questions you need to ask yourself:

(1) What kind of information do I need?

(2) Who is most likely to possess that information?

(3) Do the intended recipients of the request have some motivation to avoid providing the requested information? If so, how might they successfully do so, and what can I do to prevent that result?

In this chapter, our goal is not to construct a complete discovery plan, but to get you started on thinking about how the process works, and to help you think about discovery as a kind of legal writing. Thus, in the rest of this discussion, we focus on discovery requests to the hotel regarding its provision of security generally, and particularly on the night of the attack on the Smiths. We begin with interrogatories, and then discuss requests for the production of documents and for admissions.

You should be aware that each type of discovery request has certain requirements or conventions regarding format. The applicable procedural rules may specify particular information that must be provided to the recipient of a discovery request. All discovery requests include a caption identifying the case that is the subject of the discovery. Different law offices have different approaches to such things as the definitions and instructions that generally accompany discovery requests. You should read the applicable rules carefully, and obtain copies of documents that have been used previously in your office in similar cases. Be sure that the discovery requests you prepare conform to all expectations.

[1]   Interrogatories

Interrogatories are usually phrased as imperatives rather than questions, because a question may give the respondent more opportunity to maneuver.[2] Thus, you might ask the manager of the Palm Court Hotel: "Do you know if a security guard was on duty the night of May 31, 1997?" If he or she answered "no," you would still not know whether a security guard was on duty. An affirmative directive to provide information is more likely to produce an accurate response.

Choose your words carefully, so the respondent will understand precisely what you are asking for. If the recipient understands clearly, he or she must provide the requested information if he or she has it. In the previous example, the inclusion of the phrase "do you know" gave the recipient a means of avoiding the question. If the request had said, "state whether a security guard was on duty between the hours of 5:00 p.m. and midnight on May 31, 1997," the manager would have no choice but to obtain the required information and answer "yes" or "no." This time, you would know what the answer meant.

Interrogatories may seek the identity of potential witnesses or information about relevant facts that is within the control of the responding party. For example, interrogatories in the Palm Court Hotel case might include:

(1)   Identify any security personnel who were on duty on May 31, 1997, between the hours of 5:00 p.m. and midnight.

(2)   Provide the name and address of your Director of Security, or the individual responsible for designing or coordinating your security program.

(3)   Provide the dates of all criminal activity, reported or unreported, on the premises of the Palm Court Hotel within one year before May 31, 1997. For each incident, describe the nature of the criminal activity involved, and indicate whether a police report was prepared.

Compare the above interrogatories with these:

---

[2] The advice in this chapter is generally derived from Thomas Mauet's book, *Pretrial*, 3d ed. (Little, Brown, 1995). Readers who wish to study discovery requests in greater detail should consult Mauet's book, or another similar source.

(1)   Did you employ any security measures at the Palm Court Hotel on May 31, 1997?

(2)   Were you aware of any criminal activity on the Palm Court Hotel's premises within a year of May 31, 1997?

These last two interrogatories are much less likely to produce any useful information than the preceding three. You should immediately notice that they are questions requiring only a "yes" or "no" answer, which is not at all helpful. Even if the writer of the first interrogatory requested that the recipient describe the security measures, the interrogatory leaves the respondent complete discretion in defining the term "security measures," and the respondent is likely to do so in a way that is not necessarily what the drafter of the interrogatory had in mind. For example, the respondent might answer "yes," and mention the observation ports in the doors of the guest rooms, the fact that the doors were of steel, that they were spring-locked, and that the doorknobs were equipped with anti-picking devices. This answer could make the hotel sound quite security-conscious, but it would not address the problem that Mr. Smith had to open the door to find out who had knocked on it, which is important to the claim of inadequate security.

EXERCISE

Draft five additional interrogatories to the Palm Court Hotel concerning security measures.

[2]   Requests for Production of Documents

These requests may be served on the responding party at the same time as interrogatories. You also may serve them as a follow-up to interrogatories, after you have obtained enough information to know what types of documents are likely to be available and in whose possession they are likely to be. Again, you should choose your words carefully, so the recipient of the request will be able to identify the documents you seek, and will not be able to point to any ambiguity in the request as a reason not to produce the documents. Be as clear and specific as you can. Here are some of the documents you might request from the Palm Court Hotel:

- All police or other written reports of criminal activity on the premises of the Palm Court Hotel between May 31, 1996 and May 31, 1997.

- All time records of security guards employed by the Palm Court Hotel between May 31, 1996 and May 31, 1997.

Do not make document requests such as these:

- All documents relating to security measures provided by the Palm Court Hotel.

- All documents showing knowledge of criminal activity on the premises of the Palm Court Hotel.

These requests are vague in several respects: they do not specify a particular time frame, they allow the respondent to define terms such as "security measures" and "knowledge," and they provide the respondent with a basis for an objection on the grounds of undue burden. At a minimum, you may find yourself poring over documents that have no relevance to your case and wasting your valuable time and resources. For example, in response to the first request, the hotel might produce boxes containing, among other things, every receipt for a doorknob or every repair order for a lock since the hotel was built. You would spend many hours trying to find the documents relating to the specific security measures and the time period in which you are interested.

EXERCISE

Draft three additional requests for production of documents for the Palm Court Hotel concerning security measures.

[3] Requests for Admission

As noted previously, the stakes in responding to requests for admission are high. Therefore, you should be particularly careful to phrase these requests in a way that cannot be misunderstood, deliberately or otherwise. Ask the responding party to admit specific facts that are within its control, and that it cannot deny in good faith if they are true. You can use the admitted facts later, in conjunction with other facts you are able to prove, to lead the trier of fact inexorably to the overall legal or factual conclusion you must establish in order to win your case.

The necessary precision can best be accomplished by drafting simple requests for the admission of straightforward facts, one at a time. For example, you could ask that the Palm Court Hotel admit that each of the following facts is true:

- There was no security guard on duty on the premises of the Palm Court Hotel on May 31, 1997 between the hours of 5:00 p.m. and midnight.

- There were no safety chains on the doors to any guest rooms in the Palm Court Hotel on May 31, 1997.

- There were no exterior lights on any of the buildings of the Palm Court Hotel on May 31, 1997.

While the natural inclination of the recipient of a request for admission may be to resist admitting any fact that might be damaging, the Federal Rules impose strong and specific obligations on the respondent. Rule 36(a) of the Federal Rules of Civil Procedure describes the obligations of the respondent to a request for admission this way:

> The answer shall specifically deny the matter or set forth in detail the reasons why the answering party cannot truthfully admit or deny the matter. A denial shall fairly meet the substance of the requested admission, and when good faith requires that a party qualify an answer or deny only a part of the matter of which an admission is requested, the party shall specify so much of it as is true and qualify or deny the remainder. An answering party may not give lack of information or knowledge as a reason for failure to admit or deny unless the party

states that the party has made reasonable inquiry and that the information known or readily obtainable by the party is insufficient to enable the party to admit or deny. A party who considers that a matter of which an admission has been requested presents a genuine issue for trial may not, on that ground alone, object to the request; the party may, subject to the provisions of Rule 37(c), deny the matter or set forth reasons why the party cannot admit or deny it.

Thus, if you phrase your requests for admission concretely and simply, as are the examples above, you should be able to obtain the desired admissions. If you do, you will be able to eliminate time-consuming and unnecessary proof of the admitted facts at trial.

Compare the earlier requests for admission with these:

- Mr. Smith was unable to see who was outside his room without opening the door.

- A security guard could have prevented the attack on the Smiths.

While these are the conclusions you want the trier of fact to draw from the evidence you intend to present at trial, and perhaps even from the facts you can get the Hotel to admit before trial, the Hotel is not likely to agree with your conclusions. It should be able to deny these requests for admission within the requirements of Rule 36, because it cannot possibly know what Mr. Smith was able to do, or what a security guard on duty that night could have accomplished. Additionally, these requests for admission reveal more about your strategy than is necessary at this point. You should stick to facts in your discovery requests, and save your arguments for when they will have more impact - i.e., before the trier of fact.

EXERCISE

Draft five additional requests for admission for the Palm Court Hotel concerning security measures.

As with all actions you take in an adversary system, you must think strategically about discovery requests. Do not think only about what you hope to accomplish, but plan on how to accomplish your goal when the opposite party's goal is likely to be precisely contrary to yours. Make discovery requests that are clear and precise, and ask for information that the other party must have and can have no legitimate excuse for not providing. You then give yourself the tools for accomplishing your ultimate goal, which is to win your case. Although the other party will not willingly build your case for you, you may be able to give that party no choice but to supply you the necessary building blocks.

CHAPTER **20**

WRITING PERSUASIVELY

§ 20.01 Introduction

With appellate briefs, we move from expository writing to persuasive writing. When you represent a client and argue to a court, you must do more than state the facts, explain the law and predict how a case will be resolved. You cannot merely present information to a court and rely on it to make a decision. You also must persuade the court to find in your client's favor.

Persuasion requires constructing a clear, concrete, and tightly written argument that presents your client's case in the best light. Learning to write persuasively is not a matter of mastering a grab bag of gimmicks or tricks. It also is not a matter of using exaggerated rhetoric. Lawyers and judges have seen all the tricks and flourishes too many times. If you rely on these devices, you will impress no one.

The chapters that you have read so far teach you how to write clearly and concretely, and how to construct a legal analysis. The following chapters teach you not only the mechanics of brief writing, but also how to write persuasively. You will learn that you must construct every part of the brief in a way that advances your client's position.

This chapter summarizes the methods of persuasion that the other chapters discuss. By presenting these methods in a single chapter, we offer you an overview and reinforce the thesis that persuasive methods are not simply a number of isolated techniques, but share a common theme. To reiterate, persuasive writing consists of constructing a well written, well reasoned analysis that puts your client's best foot forward.

Here is an outline of this chapter's lessons:

(1) Make your argument clear and credible.

(2) Write a well organized argument.

(3) Adopt a persuasive writing style.

(4) State your facts persuasively.

(5) Use equity and policy arguments.

(6) Use precedent persuasively.

§ 20.02   Make Your Argument Clear and Credible

[1]   Make Your Argument as Simple as Possible

When you write a law school exam, you expect to get credit for identifying and discussing the critical issues. You also expect extra points for discussing issues that are barely arguable or exceptionally complicated, but that would be extremely artificial if raised in a "real world" legal argument. When you include complicated, artificial arguments in a brief, you cannot expect the rewards that you gained in law school. These arguments will distract the reader from the arguments with real persuasive power. They also may detract from your credibility. Stick to the arguments that have the best chance of winning.

You also can expect to hurt your case if you make your critical arguments sound unnecessarily complicated. You are more likely to persuade the reader with arguments that seem logical and simple and sound like common sense. Stick to your main arguments and write them so that they are easy to understand.

A busy judge has many cases to consider and many briefs to read. He or she does not have the time or patience to digest peripheral arguments or even major arguments that are not stated clearly. Thus, unnecessary complexity hurts your client.

Here is a simple method for rooting out complexity. Try to state your argument to a legal associate in a very few sentences. If he or she cannot follow your train of thought, revise your words and presentation and try again.

A major part of advocacy is to place your client's arguments in clear focus: What does your client want and why? Bringing the argument into focus requires striving for simplicity.

[2]   Write in a Persuasive but Credible Style

Some lawyers try to be persuasive by overstating their cases and by using emotionally charged verbs, adjectives, and adverbs. This tactic inevitably marks the practitioner as an amateur. Other lawyers state their cases without adding a persuasive edge of any kind. Their style also does the client a disservice. Strive for a style that is assertive, but reasoned and even a little understated.

Consider this excerpt from a brief:

> Next we have Wilmer's ludicrous explanation of the circumstances surrounding his secret taping of various people at the dental school. Instead of coming clean and admitting that he was gathering information for his malpractice case, Wilmer asks the court to swallow his tall tale about how he was merely furthering his education.

The writer has overwritten. Words like "ludicrous" and "swallow his tall tale" do not have the effect for which the writer is striving. Judges have seen too much of this hyperbole to find it persuasive.

Compare this version:

> Wilmer admits that he secretly taped various people at the dental school, but states that he was furthering his education.

Here, the writer has underwritten and does not advance the client's position. To be persuasive, strive for a style somewhere between these extremes. For example:

> Wilmer admits that he secretly taped various people at the dental school. However, he offers a curious explanation. He denies that he was gathering information for his malpractice case and instead, claims that he was furthering his education.

Here is another acceptable revision:

> Wilmer admits that he secretly taped various people at the dental school. However, he denies that he was gathering information for his malpractice case and instead, claims that he was taping for an educational purpose. He has not been terribly specific about how he would use the tapes to further his education.

These two revisions illustrate the proper tone. In the first revision, the writer draws attention to Wilmer's unbelievable explanation by terming it "curious." "Curious" adds flair, but not too much. In the second revision, the writer adds a final sentence to subtly highlight the improbability of the proffered explanation. In both, the writer juxtaposes Wilmer's explanation with what is apparently the real reason. As a result, the writer furthers the client's cause by painting the opposing litigant as untruthful and even pathetically comical.

§ 20.03   Write a Well Organized Argument

[1]   Structure Your Argument

An important key to persuasive writing is producing a document with a structure that is readily apparent. You want the reader to follow your argument as effortlessly as possible. Forego stream-of-consciousness writing in favor of organization.

The key to organization is to write according to an outline and to put your conclusions first. Even if you are not the type of writer who is comfortable outlining first and then writing, you still can write first and then organize your result so that it fits an outline. That is, write the outline after you have finished and then, where necessary, reorganize according to the outline.

After you have written your first draft, make sure that you begin the discussion of each argument with a conclusion that applies the legal argument to the facts of your case. Briefly outline your argument in the first paragraph so that the court has a "road map" of where you are going. Review your paragraphs for topic sentences. In most paragraphs, you will want the topic sentence at the beginning.

[2]   Put Your Best Arguments First and Develop Them More Fully

When we read a document, we usually pay more attention at the beginning. After a while, our interest wanes. In addition, as readers, we expect the important arguments to come first and to be developed in proportion to their importance. The lesson is clear. Place your most persuasive arguments first and allocate more space to them.

For example, suppose you are opposing the argument that a statute requires your client to give a neighbor an easement over her property. You have three arguments. First, the statute is unconstitutional. Second, in this case, the terms of the statute do not require granting an easement. Third, the neighbor did not follow the procedure the statute prescribes. Because courts are extremely reluctant to declare statutes unconstitutional, either your second or third argument probably gives you the best chance of winning. Decide which is your best argument and develop it fully. Then set out your second argument and give it less space. Finally, set out your argument on constitutionality and allocate it the least space.

As with all rules, there are exceptions. Sometimes you will decide to put your second best argument first, because it sets a good stage for your best argument. Then you will include your best argument. Nonetheless, in the overwhelming number of cases, you will do well to put your best argument first.

§ 20.04   Adopt a Persuasive Writing Style

[1]   Be Concrete

When you argue for a client, you are not arguing for an abstract legal principle. You are seeking a holding that has practical consequences. In the same manner, judges are not interested in debating legal abstractions; they are interested in resolving specific disputes. The lesson: write about your case in concrete terms. In doing so you drive home the fact that your case is not an academic debate, but a conflict involving real people, particularly your client.

Consider this sentence:

The unforeseeability of the event absolved the defendants of liability.

This sentence is abstract. It could be about anyone. If you include facts about the relevant events, you make the issue concrete and compelling:

Because it was unforeseeable that a twenty-year-old trespasser would dive head first from a lifeguard chair into a shallow pool, the defendant is not liable.

Here is another example:

A reasonable adult in plaintiff's position would recognize that the attempt to execute a head-first, straight dive into the lake without prior awareness of the depth of the waters might result in severe injury from the collision of one's head on the lake bottom.

Compare this revision:

A reasonable adult like the plaintiff would know that if he dived straight down and head-first into a shallow lake without knowing its depth, he could hit his head on the lake bottom and become paralyzed.

In the revision, the changes are subtle, but telling. They make the sentence far more concrete and persuasive.

[2]   When You Want to Emphasize a Word or Idea, Place it at the End of the Sentence

In a sentence, the beginning and the end are the best places to put information that you want to emphasize. Use the beginning of the sentence for information already familiar to the reader, usually the subject. Also use the beginning for information that the reader expects or can understand easily. Use the end for new information that you want to emphasize.

Suppose you are arguing about which law applies to your case, Missouri law or federal law. If you are arguing in favor of applying Missouri law, you might write this sentence:

Missouri law, not federal law, governs this case.

Although this sentence states your position, it does not make the best use of the end of the sentence. You will make your point more emphatically if you end with "Missouri law." Therefore, you should rewrite the sentence this way:

This case is governed not by federal law, but by Missouri law.

Although this revision forces you to use the passive voice, the loss of the active verb is far outweighed by the power of placing "Missouri law" at the end of the sentence.

The same principle applies to sentences with more than one clause. Consider this sentence:

The court barred the plaintiff's complaint as a matter of law, because the plaintiff failed to notify the bank of the forgery within the time prescribed by the statute.

Suppose you want to emphasize that the court barred the complaint as a matter of law. You would rewrite the sentence this way:

Because the plaintiff failed to notify the bank of the forgery within the time prescribed by the statute, the court barred the plaintiff's complaint as a matter of law.

By placing the main clause at the end of the sentence, you stress the idea that you want to emphasize.

[3]   When Appropriate, Use the Same Subject for a Series of Sentences

By using the same subject for a series of sentences, you make it clear that you are telling the story of the subject. As a result, you give your sentences unity and direction.

Consider this paragraph from the brief of a convicted criminal defendant arguing ineffectiveness of counsel:

The client and the defense counsel did not meet until one hour before the trial. As a result, there was never the personal exchange between the two parties so necessary to a strong defense. The defense counsel never had the opportunity to observe her client. Thus there was no opportunity to judge his mannerisms and overall appearance, the fact being that the defendant, being somewhat quiet and shy, would not make a strong witness at trial. When he testified at trial, he did not come across well to the jury. The tactical error of placing him on the stand could have been avoided if more time had been spent with the defendant and a personal interview had been conducted.

The argument becomes much more compelling when the defense counsel becomes the subject of every sentence and of virtually every clause:

> Until one hour before the trial, the defense counsel never met with the defendant and thus never had the personal exchange so necessary to a strong defense. Because she had never had the opportunity to observe her client, she could not judge his mannerisms and overall appearance. She therefore did not know that her client was somewhat quiet and shy and, at trial, would not come across well to the jury. By placing her client on the stand, the defense counsel made a tactical error that she could have avoided by taking the time to conduct a personal interview.

The rewrite makes it clear that the writer is discussing the failings of the defense counsel and detailing what she did and failed to do. As a result, the writer is presenting a persuasive argument for ineffectiveness of counsel.

§ 20.05   State Your Facts Persuasively

At the beginning of your brief, you will have the opportunity to present the facts from your client's perspective. Judges expect your statement of the facts to be straightforward and accurate. They dislike rhetoric here and will form a negative opinion of your credibility if you attempt to mislead them by distorting or omitting critical facts. Therefore, you must present an objective narrative.

Nonetheless, you still must write the facts as an advocate. Here is how. Stress the facts that favor your case and de-emphasize those that hurt it. Instead of stating your own opinions about the facts, report that someone else offered those opinions. In this way, you are stating a fact — what someone else stated —not your opinion.

This excerpt from a brief furnishes a good example. The plaintiff dived into a pool with only three feet of water and suffered severe injuries. The writer represents the defendant, the manufacturer of the pool.

> The plaintiff claimed that he perceived the water depth to be six feet and not its actual depth of three feet. At trial, several experts testified that this misperception was significant to their conclusion that the plaintiff caused the accident. As Dr. Luna, one of the experts, testified, if the plaintiff believed that the water was six feet deep, "his mental and physiological processes involving visual perception and judgment of his surroundings were impaired by his ingestion of alcohol and hallucinogens."

In this example, the writer makes the essential point without rhetoric or value-laden adjectives or adverbs. She does not call the plaintiff irresponsible or label him dissolute. She does not berate the opposing lawyer for pursuing a frivolous lawsuit. The writer simply reports the plaintiff's assertion and then reports the testimony of experts hired by the defendant.

(Matthew Bender & Co., Inc.)   (Pub. 676)

The quotation from Dr. Luna is part of a sentence objectively reporting what happened at trial. Instead of quoting an expert, the writer might have stated the opinion as her own: "If the plaintiff believed that the water was six feet deep, his mental and physiological processes involving perception and judgment of his surroundings clearly were impaired by his ingestion of alcohol and hallucinogens." However, by placing the opinion in the mouth of another person, an expert, the writer makes it far more persuasive. (In the alternative, she might have attributed the opinion to Dr. Luna and then paraphrased his words in order to make the sentence better stylistically.) As you can see, it is possible to state facts in an objective manner and still write as an advocate.

§ 20.06 Make Equity and Policy Arguments

In most cases that go to trial and certainly in most cases on appeal, both parties have sound legal arguments. Therefore, the advocate must argue more than the law. You also need to argue the equities and social policy. To argue the equities means to argue that your client is the most sympathetic litigant and should win as a matter of justice. To argue policy means to argue that the legal holding you seek has good ramifications for society and your opponent's does not.

Here is an example. Suppose you represent a child whose mother was seriously injured in an accident. You are suing the party that caused the accident for loss of parental consortium. In other words, you are arguing that the child should recover for losing the companionship and affection of the parent.

To argue the equities, you would enumerate the ways in which the child has suffered. You would mention activities that the child and mother used to share. You might quote the child reflecting on her loss. You thus would paint a picture of a child deserving to recover.

To argue policy, you would assert that as a general principle, the court should recognize the right of a child to sue for loss of parental consortium and should be liberal in finding that the loss has occurred in specific cases. Your policy argument might read like this:

> The importance of a child's feelings and emotions merit more than lip service. The loss of a parent is a devastating injury at least as important as a spouse's loss of consortium, which this jurisdiction recognizes. For these sorts of injuries, tort law is the appropriate avenue of redress.

Thus, while an equitable argument focuses on the particulars of a case, a policy argument generalizes. In the illustration, the policy argument states that recognizing this cause of action is desirable, that it is very similar to another tort that the jurisdiction already permits, and that its recognition is consistent with the development of tort law.

§ 20.07 Use Precedent Persuasively

Judges prefer that their decisions be consistent with past decisions of their court. They also must be persuaded that their decisions are consistent with those of any higher court. Therefore, invoking favorable precedent is a powerful tool of persuasion.

The difficulty arises when the earlier case does not support your position or it is unclear whether or not the case supports it. You might argue that the earlier case was wrongly decided. However, such an argument is at cross purposes with the desire to claim consistency with existing case law. Therefore, an argument rejecting precedent should be an alternative argument of last resort. Your first argument should be that existing law supports your position or at least is consistent with it.

[1] Argue that Adverse Precedent is Consistent with Your Argument

To harmonize adverse precedent, argue that the contrary case is distinguishable from your case on its facts or that it does address the issue in your case. If possible, go one step further and argue that the policy underlying that opinion is the one you are advancing.

Return to your argument that the court should recognize a cause of action for a child's loss of parental consortium. Suppose that in another case, the same court rejected the argument. There, the court stated that because the parent will receive compensation from the defendant, that compensation probably will give ample recovery to both parent and child. Therefore, according to the court, permitting a separate recovery for the child would be unfairly duplicative.

If, in that case, the only plaintiff was the child, and in your case, the child's claim is joined with the parent's claim, you can distinguish the cases. Argue that the previous case's holding dealt only with cases in which the actions of parent and child were not joined at trial. Argue that if the same jury is deciding the claims together, the risk of a duplicative recovery is very small. Then argue that, in both cases, the underlying goal is just compensation. Here, you are advancing this goal in a situation that will not result in overcompensation. With this argument, you distinguish the adverse precedent and also argue that you are furthering the same goal that motivated that decision.

[2] Interpret Precedent Narrowly or Broadly, As Appropriate

As you have learned in law school, a holding is open to more than one interpretation. When you are dealing with precedent, select the interpretation that furthers your case. Depending on the facts of your case, this endeavor may require you to interpret the holding narrowly or broadly.

Suppose you are arguing that an adult should be able to recover for the loss of consortium of a parent. Suppose your jurisdiction has an earlier case permitting a minor child to recover for loss of parental consortium. Opposing counsel would interpret the holding narrowly to permit the cause of action only when the plaintiff is a minor child. However, you would interpret the holding broadly to permit any child to recover.

The way you deal with precedent is illustrative of the way you make a persuasive legal argument. Interpret the law and facts in a way that is both credible and in your client's best interest.

CHAPTER 21

WRITING PRE-TRIAL MOTIONS

§ 21.01 Purposes of Motions

Pre-trial motions are filed in an effort to persuade the court to make a decision in the early stages of a case. The decision requested may be to dismiss the case entirely, to decide it without trial, or to resolve a discovery dispute between the parties. Although there are other types of motions that may be filed, we will focus on these three as representative of common motions. Motions involve advocacy; you are trying to persuade the court to do something, and should follow all the advice about advocacy writing that is offered elsewhere in this book.

§ 21.02 Form of Motions

There is no set format for writing motions. You should get sample motions from other lawyers in your office or look at motions that have previously been filed in the court for which you are writing your motion. In most courts, the motion itself is a simple statement of the basis upon which relief is requested. The motion may be supported by a memorandum that sets forth the legal arguments in support of the motion, and by other documents appropriate to the motion, such as affidavits. All memoranda, or briefs, in support of motions should include a statement of the relevant facts and an analysis of the relevant law. There is a sample motion for summary judgment in Appendix V.

§ 21.03 Motions to Dismiss

Under Rule 12(b)(6) of the Federal Rules of Civil Procedure a defendant may move to dismiss a complaint on the grounds that it fails to state a claim upon which relief can be granted. Most, if not all, states permit a similar motion—sometimes called a demurrer—that allows a defendant to attempt to get a defective complaint dismissed. Under this standard, the defendant must demonstrate that even if plaintiff can prove all the facts alleged in the complaint, there is no basis for legal relief. In ruling on such a motion, the court will interpret the facts in the light most favorable to plaintiff. Motions to dismiss may also be granted when the plaintiff fails to allege some crucial element of the cause of action. In such a case, the court may dismiss the complaint with leave to amend, so the plaintiff can correct the defect.

In our case against the dating service on behalf of Susan Starkey (See Chapter 15), let us assume that you filed a complaint for negligence. Assume also that the dating service filed a motion to dismiss for failure to state a claim, alleging that it had no duty to protect persons in Susan's position, and therefore there is no basis for recovery. You should have researched the applicable law before filing the complaint, and you should have legal support for your argument in favor of such a duty. Your response to the motion should focus on establishing the duty to protect; you should not try to win your whole case on the motion, because you will need to establish the facts in support of your argument that the duty to protect was breached and that the breach was the proximate cause of Susan's damages; that is, the failure of the dating service to adequately screen its clients led to Susan's stalking and emotional distress. This will require witness testimony and other evidence. The point here is that only purely legal arguments can be resolved in the context of the motion to dismiss. If the court needs to find facts in order to resolve the question presented, the case must go on. If the motion to dismiss raises factual issues, that may be reason enough to deny the motion.

EXERCISE

Write a few paragraphs explaining why a motion to dismiss should not be granted in the Starkey case. Focus on the facts you would like to prove and how they fit into your negligence claim, especially the issue of the dating service's duty to its customers. Write these paragraphs as if they would go into your response to the motion to dismiss. In other words, your audience is the judge who will decide the motion. Remember that the judge will interpret the facts in the light most favorable to your client in deciding the motion. You do not need to cite cases; write the paragraphs as if they were a summary of your arguments in the response to the motion.

§ 21.04 Motions to Compel Discovery

Under Federal Rule of Civil Procedure 37(a), a party may move to compel discovery when the opposing party does not respond to a discovery request and the parties cannot work out the dispute themselves. For example, under Rule 37(a)(2)(B),

If a deponent[1] fails to answer a question propounded or submitted under Rules 30 or 31, or a corporation or other entity fails to make a designation under Rule 30(b)(6) or 31(a), or a party fails to answer an interrogatory submitted under Rule 33, or if a party, in response to a request for inspection submitted under Rule 34, fails to respond that inspection will be permitted

---

[1] The term "Deponent" refers to the person being questioned in a deposition.

as requested or fails to permit inspection as requested, the discovering party may move for an order compelling an answer, or a designation, or an order compelling inspection in accordance with the request. The motion must include a certification that the movant has in good faith conferred or attempted to confer with the person or party failing to make the discovery in an effort to secure the information or material without court action. When taking a deposition on oral examination, the proponent of the question may complete or adjourn the examination before applying for an order.

Under Rule 37(a)(3), an evasive or incomplete answer may be treated as a failure to respond. Available sanctions under Rule 37(a)(4) include the expense of filing or opposing the motion, including attorney's fees.

Assume that you served a request for production of documents on the dating service, and that the dating service refused to produce Partlow's file in response to your specific request, claiming confidentiality. Note that under Rule 37 you are required to confer with the dating service to attempt to obtain the material without court action. If you try to work the matter out but are unsuccessful, you may move to compel the production of the file. You would need to research the issue of confidentiality raised by the dating service, and establish that under the law the service is not entitled to keep the file from you. You would make this argument in your memorandum in support of the motion.

Because the rule requires that you confer with the defendant, you should state in your motion that you have made the attempt to confer, and you should probably detail the attempts you made in your memorandum in support of the motion. It is always a good idea to put in writing all efforts you have made to comply with prerequisites to obtaining a hearing on the merits.

§ 21.05 Motions for Summary Judgment

Rule 56 of the Federal Rules of Civil Procedure provides that either party may move for summary judgement. Rule 56(c) states that the motion will be granted "if the pleadings, depositions, answers to interrogatories, and admissions on file, together with the affidavits, if any, show that there is no genuine issue as to any material fact and that the moving party is entitled to a judgment as a matter of law." This means that, as in the case of the motion to dismiss, if the question before the court is one of law, the case may be decided upon motion. The difference between a motion to dismiss and a motion for summary judgment is that the motion for summary judgment generally includes some supporting factual material such as responses to discovery or affidavits, while the motion to dismiss focuses solely on the complaint.

Let us go back to Susan Starkey's case. If counsel for the dating service files a motion for summary judgment alleging that there was no breach of the duty to protect persons in Susan's position because the screening procedures were adequate, and attaches an affidavit from an employee of the service outlining those procedures, you would simply respond that the motion raises a genuine issue of material fact. Regardless of the screening procedures employed by the dating service, you would want the opportunity to prove that those procedures either were inadequate or that they were not followed. The only way to prove these things is to cross examine the employees of the dating service, and perhaps to hire an expert to testify that the service's procedures did not meet the standards of the industry.

The key to responding to any motion is to limit your argument to what you need to establish to overcome the motion. Many lawyers succumb to the temptation to argue the entire case at the motion stage, which only confuses the issue and may make it less likely that the motion will be decided in your favor. Thus, if in responding to the dating service's motion for summary judgment, you choose to argue the inadequacy of the screening procedures and the damages Susan suffered, you might actually suggest to the court that you think the case is ready for decision, when all you really want at this stage is the chance to prove your case in court. Understanding the standard in the applicable rule is critical. Read carefully, and argue only what you need to in order to defeat the motion.

Note that the parties in some cases may actually agree upon the facts, in which case both parties may be content to submit the case for decision by summary judgment, and avoid the time and expense of a trial. This will probably be the exceptional case, but if there are no genuine issues of fact to be proved at trial, you may very well win the gratitude of the court by stipulating to the facts and submitting the case for a decision on the law.

EXERCISE

Write a few paragraphs explaining why Susan Starkey's case cannot be decided on summary judgment. Explain the genuine issues of material fact that must be addressed at trial. Again, assume that you are writing for the judge who will decide the motion, and do not cite cases. Focus on the basis for the motion, and what you need to establish to persuade the judge to deny the motion.

§ 21.06 Ethical Considerations in Motion Practice

As an officer of the court, you should never file a frivolous claim, or make a frivolous argument. Your factual and legal support for your argument must be sufficient to justify taking up the time of the court and other parties to the matter. Rule 11 of the Federal Rules of Civil Procedure provides that pleadings and motions must be signed by the attorney of record. When you sign a pleading or motion, you represent that to the best of your "knowledge, information, and belief, formed after an inquiry reasonable under the circumstances,—

(1) it is not being presented for any improper purpose, such as to harass or to cause unnecessary delay or needless increase in the cost of litigation;

(2) the claims, defenses, and other legal contentions therein are warranted by existing law or by a nonfrivolous argument for the extension, modification, or reversal of existing law or the establishment of new law;

(3) the allegations and other factual contentions have evidentiary support or, if specifically so identified, are likely to have evidentiary support after a reasonable opportunity for further investigation or discovery; and

(4) the denials of factual contentions are warranted on the evidence or, if specifically so identified, are reasonably based on a lack of information or belief."

Fed. R. Civ. P. 11(b). Violators of this rule are subject to monetary and other sanctions. If you believe that another attorney has submitted papers to the court in violation of this rule, you may move for sanctions.

§ 21.07 Checklist for Motions

_____ Before filing or responding to any motion, make sure that you understand the standard upon which the motion will be decided. Read the Rule!

_____ Research the applicable law.

_____ Find sample motions of the type you will be filing for the court in which you will be filing the motion. You may want to make copies for your files.

_____ Prepare your memorandum in support of the motion to carefully articulate the factual and legal basis upon which the court may grant you the relief you seek. Argue no more than necessary to obtain that relief, but make sure that you have met the standard set forth in the applicable rule. Do not try your case at the motion stage!

_____ When responding to a motion, carefully focus your argument on what you need to establish to overcome the motion. Do not argue your entire case and confuse the issue.

PART V

TRIAL AND APPEAL

CHAPTER 22

DRAFTING JURY INSTRUCTIONS

§ 22.01 The Problem with Jury Instructions

Suppose that you are a juror in a civil action and that you have no training in law. You have heard the evidence in an action for abuse of process, and now the judge is reading jury instructions to you. You listen intently and hear this passage from the jury instructions:

> There is evidence tending to show that the defendant, in causing to be issued a criminal indictment, did so to attain an ulterior object that such process is not designed by the law to achieve and that he made use of the process to attain this objective.

Would you be able to understand this passage? You might have difficulty with some of the terminology. Hopefully, somewhere during the trial, you learned what a criminal indictment is. However, you still may be unclear exactly what "process" means. You also might have difficulty with a word like "ulterior" and perhaps "objective," because they are not words that you normally use or confront. You also might find your understanding hampered by stilted language, such as "in causing to be used a criminal indictment." Moreover, you may have trouble with the clause beginning "in causing . . ." because it disrupts the flow of the sentence by intervening between the actor, "defendant," and the verb phrase, "did so."

In most cases, you could not clear up your confusion by slowly reading through the instructions later, because most judges will not give you a copy. At best, during your deliberations, you can ask the judge to read a section of the instructions to you again.

This example illustrates a common problem with jury instructions: often they are incomprehensible to their audience—the lay people who comprise the jury. If the instructions prove a mystery to the jurors, the jurors may prove unable to do justice. Thus writing and delivering understandable jury instructions is a vital responsibility of the bench and bar.

At first glance, the existence of confusing jury instructions might seem puzzling. After all, a few states like Alaska and Michigan have issued plain English pattern jury instructions, as have the federal district courts in a few circuits. However, the difficulties are more understandable when we examine the two reasons that impede progress.

First, many lawyers and judges have had insufficient schooling in plain English writing to know how to draft an instruction that most lay people could understand. Even sympathetic members of the bar find translating classic "lawyer talk" into "lay talk" to be a daunting task.

Second, in arriving at a jury instruction, the judge and lawyers are trying to arrive at an accurate statement of the law that can withstand the scrutiny of an appellate court. After a jury issues a verdict, the losing party may challenge the verdict by arguing that the jury instruction misstated the law. To avoid the possibility of an appeals court overturning a verdict, a judge will want to issue an instruction that an appeals court has previously approved. Alternatively, a judge will want to use an instruction that defines the law with words that an appeals court has used approvingly. Even if the approved instruction or approved definition is confusing, the judge will be inclined to use it and pass on the difficulties to a new generation of jurors.

As with all complex issues, we can only do our best. As we shall see, the plain English lessons that we teach in this book go a long way toward improving jury instructions.

§ 22.02 How Lawyers Draft Jury Instructions

As a lawyer, rarely will you have to sit down with a blank sheet of paper and draft a jury instruction. Instead, you will have available jury instructions from a variety of sources. Your jurisdiction may have pattern jury instructions, that is, a compilation of suggested jury instructions, usually court approved. You also may have instructions that courts have given in other, similar cases. In addition, you may consult some of the treatises that include collections of jury instructions. Thus you will often begin with a jury instruction from one of these sources and then revise it.[1]

In creating or revising a jury instruction, you have four goals. First, you want the instruction to be comprehensible to the typical juror. Second, you want it to accurately state the applicable law. Third, you want it to help explain the facts and evidence as the law applies to them. Fourth, you want to emphasize the facts and law that make your arguments persuasive.

---

[1] In this chapter, we use sample jury instructions (usually in modified form) taken from Graham Douthwaite, *Jury Instructions on Medical Issues* (4th ed. 1992); Ronad W. Eades, *Jury Instructions on Damages in Tort Actions* (3d ed. 1993); Amiram Elwork et al., "Making Jury Instructions Understandable: A Psycholinguistic Study of Jury Instructions," 79 Colum. L. Rev. 1306 (1979); Jamison Wilcox, "The Craft of Drafting Plain-Language Jury Instructions: A Study of a Sample Pattern Instruction on Obscenity," 59 Temp. L.Q. 1159 (1986).

In this chapter, we focus on one of these goals: making the instruction comprehensible to the typical juror. As a guide, we offer four principles:

    (1) Simplify the Sentence Structure

    (2) Explain or Avoid Legal Terms and Complex Words

    (3) Employ a Plain English Writing Style

    (4) Stylize the Instructions to Fit Your Case

§ 22.03　Simplify the Sentence Structure

Suppose that you are a juror in a personal injury action. At the conclusion of the trial, you listen to the jury instructions and hear this sentence:

> There is evidence tending to show that the person injured was also at fault in bringing about the occurrence which is the cause of the injury.

As the judge reads this sentence, you probably will find it hard to follow. The first part of the sentence might not be too difficult: "There is evidence tending to show that the person injured was also at fault in bring about the occurrence." However, when you try to understand the last clause, you may well lose track of the sentence's meaning. The idea in the last clause adds too much complexity for you to handle.

Compare this sentence:

> Some of the evidence tends to show that the occurrence causing the injury may have been partly the fault of the plaintiff.

This sentence is easier to understand. Although it communicates the same message as the original, it sets out the parts of the message in an order that is easier for the juror to grasp. It also does not end with a clause that requires the listener to rethink the earlier parts of the sentence. Thus a slight revision simplifies the sentence structure and makes the instruction more comprehensible.

It is possible to increase comprehensibility even more by using two sentences:

> The evidence has described the occurrence causing the injury. Some of the evidence tends to show that the occurrence may have been partly the fault of the plaintiff.

Using two sentences introduces the ideas in the same order as before, but at a slower pace. Thus, even though two sentences require more words, they further the goal of reducing complexity.

Here is another example. Suppose that you are a juror in a medical malpractice action. You are listening to jury instructions on how to evaluate expert testimony. As you listen, you hear this sentence:

In weighing the testimony of the expert witnesses, you should consider the extent of the familiarity of each one of these expert witnesses with the standards required in such communities as that in which the defendant was practicing at the time of the alleged injury.

The sentence is not impossible to understand. However, as you listen to the judge read it, you might wish the judge would read it two or three more times so that you would be sure to grasp its meaning. A little editing could free the sentence from some of its complexity. Here is a rewrite:

In weighing the testimony of the expert witnesses, you should consider what standards of skill and care they are familiar with. In particular, are they familiar with the standards required in communities like the one in which the defendant was practicing when the alleged injury occurred?

§ 22.04   Explain or Avoid Legal Terms and Complex Words

Before you entered law school, you probably had no idea what "probable cause" meant. It took much study and several law school classes to unravel its meaning. Imagine the difficulty of explaining the concept to a lay juror in a sentence or two. Here is one such effort:

A proximate cause of an injury is a cause which, in natural and continuous sequence, produces the injury, and without which the injury would not have occurred.

Some researchers attempted to make the instruction more understandable by changing it in two ways.[2] First, they omitted unnecessary terminology by omitting the word "proximate" and inserting the word "legal." They had discovered that jurors, unfamiliar with "proximate cause" often heard "approximate cause" or some other phrase. Second, they tried to better explain the notion of causation by describing it as "something that triggers a natural chain of events." Their modified instruction read this way:

A legal cause of an injury is something that triggers a natural chain of events that ultimately produces the injury. Without a legal cause, the injury would not occur.

The language about triggering a natural chain of events improved comprehension. However, many of the research subjects misinterpreted "legal cause" as the opposite of an "illegal cause." This unexpected result leads to the suggestion to use the word "cause" and explain that the law has its own definition of "cause."

The lesson of this research is clear. Take care to explain legal terms of art carefully and, when possible, avoid specialized terminology. In addition, beware of the homonym, a word that sounds like another word—for

---

[2] See Charrow & Charrow, supra note 1, at 1352-53.

example, "a proximate" and "approximate" or "a legal" and "illegal." With oral communication, they become an unexpected pitfall.

Here is another example. Again suppose that you are a lay juror and, as part of the jury instructions, you hear these sentences:

> The plaintiff seeks to recover compensation for an injury sustained by her child. Under the law of this state, the plaintiff may recover that proportion of the damage sustained that is not the result of her fault.

For the law student, these sentences would be relatively easy to understand. However, the law student may have forgotten the time when a phrase like "recover compensation" or a word like "damage" (meaning a monetary amount) would have been puzzling. The student also may fail to remember when a word like "sustained" (meaning "suffered") was recognizable, but not a part of the daily vocabulary.

These sentences are more comprehensible to the juror when familiar words replace the problematic ones:

> The plaintiff seeks money to compensate for the injury that her child suffered. Under the law of this state, the plaintiff may get compensation for the portion of the injury that is not the result of her fault.

§ 22.05   Employ a Plain English Writing Style

Although this book contains many lessons on writing style that would improve jury instructions, three rules seem to be the most helpful:[3]

(a) Use Verbs Instead of Nouns

(b) Favor the Active Voice

(c) Avoid Subordinate Clauses Using the Passive Voice

[1]   Use Verbs Instead of Nouns

Consider this jury instruction:

> If you find from the evidence that the defendant hospital was negligent in a failure to provide equipment adequate for the treatment of the plaintiff, and, if you find that such failure was the cause of the injuries that the plaintiff claims, your verdict must be for the plaintiff.

Words like "failure" and "treatment" are called nominalizations, that is, words in the form of nouns instead of verbs. Here, the verb counterparts are "fail" and "treat." While there is nothing inherently wrong with using a nominalization, it is best to use a verb instead. Verbs give action to a sentence. They make a sentence interesting and easier to understand. For example, here is a rewrite of the jury instruction that uses several verbs instead of nominalizations.

---

[3] See id. at 1366.

If you find from the evidence that the defendant hospital negligently failed to provide equipment adequate to treat the plaintiff and, if you find that this failure caused the injuries that the plaintiff claims, you must decide for the plaintiff.

The rewrite replaces four nouns with verbs. By increasing the number of verbs, we make the sentence more action-oriented and easier to comprehend.

Here is another example. This passage from an instruction addresses a complex issue in a products liability action:

Watering down the substance of the warning so as to give false assurance to the medical profession that a drug is capable of safe administration and thus causing an unreasonable minimization of the reasonably foreseeable danger in the use of the product amounts to an inadequate warning.

Although this sentence is grammatically correct, it takes some effort to read and understand it. In large part, the problem is that the sentence has too few verbs to energize it. See how much easier the passage is to understand when we change a number of nouns into verbs:

If you find that the manufacturer watered down the substance of the warning and thus falsely assured the medical profession that it could safely administer the drug, then you may find that the manufacturer unreasonably minimized the reasonably foreseeable dangers in using the product. If you so find, then you have found that the manufacturer inadequately warned the medical profession.

As you see, the revised version is noticeably longer than the original. When you trade nominalizations in for verbs, you often find that your new version is longer. However, although shortness is an admirable goal, writing easily understandable sentences is a more important one.

[2] Favor the Active Voice

Although the passive voice is sometimes appropriate, the active voice usually will make your writing easier to understand. In part, the active voice makes a sentence more comprehensible, because it usually requires explicitly identifying the subject and placing the subject before the verb.

Consider this sentence from a jury instruction:

In determining whether the defendant should be held liable for deviating from the standard of skill and care, due consideration should be given to the state of medical knowledge about the subject matter at the time of the alleged malpractice.

In trying to understand this sentence, the juror must answer two related questions. First, who will be determining whether to hold the defendant liable? Second, who should be giving due consideration to the state of medical knowledge? Now consider this revision:

> When you determine whether or not to hold the defendant liable for deviating from the standard of skill and care, you should give due consideration to the state of medical knowledge about the subject matter at the time of the alleged malpractice.

Now the subject "you" makes it very clear who the actor is: it is the juror. In addition, the active voice gives some vitality to the instruction.

[3]　Avoid Subordinate Clauses Using the Passive Voice

Your first question may well be: What is a subordinate clause that uses the passive voice? A subordinate clause is a clause that is not the main clause in the sentence; that is, it could not stand alone as a complete sentence. It usually begins with "that" or "which." In the second sentence of this paragraph, the subordinate clause is: "that is not the main clause in the sentence."

A subordinate clause with a verb in the passive voice can be particularly difficult to understand. Consider this example:

> If you determine that the defendant is liable for the wrong, the damages for which the defendant can be required to compensate the plaintiff are only those damages that the plaintiff has shown to directly result from the wrong.

The clause "for which the defendant can be required to compensate the plaintiff" is a subordinate clause using the passive voice. As you can see, although it is not impossible to understand, it does give the reader pause. Imagine the challenge it would pose for the listening juror. Revising the instruction is not difficult:

> If you determine that the defendant is liable for the wrong, the defendant must compensate the plaintiff for only those damages that the plaintiff has shown to result directly from the wrong.

As you can see, simplifying the construction of the sentence remedies the problem. The larger lesson is to avoid complex sentence structures in favor of their simpler counterparts. You can do so without changing the meaning of the instruction.

§ 22.06　Stylize the Instructions to Fit Your Case

Suppose that you are a juror in a personal injury case that turns on the concept of negligence per se. You might hear this instruction:

> If you find that the defendant's conduct violated a law, then you must find that the defendant was negligent.

Although this instruction may give you the information you need, think how much more helpful you would find an instruction that makes reference to the facts of the case:

The motor vehicle code of this state provides that traffic facing a red signal must stop and remain standing until there is a signal to proceed. Ms. Plaintiff has offered evidence that Ms. Defendant did not stop at the red traffic signal as required by the motor vehicle code. If you find that the traffic signal was red and that Ms. Defendant did not stop, then I instruct you that Ms. Defendant's conduct was negligent.

As you can see, it is better to discuss the law concretely instead of abstractly.

Here is another example. In a personal injury case, you, the juror, might hear this instruction:

You shall award damages for the wages lost by Mr. Roberts.

You might have a better chance of awarding accurate damages if the judge supplemented the instruction with these words:

You have heard testimony that Mr. Roberts was employed at the time of his injuries and that his salary was $500 per week. You have heard testimony as well that as a result of his injuries he was unemployed for 12 weeks. This totals $6,000. If you find that evidence to be correct, then you should award Mr. Roberts $6,000 for lost wages.

The lesson is clear. Stylized instructions bring home the message to the juror far more clearly than do all-purpose instructions.

However, there is a caveat. When you stylize an instruction, you may slant it for or against one of the parties. As an advocate, you may wish to introduce a bias that favors your client. You are free to advance your client's interests within reason. However, you run the risk that the judge might detect an unacceptable bias in your proposed instruction and refuse to use it. Thus, stylizing requires you to take particular care in avoiding unfairness.

The struggle to make jury instructions readily understandable to jurors has been uphill. However, plain English advocates are making some progress. As an emerging generation of lawyers receives schooling in the importance of writing clearly and in the techniques to use, we can look forward to increasing success.

EXERCISES

1. Please review the sample jury instruction at the beginning of this chapter. Please rewrite it to make it more understandable to a lay juror.

2. Here is a definition of "obscenity" from a typical pattern jury instruction. Please revise it to make it more understandable.

Although the indictment includes the words of the statute, namely, the adjectives "obscene," "lewd," "lascivious," "indecent," and "filthy," the gist of the offense alleged in the indictment is the charge that the defendant wilfully misused the United States mail for the delivery of obscene photographs or pictures.

"Obscene" means something which deals with sex in a manner such that the predominant appeal is to prurient interest; which, by the current standards of the community as a whole, and which, taken as a whole, lacks serious literary, artistic, political, or scientific value.

An appeal to prurient interest is an appeal to a morbid interest in sex, as distinguished from a candid interest in sex.

3. The case at trial is the criminal prosecution of Mr. Collins. Please stylize this jury instruction to make it less abstract and more understandable:

You are instructed that a defendant in a criminal action is presumed to be innocent until the contrary is proved; and in case of reasonable doubt as to his guilt, he is entitled to be acquitted.

CHAPTER 23

INTRODUCTION TO WRITING BRIEFS

§ 23.01   What Is a Brief?

A brief is a written argument that a lawyer submits to a court. Briefs may be written in support of motions, as we discussed in Chapter 21, to define issues for trial, or on appeal. Trial briefs do not generally follow any specific format, and may not be submitted in every trial. In an appellate brief, the lawyer argues that the appellate court should reverse or affirm the lower court's decision, or asks for whatever other relief is appropriate. A court uses briefs to define the issues it will decide, to learn about the facts and the law, and to determine who should win.

Unlike a memorandum, which is an objective document, a brief is a persuasive document. Therefore you should write it in a way that will encourage the court to reach a decision favoring your client.

Although you should seek to convince the court that your client should win, do not overstate your case. Be sure to include a discussion of any adverse facts or cases. To win, you must not only argue that the law, policy, and equity support your client's argument, but also face up to damaging facts and contrary cases. You must downplay the significance of the facts and distinguish the cases. If you ignore adverse information, you will be embarrassed when your opponent brings it to the court's attention.

Write the brief persuasively, even the Statement of Facts. Argue that equity and policy, as well as the law, support your client's case. Chapter 5 describes how to make equity and policy arguments and gives an example of each. Because appellate briefs are the most complicated, and involve the most precise rules, we focus on appellate briefs in the next few chapters. You should follow the rules articulated in this book for writing persuasively and for presenting the facts and analysis when writing any brief. You should try to get information from the court or from experienced lawyers who have written similar briefs if you seek guidance regarding the format or desired content of other types of briefs.

Before writing an appellate brief, read the Record. The Record usually consists of documents and exhibits filed in the lower court, transcripts of depositions, trial testimony and arguments before the lower court, docket entries, and the lower court's orders and opinions. The Record defines the issues you may raise on appeal because you can argue only issues raised in the proceedings before the lower court. The Record also limits the facts on which you can rely in your brief, because you can rely only on facts that are in the record. Chapter 25 describes the record in more detail.

§ 23.02 Procedural Rules for Appellate Briefs

Appellate courts promulgate their own rules of appellate procedure. You must follow these rules when you write an appellate brief. These rules regulate the appearance, length, and content of appellate briefs.

Many appellate courts have rules governing paper size, paper color, size of margins, size of type, line spacing, type of binding, numbering of pages, and the format of the Title Page. As a general rule, each part of an appellate brief must begin on a new page. For example, even if the Table of Contents takes up only half of a page, you cannot put the Table of Authorities on the same page. You must begin the Table of Authorities on the next page.

Many appellate courts also limit the length of appellate briefs. Judges do not have the time to read long briefs. The shorter your brief is, the more likely it is that the judge will read all of it. Even if the appellate court's rules allow you to write a fifty-page brief, write one that is as short as possible.

All appellate courts require appellants to file their briefs first because the appellant is appealing the lower court's order. The appellee then files a brief that responds to the appellant's brief. Most appellate courts allow the appellant to file a reply brief to the appellee's brief.[1]

Most appellate courts require that appellants include the following parts in their briefs:

(1) Title Page

(2) Table of Contents

(3) Table of Authorities

(4) Statement of Jurisdiction

(5) Questions Presented

(6) Constitutional and Statutory Provisions

(7) Statement of Facts

(8) Summary of Argument

(9) Argument

(10) Conclusion

(11) Appendix (all or part of the Record).

---

[1] If the parties have the right to appeal a lower court's decision, the party who initiates the appeal is called the appellant and the opposing party is called the appellee. When review of a lower court's decision is discretionary, the party seeking such review is called the petitioner and the opposing party is called the respondent.

Although the appellee's brief has most of the same parts, most appellate courts do not require the appellee to include a Statement of Jurisdiction, Questions Presented, or a Statement of Facts. The appellee, however, is allowed to, and should, include its own version of the Questions Presented and a Statement of Facts.

§ 23.03   The Parts of a Brief

This section briefly describes the parts of a brief that most appellate courts require. Chapters 25, 26, and 27 describe the parts of the brief in greater detail.

[1]   The Title Page

The Title Page contains sufficient information to identify the case and who filed the brief. The Title Page usually sets out the names of the appellate and lower courts, the names of the parties, the numerical designation for the case, and the name of the attorney who is filing the brief.

[2]   Table of Contents

The Table of Contents tells the court the pages on which it will find each part of your brief. The Table of Contents provides a summary of your argument because it consists of the headings and sub-headings of your argument in sentence form.

[3]   Table of Authorities

The Table of Authorities tells the court the pages on which it will find the cases, constitutional provisions, statutes and secondary authorities you cite in your brief. The citation format in the Table of Authorities must be as accurate and complete as the citation format you use in the Argument section of your brief.

[4]   Jurisdictional Statement

The Jurisdictional Statement tells the court what authority confers jurisdiction on the court to hear the appeal.

[5]   Questions Presented

This section frames the issues for the court. Frame the issues persuasively so that they suggest the answers you want the court to reach, but do not be argumentative.

[6]   Constitutional and Statutory Provisions

This section sets out the text of the constitutional and statutory provisions you cite in your brief. Do not set out the text of the jurisdictional authority you cite in the Jurisdictional Statement.

[7]   Statement of Facts

This section sets out a clear and concise statement of the facts relevant to the Argument section of the brief. Write the facts in a light most favorable to your client, but do not omit adverse facts. Include references to the record but do not include arguments, conclusions of law, or citations in this section.

[8] Summary of Argument

This section sets out a clear, concise, and persuasive summary of your argument. In this section, summarize your primary and most compelling arguments.

[9] Argument

The Argument section is the heart of the brief. In this section, analyze the pertinent legal authorities and apply them to the facts of the case. Divide the Argument into as many subsections as there are issues and subissues. Unlike the Discussion section of a memo, which is objective, the Argument section of a brief is persuasive. Argue equity and policy as well as the law. You must discuss adverse facts and cases.

§ 23.04 The Hallmarks of a Well-Written Brief

The hallmarks of a well-written brief are the same as the hallmarks of a well written memo, which are set out in § 12.04, *supra*. They are:

(1) Clear writing style;

(2) Good organization;

(3) Thorough research;

(4) Good judgment;

(5) Writing for the reader;

(6) Precision and clarity;

(7) Creativity; and

(8) Correct citation format.

There are certain strategic differences between memos and briefs. Your primary audience is the court, not the assigning attorney. Therefore, a brief is persuasive, not objective. The judges will not have read the case file or the applicable law before they read your brief. They usually will know less about the facts and the law than you do. For this reason, be very careful to discuss the facts and the law clearly and thoroughly.

CHAPTER 24

APPELLATE PROCESS AND STANDARD OF REVIEW

§ 24.01   Introduction

Writing appellate briefs requires an understanding of the appellate process. The structure and ground rules of that process affect your ability to present an effective legal argument. In this chapter, we discuss in broad terms how cases come up on appeal, the record on appeal, and standards of review, that is, the tests an appellate court uses to evaluate the decision below. The discussion focuses primarily on the civil appellate process. If you are handling a criminal appeal, you should check and follow the applicable rules.

§ 24.02   How Cases Come Up on Appeal

Although each state court system and the federal system has its own rules on the proper procedure for taking an appeal, all systems share important similarities. Once a court or jury decides a case, the losing party may take an appeal to the appellate court. In a state with an intermediate appellate court, most appeals to that court are a matter of right. In most civil cases, the court of last resort, often called the state supreme court, has discretion in deciding whether to hear an appeal.

In general, the losing party can take an appeal from a final judgment, that is, a decision that disposes of the entire case. A final judgment might arise when a trial ends or when the court decides the case on a motion, for example, a motion for summary judgment. However, in certain instances, an appellant may take an appeal from an interlocutory order. An interlocutory order does not determine the final result of an action, but decides only some intervening matter, such as the grant or denial of an injunction. An appeal from an interlocutory order must follow procedural rules specifically applicable to interlocutory appeals.

§ 24.03   The Record on Appeal

In reviewing the proceedings of the court below, the appellate court relies on the record. Rule 10(a) of the Federal Rules of Appellate Procedure sets out a typical definition of the record: "the original papers and exhibits filed in the district court, the transcript of the proceedings, if any, and a certified copy of the docket entries prepared by the clerk of the district court." Reliance on the record assures that the appellate court will base its decision on only those matters presented to the district court, including both factual and legal questions.[1]

As a general rule, the court will not independently review the record for errors, but will rely on the parties to identify and brief any errors that should be reviewed. When you make your arguments on appeal, you must point to a specific reference in the record to justify each argument. In your brief, you must make constant references to the record so that the court can easily locate the parts of the record on which you are relying. If you fail to make sufficient precise references, you force the court to sift through the often voluminous stack of paper that comprises the record or you run the risk that the court will reject your argument as unsupported by the record. Such a failure will hardly endear you to the court or your client. For examples of citations to the record, please look at the sample briefs in Appendix V. For a further discussion of the record, see § 25.01.

§ 24.04 The Standard of Review

In deciding an appeal, a court cannot simply ignore the decision of the court below. The appellate court may decide only issues that the parties properly identified and objected to as erroneously decided at the trial level. This requirement allows the trial court to correct errors immediately, or at least gives the appellate court the benefit of the trial court's thinking on the issue. In addition, only issues or findings that are necessary to the trial court's decision may be appealed.

The test the appellate court must apply in passing on the lower court's decision is called the standard, or scope, of review. The standard of review varies depending on the jurisdiction and the type of case. You will explore the various types of review in detail in Civil Procedure. Our goal is to briefly introduce you to the most typical standards: clearly erroneous, abuse of discretion, and *de novo* review. These standards are part of a continuum, from extreme deference to the trial court on fact findings because of the trial court's firsthand exposure to evidence at trial, to little or no deference on purely legal questions.

[1] Clearly Erroneous

The most deferential standard for review of a trial court's decision is the "clearly erroneous" standard.[2] The standard is set forth in Rule 52(a) of the Federal Rules of Civil Procedure: "[f]indings of fact, whether based on oral or documentary evidence, shall not be set aside unless clearly erroneous, and due regard shall be given to the opportunity of the trial court to judge of the credibility of the witnesses." The rationale for this standard is clear. Because findings of fact are based on in-court

---

[1] The appellate court may sometimes consider new legal theories or arguments on appeal, but only if those arguments can be resolved based on the facts found at trial.

[2] Jury findings are accorded even more deference. The standard is the same as that employed in deciding motions for directed verdict or for judgment notwithstanding the verdict: whether a reasonable jury could have reached the verdict. Gene R. Shreve and Peter Raven-Hansen, *Understanding Civil Procedure*, 444-45 (2d ed. 1994).

proceedings where the trial court can make judgments on the credibility and competence of witnesses after seeing them first-hand, these judgments are due substantial deference. Because the trial court has a greater familiarity with the case, the appellate court may not independently determine the weight or credibility of the evidence, or assess the inferences drawn from the facts by the trial court.[3]

The Supreme Court described the standard this way: 'A finding is clearly erroneous' when although there is evidence to support it, the reviewing court is left with the definite and firm conviction that a mistake has been committed.'[4] This standard obviously places quite a difficult burden on the appellant's attorney.

[2] Abuse of Discretion

Slightly farther along the deference continuum, and more difficult to define, is the abuse of discretion standard. This standard applies to matters that are within the discretion of the trial court because they are "largely ad hoc and situation-specific."[5] This standard is tolerant of mistakes that may be made by a trial court in the exercise of its acknowledged discretion. Trial courts have a great deal of discretion on issues relating to trial management, such as joinder, discovery, sanctions, and the grant or denial of a motion for a new trial.

The scope of the trial court's discretion in a particular instance will depend on and must be evaluated in the context of the source of its discretion. For example, Rule 35 of the Federal Rules of Civil Procedure gives the trial court discretion to order a mental or physical examination of a party "for good cause shown," when the mental or physical condition of the party is "in controversy." Such an order would normally be accorded great deference on appeal, but in *Schlagenhauf v. Holder*, 379 U.S. 104 (1964), the Supreme Court found abuse of discretion in a case where the trial court ordered that a defendant be examined in each of four medical specialties — internal medicine, ophthalmology, neurology, and psychiatry. There was nothing in the record to support any examination other than a visual examination, so the Court vacated the judgment of the district court and remanded for reconsideration and further proceedings.

The abuse of discretion standard "varies in intensity with the breadth of discretion. Accordingly, abuse of discretion really occupies a band in the middle of the spectrum of intensity of review, its precise locus in any particular case depending upon the nature of the discretionary order under review."[6] If abuse of discretion is the standard for the case you are appealing, you will need to research similar cases in order to understand and argue precisely how the standard should be applied in your case.

[3] *De Novo* Review

The least deferential standard of review is applied to pure questions of law, or to mixed fact-law questions.[7] The appellate court is at no disadvantage in deciding

---

[3] Jack H. Friedenthal, Mary Kay Kane, and Arthur R. Miller, *Civil Procedure* 601-02 (1985).

[4] *United States v. U S. Gypsum Co.*, 333 U.S. 364, 395 (1948).

[5] Shreve and Raven-Hansen, *supra*, at 445.

[6] *Id.* at 446.

[7] Friedenthal, et al., *supra*, at 600, 602.

these types of questions, because it has the same access to relevant information that the trial court had. By making *de novo* decisions, the appellate court fulfills one of its primary functions: to provide guidance to the lower courts by ruling on questions of law.[8]

The *de novo* standard comes into play, for example, in reviewing pretrial motions. To illustrate, Rule 56(c) of the Federal Rules of Civil Procedure sets out the standard to apply when the federal district court grants a motion for summary judgment. According to the rule, summary judgment is proper when it appears that "there is no genuine issue as to any material fact and that the moving party is entitled to a judgment as a matter of law." The appellate court reads the record in the light most favorable to the party against whom the summary judgment was granted. Because the lower court heard no witnesses and weighed no evidence, the appellate court has no findings of fact to review. It therefore may decide the issue *de novo*. As you would expect, this standard is the one most favorable to the appellant.

[4] The Importance to the Practitioner

As you can see, the appellate lawyer must know what standard of review the court should employ and should think strategically in presenting the appropriate standard to the court. If you represent the appellant, it is to your advantage to be able to characterize the issue on appeal as a question of law, or of mixed fact and law. If you succeed, the standard of review will be *de novo*.[9] Conversely, if you represent the appellee, you want to characterize the issue as one of fact, or at least as one subject to the trial court's discretion. That way, the appellate court will be forced to give greater deference to the opinion of the trial court. Not surprisingly, complicated analysis and legal research may be required to distinguish the mixed fact-law question from the purely factual question.

Your understanding of the standard of review will also affect the way you argue and emphasize different aspects of the record. If you are representing the appellee and the court must find the decision below to be clearly erroneous in order to overturn it, you should stress the evidence that supports the trial court's decision and argue that the appellate court must defer to the judgment of the lower court. On the other hand, if you are representing the appellant and the court may hear the case *de novo*, you should point out that the decision below carries no weight and then make as few references to it as possible. Present the argument as if you are making it for the first time.

§ 24.05 Available Forms of Relief

When the appellate court completes its review, it has the discretion to take certain specific actions. It may reverse or vacate the decision below, remand the matter to the lower court for further proceedings, or affirm. As an appellate attorney, you must tell the court precisely what action you want it to take. You may want the court to

---

[8] *Id.* at 601.

[9] *Id.* at 602.

take different actions on different issues. If you fail to be precise about the relief you seek, the court can only guess at what your client wishes.

CHAPTER 25

THE APPELLATE BRIEF: THE INTRODUCTORY PARTS

§ 25.01 Using the Record

You must have authority for every fact you state in your brief. Your authority for facts and for the history of your case is the "Record." Although some courts call the Record the "Appendix," in this book, we use the term "Record." The Record consists of docket entries, trial transcripts, deposition excerpts, and pleadings filed in the court below. You will make many references to the Record in your Statement of Facts. You will also refer to the Record every time you repeat a fact in the Argument section of your brief and every time you refer to any event or filing of documents in the proceedings in lower courts.

An attorney prepares the Record before writing the brief. In practice, attorneys for the opposing parties on appeal usually agree to the contents of the Record. In the law school situation, the instructor gives students the Record from which to write the brief. The Record is the "reference book" for your brief. You must not rely on any fact that is not in the Record.

Rules of court usually tell you what you must include in the Record. For example, the rules may require all docket entries from the lower courts and all orders and opinions from the lower courts. You also should include in the Record all relevant pleadings in your case and relevant excerpts from depositions and trial transcripts.

When you prepare the Record, put all items in the order the court rules specify. If the court rules specify that you arrange items in groups, arrange the items within that group in order. Put other items, such as testimony, in the order that you think is logical. The Record is bound into a volume, or, in many cases, several volumes. The pages of the Record are then numbered sequentially as "R-1," "R-2," "R-3," and so forth. (If the Record is called "Appendix," the pages are numbered "A-1," "A-2," and so forth.)

When you write your brief, make references to the pages containing the facts that you include. For example:

> The defendant hit the plaintiff. (R. 35-37.) The plaintiff then skidded off the road. (R. 107-111.) The plaintiff's car was totally destroyed. (R. 103.)

If you have stated a fact that appears on several pages in the Record, make references to all pages on which that information appears:

> The defendant hit the plaintiff. (R. 35-37, 86-89.) The plaintiff then skidded off the road. (R. 107-111, 332, 345-346.) The plaintiff's car was totally destroyed. (R. 103, 111, 462-465, 503.)

Do not include any fact in your brief that the Record does not substantiate. Do not assume any facts that are not in the Record. The court that reads your brief will rely only on facts in the Record. It is also very important that all your Record references be accurate because the court will refer to the pages of the Record you cite.

Skim the sample briefs in Appendix V and notice that the writers have made Record references throughout their briefs.

§ 25.02 The Title Page

The Title Page of your brief gives the court necessary information. Look at the Title Pages of the sample briefs in Appendix V. The Title Page in your brief must conform to the rules of the court with which you file your brief.

There are many ways to type Title Pages of briefs. The one you choose should be pleasing to the eye and easy to scan for the necessary information it contains. Some courts require typeset briefs.

A typical Title Page contains:

(1) The exact name of the appellate court with which you are filing your brief;

(2) The term in which the court is to consider your appeal, including the month and the year;

(3) The docket number for the case;

(4) The names of the parties with the appropriate appellate designation ("appellant," "appellee," "petitioner," or "respondent");

(5) The exact name of the court from whose order you appeal;

(6) Identification of the party: "Brief for Appellant," "Brief for Appellee," "Brief for Petitioner," or "Brief for Respondent";

(7) The name and address of the attorney writing the brief; and

(8) The name and address of the attorney representing the opposing party (optional).

If court rules tell you how to prepare a Title Page, follow those rules exactly.

§ 25.03 Table of Contents

The Table of Contents is a "road map" for the court and the opposing counsel. This section is the first summary of your argument. It also serves as a reference tool. You must be sure that the page references are accurate and that the headings of the arguments in the Table of Contents are exact duplicates of the headings in your brief. For a discussion of brief headings, see Chapter 27.

Read the Tables of Contents for the briefs in Appendix V. Notice that the argument headings summarize the writer's arguments.

§ 25.04   Table of Authorities

The Table of Authorities is a listing of all legal authorities you have used in your brief. The first and most important part of this table is the listing of cases.

In compiling the Table of Authorities, follow the rules of the court for which you are writing the brief. Some rules require that you list cases alphabetically and by court—all United States Supreme Court cases in alphabetical order, all United States Court of Appeals cases in alphabetical order, and so forth. Others require a single alphabetical listing of all cases from all courts.

Follow the Bluebook for citation form, including the procedural history of cases. Again, accuracy is most important. The court and opposing counsel will rely on the accuracy of the page numbers in your Table to find the location of the authorities in your brief. When you prepare your brief, checking these page references is the last thing you should do, because they can change at any time.

When a writer uses an authority many times throughout a brief, the Latin word *"passim"* can replace page numbers in the Table of Authorities; it indicates that the authority is "everywhere." Be very careful about using this term, and do not use it in the Table of Authorities unless you actually use the authority "everywhere." For example, you may have cited a case on virtually every page. In this situation use *"passim."* However, if you use a reference only a few times, *"passim"* is inappropriate, and you should list all the pages on which that reference appears.

In the Table of Authorities a listing of statutes and constitutional authorities usually follows the listing of cases. Be thorough, list every statute and constitutional provision you have used in your brief, and follow the Bluebook for citation form.

After the listing of statutes and constitutional authorities, list all "secondary" sources you have cited in your brief. These include legal periodicals, treatises, restatements of the law, and other sources that are neither cases, statutes, nor constitutional provisions.

Again, list every authority you use, write accurate citations, and number the pages accurately. The court will use the page references to authorities while reading your briefs. A common question the court asks during oral argument of a case is "Where can I find that case in your brief?" Save yourself the embarrassment of referring the court to the wrong page. And remember: The court will get its first impression of the accuracy of your brief from the Table of Authorities section. If this section is inaccurate, the court may question the rest of your work. Attention to detail is very important.

§ 25.05   Jurisdictional Statement

Read the jurisdictional statements in the sample briefs in Appendix V. You can follow those formats generally.

This section of your brief tells the court what authority permits the court to consider your case. Cite the authority, but do not quote it. It is not a statement of a statute governing the substance of your case, but a statement of a statute, a rule of court, or a constitutional provision authorizing the appellate court to hear the kind of case you are appealing. This statement tells the court that your case is in the right court.

A colleague may tell you to appeal a certain kind of case to a certain court. However, you cannot rely on word of mouth. Find the provision of law specifically stating that the court in which you are bringing your appeal is the right one to consider your case.

§ 25.06   Questions Presented

The Questions Presented section is one of the most important sections of the brief. It frames the questions you want the court to answer and frames those questions in a way that encourages the court to decide them in your favor. The number of Questions Presented must correspond to the number of major headings in your brief.

Courts often give you specific rules about this section of the brief; however, most rules are the same:

(1) State the questions clearly and concisely.

(2) Avoid specific names, dates, and locations unless they help clarify the issues and are persuasive.

(3) Let the court know precisely what your case involves.

Writing the Questions Presented by your case is an art in itself. You can master this art only through practice. Writing the Questions Presented section is not a mechanical effort, but one to which you should devote a significant amount of time.

Here are examples of issues stated in different ways to illustrate what to say and what not to say in Questions Presented.

Bad: Whether Mr. Barnes proved his case of adverse possession.

Better: Does an adverse user satisfy the "continuous" and "exclusive" use elements needed to establish adverse possession to severed mineral rights by mining at times that are economically feasible and allowing neighbors to mine coal for personal use at other times throughout the statutory period?

Comment: In the first example the question is too broad and could refer to any adverse possession case. The second statement of the question includes the specifics of the case in question. Note that when you begin the question with "whether," you should end with a period, and, when you begin with a word like "does" or "can," you should end with a question mark.

Bad: Did the trial court err in admitting the evidence the officers obtained through the search?

Better: Did the trial court err in admitting evidence voluntarily given to the police by the minor child, when the child obtained it as a result of his independent search of the property and without police direction?

Comment: The first example is too general and says nothing about the particular case. The second statement of the question states the important facts concisely and clearly.

In addition to writing the questions presented with particularity and sufficient information, write your issues persuasively in your client's behalf. Here is how counsel on each side of the case might write the first example above.

> *Plaintiff's phrasing of the question:* Can a land user satisfy the "continuous" and "exclusive" use needed to establish adverse possession to severed mineral rights by mining at times that are economically feasible and consistent with local custom, and allowing neighbors to mine coal for personal use only at other times throughout the statutory period, particularly when he acted at all times and in all other ways as a true owner would have acted?

> *Defendant's phrasing of the same question:* Whether sporadic mining of a property only at convenient times while allowing others to use the property at their will was insufficient evidence of the continuity and exclusivity required to deprive the record owner of his superior rights to the minerals on the land.

Comment: The first statement of the adverse possession question suggests that the plaintiff has acquired rights by meeting legal requirements, and the second statement of the same question suggests that plaintiff failed to fulfill the legal requirements and should not deprive the record owner of mineral rights. Some readers may find the phrasing of the questions too argumentative. For a less argumentative version of the plaintiff's question, omit the words "only" and "particularly." For a less argumentative version of the defendant's question, omit the word "only" and substitute "sufficient" for "insufficient."

Here is how counsel on each side of the case might write the second example above.

> *Prosecution's phrasing of the question:* Whether the trial court was correct in admitting evidence when the child who provided the evidence voluntarily conducted a search of his home, with no direction from the police, and voluntarily offered that evidence to the police.

> *Defendant's phrasing of the question:* Whether the trial court erred in admitting evidence provided by a child, who, at the direction of the police, searched his own home and provided the evidence after further prompting by the police.

Comment: The prosecution's phrasing of the question first suggests that the trial court was correct, then places the child's activity on the child's shoulders and not on the police. It suggests that no police search occurred and that the search was an appropriate private search resulting in admissible evidence. The defendant's phrasing suggests that the trial court erred in admitting the evidence. It suggests that the child obtained the evidence only at the direction of the police in violation of the defendant's constitutional rights.

§ 25.07 Text of Constitutional, Statutory, and Regulatory Provisions

This section of the brief contains the text of the constitutional, statutory, and regulatory provisions you use in your brief. See the examples of this section in the briefs in Appendix V.

Do not include the text of any of these provisions if you do not rely on them in your argument. For example, do not include the statute or rule you use in your jurisdictional statement unless that authority is at issue in your case. If you make reference to a provision that is not at issue in your case, do not include its text.

Do not include full texts of provisions when only parts of those provisions are at issue. A statute, for example, may be very lengthy and may contain much language that has nothing to do with your case. Use only relevant portions as long as those portions make sense standing alone. Follow the Bluebook for correct citation format.

EXERCISES

(1) Using the information provided, prepare a Title Page for a brief. Type it the way it would appear in final form. Follow the format of the briefs in Appendix V.

 (1) The appellate court is the Supreme Court for the State of Ohio.

 (2) The term of court is January of 1998.

 (3) The docket number for your case is No. 96-43360.

 (4) The appellee is the State of Ohio.

 (5) The appellant is Elyse Keaton.

 (6) The case is on appeal from the Court of Appeals for the State of Ohio.

 (7) The brief is for the appellee.

 (8) You are the attorney for the appellee. Your address is 106 Main Street, Centerville, Ohio 90207. Your phone number is (302) 777-7777.

 (9) Mary Smith is the attorney for the Appellant, and her address is 100 Main Street, Centerville, Ohio 90207. Her phone number is (302) 555-5555.

(2) Prepare a Table of Contents from the following information. Conform to the format in the sample briefs in Appendix V. Omit page numbers.

 (1) Conclusion

 (2) Argument headings:

  1. The state did not violate the defendant's Fourth and Fourteenth Amendment rights, and the cocaine is admissible because the police

found it as a result of a legal private search by defendant's child, without government involvement; and the child gave the evidence voluntarily to the police

A. Officer Rambo did not direct Alex's search

    1. The interaction between Alex and Officer Rambo did not give rise to an agency relationship

    2. Alex conducted his search without Officer Rambo's knowledge, and he completed it before he notified Officer Rambo

B. Alex was not acting as Officer Rambo's agent when he gave Officer Rambo the evidence

C. Even if the search and seizure was subject to the Fourth Amendment, Alex's consent constitutes an exception to the warrant requirement

    1. Alex had authority to consent

    2. Alex voluntarily and knowingly consented to the search and seizure of the evidence

II. Neither a husband-wife privilege nor a parent-child privilege provides a basis for defendant to exclude her child's testimony since neither would be available to defendant under Ohio law, the law of other courts and legislatures, or social policy

A. Ohio law clearly prohibits defendant from invoking the husband-wife privilege

B. The Ohio statute does not authorize a parent-child testimonial privilege, and the court should not recognize such a privilege where a child voluntarily testifies about a communication his mother made in his presence regarding her criminal activities

(3) Summary of the Argument

(4) Table of Authorities

(5) Statement of the Case

(6) Constitutional and Statutory Provisions

(7) Statement of Jurisdiction

(8) Questions Presented

(3) Prepare a Table of Authorities from the following information. Omit page numbers. Use correct citation form. Follow the format in the sample briefs in Appendix V.

Ohio Rev. Code Ann. § 2317.02 (Anderson 1991)

Weis v. Weis, 147 Ohio State 416, 72 N.E.2d 245 (1947)

State v. Morris, 42 Ohio State 2d 307, 329 N.E.2d 85 (1978)

Three Juveniles v. Commonwealth, 455 N.E.2d 1203 (Mass. 1983)

Idaho Code § 9-203(7) (1990)

United States v. Matlock, 415 U.S. 164 (1974)

Arnovitz v. Wozar, 9 Ohio App. 2d, 222 N.E.2d 660 (1964)

Belichick v. Belichick, 37 Ohio App. 2d 95, 307 N.E.2d 270 (1973)

Martin J. McMahon, Annotations, Presence of Child at Communication Between Husband and Wife as Destroying Confidentiality of Otherwise Privileged Communication Between Them, 39 American Law Reports Annotated 4th 481 (1985)

Fourth Amendment, United States Constitution

In re Terry, W., 130 California Reporter 913 (Ct. App. 1976)

Mapp v. Ohio, 367 U.S. 643 (1961)

Jeffrey Begens, Comment, Parent-Child Testimonial Privilege: An Absolute Right or an Absolute Privilege?, 11 University of Dayton Law Review 709, 1986

Oregon v. Scott, 729 P.2d 585 (Or. Ct. App. 1986)

Herbert v. Maryland, 269 A.2d 430 (Md. Ct. Spec. App. 1970)

Ohio Const. amend. IV, § 1

(4) Write a Jurisdictional Statement based on the following information:

This case is an appeal to the Supreme Court for the State of Ohio.

A statutory section governs jurisdiction for this appeal: Section 2505.28 of the Ohio Revised Code Annotated (Anderson 1991).

(5) Rewrite the following facts into a question presented two ways: for the plaintiff/appellant and for the defendant/appellee.

Mr. Hale is a tenant, and Ms. Petrie is his landlady. Mr. Hale's apartment is in New Jersey. A few months ago a robber attacked Mr. Hale in the parking garage of his apartment complex and robbed him at gunpoint. The robber also beat Mr. Hale, causing him injuries and a broken arm.

Mr. Hale sued Ms. Petrie for negligence for her failure to provide adequate security in the parking garage. Although a guard was usually stationed in the garage, that guard was off-duty at the time of the criminal attack. Ms. Petrie contended in the trial court that, in New Jersey, she had no duty to protect her tenants from criminal attacks and was therefore not negligent. She also argued that, even if she had a duty, she provided sufficient security and that she had fulfilled any duty she had by taking reasonable steps to provide security. Her argument won in the court below. Mr. Hale now appeals that decision and argues that, once Ms. Petrie undertook to provide security, she also undertook to provide reasonable security but failed to do so.

(6) Suppose you are working on a case concerning a confidential communication to a priest. Prepare the text of the relevant statutory provision from the following statute as if you were preparing this text for a section on Constitutional and Statutory Provisions for a brief.

Section 2317.02 of the Ohio Revised Code Annotated (Anderson 1991), *Privileged Communications and Acts*, provides in relevant part:

> The following persons shall not testify in certain respects:
>
> A) An attorney, concerning a communication made to him by his client;
>
> B) A physician concerning a communication made to him by his patient;
>
> C) A clergyman, rabbi, priest, or minister, concerning a confession made, or any information confidentially communicated, to him for a religious counseling purpose;
>
> D) Husband or wife, concerning any communication made by one to the other, or an act done by either in the presence of the other, during coverture, unless the communication was made, or act done, in the known presence of hearing of a third person competent to be a witness;
>
> . . . .
>
> G) A school guidance counselor . . . professional counselor, counselor assistant, social worker, social work assistant or independent social worker concerning a confidential communication made to him by his client.

CHAPTER **26**

THE APPELLATE BRIEF: STATEMENT OF FACTS; SUMMARY OF ARGUMENT

§ 26.01 Statement of Facts

The Statement of Facts, also called the Statement of the Case, should include all the facts that the court needs to know to decide the case. Turn to the Statements of Fact in the briefs in Appendix V to get an idea of what the Statements look like.

For the attorney, the Statement has a purpose in addition to furnishing information. Use the Statement to set the stage for your argument. Tell the truth, be complete, but put your best foot forward. This part of the brief offers still another opportunity for advocacy.

Organize the facts and state them clearly so that the court can readily understand them. You are writing a Statement of Facts; therefore, state the facts truthfully and write without editorializing. Nonetheless, write so that the court sees your client in the most favorable light possible. The following pages show you how to perform this feat.

Here are three rules for writing the Statement of Facts:

1. Tell what happened.

2. Tell the truth, but put your best foot forward.

3. Hold the court's attention.

To illustrate our discussion of these rules, we will examine excerpts from the Statements of the Petitioners and Respondents in *New Jersey v. T.L.O.*, 469 U.S. 325 (1985). In this case, a high school vice-principal searched the purse of T.L.O., a student, and found marijuana. New Jersey began a delinquency proceeding against the student.

The issue was whether the Fourth Amendment's exclusionary rule should apply when a public school teacher or official illegally seizes evidence from a student. As you may know, the Constitution's Fourth Amendment forbids unreasonable searches and seizures by government officers. Under the exclusionary rule, evidence obtained during an unconstitutional search is inadmissible in court.

In *T.L.O.*, the trial court and the intermediate appellate court ruled that the evidence was admissible. The New Jersey Supreme Court, however, ruled that the exclusionary rule applied to the search and that the evidence therefore was inadmissible. Before the United States Supreme Court, New Jersey was the petitioner, and T.L.O. was the respondent.

[1] Tell What Happened

In the Statement of Facts, you are telling a story. Tell the story so that the reader can follow along with the least amount of effort.

An important part of the story is the case's procedural history: how the case started and what decisions the courts below have issued. A court will want this information readily available. Some attorneys set it out as a short, separate section of the brief. Others include it as an introductory subsection of the Statement of Facts, and still others weave pieces of it into the Statement of Facts as the pieces naturally arise in the course of the story. You should use the method that works best for you in a particular case. If the procedural history is brief and uncomplicated, you might state it in the opening sentences of the Statement of Facts. If it is complicated, you might set it out as a subsection of the Statement or as a completely separate section labeled "Procedural History." If you choose the latter method, you also might discuss the lower court decisions near the end of the Statement.

You will help the court to follow the story if you call the parties by their names and do not refer to them as "petitioner" and "respondent." Think of the times when you have read a court opinion and the court called the litigants "appellant" and "appellee." Remember how difficult it was to recall which label went with which litigant. In the *T.L.O.* case, call the juvenile "T.L.O." as opposed to "respondent." Call the petitioner either "New Jersey" or "the State."

Most of the time, you will want to tell the story chronologically. The historical approach is easy to follow. To illustrate, here are the opening paragraphs of the Statements of Facts in the *T.L.O.* briefs. The first excerpt comes from the brief of the petitioner, New Jersey:

> On the morning of March 7, 1980, a teacher of mathematics at Piscataway High School entered the girls' restroom and found the juvenile-respondent T.L.O. and a girl named Johnson holding what the teacher perceived to be lit cigarettes. (MT20-1 to 25).[1] Smoking was not permitted and the girls were thus committing an infraction of the school rules. The girls were taken to the principal's office where they met with Theodore Choplick, the assistant vice-principal. (MT21-1 to 3; MT21-24 to 22-11; MT31-18 to 20; MT33-20 to 34-10).

The second excerpt comes from T.L.O.'s brief:

> On March 7, 1980, a search was made by Mr. Choplick, vice principal of Piscataway High School, of a purse belonging to T.L.O., a student at the school. Ms. Chen, a teacher, had made a routine check of the girls' restroom. She observed T.L.O. and another girl smoking tobacco cigarettes. (MT 20-7 to 25)

---

[1] "MT" refers to the transcript of the motion to suppress heard before the Juvenile and Domestic Relations Court on September 26, 1980.

"T" refers to the transcript of trial on March 23, 1981, the transcript of the juvenile's plea of guilty to other complaints on June 2, 1981, and the transcript of sentencing on January 8, 1982, all contained in one volume.

> Although smoking by students was permitted in designated areas, it was not allowed in the restrooms. (MT 33-20 to MT 34-6) Ms. Chen accompanied both girls to Mr. Choplick's office, where she advised him of the infraction. (MT 21-1 to MT 22-23)

In each paragraph, the attorneys told the story in chronological order in a way that is easy to follow. T.L.O.'s Statement began with a sentence not in chronological order, because the sentence offered a desirable way to begin the story. Which paragraph do you prefer? Note that both attorneys documented their facts by making reference to the record. You are expected to furnish this documentation as a convenience to the court.

In telling the story, keep the narrative moving. Stay on point and omit irrelevant information. You should include facts that help make your client's case sympathetic, even if they are not essential to your legal argument. Here is the second paragraph from New Jersey's Statement of Facts:

> Mr. Choplick asked the two girls whether they were smoking. Miss Johnson acknowledged that she had been smoking, and Mr. Choplick imposed three-day attendance at a smoking clinic as punishment. (T49-24 to 50-7). T.L.O. denied smoking in the lavatory and further asserted that she did not smoke at all. (MT27-10 to 17). Mr. Choplick asked T.L.O. to come into a private office. (MT27-14 to 21; MT30-22 to 31-17).

T.L.O.'s brief does not contain a comparable paragraph. It offers a single sentence: "Upon being questioned, T.L.O. denied that she smoked." Do you understand why New Jersey's attorneys decided to include the additional information?

Here is another example. T.L.O.'s brief describes the juvenile court's disposition in the following words: "On January 8, 1982, a probationary term of one year was imposed." Here is how the New Jersey brief describes the disposition: "On January 8, 1982, T.L.O. was sentenced to probation for one year with the special condition that she observe a reasonable curfew, attend school regularly and successfully complete a counselling and drug therapy program." Arguably, the New Jersey brief includes more information than a court would need to make a decision about the applicability of the exclusionary rule. The additional information, however, helps place the state in a more favorable light. New Jersey's attorneys were correct in including it.

[2] Tell the Truth, But Put Your Best Foot Forward

In writing your Statement of Facts, you must tell the truth and not otherwise mislead the court. If the court discovers that you have been less than truthful, you lose your credibility, severely damage your client's case, and hurt your reputation as a trustworthy attorney. Still, you should state your case in the most favorable way possible. Write in an objective, noneditorial style, but emphasize the facts that help your client's case. Here is an excerpt from the New Jersey brief:

> Once inside this office, Mr. Choplick requested the juvenile's purse, and she gave it to him. (MT27-24 to 28-7). A package of Marlboro cigarettes was

visible inside the purse. (MT28- 9 to 11). Mr. Choplick held up the Marlboros and said to the juvenile, "You lied to me."

This excerpt paints the picture by using facts, rather than adverbs, adjectives, or editorial statements. Instead of explicitly calling T.L.O. a liar—an editorial statement—New Jersey's attorneys furnish facts that permit the Court to reach this conclusion. The Statement adds emphasis by quoting the vice-principal. Quoting another person's judgmental words is more effective than employing your own editorial words. In a Statement of Facts, employing your own editorial words is inappropriate.

As another illustration, consider how T.L.O.'s brief describes the items that Mr. Choplick found in the purse:

> Looking further into the handbag, he found a metal pipe, and one plastic bag containing tobacco or some similar substance.[3] (MT29-10 to 16) He also found a wallet containing "a lot of singles and change," and inside a separate compartment of the purse, two letters and an index card.

Compare the description in New Jersey's brief: "There he found marijuana, drug paraphernalia, $40 in one-dollar bills and documentation of T.L.O.'s sale of marijuana to other students." Each statement tells the same story, uses objective words, offers accurate information, and yet favors the respective client.

Writing the Statement of Facts may require you to deal with information adverse to your client. You already have seen some examples of ways to confront the problem. For another example, compare the following accounts of T.L.O.'s encounter with the police. Here is the account in New Jersey's brief:

> T.L.O.'s mother acceded to a police request to bring her daughter to police headquarters for questioning. (T18-12 to 18). Once at headquarters, T.L.O. was advised of her rights in her mother's presence and signed a *Miranda*[4] rights card so indicating. (T20-3 to 21). The officer then began to question T.L.O. in her mother's presence. (T23-4 to 6). T.L.O. admitted that the objects found in her purse belonged to her. She further admitted that she was selling marijuana in school, receiving $1 per "joint," or rolled marijuana cigarette. T.L.O. stated that she had sold between 18 and 20 joints at school that very morning, before the drug was confiscated by the assistant principal.

Compare the account in T.L.O.'s brief:

> The local police transported T.L.O. and her mother to headquarters. Upon arrival, Officer O'Gurkins advised the juvenile of her *Miranda* rights. (T20-7 to T21-3). When Mrs. O. indicated that she wanted to have an attorney present during the questioning, she was permitted to telephone the office of her lawyer. (T34-10 to 24). He was not available, so the officer proceeded with the interrogation. According to Mrs. O., at no time did her daughter state that she had sold marijuana. (T35-15 to 22).

---

[3] At trial it was stipulated that the bag contained 5.40 grams of marijuana. (T12-17 to 25). [Would you have advised the writer to place this information in a footnote?- -Ed.]

[4] Miranda v. Arizona, 384 U.S. 436 (1966).

Officer O'Gurkins admitted that although it was standard practice in juvenile matters to reduce incriminating statements to writing, he did not follow this procedure with T.L.O. (T24-12 to 18). He nevertheless maintained that T.L.O. had confessed that she had been selling marijuana in school for a week. (T22-2 to 17). He conceded that T.L.O. explained to him that the $40.98, which was found in her purse, constituted the proceeds from her paper route, which she had collected the night before.

The New Jersey brief seems to deal with some adverse facts by omitting them. Controversy exists over whether T.L.O. admitted to selling marijuana. From a technical perspective, the controversy is not pertinent to the issue before the Supreme Court. Nonetheless, the possible innocence of T.L.O. on the selling charge may affect the Court's perception of the case. T.L.O.'s brief discusses the controversy. The Court might think less of New Jersey's brief for ignoring it. The New Jersey brief could have alluded to the matter without turning it into a major issue. It might have begun the critical sentence this way: "According to the officer, T.L.O. admitted that she was selling. . . ." It also might have included an additional sentence: "Her mother later denied that T.L.O. made this admission." The lesson is that you can own up to adverse facts without waving them about.

Another way to use facts to your advantage is to summarize or quote favorable opinions of the court below. These opinions are powerful support for your arguments. Use them. If a majority opinion goes against you, mention the opinion and then focus on the dissent. In either case, you have the opportunity to make your arguments while still writing objectively. You summarize the favorable words of a third party, a court. This summary is still one more presentation of your argument. In *T.L.O.*, for example, New Jersey's Statement of Facts summarizes the adverse holding of the state supreme court in a single sentence. T.L.O.'s Statement, however, spends four paragraphs summarizing the majority opinion.

[3]   Hold the Court's Attention

Both New Jersey and the T.L.O. Statements of Fact hold the reader's interest. They tell the story in chronological sequence. They omit needless information. They use a concrete writing style. They refer to T.L.O.'s cigarettes as "Marlboros," as opposed to "tobacco cigarettes." New Jersey's Statement quotes the vice-principal: "You lied to me." It also states that Mr. Choplick found "$40 in one-dollar bills" as opposed to "$40" or "some money." The attorneys writing these Statements followed the rules of good writing style that you have learned. In these Statements, the most important rules of style are using the active voice, keeping sentences and words simple and concrete, and avoiding the inflammatory rhetoric that marks the advocate as an amateur.

EXERCISE

Here is a paragraph from T.L.O.'s Statement of Facts. Rewrite it to improve it stylistically so that it holds the reader's attention better.

An appeal was taken and decided on June 30, 1982. *In re T.L.O.*, 448 A.2d 493 (N.J. Super. Ct. App. Div. 1982). Two judges affirmed the denial of the motion to suppress the evidence secured by the search of the juvenile's purse, adopting the reasons set forth in the opinion of the trial court. However, they found that the record was inadequate to determine the sufficiency of the *Miranda* waiver which was allegedly made by the juvenile after her mother's unsuccessful attempt to summon counsel. *Id.* at 493. They therefore vacated the adjudication of delinquency and ordered a remand for further proceedings in light of the principles enunciated in *Edwards v. Arizona*, 451 U.S. 477 (1981) and *State v. Fussell*, 174 N.J. Super. 14 (App. Div. 1980). *Id.* One judge dissented, indicating that he would suppress the evidence found in T.L.O.'s purse because the search had been unreasonable. *Id.* at 495.

§ 26.02 Summary of Argument

In the Summary of Argument, you summarize your argument. According to United States Supreme Court Rule 34(h), the Summary is a "succinct, but accurate and clear condensation of the argument made in the body of the brief. It should not be a mere repetition of the headings under which the argument is arranged." Please read the Summaries of Argument in the briefs in Appendix V. As you can see, the Summary rarely is more than one or two pages.

This part of the brief is your chance to give the court a summary of your argument. It may be all some judges read before they hear your oral argument. Because of its importance, spend the time necessary to make it readable and persuasive. When a judge turns to your Summary, he or she probably knows very little about your case. Therefore write the Summary for an intelligent, but uninformed audience.

The task is harder than you may think. After spending weeks or months grappling with a case, you may have difficulty in accurately reducing your analysis to a page or two. Stick to your main arguments and save the subtle points for the body of the brief.

Use the Table of Contents as an outline for the Summary. Write a topical sentence stating a point of your argument at or near the beginning of each paragraph. Then flesh out the outline a bit. If you cite any cases at all, cite only those that are essential to making your Summary understandable. For example, you might cite the major case that you are distinguishing or relying on.

EXERCISE

Please read the following excerpt from the Summary of Argument in T.L.O.'s brief. Then write an outline of the summary. Note also how the writer fleshed out the argument. What suggestions do you have for improvement?

Assuming *arguendo* that the decision of the New Jersey Supreme Court does present a federal question for adjudication, petitioner's contention that the exclusionary rule need not be applied to the fruits of the illegal search at issue in this matter is clearly erroneous. The Fourth Amendment protects against unreasonable searches conducted by any governmental agency. Because public school personnel are employed by the state, act with state authority, and are responsible for carrying out state laws and regulations, their conduct constitutes governmental, rather than private, action. Thus the search of T.L.O. by the vice-principal comes within the ambit of the Fourth Amendment.

While petitioner is correct in asserting that this Court has not found the exclusionary rule to be constitutionally required in the case of every Fourth Amendment violation, those instances where it has not been applied have involved limited, peripheral uses of the evidence so obtained. This Court has not permitted the fruits of an illegal search to be introduced into evidence on the prosecution's case-in-chief in a criminal proceeding, as the State seeks to do in the present matter. In such circumstances, application of the rule is mandatory.

Even if petitioner is correct in maintaining that a balancing test — weighing the benefits of deterrence against the societal costs resulting from implementation of the rule — is constitutionally permissible to determine if the exclusionary rule should be applied in the present circumstances, it is clear that the expected benefits would outweigh the anticipated detriments. First, educators do have an interest in the successful prosecution of juvenile delinquency proceedings and would be deterred from conducting unreasonable searches by the knowledge that the resulting evidence would be excluded. Second, if evidence illegally secured by educators was not admissible at trial, the police would be deterred from instigating teachers to conduct illegal searches in order to provide otherwise obtainable evidence on "a silver platter." With regard to societal costs, statistical studies have shown that relatively few prosecutions are dismissed because of Fourth Amendment problems. School surveys do not support the conclusion that the crime rate in schools is rising or that an increase in searches by school personnel would be a significant factor in reducing the present rate.

Petitioner has demonstrated no alternatives to the exclusionary rule which would effectively deter violations of the Fourth Amendment rights of students. In addition, the exclusionary rule serves constitutionally recognized purposes other than deterrence: it protects the imperative of judicial integrity, and teaches respect for constitutional rights.

CHAPTER **27**

THE APPELLATE BRIEF: ARGUMENT AND CONCLUSION

§ 27.01   The Argument

The Argument is the heart of the brief. Its purpose is to persuade the court that your arguments rest on the applicable law and mandate a decision favorable to your client. While the other portions of the brief are important, you generally will win or lose your case on the substance of the Argument. The Argument section must be written persuasively and forcefully. It must be interesting enough to hold the attention of the court, and convincing enough to warrant a decision in your client's favor. This chapter instructs you how to structure and prepare the substance of an effective argument.

[1]   Structuring the Argument

[a]   Use Headings

A heading is a concise, persuasive statement of a conclusion that you want the court to accept with respect to a segment of your argument. Headings appear both in the Table of Contents and in the body of the Argument at the beginning of different sections and subsections; they should be identical in both places. For examples of headings, turn to Appendix V and examine the sample briefs. Here is an additional example:

I.   NALLY'S TAPE-RECORDED STATEMENTS ARE ADMISSIBLE IN EVIDENCE.

    A.   *Because Nally Contradicted His Taped Statements, the Taped Statements Are Admissible Under the Hearsay Exception for Prior Inconsistent Statements.*

    B.   *Because Nally Testified About These Statements at the First Trial, They Are Admissible Under the Hearsay Exception for Judicial Admissions.*

As you can see, the headings divide the Argument into major sections, and subheadings further divide those sections. Together, the headings and subheadings create an outline of your argument. You can feel confident about your headings when you list them in the Table of Contents and they present a logical, compelling summary of your argument.

Headings, then, are an essential tool in writing an organized, logical, and therefore persuasive argument. They give the court guidance in understanding your arguments and their logic. If you write persuasive headings, they should help persuade the court to rule in your client's favor.

[b] How to Write the Headings

The Questions Presented provide the foundation for the headings. To draft the headings, prepare a list of the specific conclusions the court must adopt to decide the case in your client's favor and identify the reasons that support those conclusions. These conclusions will become the arguments made in the headings and should serve as an excellent outline for drafting the brief. Make a separate list for each question presented. Then outline the necessary conclusions.

The order in which you present your conclusions or arguments is important. First, present your arguments in the same order as your Questions Presented so that the court will find it easy to follow you. Second, arrange your arguments for each Question Presented in a logical order, keeping related parts of the argument together. Third, begin with your strongest argument, unless doing so would strain the logic of the discussion. Your strongest argument is the one with which the court is the most likely to agree, based on your knowledge of its prior decisions and its members' predilections. It is not necessarily the one about which you feel the most strongly.

Once you have decided on the necessary conclusions and their order, you are ready to write the headings. Headings should be an integral part of the Argument. They are more than section titles. A heading is a statement of the argument to follow. It should be a complete sentence and be affirmative, persuasive and specific. It should not, however, be so partisan that it sounds unreasonable. Do not make arguments you cannot support.

Each Question Presented usually warrants only one major heading. If a Question has several subparts, write one general major heading. Then use the subparts to write minor headings. Place a Roman numeral before each major heading and a capital letter before each minor heading. Capitalize the first word and the first letter of all words except articles, conjunctions and prepositions, and underline each such minor heading. State the elements of the argument supporting a minor heading in subheadings preceded by numerals indicating their positions under the minor heading. Capitalize only the first word of subheadings and do not underline it. Always use a period after a heading, whether it is a major heading, a minor heading or a subheading. However, when you list a heading in your Table of Contents, you need not place a period at the end. Single-space your headings. Do not use minor headings or subheadings unless you use two or more of them. The headings should look like this:

    I. FIRST MAJOR HEADING.

        A. *First Minor Heading.*

        B. *Second Minor Heading.*

           1. First subheading.

2.   Second subheading.

3.   Third subheading.

II.   SECOND MAJOR HEADING.

Each heading is the thesis sentence for the part of the argument it introduces. As such, a well written heading identifies the legal issue or rule of law involved, indicates your position on the issue and sets out the reasoning supporting that position by relating the rule to your specific factual situation. It thus includes both the law and the facts of your case. Parties are often identified by name in headings. When minor headings and subheadings are used, the major heading need include only your conclusion regarding the application of a rule of law to your particular facts, since the minor headings and subheadings will set out the reasons for that conclusion. The more specifically you state the question, the rule, your reasoning and the facts, the more persuasive the headings will be. Framing a heading, however, remains a balancing process requiring good judgment and common sense. While the heading must contain sufficient information to effectively summarize the argument, it must also be easily comprehensible.

Here are a few examples of the types of headings that result when the writer does not adhere to the principles of effective heading drafting:

The elements of the foreseeability test.

Comment: Avoid general topical phrases that could be applicable to any number of cases.

Only blood relatives are permitted to recover for negligent infliction of emotional distress.

Comment: Avoid stating an abstract legal proposition by failing to show its relevance to your case. A better heading would be:

Because the appellant is not a blood relative of the injured person, she may not recover for negligent infliction of emotional distress.

Appellant fails to state a cause of action for negligent infliction of emotional distress since her claim does not fall within the parameters of the *Sinn v. Burd* foreseeability test.

Comment: Avoid using case and statutory citations as shorthand references to the applicable legal principle unless the reader would be familiar with them (*e.g. Miranda*). A better heading would be:

The appellant fails to state a cause of action for negligent infliction of emotional distress because she was not near the scene of the accident and was not closely related to the injured person.

[c] Using Headings as an Advocate

Seek to advocate your position, to make your basic arguments, through the headings. When you write a heading, use persuasive sentence structure and language. How you phrase a heading will depend on which side you represent.

Consider the following headings as they appeared in the Tables of Contents of two student briefs.

As drafted by counsel for the appellant:

I.   PAULA DIGIACOMO'S CLAIM FOR NEGLIGENT INFLICTION OF EMOTIONAL DISTRESS SATISFIES THE FORESEEABILITY TEST ADOPTED BY THIS COURT

    A.   Ms. DiGiacomo's Presence at the Scene Within Seconds After the Farmer's Bat Struck Henry's Head Satisfies the Requirement of Physical Proximity

    B.   Ms. DiGiacomo, Hearing the Crowd's Screams After Seeing Farmer Lose His Bat, Sensed a Contemporaneous Threat of Danger to Henry

    C.   Ms. DiGiacomo's Long-term Commitment to Henry Qualifies Her as Having a Close Relationship with Him Deserving of Legal Protection

    D.   Ms. DiGiacomo's Loss of Sleep, Need for Medication, and Frequent Visits to Her Psychiatrist Present Physical Manifestations of Emotional Distress

As drafted by counsel for the appellee:

II.   THE COURT BELOW CORRECTLY AFFIRMED THE SUMMARY JUDGMENT ORDER FOR THE APPELLEE BECAUSE APPELLANT DIGIACOMO CANNOT SATISFY THE REQUISITE FACTORS OF THE FORESEEABILITY TEST AND THEREFORE FAILS TO STATE A VALID CAUSE OF ACTION FOR NEGLIGENT INFLICTION OF EMOTIONAL DISTRESS

    A.   The Appellant's Relationship as an Unmarried Cohabitant with the Victim Does Not Satisfy the Requirement that the Appellant Be Closely Related to the Injured Party

    B.   The Emotional Distress Alleged by the Appellant Could Only Have Resulted from Her Observation of her Cohabitant's Condition upon Arriving at the Scene of the Accident as the Appellant Neither Witnessed Nor Sensorially and Contemporaneously Observed the Accident as It Occurred

    C.   The Appellant Has not Alleged or Suffered Any Bodily Harm or Severe Physical Manifestation of Emotional Distress as a Result of the Accident

Note how each version uses identical facts but offers a different perspective on the same arguments, yet both are persuasive.

[d] How Many Headings?

Headings should reflect your organization and simplify it by providing logical breaks in your argument. A well-written brief containing carefully drafted and logically placed headings will lead the reader easily from one point to the next. Too few headings will result in an argument that is difficult to follow and often poorly organized. Too many headings will interrupt the flow of the argument and may draw attention to insignificant or weak arguments. With these considerations in mind, use your judgment.

[e] Final Considerations

When you have formulated your point headings, write them out in outline form as they will appear in the Table of Contents. Then ask yourself whether they conform to the principles discussed in this section. Are they complete? Does each point follow logically from the ones preceding it? Is the phrasing persuasive but reasonable? Is each heading readable? Only if you can answer each question affirmatively should you be satisfied with this crucial part of the Argument section.

[2] Preparing the Substance of the Argument

To be an effective advocate, you must be coherent and credible. The presentation of your argument may be as important as the substance of your argument. Your research must be complete, your organization clear, your argument logical, and your writing precise.

[a] General Considerations

[i] Understanding the Appellate Process

Remember that the judges are the ones who must be persuaded. In every appellate case, the judges seek to render a decision that is both fair and consistent with precedent. Write your brief with these dual concerns in mind. To achieve a favorable result, write a brief that is clear, interesting, complete and reliable. Be honest about the law. Persuade with the strength of your arguments. Avoid excessive partisanship and statements without support. Never omit or distort the applicable law. If you do so you will sacrifice your credibility, an essential element of a successful appeal.

[ii] Familiarity with the Record

The record is your sole source of information about the case. To prepare an effective argument, you must have a clear and thorough understanding of the record. Read it carefully several times. Be certain that you understand the arguments and facts presented to the lower court, as well as the legal issues raised on appeal.

[iii] Research: Do It Right But Know When to Stop

A carefully crafted and persuasive argument begins with thorough research. For an approach to doing research, review Chapter 6.

Here are some tips. Think through the legal question. Approach it from a number of perspectives. Be creative in using the indexes to the digests. Look under a variety of topical headings. You and the index's publisher may list a topic under very different headings. Keep track of what you have researched and how you arrived at each source. Do not rely on headnotes. Read a case critically before relying on it. Shepardize each case you intend to cite. Make certain your research is current — check the pocket parts.

How do you know when to stop? Stop researching when you begin to find the same cases again and again. You should know when you have reached the point of diminishing returns.

Students sometimes engage in excessive research for two reasons. First, they keep searching for the one case that will give them a definitive answer to the legal issue. However, if you fail to find such a case early on in your research, there probably is no such case. In law school assignments, most problems have no definitive answer and no dispositive case.

Second, students keep researching because they are avoiding the next step, organizing the material and starting to write. Avoiding this pitfall requires being honest with yourself and recognizing that doing excessive research will deprive you of the time you need to finish your brief before the deadline. Drafting an effective argument is not an easy task. Be certain that you leave yourself enough time to do it well and expect that it will take longer than you anticipate.

[iv] Compliance with the Rules of Court

To be an effective advocate, you must be credible. One of the simplest ways to establish your credibility is to comply with the rules of court concerning briefs.[1] Failure to comply will not reflect well on you and may have a major adverse effect, such as dismissal of your client's case.

[v] Simplicity in Substance and Style

Perhaps the single most important attribute of an effective argument is simplicity in substance and style. Limit the arguments presented to the court and make them as uncomplicated as possible. If your outline is too long and complicated, rethink it. Adhere to the plain English writing style discussed in Chapters 8 and 9. Most courts have a heavy volume of cases and therefore have limited time to spend on any particular case. You are more likely to capture and hold the court's attention with a brief that is straightforward in both substance and style.

[b] Formulating the Arguments

Formulating the arguments you will make is a dynamic process involving analysis and evaluation of legal authority. You should consider not only the arguments suggested by your research, but also those that you develop based on your own insight into and understanding of a particular issue. Think carefully about the kinds of arguments that would be most effective for your client.

There are six distinct types of arguments you can make:

---

[1] All appellate courts have rules about brief format, content, and length. Your legal writing program most likely has rules that govern the briefs you write for it.

(1)   arguments based on legal precedent;

(2)   arguments by analogy to similar situations;

(3)   arguments based on public policy;

(4)   arguments based on a "parade of horribles," *i.e.*, the potential consequences of a precedent-setting decision against you;

(5)   arguments based on common sense notions of justice and fair play; and

(6)   arguments that stress certain sympathetic facts and rely on the emotional
appeal of your case.

Consider all six types of arguments when formulating your position. Use the ones
that seem most persuasive in your particular case.

[c]   The Organization and Substance of the Arguments

When your appeal raises several independent issues, begin the argument section
of your brief with the strongest issue. Similarly, where you have formulated several
arguments in support of your position on an issue, start with the most compelling
argument, unless logic dictates otherwise. Your brief will be more persuasive if the
strongest issues and arguments are presented first. The court's attention and time
are limited. Beginning a brief with a strong argument will ensure that at least that
argument will be read. Starting with a compelling argument will impress the court
with the soundness of your legal position and enhance your credibility. In addition,
the less persuasive issues and arguments are more compelling when they seem to
support the stronger issues and arguments. Some advocates put the weakest
argument last, while others bury them in the middle.

An effective argument generally has five components. These components suggest
an organization for discussion of each argument.

First, open the discussion of the argument with a fact-specific conclusion, even
though you may, to a certain extent, be repeating what is contained in the heading.
Do not begin with a broad statement of black letter law. If you do so, you risk losing
the court's attention. Opening with an affirmative, specific statement is more
persuasive and more likely to hold the court's interest.

Second, state the specific legal question raised by the argument under discussion
and provide an answer, indicating how the applicable rule of law will apply to your
facts. By doing so you are, in effect, giving the court a "road map" of your argument.
With the aid of a "road map," the court will know where the discussion is leading.
Knowing where the discussion is leading is invaluable to understanding it and a
prerequisite to being persuaded by it. If the court does not grasp your argument on
the first reading, that argument is most likely lost as the court will not take the time
to grapple with it. If the discussion requires more than one reading, the fault lies
with the writer.

Third, give a full discussion of the authorities on which you rely. Unless you are
citing a case only for a general legal proposition, be certain that you provide the
reader with the relevant facts, the court's holding and its rationale. Failure to
sufficiently develop a case you cite will rob it of its persuasive value and frustrate

the court. Remember that your role here is that of an advocate. Sometimes your discussion of a case will require a paragraph, other times it will require only a sentence or a parenthetical. Present relevant authority in the light most favorable to your position but never mislead the court. Stress those portions of the opinion that are helpful to your argument, but do not take statements out of context.

Fourth, apply, explain, or relate that analysis to the facts of your client's case. Effective argument requires that you take your facts and work them into the authorities you have cited. Develop them in the context of the facts, the rationale, the policies or the rules those authorities set out. In this section of the brief you must argue — you must comment, compare, distinguish, find controlling, highlight, explain away. Demonstrate to the court why it should decide the case in favor of your client and how it can do so in a manner consistent with existing precedent. Remember to cite the Record each time you refer to the facts of your case.

Fifth, when appropriate, restate your specific conclusion in regard to the argument under discussion.

This sample argument illustrates the suggested organization:

> The appellant, Ms. DiGiacomo, cannot state a claim for negligent infliction of emotional distress because she fails to meet the first and second prongs of the foreseeability test in *Sinn v. Burd*, 486 Pa. 146, 173, 404 A.2d 672, 686 (1979). The first and second prongs require, respectively, that the plaintiff be near the scene of the accident and that the shock result from a direct emotional impact upon the plaintiff from the sensory and contemporaneous observance of the accident. Here, the appellant was neither near the scene of the accident nor was her shock the result of a sensory and contemporaneous observation of the accident.

> When invoking the *Sinn* foreseeability test, this state's highest court considers both prongs simultaneously and then strictly construes both. See *Brooks v. Decker*, 512 Pa. 365, 516 A.2d 1380 (1986); *Mazzagati v. Everingham*, 512 Pa. 265, 516 A.2d 672 (1986). Consequently, the court has refused to recognize a cause of action when, as here, the plaintiff comes upon the accident scene immediately after the accident has occurred. As recently as October 1986, the Pennsylvania Supreme Court held against the plaintiff in two such cases. *Brooks*, 512 Pa. at 368, 516 A.2d at 1382; *Mazzagati*, 512 Pa. at 268, 516 A.2d at 679.

> Two Pennsylvania cases particularly illustrate why Mrs. DiGiacomo was not a contemporary observer. In the first case, *Brooks*, a father, returned to his home in the afternoon and was passed by an ambulance. After the ambulance turned up the street to his house, it stopped at a crowd of people. As the father approached, he noticed his son's bicycle lying on the ground and discovered that his son had been in an accident with an automobile. The father accompanied his son to the hospital where the boy lay comatose for ten days and then died. 512 Pa. at 366, 516 A.2d at 1381. This Court dismissed the claim for negligent infliction of emotional distress, because the parent did not witness the injury causing the accident. *Id.* at 367, 516 A.2d. at 1382.

As in *Brooks*, Ms. DiGiacomo did not actually witness the defendant's negligent act. The act was completed when the bat struck its victim. Witnessing the bat leave the defendant's hands and hearing the crowd's uproar was analogous to Mr. Brooks seeing the ambulance turn down his street and then seeing his son's bicycle on the ground.

In the second case, *Bliss v. Allentown Public Library*, 497 F. Supp. 487 (E.D. Pa. 1980), a federal court applying Pennsylvania law permitted a mother to recover, even though she was not looking at her child at the exact moment a statue fell on him. The court held that the mother was a percipient witness, because she observed her child immediately before the accident and heard the statue fall. She absorbed the full impact of the accident as if she had personally witnessed it. *Id.* at 489. There were no intermediary forces lessening her shock in witnessing her child's condition. *Id.*

The facts in that case differ from the facts here. In *Bliss*, the mother knew where her child was located and heard the accident happen. In contrast, Ms. DiGiacomo was unaware of her boyfriend's location before the accident. She was unaware that he had been struck by a bat. She heard the crowd roar, but she did not know that it was because of an injury to her boyfriend. As was true of the father in *Brooks*, Ms. DiGiacomo had no sensory and contemporaneous perception of the accident.

This Court's test is not unique to Pennsylvania. The facts of the instant case most closely resemble those of *Scherr v. Las Vegas Hilton*, 214 Cal. Rptr. 343 (Ct. App. 1985). In *Scherr*, the plaintiff watched live news coverage of a hotel fire and knew that her husband was in the hotel at the time of the fire. Because she did not witness her husband's injuries and did not know with certainty that he was being injured at that time, she could not recover for negligent infliction of emotional distress. *Id.* at 910-11, 214 Cal. Rptr. at 394-95. The court held that the "decisive question . . . is whether plaintiff, through whatever medium, received a sudden and severe shock by *actually* and *contemporaneously witnessing* not just the fire but the *infliction of injuries* upon her husband." *Id.* (emphasis in original).

By simply witnessing the throwing of the bat, Appellant DiGiacomo did not know with any certainty that her boyfriend was in danger, let alone injured. The cry of the crowd provided no greater certainty. Therefore, like the wife in *Scherr*, the appellant was neither physically proximate to the scene of the accident nor was her shock the result of sensory and contemporaneous observation of the accident.

As these cases demonstrate, the appellant cannot state a claim for negligent infliction of emotional distress. She fails to meet well-established elements of the foreseeability test set forth by the Pennsylvania Supreme Court.

Review the sample briefs in Appendix V for additional illustrations of effective organization of the argument.

[d]   What to Avoid

Year after year, legal writing instructors see students make the same errors in organizing and presenting their arguments. In the world after law school, judges see the same errors. These errors are both well known and easy to avoid. You can find a discussion of them in § 9.03. Take the time to review that discussion. To refresh your memory, you are on the way to writing a well-crafted brief if you:

(1)   Avoid the "Digest" Approach

(2)   Avoid the "Historical Development of the Law" Approach

(3)   Avoid the Use of Too Many Quotations From Legal Authorities

(4)   Avoid the "Abstract Writing" Approach

(5)   Avoid the "Law Discussion Only" Approach.

[e]   Using Precedent

In writing the argument portion of the brief, you must select the authorities on which you will base your argument.

[i]   Hierarchy of Precedent

When choosing authorities, select those that have the greatest precedential value. Binding precedent is case law from the jurisdiction whose law is controlling, particularly from the highest court in that jurisdiction or sometimes from the court that is hearing your case. Therefore, these cases have the greatest relevance. Although decisions from lower courts are not binding, they still will be persuasive. Recent cases are generally more desirable than old cases. If you are in state court, federal court decisions interpreting the law of the controlling jurisdiction are not binding, but generally provide very persuasive authority.

You often will find that there is no binding authority directly on point, that the courts in your jurisdiction have not decided the issue, or that the case is one of first impression. In such a situation, you must rely on the decisions of other courts, decisions that are not controlling. Seek to persuade the court that those decisions are based on sound policy considerations and are compatible with your jurisdiction's existing body of law.

The law of some states will be more persuasive than that of other states. Generally those states that are geographically closer to your state will have case law that is similar to that of your jurisdiction. This case law will provide you with strong arguments urging the adoption of your client's position. Certain states tend to be in the forefront of developing areas of the law and may provide you with authority for your argument. You may also make an argument based on a trend in the developing law. Suggest to the court that the conclusion reached by a number of other jurisdictions is proper and warrants adoption.

[ii]   Handling Adverse Precedent

In researching your argument, you will encounter decisions adverse to your position. Both ethical and practical reasons dictate that you discuss adverse decisions in your argument. The ethical reason stems from your obligation as a lawyer. The

A.B.A. Model Code of Professional Responsibility requires that "legal authority in the controlling jurisdiction directly adverse to the position of [your] client . . ." be disclosed,[2] while the A.B.A. Model Rules of Professional Conduct state that "[a] lawyer shall not knowingly . . . fail to disclose to the tribunal legal authority in the controllingjurisdiction known to the lawyer to be directly adverse to the position of the client and not disclosed by opposing counsel. . . ."[3] The practical reason should be apparent. If you have found adverse authority it is likely that your opponent has found it as well. It is far more desirable to address and minimize the adverse authority in the context of your argument than to allow your opponent to argue it from the opposite side. Your position will be far more credible if your argument is complete and includes adverse decisions. Seize any opportunity to explain why the authority should not be followed.

There are several ways to effectively harmonize adverse precedent. You might distinguish it on the facts of the case. You might argue that the policy goals stressed in the adverse case mandate a different result in your case. Suggest that a decision in favor of your opponent would set an unfortunate precedent with negative consequences. If the case is the most recent pronouncement of a well established legal rule, you might want to argue that your case requires an exception to that rule. You might be forced to argue that the case is an aberration and was wrongly decided. Use this tactic only as a last resort. It is an admission that you cannot harmonize the precedent. This argument may be ineffective when there are other decisions espousing the same position.

When you are the appellant, consider as adverse authority the decision from which you are appealing. Seek to harmonize it by pointing out its errors or omissions. Counsel for appellee will stress the decision as favorable and argue that it is sound.

[iii]   Rebuttal of Opposing Arguments

Seek to defuse the impact of the opposing arguments by criticizing them in one or several of the ways outlined in this chapter. Do not make conclusory statements that characterize your opponent's position as wrong. A broad dismissal suggests to the court that you cannot counter the position adequately and will adversely affect your credibility.

Resist the temptation to devote too much attention to your opponent's cases and arguments. The tone of your argument must remain affirmative and not convey a defensive posture. Use paragraph structure to your advantage. Never start an argument with a rebuttal of your opponent's position or the adverse cases. Do not devote a lot of time to your opponent's position or elaborate on the adverse cases. Doing either will focus undue attention on the opposing arguments and detract from the importance of your own arguments. Your argument should recognize that there is another position, address and dispose of it briefly, and move on.

---

[2] Model Code of Professional Responsibility EC 7-23 and DR 7-106.

[3] Model Rules of Professional Conduct Rule 3.3.

[iv]   Parentheticals, String Cites, Signals, Quotations, and Footnotes

Use the authorities on which you rely to persuade the court that your client's position is correct. After you have fully discussed the cases that are critical to your argument, you may want to cite additional cases that have arrived at similar conclusions based on analogous facts. Those cases may not warrant full discussion but you may want to include them to bolster your position. In this situation include a parenthetical after your citation of the case. Your parenthetical abstractions of the case should not be more than one sentence but should contain a brief summary of the relevant aspects of the case.

> See *Pearsall v. Emhart Industries*, 499 F. Supp. 207 (E.D. Pa. 1984) (woman who arrived home to find firefighters attempting to control the blaze engulfing her house and who saw the unconscious bodies of her husband and children was a contemporaneous observer); *Corso v. Merrill*, 119 N.H. 647, 406 A.2d 300 (1979) (mother who heard and immediately witnessed a car accident involving her daughter contemporaneously observed the accident).

Signals such as *see, accord*, and *contra*, can be used effectively in the argument. You might use a signal and a parenthetical to cite an adverse case, depending on how much discussion the case requires. Such a brief reference will demonstrate to the court that you have considered the case but will reduce its impact.

Avoid string citations, except perhaps where you are seeking to demonstrate the long-standing acceptance of a rule or an emerging trend in the law. String citations add nothing to your analysis. The court does not read them. Moreover, they are a distraction and break the flow of your argument. String cites suggest to the court that you think it is responsible for locating and reading the cited cases.

Exercise restraint when using quotations. Occasionally a judge will have phrased a certain point very effectively, and you will want to use a quotation. Most often your argument will be better if you paraphrase the opinion. Avoid long block quotes. Readers will often skip them entirely. If you must use them, use them very sparingly and delete all of the language that is not relevant by using ellipses indicated by three periods. *The Bluebook: A Uniform System of Citation*, Rule 5.3 (16th ed. 1996).

Use footnotes sparingly. Generally, if the thought is worthy of a footnote, you can fit it into your argument. Footnotes are undesirable because they interrupt the flow of the argument.

Use underlining or other methods of emphasis only very rarely. They are distracting. Rely on language and structure to emphasize a particular word or phrase.

[f]   Writing Persuasively

When drafting your argument, keep in mind the general principles of clear and effective legal writing. Take the time to review Chapter 19. In addition, take note of the following points.

[i]   Control Tone

Carefully control the tone of your brief because it affects the court's reaction to the substance of your arguments. Seek to establish an assertive tone. Make strong arguments, but do not overstate your position. Be scrupulously accurate. Do not use colloquialisms. Avoid informality and the use of abbreviations. Do not sound stuffy or pompous. Beware of humor, as an attempt at humor may annoy the judges. Sarcasm is always inappropriate, as is insulting or attacking the integrity of opposing counsel or the parties to the lawsuit. Do not adopt an arrogant tone — it will annoy and alienate a judge who may be favorably inclined to your opponent's arguments. Refer to the judges as "the court", opposing counsel as "counsel for appellant (or appellee)". Personalize your clients by referring to them by name, while referring to opposing counsel's client as "the appellant" or "the appellee." Never refer to the court as "you" or yourself as "I."

[ii]   The Final Touches

Rewrite, edit and polish your argument. Make sure your language is clear, strong and concise. Eliminate unnecessary words. Ask yourself whether your arguments are tightly reasoned. As you examine your brief, try to read it through the eyes of the judges that will decide the case. Will they find it easy to understand and persuasive?

Proofread your argument. Typographical errors may cause the court to question how careful you were in constructing the substance of the argument.

§ 27.02   The Conclusion

The Conclusion is a separate section of the brief and states precisely what action the party wants the appellate court to take. Here are two typical Conclusions:

> Wherefore, for the above reasons, appellees respectfully submit that the judgment of the court below should be affirmed.

> For the reasons discussed above, we respectfully request that the judgment of the court below be reversed and the case remanded with instructions to dismiss the complaint against the appellant.

Because a wide variety of relief is available, you must specify the relief you seek. Do not assume the court will know what relief is sought. You will annoy the court by forcing it to guess and you risk not having the desired relief ordered. The Conclusion is not a summary of the arguments presented in the brief. Such a summary should be included at the end of the Argument section. The Conclusion should never consist of more than a short paragraph and may be only one sentence. Close the brief with "Respectfully submitted," and your signature as counsel.

For more illustrations, review the sample briefs contained in the Appendix.

§ 27.03   A Checklist

In writing and revising a brief, some lawyers and law students find it helpful to use a checklist. A good checklist lists the important mechanical and stylistic rules that the writer should follow. You may find this checklist useful.

I.   Title Page: Does the Title Page conform to the rules of the court?

II. Table of Contents

    A.   When you read the headings, do they present a good summary of the Argument?

    B.   Are the headings exactly the same as they appear in the Argument?

    C.   Are the page numbers accurate? Is the brief within the page limitation that the court rules prescribe?

III. Table of Authorities

    A.   Does the Table include all the authorities you cite in the Argument? Have you excluded the citations in the Jurisdictional Statement, unless jurisdiction is an issue in the Argument?

    B.   Have you listed the authorities in the order that the court rules require? If court rules do not prescribe an order, have you listed them in a conventional way: for example, cases alphabetically, then constitutional provisions and statutes, then other authorities?

    C.   Are the page numbers accurate?

    D.   Is your citation form accurate? When required, have you included a case's prior or subsequent history?

IV. Jurisdictional Statement: Have you cited the authority that gives jurisdiction to the court?

V.   Questions Presented

    A.   Does the number of Questions Presented correspond to the number of major headings in your brief?

    B.   When you read each Question, do you find it comprehensible?

    C.   Is each Question framed in a way that, while not argumentative, encourages the Court to answer it affirmatively and in your favor?

    D.   Does each Question include sufficient specifics of your case without including too much detail?

VI. Constitutional, Statutory, and Regulatory Provisions

    A.   Have you included the relevant text of all provisions at issue in the Argument? Have you excluded the statute or rule in the Jurisdictional Statement unless it is at issue in your Argument?

    B.   Have you included only the pertinent parts of provisions, as opposed to the full texts?

    C.   Are the citations in proper form?

VII. Statement of Facts

    A.   Have you documented the facts with references to the record?

    B.   Have you stated the facts truthfully?

    C.   Have you avoided editorializing and using value-laden modifiers?

    D.   Have you put your best foot forward and told the story from your client's perspective?

    E.   If a court below or a dissenter supported your position, have you emphasized that fact?

    F.   Have you organized the facts and stated them so that the court can readily understand the story you are telling?

    G.   When appropriate, have you used a chronological sequence?

    H.   Have you employed a concrete writing style?

VIII.   Summary of Argument

    A.   Is the Summary succinct, but accurate?

    B.   Does the Table of Contents serve as an outline of the Summary?

    C.   Have you avoided citing cases unless they are essential to making the Summary accurate?

    D.   Have you stuck to your main arguments and saved the subtle points for the Argument?

    E.   Will the Summary be comprehensible and persuasive to an intelligent, but uninformed audience?

IX.   The Argument

    A.   Are your headings effective?

1.   Have you structured the Argument with sufficient headings and subheadings, but not too many?

2.   Do the headings correspond exactly to the headings in the Table of Contents?

3.   Is each heading a complete sentence?

4.   When appropriate, does each heading make specific reference to the facts in your case?

5.   Have you written the headings to be persuasive and advance your argument as opposed to just stating the law?

    B.   Have you adhered to a plain English writing style?

    C.   Have you chosen your arguments with care?

1.   Have you used your strongest arguments?

2.   Have you placed your strongest arguments first when it is logical to do so?

3.   Have you given your stronger arguments proportionately greater space?

4.   Have you made your arguments as uncomplicated as possible?

    D.   Have you presented each argument clearly and persuasively?

1.   Have you begun the discussion of each argument with a fact-specific conclusion and an answer to the specific legal question that you are addressing so that the

court knows where your argument is going? Have you briefly outlined your argument in the first paragraph so that the court has a "road map?"

2. Have you given a sufficiently full discussion of the authorities on which you rely, including the facts of decided cases when appropriate?

3. Have you applied, explained, or related your analysis to the facts of your case?

4. At the end of your discussion, have you restated that your argument leads to the specific conclusion you advocate?

5. Have you made your argument as persuasive as possible?

     E.   Have you dealt with adverse arguments?

     F.   Have you made the best use of authority?

1. Have you used proper citation form?

2. Have you relied primarily on authorities with the greatest precedential value?

3. Have you dealt with adverse precedent?

4. When cases have not needed extended discussion, have you briefly summarized them in parentheticals?

5. Have you used proper citation signals?

6. Have you avoided string citations?

7. Have you exercised restraint in using quotations and footnotes?

     G.   Have you written in an assertive tone that does not overstate your position?

   X.   Conclusion

     A.   Have you specified the precise relief you seek?

     B.   Have you closed the brief with "Respectfully Submitted" and your signature as counsel?

EXERCISE

Suppose you are the legal writing instructor. What comments would you have on the argument below? Assume the other prongs of the test have already been discussed.

Ms. DiGiacomo's Long-term Commitment to Henry Qualifies Her as Having a Close Relationship With Him Deserving of Legal Protection.

According to the third prong of the "foreseeability" test, the bystander and the victim must enjoy a "close relationship." *Sinn*, 486 Pa. at 171, 404 A.2d at 684. Henry and Ms. DiGiacomo have such a relationship.

In *Butcher v. Superior Court*, 188 Cal. Rptr. 503 (Ct. App. 1983), a court, in an action for loss of consortium, held that an unmarried cohabitant may present an actionable claim upon a showing that the nonmarital relationship is both "stable and significant." Although *Butcher* was an action for loss of consortium, several California courts have since adopted the *Butcher* standard as appropriate in actions for negligent infliction of emotional distress.

Ledger v. Tippitt, 210 Cal. Rptr. 814 (Ct. App. 1985), presents the case of an unmarried woman who witnessed the death of her boyfriend. Before the murder of her boyfriend, plaintiff and the deceased had lived together for two years. *Id.* at 815. In reaching its decision, the court held that it would be unfair to deny Ms. Ledger recovery simply because she had not gone through the formality of a marriage ceremony. *Id.* at 825. In doing so, the court reapplied the reasoning of *Butcher*, pointing to the fact that the incidence of cohabitation outside marriage had increased 800 percent between 1960 and 1970. *Id.* at 816. This trend, dispositive in *Ledger*, has continued to the present, as nearly 2,000,000 unmarried couples presently maintain households in the United States. U.S. Bureau of the Census, Current Population Reports, Series P-20, No. 410, *Marital Status and Living Arrangements: 1985*, U.S. Government Printing Office, Washington, D.C., 1986.

In *Garcia v. Superior Court*, 215 Cal. Rptr. 189 (Ct. App. 1985), an unmarried woman witnessed the death of her boyfriend in a vehicular collision. The court held that the issue was one of foreseeability. "The issue of law here is simply this: Is it foreseeable in contemporary society that injury to an adult may result in emotional trauma to another adult with whom the injured party is cohabiting without benefit of marriage?" *Id.* at 192. By adopting the *Butcher* "stable and significant" test, the court has answered its own question in the affirmative.

In *Eldon v. Sheldon*, 210 Cal. Rptr. 755 (Ct. App. 1985), a plaintiff witnessed the death of his nonmarital partner after she had been thrown from their vehicle in a collision. The court denied recovery of the plaintiff's claim for negligent infliction of emotional distress, reasoning that the "close relationship" prong should be construed narrowly. *Id.* at 759. In its view, to allow such a claim would reject *Dillon*'s assertion that "remote and unexpected" claims be denied. *Id.* Yet, in reasoning so, the *Eldon* court failed to consider the fact that such relationships are no longer "remote" nor "unexpected" given the decisions in *Ledger* and *Garcia*.

In *Kratzer v. Unger*, 17 D. & C.3d 771 (Bucks Co. 1981), a foster parent heard the defendant's vehicle strike her foster child. In a subsequent suit for infliction of emotional distress, the court found no barrier to her recovery as a foster parent relationship parallels that of a natural parent relationship. *Id.* at 773. The court held that "[t]he technical nomenclature ascribed to the relationship is not as important as the closeness of feelings between the participants." *Id. Accord Mobaldi v. Regents of University of California*, 127 Cal. Rptr. 720 (Ct. App. 1976), *disapproved on other grounds, Baxter v. Superior Courts*, 563 P.2d 871 (1977). Similarly, in *Lafferty v. Manhasset Medical Center Hospital*, 425 N.Y.S.2d 244 (Sup. Ct. 1980), a daughter-in-law recovered under similar reasoning as did a foster grandchild in *Leong v. Takasaki*, 520 P.2d 758 (Haw. 1974).

Given the strength of their relationship, the *Butcher* "stable and significant" standard establishes Ms. DiGiacomo's claim for the emotional trauma she experienced upon arriving on the scene to find Henry's lifeless body. Further, as Henry and Ms. DiGiacomo's relationship parallels the close relationships indicated above between foster parent/child, daughter-in-law/mother-in-law, and foster grandchild/ grandparent, Ms. DiGiacomo's recovery is reasonable.

PART VI

THE ORAL ARGUMENT

(Pub. 676)

CHAPTER 28

BASIC PRINCIPLES OF ORAL COMMUNICATION

§ 28.01   Introduction

There are several aspects of any oral presentation that should be carefully thought out or practiced in advance of the presentation itself. This chapter asks you to think about the appellate argument the same way you would think about any other spoken presentation. We attempt to teach you some basic principles that should guide your preparation every time you are asked to speak, whether to a court, clients, other attorneys, or community groups. In Chapter 29, we will discuss in detail the steps that arc unique to preparing for and presenting an appellate oral argument.

Knowing how to talk is not the same thing as knowing how to speak effectively; our goal is to help you do the latter. Inadequate preparation and poor presentation can so distract from a message, even a very important one, that the impact of the message can be virtually destroyed. If you think about speeches and presentations you have sat through that have not kept your attention, you should understand very quickly that communication is impossible where the receiver is not functioning as such. Your aim should be to have your audiences hanging on your every word, or, if not, at least processing *most* of the information you are trying to convey.

§ 28.02   Consider the Audience

If the purpose of speaking is the communication of ideas, audience evaluation is critical. How can you judge how best to communicate your thoughts to a particular audience if you have not considered who your audience is and what preconceptions they might bring to the topic and your position on that topic?

[1]   Do Your Homework

In the appellate context, you will seldom be faced with individuals on the bench who are unknown quantities. Your judges will likely have written opinions that you can read before you go into court. If they have written opinions on related issues, it would almost be negligence not to read them. Even if they have not written opinions in similar cases, you might gain some insight into the judges' styles of reasoning by reading unrelated opinions. You do not need to spend several days in this process, but it should be well worth your time to spend a few hours at it.

You should also try to find someone who has previously argued in front of these judges. Ask about the judges' styles of questioning, the types of arguments they seem to find persuasive, and the types of issues they like to focus on in reaching their decisions. Find out whether the judges concentrate on the facts of the cases in front of them, or on policy implications for the future. When you have this kind of information, you can structure your argument accordingly.

If time and circumstances permit, you should also consider going to court and listening to someone else argue in front of the same judges. Try to get a feel for the judges' reactions to various arguments and approaches, and think about what you might do to obtain the reaction you are seeking to your argument.

[2] Adapt to Your Audience

Once you have developed a sense of what might persuade your audience, you need to think about how to accomplish that goal. The first thing you should consider is the image you want to present. If you have previously appeared before this court, you may already have established a certain ethos or credibility that will help you convey your message. If not, you need to determine how to suggest to the court a level of competence that will make the judges receptive to your arguments. Adequate preparation and a professional demeanor, which we will discuss in greater detail later, are good ways to accomplish this.

In order to persuade an audience, you must give them a reason and the means to identify with your position. You can do this most effectively if you can establish common ground between you and the audience. Convince the audience that you are all on the same side, or at least that you have in some way attempted to adapt to your audience's perspective on the issues being discussed. If you have made some effort to ascertain your audience's attitude toward the topic before making your presentation, you will find this a lot easier to do.

If you sense, or have learned, that your audience's attitude toward the topic is different from yours, try to figure out the source of their attitude. If you understand where it comes from, your chances of changing it may improve if you can address the root cause. You should recognize, however, that extreme attitudes cannot usually be changed greatly or quickly, and that an attitude that has been expressed publicly, *e.g.*, in an opinion, article or speech, will be more resistant to change than an attitude that has not been committed to in that manner.

There are strategies that can be employed to change audience attitudes. You can attempt to persuade the audience that circumstances have changed sufficiently that the original attitude is no longer appropriate. If there has been no change in circumstances, you may be able to persuade the audience that they were previously misinformed, or that they had not been made aware of all the available facts. Or, you can point out that the situation you are discussing is sufficiently distinct from previous situations that it calls for a different result. If you are trying to "scare" your audience into changing their attitude, you should know that attitudes are generally changed more easily by moderate than by strong anxiety appeals.

§ 28.03   Consider the Setting

When we use the term "setting" in this context, we are referring to both the physical surroundings in which the presentation will be made, and the occasion, or reason for convening the speaker and the audience. Spending a little time understanding the expectations created by these contextual factors will help you prepare a more effective presentation.

[1]   Study the Physical Surroundings in Advance

You should, if at all possible, take the time to visit the courtroom or other location in which you will be "performing." If you have a sense of the size of the space, its acoustical properties, and the location of any furniture or other objects that will be present when you speak, you can prepare in advance to deal with any problems that might be caused by any of these factors. For example, if the podium is too high or too low, find out whether it can be adjusted, as many of them can, by the simple push of a button. If you can manipulate the physical environment to make yourself more comfortable, you should do so, because greater comfort will mean greater confidence and, in all likelihood, a stronger presentation.

Another factor to consider is the time of day at which you will be speaking — are people likely to be tired because your turn comes at the end of a long day, or might they forget your message because it appeared in the middle of a long parade of other speakers? If you sense that these types of factors might create a problem for you, you can try to come up with ways of making your presentation stand out, such as an especially strong opening or closing statement. If you arrive early, you may even be able to make last-minute adjustments in your prepared material to account for the mood of the audience at that particular day and time.

If you need some sort of visual aid to make your presentation, you must plan for it in advance. Check to find out whether the courtroom has an easel, or whatever else you might need. If not, find out whether one can be brought in, or whether you should supply the necessary equipment yourself.

[2]   Understand the Occasion

The reasons an audience convenes will largely determine the audience's expectations of what the speakers will say and of how they will conduct themselves. You should be sure that your understanding of the occasion and the audience's understanding are the same. Ask questions to be sure that you are aware of any traditions and conventions that must be followed if you are to avoid surprising the audience in a way that will detract from your message.

In an appellate courtroom, for example, the expectation is that you will behave with proper formality and deference. If you go in expecting to dazzle the judges with the type of flamboyance and histrionics that might be more appropriate for a jury, you are not likely to make a favorable impression, or to be taken as seriously as you need to be.

§ 28.04 Structure Your Argument for Maximum Effect

You should plan the structure of your presentation to reinforce your intended message. Remember that, from your audience's perspective, your meaning will come across sequentially and cumulatively. Thus, you want to be sure that the sequence of your ideas is logical and that the cumulative effect of your presentation is persuasive. Your ideas should progress in a manner that the audience can follow and be tied together appropriately, even explicitly where that will enhance understanding.

[1] Structural Strategy

It is useful to have some basic understanding of human psychology and memory when deciding how to structure an argument for maximum persuasive effect. Most of you have probably read or heard about "primacy" and "recency" as factors to be considered in the placement of arguments. These concepts refer to the likelihood that audiences will remember best the ideas they hear first and last, when their attention is most focused on the presenter.

You should also consider whether you want to present your arguments in ascending order of impact, saving the best for last, or descending order, starting with your strongest point. Because both primacy and recency will work in most contexts, you should try to start *and* end on a strong note, and bury your weaker points in the middle, where they will be the least detrimental.

Virtually all appellate advocates will tell you to start with your strongest argument, for the simple reason that you may never get beyond your first argument if the judges have many questions. Because an appellate argument is not a "set piece," where you have total control over the presentation, but rather a dialogue between you and the court, you must plan your strategy accordingly.

[2] Methods of Proof

There are two primary approaches to proving a proposition: the direct approach, from proposition to proof, and the indirect approach, which gradually builds up the building blocks of proof until the proposition being proved becomes the inevitable conclusion. The latter method is somewhat more difficult, but often more effective, particularly when dealing with a skeptical or hostile audience. The reason this method works better for such audiences is that they may decide not to listen to the proof after they hear a proposition stated with which they disagree. If they do not know what the proposition is until they have heard the proof, you may be able to keep their minds open longer.

Even so, most legal arguments will work from proposition to proof because that is the expected approach. Judges may get frustrated if they do not understand immediately where an argument is going and what an attorney is trying to prove. Because the judges have the right to interrupt at any point, the attorney trying to prove a point by indirection would probably have to be doing so in an especially fascinating manner to avoid an irritated, "Counsel, where is this going?"

Part of your proof should consist of anticipating and defusing adverse arguments. You do not need to deal with every possible argument that might be made against your position, but if you know that an opposing argument will be made, or that those who disagree with you do so for a particular reason, it is foolish not to address that point. Pretending something does not exist is not the best way to make it disappear, and it does nothing for your credibility or persuasiveness. Why should your audience believe your arguments if you ignore theirs?

Raising and then explaining away the negative arguments is known as the "straw man" approach to proof. It is called that because you are setting up the straw man arguments just to knock them down, demonstrating all the while how insubstantial they were in the first place. Just make sure that in the course of dealing with the "straw men," you do not inadvertently make them seem more substantial than your opposition would have been able to, or that you do not create new arguments against your position that might not have come up at all.

[3]   Organizational Patterns

There are many ways to structure an argument, and you must figure out which approach makes the most sense for each project you undertake. The most important aspect of the choice, however, is that you make one. Structure does not take care of itself; you must make conscious decisions about what structure is most likely to enhance the message you are trying to convey. Here are several possibilities to consider.

[a]   Chronological

This approach to structure makes the most sense when you are relating a story, and the exact sequence of events is important to the audience's understanding of the story. In the context of the appellate argument, a chronological organization will probably be useful in your presentation of the facts of the case you are arguing.

[b]   Cause to Effect

If you are trying to establish a causal relationship between two events, as you might be in a negligence case where proximate cause is an issue, you should be sure to structure the argument so that the causal link will be apparent to the audience. This will usually require you to begin with the statement of the cause, and then move on to the result, demonstrating the unbroken nature of the chain of events you are describing.

[c]   Problem to Solution

If you are arguing for a change in an existing rule, this structure will probably be useful. It is one of the most common approaches to persuasion. Begin by developing the need for change; discuss the harmful consequences of the current rule, being sure to connect those harms directly to the rule you seek to change. Once you have thoroughly proved that a change is necessary, move on to the solution you propose.

In order to make this structure really effective, you must establish a strong link between the benefits of your proposal and the harms you previously identified. In other words, now that you have made the case for change, you must convince your audience that your change is the right one, and that it will solve all the problems previously identified. Many speakers simply present their proposal and assume the audience will immediately see that it is the perfect answer. This is very rarely persuasive — you run the risk that the audience will not find your solution as obvious as you do, and will begin to think about other alternatives.

If you do a good job of convincing the audience that change is necessary, you will have created the perfect atmosphere for receptivity to your proposal. Do not waste that opportunity by failing to make explicit connections between your solution and the need for change; you may not get another chance!

[d] Pro vs. Con

You may occasionally be in the position of offering an evaluation of which of two proposals is more likely to effect a desired result, or of defending a proposal that you know has encountered strong opposition. If so, this might be the structure to choose. Where the positions on both sides are clearly defined, it will make sense to the audience that you choose to address those positions sequentially.

Your only remaining decision is whether to address the "pro" or the "con" first. This will depend on the context of the argument, and probably on which side you think is stronger — for example, if you think the audience is hostile to the proposition you support, you may want to deal with the 'con' arguments first. If you can effectively negate those, the audience may be more receptive to hearing why you support the other side.

[e] Topical

When you have several issues to address, you will generally take a topical approach to structure, presenting the various topics in any order that seems appropriate. It is here that issues of primacy and recency, and ascending versus descending order, arise. If there is a sequence that is naturally logical — for example, if one argument must be developed first to provide context for another, you should present the arguments in that order. Similarly, if you are making arguments in the alternative, or if one argument is conditional upon the acceptance of another, you should take that into consideration when structuring the overall presentation.

[4] Introductions, Conclusions, and Transitions

These are important parts of the structure of any spoken presentation. We have included them last in this discussion because that is probably when you should think seriously about them. The conclusion obviously belongs at the end of the speech, but you should also construct your introduction *after* you have completed your substantive analysis. It is at that point that you will have the best idea of the tone you are attempting to create and of the central theme of your argument. Both of these should be reflected in the introduction.

The introduction and the conclusion should be short, pithy, and as powerful as you can make them, consistent with the subject of your argument. These are the first and last impressions you will leave with the audience, and you want them to be strong ones. You should identify the one idea you would like the audience to take away from your presentation (assuming that that is all you can realistically expect them to take away), and that idea should be reflected in the introduction and conclusion. Ideally, the conclusion will echo the introduction in some interesting way, so that the central idea will be reinforced.

Transitions should also be consciously considered after you have constructed the argument. The reason you move from one argument to another, or the relationships between arguments, will often seem obvious to you, and thus you will not feel the need to state them as you develop the argument. After you have created the body of the argument, look at it as objectively as you can, and ask yourself whether the audience will see the flow of the argument as well as you do. Even if you think they will, you should probably add at least brief transitions between major points. Remember that the audience has to process your message aurally; any help you can offer to make that message clearer will almost certainly be appreciated.

§ 28.05   Write For Sound Appeal

Remember, as you draft the language you intend to speak, that writing words to be spoken requires a different style from writing words that will be read in silence. You have additional tools at your disposal to enhance the impact your words will have on the audience. Try to hear the words as you write them, and to picture how the delivery will go. What facial expressions will accompany your words? How will you use your hands to support your message? What will your volume and vocal inflection reveal about the importance of what you are saying? What tone will most enhance your message? Language shapes perceptions; use your knowledge of this fact to encourage or discourage particular responses.

[1]   Useful Tools

There are several ways you can maintain audience interest in your spoken message. Some of them are relatively simple and quite effective if used in appropriate contexts. Others may require more conscious effort on your part to use them effectively. Here is a list of some of the ways you can keep an audience listening and wanting to hear more.

[a]   Humor

Humor can be a very good way to involve your audience in your message from the start. This is probably why so many speakers begin their presentations with a joke. Be sure that what you say really is funny, and that it is appropriate to the audience. Also remember that subtle humor is often more effective than obvious humor; surprise is an important element of good humor.

[b] Novelty

Novelty may also be a way to catch your audience's attention early on. If you have a different approach to an old topic, or if you are discussing something with which the audience is not familiar, you can use the interest that most of us have in new things to your advantage. Choose an interesting way to alert the audience to the fact that you are presenting them with new information, and you may very well be able to keep their attention longer.

As with anything else, though, do not get carried away; novelty for its own sake will wear thin very quickly. Be sure that your approach is actually novel, present it in a way that is appropriate to the audience and the topic, and avoid "cuteness" that may only succeed in turning the audience off.

[c] Conflict

You may be able to use the element of surprise in another way. If your topic lends itself to the creation of conflict, for example between light and serious tones, a sudden shift can catch the audience off guard and make them sit up and take notice. Thus if you can begin with a humorous approach, and then move unexpectedly into an aspect of the topic that is decidedly not funny, you may shock the audience into listening more carefully than they might otherwise. This is a manipulative approach to getting your message across, but if handled adroitly, it can be quite effective.

[d] Suspense

This is a difficult technique to use effectively, particularly in a legal setting, but if done well it can really add to the impact of a message. You can use suspense in the introduction to your presentation by finding an interesting but somewhat ambiguous way of leading into your topic. In order not to lose or frustrate the audience, make certain that your mysterious introduction is genuinely fascinating, and it should not go on for too long.

You may find it more effective to at least signal your topic early on, but leave the audience wondering exactly what your approach or perspective is. It can be a very effective means of persuading a hostile or skeptical audience to begin by articulating the arguments for your opponents and suggesting that you understand them, and then suddenly revealing your true position on the issue. Once again, the element of surprise proves useful in keeping the audience involved in the presentation.

Be very sure that you understand the expectations of your audience before you try this technique in a legal setting. In the appellate context, where presentations tend to assume nearly identical guises, and where the judges can interrupt you if they get frustrated, too much suspense could be detrimental to the persuasiveness of your argument. With a jury, however, appropriate use of this technique could be quite powerful.

[e] Emphasis

In a spoken presentation, you have many opportunities to suggest appropriate emphasis. The voice, hands, and face can all be used to guide the audience to the conclusion that what you are saying at any given moment is particularly important. You should also recognize that the audience will generally expect that important information is more likely to appear at the end of sentences than at the beginning. The beginning of a sentence is expected to contain contextual information that will help the listeners orient themselves in the message, and prepare themselves for what is to follow. What follows is a powerful example of the effect an understanding of this simple expectation can have on the impact of a message. Read this excerpt and think about how you would react to it as a listener.

I have refrained directly from criticizing the President for three years. Because I believe that Americans must stand united in the face of the Soviet Union, our foremost adversary and before the world, I have been reticent. A fair time to pursue his goals and test his policies is also the President's right, I believe. The water's edge is the limit to politics, in this sense. But this cannot mean that, if the President is wrong and the world situation has become critical, all criticism should be muted indefinitely.

A fair chance has been extended the President, and policies that make our relationship with the Soviet Union more dangerous than at any time in the past generation no longer deserve American support and support cannot be expected.

Reagan administrative diplomacy has had this grim result: We could face not the risk of nuclear war but its reality if we allow present developments in nuclear arms and United States-Soviet relations to continue.

This is an excerpt from a campaign speech by Walter Mondale. It seems very flat, and leaves the reader wondering what exactly the speaker was trying to accomplish. If we simply restructure the sentences, leaving the meaning and vocabulary virtually intact, here is the result[1]:

For three years, I have refrained from directly criticizing the President of the United States. I have been reticent because I believe that Americans must stand united before the world, particularly in the face of our foremost adversary, the Soviet Union. I also believe a President should be given fair time to pursue his goals and test his policies. In this sense, politics should stop at the water's edge. But this cannot mean that all criticism should be muted indefinitely, no matter how wrong a President may be or how critical the world situation may become.

President Reagan has had his fair chance, and he can no longer expect Americans to support policies that make our relationship with the Soviet Union more dangerous than at any time in the past generation.

This is the grim result of Reagan administrative diplomacy: If present developments in nuclear arms and United States-Soviet relations are permitted to continue, we could face not the risk of nuclear war but its reality.

---

[1] This example is taken from George Gopen, *The Common Sense of Writing: Teaching Writing from the Reader's Perspective* (unpublished 1990); he, in turn, got the example from Joseph M. Williams, and asked us to acknowledge that fact.

By simply restructuring the sentences to place emphasis on the appropriate information, we end up with something that actually sounds as though it might belong in a campaign speech.

[f]   Theme

One of the most important tools for effective speaking is the creation and emphasis of a central theme for any presentation. Find a way to tie your ideas together, to relate them to a single overarching principle, and be sure to clearly identify that theme for your audience and to refer to it wherever appropriate to emphasize its importance. Choose a tone for your presentation that reinforces this central theme (*i.e.*, solemn, ironic, indignant, *etc.*) You should never assume that any audience will remember every subpoint of an argument, but if they walk away understanding the main goal you were trying to accomplish and why that goal is important, you will have achieved something to be proud of.

[g]   Language

Remembering always that your audience cannot go back for another look at something that was not immediately clear, keep your language concrete, precise, active, colorful, and simple. Most people will process information more efficiently if they can conjure up a visual representation of it. You can help your audience do this by using concrete analogies and examples to clarify points that might otherwise seem abstract. Here are some specific examples of stylistic devices that speakers have used to good effect in many contexts.

[i]   Rhetorical Questions

Asking questions to which you do not expect an answer can, if used sparingly, be a very effective means of keeping your audience involved in your presentation. Your goal is to frame the question in such a way that it suggests the desired answer, but leaves enough room for thought that the audience will feel that they have arrived at the answer on their own, and thus feel a sense of commitment to it. You should, of course, be a little extra careful about using this technique with an appellate bench — you do not want the judges to feel that you are trying to usurp their role!

[ii]   Repetition

Strategic use of repetition, whether of sentence structure (*e.g.*, antithesis), words, or sounds (*e.g.*, alliteration), can be an effective signal of emphasis or simply a means of increasing the memorability of what you say. Part of the reason so many people remember and quote speeches by John F. Kennedy and Martin Luther King is because they used repetition so powerfully. You should, however, be careful to avoid monotony, which will almost certainly result from an overuse of this technique.

[iii]   Imagery

As mentioned above, giving your listeners the ability to "see" what you are saying will help them process and retain the message. There are several ways to do this, all involving comparisons, sometimes literal, sometimes of very dissimilar things.

The literal analogy is the most direct comparison, and tries to identify similarities between things or ideas that will help clarify a point. The more figurative similes and metaphors make comparisons between very different things in order to create a picture in the listener's mind that will suggest meaning quickly and powerfully. A simile is a comparison that actually uses the words "like" or "as," while a metaphor implies the comparison.

Martin Luther King's "I Have A Dream" speech is one of the strongest and most effective uses of metaphors you are likely to see; it creates an entire landscape in your mind through the simple use of words. Most of us cannot use metaphors nearly so well. They should be used sparingly and carefully; if you create a metaphor that is too startling or confusing, you run the risk of distracting your listeners as they struggle to deal with the visual image you have created.

Personification is another type of comparison that can be used effectively to create a lasting image in the mind of the listener. This is the giving of human traits to inanimate or intangible objects, as by suggesting that an institution is "ill" or that an idea "limps." Again, you should be careful not to create images that are so strange the audience will spend substantial time puzzling over them, or laughing where you did not intend humor.

[2] Not So Useful Tools

As you can see, there are many ways you can enhance your message by making it more fun for the audience to listen to you. Similarly, there are some ways you can detract from the message and irritate the audience so that they may decide to stop listening, or at least become less receptive to your message. For example, the inclusion of slang, foreign phrases, vulgarity, euphemisms, or triteness might have this kind of effect, ranging from distraction to active annoyance.

Another tactic speakers sometimes resort to, particularly in the political arena, is name-calling. By this, we do not mean only the obvious mud-slinging type of name-calling, but also the more insidious, intellectually dishonest use of labels in place of analysis. When a speaker knows that a particular word will generate an emotional reaction, such as the word "quota" in a discussion of affirmative action, it may be tempting to simply use the word and thereby short-circuit a genuine examination of the topic under discussion. This technique may get results — it is always easier, both for the speaker and the listeners, to oversimplify an issue and thus discourage reason and evaluation — but it does so inappropriately.

Particularly in a courtroom setting, where your listeners are intelligent and at least somewhat informed, you should respect them enough to offer a straightforward and thoughtful analysis of the topic you are discussing. You should say what you mean, and not shy away from the difficult questions. If your audience is paying any attention at all, attempts to avoid the real issues are likely to be challenged and will cost you valuable credibility. There is simply no reason to take this kind of risk.

§ 28.06 Apply the Fundamentals of Good Public Speaking

Delivery is the final element of any spoken presentation. When you have worked so hard to prepare your argument, it would be very unfortunate to diminish the impact of your efforts by not delivering the message effectively. Here are some suggestions about how to achieve maximum influence as a messenger.

[1] Maintain Eye Contact

Maintaining eye contact with an audience is difficult for inexperienced or nervous speakers, but it is essential. In a courtroom, look the judges in the eye rather than at your notes or the ceiling. Eye contact lets the judges know you are interested in what they have to say. It also helps keep them interested in what you are saying.

[2] Be Heard

Speak loudly and clearly enough that everyone in the room can hear you. Project but do not yell. Speaking at an appropriate volume suggests confidence in your position. If you speak so that everyone can hear you easily, you help insure that your audience will understand your argument. You also increase the likelihood that your audience will find your argument persuasive.

[3] Do Not Read

Reading will cause you to speak too fast and make you more difficult to understand. It suggests a lack of preparation, and even a lack of interest in your argument. In addition, you will lose eye contact with the bench, and the judges' interest in your argument may decrease.

[4] Use Emphasis

Sounding like you are interested in your arguments and believe them makes it more likely that your audience will find you persuasive. It is difficult to listen to someone who speaks in a monotone. We are not suggesting that you try to be flamboyant, but merely that you modulate your voice appropriately for the point you are making.

[5] Use the Pause

Silence is often anathema to someone who is unused to speaking in public. As you develop experience and expertise in speaking to an audience, you will learn to use a well-timed pause to provide emphasis. A pause while you ponder a question or collect your thoughts can ensure that what follows the pause is more fluent and persuasive.

[6] Use Appropriate Gestures

Not all people use their hands while speaking. If you are not comfortable using hand gestures, do not try them for the first time in the pressure-filled environment of a courtroom. If, however, it is natural for you to use your hands to add appropriate emphasis to your presentation, do so in your oral argument. Be careful not to use your hands excessively.

[7] Watch Your Posture

The courtroom is a formal setting. Do not lean excessively on the podium. You may rest your hands on the podium, but not your elbows. Do not argue with your hands in your pockets or on your hips. Casual poses may suggest a lack of respect for the court and at the very least are likely to be distracting. Do not pace or rock back and forth. Stand in one place and maintain an upright, respectful posture.

CHAPTER 29

THE APPELLATE ARGUMENT

§ 29.01 Introduction

This chapter teaches you specifically how to make an oral argument in appellate court. Although most attorneys do not find themselves in appellate court very often, the skills you learn in presenting an oral argument will be useful in other areas of practice. Attorneys also argue motions to the trial court and appear before various administrative agencies that may require argument.

Oral argument is the culmination of an attorney's efforts in an appeal. It complements the brief. You cannot expect, however, to present an argument every time you file a brief, because the court has discretion about whether to grant oral argument. If you get a chance to argue, view it as a golden opportunity. You will have no other in-person, one-on-one contact with the judges who will decide whether you win or lose.

The oral argument provides you with an opportunity to interest the court in particular arguments presented in the brief and to convince the court that your client's position is correct. Generally, the argument is more provocative, more personal and more lively than the brief. The oral argument affords an opportunity to answer the court's questions and address its concerns. Time is limited and therefore precious, which means that precision in presenting the argument is crucial.

Most lawyers will tell you there is very little chance you will win a case at oral argument that you otherwise would have lost. They will also tell you that you can lose a case based on your argument. On the other hand, some experts, including Justice Kennedy of the Supreme Court, will tell you that many cases are decided at oral argument.[1]

Many first-year law students view oral argument as an ordeal to be endured. Because the experience is new and the process unknown, the prospect of oral argument makes students nervous. Fortunately, despite their initial misgivings, most students find that the actual experience is worthwhile and even fun.

---

[1] Justice Kennedy, in his address as part of the Enrichment Program at the George Washington University National Law Center, February 6, 1990.

§ 29.02   The Setting of the Oral Argument

The appellate oral argument usually is conducted before a panel of three judges. The court allots each side a specified amount of time in which to present its argument. The attorney addresses the bench from behind a podium. The appellant presents the first argument and may reserve time for rebuttal. The appellee argues after the appellant and does not present a rebuttal. If two teams are arguing in a first year legal writing or moot court program, both appellants argue, followed by both appellees. The appellant delivers the rebuttal after the appellee has argued. The judges may interrupt at any time with questions.

As a matter of protocol, rise when the judges enter the room and remain standing until the judges have seated themselves. The court then calls the case and may ask whether counsel is prepared. After you indicate your readiness to proceed, step to the podium and begin your argument. Refer to any judge to whom you are speaking as "Your Honor." Refer to your opponent as "opposing counsel" or "counsel for appellant" (or appellee).

§ 29.03   Preparing the Oral Argument

The key to a successful oral argument is preparation. If you are prepared, you will be confident and you should be able to address any concerns raised by the judges to their satisfaction. In preparing your argument, remember that time is limited, so you must state your arguments in general terms. Focus on policy and equity rather than the details of case law.

The judges' questions will probably force you to deviate from your prepared outline. You should be sufficiently prepared that you can shift back and forth from one part of your argument to another as necessary. The judges may not wish to follow your structure and you should be prepared to accommodate them. Also, you must think through the consequences of your arguments and the relief you want the court to grant. Judges will want to know precisely what you want them to do and what effect your preferred result will have on future cases. Here are seven rules to help you achieve the required degree of preparation.

[1]   Know the Record

You must have all information about what happened in your case at your fingertips. This information includes not only the facts that gave rise to the cause of action, but also the entire procedural history of the case, including discovery. You will present a brief history of the case as part of your argument, but you must be able to answer the court's questions about any additional facts. The judges may doubt the accuracy of other aspects of your argument if you cannot tell them what happened previously in your own case.

[2]   Study the Authorities

Although you usually do not focus primarily on details of decided cases in presenting your argument, you must be able to answer questions about the major cases cited in your brief or in your opponent's brief and to use such cases in response to questions where appropriate. You must know the facts, holdings and rationales of all such cases. The court will expect you to be able to apply them to the facts of your case.

[3] Know the Arguments

You must be familiar with all arguments raised in your brief. For purposes of oral argument, however, select a maximum of three major arguments to present to the court. Use the organization of your brief as a guide. As explained in Chapter 28, try to begin with your strongest argument. This will help capture the judges' attention and set the tone for the rest of the argument. Also, the judges might ask so many questions that you never reach your second argument. You must, however, be prepared to answer questions about your weaker arguments, because the judges may focus on those arguments. Also, remember that if your strongest argument does not logically come first, you may not be able to begin with it.

Be flexible about the order in which you present your arguments and be prepared to adapt your argument to what happens in the courtroom. For example, if you are the appellee, listen carefully to the questions the court asks the appellant. If the court focuses on a particular issue, you may want to begin by presenting your argument on that issue.

[4] Outline Your Arguments

An outline is an essential part of preparing for an oral argument. Even if you do not use your outline during the argument, preparing one ahead of time will give your presentation clarity and structure. The outline should present the high points of your argument. When deciding how much detail to include in your outline, use the rule of thumb that you should have enough prepared material to occupy approximately half your allotted time. For a fifteen-minute argument, prepare an outline that should take you approximately eight minutes to present. Some people feel more prepared if they put virtually every word they intend to say on paper beforehand. Others prefer a sketchy outline that allows greater flexibility of word choice at the time of the argument. As a general rule, you should try to go to the podium with the fewest words on paper that will allow you to feel comfortable that you can remember your key points. Regardless of which approach you choose, keep your arguments simple and straightforward and use only minimal references to details such as case names in preparing your outline.

[5] Prepare Argument Aids

After preparing your outline, think about the kind of notes and other aids you are likely to need while presenting your argument. You may choose to use the outline or you may find that some other form of prompting is more helpful to you. Many appellate advocates suggest putting your outline on the inside of a manila folder so that the entire argument is laid out in front of you. This approach makes referring to various parts of the argument in response to questions easier. If you are shuffling through loose papers to find needed information, you may distract the bench. Locating a particular part of your argument under pressure can be difficult.

When you go to the podium, take your brief, your outline and notes or cards that summarize the relevant cases. The case notes should provide a short summary of the facts, holding, and rationale of each case about which you can reasonably expect questions during the argument.

Take your argument aids to the podium with you, but do not read from them. Use the argument aids only to remind you of the points you wish to raise with the court. Forcing yourself to speak without heavy reliance on notes will facilitate the all-important eye contact with the bench. One way to accomplish this is to follow the general rule stated above, and have only as many words in front of you as you really need to remember the key points you intend to make. For example, use important words and phrases rather than full sentences.

[6] Rehearse the Argument

Although some people may feel a bit foolish practicing an oral argument, it is an essential exercise. If you are not accustomed to public speaking, practice in front of a mirror. You will be able to see how effective your facial expressions and hand gestures are. You also may want to practice in front of other people—your friends, family, or your partner if you are arguing as part of a team. The best way to gauge your effectiveness as a public speaker is to videotape your performance. Although videotaping is obviously not always a practical alternative, it definitely is an educational experience.

An important part of rehearsing the argument is anticipating questions the judges are likely to ask. Prepare for:

(1) questions about the facts of your case;

(2) questions about the facts of cases cited in the briefs filed with the court;

(3) questions about arguments raised by your opponent;

(4) questions about arguments you intend to make but have not raised yet—that is, questions that require you to deviate from your prepared outline; and

(5) questions about the ramifications of your arguments and the rule or rules you are asking the court to adopt; understand and be able to articulate the policies behind the options available to the court and know your "bottom line"—what are the precise parameters of your arguments and the rule(s) you are advocating?

Although you cannot possibly predict every question the judges will ask during the argument, you will give a much more polished and persuasive presentation if you have anticipated and rehearsed answers to the majority of questions you receive.

[7] Advise the Court and Your Opponent of New Information

Information or case law relevant to your case sometimes becomes available after you file your brief. You have an affirmative obligation to advise the court of any new case law that may be dispositive. If you decide that it is necessary to provide newly discovered case law to the court, do so before the argument and send a copy to your opponent at the same time. Not only is this practice a matter of courtesy, it also prevents the court from becoming distracted by reading a document you hand up during your argument.

§ 29.04   The Structure of the Oral Argument

[1]   Basic Argument Structure

The oral argument, whether presented by appellant or appellee, usually conforms to a basic framework that contains a number of elements:

(a) The opening statement. The opening statement usually begins with the phrase "[m]ay it please the court," briefly introduces counsel and the party represented by counsel, and reserves time for rebuttal if desired. For example, in the case of *Ace Trucking Co. v. Skinflint Insurance, Inc.,* counsel for appellant Ace Trucking Co. might begin:

> May it please the court, my name is Nancy Schultz, my co-counsel is Annemiek Young, and we represent Ace Trucking Company. We would like to reserve four minutes for rebuttal, with two minutes deducted from each of our arguments.

Then give a brief summary of what the case is about, provide a short procedural history and indicate the relief requested. Your summary offers a good opportunity to explain briefly to the court why your client deserves to win and to set the tone for the rest of your argument.

(b) The statement of the facts. The statement of the facts should be short, accurate and persuasive. Frame it to present your point of view and the merits of your client's case. It must not be misleading, however, or you will lose credibility with the court. You should emphasize helpful facts, but you must appear fair. Do not omit adverse facts, but they can be "toned down" if not helpful to you.

The first statement of facts on each side should cover all important facts. It is not absolutely necessary for the appellee to present the facts, but you probably should not pass up the opportunity to tell your client's story in your own way. As appellee, you probably will choose not to give a full rendition of the facts, but instead to discuss facts that the appellant omitted or failed to discuss fully. If you are presenting an argument as part of a team, the second person to argue on each side may want to highlight only a few facts that are especially important to that person's argument. Sometimes the court may ask you to omit the facts.

(c) The argument. Present the argument section in two parts:

(i) outline of the legal arguments, and

(ii) presentation of the arguments.

Providing the bench with a brief outline, or 'roadmap,' of the arguments you intend to make indicates to the judges which arguments you believe are worthy of oral argument and advises them of the order in which you will be making those arguments. An outline enables you to at least mention all of the arguments you have selected, albeit broadly, and may encourage the court to defer its questions until the appropriate time. If you are arguing as appellee and will be presenting arguments in an order different from that used by your opponent, it may be wise to advise the court of that fact.

Some advocates may tell the court that they intend to rely on their briefs for arguments not specifically addressed at oral argument. This practice is questionable because it may encourage the judges to ask questions on a topic you have not prepared in depth or on which you would prefer not to spend valuable argument time.

Present your arguments as you have outlined them. State conclusions first, then support them with facts and law. During your argument, refer to your client by name. This practice both humanizes your client and helps the court keep the parties straight. When referring to the opposing party, most advocates use an appropriate party designation such as "appellant" or "appellee."

(d) The conclusion. When your time has run out, finish your sentence and sit down. Before concluding, make sure you have answered any pending question to the questioner's satisfaction. If you finish your argument before your time has run out, do not keep talking just to fill the time. Present your conclusion and sit down. Conclude your oral argument by providing the court with a short, "punchy" statement of why your client deserves to win and is entitled to the requested relief. Depending upon how your argument has progressed and the time remaining, the conclusion may be a single sentence or it may be more detailed. You should prepare both. If, when time runs out, you have not had an opportunity to conclude, you must ask the court for permission to do so. The court may or may not grant such permission. Finally, before you sit down, thank the court.

[2] Rebuttal

If, as appellant, you choose to reserve time for rebuttal, be prepared to use that time efficiently and effectively. If you are arguing as part of a team, usually one member of the team will present the entire rebuttal for the side and should be prepared to discuss any issues raised during the argument. In two to five minutes, you cannot rebut every argument made by your opponent. You also may not use this time to raise new issues. Select one or two major points made during the argument that you feel most require clarification or rehabilitation. Remember that your rebuttal is the last thing the judges will hear before they decide your case. Choose your arguments accordingly.

There are other effective ways to use rebuttal time. Listen carefully to your opponent's argument. Your opponent may make statements or mistakes that you can use to your advantage. If you do not have one or two major points that need reinforcing, you may want to use the time to give the court a brief and powerful summary of the reasons your client deserves to win. Some advocates choose to use the time to answer an important question they were unable to answer when the court asked it during the argument.

It may be worthwhile to prepare several possible rebuttals ahead of time. Canned rebuttals, however, are no substitute for listening to your opponent's argument. Tailor your rebuttal to the argument the court actually hears. It also is acceptable to waive your rebuttal if you are satisfied with the way the argument has progressed. The judges are likely to appreciate the time savings, and you send a distinct message of confidence when you waive rebuttal. If, however, you have reserved substantial time for rebuttal, perhaps five minutes or more, you may want to use the time to at least summarize your major arguments for the court. Always close your rebuttal with a request for the specific relief you seek from the court.

§ 29.05   Questions From the Judges

Throughout your argument the judges are likely to interrupt with questions. Questions from the court are desirable because they signal the judges' interest and involvement in the matter. Questions from the bench reveal to you what the judges' concerns are and permit you to tailor your argument to be responsive to those concerns. Oral argument is your only opportunity to directly address the concerns of individual judges. Do not be disturbed if the questions from the bench take you out of your prepared sequence. You use your allotted time most effectively by focusing on those matters about which the court is undecided. Do not consider every question as an attack on your position. Some questions are designed to support your view. If you are asked a helpful question, try to recognize it and use it to your advantage.

As noted previously, the types of questions the judges ask will vary. A judge might seek information about the facts or raise policy considerations. He or she could ask about the authorities upon which you or your opponent rely for support. You might be asked about the ramifications of a particular legal argument. If you have formulated answers to a variety of questions in advance, you should be able to use most questions to advance your argument.

To handle questions from the bench effectively, remember six basic rules:

1. Listen to the question very carefully. To respond to it, you must fully understand the judge's concerns. Never cut a judge off in the middle of a question.

2. Be sure you understand the question. If you did not understand the question, ask the court to repeat it. If you think you understand the question but are not certain, begin your answer by restating the question.

3. Think before you speak. If you need to think about the question before you can effectively answer it, do so. A brief pause will indicate to the court that you are considering the question and formulating a precise and thorough response.

4. Be responsive. Answer the question directly. Some first-time advocates have a tendency, particularly early in the argument, to give long, rambling answers that cover much more ground than the question requires. Such an

answer may obscure the point you need to make and may bore or confuse your listeners. It also may suggest new questions to the judge.

Do not hedge when answering a question, or the judge may think that you are being evasive. If the question seeks information you do not have, say so. If you cannot answer a question for other reasons, it sometimes helps to fall back on a general statement of your fundamental argument on the issue. Do not overuse this device. Seek to explain and clarify your position to the judge's satisfaction. When you feel that you have answered the question and additional inquiries are not immediately forthcoming, move on. Do not wait for a signal from the bench giving you permission to proceed.

5. Be an advocate. Use your responses to the court's questions as a vehicle to present and advance your argument, even if you must depart from the order set out in your outline. If you are interrupted by a judge, be polite and answer the question immediately. Never ask the judge to wait until later in your argument for an answer. Once the court is satisfied with your answers and you have fully presented your arguments on a particular issue or point, make a smooth transition to the next issue or point. Try to get your argument back on track if it has been disrupted by questioning, but if you have fully discussed a point in response to questions, do not go back and present the argument again from your outline. You will waste valuable time and confuse the bench, and you may invite new questions that will force you back into issues you would rather not spend any more time on.

6. Prepare in advance for questions. At the risk of repeating ourselves yet again, good preparation is the key to answering questions. A thorough understanding of your case will permit you to spot both your weak points and your opponents' strong ones. These areas will be the source of many questions from the bench.

Be prepared for a wide variety of personalities on the bench. Some benches take on personalities themselves, which may range from "cold" benches that ask very few questions to "hot" benches that rapidly fire questions at you. Sometimes the judges are not prepared and may not even have read your brief. Others may have read only parts of it. You may get very few questions or an unending stream of questions. You may get thoughtful, probing questions or questions that seem completely irrelevant. Your role in the argument is to address the particular concerns of the court, whatever they may be, and to answer all questions to the best of your ability.

§ 29.06 Oral Argument Checklist

_____ Identify and articulate the fundamental reason or reasons your client deserves to win; prepare a short explanatory statement for use during the argument.

_____ Select the two or three major points you intend to make during the argument, and decide upon the order in which they will be presented.

_____ Think through the implications of your major arguments, and identify the policy goals served by those arguments.

_____ Identify key facts, and prepare a short statement of your client's perspective on those facts, if they are helpful to your case.

_____ Prepare your introduction, conclusion, and road map.

_____ Anticipate questions, and formulate answers to any questions you can be reasonably sure the judges will ask.

_____ Know the facts, holdings and rationales of any important cases relied upon by you or your opponent(s).

_____ Prepare your argument aids, remembering to keep them as short as you can.

APPENDIX I

CITATION FORM

Revised to conform to the sixteenth edition of **The Bluebook: A Uniform System of Citation (1996)**

This Appendix contains five lessons that teach you how to cite legal authorities in conformity with *The Bluebook: A Uniform System of Citation* (16th ed. 1996), also known as "the Bluebook." Please turn to Chapter 1 of this book and read again § 1.05 on citation form.

These five lessons do not cover all the intricacies of the Bluebook. They cover the rules you need to cite most materials that you will use in your first year legal writing course. Once you have completed the lessons, you will know how to use the Bluebook when you have a question about citation form. You will feel comfortable in referring to the table of contents or index to find the appropriate rules and illustrations. You also will have a sense of the typical problems that arise in citing authorities.

You should come to realize the advantages of using the Bluebook in conjunction with a recent issue of a quality law review. By comparing the citations in the law review's footnotes with the Bluebook's rules, you should be able to ascertain the correct citation form. Be careful to use a law review that conforms to the sixteenth edition of the Bluebook. Note, however, that typeface conventions are different for law reviews and the rules for abbreviating case names sometimes differ. You will learn about these differences in the Introduction and Lesson One.

To complete these lessons, you must refer to the Bluebook repeatedly. Requiring you to use the Bluebook is part of our teaching strategy. Our goal is not to explain the rules in plain English, but to teach you how to use the Bluebook. You learn by using the Bluebook. For your convenience, we have written the lessons so that you need not use a law library to complete them.

The Bluebook prescribes certain rules for law reviews and slightly different rules for practitioners. In this course, you will be drafting the documents that practitioners draft. Therefore, we will follow the rules set forth in the "Practitioners' Notes," pages 10-19.

SUMMARY OF THE LESSONS

INTRODUCTION: A Note on Typeface

LESSON ONE: Citing State Cases; Abbreviating Case Names; A Word of Encouragement

LESSON TWO: Citing United States Supreme Court Cases and Other Federal Cases; More Rules on Citing Cases

LESSON THREE: Bluebook Style

LESSON FOUR: Citing Constitutions and Statutes

LESSON FIVE: Citing Books and Periodicals

EXPANDED DESCRIPTION

INTRODUCTION:	A Note on Typeface
LESSON ONE:	Citing State Cases; Abbreviating Case Names; A Word of Encouragement

    A. State Cases

        1. Citation Form
        2. Summary
        3. Problems
        4. Exercise

    B. Case Names

        1. Introduction
        2. Problems I
        3. Problems II

    C. A Word of Encouragement

LESSON TWO:	Citing United States Supreme Court Cases and Other Federal Cases; More Rules on Citing Cases

    A. Supreme Court Cases

    B. Other Federal Cases

        1. United States Court of Appeals
        2. District Courts

    C. Exercise

    D. More on Citing Cases

        1. Cases on Electronic Databases
        2. Prior and Subsequent History

            (a) Multiple Decisions Within a Single Year
            (b) Different Case Names on Appeal

        3. Exercise

C. Short Citation Forms for Books and Periodicals

INTRODUCTION: A NOTE ON TYPEFACE

Most examples in the Bluebook use the typefaces that a law review uses. In writing memoranda and briefs, type citations in Roman type. Compare the inside front pages of the Bluebook with the inside back pages. For a full explanation, see pages 11-13 of the Bluebook. These pages are within a section of light blue pages called Practitioners' Notes. The rules within these pages are the ones we will follow in drafting legal memoranda and court documents.

Here is how to adapt the citations you find in law reviews to your typewriter or word processor.

1. When a law review uses italics, use Roman type and underline.

2. When a law review uses large and small capital letters, use upper case Roman letters for the large capitals and lower case Roman letters for the small capitals. In the case of a book title, underline as well.

3. When the name of a court case appears in a memorandum, brief, or letter, underline it and any procedural phrases, such as "cert. denied" and "ex rel."

4. When in doubt, consult the inside back cover of the Bluebook and pages 11-13.

5. If your typewriter or word processor cannot print the section symbol (§), type "sec." When "section" is the first word of a sentence, spell it out. (Rule 6.2(b), p. 49)

LESSON ONE: CITING STATE CASES; ABBREVIATING CASE NAMES; A WORD OF ENCOURAGEMENT

A. State Cases

1. Citation Form

Please begin by skimming pages 5-6 and 55-68 of the Bluebook for an overview. The best way to learn how to cite a case in a state court is to examine a citation and see what information it contains. Here is a citation to a case decided by the Utah Supreme Court.

State v. Hunt, 607 P.2d 297 (Utah 1980)

The "P.2d" tells us that the case is in the Pacific Reporter, second series, usually called the "Pacific Second."

If you do not know what a case reporter is, consult the course materials for your Legal Research course and visit the library to have a look. The case is in volume 607, and the opinion begins on page 297. The state's name without any reference to a particular state court means that the highest court in the state decided the case. See Rule 10.4(b) (p. 64) in the Bluebook. The year is the year that the court handed down the decision. It is not necessarily the year that the court heard the case argued.

The United States Jurisdictions Table, beginning on page 165 of the Bluebook, gives information on how to cite cases from specific jurisdictions. Please turn to page 221. The information on Utah tells which reporter to cite. We are examining a 1980 case. The Bluebook therefore requires a cite to the Pacific Second. We could not cite to the Utah Reports, because the series ceased publication in 1974. The Utah Reports was the state's official reporter. Utah published it as the official record of its state's supreme court decisions. Pacific Second is the unofficial reporter, because it is published by a commercial enterprise, the West Group.

Here is a citation to a Pennsylvania case.

Liss v. Medary Homes, 388 Pa. 139, 145, 130 A.2d 137, 140 (1957)

Please turn to page 210 of the Bluebook. Here we learn that "Pa." stands for Pennsylvania State Reports, which contains decisions of the Pennsylvania Supreme Court. It is the official state reporter for the court. In the previous example, we learned that the Utah Supreme Court has had no official reporter since 1974; that is, the state no longer publishes a official record of the state's supreme court opinions. Therefore we cited only the unofficial reporter. When a state has an official reporter, the Bluebook instructs us to cite to it and to the regional unofficial West Reporter when we are including the case in a document we are submitting to a Pennsylvania state court. The last three lines on page 210 and the first two lines on page 211 give this instruction and tell us the order in which to cite the reporters.

If we were submitting the document to a court other than a Pennsylvania court or if we were writing an interoffice memorandum, we would omit the citation to the Pennsylvania State Reports. The cite would look like this:

Liss v. Medary Homes, 130 A.2d 137, 140 (Pa. 1957)

Suppose we are including the case in a brief we are submitting to a Pennsylvania court. The cite then would include reference to both the Pennsylvania State Reports and the Atlantic Second. Citations to more than one reporter are called parallel citations. Note that information on the Atlantic Reporter appears as the last entry in the section on citing cases by the Pennsylvania Supreme Court.

In the examples above, two page numbers follow the name of each reporter. In each instance, the first is the first page of the court decision in the respective reporter. The second indicates that the writer is referring to specific language in the opinion. The language appears on page 145 of the Pennsylvania State Reports and on page 140 of the Atlantic Second. Reference to a specific page is called a pinpoint cite. Whenever you give a pinpoint cite, give the appropriate page number for each reporter in the citation.

The cite to "Pa." tells us that the state supreme court decided the case, because the Pennsylvania State Reports includes only opinions by that court. Therefore we do not include the name of the state in the parenthesis with the date of decision. Include the jurisdiction and the court's name only when the reader otherwise cannot determine this information from the rest of the citation. See Rule 10.4(b) (p. 64).

Here is one more illustration. Suppose we are including this case in a document that we are submitting to a New York state court:

Clark v. Geraci, 29 Misc. 2d 791, 208 N.Y.S.2d 564 (Sup. Ct. 1960)

Please turn to page 200. Because the cite is to a case in the Supreme Court, the information on "other lower courts" is pertinent. (In New York, the Supreme Court is not the state's highest court.) As in the previous illustration, the case has parallel citations. The Bluebook tells us to cite to Misc. 2d first and then to N.Y.S.2d. If you were to look at the reporters included in the cite, you would discover that each reporter includes cases from a variety of courts. The names of the reporters alone would not tell you that a New York Supreme Court decided the case. Therefore the citation states the court's name explicitly.

Note that there is a space before the "2d" in the cite to Miscellaneous Reports, Second Series, and there is no space before the "2d" in the cite to the New York Supplement, Second Series. Rule 6.1(a) (p. 47) governs. When in doubt, follow the example in the Bluebook.

If we were including this case in a brief we were submitting to a court in California, for example, or in an interoffice memorandum, we would cite only to N.Y.S.2d:

Clark v. Geraci, 208 N.Y.S.2d 564 (Sup. Ct. 1960)

2. Summary

Here is a summary of what you have learned thus far about citing state court cases.

1. Cite the reporters that the United States Jurisdiction Table directs you to cite. Give parallel citations when required. Include the volume and the page number on which the decision begins. When referring to a specific page in the opinion, give a pinpoint cite and include the parallel page number for each reporter in the citation.

2. If the names of the cited reporters do not indicate the court unambiguously, include the name of the court in the parenthesis with the date. Indicate the state's highest court by including only the abbreviated name of the state. Indicate a lower court by using the designation that the Bluebook requires.

3. Include the date on which the court handed down the decision, not the date on which the attorneys filed or argued the case.

3. Problems

Next, we will complete three citation problems.

Problem I

Assume you are including this citation in a brief you are submitting to a Pennsylvania state court. The case name is Valley Trust Co. v. Lapitsky. The Pennsylvania Superior Court decided the case in 1985. The opinion appears in the Pennsylvania Superior Court Reports, volume 339, page 177. It also appears in volume 488 of the Atlantic Second at page 608.

Begin by turning to page 210 to see how to cite Pennsylvania Superior Court cases. The Bluebook requires references to both reporters, first the "Pa. Super." and then the "A.2d." The citation to Pa. Super. implicitly communicates the name of the court, because the reporter includes only cases that the Pennsylvania Superior Court has decided. We therefore do not include the court's name in the citation. The correct citation is:

Valley Trust Co. v. Lapitsky, 339 Pa. Super. 177, 488 A.2d 608 (1985).

Problem II

Assume you are including the citation in a brief you are submitting to a federal court. The Oklahoma Court of Criminal Appeals decided *Garner v. State*

in 1972. The case appears in volume 500 of the Pacific Second and begins on page 1340.

Please begin by turning to page 209. Whether we are including the citation in a brief to a federal court or to an Oklahoma state court, the Bluebook tells us that we must cite only to "P.2d." "Okla. Crim." stopped publication before 1972. A citation to P.2d alone would create ambiguity about the name of the court. That reporter includes court opinions from a variety of states as well as from the Oklahoma Supreme Court. We therefore must include the name of the court in the citation. The Bluebook gives us the abbreviation to use. The correct citation is:

Garner v. State, 500 P.2d 1340 (Okla. Crim. App. 1972)

Problem III

Assume you are including this citation in a brief that you are submitting to a California state court. The California Supreme Court decided *Kapellas v. Kofman* in 1969. It appears in three reporters: volume 1 of California Reports, Third Series, beginning on page 20; volume 459 of Pacific Second, beginning on page 912; and volume 81 of the California Reporter, beginning on page 360. In your citation, you want to refer to specific language located on page 35 of the first reporter, pages 921-22 of the second, and pages 369-70 of the third.

Please begin by turning to page 173. The Bluebook tells us to include references to all three reporters in a particular order: first, Cal. 3d, next, P.2d, and finally, Cal. Rptr. Only California Supreme Court cases appear in Cal. 3d. You can determine this fact by looking at the reporter or by employing deductive logic as you read pages 173-4. The reference to this reporter implicitly identifies the court. We therefore do not state the court's name explicitly. The correct citation is:

Kapellas v. Kofman, 1 Cal. 3d 20, 35, 459 P.2d 912, 921-22, 81 Cal. Rptr. 360, 369-70 (1969).

If you were including this citation in an interoffice memorandum or a brief to an Illinois state court, the correct citation would be

Kapellas v. Kofman, 459 P.2d 912, 921-22 (Cal. 1969)

4. Exercise

Here is the information needed to write the citations for four cases. Please write the citations in Bluebook form.

(a) You plan to include this case in a brief you will submit to the New York Court of Appeals. The New York Supreme Court decided Doe v. Roe in 1977. The decision appears in volume 400 of the New York Supplement, Second Series, at page 668 and in volume 93 of the New York Miscellaneous Reports, Second Series, at page 201.

(b) You plan to include this case in a brief you will submit to the Washington Court of Appeals. The Washington Court of Appeals decided Eddy v. Moore in 1971. The decision appears in volume 5 of the Washington Appellate Reports at page 334 and in volume 487 of the Pacific Second at page 211.

(c) You plan to include this case in a brief you will submit to the Texas Court of Appeals. The Texas Supreme Court decided Humber v. Morton in 1968. The decision appears in volume 426 of the Southwestern Second at page 554 and in volume 25 of the American Law Reports, Third Series, at page 372.

(d) You plan to include this case in a brief you will submit to the Illinois Appellate Court. The Illinois Appellate Court decided Edmonds v. Heil in 1948. The case appears in volume 333 of the Illinois Appellate Court Reports, beginning on page 497, and in volume 77 of the Northeastern Second, beginning on page 863. You want to give a pinpoint cite to language appearing on page 501 in the first reporter and page 866 in the second.

(e) Please refer to Exercise 4(d). You plan to include the pinpoint cite to Edmonds v. Heil in a brief you will submit to an Ohio court.

B. Case Names

1. Introduction

The rest of Lesson One teaches you how to abbreviate the names of cases. Please begin by skimming Rule 10.2 in the Bluebook (p. 56-61).

The Bluebook's policy is to keep case names as short as possible without creating confusion. For example, if the case's full name is *Donna Doe v. Roberta Roe*, the Bluebook requires omitting the first names. The shortened result is *Doe v. Roe*.

In legal documents, a case name may appear in a textual sentence. It also may appear simply as a citation and not as part of a textual sentence. The opening paragraphs of Rule 10.2 (p. 56) offer an illustration of each instance. In all instances, the Bluebook employs the same rules for abbreviating the case name with one exception. When the case name appears as a citation and not as part of a textual sentence, the Bluebook requires greater abbreviation. See the opening paragraphs of Rule 10.2 (p. 56) and Rule 10.2.2 (p. 61).

2. Problems I

Read the opening paragraphs of Rule 10.2.1. Then please read Rules 10.2.1(a), (c), (d) & (e) and Rules 10.2.2(a) & (b). Here are six case names. Please rewrite them so that they conform to the Bluebook rules. Rewrite them as they would appear in a textual sentence and then as they would appear in a citation not part of a textual sentence. The answers follow. Please do not look at them until you complete the exercise. If you ignore these directions, you will learn far less.

(a) Francis Gryger v. C.J. Burke, Warden, Eastern State Penitentiary

(b) State Life Insurance Company, et al. v. Board of Education

(c) John Rocco v. The Johns-Manville Corporation

(d) Northern Pipeline Construction Company v. Marathon Pipeline Co.

(e) San Antonio Independent School District v. Rodriguez

(f) Federal Communications Commission v. Pacifica Foundation

The Answers

(a) Both text and citation: *Gryger v. Burke*

(b) Text: *State Life Insurance Co. v. Board of Education*

   Citation: *State Life Ins. Co. v. Board of Educ.*

(c) Both text and citation: *Rocco v. Johns-Manville Corp.*

(d) Text: *Northern Pipeline Construction Co. v. Marathon Pipeline Co.*

   Citation: *Northern Pipeline Constr. Co. v. Marathon Pipeline Co.*

(e) Text: *San Antonio Independent School District v. Rodriguez*

   Citation: *San Antonio Indep. Sch. Dist. v. Rodriguez*

(f) Text: *FCC v. Pacifica Foundation*

   Citation: *FCC v. Pacifica Found.*

3. **Problem II**

Please read Rules 10.2.1(b), (f), (g), (h), (i) & (j). Also keep in mind the rules you have studied already. Here are eight case names. Please rewrite them so that they conform to the Bluebook as they would appear in both textual sentences and citations. The answers follow. Again, please complete the exercise before you look at the answers.

(a) Cole v. Housing Authority of Newport

(b) Korematsu v. United States

(c) In the matter of Gault

(d) Rose & Crown, Limited v. Shaw Enterprises, Inc.

(e) Republic Investment Company v. Naches Hotel Co.

(f) Commissioners of Lewes v. Breakwater Fisheries

(g) U.S. ex rel. Ricketts v. Lightcap

(h) Tuttle v. W.T. Grant Co.

The Answers

(a) Text: *Cole v. Housing Authority*

Citation: *Cole v. Housing Auth.*

(b) Both text and citation: *Korematsu v. United States*

(c) Both text and citation: *In re Gault*

(d) Text: *Rose & Crown, Ltd. v. Shaw Enterprises, Inc.*

Citation: *Rose & Crown, Ltd. v. Shaw Enters., Inc.*

(e) Text: *Republic Investment Co. v. Naches Hotel Co.*

Citation: *Republic Inv. Co. v. Naches Hotel Co.*

(f) Both text and citation: *Commissioners of Lewes v. Breakwater Fisheries*

(g) Both text and citation: *United States ex rel. Ricketts v. Lightcap*

(h) Both text and citation: *Tuttle v. W.T. Grant Co.*

C. **A Word of Encouragement**

Are you expected to memorize the intricacies of the rules we have just discussed? Of course not. If you did, you would forget them in a matter of days. Your goal is to learn what the rules are in general terms and what specific problems frequently crop up. When you are writing citations in the future, you will have the Bluebook at your elbow. As you formulate a cite, you will recognize that the Bluebook probably has an applicable rule, and you will turn to the appropriate page. Learn as much as you can now. Close attention to these lessons will save you enormous amounts of time in the future.

LESSON TWO: CITING UNITED STATES SUPREME COURT CASES AND OTHER FEDERAL CASES; MORE RULES ON CITING CASES

A. Supreme Court Cases

The method for citing Supreme Court and other federal cases is essentially the same as for citing state court cases. Please begin by reading the material about Supreme Court citations on page 165. Then please read the material dealing with federal cases in Rules 10.3.2 (p. 62) and 10.4(a) (p. 63).

When you cite a Supreme Court case, include a reference to only one reporter. If the case already appears in the official reporter, United States Reports (U.S.), cite to it. Otherwise, cite to West's Supreme Court Reporter (S. Ct.). If it has not yet appeared there, cite to Lawyer's Edition (L. Ed.). If it has not yet appeared there, cite to United States Law Week (U.S.L.W.). As an example, the proper cite to *Red Lion Broadcasting Co. v. FCC* is:

Red Lion Broadcasting Co. v. FCC, 395 U.S. 367 (1969)

An incorrect cite would be:

Red Lion Broadcasting Co. v. FCC, 395 U.S. 367, 89 S. Ct. 1794, 23 L. Ed. 2d 371 (1969).

You see this latter form frequently. Because it contains citations to three reporters and, therefore, furnishes three sources for the same case, it serves as a convenience for the reader. Do not use this form when you must conform to the Bluebook.

If the case had not yet appeared in the official reporter, the proper cite would be:

Red Lion Broadcasting Co. v. FCC, 89 S. Ct. 1794 (1969)

If the case had not yet appeared in the Supreme Court Reporter, the proper cite would be:

Red Lion Broadcasting Co. v. FCC, 37 U.S.L.W. 4509 (U.S. June 9, 1969)

The "U.S." in parentheses indicates that the citation is to the Supreme Court Section of United States Law Week. See Rule 10.4(a) (p. 63).

When you cite to *U.S. Law Week* or any similar commercial service, include the month, day, and year of the decision. See the opening sentence of Rule 10.5 (p. 64).

When you cite a case in the first ninety volumes of the *United States Reports* (before 1875), include the editor's name in the cite as well as the volume of his series. See Rule 10.3.2 (p. 62). For the correct abbreviations of the editors' names, see page 165 of the Bluebook. Here are examples:

Swift v. Tyson, 41 U.S. (16 Pet.) 1 (1842)

Watson v. Jones, 80 U.S. (13 Wall.) 679 (1872)

Note that in each instance you are citing one volume and not two parallel volumes.

B. Other Federal Cases

Please begin by reviewing Rule 10.4(a) (p. 63) and page 165.

1. United States Courts of Appeals

Virtually all cases of the United States Courts of Appeals that you will be citing appear in the Federal Reporter, First, Second or Third Series (F.,F.2d or F.3d), except for very early cases. The Bluebook has rules for citing earlier cases as well as cases decided by the old Circuit Courts. See page 165. Always identify the particular court:

Sykes v. United States, 444 F.2d 928 (D.C. Cir. 1971)

Riley v. City of Chester, 612 F.2d 708 (3d Cir. 1979)

Note that the Bluebook abbreviates the Second Circuit as "2d Cir.," the Third Circuit as "3d Cir.," and the Fourth Circuit as "4th Cir."

2. District Courts

In most instances, you will cite to the Federal Supplement (F. Supp.), the preferred reporter. Some cases, however, do not appear in this reporter. For those cases, cite to another reporter. See Rule 10.3.1(b) (p. 61) and page 165. In each citation, identify the particular district court. See rule 10.4(a) (p. 63) and page 167. Here are examples.

Reichenberg v. Nelson, 310 F. Supp. 248 (D. Neb. 1970).

Caton v. Barry, 500 F. Supp. 45, 48 (D.D.C. 1980).

County of Suffolk v. Secretary of the Interior, 76 F.R.D. 469 (E.D.N.Y. 1977).

Note the spacing in the abbreviations of the district court names. See Rule 6.1(a) (p.47). See also the examples in Rule 10.4(a) (p. 63).

C. Exercise

Please rewrite these six citations in correct Bluebook form. Note: The case names are in correct form.

(a) *Gertz v. Robert Welch, Inc.*, 418 U.S. 323, 94 S. Ct. 2997, 41 L. Ed. 2d 789 (1974)

(b) *Smith v. Orton*, 21 Howard 241, 242, 62 U.S. 241 (1858)

(c) *Rhoades v. Powell*, 644 Federal Supplement, 645 (United States District Court, Eastern District, California, Sept. 5, 1986)

(d) *United States v. Hubbard*, 493 F.Supp. 202 (D. D.C. 1979)

(e) *Accuracy in Media, Inc. v. FCC*, 521 F. 2d 288 (D.C.Cir. 1975)

(f) *Chuy v. Philadelphia Eagles Football Club*, 595 F.2d 1265, 1280 (3rd. Cir. 1979)

D. More on Citing Cases

In this section, you will learn how to cite unpublished cases that appear on electronic databases such as LEXIS and WESTLAW. You also will learn how to cite a case's prior and subsequent history.

1. Cases on Electronic Databases

Sometimes a case does not appear in a reporter, but appears on an electronic database such as LEXIS or WESTLAW. Rule 10.8.1(a) (p. 68) explains how to cite such a case. The cite includes the name of the case, its docket number, its WESTLAW or LEXIS identification number, its screen or page number, the court, and date of decision. The Bluebook offers several examples.

2. Prior and Subsequent History

Please begin by reading Rules 10.7 & 10.7.1. (p. 65-66) as well as Table T.9 (p. 292). A citation must include a case's subsequent history, that is, subsequent court decisions on the same case. There are three exceptions. First, omit denials of certiorari and denials of similar discretionary appeals unless either (a) the decision is less than two years old or (b) the decision is particularly relevant. Second, omit the history of the case on remand and any denial of rehearing unless this information is relevant to a point you are making. Third, omit any disposition withdrawn by the deciding authority, such as an affirmance followed by reversal on rehearing. Here are citations that include subsequent history:

Afroyim v. Rusk, 361 F.2d 102 (2d Cir. 1966), *rev'd*, 387 U.S. 253 (1967)

United States v. Eller, 208 F.2d 716 (4th Cir. 1953), *cert. denied*, 347 U.S. 934 (1954)

Note that all parenthetical expressions, such as *rev'd* and *cert. denied*, are italicized, whether the citation is part of a textual sentence or stands alone. P.1(d) (p. 13); Rule 10.7.1(a) (p. 66).

Omit a case's prior history unless (1) it is relevant to a point you are making or (2) the earlier decision is necessary to intelligibly describe the issues in the case you are citing. Here are citations that include prior history:

Troy, Ltd. v. Renna, 727 F.2d 287 (3d Cir. 1984), *rev'g* 580 F. Supp. 69 (D.N.J. 1982).

In re Burrus, 403 U.S. 528 (1971), *aff'g* 275 N.C. 517, 169 S.E.2d 879 (1969).

(a) **Multiple Decisions Within a Single Year**

Please read Rule 10.5(d) (p. 65). This rule applies when you include a case's prior or subsequent history. When different decisions are in the same year, include the year only at the end of the citation.

> *Haelan Laboratories v. Topps Chewing Gum, Inc.*, 202 F.2d 866 (2d Cir.), *cert. denied*, 346 U.S. 816 (1953).

> *Volkman v. Miller*, 52 A.D.2d 146, 383 N.Y.S.2d 95, *aff'd*, 41 N.Y.2d 946, 363 N.E.2d 355, 394 N.Y.S.2d 631 (1977).

The next citation includes three opinions. The latter two appeared in the same year.

> *Foremost Int'l Tours, Inc. v. Qantas Airways, Ltd.*, 478 F. Supp. 589 (D. Haw. 1979), *aff'd*, 629 F.2d 867 (9th Cir.), *cert. denied*, 454 U.S. 967 (1981).

(b) **Different Case Names on Appeal**

Please read Rule 10.7.2 (p. 67). When you write the citation of a case that has a different name in its prior or subsequent history, the general rule requires giving both names. The rule, however, makes broad exceptions. In general, include both names only when the names are different, not just in reverse order. Even when the names are different, do not include both when the citation in which the difference occurs is a denial of cert. or of a rehearing. In the next three examples, the rule requires including both names.

> *Rosenfeld v. Lent*, 353 F. Supp. 23 (D. Mass.), *aff'd sub nom. Healy v. Lent*, 449 F.2d 232 (1st Cir. 1971).

> *Barlow's, Inc. v. Usery*, 424 F. Supp. 437 (D. Idaho 1976), *aff'd sub nom. Marshall v. Barlow's, Inc.*, 436 U.S. 307 (1978).

> *Marshall v. Barlow's, Inc.*, 436 U.S. 307 (1978), *aff'g Barlow's, Inc. v. Usery*, 424 F. Supp. 437 (D. Idaho 1976).

In the last two examples, one requires the phrase "sub nom.," and the other does not. Read Rule 10.7.2 (p. 66) to understand why.

Exercise

Please rewrite these citations so that they are correct. Please include citations to prior and subsequent history. Rewrite them as citations as opposed to parts of textual sentences. Hint: see Rule 10.2.2 (p. 61).

> (a) United States v. Haaf, 532 F.2d 368 (5th Cir. 1977, *vacated and remanded*, Haaf v. United States, 434 U.S. 1030 (1978).

> (b) Luskey v. Steffron, Inc., 461 Pa. 305, 336 A.2d 298 (1975), *affirmed on rehearing*, 469 Pa. 377, 366 A.2d 223 (1976), *cert. denied sub nom.*

Steffron, Inc. v. Luskey, 430 U.S. 968 (1977). Assume you are citing this case in a brief you will submit to a Pennsylvania court.

(c) *In re* Dino, 359 So. 2d 586 (La. 1978), *cert. denied* 439 U.S. 1047 (1978).

(d) Community Blood Bank v. Russell, 196 So. 2d 115 (Fla. 1967), *aff'g sub nom.* Russell v. Community Blood Bank, 185 So. 2d 749 (Fla. Dist. Ct. App. 1966).

(e) *In re* Establishment Inspection of Gilbert & Bennett Mfg. Co., 589 F.2d 1335 (7th Cir. 1979), *cert. denied sub nom.* Chromalloy American Corp. v. Marshall, 444 U.S. 884 (1979).

LESSON THREE: BLUEBOOK STYLE

In this lesson, you will learn about signals; order of authority within a signal; short forms and cross-references; parentheticals; abbreviations, numbers, and signals; and quotations.

A. **Signals and Their Order of Importance**

A signal is a phrase that appears at the beginning of a citation to indicate how much persuasive authority the cited material carries. Please read Rules 1.2 & 1.3 (pp. 22-24). Here is an excerpt from an appellate brief. Note how it uses signals to indicate the weight of various authorities. Be sure you understand the meaning of each signal and the reason the signals appear in this particular order.

> "[In its] review, the court may substitute its judgment for that of the [fact-finder]." *Helvering v. Tex-Penn Oil Co.*, 300 U.S. 481, 491 (1937); *accord Bogardus v. Commissioner*, 302 U.S. 34, 39 (1937); *Helvering v. Rankin*, 295 U.S. 123, 131 (1935); *cf. United States v. General Motors Corp.*, 384 U.S. 127, 141 n.16 (1966); *United States v. United States Gypsum Co.*, 333 U.S. 364, 396 (1948). *But see Commissioner v. Duberstein*, 363 U.S. 278, 289 n.11 (1960).

Note the use of semicolons and periods. The writer cites several supporting authorities and introduces different ones with different signals. All the supporting authorities are treated as part of a single sentence. A semicolon appears between each authority and before each new signal. Contrary authorities are treated as part of a separate sentence. See Rules 1.1(a)(1) (p. 21), 1.3 (p. 24) & P.2 (p. 13).

B. **Order of Authority Within a Signal**

1. **The Rule**

Please read Rule 1.4 (p. 25). Here is an edited excerpt from an appellate brief. Be sure you understand why the cases appear in this particular order. Note: when you cite two cases that the same court decided, list the cases in reverse chronological order.

> *See Gertz v. Robert Welch, Inc.*, 418 U.S. 323 (1975); *Rosenbloom v. Metromedia, Inc.*, 403 U.S. 29 (1971); *Time, Inc. v. Pape*, 401 U.S. 279 (1971); *Greenbelt Cooperative Publishing Ass'n v. Bresler*, 398 U.S. 6 (1970); *Rosenblatt v. Baer*, 383 U.S. 75 (1966); *Garrison v. Louisiana*, 379 U.S. 64 (1964); *New York Times Co. v. Sullivan*, 376 U.S. 254 (1964).

Here is another example. Please assume it comes from a brief filed with a Michigan court.

> *In re Gault*, 387 U.S. 1 (1967); *People v. Chapman*, 301 Mich. 584, 4 N.W.2d 18 (1942); *In re Mundy*, 85 A.2d 371 (N.H. 1952); *In re Moulton*, 77 A.2d 26 (N.H. 1950).

Here is a final example. It cites a Restatement, two books, and three law review articles. To understand the order of citation, please review Rule 1.4(i) (p.27).

> *See* Restatement (Second) of Torts § 580A comment g (1977); Thomas I. Emerson, *The System of Freedom of Expression* 535-37 (1970); Robert D. Sack, *Libel, Slander, and Related Problems* 538, 560 (1980); David A. Anderson, *Libel and Press Self-Censorship*, 53 Tex. L. Rev. 422, 467-68 (1975); James L. Oakes, *Proof of Actual Malice in Defamation Actions: An Unsolved Dilemma*, 7 Hofstra L. Rev. 655, 707-09 (1979); David W. Robertson, *Defamation and the First Amendment: In Praise of* Gertz v. Robert Welch, Inc., 54 Tex. L. Rev. 199, 249-50 (1976).

In the citation to the last law review article, note that the name of the case is not italicized. See the first illustration in Rule 16.5.1(a) (p. 115).

2. Exercise

Please rewrite these citation sentences so that the signals and authorities appear in proper order. Assume the excerpt comes from a brief filed with a California court.

> *Kline v. 1500 Mass. Ave. Apartment Corp.*, 439 F.2d 477 (D.C. Cir. 1970). *See also* Peter S. Selvin, *Landlord Tort Liability for Criminal Attacks on Tenants: Developments Since* Kline, 9 Real Est. L.J. 311 (1981); Comment, *The Landlord's Emerging Responsibility for Tenant Security*, 71 Colum. L. Rev. 275 (1971); Benjamin N. Henszey & Eileen D. Weisman, *What Is the Landlord's Responsibility for Criminal Acts Committed on the Premises?*, 6 Real Est. L.J. 104 (1977). *See Abbott v. New York Pub. Library*, 32 N.Y.S.2d 963 (App. Div. 1942); *Morris v. Barnette*, 553 S.W.2d 648 (Tex. Civ. App. 1977); *Eastep v. Jack-in-the-Box, Inc.*, 546 S.W.2d 116 (Tex. Civ. App. 1977); *Cf. Wallace v. Der-Ohanian*, 199 Cal. App. 2d 141, 18 Cal. Rptr. 892 (1962). *But cf.* Restatement (Second) of Torts § 314 (1966).

Note: In 1971, the *Columbia Law Review* did not disclose the names of students who wrote comments.

C. Short Forms and Cross-References

1. The Rules

Please read Rules 3.6, 4.1, 4.2 (pp. 39-43), P.4 (p. 15),and Rule 10.9 (p. 70). Pay particular attention to the examples. Conform to the format that they illustrate.

Do not use *ibid.* instead of *id.*. Use *id.* only when you are referring to the immediately preceding authority and that authority is not part of a string cite including other authority. *Id.* means "the same." *Id.* means you are citing the same authority that you cited just previously. Suppose you cite a case, then cite a statute, and now want to cite the case again. You cannot use *id.* to cite the case, because the case is not the authority that you cited just previously.

Do not use supra to refer to cases except in rare instances, for example, when the name of the case is extremely long. See Rule 4.2. (p. 41). For examples of *supra* in connection with books and articles, see P.4(d) (p. 16).

Practioners' Note 4 (p. 15) explains how to give shortened cites to cases. You usually will use shortened cites when you already have cited the case and want to cite it again and cannot use id. Be sure to study the examples (p. 15-16). The next illustration demonstrates these rules at work.

In *Presbyterian Church in the United States v. Mary Elizabeth Blue Hull Memorial Presbyterian Church*, 393 U.S. 440 (1969), the Court asserted: "States, religious organizations, and individuals must structure relationships involving church property so as not to require the civil courts to resolve ecclesiastical questions." *Id.* at 449. In *Maryland & Virginia Eldership of the Churches of God v. Church of God at Sharpsburg, Inc.*, 396 U.S. 367 (1970), the Court approved a state court decision purporting to apply neutral principles. *See id.* at 368. The phrase "neutral principles" first appeared in the 1969 case. 393 U.S. at 449. Neither *Presbyterian Church* nor *Sharpsburg*, however, offered a detailed explanation of the neutral principles methodology.

Note: Please review Rule 10.2 (p. 56). It requires us to distinguish between (1) a case used as part of a textual sentence and (2) a case used in a citation sentence or a citation clause. For examples of cases as parts of textual sentences, see the first two illustrations in Rule 10.2 (p.56). For examples of citation sentences and clauses, see the third example in Rule 2.2 (p. 56) and the examples in P.2 (p. 14).

When a case name is part of a textual sentence, we use a limited number of abbreviations. Rule 10.2.1 (p.56). When a case appears in a citation sentence or a citation clause, we use still more abbreviations. Rule 10.2.2 (p. 61). In the first sentence of the last example, *Presbyterian Church* is part of a textual sentence even though it contains the citation to the case. In contrast, "Id. at 449" is a citation sentence. It stands as a separate sentence and, therefore, is not part of a textual sentence. The first mention of *Sharpsburg* is in a textual sentence. Therefore, we do not abbreviate "Virginia" in that sentence. If the case's name appeared in a citation sentence, we would abbreviate "Virginia"—for example: *See, e.g., Maryland & Va. Eldership of the Churches of God v. Churches of God at Sharpsburg, Inc.*, 396 U.S. 367 (1970).

2. **Exercise**

Please revise the citations so that they are in proper Bluebook form.

(a) For a comprehensive treatment of state laws governing the corporate status of churches, see Paul G. Kauper & Stephen C. Ellis, *Religious Corporations and the Law*, 71 Mich. L. Rev. 1499 (1973). If a statute required a church to deviate from its religious beliefs regarding internal church affairs, the legislation would be vulnerable to attack under the free exercise clause. Kauper & Ellis, supra at 1566-88.

(b) *See Conflicts of Interest on the American Campus*, The Economist, May 22, 1982, at 107 [hereinafter *Conflicts*].

(c) A court may not reject the determination of thechurch's highest authority by finding that it acted beyond its jurisdiction or failed to comply with church laws. *Serbian E. Orthodox Diocese v. Milivojevich*, 426 U.S. 696, 712-13 (1976). Dicta in *Gonzalez v. Roman Catholic Archbishop*, 280 U.S. 1 (1929) stated that a court need not defer to church authorities when fraud, collusion or arbitrariness is charged. *Ibid.*, at 16. *Serbian* declared that inquiry into allegations ofarbitrariness entails an unconstitutional examination of church procedural or substantive law. 426 U.S. 696, at 713. *Serbian* made clear that it was not evaluating the constitutionality of inquiries into fraud or collusion. *See Serbian* at 713 n.7.

(d) [Use short forms where needed.] In *Pacific States Telephone & Telegraph v. Oregon*, 223 U.S. 118 (1912), the Court refused to examine the constitutional validity of an initiative-enacted statute imposing a license fee on telephone and telegraph companies. In response to company claims that the guaranty clause prohibits such majoritarian excesses, the Court vigorously argued that the issue fell beyond the reach of judicial authority. *Pacific States Telephone & Telegraph v. Oregon*, 223 U.S. 118, 150 (1912). In another case decided the same day, the Court extended the political question doctrine to initiatives at the municipal level. *Kiernan v. City of Portland*, 223 U.S. 151, 164 (1912). In the former case, the Court relied heavily on *Luther v. Borden*, 48 U.S. (7 How.) 1 (1849). *Pacific States Telephone & Telegraph v. Oregon*, 223 U.S. 118, 140-51 (1912). In the 1849 case, the Court refused to determine which of two competing state governments had lawful authority in Rhode Island. *Luther v. Borden*, 48 U.S. (7 How.) 1, 46 (1849).

D. Parentheticals

Please read Rule 10.6 (p. 65). Parentheticals offer a helpful way to furnish explanatory material in a few words. You particularly will appreciate parentheticals when you have a page limit on your memo or brief and need to condense information as much as possible.

E. Abbreviations, Numbers, and Symbols

1. The Rules

Please read Rules 6.1 and 6.2 (p. 47-50). As you can see, the rules are very specific. Be especially sure to:

(a) follow the rules for abbreviations,

(b) follow the rules for spacing and using periods,

(c) know when to use numerals and when to spell out numbers, and

(d) remember to spell out the first word of any sentence.

2. Exercise

Please conform these sentences to Bluebook style.

(a) [in a footnote] The top ten percent includes 13 journals.

(b) [in text] Of these 8 journals, 5 were among the eight that courts cite most frequently.

(c) [in text] The bottom fifty percent of cited journals accounted for 9 percent of all citations.

(d) 100 percent of the books were cited.

(e) [in text that refers to a state statute] The statute's critical provision is § 104 (a).

F. Quotations

1. The Rules

Please read Rules 5.1, 5.2, 5.3 and 5.4 (p. 42-46). Be sure you know:

(a) when and when not to use a block quote;

(b) how to use brackets to substitute words and letters in a quote; and

(c) how to use periods to mark the omission of words, how many periods to use, and when to leave a space before a period.

2. Exercise

Treat the next passage as a quotation. Rewrite it omitting all italicized words. Follow the Bluebook rules for indicating the omissions.

These limitations aside, public interest groups and other special interests do not necessarily indicate their priorities in selecting the proceedings to which they devote their limited resources.

Different types of proceedings require different types of commitments. A group, *for example*, may be concerned with the anticompetitive effects of a corporate reorganization. It may, however, forego a challenge, because participation would consume resources that could yield greater impact if spent on *less demanding*, lower priority projects. No invisible hand insures that groups with limited resources will distribute their efforts in direct proportion to the relative importance that an issue holds *for them*.

(Matthew Bender & Co., Inc.)   (Pub.676)

G. Citing to the Internet

Rule 17.3 offers suggestions for citing to electronic sources and databases. Rule 17.3.3 points out that Internet sources are transient and should not be cited unless other sources are not available. The Rule does offer some guidelines for citing to Internet sources. As more and more legal sources become accessible on the Internet, the frequency with which legal writers will cite to Internet sources will increase. At the moment, there are active debates over citation form, and whether "vender-neutral" citations (in other words, citations that do not refer to published books, LEXIS or WESTLAW) should be allowed. It is likely that acceptable citation forms and sources will change dramatically while you are in law school.

LESSON FOUR: CITING CONSTITUTIONS AND STATUTES

A. Constitutions

1. Citation Form

Please read Rule 11 (p. 73). As you can see, the citation form for constitutions is simple. When citing a state constitution, use the abbreviation for the state's name that appears in Table T.10 (p. 271).

2. Exercise

Please provide the proper citation for each of these constitutional provisions.

(a) Section one of amendment 13 to the federal constitution.

(b) Article 3, section 9 of the Pennsylvania Constitution.

(c) The second indented paragraph of § 4 of amendment XXV of the federal constitution, ratified July 5, 1971. Hint: see Rule 3.4 (p.37).

(d) Preamble to the Alaska Constitution, operative Jan. 3, 1959.

B. Statutes

1. Citation Form

Often the first page in a volume of statutes offers a citation form for the statutes and tells you to follow it. Please ignore this information. The suggested citation form comes from the publisher and rarely conforms to the Bluebook. Follow the Bluebook.

Here is a typical citation to a statute.

29 U.S.C. § 701 (1988).

"U.S.C." refers to the United States Code, the official compilation of federal statutes. Cite to the U.S.C. whenever possible. See page 168 of the Bluebook. See also the opening paragraphs of Rules 12.2.1 (p. 74) and 12.3 (p. 76). The numeral appearing before U.S.C. tells us that § 701 appears in title 29. A title is not the same thing as a volume. A title is a subdivision of a set of statutes. A title may require several volumes or less than one volume.

The date is the year appearing on the spine or title page of the volume in which the statute appears. See Rule 12.3.2 (p. 78). NOTE: In this lesson, these dates often are inaccurate. Publishers frequently issue new volumes and thus change dates. The resulting changes make accurate dates an impossibility.

Suppose § 701 did not yet appear in the U.S.C. In that case, cite an unofficial compilation. See the opening paragraph of Rule 12.2.1 (p. 74). To determine the preferred unofficial compilations for various jurisdictions, refer to Table T.1 in the Bluebook. For federal statutes, the unofficial compilations are U.S.C.A. and U.S.C.S. In our example, the cite would be either:

29 U.S.C.A. § 701 (West 1988)

or

29 U.S.C.S. § 701 (Law. Co-op. 1988).

In each case, the parenthetical includes the name of the publisher as well as the date of the volume.

Suppose § 701 does not yet appear in the main volume of U.S.C., but appears in a supplementary volume designed to update the main volume. If the supplementary volume is called Supplement I and carries the date 1989, the proper citation would be

29 U.S.C. § 701 (Supp. I 1989).

See Rules 12.3.1(e) (p. 77) and 3.2(c) (p. 34).

Suppose § 701 does not yet appear in the U.S.C. or its supplements, but instead appears in the pocket parts to the respective volumes of U.S.C.A. and U.S.C.S. If each pocket part carries the date 1991, then the proper cite is either

29 U.S.C.A. § 701 (West Supp. 1991)

or

29 U.S.C.S. § 701 (Law. Co-op. Supp. 1991).

2. Summary

You now know the basics of citing a statute appearing in a code.

(a) Cite to the official statutory compilation if possible. Otherwise cite to the preferred unofficial compilation. Look to Table T.1 to find the proper statutory compilation and proper citation form. *Warning*: Sometimes the code volume instructs the reader to use a citation form that differs from the Bluebook's prescribed form. Use the Bluebook form.

(b) If the provision or part of it appears in the supplement or pocket part, indicate this fact by following proper Bluebook form.

3. Exercise

Please write citations for these statutory provisions.

(a) Section 3553(a)(2) of title 18 of the United States Code. It appears in Supplementary Volume II, which was published in 1984.

(b) Section 367(f) of the California Penal Code. It appearsin the 1989 pocket part of West's Annotated California Code.

(c) Section 292(21) of the Executive Laws in the New York state statutes. In the compilation published by McKinney, it appears in a volume issued in 1976.

(d) Section 495 of title 21 in Vermont's statutes. The section appears in a pocket part dated 1985.

4. Session Laws

When a statute has not yet appeared in a code or supplement or pocket part to a code, cite to the official session laws, if available. Otherwise cite to the unofficial session laws. Most libraries shelve a jurisdiction's session laws with its statutory codes. For the rules on citing session laws, please read Rule 12.4 (p. 78). To find the proper citation form for a particular jurisdiction's session laws, please consult Table T.1.

5. Uniform Acts and Restatements

The Bluebook has simple rules for citing uniform acts, model acts, and restatements. See Rules 12.8.4 and 12.8.5 (p. 84.)

Restatement of Property § 370 (1944).

Restatement (Second) of Torts § 820 (1977).

Unif. Land Transactions Act § 2-104 (1977).

6. Short Citation Forms for Statutes

Once you give the full citation for a statute, you can use a short form when you cite the statute again in the same general discussion. The short form must identify the statute clearly. See P.4(b) (p. 16). Rule 12.9(b) (p. 86) gives examples of short citation forms. Follow the examples in the column entitled "Short forms." You also may use *id.* when appropriate. See Rule 4.1 (p. 40). Here is an example.

The Deficiency Judgment Act applies only to the judgment creditor who buys the debtor's property in an execution proceeding. 42 Pa. Cons. Stat. § 8103(a) (1982). To collect a deficiency judgment, the mortgage lender who has purchased the property first must obtain a personal judgment against the debtor. *See McDowell Nat'l Bank v. Stupka*, 310 Pa. Super. 143, 147-49, 456 A.2d 540, 542-43 (1983). The lender then must petition the court to fix the property's fair market value in accordance with the Act. 42 Pa. Cons. Stat. § 8103(a). The petition must be filed within six months of the sale. *Id.* § 8103(d). Section 8103(c) of the Act requires the petitioner to assert the property's fair market value.

LESSON FIVE: CITING BOOKS AND PERIODICALS

Books and articles in periodicals, such as law reviews, are the secondary sources that lawyers cite most frequently. The Bluebook's citation rules for these sources are fairly simple.

A. **Books**

1. **Citation Form**

Please read through Rule 15 (p. 103-112). As you can see, the main elements of a book citation are the author's full name, the book's title, the page that you are citing, and the date of publication. Here are three examples:

Bernard Bailyn, *The Ideological Origins of the American Revolution* (1967).

Clinton L. Rossiter, *Seedtime of the Republic* (1955).

Walton H. Hamilton & Douglass G. Adair, *The Power to Govern* (1937).

2. **Author**

Include the author's full name as it appears in the book. If the book has two authors, include both. If it has more than two, include the first author's name followed by "et al." See Rule 15.1.1 (p. 103).

G.K. Chesterton

J. Hector St. John de Crevecour

Edmund S. Morgan & Helen M. Morgan

Archibald Cox et al.

If the author is an institutional author, use the author's complete name. See Rule 15.1.3 (p. 104). Note that the rule permits some abbreviation of the institutional author's name. See Rule 15.1.3(c) (p. 104).

Lawyers Comm. for Human Rights, *Crisis in Crossroads: A Report on Human Rights in South Africa* (1988).

Criminal Justice Section, American Bar Ass'n, *Drunk Driving Laws & Enforcement: An Assessment of Effectiveness* (1986).

3. **Editor**

If a book has an editor instead of an author or in addition to an author, follow Rule 15.1.2 (p. 101). Here are two illustrations:

America in Crisis (Daniel J. Aaron, ed., 1952)

The Era of the American Revolution (Richard B. Morris ed., 1939).

To cite an article or essay within an edited collection, see Rule 15.5.1 (p. 107). Italicized the names of articles and essays in collections. See P.1(b) (p. 12). Here are two examples:

> J. Allen Whitt, *The Arts Coalition in Strategies of Urban Development, in The Politics of Urban Development* 144, 147 (Clarence N. Stone & Heywood T. Sanders eds., 1987).

> A. Leo Levin, *Lessons for Smaller Circuits, Caution for Larger Ones, in Restructuring Justice* 331, 338 (Arthur D. Hellman ed., 1990).

4. **Multivolume Works**

When citing a multivolume work, include the volume number and only the author of the volume cited. See Rules 15.1 (p. 103) and 3.2(a) (p. 33).

> 2 Ellen W. Wertheimer, *Appeals to the Third Circuit* 481 (1986).

> 3 *Documentary History of the First Federal Congress of the United States of America: March 4, 1789-March 3, 1791* 43-44 (Linda Grant De Pauw, ed. 1977).

5. **Sections and Paragraphs**

When citing a book organized by section numbers or paragraphs, consult Rule 3.4 (p. 37) and include the section or paragraph. Include the page number as well if useful in locating the specific matter cited within the section or paragraph. Here are two examples:

> Edward W. Cleary, *McCormick on Evidence* § 12, at 31 (3d ed. 1984).

> Leonard Packel & Anne Bowen Poulin, *Pennsylvania Evidence* § 803.2 (1987).

6. **Special Citation Forms**

Certain books have special citation forms. See Rules 15.7 (p. 109) and 16.5.5. (p. 118). Please pay particular attention to the latter rule. Be sure to study the rule on citing unpublished materials. Rule 17.1 (p. 121). When a published work reprints an unpublished work, include a cite to the published work as well. See Rule 17.1 (p. 121) and 15.5.2(a) (p. 108).

> Letter from J. Skelly Wright to Edward H. Rabin (Oct. 14, 1982), in Edward H.Rabin, *The Revolution in Residential Landlord-Tenant Law: Causes and Consequences*, 69 Cornell L. Rev. 517, 549 (1984).

7. **Exercise**

Please provide the proper citations.

> (a) Page 7 of *The Tolerant Society* by Lee C. Bollinger, published in 1986.

> (b) Page 702 of paragraph 702[03] to volume 3 of *Weinstein's Evidence* by Jack B. Weinstein and Margaret A. Berger. Please cite the edition published in 1981.

(c) An article by Lawrence M. Friedman, entitled "The Law Between the States: Some Thoughts on Southern Legal History." It appears in "Ambivalent Legacy: A Legal History of the South" at page 30. The book was published in 1984, and the editors were David J. Bodenhamer and James W. Ely, Jr.

(d) Section 860 of the article on Corporations in American Jurisprudence, Second Series, volume 18A, published in 1985. The title of the section is "Enforcing contribution in state of incorporation or foreign jurisdiction."

(e) An annotation entitled "Baseball Player's Right to Recover for Baseball-Related Personal Injuries from Nonplayer," beginning on page 664 of volume 55 of American Law Reports, Fourth Series, published in 1987. The author is Karen L. Ellmore.

B. **Periodicals**

1. **Citation Form**

Please skim Rule 16 (p. 112-20) and give particular attention to the examples in Rule 16.1. (p. 113). As you can see, articles in periodicals have a simple citation form. The only moderate difficulty lies in properly abbreviating the periodical's name. A citation usually includes the author's full name, the article's full title, the periodical's volume number, the name of the periodical properly abbreviated (see Table T.13, p. 299), the number of the first page of the article, and the year of publication. If you are referring to a particular page of the article, include it after including the number of the first page of the article. Here are two typical citations to law reviews.

Richard C. Turkington, *Legal Protection for the Confidentiality of Health Care Information in Pennsylvania: Patient and Client Access; Testimonial Privileges; Damage Recovery for Unauthorized Extra-Legal Disclosure*, 32 Vill. L. Rev. 259, 391 (1987).

Louis J. Sirico, Jr. & Jeffrey B. Margulies, *The Citing of Law Reviews by the Supreme Court: An Empirical Study*, 34 UCLA L. Rev. 131, 133 (1986).

2. **Student Works**

Please see Rule 16.5.1 (p.115). In a student work, include the author's full name, if given, and use the designation that the periodical employs, such as Note or Comment.

Lisa Bazemore, Note, *Employment Discrimination Against Cancer Victims: A Proposed Solution*, 31 Vill. L. Rev. 1549 (1986).

Michael L. Marowitz, Comment, Birkenfield v. City of Berkeley: *Blueprint for Rent Control in California*, 7 Golden Gate U.L. Rev. 677,

702 (1977). Note again that you do not italicize the name of a case when it appears in the title of an article. See the first illustration on p. 115.

3. Volume Number

Some journals use the year of publication as the volume number. In this case, do not put the year at the end of the cite. See Rule 16.2 (p. 113).

Michael J. Brophy, Comment, *Statutes of Limitations in Federal Civil Rights Litigation*, 1976 Ariz. St. L.J. 97.

4. Pagination

If each issue of a periodical is paginated separately--that is, the first page of each issue is page 1--follow Rule 16.3 (p. 114). Be sure to omit the volume number.

An Array of New Tools Against Inherited Diseases, U.S. News & World Rep., Apr. 22, 1985, at 75.

Rick Johnson, *A Strategy for Service--Disney Style*, J. Bus. Strategy, Sept-Oct. 1991, at 38, 39.

5. Newspaper Articles

When citing a newspaper, follow Rule 16.4 (p. 114).

Dan Mirvish, *The Next Boat to Burundi*, N.Y. Times, August 25, 1991, § 5, at 31.

Suzanne Sczubelek, *Easing Town vs. Gown Tensions*, Phila. Inquirer, Sept. 19, 1991, at 30-M.

6. Exercise

Please provide the correct citations.

(a) "Impact of the Tax Act of 1986 on Legal Education and Law Faculty," by Christopher R. Hoyt, in the Journal of Legal Education, volume 36, No. 4, at page 568 (December 1986).

(b) "Social Host Liability in Massachusetts for the Torts of Drunken Drivers," by Peter W. Adler and David M. McCarthy, in the Massachusetts Law Review, volume 72, No. 2 (June 1987), at page 70.

(c) A student casenote by Pamela Tobin on Belasco v. Pittsburgh Board of Education, in the Temple Law Quarterly, vol. 60, No. 2, Summer 1987, at page 361. (Hint: see Rule 16.1 (a) (p. 114).

(d) An article entitled "PE Says N-plant Shutdown May Last for Weeks," by Dan Stets in the Philadelphia Inquirer, on Tuesday, April 7, 1987, on page 1-A, beginning in the first column.

C. Short Citation Forms for Books and Periodicals

Once you give the full citation for a book or periodical, you can use a short form for subsequent cites. The short form must identify the book or periodical unambiguously. If all short forms are ambiguous, repeat the full cite. For examples of short forms, see P.4 (d) (p. 16) and Rules 15.8.1 (p. 108) and 16.6 (p. 119). Note the use of "hereinafter." Here is an illustration:

Jefferson believed that people lacking an innate moral sense could gain it through education and practice. *See Report of the Commissioners for the University of Virginia* (1818), *reprinted in The Portable Thomas Jefferson* 332, 336 (Merrill D. Peterson ed., 1975) [hereinafter *Rockfish Gap Report*]. For Jefferson, only that aspect of religion that deals with morality is true religion. Letter from Thomas Jefferson to John Adams (May 15, 1817), *in* 15 *Writings of Thomas Jefferson* 108, 109 (Andrew A. Lipscomb, ed. 1904); *see* Robert M. Healey, *Jefferson on Religion in Public Education* 159-61 (1962). He had antipathy toward organized religion, in part, because he thought it corrupts society whenever it joins forces with secular government. *E.g., Rockfish Gap Report, supra*, at 337. Though he advocated that Virginia's proposed university have no professor of divinity, he wished other professors to teach morality and proofs of the existence of God, that is, matters common to all sects. *Id.* at 337-43. Yet he disliked theological speculation and even thought it could make people immoral by encouraging them to rely on nonrational doctrines instead of reason. *See* Healey, *supra*, at 162.

APPENDIX **II**

PLEADINGS

ATTORNEY OF RECORD
IDENTIFICATION NO.
M. Noel Lerner
11240 Stillwell Dr.
Riverside, CA 92505
1-909-689-9728
Attorney for Plaintiff

SUPERIOR COURT OF CALIFORNIA
COUNTY OF ORANGE

REVEREND TOMMY SMITH
1240 S. STATE COLLEGE
BLVD.
ANAHEIM, CA
        Plaintiff

v.

**BOARD OF TRUSTEES
SALVATION BAPTIST
CHURCH**
1240 S. STATE COLLEGE
BLVD.
ANAHEIM, CA
        Defendant

NO. 96-00000

NOVEMBER TERM, 1996

**COMPLAINT FOR -PUBLIC
DISCLOSURE OF PRIVATE
FACTS**

STATEMENT OF FACTS FOR ALL CAUSES OF ACTION

Plaintiff argues:

1. Plaintiff is Reverend Tommy Smith, an adult individual who resides at 1240 S. State College Blvd., Anaheim, CA.

2. Defendant is the Board of Trustees of the Salvation Baptist Church, with offices located at 1240 S. State College Blvd., Anaheim, CA.

3. On or about 6/19/95, plaintiff entered into an employment contract with the Salvation Baptist Church, 1234 Main St., Mission Viejo.

4. Under the employment contract, plaintiff's duties were to function as minister and run the day to day operations of the church.

5. On or about 4/17/96, defendant held a meeting of part of the congregation of the church. At this meeting, a vote of 101-7 was taken, to terminate the employment of plaintiff.

6. The Board told the congregation that plaintiff was having extramarital affairs and was guilty of adultery.

7. Before this disclosure the information regarding plaintiff's extramarital affairs was private, that is, not known to the public.

8. Fifty members of the congregation have sworn affidavits about the public statements made by the Board about plaintiff. The members include statements that they did not know about plaintiffs extramarital affairs before the Board's statements. The members also state that the outcome of the vote was influenced by the public statements made by the Board about plaintiff to the congregation. These original sworn affidavits are attached to this complaint and marked as Exhibits 1-50.

9. On or about July 10, 1996, a second meeting was held. As a result of this meeting the congregation reinstated plaintiff by a vote of 259-196.

10. Plaintiff has suffered damage to his reputation both personally and professionally.

11. Plaintiff has also suffered damage to his ability to be employed as a minister because of the highly personal and intimate nature of the disclosure of the extramarital affairs.

CAUSE OF ACTION

RIGHT OF PRIVACY – PUBLIC DISCLOSURE OF PRIVATE FACTS

12. Plaintiff incorporates by reference paragraphs 1 through 11 of this Complaint.

13. On or about 4/17/96, defendant made a public disclosure of a private fact about plaintiff to members of the congregation. The private fact was the extramarital affairs of plaintiff.

14. Prior to this date, the congregation had not known of this fact.

15. The defendant disclosed the fact either with knowledge that it was highly offensive or with reckless disregard of whether it was highly offensive or not. The fact made known was an intrusion into plaintiffs most intimate and private sexual affairs.

16. The public disclosure of this fact caused plaintiff to sustain injury to his reputation, damage to his emotions, and harm to his employability as a minister.

Wherefore, Plaintiff demands that this Court enter judgment in his favor and against defendant in an amount in excess of $10,000, exclusive of interest and costs.

_____

Attorney for Plaintiff

VERIFICATION

I, Reverend Tommy Smith, state that I am the plaintiff in this action and verify that the statements made in the foregoing complaint are true and correct to the best of my knowledge, information, and belief.

_____
Date

_____
Reverend Tommy Smith

CERTIFICATION OF MAILING

I, Noel Lerner, certify that I personally placed a copy of this complaint in the student mailbox of Kimchi Huynh, on November 22, 1996.

I certify this under penalty of perjury.

———————

Date

————————————————————

Noel Lerner

ATTORNEY OF RECORD:
IDENTIFICATION NO.

_____

ALAN and LINDA SHERMAN
123 BIRCH STREET
PHILADELPHIA, PA,
   Plaintiffs
    v.
KATHRYN JONES
UNIT 14
130 ELM STREET
PHILADELPHIA, PA,
   Defendant

Attorney for Plaintiffs COURT
OF COMMON PLEAS
PHILADELPHIA COUNTY
CIVIL ACTION — LAW APRIL
TERM, 1993 NO. 0000

COMPLAINT IN ASSUMPSIT

1. Plaintiffs are Alan and Linda Sherman, adult individuals who reside at 123 Birch Street, Philadelphia, PA.

2. Defendant is Kathryn Jones, an adult individual who resides at Unit 14, 130 Elm Street, Philadelphia, PA.

3. On or about December 3, 1991, plaintiffs entered into an agreement with defendant Jones to purchase real estate ("the property") owned by her at Unit 14, 130 Elm Street, Philadelphia, PA. A true and correct copy of this agreement is attached to this complaint and marked as Exhibit "A."

4. Under the agreement, plaintiffs paid the sum of ten thousand ($10,000) dollars to Creampuff Real Estate, Inc. ("Creampuff"), as a down payment on the property for Creampuff to deposit in an interest bearing escrow account.

5. At all pertinent times, Creampuff acted as defendant Jones's agent, the defendant having agreed that Creampuff was to receive a six percent commission for procuring plaintiffs to buy the property.

6. Under paragraph 19 of the agreement, plaintiffs' duty to proceed to settlement was expressly subject to their ability to obtain a mortgage commitment within sixty days at a cost of no more than three percent of the principal ("three points"). Failing to obtain such a commitment, at plaintiffs' option, plaintiffs were to receive all deposit monies and the agreement was to become null and void.

7. At Creampuff's insistence, plaintiffs proceeded with due diligence to apply to Security Mortgage Service Company for a mortgage that would meet the terms of the agreement.

8. As of February 1, 1992, however, sixty days elapsed with no commitment. On February 17, 1992, plaintiffs received a written commitment, dated February 12, 1992. A copy of the commitment is attached and marked as Exhibit "B."

9. The commitment offered plaintiffs a mortgage which would cost them four points rather than the maximum of three points set forth in that paragraph 19 of the agreement.

10. The commitment further required plaintiffs to meet special conditions that paragraph 19 of the agreement did not contemplate, namely (a) evidence of sale or lease of their present residence, and (b) proof of 1991 income of $110,997.

11. Upon receipt of the commitment, plaintiffs asked the mortgage company to remove the special conditions, but Security refused to.

12. In view of the circumstances in paragraphs 9-11 above, plaintiffs on February 25, 1992, sent a letter to defendant Jones notifying her that they could not meet the terms of the commitment and that they desired the return of their deposit with interest. A copy of the letter is attached and marked Exhibit "C."

13. Despite the request, by letter dated February 25, 1992, defendant Jones refused to return plaintiffs' deposit, and despite many subsequent requests, persists in her refusal. She additionally has directed Creampuff not to release the funds.

COUNT I

14. Further, by letter dated March 3, 1992, Creampuff notified plaintiffs they would not return the deposit unless the parties agreed or the court so directed.

15. Paragraphs 1-14 above are incorporated as though set forth at length.

16. Defendant Jones is liable to plaintiffs in the amount of ten thousand ($10,000) dollars, together with interest from December 3, 1991.

WHEREFORE, plaintiffs demand judgment in their favor and against defendant Jones in the amount of ten thousand ($10,000) dollars, together with interest from December 3, 1991, and costs of suit.

COUNT II

17. Paragraphs 1-14 above are incorporated as though set forth at length.

18. Defendant Jones' refusal to return plaintiffs' money has at all times been willful, malicious, and utterly without foundation in law.

19. Defendant Jones is liable to plaintiffs for punitive damages.

WHEREFORE, plaintiffs demand punitive damages against defendant Jones in an amount not in excess of twenty thousand ($20,000) dollars.

COUNT III

20. Paragraphs 1-14 above are incorporated as though set forth at length.

21. On April 13, 1992, plaintiffs notified defendant by hand-delivered letter that unless defendant returned the deposit by April 15, they could not pay their income taxes on time and expected to be liable for penalties and interest.

22. Defendant is now liable to plaintiffs for consequential damages since plaintiffs could not pay taxes on time.

WHEREFORE, plaintiffs demand judgment in their favor and against defendant for consequential damages calculated from April 15, 1992, until time of judgment.

_____

Attorney for Plaintiff

ATTORNEY OF RECORD:
IDENTIFICATION NO.

———————————————

ALAN and LINDA SHERMAN,
Plaintiffs, v.
KATHRYN JONES,
Defendant

ATTORNEY FOR DEFENDANT
COURT OF COMMON PLEAS,
PHILADELPHIA COUNTY,
PENNSYLVANIA CIVIL
ACTION–
LAW DIVISION
APRIL TERM, 1993 No. 231

———

ANSWER, NEW MATTER, AND COUNTERCLAIM OF DEFENDANT KATHRYN JONES TO PLAINTIFFS' COMPLAINT

———

ANSWER

Defendant Kathryn Jones, by her counsel, answers plaintiffs' complaint as follows:

1. Admitted.

2. Admitted.

3. Admitted.

4. Admitted.

5. Admitted in part and denied in part. Defendant admits that Creampuff was to receive a six percent commission for procuring a satisfactory purchaser (not necessarily plaintiffs) for the property. Counsel advises defendant that she need not respond to the remaining allegations in this paragraph because those allegations constitute conclusions of law which operation of law deems denied.

6. Counsel advised defendant that she need not respond to the allegations in this paragraph because those allegations constitute conclusions of law which operation of law deems denied. Furthermore, the document speaks for itself. In any event, defendant specifically denies that plaintiffs' duty to proceed to settlement was subject to their ability to obtain a mortgage commitment "at a cost of no more than three percent of the principal ("three points')." On the contrary, paragraph 19 of the agreement provides that the commitment "shall not require the Buyer to pay more than three percent of the principal amount as 'points' or a 'commitment fee.'"

7. Defendant is without knowledge or information sufficient to form a belief as to the truth of the averments of paragraph 7 of the complaint because the means of proof are within the exclusive control of adverse parties or hostile persons, and defendant demands proof of them.

8. Admitted in part and denied in part. Defendant admits that plaintiffs received a commitment dated February 12, 1992, and that a copy of that commitment is attached to the complaint and marked as Exhibit "B." As to the remaining allegations of paragraph 8 of the complaint, defendant is without knowledge or information sufficient to form a belief as to the truth of these averments because the means of proof are within the exclusive control of adverse parties or hostile persons, and demands proof of them.

9. Defendant specifically denies that the commitment offered plaintiffs a mortgage which would cost them four points rather than the maximum of three points set forth in paragraph 19 of the agreement. On the contrary, the commitment expressly provided that the buyer pay three percent of the principal amount as "points" or as a "commitment fee."

10. Counsel advises defendant that she need not respond to the allegations in this paragraph because those allegations constitute conclusions of law which operation of law deems denied. Furthermore, the document speaks for itself. In any event, the commitment does not require proof of 1991 income of $110,997. On the contrary, the commitment merely requires that plaintiffs substantiate the income that plaintiffs claim on their application for the commitment by providing a "1991 IRS return substantially supportive of income claimed on application of $110,997.00 OR complete **AUDITED** profit and loss for 1991 on both businesses supporting same income figure." Also, defendant specifically denies that any requirement as to "evidence of sale or lease of [plaintiffs'] present residence" is a "special condition not at all contemplated" by the agreement. On the contrary, such an occurrence is a normal, expected, and understood condition in such circumstances.

11. After reasonable investigation, defendant is without knowledge or information sufficient to form a belief as to the truth of the averments of paragraph 11 of the complaint, and demands proof of them.

12. Admitted in part and denied in part. Defendant admits that plaintiffs sent the letter described, and that the letter indicated that plaintiffs could not or would not accept the commitment and desired the return of the deposit, with interest. Defendant also admits that a copy of the letter is attached to the complaint as Exhibit "C." Defendant is without knowledge or information sufficient to form a belief as to the truth of the remaining averments of this paragraph because the means of proof are within the exclusive control of adverse parties or hostile persons, and defendant demands proof of them.

13. Denied as stated. Defendant admits that her counsel, by letter dated February 26, 1992, indicated that plaintiffs would be held liable under the agreement between the parties, based on previous indications defendant received that plaintiffs had obtained an acceptable commitment and defendant's detrimental reliance on those indications. Defendant further admits that her husband informed Creampuff that any release of the deposit would be in violation of the agreement between the parties.

14. Admitted.

COUNT I

15. Paragraphs 1 through 14 of this answer are incorporated by reference.

16. Counsel advises defendant that she need not respond to the allegations in this paragraph because those allegations constitute conclusions of law which operation of law deems denied. In any event, defendant specifically denies that defendant is liable to plaintiffs in the amount of $10,000, together with interest, from December 3, 1991. On the contrary, defendant is not liable to plaintiffs.

COUNT II

17. Paragraphs 1 through 14 of this answer are incorporated by reference.

18. Defendant specifically denies that her refusal to return plaintiffs' money has at all times been willful, malicious, and utterly without foundation in law. On the contrary, defendant has at all times acted properly and within her legal rights and has acted in conformance with a good faith belief as to her legal rights.

19. Counsel advises defendant that she need not respond to the allegations in this paragraph because those allegations constitute conclusions of law which operation of law deems denied. In any event, defendant specifically denies that she is liable to plaintiffs for punitive damages. On the contrary, defendant is not liable to plaintiffs.

COUNT III

20. Paragraphs 1 through 14 of this answer are incorporated by reference.

21. Admitted in part and denied in part. Defendant admits that her counsel received the letter described indicating that plaintiffs sought the return of the deposit by April 15 in order to have the money to pay their income taxes. Defendant is without knowledge or information sufficient to form a belief as to the truth of the averment that plaintiffs were unable to pay their income taxes on time and expected to be liable for penalties and interest because the means of proof are within the exclusive control of adverse parties or hostile persons, and defendant demands proof of them.

22. Counsel advises defendant that she need not respond to the allegations in this paragraph because those allegations constitute conclusions of law which operation of law deems denied. In any event, defendant specifically denies that she is now liable to plaintiffs for consequential damages since plaintiffs were unable to pay their taxes on time. On the contrary, defendant is not responsible for any alleged inability of plaintiffs to pay their income taxes on time and is not liable to plaintiffs.

NEW MATTER

23. Creampuff, through its employee Sharon Sellit, acted for plaintiffs as their agent.

24. Throughout the month of February, plaintiffs or their representatives visited the property for the purpose of taking measurements and also performed other actions consistent with an intent to make settlement under the agreement.

25. On or about February 22, 1992, Sharon Sellit indicated to defendant that plaintiff Linda Sherman had instructed that carpet tacking remaining on the floor after carpeting was removed pursuant to the agreement between the parties should be left there.

26. In reliance on the above, and in reliance on other indications from plaintiffs and their agents that plaintiffs had accepted or intended to accept the commitment, that the agreement was still in force, and that plaintiffs intended to make settlement under the agreement, defendant continued to act, at her own expense, pursuant to her agreement with plaintiffs.

27. Based on the above, plaintiffs are estopped from asserting: (1) that the commitment was not in conformity with the agreement; and (2) that the agreement became null and void.

28. Based on the above, plaintiffs have waived the requirements and conditions of paragraph 19 of the agreement as a basis for failing to fulfill their obligations under that agreement.

WHEREFORE, defendant Kathryn Jones requests an order dismissing plaintiffs' complaint.

COUNTERCLAIM

COUNT I

29. Paragraphs 1 through 28, above, are incorporated by reference.

30. Plaintiffs have breached the agreement by failing to make settlement as the agreement requires.

31. As a result of plaintiffs' breach, defendant is entitled to the $10,000 deposit as liquidated damages under paragraph 10 of the agreement.

WHEREFORE, defendant Kathryn Jones requests an order awarding her the sum of $10,000, plus interest and costs.

COUNT II

32. Paragraphs 1 through 31 are incorporated by reference.

33. Based on the above, plaintiffs have made misrepresentations of material facts for the purpose of inducing defendant to act or to refrain from acting in reliance on those misrepresentations.

34. Alternatively, plaintiffs' misrepresentations were negligent or fraudulent.

35. Defendant acted and refrained from acting in reliance on plaintiffs' misrepresentations.

36. As a result, defendant has sustained damages totaling $19,099.72.

WHEREFORE, defendant KATHRYN JONES requests an order awarding her $19,099.72, plus interest and costs.

Attorney for Defendant
Kathryn Jones

AFFIDAVIT

Commonwealth of Pennsylvania }   ss
County of Philadelphia

KATHRYN JONES, being duly sworn according to law, deposes and says that she is Defendant in this action and that the facts set forth in the foregoing answer, new matter, and counterclaim are true and correct to the best of her knowledge, information, and belief.

_____

Kathryn Jones

Sworn to and subscribed
before me this 27th day
of September, 1992.

_____

Notary Public

My Commission Expires:

ATTORNEY OF RECORD
IDENTIFICATION NO. 0000

| ALAN and LINDA SHERMAN,
Plaintiffs,
v.
KATHRYN JONES,
Defendant
CREAMPUFF REAL ESTATE,
INC.,
Additional Defendant | ATTORNEY FOR DEFENDANT
COURT OF COMMON PLEAS
PHILADELPHIA COUNTY,
PENNSYLVANIA CIVIL
ACTION —
LAW DIVISION APRIL TERM,
1993 No. 231 |

———

DEFENDANT'S COMPLAINT AGAINST
ADDITIONAL DEFENDANT

———

1. Plaintiffs have sued defendant contending that defendant wrongfully has refused to return $10,000 plaintiffs deposited as a down payment toward the purchase of real estate located at Unit 14, 130 Elm Street, Philadelphia, PA. A copy of plaintiffs' complaint is attached as Exhibit "A."

2. Defendant has filed an answer to plaintiffs' complaint in which defendant (a) denies any liability to plaintiffs and (b) asserts counterclaims against plaintiffs. Copies of defendant's Answer, New Matter, and Counterclaim are attached.

3. Additional defendant, Creampuff Real Estate, Inc. ("Creampuff"), is a corporation organized and existing under the laws of Pennsylvania with an office at 456 Maple Street, Philadelphia, PA.

4. Creampuff is holding as escrow agent the $10,000 deposit that is the subject of plaintiffs' complaint under the Agreement of Sale between plaintiffs and defendant.

5. Creampuff, through its employee Joan Buyit, acted as defendant's agent for purposes of the sales transaction.

6. Creampuff, through its employee Sharon Sellit, also acted as plaintiffs' agent in this transaction.

7. Plaintiffs' obligation to make settlement under the Agreement of Sale was contingent on the receipt by plaintiffs of a mortgage commitment that was to meet certain conditions specified in the Agreement of Sale.

8. Creampuff represented to defendant that plaintiffs had obtained a mortgage commitment that met the conditions specified in the Agreement of Sale.

9. Creampuff also represented to defendant that plaintiffs had accepted the mortgage commitment and intended to make settlement under the Agreement of Sale.

10. Prior to February 25, 1992, and in reliance on Creampuff's representation, defendant removed carpeting from the premises and took other action and incurred expenses in preparation for settlement under the Agreement of Sale.

11. Creampuff advised plaintiff prior to February 25, 1992, not to inform defendant that plaintiffs refuse the mortgage commitment.

12. On February 25, 1992, Joan Buyit indicated to defendant for the first time that there was "a problem" with the plaintiffs' commitment.

13. Plaintiffs refused to make settlement under the Agreement, allegedly because the mortgage commitment they received did not meet the conditions specified in the Agreement of Sale. Complaint, paragraphs 9-10.

14. Plaintiffs have also alleged that they never accepted the mortgage commitment. Complaint, paragraphs 11-12, and Exhibit "C" to complaint.

Count I

15. Paragraphs 1-14 of this complaint against additional defendant are incorporated by reference.

16. Based on the above, Creampuff is alone liable to plaintiffs or, in the alternative, is liable over to defendant in indemnity or contribution for any amounts which may be adjudged against defendant.

WHEREFORE, Defendant Kathryn Jones demands judgment against additional defendant Creampuff for any amounts that may be adjudged against defendant and in favor of plaintiffs.

Count II

17. Paragraphs 1-14 of this complaint against additional defendant are incorporated by reference.

18. In the event the mortgage commitment did not meet the conditions set out in the Agreement of Sale, which defendant specifically denies, then Creampuff misrepresented that fact to defendant.

19. Creampuff additionally misrepresented plaintiffs' intention to accept the mortgage commitment.

20. Creampuff further misrepresented plaintiffs' intention to make settlement under the Agreement of Sale.

21. Creampuffs' actions violated the Real Estate Licensing Act, 63 Pa. Cons. Stat. § 455.604 (1976).

22. Based on the above, Creampuff has made misrepresentations of material facts for the purpose of inducing defendant to act or to refrain from acting in reliance on those misrepresentations.

23. Alternatively, Creampuff's misrepresentations were negligent or fraudulent.

24. Defendant acted and refrained from acting in reliance on Creampuff's misrepresentations.

25. By reason of its misrepresentations to defendant, Creampuff is liable directly to defendant for any damages that defendant does not recover from plaintiffs under defendant's counterclaim against plaintiffs.

26. As a result of Creampuff's misrepresentations, defendant has sustained damages totaling $19,099.72, plus interest, costs, and defendant's reasonable attorney's fees.

Count III

27. Paragraphs 1-26 of this complaint against additional defendant are incorporated by reference.

28. Based on the above, Creampuff has breached its duty as an agent of defendant to act with standard care and with the skill that is standard in the locality for the kind of work which Creampuff was employed to perform.

WHEREFORE, Defendant Kathryn Jones demands judgment against additional defendant Creampuff for $19,099.72, plus interest, costs, and defendant's reasonable attorney's fees.

Count IV

29. Paragraphs 1-26 of this complaint against additional defendant are incorporated by reference.

30. Based on the above, Creampuff has breached its duty to defendant not to act on behalf of an adverse party in a transaction connected with its agency without defendant's knowledge.

31. Alternatively, Creampuff has breached its duty to act with fairness to each of its principals and to disclose to each all facts which it knew or should have known would affect reasonably the judgment of each in permitting the dual agency.

WHEREFORE, Defendant Kathryn Jones demands judgment against additional defendant Creampuff for $19,099.72, plus interest, costs, and defendant's reasonable attorney's fees.

_____

Attorney for Defendant
Kathryn Jones

THE STATE OF TEXAS COUNTY OF HARRIS	KNOW ALL MEN BY THESE PRESENTS:

BEFORE ME, the undersigned authority, personally appeared KATH-RYN S. JONES, known to me to be a credible person, and after being duly sworn, upon oath deposed and stated the following:

"That the allegations in the complaint against the additional defendant are true and correct to the best of my knowledge, information, and belief."

Further deponent sayeth not.

_____

Kathryn S. Jones

SWORN TO AND SUBSCRIBED BEFORE ME by KATHRYN S. JONES on this _____ day of November, 1992, to certify which witness my hand and seal of office.

_____

Notary Public in and for
The State of TEXAS

My Commission Expires:

_____

IN THE UNITED STATES DISTRICT COURT
FOR THE EASTERN DISTRICT OF PENNSYLVANIA

QUALITY PRODUCTS CORPORATION, Plaintiff v. MIDDLEMAN STEEL COMPANY, Defendant and Third-Party Plaintiff v. HEAVY METALS COMPANY, Third-Party Defendant	Civil Action No. 75-4113

PLAINTIFF'S COMPLAINT AGAINST THIRD-PARTY DEFENDANT, HEAVY METALS COMPANY

---

1. Plaintiff, Quality Products Corporation ("Quality") is a Delaware corporation having its principal place of business in New York, New York.

2. Third-Party Defendant, Heavy Metals Company ("Heavy Metals"), is a Pennsylvania corporation having its principal office and place of business in Philadelphia, Pennsylvania.

3. Jurisdiction of this claim is based upon the diversity of citizenship of the plaintiff and third-party defendant, under Title 28, United States Code, Section 1332.

4. The amount in controversy in this claim exceeds $10,000 exclusive of interest and costs.

5. Plaintiff incorporates by reference, as if set forth separately and in full, the allegations in paragraphs 5-11 of its Complaint in this action, which plaintiff filed with the Court on October 20, 1985, and a copy of which was served upon Middleman on or about December 18, 1985.

COUNT I

6. In or about November and December, 1984, defendant, Middleman Steel Company ("Middleman"), made a contract with Heavy Metals to purchase certain quantities of steel, which Middleman afterward sold to Quality as abrasion-resistant steel. The terms of their contract required that the quantities of steel Middleman purchased from Heavy Metals were to be abrasion-resistant steel.

7. At the time of the contract for the sale of the quantities of steel to Middleman, Heavy Metals knew that Middleman was a steel warehouse, engaged in the business of reselling steel to others, and that the steel Heavy Metals sold would come to rest in the hands of an ultimate consumer, who would be some person or company other than Middleman.

8. Quality was the ultimate consumer of the steel Heavy Metals sold to Middleman and is a third-party beneficiary of the contract between Middleman and Heavy Metals, and of all warranties, express and implied, on the part of Heavy Metals in that contract.

9. The steel that Heavy Metals sold to Middleman for resale to Quality under the contract was not abrasion-resistant steel, but was steel of different and inferior physical and chemical properties.

10. By failing to deliver to Middleman abrasion-resistant steel as Middleman had ordered, Heavy Metals breached the contract, and the express and implied warranties in that contract, causing loss and damage to Quality as alleged in its Complaint.

WHEREFORE, plaintiff demands judgment in its favor against third-party defendant Heavy Metals Company for all sums which Quality had to expend as a result of the third-party defendant's breaches, plus interest and costs.

COUNT II

11. The allegations in paragraphs 1-10 are incorporated by reference.

12. Heavy Metals is engaged in the business of selling the steel it sold to Middleman and afterwards that Middleman sold to Quality.

13. Heavy Metals expected that the steel that it sold to Middleman could reach the user or consumer without substantial change in the condition in which it was sold, and the steel did reach Quality in that condition.

14. The steel Heavy Metals sold to Middleman was in a defective condition because it was not abrasion-resistant steel as Heavy Metals represented it to be, and was unreasonably dangerous to plaintiff's property.

15. As a result of the defective condition of the steel, plaintiff suffered damage to its property in that the machinery plaintiff manufactured from the steel became inoperative and required the expenditure of large sums for repairs.

WHEREFORE, plaintiff demands judgment in its favor against third-party defendant Heavy Metals Company for all sums which Quality had to expend as a result of the third-party defendant's sale of the steel, plus interest and costs.

COUNT III

16. The allegations in paragraphs 1-15 are incorporated by reference.

17. Heavy Metals failed to exercise reasonable care in supplying steel to Middleman under the contract in Count I by delivering steel that was labeled erroneously and described as abrasion-resistant steel when it was not abrasion-resistant steel.

18. As a result of Heavy Metals' negligence in delivering steel to Middleman knowing that Middleman was to resell the steel to another, Quality suffered damages by having to expend large sums of money to repair machinery components manufactured of the steel Heavy Metals delivered.

WHEREFORE, plaintiff demands judgment in its favor against third-party defendant Heavy Metals Company for all sums which it had to expend as a result of the third-party defendant's negligence, plus interest and costs.

COUNT IV

19. The allegations in paragraphs 1-18 are incorporated by reference.

20. Heavy Metals knowingly and willfully supplied non-abrasion-resistant steel to Middleman, which had ordered the steel as abrasion-resistant, and misrepresented the character of the steel it shipped as abrasion-resistant, when it knew full well that the steel did not have the physical and chemical properties of abrasion-resistant steel.

WHEREFORE, plaintiff demands judgment in its favor against third-party defendant Heavy Metals Company for all sums that it had to expend as a result of the third-party defendant's willful delivery of nonconforming steel, plus interest and costs, plus punitive damages.

_____

Attorney for Plaintiff

IN THE UNITED STATES DISTRICT COURT
FOR THE SOUTHERN DISTRICT OF FLORIDA

UNITED STATES OF
AMERICA,
        Plaintiff,

        v.

THE GOOD CORPORATION,
        Defendant

CIVIL NO. 78-6789

———

ANSWER

———

Defendant, the Good Corporation, answers the Complaint as follows:

FIRST DEFENSE

1. Defendant admits that plaintiff seeks to bring this action under the statutory sections alleged but denies that it has violated any provision of the Federal Trade Commission Act or any rule issued by the Commission and denies that the plaintiff is entitled to recover civil penalties or obtain any other relief.

2. Defendant denies the allegations in paragraph 2.

3. Defendant denies that venue in the Southern District of Florida is proper.

4. Defendant denies the allegations in paragraph 4 and further states that they constitute conclusions of law that require no answer.

5. Defendant denies the allegations in paragraph 5 and further states that it does not know what the term "purchase money loan" means as used in the Complaint and that these allegations constitute conclusions of law which require no answer.

6. Defendant admits the allegations in paragraph 6.

7. Defendant admits that the Federal Trade Commission purported to issue a Trade Regulation Rule concerning Preservation of Consumers' Claims and Defenses on November 18, 1985, and that this Rule purported to become effective on May 14, 1986; but defendant alleges that the Rule is invalid and of no force and effect, was improperly promulgated, and is in excess of the statutory authority of the Federal Trade Commission.

8. Defendant admits the allegations of paragraph 8.

9-65. Defendant denies the allegations contained in paragraphs 9-65 and further states that they constitute conclusions of law which require no answer.

SECOND DEFENSE

66. The Complaint fails to state a claim on which relief may be granted.

THIRD DEFENSE

67. This Court lacks jurisdiction over the subject matter of any claim in the Complaint.

FOURTH DEFENSE

68. The applicable statute of limitations bars plaintiff's claim in whole or in part.

FIFTH DEFENSE

69. The doctrine of laches bars plaintiff's claim in whole or in part.

SIXTH DEFENSE

70. The Federal Trade Commission did not comply with the procedures the law requires when it promulgated the Rule concerning Preservation of Consumers' Claims and Defenses.

SEVENTH DEFENSE

71. The Federal Trade Commission did not have statutory authority to promulgate the Rule concerning Preservation of Consumers' Claims and Defenses.

EIGHTH DEFENSE

72. The Rule concerning Preservation of Consumers' Claims and Defenses is an unlawful and unauthorized attempt by the Federal Trade

Commission to regulate banks and banking institutions, which the Federal Trade Commission Act forbids the FTC from doing.

NINTH DEFENSE

73. The Rule concerning Preservation of Consumers' Claims and Defenses is vague, unspecific, confusing, and misleading, and is therefore void and unenforceable.

TENTH DEFENSE

74. The Rule concerning Preservation of Consumers' Claims and Defenses is vague, unspecific, confusing, and misleading; and defendant and all Credit Unions identified in the Complaint attempted in good faith to comply with it.

ELEVENTH DEFENSE

75. The Rule concerning Preservation of Consumers' Claims and Defenses attempts to regulate defendant based upon acts of others who are not within the control of defendant, in violation of the United States Constitution.

TWELFTH DEFENSE

76. Substantial evidence in the rule-making proceeding did not support the Rule concerning Preservation of Consumers' Claims and Defenses.

THIRTEENTH DEFENSE

77. Defendant has not engaged in an "unfair or deceptive act or practice" within the meaning of Section 5 of the Federal Trade Commission Act.

FOURTEENTH DEFENSE

78. Defendant did not accept the proceeds of purchase money loans with actual knowledge or knowledge fairly implied on the basis of objective circumstances that such acceptance was unfair or deceptive and prohibited by the Rule concerning Preservation of Consumers' Claims and Defenses.

FIFTEENTH DEFENSE

79. At the time that defendant made any alleged sale of a used car, defendant had no knowledge, and no reason to know, that the purchaser had executed a consumer credit contract that did not contain the notice in the Rule concerning Preservation of Consumers' Claims and Defenses.

SIXTEENTH DEFENSE

80. No person has sustained any injury because of the matters alleged in the Complaint.

SEVENTEENTH DEFENSE

81. Defendant at all times exercised reasonable care and diligence to insure that any consumer credit contract executed in connection with the purchase of a used car as alleged in the Complaint contained the notice in the Rule concerning Preservation of Consumers' Claims and Defenses.

EIGHTEENTH DEFENSE

82. Upon information and belief, defendant alleges that this action is frivolous and without merit and that plaintiff brought it under pressure from special interest groups that compete with defendant in the sale of used cars.

WHEREFORE, defendant, The Good Corporation, demands judgment in its favor and requests that the Court dismiss the Complaint and grant to defendant the costs of this action and reasonable attorneys' fees, together with such other and further relief as may be just and proper.

Attorney for Defendant

By _____

APPENDIX III

CLIENT LETTERS

ADAMS & ASSOCIATES, STUDENTS OF LAW

12510 Inglenook Lane * Cerritos, CA 90703 * (888) 41 ADAMS * Fax (562) 809-2653

February 11, 1997

Ms. Mary Louise Solomon
1240 South State College Blvd.
Anaheim, CA 92806

Re: Surrogate Contract between Mary Louise Solomon and James Kelk

Dear Ms. Solomon:

Thank you for choosing Adams & Associates to represent you. We are mindful of the importance of this matter and we will do our best to justify the confidence you have placed in us. The purpose of this letter is to acquaint you with how we see your case, what you may expect to happen and what you need to do to assist us as we move forward. We work for you, so if you have questions, or you think there are things we should know, please do not hesitate to contact our office. If we are not available when you call, please leave a message and we will get back to you as soon as we can. We will be providing you with a monthly itemized statement of your account with us and any amounts we are subtracting from your retainer.

Before proceeding further, there are a couple of items that require your immediate attention. First, please sign the enclosed Substitution of Attorney letter, return it to us in the envelope provided and keep the second copy for your files. We cannot act on your behalf if you have not released your prior attorney from any obligations to you. Second, it is imperative that you keep an accurate record of all of your expenses associated with the pregnancy. Please use the enclosed expense form to keep track of your mileage to and from the doctor, and any other expenses you incur as a result of your pregnancy, such as maternity clothes.

According to information you provided during our initial consultation, you entered into a contract with James Kelk, in which you agreed to be artificially inseminated, and to conceive and deliver a child. Mr. Kelk promised, among other things, to pay all medical and collateral expenses, and to give you

$15,000 upon surrender of custody of the child to him. You have abided by all the terms and conditions of the contract up to this point and are in your twentieth week of pregnancy.

Recently, your husband contacted the Kelks and informed them that your father was an alcoholic and that your mother was addicted to pain killers, facts that you confirmed were true. Now the Kelks have decided that they do not want the baby and wish to terminate the contract, despite the fact that you have no history of drug or alcohol abuse, and that tests conducted on your fetus offer no evidence of any problems with the baby. In seeking legal counsel, your goal is to have the Kelks perform the contract, *i.e.*, do what they promised to do, including taking custody of the baby after it is born. Based on what you have told us and on our preliminary research, and with the understanding that we cannot guarantee the outcome of your case, we believe we have a reasonably good chance to either force the Kelks to pay the monies promised under the contract, or to pay any expenses and losses you might incur involving the pregnancy. We do not believe that we would be successful in forcing the Kelks to take custody of the baby.

In contract law, breach of a contract is the same as breaking one's promise. The law offers various remedies to the injured party (the party who is willing to perform on her promise). The basic goal of the courts in contract disputes is to put the parties in the same positions they were in before they entered into the contract. Usually, this involves the court either ordering the breaching party to perform as agreed in the contract, or the awarding of monetary compensation to the injured party for any expenses incurred or losses sustained as a result of the contract not being fulfilled.

Ordinarily, the law requires that a breach of the contract must occur before a legal remedy may be sought. At this point, the Kelks have not legally breached the contract, because they have performed the promises that are already due under the terms of the contract, *i.e.*, paid expenses to the fertility clinic, and the costs of the medical evaluations, etc. Normally, we would have to wait until the Kelks actually broke one of their contract promises before we could take any action. However, by verbally telling you that they did not want the baby, the Kelks may have committed an "anticipatory repudiation of the contract." This is like reneging on a promise before the time when you are required to carry out that promise. We would need to prove, either through the Kelks' own admission, or through other acts on their part, that they do not plan to make good on their contract promises to you.

Assuming that we can prove that the Kelks committed an "anticipatory repudiation of the contract," there are three possible responses we would advise. First, we can urge the Kelks to perform on the contract --to cancel or undo their repudiation. Second, if they still insist they do not want custody of the baby, we can try to negotiate a settlement that would be agreeable to both you and the Kelks. Third, we can immediately file an action to try and force performance of the contract or recover any damages that may be appropriate.

We recommend first sending a letter to Mr. and Mrs. Kelk urging them to honor the contract. They may have been overreacting to the information provided by your husband and may have reconsidered their position. This is the preferred approach because it accomplishes your goal and avoids the more costly alternatives. We have enclosed a copy of the letter we will send as soon as you give us the go ahead.

If the Kelks refuse to reconsider and remain steadfast in their position that they do not want the baby, then we can still attempt to negotiate with them for a mutually agreeable alternative to the enforcement of the entire contract. Of course you would have to approve any final agreement we negotiated. The advantage to you of solving this disagreement through negotiation is that the outcome may be the same as through litigating the matter but it would be resolved more quickly and at considerably less cost to you.

Should the initial negotiations fail to generate an acceptable outcome, we recommend filing an action in Superior Court for anticipatory repudiation of the contract. Based on the information you provided us and our preliminary research, we believe that filing an action would be a prudent approach and that there is a reasonable chance of prevailing. With that said, we must caution that there are no guarantees that we would win the action.

Although we would file the action in Superior Court, if you so directed us, we recommend that we enter into non-binding arbitration, rather than court litigation. There are three reasons for this strategy. First, we can arrange an arbitration hearing much quicker than we can obtain a hearing date in our crowded court system. This means that if we are successful at arbitration, we can receive a judgment that would cover your expenses including attorney's fees, thereby minimizing any financial burden to you. Second, it is far less costly to you than a protracted court battle. Third, we may have a better opportunity for a ruling in our favor. There has never been a case in California quite like yours and, in general, the law surrounding surrogate contracts is very unsettled. For a number of legal reasons too complex to discuss here, how the courts would treat our case is unpredictable. In addition, an outcome in our favor in court would almost certainly result in an appeal, which would increase the costs and the length of time to a final outcome. Because the arbitration proposed is non-binding, neither side has to abide by the decision of the arbitrator. However, having heard the other side's arguments, we will have a better idea of our chances of winning at trial if we are forced to litigate.

Thus far we have focused only on the monetary issues of your agreement with the Kelks. We realize that you want the Kelks to also honor their commitment to take custody of the baby upon its birth. However, as we mentioned before, it is our opinion that the courts would be unwilling to force Mr. and Mrs. Kelk to take custody of the child. Should you wish to put the baby up for adoption, that will be a separate issue with which our family law specialist can help. Should you decide to keep the baby, it is very likely that Mr. Kelk, as the child's natural father, would be responsible for part of the child's financial support, until he or she attains the age of eighteen. Again, that is a separate action and would be handled by our family law specialist.

To recap, upon your approval, we will send a letter to Mr. and Mrs. Kelk asking them to reconsider their position and honor the contract. If that proves unsuccessful, we will negotiate to arrive at a mutually agreed upon settlement, and failing that, we will file an action and seek to enter into arbitration. Should arbitration fail to produce the desired results, then we will go forward with a litigated action in Superior Court.

Please contact our office no later than Friday, February 14, 1997, to inform us of your decision regarding the letter to the Kelks. Also, please mail the Substitution of Attorney letter immediately. We will keep you informed of further developments in your case.

Sincerely,

Richard G. Adams
Sr. Student

encl: Substitution of Attorney Letter (2)
        Letter to Mr. & Mrs. Kelk
        Expense Sheet

ADAMS & ASSOCIATES, Students of Law

*12510 Inglenook Lane * Cerritos, CA 90703 * (888) 41 ADAMS * Fax (562) 809-2653*

February 11, 1997

Mr. Yves Bordeaux, Esq.
Law Offices of Yves Bordeaux
2323 Main St., Suite 200
Orange, CA 92666

Reference: Surrogacy Contract 6/1/96 between James Kelk and Mary Louise Solomon

Dear Attorney Bordeaux:

Please be advised that effective immediately I have retained the legal services of Adams & Associates to pursue my claims related to the above referenced contract.

Accordingly, please forward my file to my law student, Richard G. Adams as soon as possible. Your cooperation will be appreciated.

Sincerely,

Mary Louise Solomon

ADAMS & ASSOCIATES, Students of Law

*12510 Inglenook Lane * Cerritos, CA 90703 * (888) 41 ADAMS * Fax (562) 809-2653*

February 11, 1997

Mr. & Mrs. James Kelk
12345 Orange Avenue
Orange, CA 95555

Re: Surrogacy Contract between James Kelk and Mary Louise Solomon

Dear Mr. & Mrs. Kelk:

Please be advised that our firm has been retained by Ms. Mary Louise Solomon relative to the surrogacy contract entered into on October 6, 1996, by Mr. James Kelk. Ms. Solomon has informed this firm that you no longer wish to take post-natal custody of the child that is the subject of the aforementioned contract, and of which Mr. Kelk is the legal father.

We believe Ms. Solomon would prevail in legal enforcement of the financial terms of her contract with Mr. Kelk. However Ms. Solomon does not wish to engage in protracted litigation to resolve this matter unless absolutely necessary. To avoid litigation, which could ultimately prove very costly to you, we respectfully request that you reconsider your position. Please indicate in writing via a letter to this office, your intention to honor all of the promises you made in the aforementioned contract.

If you have any questions, please contact me. If you have employed an attorney, then please have that person contact my office. Communicating directly with you is inappropriate if you are represented by counsel.

Sincerely,

Richard G. Adams
Student at Law

EXPENSES RELATED TO BABY

Date	Miles to Doctor	Miles from Doctor	Total Miles	Medical Expenses	Personal Expenses

RACHEL GOLDSTEIN
ATTORNEY AT LAW
426-1/2 BEGONIA AVENUE
CORONA DEL MAR, CALIFORNIA 92625
TELEPHONE: (714) 675-3242; FACSIMILE: (714) 675-3243

November 12, 1997

Mr. Dana Clark
Dana's Restaurant
101 S. Imperial Highway
Anaheim, CA 92807

Re: Ms. Julia Kidd's Right of Publicity Claims Against You

Dear Mr. Clark:

Thank you for meeting with me in my office on October 8, 1997. This letter is a follow-up to our meeting. It restates my understanding of the facts, addresses your concerns regarding whether famous chef and T.V. personality Julia Kidd can take legal action against you for airing a T.V. commercial that features an actress resembling her, and proposes a course of action for your review and consideration.

First of all, I want to be sure I have the facts of your case straight. Based on our discussion, I understand the facts to be as follows: you are the owner and chef of Dana's, a two-year-old restaurant in Anaheim, California. In or about January, 1997, you paid an ad agency to create a t.v. commercial (ad) that would promote your restaurant. The ad, which began airing in Los Angeles in or about March, 1997, appears on Channels 5, 13, and 50.

The ad you approved features an actress resembling famous cooking show chef and T.V. personality Julia Kidd. The actress stands in a kitchen and says, "You know me". The actress never says she is Julia Kidd in the ad and there is no disclaimer on the ad. The ad agency titled the ad copy "Julia Kidding" for its own internal reference. You estimate the ad has increased business by fifty percent.

On October 1, 1997, you received a letter from Ms. Kidd's attorney warning you that Ms. Kidd will pursue legal action against you if you do not pull the ad by November 30th. The letter also demanded that you destroy all related ad material and give all your restaurant profits from the ad to Ms. Kidd.

Your primary concern is whether Ms. Kidd can bring any causes of action against you for continuing to run your ad. You want to continue running your ad because you have already paid for the ad and the ad time and the ad has increased your business. You are willing to put a disclaimer on the ad if it will protect you from liability. You have also expressed concern about whether you are required to give Ms. Kidd your profits resulting from the ad. Finally, you want to know what your options are at this time.

My research indicates that if you continue to run the ad, Ms. Kidd can pursue legal action against you under both state and federal laws. The California courts are especially protective of famous personalities' rights because there are so many celebrities living in the state. Therefore, the courts tend to looked with disfavor upon individuals who even unintentionally use a celebrity look-alike without permission to promote their goods and/or services. In addition, a jury and not a judge will decide whether the facts support Ms. Kidd's claims against you. A jury is likely to be sympathetic to Ms. Kidd because she is trying to protect her name and reputation.

Ms. Kidd can bring two state claims against you. In order for you to prevail against the first claim, you must show the actress in the commercial does not bear an exact resemblance to Ms. Kidd, you did not knowingly intend to use Ms. Kidd's likeness, or there was no direct connection between the use of the actress resembling Ms. Kidd and the promotion of your restaurant. To prevail against the second state claim, you must show the actress does not bear a close resemblance to Ms. Kidd, you did not use the actress' physical resemblance to Ms. Kidd for commercial advantage, Ms. Kidd's consent was not required, and Ms. Kidd suffered no losses resulting from the airing of the T.V. ad.

With respect to the first state claim and the issue of resemblance, the court applies a strict "likeness" standard. California courts, in particular, tend to look for an exact likeness of the person being copied rather than a close resemblance. In other words, Ms. Kidd will have to prove the actress is an exact likeness of her to prevail on this issue. You may prevail by establishing that the actress merely resembles Ms. Kidd. On the other hand, Ms. Kidd may argue the resemblance is strong enough to meet the "likeness" standard. A jury will ultimately decide if the actress' resemblance to Ms. Kidd meets the "likeness" standard by viewing the ad.

Regarding whether you "knowingly" used Ms. Kidd's likeness, you could assert that the ad agency came up with the idea and you only knowingly intended to promote your restaurant. However, Ms. Kidd can argue you were aware of the actress' resemblance to Ms. Kidd when you approved the ad and that you knew the agency labeled the ad "Julia Kidding". Ms. Kidd can also say the warning letter has formally put you on notice regarding the unauthorized use of Ms. Kidd's likeness. Again, the jury will decide if the facts support the "knowing" requirement.

Regarding the existence of a "direct connection", you could argue that no direct connection exists between the use of an actress who happens to resemble Ms. Kidd and the promotion of a restaurant because the actress does not identity herself as being a chef. However, if Ms. Kidd establishes you used her "likeness", she can establish the "direct connection" between the use of an actress who is portraying a famous chef and the promotion of your restaurant. Once again, the jury will determine if the "direct connection" requirement has been met.

Ms. Kidd is even more likely to prevail against you on the second state claim because the resemblance standard is not as strict. Under this claim, the court only requires that Ms. Kidd show you used her "identity". This broader standard considers not just physical resemblance, but the ad's total impression on the viewer. Therefore, even though you could still argue the resemblance is not close, the combination of physical resemblance, a kitchen setting and the line "You know me" is likely to be enough under this claim to show you used Ms. Kidd's identity. Ms. Kidd can show you used the actress' resemblance to Ms. Kidd for commercial advantage because the purpose of the ad was to promote your restaurant. Ms. Kidd can use the warning letter to show you did not have her consent. She can also show that she suffered lost profits because she was not paid for the ad. Finally, Ms. Kidd can show the ad damages her reputation and image because her identity has been used without her permission to endorse an unknown and, arguably, unproven restaurant that she has never visited and which is owned by a man she has never met.

Ms. Kidd can also bring a federal claim against you. To prevail against a federal claim, you must show that viewers of the ad are not likely to confuse the actress with Ms. Kidd. You may argue that viewers who know Ms. Kidd will know the actress is not Ms. Kidd. However, you have already said that people have asked you if the actress is Ms. Kidd and this evidence can be used against you. Ms. Kidd is a famous chef who has a cooking show on T.V. She will try to argue that your ad features a Ms. Kidd "look-alike" who is standing in a kitchen and telling the audience, "You know me" to indicate she is Ms. Kidd. She may also try to show that the absence of a disclaimer intentionally promotes confusion among viewers. Based on the facts of your case and the research I have done, it is my opinion that Ms. Kidd has a strong chance of prevailing against you on both state and federal claims if this case goes to trial.

You may consider joining the ad agency as an additional defendant if Ms. Kidd pursues legal action against you. You may then be able to recover some or all of your costs from the ad agency, assuming no agreement exists limiting your rights against the agency. I would need to see all documentation between you and the ad agency to determine if you have a potential claim against it.

You wanted to know if you could place a disclaimer on the ad to protect you from liability. As I already indicated to you over the phone on October

9th, Ms. Kidd's attorney rejected that idea. At that time, I also consulted another attorney who is an expert in the area of intellectual property. I relayed to you that he also advised immediately pulling the ad as requested to avoid having to pay punitive damages in addition to the regular damages you may have to pay if Ms. Kidd prevails against you in court. General damages can include compensating Ms. Kidd for using her identity. In addition, the court could make you disgorge all your profits from the ad to Ms. Kidd. The court could also make you pay punitive damages for acting in bad faith by disregarding the warning letter and continuing to run the ad, even with a disclaimer.

You also wanted to know if you are required to give Ms. Kidd all your profits resulting from the ad, as demanded in Ms. Steele's warning letter to you. You are not required to give your profits to Ms. Kidd. However, failure to make an alternative offer to Ms. Kidd may cause her to take legal action against you. I therefore suggest that you consider allowing me to negotiate a settlement on your behalf so that Ms. Kidd has no reason to pursue legal action against you.

The following settlement options may enable you to continue running the ad without risking liability. You may offer to pay Ms. Kidd a licensing fee in exchange for your being permitted to continue running the ad. Another option is to allow Ms. Kidd to modify the ad to her liking and agree to destroy the unmodified ad and all related material.

In the event Ms. Kidd is not receptive to either of these options, I suggest that you consider proposing a third settlement option. This option is not as appealing, but it will allow you to cut your losses. Such an option could include your agreeing to pull the ad, destroy all ad material and pay Ms. Kidd a licensing fee that covers the entire six month period the ad has run. This option could be proposed in the event Ms. Kidd insists on the demands made in the warning letter.

These settlement options are merely suggestions for your review and consideration. I am also happy to explore other options with you. Settlement negotiations will take approximately 20 hours and will be billed at the same hourly fee of $150.00 I quoted during our meeting. Upon your instruction, I will immediately arrange a settlement negotiation conference with Ms. Kidd's attorney.

Of course, another option you have is to continue running the ad. If you decide not to cooperate with Ms. Kidd and continue to run the ad even with a disclaimer, it is very likely that Ms. Kidd will pursue legal action against you. If you lose, you may be faced with not only paying Ms. Kidd all your profits, but also compensating her for using her identity and paying her punitive damages. You may even be forced to pay her attorney's fees in addition to my fees. I advise you to carefully consider the possible costs and consequences of not cooperating with Ms. Kidd at this time.

If you decide to pull the ad by November 30th as requested, you could replace it with a new ad. Understandably, you may not wish to consider replacing the ad because of the expense involved. Therefore, more economical alternatives are also worth exploring at this time. You could obtain free T.V., radio, newspaper and magazine publicity by inviting restaurant reviewers, dee jays and food critics to dine in your restaurant. You could also participate in food drive charities and local events, like "The Taste of Newport," to further publicize your restaurant. You could also submit articles to food magazines and even teach a cooking course.

If you have doubts about the strength of Ms. Kidd's claims, you may wish to consider having a random survey conducted on the T.V. ad to determined whether viewers are likely to identify the actress in the ad as Ms. Kidd. A random survey could give us some insight into how likely it is that a jury will identify the actress as Ms. Kidd. If you decide to enter into settlement negotiations, survey results that favor you could be used as leverage in negotiating a better settlement for you. Unfavorable results could also help you decide what to do if we cannot reach a settlement that is agreeable to you. The cost of a survey is approximately $150.00 and takes two days. Subject to your consent, I will arrange to have a random survey conducted immediately.

Mr. Clark, I recommend that you consider doing all that you can at this point to avoid what is likely to be an expensive and lengthy trial in a case that Ms. Kidd has a good chance of winning. A trial is also likely to result in negative publicity for Dana's. I understand that you want to do what you can to increase your restaurant business. I can also appreciate your not wanting to lose the cost of the ad and the ad time. However, it makes more sense to take appropriate action now while you still can to minimize your losses than to end up fighting what I believe will be an uphill battle that may ultimately cost you far more than the cost of the ad, the ad time and lost business.

Ultimately, the decision rests with you. We can discuss the options further when I see you next week. In the meantime, please feel free to call me if you have any questions. I am here to help you in any way I can.

Sincerely,

Rachel Goldstein, Esq.

Turrell, Gadol & Lamb
9000 Newport Center Place
Suite 2500
Newport Beach, California 92660

NEWPORT   Bryan Gadol

BEACH

Seal Beach   Michael Turrell

Orange   J. Matthew Lamb

October 11, 1996

VIA U.S. POSTAL SERVICE

Reverend Thomas Smith
Salvation Baptist Church
700 Glory Club Lane
Chula Vista, CA 92135

Re: *Letter of Opinion After Initial Consultation*

Dear Reverend Smith:

It was a pleasure to meet with you on August 28 to discuss the circumstances surrounding your employment at the Salvation Baptist Church. After this initial consultation, in which it was decided that you would retain our offices, I have done some preliminary research regarding your primary concerns. I also had an opportunity to discuss these matters with the attorney retained by Tony Arnold for the Board of Trustees of the Salvation Baptist Church. In this conversation some issues were raised that might also be of concern.

Before I can provide you with analysis and explanation of how the law applies to your situation, outline what our goals and priorities are, and discuss what happens next, we must have an understanding of what the relevant facts are in this matter according to you and the Trustees' attorney. If any of the following facts are wrong or need clarification, please let me know immediately to prevent us from providing improper advice. It will also be necessary for us to meet again to discuss the issues raised by the Trustees' attorney.

You are a Reverend in the Baptist religion, and have been for at least the last five years. You are currently the Reverend at the Salvation Baptist Church (the "Church"). Fred Williams, President of the Board of Trustees of the Salvation Baptist Church (the "Trustees"), recruited you from your prior position at the Newport Creek Baptist Church. According to the Trustees' attorney, you represented that you had never been sexually involved with any members at your previous church. You were hired in June, 1995, by the Trustees and given control of day-to-day operations of the Church. The structure and format of the Church is governed by the Salvation Baptist Church By-laws (the "By-laws") and the New Testament of the Bible (the "Bible").

In July, 1995, your control of the day-to-day operations of the Church was removed by Fred Williams and Tony Arnold. You believe that this was retaliation by Fred Williams and/or Tony Arnold because of two consensual relationships you had with two women church members while you and your wife were separated. Despite how Fred Williams and Tony Arnold view these relationships, you consider these two relationships to be healthy, loving relationships in accordance with the By-laws and Bible. According to the Trustees' attorney, the change in your job responsibilities was in response to the trustees becoming aware of current litigation against you stemming from relationships you had at your previous church.

During the nine months that followed you remained as the Reverend of the Church, and continued your duties, except for the day-to-day operations. Then on April 17, 1996, Fred Williams held a congregational meeting to hold a vote to determine if you should be removed as Reverend of the Church. You believe that the meeting was held in violation of the By-laws, and that the vote was swayed by Fred Williams and/or Tony Arnold discussing your sexual relations with Church members. You also believe that your reputation has been harmed by these discussions. You refused to relinquish your position after the vote.

On June 21, 1996, a court order was issued restricting you from entering the Church, and requiring you to relinquish the Church financial records to the Trustees. In response you changed the locks to the Church and refused to turn over the financial records. You also transferred money from joint church accounts into an account under your name only.

Finally, on July 10, 1996, a second congregational meeting was held to decide whether you should be reinstated as the Reverend of the Church. At this meeting you were reinstated by the Congregation. Currently, you are the Reverend of the Church, but do not have control of the day-to-day operations.

At our meeting, you stated that your primary concerns were that the Trustees had no right to remove you from your position of power, and that the Trustees had ruined your reputation within the congregation. I understand that you wish to have your control of the church day-today operations restored, and your reputation repaired.

Our ability to restore your control of the Church operations will depend on the type and character of the employment contract that you and the Trustees entered into in June, 1995. You did not make any representation in our meeting that there was a written contract, but only that the Church operations were governed by the By-laws and Bible. However, the Trustees' attorney indicated that there might be a contract. It will be necessary to review the By-laws and any such contract before making a definitive determination of your rights and potential remedies. Further, we will need to investigate the possibility that the Trustees violated the By-laws at the first meeting where you were removed.

Unfortunately, your reputation has not been harmed in any way that allows for a legal remedy. Under the law, reputational harms are called defamation. To prove defamation, we would have to prove that the statements of your sexual conduct were: (1) false and defamatory; (2) published intentionally or negligently by Fred Williams and/or Tony Arnold to third persons; (3) the third persons understood the defamatory implications applied to you; and (4) you suffered damages as a result. By your own admission you admit that you did have relationships with two members of the Church. Also, you do not have any significant proof that you were defamed by any writing showing what was stated, or by any member telling you what was spoken about you. Moreover, your damages are negligible because you still received your salary during the time you were removed, and there is no evidence that your reputation was harmed in the congregation, as demonstrated by your reinstatement.

After my conversation with the Trustees' attorney, I believe that we may have some secondary concerns. These concerns are the potential for further litigation, including a cause of action for fraud or conversion of personal property. Further, if the Trustees decide to report the alleged transfer of Church monies, the District Attorney could bring criminal charges against you for embezzlement.

First, fraud is the intentional or negligent misrepresentation or conceal-ment of a fact or facts that are intended to be relied upon by another party. The Trustees may claim that when they interviewed you for the Reverend position, you actively concealed past relationships you might have had with former congregation members, and a lawsuit regarding one of these relation-ships. Even if those facts are true, the law requires that you intentionally concealed these facts, and that the Trustees relied on your representations in reaching their decision to extend an offer of employment to you.

Second, conversion of personal property is the wrongful exercise of control over personal property of another. Conversion is only found where substantial interference with possession or right to possession occurs. In conversion cases, the damaged party is only permitted to recover the full value of the property lost. This requires that you did in fact transfer the monies from the Church accounts to your own personal account. If in fact you did transfer the money, and the Trustees were successful in bringing a conversion of personal property action, the court would only order you to return the full amount back to the Church.

Third, embezzlement is a theft crime where a person has fraudulently appropriated property entrusted to him. Indeed, the Church did entrust the money to you, and if you did in fact transfer the moneys, there may be a possibility of having to defend a criminal prosecution. However, this is dependent upon the Trustees reporting the alleged transfer to the police, and the District Attorney filing charges. Presently, if there has been no report to the authorities, this is not our primary concern.

Our goals are simple in nature, but will require diligent work and dedication on our part. First, we primarily want to work on restoring you to your position of control over the Church. We need you to provide a copy of the By-laws and both meeting notices and to outline the relevant verses of the Bible that give you authority over the Church. Second, we want to defend any potential fraud or conversion of personal property causes of action. We will need to meet and discuss in detail the circumstances of your hiring, including any and all discussions you had with any Trustee, and the nature of how you handled the Church finances and whether you did indeed transfer the monies. At that point, we will have to wait and see if the Trustees file a civil complaint. To successfully defend any embezzlement charges, we will need to meet and discuss in detail the nature of how you handled the Church finances and whether you did indeed transfer the moneys. At that point, we will have to wait and see if the Trustees file a report and the District Attorney files charges.

Finally, our next meeting will be an in-depth exploration of facts pertinent to ascertaining our goals. I would like to meet with you on or before November 30. At this meeting it will be necessary for you to bring copies of the By-laws, the meeting notices, and the court order. Also, as I outlined to you in our initial meeting, our firm does not operate on a contingency basis, but a flat billing rate. Our firm's billing rate is $350 per hour for partners, $250 per hour for associates, $125 per hour for support staff, and $95 per hour for clerical staff. Our policy is to bill in 1/10 of an hour (6 minute) increments. We will require a $5000 retainer up front at the beginning of our next meeting. The retainer will cover the first $5000 of billed time, and then you will be billed monthly from that point forward until conclusion of these matters.

I hope that our firm can earn your trust and resolve these matters to your satisfaction. Should you have any questions, please call me at (714) 288-8741. I thank you for giving Turrell, Gadol & Lamb the opportunity to handle your legal matters.

Very truly yours,

J. Matthew Lamb

APPENDIX IV

MEMORANDA

MEMORANDUM

TO: Jaded Old Partner
FROM: Eager New Associate
RE: John E. Walker, False
             Imprisonment Claim

ISSUE

Can a casino patron who is drunk and disruptive recover for false imprisonment under the law of New Jersey when security personnel detain him to "cool off" despite his repeated requests to leave?

CONCLUSION

A casino patron who is drunk and disruptive can recover for false imprisonment under the law of New Jersey when security personnel detain him to "cool off" despite his repeated requests to leave. The two requirements of false imprisonment are met because the patron was under a reasonable apprehension that the security personnel had the authority to detain him and because they did not, in fact, have such authority. There was no legal justification for the detention in this case because the patron was not cheating and had not committed a crime that the casino intended to report to the authorities.

FACTS

Our client, Mr. John E. Walker, recently visited the Empty Pockets Casino in Atlantic City, New Jersey. While there, he lost a great deal of money. Apparently believing that they had a "high roller" on their hands, casino officials instructed the waitresses on the casino floor to provide Mr. Walker with free drinks.

After accepting several free drinks and continuing to lose money, Mr. Walker became somewhat upset and began accusing the dealer and the casino of cheating and of stealing his money. He acknowledges that he was probably a bit loud and may have been annoying other patrons of the casino.

Mr. Walker was approached by two rather large men wearing suits who identified themselves as casino security guards and asked him to accompany them. Mr. Walker noticed that they were wearing identification badges that had the word "security" prominently displayed on them. Mr. Walker accompanied the men to a small room located near the casino floor, where they asked him to sit down and "cool off."

The guards remained with Mr. Walker for approximately two hours, denying his several requests to leave. At the end of this period, the guards told him he was free to go. Mr. Walker would like to know whether he can sue the Empty Pockets Casino for false imprisonment.

DISCUSSION

Mr. Walker has a cause of action for false imprisonment against the Empty Pockets Casino. Under New Jersey law, a cause of action for false imprisonment or false arrest is made out upon a showing that there was an arrest and that the arrest was without legal justification. *Barletta v. Golden Nugget Hotel Casino*, 580 F. Supp. 614, 617 (D.N.J. 1984). In New Jersey, false arrest and false imprisonment are merely different names for the same tort. *Roth v. Golden Nugget Casino/Hotel, Inc.*, 576 F. Supp. 262, 265 (D.N.J. 1983).

Mr. Walker can establish that there was an arrest in his case. He must show that his liberty was constrained as a result of force, or the threat of force, by the defendant. *Id.* New Jersey courts have held that "the assertion of legal authority to take a person into custody, even where such authority does not in fact exist, may be sufficient to create a reasonable apprehension that a person is under restraint." *Bartolo v. Boardwalk Regency Hotel Casino*, 449 A.2d 1339, 1341 (N.J. Super. Law Div. 1982).

The court in *Barletta* found that an arrest had taken place where the plaintiff was escorted to the casino security office by two security officers after an altercation between the plaintiff and another casino patron. The fact that the plaintiff accompanied the security officers under her own power did not affect her claim where she testified that she did not feel free to refuse. The court in *Roth* found an arrest under virtually identical circumstances.

Mr. Walker's situation closely parallels the cited cases. He, too, was asked to accompany security officers from the casino floor, and, by his own account, did not feel that he was in a position to refuse. Here, as in *Barletta* and *Roth*, a court should find that there was a reasonable apprehension of force.

Mr. Walker should also be able to establish that the restraint was without legal justification. There are two possible justifications for the restraint that the casino might raise, but neither of them is likely to be accepted by a court.

First, the casino might argue that the security officers were entitled to detain Mr. Walker under a broad interpretation of the New Jersey statute that allows casinos to detain patrons upon suspicion of various offenses, all of which involve cheating. N.J. Stat. Ann. § 5:12-121(b) (West 1977). Such a broad interpretation of the statute was rejected by the court in *Bartolo*. In that case the plaintiff was detained on suspicion of card counting, which the court held could not be equated with cheating. If card counting does not constitute cheating and therefore does not come within the ambit of section 5:12-121(b), being drunk and disorderly is certainly not a ground for detention under that section.

Alternatively, the casino might argue that it was entitled to detain Mr. Walker under the statutory provision that allows any person to detain another who commits a disorderly persons offense in the detainer's presence. N.J. Stat. Ann. § 2A:169-3 (West 1979). However, that statute has also been narrowly construed by the courts. In *Roth*, the court held that a disorderly persons offense must actually have occurred before an arrest without a warrant will be justified. There, the court denied defendant's motion for summary judgment because there was a genuine factual dispute as to whether plaintiff had committed the offense of criminal trespass.

It is not entirely clear whether Mr. Walker committed a disorderly persons offense, but the casino security personnel did not accuse him of committing one and took no steps to bring him before the proper authorities as is required by section 2A:169-3. Although the cases do not address the significance of the phrase "and take him before any magistrate," the previous narrow constructions of the statute would suggest that this phrase should also be read literally. Thus, the casino's failure to follow the procedure outlined by the statute should negate its claim of legal justification for the detention.

In Mr. Walker's case, the security guards simply told him that they wanted him to "cool off," and, when they were satisfied that he had done so, let him go. Such a detention is not authorized by the statutes or the decided cases. We should pursue a claim for false imprisonment on Mr. Walker's behalf.

MEMORANDUM

TO: Katie Harrington-McBride

FROM: Gregg Stepan

DATE: October 30, 1996
        Amanda Potts' case of
        retaliatory discharge,
        Case No. 96-110-0039

ISSUE

Whether, under Illinois common law, an at-will employee can recover damages for retaliatory discharge when, prior to the discharge, the employee complained to her supervisor about smoke in the workplace and petitioned other employees to support a smoke-free workplace.

CONCLUSION

Yes, under Illinois common law, an at-will employee can likely recover damages for retaliatory discharge when, prior to the discharge, the employee complained to her supervisor about smoke in the workplace and petitioned other employees to support a smoke-free workplace. Such a case could be brought under a retaliatory discharge claim because the facts show that the discharge was likely in retaliation for the employee's activities, and because protecting public health through a smoke-free workplace is likely a public policy that has been clearly mandated by the Illinois legislature but violated by the discharge.

FACTS

Amanda Potts is a 36-year-old marketing professional who was hired by Chapin Associates in April 1995 to lead a team of market specialists. Chapin is a Chicago-based marketing and public relations consulting firm. The dispute between Potts and Chapin arises over Chapin's discharge of Potts in April 1996.

Before coming to Chapin, Potts worked for Beatrice, Inc., but she wanted to quit her position with Beatrice because it required extensive travel. When she quit at Beatrice, she was earning a yearly salary of $57,000.

Upon beginning her new job at Chapin, she was dismayed to learn that two of her team members were cigarette smokers. Their cubicles joined hers and three others in a cluster. Potts was not happy and immediately asked Chapin's President, Harry Carpenter, if something could be done. Carpenter was sympathetic, but said that nothing could be done because the private offices were all taken, and team leaders were expected to have a cubicle among the team.

Two weeks later, at a staff meeting, Potts raised the issue again. She told the group that she had asked her writers to stop smoking or at least cut back, but that they refused, saying that they could not think unless they had a cigarette in hand. Reactions from those at the meeting were mixed—some agreed that smoking was disgusting, others advocated the smokers' rights, and still others thought the matter should be settled outside of staff meetings.

In November 1995, Potts received her first formal evaluation. Her work was rated as "Meets Requirements" or "Exceeds Requirements" in all categories, including Quality of Work, Time Management, and Client Relations. Potts enjoyed the work she did for Chapin and tried to make the best of the situation, but she grew progressively more angry as time passed.

In December 1995, Potts interrupted a Friday afternoon company party to take an informal poll, asking how many people agreed that smoking should be banned in the workplace. Other employees at the party seemed uncomfortable, and some began to leave, even though the party had just begun. On the following Monday, Carpenter and Ricki Hubbard, the Senior Vice President, asked Potts to meet with them to discuss the situation. They told her that her behavior was inappropriate and had to stop. She responded that her cleaning bills had increased because her clothes reeked of cigarette smoke and that she had felt ill from the smoke ever since she started working for the company. She again asked for relief but was told that no private offices were available and that she would just have to get used to the situation.

Potts decided to rally support among other employees. She hung a "NO PUFFIN" poster on the outside wall of her cubicle. She also hung an American Lung Association poster showing a diseased lung next to a healthy lung in her cubicle. She put American Cancer Association pamphlets about the dangers of smoking on an, "information exchange" table in the lunch room. She also sent an e-mail to every employee detailing the dangers of smoking and second-hand smoke. Finally, she circulated a petition to other employees asking them to join her in demanding a smoke-free workplace. She took the petition, with twenty-two signatures out of Chapin's fifty-two employees, to Carpenter on April 3, 1996. Carpenter appeared angry and refused to meet with her. Two days later, on April 5, 1996, Carpenter told Potts that her services were no longer needed at Chapin. When she asked why she was being fired, Carpenter said, "We just don't think it's working out. You'll be happier somewhere else, I'm sure."

Potts was stunned because she thought her work had been appreciated by Chapin's management. After five months of searching, Potts found a new position that pays only $51,000 and requires her to travel extensively.

The discussion that follows is in response to your request that I research whether Potts can sue Chapin for damages.

(Matthew Bender & Co., Inc.)

DISCUSSION

The Amanda Potts case is governed by the Illinois common-law claim of retaliatory discharge. As outlined by the Supreme Court of Illinois, three elements must be proven to receive damages in a retaliatory discharge case. *Hinthorn v. Roland's of Bloomington, Inc.*, 519 N.E.2d 909, 911 (Ill. 1988). They are: (1) the employee must be discharged, (2) in retaliation for the employee's activities, and (3) the discharge must violate clearly mandated public policy. *Id.* at 911. Retaliatory discharge is an exception to the at-will employment rule, which is that the employer may discharge an at-will employee for any reason or no reason at all. *Zimmerman v. Buchheit of Sparta, Inc.*, 645 N.E.2d 877, 879 (Ill. 1995). Because Amanda Potts was hired with no time duration for her employment, she is an at-will employee, *Stevenson v. ITT Harper, Inc.*, 366 N.E.2d 561, 566 (Ill. App. Ct. 1977), but her discharge likely satisfies all three of the elements of the retaliatory discharge exception.

I. The employee was discharged.

From the facts that you provided me, it seems clear that Amanda Potts was discharged when she was called into Carpenter's office on April 5, 1996 and told that her services were no longer needed. Chapin will probably not take issue with the first element.

II. The discharge was in retaliation for the employee's activities.

Whether the employee was discharged in retaliation for his or her activities is a question of fact to be decided at trial by the trier of fact. *Hugo v. Tomaszewski*, 508 N.E.2d 1139, 1141 (Ill. App. Ct. 1987). To satisfy this element, the plaintiff must necessarily show that the employer had knowledge of the activities before the discharge. *Sherman v. Kraft General Foods, Inc.*, 651 N.E.2d 708, 710 (Ill. App. Ct. 1995). The facts show that Potts met with her supervisor at least twice to discuss her problem with the smoking. Thus, Chapin was aware of the activities of Potts before the discharge. Several other facts point to Chapin's retaliatory intent. First, Potts received a formal evaluation in November 1995, in which she received markings of "meets" or "exceeds" requirements in all categories. Potts, in fact, thought her work was appreciated and was surprised to be fired. In addition, the President of Chapin, Carpenter, complained to Potts about her efforts to obtain a smoke-free workplace. For example, soon after Potts interrupted the Christmas party, Carpenter told her that she had to stop her efforts. Also, only two days after trying to submit a petition to ban smoking in the workplace, Potts was discharged. Such a short time span between the activity and the discharge has been held to establish a prima facie case of retaliation. *Hugo*, 508 N.E.2d at 1141. In short, based only on the facts that you provided, a reasonable jury would probably find that Chapin fired Potts in retaliation for her activities.

Chapin, however, may argue that it had a "valid, non-pretextual" basis for discharging Potts, and thus, no retaliatory discharge claim stands. *Hartlein v. Illinois Power Co.*, 601 N.E.2d 720 (Ill. 1992). For example, Chapin might claim that she was discharged for disrupting the workplace and as a result, she diminished Chapin's productivity and profitability.

Nevertheless, it is not likely that such an argument by Chapin would be successful. Even if the facts did support some valid reason, other than retaliation, for discharge, such a reason would most likely be pretextual in this case. A pretext as applied to retaliatory discharge has been defined as "a purpose or motive alleged or an appearance assumed in order to cloak the real intention or state of affairs." *Wayne v. Exxon Coal U.S.A., Inc.*, 510 N.E.2d 468, 471 (Ill. App. Ct. 1987). The facts already obtained point to a retaliatory basis for the discharge. Any other reason would probably be alleged to "cloak the real intention" of retaliation, as already supported by the facts. The facts show no clear evidence of Chapin's concern for productivity or profitability; rather, the facts show a prima facie case of retaliation. *Hugo*, 508 N.E.2d at 1141. Therefore, the facts we already have are sufficiently convincing that a jury would probably find that any other reason for the discharge presented by Chapin is merely pretextual.

III.   The discharge violates clearly mandated public policy.

In retaliatory discharge cases, the employee must assert that the discharge violated a clearly mandated public policy. *Palmateer v. International Harvester* Co., 421 N.E.2d 876, 878 (Ill. 1981). In this case, Amanda Potts could assert the public policy of protecting the public health through a smoke-free workplace, a policy embodied in the Illinois Clean Indoor Air Act, 410 Ill. Comp. Stat. 80/1-11 (West 1993). The Illinois courts, however, have never before allowed that particular public policy argument in retaliatory discharge cases. Nonetheless, as we analyze the Amanda Potts case, we will see that protection from smoking in the workplace is consistent with the existing judicial analysis of public policy.

The first section of this analysis will review three tests that the Illinois courts have established to define public policy, and these tests will be applied to the Amanda Potts case. The second section of the analysis will review two categories of public policy that have evolved in the Illinois retaliatory discharge cases. Again, the Amanda Potts case will be analyzed to see how it fits into these two categories. The third section of the analysis will use a case on point in California to show that protection from smoking in the workplace should be an actionable public policy. The final section of the analysis will address a pre-emption argument that Chapin might utilize to avoid expansion of the public policy doctrine.

A.   Defining public policy

To define public policy, we must look at the tests that arise in the case law on retaliatory discharge. As we apply these defining tests of public policy to the Amanda Potts case, we will see that the policy of protection from smoking in the workplace likely satisfies each defining test.

The first test is that the public policy must be "found in the State's constitution and statutes, and when they are silent, in its judicial decisions." *Palmateer v. International Harvester Co.*, 421 N.E.2d 876, 878 (Ill. 1981). Moreover, the Illinois Supreme Court further explained that to determine the public policy underlying a statutory provision we examine "the history, purpose, language and effect of the provision." *Barr v. Kelso-Burnett Co.*, 478 N.E.2d 1354, 1357 (Ill. 1985).

Amanda Potts's efforts to obtain a smoke-free workplace are embodied in the public policy declared by the Illinois legislature in the Illinois Clean Indoor Air Act, 410 Ill. Comp. Stat. 80/1-11 (West 1993). The Illinois Clean Indoor Air Act (ICIAA) became effective in July 1990, and it prohibits smoking in a public place, which includes an office workplace. *Id.* at § 4. An analysis of the language of sections 2 and 9 of the ICIAA, shows the "purpose" and "effect" of the provision. *Barr*, 478 N.E.2d at 1357.

In section 2 of the Act, the legislature stated its findings. 410 Ill. Comp. Stat. 80/2 (West 1993). Section 2 reads, "The General Assembly finds that tobacco smoke is annoying, harmful and dangerous to human beings and a hazard to public health." The language of this section embodies the motivation or purpose for the prohibition of smoking in a public place: smoking is a public hazard and is harmful to human beings. *Id.* at § 2.

The effect of this Act is found in the language of section 9, which reads, "No individual may be discriminated against in any manner because of the exercise of any rights afforded by this Act." *Id.* at § 9. From section 9, we see that the legislature created rights through the Act, and that no individual may be discriminated against for exercising these rights. The rights referred to in section 9 are not expressly defined in the statute itself, but in *Pechan v. Dynpro, Inc.*, 622 N.E.2d 108 (Ill. App. Ct. 1993), the court refers to a "right to breathe clean air in public places," in a discussion about section 9 of the ICIAA. *Id.* at 114. Thus, by examining the purpose and effect of the Illinois Clean Indoor Air Act, we find that the Illinois legislature effectuated the right to breathe clean air in public places in furtherance of a public policy protecting the public health. This Act represents a clearly mandated public policy for the state of Illinois.

A second test in determining public policy is that it "affects the citizens of the State collectively," *Palmateer*, 421 N.E.2d at 878, and not "only private interests are at stake." *Id.* at 879. In the ICIAA, the legislature found that tobacco smoke is a public health issue, 410 Comp. Stat. 80/2 (West

1993), not just a private issue. Thus, Potts's efforts to create a smoke-free workplace, while partly personal, should also be considered an effort vital to the public health. In addition, Potts' actions show that she was not just concerned about herself. Potts informed and educated others of the dangers of smoking and second-hand smoke through posters, flyers, and e-mail to all her co-workers. Also, twenty-two other employees signed a petition for a smoke-free workplace. In summary, the legislative findings in the Illinois Clean Indoor Air Act, Potts' actions showing interest in others, and co-worker interest in a smoke-free workplace, all show that this case is not just a personal matter; it is also a public matter.

Chapin, however, will likely argue that this case was actually a personal matter; it was brought about because Potts disliked cigarette smoke. Chapin will probably support its argument with the holding in *Price v. Carinack Datsun, Inc.*, 485 N.E.2d 359 (Ill. 1985). The plaintiff alleged that he was fired in retaliation for filing an insurance claim under the defendant company's group health insurance plan. The court held that the discharge of an employee for filing a health insurance claim did not fall under public policy because "the matter [was] one of private and individual grievance rather than one affecting our society." *Id.* at 361. The court further stated, "a discharge for filing a claim under which he is a beneficiary does not violate clearly mandated public policy." *Id.* at 361. Chapin will likely analogize that because in that case a private beneficiary could not invoke public policy, so too, in the Potts case, a private beneficiary should not be able to claim a violation of public policy.

Nevertheless, the *Price* case is distinguishable from the situation in Potts. In *Price*, the plaintiff pointed to the Illinois Code that regulates the health insurance industry to demonstrate public policy. *Id.* at 361. The court held that this code was "designed to govern operations of insurance companies, not insureds, such as the defendant." *Id.* at 361. In the Potts case, on the other hand, we have a more clearly applicable public policy: the Illinois Clean Indoor Air Act. Violations of this act apply to both "persons" and "corporations," 410 Ill. Comp. Stat. 80/7 (West 1993), and section 2 of the act clearly creates a public, not just private, interest, as already explained. *Id.* at § 2. In other words, the policy embodied in the ICIAA applies to all citizens, whereas the policy in *Price* only applied to insurance companies. Therefore, the public policy underlying the ICIAA in the Amanda Potts case affects the citizens of Illinois individually and collectively.

A third test in defining public policy is that "a matter must strike at the heart of a citizen's social rights, duties, and responsibilities." *Palmateer*, 421 N.E.2d at 878. As explained above, section 9 of the Illinois Clean Indoor Air Act has the effect of establishing a right of Illinois citizens to breathe clean indoor air. 410 Ill. Comp. Stat. 80/9 (West 1993). This right is established as a matter of public health. *Id.* at § 2. The legislature found that tobacco smoke is harmful, hazardous, and dangerous to human beings. *Id.* at § 2. Thus, the Potts discharge strikes at the heart of the right of an Illinois citizen to breathe clean indoor air.

B.   Categorizing public policy

In applying these three tests to various situations, the Illinois courts have applied public policy exception in two situations. *Sherman v. Kraft General Foods, Inc.*, 651 N.E.2d 708, 711 (Ill. App. Ct. 1995). First, the courts have found a violation of public policy when a citizen is fired for filing or attempting to file a worker's compensation claim. *Kelsay v. Motorola, Inc.*, 384 N.E.2d 353, 357 (Ill. 1978). Second, the courts have found a violation of public policy when a citizen is fired for reporting illegal or improper conduct, often referred to as "whistleblowing." *Lambert v. City of Lake Forest*, 542 N.E.2d 1216, 1219 (Ill. App. Ct. 1989).

In categorizing the Amanda Potts case, there are two alternatives: (1) The case could be categorized as creating a new, third category of public policy that will support a retaliatory discharge claim, or (2) the case could be categorized as another whistleblowing case. As the analysis will show, the Amanda Potts case best fits into the whistleblowing category because it is consistent with the whistleblowing cases and because its placement within an existing category avoids the expansion of the retaliatory discharge doctrine.

Amanda Potts was "blowing the whistle" on smoke in her workplace. Smoke in the workplace was prohibited under the Illinois Indoor Clean Air Act. 410 Ill. Comp. Stat. 80/4 (West 1993) Section 6 of the ICIAA provides that any person or entity "in control of a place which includes a public place shall make reasonable efforts to prevent smoking in the public place." *Id.* at § 6. In addition, under section 7 of the ICIAA, a corporation is guilty of a petty offense for violating section 4. (Section 4 prohibits smoking in a public place.) *Id.* at § 4 and § 7. Amanda Potts blew the whistle on activity that she felt was improper because it was dangerous to her health and to the health of others. Likewise, the ICIAA establishes this activity by co-workers and by Chapin as improper and illegal because it is dangerous to the public health. *Id.* at § 2. Therefore, the Potts case could fit into the existing whistleblowing category.

The situation in another whistleblowing case, *Wheeler v. Caterpillar Tractor Co.*, 485 N.E.2d 372 (Ill. 1985), is similar to Potts's situation, and provides an example of the Illinois Supreme Court's acceptance of public health as public policy. The employee in *Wheeler* repeatedly requested to be transferred to a different department because the radioactive cobalt 60 unit that he was working with could cause serious injury. *Id.* at 374. Wheeler was, in effect, blowing the whistle on improper and unsafe working conditions. *Id.* at 376. Despite the fact that Wheeler reported the unsafe conditions to the employer rather than to the authorities, *Id.* at 381, the court allowed the action and held that protecting the lives of citizens from the "hazards of radioactive material" is a public policy that is clearly mandated by legislation. *Id.* at 377.

An analogy can be drawn between the *Wheeler* case and the Potts case because the facts are very similar. Potts, much like Wheeler, repeatedly requested a change in unsafe working conditions. Potts, much like Wheeler, blew the whistle on improper and unsafe working conditions. Also like Wheeler, Potts reported the unsafe conditions to her supervisor rather than to the authorities. Thus, by analogy, Potts could argue that since the court allowed public health policy supported by legislation to support Wheeler's claim, the court should also apply public health policy in Potts's case.

Chapin, however, might argue that such an analogy would be improper. It might distinguish *Wheeler* by showing that the public policy in *Wheeler* was concerned with the protection of the lives" of Illinois citizens, *Id.* at 377, as in *Palmateer* 421 N.E.2d at 879. The public policy that Potts upholds, as embodied in the Illinois Clean Indoor Air Act, is merely concerned with the "public health." *Id.* at § 2. Thus, Chapin might argue that while protection from radioactive materials is applicable as public policy, protection from tobacco smoke should not be an allowable public policy because radioactivity is more clearly understood to be a danger to lives than tobacco smoke. Radioactivity has been clearly known to be dangerous since the atomic bombings in World War II, but the dangers of tobacco smoke are of relatively new understanding.

Nevertheless, recentness of the understanding of the danger should not be a determining factor in the public policy analysis. In *Sherman v. Kraft General Foods*, Inc., 651 N.E.2d 708 (Ill. App. Ct. 1995), an employee was discharge for reporting the existence of asbestos in the workplace. The court held that reporting asbestos in the workplace supported a public policy protecting the lives of Illinois citizens. *Id.* at 712. The dangers of asbestos, like tobacco smoke, have been relatively recently understood when compared to the dangers of radioactivity, but the court still found an actionable public policy. *Id.* at 713. While tobacco smoke is possibly a less understood danger than radioactivity, the legislature has nonetheless declared it "dangerous" and a "health hazard." 410 Ill. Comp. Stat. 80/2 (West 1993). Thus, despite Chapin's possible efforts to distinguish other whistleblowing cases, the Amanda Potts case likely fits within the whistleblowing category.

C.   Public policy in another jurisdiction

It may be persuasive to the Illinois courts to refer to other jurisdictions where a smoke-free workplace has been held to embody an important public health policy. In a case on point in California, the employee was allegedly discriminated against and eventually terminated in "retaliation -for his protesting what he considered to be hazardous working conditions caused by other employees smoking in the workplace." *Hentzel v. Singer Co.,* 188 Cal. Rptr. 159, 160 (Cal. Ct. App. 1982) In *Hentzel,* the appellate court relied on statutory declarations of public policy and reasoned:

> Achievement of the statutory objective—a safe and healthy working environment for all employees—requires that employees be free to call their employer's attention to such conditions, so that the employer can be made aware of their existence, and given opportunity to correct them if correction is needed. The public policy thus implicated extends beyond the question of fairness to the particular employee; it concerns protection of employees against retaliatory dismissal for conduct which, in light of the statutes, deserves to be encouraged rather than inhibited. *Id.* at 164.

In the *Hentzel* case, the court upheld retaliatory discharge based on a public policy of a safe and healthy working environment. In the Potts case, the public policy is also the protection of a safe and healthy workplace, and the policy is embodied, like the *Hentzel* case, in statutory declarations. As in the reasoning of *Hentzel,* Amanda Potts's conduct deserves to be encouraged rather than discouraged because whistleblowing will uphold and support the declared public policy favoring a healthy, smoke-free workplace. If the court does not allow retaliatory discharge in cases such as Potts', employees will not be willing to complain about unsafe, unhealthy working conditions caused by tobacco smoke because they might fear termination, and the public health will be compromised.

D.   Pre-emption: A way to avoid public policy expansion?

In a separate argument, Chapin might contend that the statutory remedies available under the ICLAA pre-empt any remedy that might be obtained in a common-law claim of retaliatory discharge. In other words, Chapin might argue that the remedies under the ICLAA are the exclusive remedies in such a case, and Chapin might use *Kelsay,* 383 N.E.2d at 358-359, to support such an argument. This argument would give the court a way to offer a remedy in this case but avoid the expansion of actionable public policy. Chapin might also argue this point to avoid the punitive damages that are available to Potts in a retaliatory discharge claim. *Kelsay,* 384 N.E.2d at 359.

In *Kelsay,* the plaintiff alleged that she had been terminated for filing a workmen's compensation claim. *Id.* at 355. The court allowed, for the first time, a common-law remedy of retaliatory discharge because the Worker's Compensation Act relied on for public policy did not contain any private remedy for violations of the Act. *Id.* at 358. The remedy in the Worker's Compensation Act against an employer was only penal in nature, and thus, "does nothing to alleviate the plight of employees who are threatened with retaliation." *Id.* at 359. Chapin will point out that the Illinois appellate court has allowed private remedy under the ICIAA, *Pechan*, 622 N.E.2d at 114-115, and thus, the reason for allowing a retaliatory discharge claim established in *Kelsay* does not exist in Potts' case. In short, the court has no need to expand the retaliatory discharge public policy exception to include a smoke-free workplace because Amanda Potts has no need; she can receive damages under a statutory claim for discrimination. *Pechan*, 622 N.E.2d at 114-115.

The holding in *Pechan*, however, should not necessarily be construed so broadly as to preempt retaliatory discharge in this case. Indeed, there is no exclusive language used in the *Pechan* case or in the statutory language of the Illinois Clean Indoor Air Act. *Pechan v. Dynpro, Inc.*, 622 N.E.2d 108 (Ill. App. Ct. 1993). 410 Ill. Comp. Stat. 80/1-11 (West 1993). Thus, there is no evidence that the legislature desired to limit damages to those available under the Act. Besides, in *Kelsay*, the Supreme Court also held that punitive damages are necessary "to dissuade an employer from engaging in the practice of discharging an employee for filing a workmen's compensation claim." *Kelsay*, 384 N.E.2d at 359. Neither the *Pechan* case, nor the ICIAA itself, allows for punitive damages. *Pechan v. Dynpro, Inc.*, 622 N.E.2d 108 (111. App. Ct. 1993). 410 Ill. Comp. Stat. 80/1-11 (West 1993). Thus, to preempt a retaliatory discharge claim with the remedies in the ICIAA would disallow the punitive damages that necessarily reinforce public policy. *Kelsay*, 384 N.E.2d at 359.

In conclusion, the Amanda Potts case likely satisfies all three elements of the common law claim of retaliatory discharge, which are that there (1) must be a discharge, (2) in retaliation for the employee's activities, and that (3) the discharge violates clearly mandated public policy. *Hinthom v. Roland's of Bloomington, Inc.*, 519 N.E.2d 909, 911 (Ill. 1988). The facts that have been provided likely show a discharge in retaliation for Potts' activities, and the Illinois Clean Indoor Air Act likely establishes a clearly mandated public policy that was violated by Potts' discharge. Thus, it is likely that Potts will be able to sue and collect damages from her former employer, Chapin, under a retaliatory discharge claim.

M E M O R A N D U M

TO: Katie
Harrington-McBride

FROM: Michele Mintz

DATE: November 3, 1994
Andrew
Gray: personal injury,
file no. 94-3952

ISSUE

Whether, under Ohio law, an individual, either as a social or employer host, may be held liable for injuries to a third party resulting from his intoxicated guests' negligent operation of an automobile after attending a dinner hosted by the individual where intoxicating liquor was served.

CONCLUSION

Under Ohio law, an employer host may be held liable for injuries to a third party resulting from his intoxicated guest's negligent operation of an automobile after attending a dinner hosted by the employer where intoxicating liquor was served. First, Ohio law has suggested that an employer host may be held liable for injuries to a third party resulting from the negligent acts of his guest only where it can be established that (1) the host gratuitously furnished intoxicating liquor to the guest, (2) the host knew that the guest would consume the liquor, (3) the host knew that the guest either was or would become intoxicated, and (4) the host knew that the person would probably act in such a manner while intoxicated as to create an unreasonable risk of harm to third persons. Second, Ohio law has suggested that if the intoxicated person who caused injuries to the third party was an employee of the individual who hosted the function where intoxicating liquor was served, the employer host may be held vicariously liable for injuries to a third party resulting from the negligent acts of his intoxicated employee committed within the employee's scope of employment.

FACTS

Andrew Gray, a thirty-six year old computer programmer who lives and works in Toledo, Ohio, was involved in an automobile accident while returning home from work on March 25, 1994. Gray was struck head on by another vehicle on a divided highway. The other vehicle was driven by Jerry Nolan, a forty-two year old man. Nolan's blood alcohol level was tested at the scene and he was found to be legally drunk, with a reading significantly over the minimum level for intoxication. Nolan was arrested at the scene and charged with driving under the influence.

Jerry Nolan is a senior account executive with Lux-o-lux Appliance Distributors, based in Toledo. Lux-o-lux is a $75 million a year business with over 225 employees. On the night of March 25, 1994, Nolan had been at the estate of Webster Smithers, Jr., the son of Lux-o-lux's founder and its current executive vice-president. Smithers, Jr., hosted the company's top 25 account executives and their spouses at his home on March 25, for an evening of dinner and dancing. An invitation to the dinner was considered to be a great honor by Lux-o-lux employees. Nolan, a first-time invitee, was thrilled to have been invited.

On the night of March 25, Nolan told police that he had arrived at the Smithers' estate at approximately 7:30pm. Nolan told police that he remembers mingling with his coworkers for approximately an hour while hors d'oeuvres and champagne were served. Nolan thought that he drank three or four glasses of champagne during this time. After the cocktail hour, during a six course meal, Nolan was served red and white wine and remembers having at least two glasses of each during dinner. After dinner, Nolan had a glass of dessert wine with cheese and fruit.

Following the meal, at approximately 10:00pm, the guests at Smithers' dinner congregated in the home's "Great Hall," where a "trio" played dance music. While many guests danced, Nolan used the opportunity to "schmooze" some of his colleagues. Nolan also talked with his co-workers as after dinner drinks were passed. At this time, Nolan consumed three servings of brandy while he socialized. In fact, Nolan had the opportunity to thank his host personally for the fine food, drink, and entertainment, because Smithers, Jr. always made a point of talking with each of his guests after dinner.

At approximately 11:45pm, Nolan said good-bye to his colleagues and his host and left Smithers' estate. At 11:55, Nolan's car collided with Gray's car. As a result of the accident, Gray was severely injured and was hospitalized for four weeks. Gray underwent extensive surgery and therapy. Gray will need additional surgery and will be in physical and occupational therapy for another year.

DISCUSSION

Under Ohio law, Webster Smithers, Jr. (Smithers) , as an employer host, may be held liable for the injuries caused to Andrew Gray by Jerry Nolan's negligent operation of his automobile after attending the dinner hosted by Smithers where intoxicating liquor was served.

Under Ohio law, there are several ways one might seek to hold Smithers liable for Nolan's negligence. As you have suggested, I will consider Dram Shop Act liability, social and employer host liability under the theory of direct negligence, and employer host vicarious liability under the doctrine of *respondeat superior.*

First, Ohio's Dram Shop Act provides an action "against a *seller* of liquor for injury caused by an intoxicated person to whom sale of liquor is prohibited" (Emphasis added). Ohio Rev. Code Ann. sec. 4399.01. Ohio's Dram Shop Act only imposes express liability upon commercial providers of alcohol. Smithers, as a non-commercial provider of alcohol, does not come within the express meaning of the statute.

In *Baird v. Roach*, 11 Ohio App. 3d 16, 462 N.E.2d 1229, 1231 (1983), the court noted that Ohio's Dram Shop Act applied only "to a 'Sale' of alcoholic beverages to an obviously intoxicated person . . . [T]he hospitality of serving alcoholic beverages does not offend any of the[] statutory provisions" of Ohio's Dram Shop Act. Smithers is a "hospitable server" of alcoholic beverages. As a result, Smithers, as both an employer and social host, cannot be held liable for the injuries to Gray caused by Nolan's negligence under Ohio's Dram Shop Act.

Second, under Ohio law, a social host cannot be held liable for injuries to a third party resulting from the acts of his intoxicated guest under the theory of direct negligence. In *Settlemyer v. Wilmington Veterans Post No.49, Am. Legion, Inc.*, 11 Ohio St. 3d 123, 464 N.E.2d 521 (1984), the court dismissed the plaintiff's action to recover damages for a death allegedly caused by a collision with a car driven by a woman to whom a social provider of alcoholic beverages negligently supplied alcoholic beverages. The plaintiff, administratrix of the estate of the decedent, alleged that the social provider of alcoholic beverages was negligent in that he knew or should have known that the woman was intoxicated at time he provided alcoholic beverages to her. Affirming the lower court's dismissal of the plaintiff's action, the Supreme Court of Ohio held that "the social provider of alcoholic beverages should not be held to the same duty of care as a commercial proprietor," *Id.* at 524 .

According to *Settlemyer*, the commercial proprietor "has a proprietary interest and profit motive, and should be expected to exercise greater supervision than [a provider of intoxicating liquor] in the (non-commercial) social setting." *Id.* at 524.

Reluctant to extend the statutory duty imposed by Ohio's Dram Shop Act upon the commercial proprietor of alcohol to the social provider of alcoholic beverages, the *Settlemyer* court deferred any policy modifications "designed to encompass the potential liability of social providers of intoxicating beverages [to] the sound discretion of the legislature." *Id.* at 524. As a result, under Ohio law, Smithers, as a social provider of intoxicating liquor, cannot be held liable for injuries to Gray caused by Nolan's negligence under the theory of direct negligence.

Third, under Ohio law, an employer host may be held liable for injuries to a third party resulting from the acts of his intoxicated guest under the theory of direct negligence. In *Baird v. Roach*, the Court of Appeals of Ohio suggested that the "gratuitous serving of liquor to a . . . business guest can give rise to liability on the part of the host under Ohio law . . . only where the host knew that the person to whom the liquor was furnished would consume it and either was, or would become, intoxicated and would probably act in such a manner while intoxicated as to create an unreasonable risk of harm to third persons." *Baird*, 462 N.E.2d at 1233.

Smithers, as executive vice-president of Lux-o-lux and host of the company's "top 25 account executives" dinner, gratuitously served liquor to his business guests on the evening of March 25, 1994. The facts indicate that from the time of Nolan's arrival at Smithers, estate at 7:30pm until Nolan's departure at 11:45, Smithers furnished liquor to his guests. Champagne was served with hors d'oeuvres during the cocktail hour, red and white wine was served with dinner, and desert wine and "after dinner drinks" were served after dinner.

Smithers knew that Nolan consumed intoxicating liquor. After dinner, Nolan had the opportunity to thank Smithers for the fine food, drink, and entertainment provided by Smithers. When Nolan thanked Smithers for the "fine drink", Smithers was informed that Nolan had consumed the liquor served to him.

The facts are unclear as to whether Smithers knew that Nolan either was, or would become, intoxicated. The facts, however, do indicate Smithers' knowledge of a clear and general probability of intoxication on the part of his guests. Smithers provided a seemingly endless supply of liquor between the time of his guests' arrival and their departure. After 10:00pm, and after Nolan had consumed at least 8 drinks, Nolan had the opportunity to talk with Smithers. At the scene of the accident at 11:55pm, Nolan's blood alcohol level read significantly over the minimum level of intoxication. Though the facts do not indicate that Smithers knew that Nolan either was, or would become, intoxicated, discovery may disclose that he did, as he certainly had the opportunity to acquire such knowledge.

Smithers knew that Nolan would probably act in such a manner while intoxicated as to create an unreasonable risk of harm to third persons. At 11:45pm, Nolan said good-bye to his colleagues and Smithers, and left Smithers' estate. The matter of Smithers' knowledge of Nolan's intoxication is irrelevant to the establishment of this element of Smithers' potential liability to Gray. Smithers knew that Nolan, like anyone else who was intoxicated and attempted to drive an automobile upon leaving Smithers' estate, would create an unreasonable risk of harm to third persons.

Although it is difficult to establish Smithers, knowledge of Nolan's intoxication, Smithers, as an employer host, may be held liable for the injuries to Gray caused by Nolan's negligent operation of his automobile under the theory of direct negligence.

Fourth, under Ohio law, an employer host may be held vicariously liable for injuries to a third party resulting from the negligent acts of his intoxicated guest under the doctrine of *respondeat superior.* Under the doctrine of *respondeat superior,* an employer is held vicariously liable for "injuries resulting from the conduct of his employee[] acting within the scope of [his] employment." *Cervelli v. Kleinman*, 8 Ohio App. 3d 247, 456 N.E.2d 1322, 1326 (1983)

Gray's injuries resulted from the conduct of Nolan, acting within the scope of his employment. In *Kohlmayer v. Keller*, 24 Ohio St.2d 10, 263 N.E.2d 231, 233 (1970), the Supreme Court of Ohio held that "the injuries sustained by an employee of a small business when he broke his neck while swimming at a picnic sponsored, paid for, and supervised by such employer for the purpose of generating friendly relations with its employees w[ere] sustained in the course of his employment." Quoting *Sebek v. Cleveland Graphite Bronze Co.*, 148 Ohio St. 693, 698, 76 N.E.2d 892 (1947), the *Kohlmayer* court held that in order for an employee to be acting within the scope of his employment, "it is sufficient [that] he is engaged in a pursuit or undertaking consistent with his contract of hire and which in some logical manner pertains to or is incidental to his employment."

Nolan's attendance at the dinner at Smithers' estate was within Nolan's scope of employment. Nolan's attendance at the dinner hosted by Smithers was consistent with his contract for hire and was logically related to his employment. Smithers paid for and supervised Lux-o-lux's "top 25 account executives dinner", working to improve employer-employee relations. Furthermore, an invitation to the annual "top 25 account executives dinner" at Smithers' estate was considered to be a great honor. Nolan's attendance was requested and expected by Smithers. Therefore, Nolan's attendance at the dinner at Smithers, estate was within the scope of his employment.

Nolan's consumption of intoxicating liquor at Smithers, estate was committed within Nolan's scope of employment. In *Marbury v. Industrial Commission of Ohio*, 62 Ohio App.3d 786, 577 N.E.2d 672, 674 (1989) , the court held that the activity of swimming in *Kohlmayer* that resulted in injury was committed within the employee's scope of employment because it was "an integral part of the event sponsored by the employer." Swimming facilities were provided by the employer in *Kohlmayer*. As a result, the act of swimming was considered by the *Marbury* court to be an integral part of the picnic sponsored by the employer in *Kohlmayer*. Similarly, as intoxicating liquor was provided by Smithers, Nolan's consumption of intoxicating liquor would be considered an integral part of the dinner sponsored by Smithers. Therefore, Nolan's consumption of intoxicating liquor at Smithers' estate was committed within the scope of his employment.

Under Ohio law, Nolan's negligent operation of his automobile may be considered to have been committed within Nolan's scope of employment. In *Howard v. Delco Div. of Gen. Motors Corp., Inc.*, 41 Ohio App.3d 145, 534 N.E.2d 936, 938 (1987), the court was "not satisfied that the employment relationship in Ohio [was] so paternalistic as to impose a duty upon an employer to protect Its obviously intoxicated employee from the risk that the employee will have an automobile accident after leaving work when the employee brought that risk upon himself through his own conduct, with no help or encouragement from his employer." The instant case is distinguishable from *Howard*. The risk that Nolan would have an automobile accident after leaving Smithers' estate was brought about with the help and encouragement of Smithers by Smithers' gratuitous serving of intoxicating liquor. Therefore, under Ohio law, the employment relationship of Smithers and Nolan may be extended to impose a duty upon Smithers to have protected Nolan from the risk of having an automobile accident after leaving Smithers' estate.

Under Ohio law, according to the "going and coming" rule, an employee is not considered to be acting within his scope of employment while traveling to and from work. *See id.* The District Court of Appeals in California, however, has held that the "going and coming" rule is not applicable in cases in which the "special errand" exception applies. The California court has held that if the employee is not simply going to or coming from his normal place of work, "but is coming from his home or returning to it on a *special errand either as part of his regular duties or at a specific order or request of his employer,* the employee is considered to be in the scope of his employment from the time that he starts the errand until he has returned . . ." (Emphasis added). *Boynton v. McKales*, 139 Cal. App.2d 777, 294 P.2d 733, 740 (1956). Under *Boynton*, on the evening of March 25, Nolan was on a "special errand", attending the dinner at Smithers' estate at Smithers' request. If Ohio were persuaded by California law, Nolan may be excepted from Ohio's "going and coming" rule. As a result, Nolan's negligent operation of his automobile may be considered to have been committed within the scope of his employment.

Another court has held that the "going and coming" rule is irrelevant in determining whether an employer may be held vicariously liable for the acts of his employee while going to and coming from work. In *Dickinson v. Edwards*, 105 Wash.2d 457, 716 P.2d 814 (1986), the Supreme Court of Washington avoided the "going and coming" rule in determining whether an employee was acting within the scope of his employment while traveling home from a banquet hosted by his employer. The *Dickinson* court, setting forth a new application of the doctrine of *respondeat superior,* held that since "the proximate cause of the accident, the intoxication, occurred at the time the employee negligently consumed the alcohol," the employee's destination after the function was irrelevant. *Id.* at 820. In the instant case, Nolan's intoxication occurred at Smithers' estate, before Nolan attempted to drive home. Nolan's negligent consumption of intoxicating liquor, the proximate cause of his accident with Gray, was committed within the scope of his employment. As a result, according to *Dickinson,* one need not establish that Nolan negligently operated his automobile under the scope of his employment in order to hold Smithers vicariously liable for the injuries to Gray caused by Nolan's negligence.

Under Ohio law, it is difficult to establish that Nolan's negligent operation of his automobile was committed within the scope of his employment. An Ohio court, however, may be persuaded by the holdings of the California or Washington courts which have avoided Ohio's "going and coming" rule in determining whether an employer may be held vicariously liable for the acts of his employee while going to and coming from work. As a result, Smithers, as an employer host, may be held vicariously liable for the injuries to Gray caused by Nolan's negligent operation of his automobile under the doctrine of *respondeat superior.*

Based upon the above discussion, under Ohio law, Smithers, as an employer host, may be held liable for the injuries to Gray caused by Nolan's negligence. Under the theory of direct negligence, Smithers may be held liable for the injuries caused to Gray because Smithers gratuitously furnished intoxicating liquor to Nolan, Smithers knew that Nolan consumed the liquor, Smithers might have known that Nolan was or would become intoxicated, and Smithers knew that Nolan, if intoxicated, would create an unreasonable risk of harm to third persons by driving home from Smithers' estate. Under the doctrine of *respondeat superior,* Smithers may be held vicariously liable for the injuries caused to Gray because Nolan's negligent acts were committed within the scope of his employment.

The next two memoranda appear in a slightly different format than those discussed and presented elsewhere in the book. They begin with the facts, identify the issues (both legal and nonlegal), present the analysis, then conclude with a strategy discussion that attempts to meld the legal analysis with the client's nonlegal concerns in order to arrive at a plan for handling the client's case. This approach offers a realistic approximation of the thought process an attorney should go through in planning client representation.

M E M O R A N D U M

TO: File
FROM: THOMAS DONAHOE
DATE: October 13, 1997
RE: NATASHA BORODIN – Custody and Property
             Settlement

Facts

Client Natasha Borodin began an intimate cohabitational relationship with Trudy Belson approximately seven years ago. Approximately five years ago Natasha Borodin and Trudy Belson made a videotape professing their love for one another and promising to share equally any property they acquired together during the relationship. Because same sex couples are prohibited from marrying in California, they made the tape to ceremoniously show their commitment to each other. At that time neither had acquired much property. Natasha Borodin was then an aspiring actress and Trudy Belson was a homemaking companion. Soon thereafter, Natasha Borodin began to achieve success in the movie business, starring in major box office films, and acquiring immense wealth in the process. This recently acquired property is all in Natasha Borodin's name and currently estimated at about thirty-seven million dollars. Although Natasha Borodin is a famous movie star, she has taken painstaking steps to keep her personal life private. Maintaining this privacy is critical to Natasha Borodin's career and lifestyle.

Three years ago Natasha Borodin and Trudy Belson legally adopted Amanda Belson-Borodin, born 1992. Trudy Belson provides the majority of daily care for Amanda while Natasha Borodin provides the financial support for all three. Although Natasha Borodin's work frequently takes her away, Amanda and Trudy Belson usually accompany Natasha Borodin on out of town trips. Amanda is slightly hyperactive with mild learning disabilities.

Natasha Borodin now wants to end her relationship with Trudy Belson, although she has not yet disclosed this to her. Natasha Borodin's predominant concern is maintaining as much contact with Amanda as possible, preferably through sole custody. Natasha Borodin's second priority is maintaining the privacy of her personal life. Natasha Borodin would also like to be relieved of any future payment of support to Trudy Belson.

Legal Issues

What custody rights does a same sex cohabitating parent of an adopted five year old with learning disabilities have if that parent must travel frequently to maintain her flourishing acting career?

Must an unmarried cohabitating partner divide the property she acquired equally with the other party, if they professed their love for each other and desire to share property equally on a video tape?

Analysis of Custody Issue

The California Family Code adopted the "best interest" of the child standard for courts to use in deciding which parent to award custody.

§ 3011. Best interest of child; considerations

In making a determination of the best interest of the child, . . . the court shall, among any other factors it finds relevant, consider all of the following:

(a)The health, safety, and welfare of the child.

(b)Any history of abuse by one parent . . .

(c)The nature and amount of contact with both parents. Cal. Fam. Code. § 3011 (West 1996).

Additionally, the California Family Code gives some preferences to guide the courts in applying §3011.

§ 3040. Order of preference

(a)Custody should be granted in the following order of preference according to the best interest of the child as provided in Section 3011:

(1)to both parents jointly . . . or either parent. In ordering custody to either parent, the court shall consider which parent is more likely to allow the child frequent and continuing contact with the noncustodial parent. . . . The court in its discretion, may require the parents to submit to the court a plan for the implementation of the custody order.

(b)This section establishes neither a preference nor a presumption for or against joint legal custody, joint physical custody, or sole custody, but allows the court and family the widest discretion to choose a plan that is in the best interest of the child. Cal. Fam. Code § 3040 (West 1996).

Case law is frequently relied on to interpret these statutes because "best interest" remains an ambiguous and subjective guide. Case law interpreting best interest includes thousands of cases. The statutes allow the courts immense discretion in awarding child custody. The most relevant factor courts must consider in child custody is the health, safety and welfare of the child. Natasha Borodin may assert that Amanda needs the one on one care only an expert private tutor can provide to overcome her hyperactivity and learning disability, and only Natasha Borodin has the financial resources to provide that special care. However, appellate courts have held that child custody may not be based on a parent's economic position. *In re Marriage of McGinnis*, 9 Cal. Rptr. 182 (Cal. App. 1992).

Trudy Belson will probably claim that only she can give Amanda personalized care to deal with her special needs because she does not have an outside career. However, the California Supreme Court has held that in an era where a majority of single parents must work, trial courts must not presume that a working parent is a less satisfactory parent or less fully committed to the child's care than a parent who provides full time care. *Burchard v. Garay*, 229 Cal. Rptr. 800 (Cal. 1986). But in this situation, Trudy Belson may claim that five year old Amanda, who is probably just starting school, would be better off in a stable school environment and Natasha Borodin's constant travelling would be a detriment to Amanda's welfare. In order for Natasha Borodin to prevail, she must demonstrate to the court that if given custody she has the best plan for taking care of Amanda's special needs with a private tutoring and care-giving arrangement.

The quality and quantity of contact with both parents appear as additional relevant factors a court would look at. Trudy Belson may assert that her flexible schedule would enable her to maintain custody of Amanda while assuring the court that Natasha Borodin would also be able to enjoy maximum contact with Amanda. To counter that assertion Natasha Borodin must develop a plan to show that if she is granted custody of Amanda, both parents will experience maximum contact with Amanda.

Appellate courts have indicated that best interest determinations rest on the stability and continuity of the loving relationship the child currently experiences with the parents. The length of time a child has been in the continuous, actual, physical custody of a parent is considered by most courts. *Cochran v. Cochran*, 49 Cal. Rptr. 670 (Cal. App. 1966). Trudy Belson may claim that since the couple adopted Amanda she was the primary caregiver because Natasha Borodin was engaged in a demanding acting career. However, Natasha Borodin can counter that she was an equal caregiver because facts indicate that Amanda accompanied Natasha Borodin when she was on location.

Conclusion To Custody Issue

Best interest is a somewhat subjective standard that belies a rigid definition. Of the thousands of written court opinions on the subject, expert child psychologists as well as judges differ on the best interest of the child in choosing a particular parent to have custody. The chance of Natasha Borodin gaining custody will depend on what evidence we can present to demonstrate Natasha Borodin's past stable, continuous loving relationship with Amanda, and her future plan to ensure that Amanda maintains maximum contact with Trudy Belson. Natasha Borodin's custody plan must also include treatment of Amanda's hyperactivity and learning disability. From the current facts, it would appear that Natasha Borodin has less than a twenty-five percent chance of gaining sole custody of Amanda in a legal suit.

Joint custody also appears as an option under California Family Code § 3040. Any joint custody requires some agreement between the parties for the plan to be viable and the parties must demonstrate to the court that this plan would be in the best interest of Amanda.

Property Rights Issue

No statutory law is currently available to guide courts in the distribution of unmarried cohabitants' property. The issue of unmarried parties living together, especially same sex couples, arouses extreme passion in voters, so to date the legislature has been unwilling to take on this politically sensitive issue. Therefore, property settlements of cohabiting couples outside of marriage will probably be guided by the seminal case of *Marvin v. Marvin*, 134 Cal. Rptr. 815 (Cal. 1976). In *Marvin*, the actor Lee Marvin was sued by Michelle Triola Marvin, with whom he cohabited for six years. The couple never married but orally agreed to share equally everything they acquired during the relationship. Lee Marvin agreed to financially support Michelle Marvin for the rest of her life while Michelle agreed to render her services as homemaker, housekeeper and companion to Lee as consideration.

Previous court cases never recognized cohabitation contracts as valid because the courts felt these contracts implicitly included a sexual relationship, which the courts felt was against public policy if outside of marriage. In *Marvin* the California Supreme Court recognized the enforceability of cohabitation contracts. The court declared that the fact that cohabitants engage in sexual relations does not invalidate the entire agreement unless the contract is inseparably based on the illicit sexual relationship. 134 Cal. Rptr. at 823. The court not only declared the alleged express oral agreement between the two valid, but also noted that contract principles would apply to implied cohabitation agreements as well. *Id.* at 831. Throughout the opinion, the court also emphasized the increasing number of cohabiting couples, and the increasing social acceptance of them, to support the changing public policy of recognizing cohabitation agreements.

In our case, basic contract principles would probably apply to the videotape agreement between Natasha Borodin and Trudy Belson. A court would have even stronger public policy concerns for dividing the property of Natasha Borodin and Trudy Belson because they were rearing a child together. Similar to what the California Supreme Court said would be a valid contract in *Marvin*, Natasha Borodin and Trudy Belson entered into an express agreement, where the two exchanged promises to share equally all property they acquired while cohabiting. It would appear from these facts that Trudy Belson has a right to half of Natasha Borodin's property.

California case law after *Marvin* reveals that courts have inconsistently applied *Marvin* to same sex cohabitation agreements.[1] In *Jones v. Daly*, 176 Cal. Rptr. 130 (Cal. App. 1976), a same sex couple orally agreed to share equally their efforts and earnings. For consideration, Jones agreed to be Daly's lover, companion, housekeeper and cook, while Daly agreed to financially support Jones for life. The court refused to enforce the cohabitation agreement, finding that sexual services could not be separated from the rest of the agreement. The court indicated that use of the term lover in the agreement made the contract illegal and could not be separated from the rest of the contract.

In our case, facts indicate that the videotape not only expressed the couple's promise to share property equally, but the main purpose of the tape was to allow the couple to ceremoniously profess their love for each other. Natasha Borodin can argue that a sexual relationship was implied in the contract that cannot be separated from the property division part of the contract, and therefore the object of the contract was for an illegal act, which makes the contract invalid. We could claim the expression of "love" in the tape evidenced a sexual relationship, just as the court in *Jones* found the word "lover" in the agreement to indicate an illegal contract. However, other California courts have applied *Marvin* to same sex cohabitation relationships, and severed the perceived illegal sexual parts of the contract and enforced the non-sexual part of the agreement. *Whorton v. Dillingham*, 248 Cal. Rptr. 405 (Cal. App. 1988).

One of Natasha Borodin's principal concerns is to eliminate future support to Trudy Belson. No facts indicate that Natasha Borodin expressly promised Trudy Belson anything other than an equal share of the property acquired to date. However, Trudy Belson may claim the couple entered into an implied contract for future earnings of Natasha Borodin. As indicated above, the California Supreme Court announced that implied contracts between cohabiting couples were enforceable if the cohabitants' conduct implied such an agreement. However, even in *Marvin*, when the case was remanded to find whether in fact a contract did exist between the parties, the lower court found neither an express nor implied contract. *Marvin v. Marvin*, 176 Cal. Rptr. 555 (Cal. App. 1983). Other cases also indicate courts are reluctant to order future support to an unmarried cohabitant. *Taylor v. Polackwich* 194 Cal. Rptr. 8 (Cal. App. 1983).

Conclusion To Property Rights Issue

Natasha Borodin is on weak legal ground in opposing an equal settlement of the property they acquired since the making of the videotape because

---

[1] Comments, *Applying* Marvin v. Marvin *to Same-Sex Couples: A Proposal for a Sex-Preference Neutral Cohabitation Contract Statute*, 25 U.C. Davis L. Rev. 1029, 1045-47 (1992).

Marvin permits enforcement of express contracts between unmarried cohabiting couples. However, there is enough favorable case law to make a good faith argument opposing any property distribution to Trudy Belson. This may prove useful if Natasha Borodin elects to negotiate a settlement.

Natasha Borodin need not concern herself about future support of Trudy Belson (except of course child support if Trudy Belson prevails in a custody suit). Nothing in the facts indicates Natasha Borodin promised Trudy Belson anything more than equal division of the property they acquired. A court would be reluctant to imply that Natasha Borodin contracted to support Trudy Belson after the termination of their relationship.

Non-Legal Issues

The primary non-legal issue for Natasha Borodin is the welfare of her daughter—where does the client believe Amanda will be the happiest and best cared for? Any type of custody fight would surely be detrimental to a hyperactive five year old with a learning disability. In most custody situations, two parents agreeing on something appears far better for the child than a court battle. In this case it appears that both Natasha Borodin and Trudy Belson are jointly concerned about Amanda's welfare. However, in negotiations Trudy Belson may be willing to bargain her custody rights to gain a more favorable property distribution agreement.

Another major non-legal issue for Natasha Borodin is keeping her personal life private. If Natasha Borodin chooses to fight for sole custody against the wishes of Trudy Belson a public airing of the issue would surely develop. The press would go on a feeding frenzy if a celebrity of her caliber were to air her personal life in a public courtroom, especially a unique personal life with a same sex cohabitational relationship. Trudy Belson might also threaten to disclose this to the media as a bargaining chip to advance her position. However, this position may not be self-serving for Trudy Belson because it could take future financial resources away from both herself and Amanda if Natasha Borodin's marketability is decreased due to unfavorable public response. Additionally, if no settlement is reached, a court may order all three parties in this dispute to see a psychologist, which may further complicate matters and disclose even more aspects of Natasha Borodin's personal life.

Natasha Borodin appeared reluctant to disclose why she wanted to end her relationship with Trudy Belson. The client could have any number of problems in her personal relationship. Although she seemed firm about ending this relationship, did she ever consider some type of counseling or mediation? This could be a viable alternative to ending a seven year relationship which includes a minor child. Problems in the relationship could affect the client's job performance and would surely have an effect on her future career and personal life. We must ask the client about her emotional state and how swiftly she anticipates the split in her relationship with Trudy Belson will be finalized. These non-legal issues must be discussed with the client in a sensitive way.

Strategy

This client has a particularly strong interest in settling this dispute rather than fighting a protracted court battle, because the media exposure could hurt her daughter and her career. However, we must gather all the information we can to put Natasha Borodin in the best bargaining position possible. We must also note that if our client's personal life is divulged to the public, Trudy Belson will lose the threat of disclosure as a bargaining tool in the negotiation process. From preliminary research we know that Trudy Belson has a strong legal argument for acquiring half the property. We also know that Trudy Belson has good grounds to seek sole custody of Amanda. This information needs to be discussed with the client, but we need more information from Natasha Borodin to better evaluate her situation. Pursuant to Cal. Family Code § 3040, we are required to offer a custody plan the court can implement. In order to put together a custody plan we must inquire in detail about previous living arrangements over the past three years. Where did Amanda spend the majority of her time, with Natasha Borodin or Trudy Belson? What was the quality of the time spent with Amanda? Who cared for Amanda's special needs, her hyperactivity and learning disabilities? Most importantly, how willing is Natasha Borodin to fight for custody of Amanda? The client should also be made aware of the joint custody option and how it operates.

In order to achieve the best property settlement possible we must inquire about any promises Natasha Borodin made to Trudy Belson. Did any conduct they engaged in rise to the level of an implied contract for financial support? We should view the video tape if possible to see exactly what promises the couple made to each other. With thirty-seven million dollars at stake, co-counsel with expertise in this area of family law seems appropriate and must be discussed with the client, although she may be reluctant because of her concern over confidentiality.

If further investigation to uncover additional facts proves fruitless, we should concentrate our efforts on settling this matter in the most discrete and amicable way possible.

M E M O R A N D U M

TO: Senior Partner Schultz
FROM: Associate LeToia
             Jenkins-Morgan
DATE: October 10, 1996
RE: Pastor Thomas Smith;
             file no.12874-358

FACTS

The Board of Trustees of the Salvation Baptist Church hired Pastor Smith in June, 1995. Pastor Smith's annual salary was $100,000. His duties consisted of overseeing daily operations and increasing church membership.

During his job interview with the Board of Trustees, Pastor Smith responded "no" when he was asked had he ever committed adultery. The Board received a call the following year from attorneys in northern California informing them that Pastor Smith was involved in a pending lawsuit alleging sexual misconduct. Pastor Smith admitted that the allegations were true in a deposition.

On April 17, 1996, the Board of Trustees held a congregational meeting to vote on terminating Pastor Smith. 405 households were notified, 108 members attended, and the vote was 101 to 7 in favor of termination. Pastor Smith believes that the Board's disclosure to the congregation of his sexual relationships with two female members of the church, influenced their vote in favor of his termination.

Shortly thereafter, Pastor Smith changed the locks and security codes on the church building. He also opened a new bank account in the church's name with money collected during church services. Pastor Smith was the only signatory on the account.

The Board filed suit, resulting in a preliminary injunction ordering Pastor Smith to return the security codes and money back to the Board of Trustees. The injunction also instructed the pastor to remain 500 feet away from the church at all times. The injunction was issued on June 21, 1996.

On July 10, 1996, a second congregational meeting was held regarding the reinstatement of Pastor Smith. 455 members attended the meeting and the vote was 259 to 196 in favor of reinstatement.

ISSUES

Legal Issues:

1. Did the preliminary injunction violate Pastor Smith's First Amendment right to free exercise of religion?

2. Did Pastor Smith's failure to affirmatively answer a question regarding past sexual conduct during his interview give rise to an actionable claim of fraud? If so, can the court hear the claim?

3. Did the Board of Trustees invade Pastor Smith's right to privacy by disclosing information to the congregation regarding his intimate relationships with two church members? If so, can the court hear the claim?

4. Can Pastor Smith's actions of changing the church security codes and opening a new bank account with church funds establish a claim of conversion?

Non-Legal Issues:

1. Are there any remedies available to Pastor Smith under the church constitution and by-laws to ensure job security?

2. What course of action should be taken to prevent further damage to Pastor Smith's reputation?

DISCUSSION

The fundamental subject of the disputes between Pastor Smith and the Board of Trustees is the free exercise of religion guaranteed by the United States Constitution. This guarantee does not prescribe a solution to problems arising among members of religious entities. Thus, members often seek resolution through civil courts as an alternative. While religious beliefs are protected by the Constitution, religiously motivated conduct may not be. This problem leaves the court with the task of identifying whether the authority of the church or the courts will govern disputes involving religiously motivated conduct. Pastor Smith and the Board of Trustees are trying to discover which authority will control their disputes involving possible claims for fraud, invasion of privacy, and conversion that have evolved from church related events.

The preliminary injunction issued by the court did not violate Pastor Smith's First Amendment right to free exercise of religion because the purpose of the injunction was to return property to its rightful owner. The First Amendment to the U.S. Constitution guarantees the free exercise of religion. It prohibits courts from interfering with a chruch's governance of religious matters. These matters include controversies involving church doctrine, methods of church discipline, and church administration. The majority of churches and their congregations function within local communities, therefore civil courts are given authority under the U.S. Constitution to apply rules governing property rights, torts, and criminal conduct. However, there are limitations on courts' involvement in these matters.

Higgins v. Maher, 210 Cal. App. 3d 1168, 1170 (1989) (holding that torts such as defamation and invasion of privacy must occur separate from conduct arising out of church policy in order to sever them from ecclesiastical exemptions). The purpose of the injunction was to return the security codes and money back to the Board of Trustees who were the rightful owners. Therefore, the court did not violate the pastor's First Amendment right by issuing the injunction.

Pastor Smith's response to the Board's question regarding his past sexual conduct could establish an actionable claim of misrepresentation because, when he replied "no" he had previously admitted to sexual relations with parishoners brought against him in a lawsuit by a parishoners at his previous church. The court in *Molko v. Holy Spirit Ass'n* states that the elements of fraud are: 1) misrepresentation (false representation, concealment, or nondisclosure); 2) knowledge of falsity; 3) intent to induce reliance; 4) justifiable reliance; and 5) resulting damage. *Molko v. Holy Spirit Ass'n*, 252 Cal. Rptr. 122, 129 (1988).

Pastor Smith falsely represented the truth when he answered "no" to the question regarding his past sexual conduct. The fact that he had admitted to sexual relations with parishoners at a deposition exemplifies that he had knowledge of the falsity of his statement. It can be reasonably inferred by the Board of Trustees that the pastor intended to induce reliance because disclosure of his sexual misconduct would have had an adverse effect on the decision to hire him. The fact that the Board hired the pastor suggests that it justifiably relied on the information he provided at the interview. The Board of Trustees contend that the resulting damage is the amount of salary paid to the pastor. The Board suggests that the money would still be in its possession if it had been aware of the pastor's past conduct because it would not have hired him.

Based on the merits of this case the pastor has no defense and a successful claim of fraud could be established. However, civil courts cannot hear claims involving the employment practices of a church because such claims involve the administrative functions of the church.

As mentioned before, the courts will not interfere in religious matters such as the ecclesiastical government of the church. The functions of selecting a minister, determining his salary, and assigning his duties all fall under church administration which is an ecclesiastical concern. *Higgins*, 210 Cal. App. 3d at 1174. The court states that the policy consideration behind this is that investigations and reviews regarding matters of church administration and government could invite state intrusion. This intrusion would result in the passing of control from church to state, which would render churches powerless in making decisions for themselves, free from state interference. *Id.* at 1175. The fact that civil courts will not involve themselves with disputes arising from the hiring, firing, and administration of church officials implies that even though severe problems may arise from these matters, the church itself may need to provide a remedy. *Higgins*, 210 Cal. App. 3d at 1175. Therefore, even though the Board of Trustees could establish a successful claim for misrepresentation, the court will not be able to provide a remedy because the claim itself evolved from an employment practice of the church.

Due to the Board's attempt to establish a claim of misrepresentation, I anticipate that it would like Pastor Smith permanently terminated from his position. Therefore, in addressing the Pastor's concern of job security, the issue now becomes whether there is a remedy available to the pastor under the church constitution and by-laws to ensure job security. Article III, Section 3 of the church constitution states that the pastor shall be elected by a special meeting in which a majority vote of the members present will determine the choice. This section implies that Pastor Smith's employment will always be subject to the discretion of the congregation. However, his reinstatement by the congregation at the July 10, 1996 meeting reflects that his current position is stable. The meeting also demonstrates that the misrepresentation claim was not relevant enough for the congregation to permanently terminate Pastor Smith.

The Board of Trustees invaded Pastor Smith's right to privacy by disclosing information to the congregation regarding the pastor's intimate relationships with two church members. This right was invaded because the reasonable person would find publicity of sexual behavior highly offensive, and the subject matter of an individual's sexual conduct is of a very personal nature. [2]

The majority of courts in the United States recognize rights of privacy. The law of privacy recognizes four different types of invasion. The type of invasion that is relevant to Pastor Smith's situation is the "public disclosure of private facts". The court in *Diaz v. Oakland Tribune, Inc.* applied the following test to establish a claim for public disclosure of private facts. First, the information must be publicly disclosed. Second, the information must concern a private fact. Third, the information publicized must be highly offensive to a reasonable person. Finally, the information must not be of legitimate concern to the public. *Diaz v. Oakland Tribune, Inc.*, 139 Cal.

---

[2] It should be noted that Pastor Smith is extremely concerned with the damage done to his reputation and suggested pursuing a claim of defamation against the Board. However, an essential element of defamation is that the publicized information in question must contain a false statement of fact. This allows truth to be a complete defense to civil liability for defamation. For this reason, Pastor Smith would not have a successful claim for defamation since the disclosed information is true.

App. 3d 118, 126 (Jan. 1983) (the court held that the defendant's disclosure of the plaintiff's sex change operation invaded her privacy because the information could not be considered a legitimate concern to the public just because the defendant retrieved public information confirming the plaintiff's original sex).

The fact that the Board informed the church congregation of the pastor's sexual relationships demonstrates that the information was publicly disclosed. The highly personal nature of sexual relationships can imply that a reasonable person would find disclosure of this subject matter offensive.

Whether this information was of legitimate concern to the congregation depends upon whether such conduct interfered with Pastor Smith's duties. The Board thus far has not shown that these relationships have prevented the pastor from performing his pastoral functions. Neither has there been any indication that the congregation has been directly affected. The Board could raise the issue that the congregation's vote to terminate the pastor showed that this information had an adverse effect on the congregation. However, the fact that the congregation reinstated Pastor Smith demonstrates that the initial negative effect of the information was not pertinent enough to permanently terminate the pastor.

The Board of Trustees could also contend that disclosure of the information to the congregation is not sufficient publicity to justify an invasion of privacy. In *Kinsey v. Macur*, the defendant contended that mailing letters to twenty people was insufficient publicity for an invasion of privacy. *Kinsey v. Macur*, 107 Cal. App. 3d 265, 271 (1980). The court held that although no California case has defined the number of people necessary to justify a finding of publicity, because the recipients of the information were not connected socially or professionally with the plaintiff, an invasion of privacy claim could be established. *Id.* at 272.

The present dispute can be distinguished from *Kinsey* for two reasons. First, the number of recipients privy to the information was substantially higher in our case. Second, a social and professional connection can be inferred from the relationship between Pastor Smith and the congregation since his duties included preaching to them and presiding over all the affairs of the church. Therefore, under *Kinsey* it is possible that Pastor Smith's claim for invasion of privacy will not succeed.

A contrary view was expressed in *Snyder v. Evangelical Orthodox Church* when the court held that a claim for invasion of privacy could be upheld irrespective of a social or professional connection if there was no religious purpose for the disclosure. *Snyder v. Evangelical Orthodox Church*, 264 Cal. Rptr. 640, 647 (Cal. App. 6 Dist 1989) (quoting from *Wollersheim v. Church of Scientology*, 212 Cal. App. 3d 872, 899 (1989) holding that the intentional disclosure of private information obtained during auditing sessions for non-religious purposes is not protected under the First Amendment).

The court in *Snyder* outlines the test courts should use when determining whether churches are insulated from civil tort liability. The court must ask whether a religion is involved. If so, the court must then determine whether the course of conduct alleged qualifies as a religious expression. This means that the conduct in dispute was pursuant to church policy. *Snyder*, 264 Cal. Rptr. at 645. If the conduct in dispute was not pursuant to church policy then there is no insulation from civil liability. The court notes that this distinction between whether or not the conduct in dispute was pursuant to church policy is necessary in order to protect state interests, thus warranting the burden placed on religious expression. Some compelling state interests that the court acknowledges are the maintenance of marriage and family relationships, the alienation of affections, and the tortious interference with business relationships. *Snyder*, 264 Cal. Rptr. at 646.

The first part of the test is satisfied in our situation because the church that Pastor Smith and the Board of Trustees are members of is affiliated with the Baptist religion. There is no provision in the church constitution or by-laws mandating disclosure of the officers' activities to the congregation. Therefore, it can be inferred that the Board's disclosure of information regarding Pastor Smith's sexual relationships was not pursuant to church doctrine, and is subject to the jurisdiction of civil courts. The Board's disclosure to the congregation would have been protected it if was done pursuant to church doctrine. Based on the information stated above, Pastor Smith can establish a successful claim for invasion of privacy and the courts can assert jurisdiction over this claim.

Although Pastor Smith can successfully establish a claim for invasion of privacy in a court of law, this would not be advantageous for preventing further damage to his reputation. A trial would publicize his situation even more because his actions would be discussed and evaluated in the presence of strangers. Alternative dispute resolution would be more beneficial to preventing more damage to the pastor's reputation because the dispute will involve one additional party rather than a courtroom full of strangers.

Pastor Smith's actions of changing the locks and security codes of the church's building and opening a new bank account can establish an actionable claim of conversion because he implemented these changes with the intent of preventing the owners from utilizing their property. Conversion is any act of dominion wrongfully exerted over another's personal property in denial of or inconsistent with the property owner's rights. *Enterprise Leasing Corp. v. Shugart Corp.*, 231 Cal. App. 3d 737, 747 (1991). As stated above in *Higgins*, civil courts have the authority to apply rules regarding property rights, torts, and criminal conduct. *Higgins*, 210 Cal. App. 3d at 1169.

Article IV, Section 8 of the church constitution and by-laws state that the Board of Trustees have supervision of the financial affairs of the church and they are to handle all real and personal property holdings of the church. This clearly indicates that the Board had property rights to the church's security codes, building locks, and money. Therefore, the fact that Pastor Smith took control of these property rights without authorization, and utilized the property for his own purposes establishes an actionable claim for conversion.

According to *Church of Scientology v. Armstrong*, a person is privileged to commit an act of conversion for the purpose of defending himself or a third person. *Church of Scientology v. Armstrong*, 232 Cal. App. 3d 1060, 1072 (July 1991). The court held that the respondent in this case was privileged because he believed that his life, physical, and mental well-being were threatened. *Church of Scientology*, 232 Cal. App. 3d at 1073. This case is distinguishable from the dispute at issue because Pastor Smith has not stated that his purpose for changing the locks, security codes, and opening a new account was to defend himself against any offensive or harmful conduct. Therefore, the privilege will not extend to the pastor and a successful claim of conversion can be established against him.

STRATEGY

Based on the information above, the best way to effectively resolve these disputes is through negotiation or mediation, which involves third parties assisting in the resolution process. The reason this method of resolution would be the most advantageous to Pastor Smith is because it satisfies his primary goals. Negotiating with the Board of Trustees will prevent the courts from interfering with church-related matters regardless of whether they can assert jurisdiction or not. Negotiation will also prevent further damage to Pastor Smith's reputation because the information will remain among those already aware versus the exposure the information would receive in a court room, where a substantial number of uninformed people will be privy to the Pastor's activities. Finally, this method of resolution will protect Pastor Smith against the potential civil liability that could result from his alleged commission of conversion.

APPENDIX V

BRIEFS

Here is a Motion for Summary Judgment, with supporting documents:

Inger Hultgren and Valerie Wilde, Esqs.
Hultgren & Wilde, P.C.
1789 Freedom Road, Suite 800
Libertyville, Freedonia 48295
(304) 488-3851
Bar Nos. 2294037, 9583665

IN THE
UNITED STATES DISTRICT COURT FOR THE DISTRICT OF PURITANIA
Edwardsville Division

FEDERAL COMMUNICATIONS COMMISSION, Plaintiff, v. BARRETT EDMONDSON, Defendant.	Civil Action No. 94-2837 DEFENDANT EDMONDSON'S MOTION FOR SUMMARY JUDGMENT

Defendant Barrett Edmondson moves for summary judgment on all claims in this action. Under Federal Rule of Civil Procedure 56, Edmondson is entitled to judgment as a matter of law because the undisputed facts show that: (1) Puritania does not have personal jurisdiction over Edmondson, (2) Edmondson did not violate 47 U.S.C. § 223, and (3) 47 U.S.C. § 223 is unconstitutionally vague and over broad as applied to Edmondson.

This motion is supported by the attached Memorandum of Law, Statement of Material Facts, Affidavit of Barrett Edmondson, and the entire record before the court.

February 7, 1995

Respectfully submitted,

_____

Inger Hultgren, Esq.

_____

Valerie Wilde, Esq.
Hultgren & Wilde, P.C.
1789 Freedom Road
Libertyville, Freedonia 48295

Inger Hultgren and Valerie Wilde, Esqs.

Hultgren & Wilde, P.C.

1789 Freedom Road, Suite 800

Libertyville, Freedonia 48295

(304) 488-3851

Bar Nos. 2294037, 9583665

IN THE
UNITED STATES DISTRICT COURT FOR THE DISTRICT OF
PURITANIA
Edwardsville Division

FEDERAL COMMUNICATIONS COMMISSION, Plaintiff, v. BARRETT EDMONDSON, Defendant.	Civil Action No. 94-2837 DEFENDANT EDMONDSON'S STATEMENT OF MATERIAL FACTS AND EXHIBITS SUPPORTING MOTION FOR SUMMARY JUDGMENT

For purposes of summary judgment only, Defendant Barrett Edmondson presents the following material facts:

1. Edmondson is the sole owner and operator of BarryNET, a computer bulletin board system that enables subscribers to exchange messages and communicate electronically. He operates BarryNET from a computer in his home in Freedonia. Affidavit of Barrett Edmondson ¶ 1 (Exh. A).

2. Edmondson solicits subscribers for BarryNET in only two ways: (1) through advertisements in the Easyville Daily News , and (2) through advertisements on the Internet. Individuals who wish to subscribe to BarryNET must dial in with their computers and fill out an automated sign-up form, which requests the following information: name, address, phone number, employer, age, and credit card information for billing. Edmondson calls to verify all subscription requests from persons under the age of 25, to prevent children from using their parents' credit cards without permission. Affidavit of Barrett Edmondson ¶ 2 (Exh. A).

3. Subscribers gain access to BarryNET by using a modem to connect their computers to Edmondson's computer. Edmondson charges subscribers a fee of $10.00 per month. He has sold five BarryNET subscriptions to Puritania residents, which accounts for .1% of his earnings from BarryNET. Affidavit of Barrett Edmondson ¶ 3 (Exh. A).

4. Edmondson scans both BarryNET and the Internet once a week, for approximately two hours. He has never seen any pornographic messages or material on either system. Affidavit of Barrett Edmondson ¶ 4 (Exh. A).

5. Edmondson has only been in or driven through Puritania on ten separate occasions during the past eight years. He has never contacted by telephone, computer or otherwise, any persons or businesses located in Puritania, except for the five Puritania residents who subscribe to BarryNET. Affidavit of Barrett Edmondson ¶ 5 (Exh. A).

February 7, 1995

Respectfully submitted,

_____

Inger Hultgren, Esq.

_____

Valerie Wilde, Esq.
Hultgren & Wilde, P.C.
1789 Freedom Road
Libertyville, Freedonia 48295

Inger Hultgren and Valerie Wilde, Esqs.

Hultgren & Wilde, P.C.

1789 Freedom Road, Suite 800

Libertyville, Freedonia 48295

(304) 488-3851

Bar Nos. 2294037, 9583665

IN THE
UNITED STATES DISTRICT COURT FOR THE DISTRICT OF PURITANIA
Edwardsville Division

FEDERAL COMMUNICATIONS COMMISSION, Plaintiff, v. BARRETT EDMONDSON, Defendant.	Civil Action No. 94-2837 DEFENDANT EDMONDSON'S MEMORANDUM OF LAW IN SUPPORT OF MOTION FOR SUMMARY JUDGMENT

I.   INTRODUCTION

The Court should grant defendant, Barrett Edmondson's, Motion for Summary Judgment of the Federal Communications Commission's claims against him under 47 U.S.C. § 223, for both procedural and substantive reasons. First, summary judgment is warranted because the United States District Court for the District of Puritania lacks both specific and general jurisdiction over Edmondson. Second, the undisputed facts show that Edmondson did not violate 47 U.S.C. § 223. Third, summary judgment is proper because 47 U.S.C. § 223 is unconstitutional as applied to Edmondson.

II.   ARGUMENT

   A.   THE UNITED STATES DISTRICT COURT FOR THE DIS-
        TRICT OF PURITANIA LACKS PERSONAL JURISDICTION
        OVER EDMONDSON BECAUSE EDMONDSON DOES NOT
        HAVE SUFFICIENT CONTACTS WITH PURITANIA.

   1.   *Edmondson did not purposefully avail himself of the benefits of
        Puritania and therefore does not have minimum contacts with
        Puritania as required for specific jurisdiction.*

Under the minimum contacts test set forth in *International Shoe Co. v. Washington,* courts may not assert specific jurisdiction over non-resident defendants unless jurisdiction under the circumstances is sanctioned by the forum state's long-arm statute, and defendants have "minimum contacts" with the forum state such that the assertion of jurisdiction will not violate the Fourteenth Amendment's due process clause. *International Shoe Co. v. Washington,* 326 U.S. 310 (1945). As Puritania's long-arm statute grants jurisdiction ". . . on any basis not inconsistent with the Constitution of this state or of the United States," the jurisdictional inquiry in this case may proceed directly to the question of minimum contacts. 5 Pur. Code Civ. Pro. § 410.10 (Deering 1994). In conducting minimum contacts analyses, courts must focus on the "relationship among the defendant, the forum, and the litigation." *Shaffer v. Heitner,* 433 U.S. 186, 204. Thus, in evaluating whether a defendant has minimum contacts with the forum state, courts must consider: 1) The relatedness of the defendant's conduct to the claim, 2) the nature and quality of the defendant's contacts with the forum state, and 3) the degree to which the defendant purposefully availed himself of the benefits of the forum state. *See Burger King Corp. v. Rudzewicz,* 471 U.S. 462 (1985); *World-Wide Volkswagen v. Woodson,* 444 U.S. 286 (1980).

    a.   Because Edmondson's only contacts with Puritania were effected through the operation of his computer bulletin board system, "BarryNET," in Freedonia, Edmondson had only non-physical contacts with Puritania.

The United States Supreme Court has established that a defendant need not have physical, in-state contacts with a given state in order to have "minimum contacts" with that state. Minimum contacts may exist where the defendant's out-of-state activities produce certain "effects" in the forum state, which effects give rise to the plaintiff's claim. *Keeton v. Hustler Magazine,* 465 U.S. 770 (1984) (where the defendant's only related contacts with the forum state were through the circulation of magazines in that state).

However, where the defendant's effects-producing activities did not occur within the forum state, the court may not assert jurisdiction over the defendant unless the defendant "purposefully directed" his activities at the forum state. *Burger King Corp. v. Rudzewicz,* 471 U.S. at 476. Absent such evidence, the "purposeful availment" requirement for minimum contacts cannot be met in cases concerning non-physical contacts. *Id.* The record shows that Edmondson did not have any physical contacts with the forum state, Puritania. Instead, Edmondson engaged in the following activities from outside of Puritania: ownership and operation of a computer bulletin board system from his home in Freedonia and sale of access to this system to various individuals, including five Puritania residents. (Edmondson Aff.) Thus, Edmondson's out-of-state activities may not amount to minimum contacts with Puritania unless Edmondson in some way purposefully directed these activities at Puritania.

    b.   Because Edmondson did not actively solicit residents of Puritania to subscribe to BarryNET, he did not purposefully direct his activities at Puritania.

As there is currently no case law discussing personal jurisdiction over computer bulletin board operators, this case requires an especially careful inquiry into the facts of Edmondson's situation. Computer bulletin board systems possess characteristics similar to those of telephone networks. Like telephone networks, computer bulletin board systems act as a conduit for the exchange of communications between users of the system. Eric C. Jensen, *An Electronic Soapbox: Computer Bulletin Boards and The First Amendment*, 39 Fed. Com. L.J. 217, 250 (1987). Computer bulletin board users dial into the system from their computers to send and receive written messages of their own choosing. Thus, in contrast to television, radio, newspaper and magazine providers, who choose which types of shows, broadcasts and articles they will disseminate, telephone and computer bulletin board operators do not determine the content of the communications transmitted on their systems. Note, *The Message in the Medium: The First Amendment on the Information Superhighway*, 107 Harv. L. Rev. 1062, 1092 (1994).

However, there are very few cases concerning the liability of telephone network providers for harmful communications made by telephone network users, and there are no cases applying the minimum contacts test to telephone providers under such circumstances. *See* Phillip H. Miller, Note, *New Technology, Old Problem; Determining the First Amendment Status of Electronic Information Services*, 61 Fordham L. Rev. 1147, 1163 (1993). Thus, the telephone network/computer bulletin board system analogy does not lead to a standard by which to judge Edmondson's contacts. Nevertheless, this comparison serves to underscore the major difference between computer bulletin board operators and other communication media; the computer bulletin board operator does not control or endorse the messages and materials which are transmitted through his system. Courts have refused to hold telephone companies liable at all for the communications of their users. *See Sable Communications of Cal., Inc. v. FCC*, 492 U.S. 115 (1989) (holding the defendant, dial-a-porn service, rather than the telephone company subject to sanctions for transmitting content that violated 47 U.S.C. § 223); *Anderson v. N.Y. Telephone Co.*, 320 N.E.2d (N.Y. 1974) (holding that defendant, telephone company, which didn't intentionally transmit libelous communications could not be held liable for doing so). Thus, at the very least, the fact that Edmondson was not responsible for the existence of the allegedly obscene materials found on BarryNET, and did not intentionally transmit these materials, indicates that a much greater showing of purposeful availment should be required to establish that he has minimum contacts with Puritania.

However, it is not necessary in this case to determine what this greater showing would entail because even under the standards applied to newspaper and magazine editors, who are responsible for the content of their communications, Edmondson has not purposefully directed his activities at Puritania. In several defamation cases, courts have considered whether non-resident magazine and newspaper publishers and editors were subject to the jurisdiction of the states in which they solicited and maintained subscribers. In these cases, the courts primarily considered factors such as the number of subscriptions maintained in the forum states, and the manner in which subscriptions were solicited, in determining whether the defendants purposefully directed their activities at the forum states. *E.g. Army Times Publishing Co. v. Watts* 730 F. 2d. 1398 (11th Cir. 1984); *Putnam v. Triangle Publications, Inc.*, 96 S.E. 2d 445 (1957 N.C.).

Courts have particularly stressed the significance of the manner in which defendants solicited subscriptions from residents of the forum state. Indeed, statistical evidence as to subscriptions maintained in the forum state cannot by itself prove that the defendant purposefully directed his publications at that state. In *Putnam v. Triangle Publications, Inc.*, the North Carolina Supreme Court explained that although some North Carolina residents subscribed to magazines published by the defendant, the defendant was not subject to the Court's jurisdiction because the defendant had not actively solicited North Carolina residents. Instead, ". . . subscriptions [were] solicited from outside the state by mail and by coupons attached to the magazines. No sales to subscribers [were] solicited within the state of North Carolina." *Putnam v. Triangle Publications, Inc.* 96 S.E. 2d at 448.

In contrast, the fact that the defendant newspaper publisher actively solicited residents of the forum state to subscribe to its publication weighed heavily into the Court's decision to find personal jurisdiction over the defendant in *Army Times Publishing Co. v. Watts*. In this case, the defendant, publisher of a weekly newspaper covering military issues, solicited new and renewal subscriptions in Alabama by making numerous telephone calls to Alabama residents. Although the number of newspapers sold in Alabama was small and constituted only 2.1% of the newspaper's total circulation, the Court found that the defendant "could reasonably anticipate being 'haled into court' in Alabama." *Army Times Publishing Co. v. Watts* 730 F.2d at 1400 (citing *World-Wide Volkswagen Corp. v. Woodson*). The key factor underlying the Court's decision was that ". . . the defendant *actively* undertook efforts to maintain its Alabama readership" by seeking to ". . . penetrate and exploit the various pockets of federal civilian and military personnel" in Alabama. *Army Times Publishing Co. v. Watts*, 730 F.2d at 1400 (emphasis added).

Computer bulletin board operators can be analogized to newspaper and magazine publishers insofar as they provide their services to individuals on a subscription basis. Computer bulletin board operators essentially sell "subscriptions" to their services by charging user monthly fees for access to their computer bulletin boards. Thus, a computer bulletin board operator may be subjected to a state's jurisdiction only when he has *actively* solicited subscribers from that state. In the case at issue, Edmondson has sold only five BarryNET subscriptions to Puritania residents, and derives only .1% of his total BarryNET earnings from these sales. (Edmondson Aff.) More importantly, however, he did not actively solicit these Puritania residents to purchase BarryNET subscriptions. Instead, Edmondson merely placed an advertisement for BarryNET on the Internet and in a local Freedonia newspaper, neither of which are specifically directed at Puritania. (Edmondson Dep. at 4) These solicitation activities do not rise to the level of purposefulness required in the aforementioned newspaper and magazine defamation cases, as they fail to show that Edmondson was attempting to "penetrate" or "exploit" the Puritania computer bulletin board market.

Thus, although a higher standard should be applied in assessing Edmondson's contacts with Puritania because he acts merely as a conduit for communications, Edmondson does not have minimum contacts with Puritania even under the standard applied to newspaper and magazine publishers.

2. *Because Edmondson did not engage in substantial or continuous and systematic activities in Puritania, the United States District Court for the District of Puritania may not assert general jurisdiction over Edmondson.*

A defendant may be hauled into a state's courts to defend against causes of action unrelated to his conduct there if his activities in the state are "substantial" or "continuous and systematic." *Perkins v. Benguet Consol. Mining Co.*, 342 U.S. 446-447 (1952). The record shows that Edmondson has "only been in or driven through Puritania on ten separate occasions during the past eight years" and "has not contacted any persons or businesses located in Puritania, except for the five Puritania residents who subscribe to BarryNET." (Def.'s Statement of Material Facts and Exs. at ¶ 5.) These contacts cannot be characterized as "substantial" or "continuous and systematic" and therefore do not give rise to general jurisdiction.

B. EDMONDSON DID NOT VIOLATE 47 U.S.C. § 223(b) BE-CAUSE THE MATERIALS UPLOADED AND DOWN-LOADED FROM EDMONDSON'S COMPUTER BULLETIN

BOARD SYSTEM ARE NOT OBSCENE UNDER APPLICABLE COMMUNITY STANDARDS FOR OBSCENITY.

1. *The applicable community standards for obscenity and indecency are those of Edmondson's state of residence, Freedonia.*

While courts have held in actions brought against "dial-a-porn" companies under 47 U.S.C. § 223(b) that the community standards of the communities receiving allegedly obscene materials may be used in determining whether these materials are in fact obscene, this rule can not be applied in actions brought against computer bulletin board operators. *See Sable Communications of Cal., Inc. v. FCC*, 492 U.S. 115 (1989). Adherence to this community standards rule in cases concerning computer bulletin board operators would have unacceptable effects on free speech, which adherence to the rule does not have in dial-a-porn cases.

The differences in the rule's free speech implications in the dial-a-porn and computer bulletin board contexts derive from significant differences in the way in which the two services function. First, dial-a-porn operators, who provide a service through which individuals may dial in on their telephones for sexually explicit messages, are ". . . free to tailor [their] messages, on a selective basis, if [they] so choose[ ], to the communities [they] choose[ ] to serve." *Id.* at 125. Bulletin board operators, however, do not create the messages which are received on their systems and furthermore have extremely little ability to control and edit the messages of their users. As Jonathan Gilbert explains in his law review article, *Computer Bulletin Board Operator Liability for User Misuse*, there are no feasible ways for a computer bulletin board operator to eradicate user misuse without seriously undermining the beneficial purposes of this medium as a forum for public debate. Jonathan Gilbert, *Computer Bulletin Board Operator Liability for User Misuse*, 54 Fordham L. Rev. 439. Monitoring and editing of all user messages to ensure that no messages which might be obscene in any given state are distributed is simply an impossible task. *See Id.* Thus, to protect himself from the increased possibility of liability under 47 U.S.C. § 223(b), created by application of many different community standards for obscenity, Edmondson would be forced to limit the sale of BarryNET subscriptions to states where he knows that community standards are less strict.

Second, application of this rule has farther-reaching free speech implications in the context of BarryNET, because this computer bulletin board system, unlike dial-a-porn hotlines, provides a forum for expression of a wide variety of speech. The restrictive measures which Edmondson would be forced to take would therefore not only prevent individuals from exchanging pornographic materials on the system, but would prevent them from communicating on more legitimate topics by depriving them of the advantages of the system altogether.

Such restrictive results would run counter to our country's strong national commitment to the free expression and communication of ideas, and therefore should not be promoted by the law. *See* Gilbert, *supra* at 446. The United States Supreme Court has enunciated this commitment to promoting free speech on numerous occasions. *N.Y. Times Co. v. Sullivan*, 376 U.S. 254, 269-70 (1964) ("Thus, we consider this case against the background of a profound national commitment to the principle that debate on public issues should be uninhibited, robust, and wide open."); *Roth v. U.S.*, 354 U.S. 476, 484 (1957) ("Protection given speech and press was fashioned to assure unfettered interchange of ideas. . ."). Thus, a new community standards rule should be applied in cases involving computer bulletin board operators, which would grant them a greater sense of security and give them less of an incentive to take such undesirable actions to restrict free speech. The community standard of the community in which the computer bulletin board operator resides should be applied, as it would give the operator notice of the applicable standard and the operator to decide which community standard he wishes to operate under. Thus, the community standard of Edmondson's residence, Freedonia, should be applied in this case.

2. *The materials uploaded and downloaded from defendant's computer bulletin board system are not obscene under Freedonia's community standards.*

Finally, the statute section under which the Federal Communications Commission has brought suit, 47 U.S.C. § 223(b), only concerns *obscene* communications. Thus, because the materials exchanged on Edmondson's computer bulletin board system were merely *indecent* under Freedonia's community standards, Edmondson has not violated 47 U.S.C. § 223.

C. IT WOULD BE UNCONSTITUTIONAL FOR EDMONDSON TO BE HELD TO THE STANDARD OF OBSCENITY SET FORTH IN THE *MILLER* DECISION OR 47 U.S.C. at 223.

1. *The policy reasons set forth by the court in Miller are not applicable in Edmondson's case because BBS users are not unwilling recipients or juveniles.*

The Supreme Court has distinguished between the constitutional protection of "indecent" and "obscene" speech. The former is afforded First Amendment protection; the latter is not included in the First Amendment's freedom of speech doctrine. *Miller v. California*, 413 U.S. 15 (1973).

In *Miller v. California*, the court treated the issue of whether a person should be held criminally liable for sending sexually explicit materials to other persons who had no interest in receiving such materials. *Id.* at 18. The court held that obscene material is not protected by the First Amendment, and should therefore result in criminal liability for anyone who violates a state's obscenity statute. Moreover, the court established a three-part test to determine whether material should be labeled "obscene." "The basic guidelines for the trier of fact must be (a) whether the "average person, applying contemporary community standards" would find that the work, taken as a whole, appeals to the prurient interest, (b) whether the work depicts or describes in a patently offensive way, sexual conduct specifically defined by the applicable state law, and (c) whether the work, taken as a whole, lacks serious literary, artistic, political, or scientific value." 413 U.S. at 15.

The stringent guidelines established by the court for determining whether speech is obscene were justified on the basis of two public policy arguments. First, the court expressed its concern regarding the effect of obscene materials on youngsters and those who do not wish to be exposed to such material. "The States have a legitimate interest in prohibiting dissemination or exhibition of obscene material when the mode of dissemination carries with it a significant danger of offending the sensibilities of unwilling recipients or of exposure to juveniles." *Id.* at 19. Second, the court adopted the position set forth by the court in *Roth v. United States*: "Such utterances are no essential part of any exposition of ideas, and are of such slight social value as a step to truth that any benefit that may be derived from them is clearly outweighed by the social interest in order and morality. . ." 413 U.S. at 21. Therefore, the *Miller* court reasoned that the possible benefits that might result from the complete exposition of ideas are far outweighed by the risk of social disorder that might result if obscene materials were afforded First Amendment protection.

The *Miller* court's justifications raise a multitude of troubling issues that need to be addressed. First, it is possible that the court's policy concerns do not always warrant preclusion of First Amendment protection to speech that is labeled "obscene." In many cases, measures are taken to ensure that neither "unwilling recipients" nor juveniles receive "obscene" material. Those who wish to receive "obscene" material should not be prevented from doing so, in the state's interest of protecting those who are "unwilling recipients." Second, it is not always clear what obscenity statutes prohibit. It is difficult for society to understand what it means for speech to be labeled "obscene." Furthermore, there is a question as to whether the standards for obscenity should be set by the courts or by the legislature. Although the Court has designated "obscene" speech as unworthy of First Amendment protection, it is not clear when this doctrine will apply.

2. *47 U.S.C. § 223 is unconstitutionally vague and overly broad and is therefore inapplicable to Barrett Edmondson's conduct.*

A statute is unconstitutionally "vague" when it "fails to draw reasonably clear lines between the kinds of . . . treatment that are criminal and those that are not." *Smith v. Goguen*, 415 U.S. 566 (1973). An "overly broad" statute is one "which does not aim specifically at evils within the allowable area of state control but, on the contrary, sweeps within its ambit other activities that in ordinary circumstances constitute an exercise of freedom of speech . . . resulting in a continuous and pervasive restraint on all freedom of discussion that might reasonably be regarded as within its purview." *Thornhill v. Alabama*, 310 U.S. 97(1940). Under section 223(b)(1)(A) of 47 U.S.C. § 223, it is difficult to determine exactly what kind of conduct the statute prohibits. This results in an unconstitutional "chilling effect" on protected speech. This section of the statute states: "Whoever knowingly — within the United States, by means of **telephone**, makes (directly or by recording device) any obscene communication for commercial purposes of any person, regardless of whether the maker of such communication placed the call . . . shall be fined. . .." 47 U.S.C. § 223 (1994). This portion of the statue is vague and overly broad in three respects: its use of the word "telephone," "maker," and "call."

It is unclear from the legislature's use of the word "telephone" whether the statute applies to users of telephones only, or to users of telephone lines as well. If it applies only to users of telephones, then the statute is not applicable to those people who use telephone lines/modems to gain access to computer communication. In this manner, the statute could be creating a "chilling effect" by curbing speech that is currently protected by the Constitution. This would be unfair to Barrett Edmondson and other members of the computer community who are particularly affected by the statute.

The interpretation of the word "maker" is dependent upon the context in which the word is used. Applied to different situations, the word "maker" will apply to different people. For example, the "maker" of a telephone call will presumably be the person who dials another person's number. However, if we apply the word "maker" to electronic communication, it is unclear as to whom the statue applies. It may apply to the person who logs onto his/her computer to communicate with another. It may also refer to the person who creates and operates a Bulletin Board System. The ambiguities that arise in applying the statute to users of telephone lines for electronic communication suggest that the statute was not created to cover members of the computer community.

The use of the word "call" implies the spoken, rather than the written word. However, people who communicate by computer do not "speak" to each other; they "write" to each other. This also suggests that the legislature probably did not intend for the statute to apply to computer communication. The uncertainty inherent in the statute will again cause a "chilling effect," causing users of electronic communication to curb their speech unnecessarily.

D. IT WOULD BE UNCONSTITUTIONAL FOR EDMONDSON TO BE HELD TO THE STANDARD OF CARE OF A "PROVIDER" OF SEXUALLY EXPLICIT MATERIAL BECAUSE IT WOULD VIOLATE HIS DUE PROCESS RIGHTS.

1. *Barrett Edmondson should not be held to the same standard of care as the* **provider** *of a dial-a-porn because Edmondson does not* **provide** *sexually explicit material to the public.*

The constitutionality of 47 U.S.C. § 223 was addressed in *Sable v. FCC*, 492 U.S. 115 (1989), following the 1988 amendments to the statute. Sable Communications, Inc., a company that began offering sexually oriented prerecorded telephone messages through the Pacific Bell telephone network, challenged the obscenity provisions of the amended statute under the First and Fourteenth Amendments to the Constitution. *Id.* at 118.

The court in *Sable* held that the statute "does not unconstitutionally prohibit the interstate transmission of obscene commercial telephone messages." *Id.* At 115. This holding was justified on two grounds. First, the protection of the First Amendment does not extend to obscene speech. Second, no constitutional barrier existed under *Miller* that would prevent Sable from tailoring its messages to the communities it chose to serve. The court reasoned that as the **provider** of "dial-a-porn" messages, Sable should bear the burden of complying with the prohibition on obscene messages. 492 U.S. at 125.

Edmondson should not be held to the same standard of responsibility as the company that provides obscene material to the public over the telephone. The facts of *Sable* are readily distinguishable from the facts of the present case: Edmondson does not **provide** the public with sexually explicit material; his business is simply to act as the medium through which people may distribute information to each other. Therefore, even if obscene material should not be protected by the First Amendment, the *Sable* holding should not apply to the case at bar. Because it would violate his Due Process Rights, Edmondson should not be held to the same standard of care as the corporation that provides the public with sexually explicit material.

2. *The test of "knowledge" established in Cubby v. CompuServe should be applied to Edmondson in his capacity as "distributor" rather than "provider" of sexually explicit material.*

In *Cubby, Inc. v. CompuServe, Inc.*, 776 F. Supp. 135 (S.D.N.Y. 1991), the court addressed a corporation's liability for distributing defamatory statements, when that corporation provides computer services, electronic bulletin boards, and interactive on-line conferences to its subscribers. Because the court found that CompuServe was a "distributor" rather than a "publisher" of information, it held that the company would not be liable if it neither "knew nor had reason to know" of the defamation. *Id.* at 139. As a result, the court granted the defendant's motion for summary judgment.

The court justified its holding in *Cubby* based on the burden that the distributor would encounter if it were required to monitor every publication it distributed. The court cited *Smith v.California*, 361 U.S. 147, 152-53, in analogizing the provider of on-line computer services to a bookshop owner. "In *Smith*, the Court struck down an ordinance that imposed liability on a bookseller for possession of an obscene book, regardless of whether the bookseller had knowledge of the book's contents. The Court reasoned, 'it would be altogether unreasonable to demand so near an approach to omniscience.' " 776 F. Supp. At 139.

In his capacity as bulletin board operator, Edmondson might have encountered sexually explicit material on his system. However, this does not establish that he was aware of all material on the system. Edmondson stated during deposition that he verified credit card numbers, not to prevent minors from obtaining access to obscene material on his system, but to prevent minors from using their parents' credit cards without permission. This suggests that Edmondson was unaware of the prevalence of obscene material on the BBS.

Edmondson should be held to the same standard of liability as CompuServe in *Cubby*. If Edmondson were held civilly liable for all obscene statements printed on his bulletin board system, it would preclude First Amendment protection of distributors of publications.

III. CONCLUSION

For the following reasons, the defendant's motion for summary judgment should be granted by the court. First, Edmondson does not have sufficient contacts with Puritania to warrant that state's personal jurisdiction over him. Second, the applicable community standards for obscenity suggest that Edmondson did not violate 47 U.S.C. § 223(b). Third, it would be unconstitutional for Edmondson to be held to the standards of obscenity set forth in 47 U.S.C. § 223. Lastly, it would violate Edmondson's Due Process rights if he were held to the same standard of care as the "provider" of sexually explicit material.

EXHIBIT A

AFFIDAVIT OF BARRETT EDMONDSON
IN SUPPORT OF MOTION FOR SUMMARY JUDGMENT
Chastity County Puritania

Barrett Edmondson, under oath swears to the following information from personal knowledge:

1. I am the sole owner and operator of BarryNET, a computer bulletin board system that enables subscribers to exchange messages and communicate electronically. I operate BarryNET from a computer in my home in Freedonia.

2. I solicit subscribers for BarryNET in only two ways: (1) through advertisements in the Easyville Daily News, and (2) through advertisements on the Internet. Individuals who wish to subscribe to BarryNET must dial in with their computers and fill out on automated sign-up form, which requests the following information: name, address, phone number, employer, age, and credit card information for billing. I call to verify all subscription requests from persons under the age of 25, to prevent children from using their parents' credit cards without permission.

3. Subscribers gain access to BarryNET by using a modem to connect their computers to my computer. I charge subscribers a fee of $10.00 per month. I have sold five BarryNET subscriptions to Puritania residents, which accounts for .1% of my earnings from BarryNET.

4. I scan both BarryNET and the Internet once a week, for approximately two hours. I have never seen any pornographic messages or material on either system.

5. I have only been in or driven through Puritania on ten separate occasions during the past eight years. I have never contacted by telephone, computer or otherwise, any persons or businesses located in Puritania, except for the five Puritania residents who subscribe to BarryNET.

I swear under oath that the foregoing is true:

_____

Barrett Edmondson

_____

Date

Here is a pair of briefs on opposing sides of the same issue. The briefs were written for a state appellate court.

IN THE
SUPERIOR COURT OF PENNSYLVANIA

———

March Term, 1987

———

No. 19

———

ST. MARY'S HOSPITAL,
Appellant

v.

ADMINISTRATORS OF THE ESTATE OF CHARLA LOUIS,
Appellees

———

On Appeal from the Court of Common Pleas
of Berks County, Pennsylvania

———

BRIEF FOR APPELLANT

———

Robert M. Maxwell, Jr.
Lorijean Golichowski Oei
Attorneys for Appellant

TABLE OF CONTENTS

[Illustrative page references are to original document.]

TABLE OF CITATIONS

CASES   PAGE

STATEMENT OF JURISDICTION

The Superior Court of Pennsylvania has jurisdiction over this matter pursuant to 42 Pa. Cons. Stat. Ann. section 742 (1981).

QUESTIONS PRESENTED

I. Should not Workmen's Compensation be the exclusive remedy for injuries sustained by an employee in the course of her employment from an attack by a third person when no relationship between the third person and employee existed prior to the attack?

II. Can a hospital be held liable under a negligence theory for an attack on an employee by a third party where the hospital employed a security force which conducted a systematic security program and where there was no history of criminal conduct occurring on the premises that would have alerted the hospital to the likelihood of danger to its employees?

STATUTORY PROVISIONS

Pa. Stat. Ann. tit. 77 section 411(1) (1986) *"Injury," "personal injury," and "injury arising in the course of his employment" defined*

(1) The terms "injury" and "personal injury," as used in this act, shall be construed to mean an injury to an employee, regardless of his previous physical condition, arising in the course of his employment and related thereto, and such disease or infection as naturally results from the injury or is aggravated, reactivated or accelerated by the injury; and wherever death is mentioned as a cause for compensation under this act, it shall mean only death resulting from such injury and its resultant effects, and occurring within three hundred weeks after the injury. The term "injury arising in the course of his employment," as used in this article, shall not include an injury caused by an act of a third person intended to injure the employee because of reasons personal to him, and not directed against him as an employee or because of his employment; but shall include all other injuries sustained while the employee is actually engaged in the further-ance of the business or affairs of the employer, whether upon the employer's premises or elsewhere, and shall include all injuries caused by the condition of the premises or by the operation of the employer's business or affairs thereon, sustained by the employee, who, though not so engaged, is injured upon the premises occupied by or under the control of the employer, or upon which the employer's business or affairs are being carried on, the employee's presence thereon being required by the nature of his employment.

Pa. Stat. Ann. tit. 77 section 481(a) (1986) *Exclusiveness of remedy; actions by and against third party; contract indemnifying third party*

(a) The liability of an employer under this act shall be exclusive and in place of any and all other liability to such employees, his legal representative, husband or wife, parents, dependents, next of kin or anyone otherwise entitled to damages in any action at law or otherwise on account of any injury or death as defined in section 301(c)(1) and (2) or occupational disease as defined in section 108.

STATEMENT OF THE CASE

Charla Louis was working on the night shift in the Medical Records Office of St. Mary's Hospital on July 25, 1982. In the early morning hours on that date, George Knapp, a hospital security guard, discovered Michael Bronstein wandering toward the vending machine area (R. 80 – R. 83). Knapp stopped Bronstein and asked him what he was doing (R. 86 – R. 87). Bronstein replied that he was going home (R. 104). Knapp escorted Bronstein out of the building. On the way out of the Hospital, Knapp and Bronstein passed the Medical Records Office where Louis was working. Knapp, in his deposition, testified that "there is no way that he [Bronstein] could have seen her or she [Charla Louis] seen him as he was walking down the hall" (R. 105). Knapp also stated that he did not see Charla Louis as he was walking down the hallway escorting Bronstein out of the Hospital (R. 112). Knapp made sure the doors through which Bronstein exited were secured (R. 116) and then checked on Louis at the Medical Records Office, informing her that he would be back on a later round (R. 118, 119). In addition, Knapp stated at the deposition that Louis never indicated that she knew Bronstein or had ever seen him (R. 121).

Later that night, at approximately 3:00 a.m., Bronstein managed to reenter the Hospital. He found Louis, forced her to leave the building, attempted to rape her and, when she resisted, stabbed her to death. At approximately 4:00 a.m., a side door of the Hospital was found propped open (R. 47 – R. 50).

At Bronstein's trial, a fellow prisoner, David P. Strong, testified that Bronstein had confessed to Louis' murder. Strong testified that Bronstein told him:

Well, you see, that night I [Bronstein] was really horny and I went into the hospital *hoping I could find a nurse or somebody who would be alone or isolated*, and I would have the opportunity to do it to her . . . I went in the hospital, I was in there about five minutes when I came across an office where there was a young lady there working (R. 73) (emphasis added).

At the trial, Bronstein testified that he did not know Charla Louis and had never seen her before (R. 85-87).

Linda Bach, a friend of Louis, stated she had seen Louis two weeks prior to the murder and that Louis said that work was fine except that "she said somebody was hassling her up there or something, and she didn't say what it was . . . " (R. 3). Bach did not inquire any further into the meaning of this statement and she stated she did not know if the person "hassling" Louis was somebody who worked at the Hospital or not (R. 4).

Charla Louis' Estate filed a civil action in April of 1983, asserting a claim for wrongful death and a survival action based upon the alleged negligence of St. Mary's Hospital. The complaint was amended on May 17, 1983. Preliminary objections were overruled, and St. Mary's Hospital filed its Answer and New Matter on September 7, 1983; the Estate replied on September 16, 1983. The Estate answered requests for admissions and interrogatories. Linda Bach was deposed on May 29, 1985. All discovery was initiated by St. Mary's Hospital.

The case had been pending for thirty months when St. Mary's Hospital advised the Estate of its intention to move for summary judgment and requested that the Estate identify any further discovery that would be required. In three weeks, the Estate made no response. The court below denied the Hospital's motion for summary judgment on the undisputed facts set forth and held that the Estate's action was not barred by the Workmen's Compensation Act, that the attack was for reasons personal to the assailant, and that the hospital was negligent in providing security to its employees (R. 4, 12). Summary judgment was granted in favor of the Estate with the measure of damages to be determined at trial (R. 12).

SUMMARY OF ARGUMENT

Michael Bronstein entered St. Mary's Hospital where Charla Louis was working, forced her to leave the hospital, and killed her after attempting to rape her. Workmen's Compensation should be the exclusive remedy for Charla Louis' Estate in accordance with the Pennsylvania legislature's intent that Workmen's Compensation be the sole remedy for injuries incurred during one's employment.

There is a narrowly defined exception to the exclusive nature of Workmen's Compensation which permits plaintiffs to pursue a common law tort remedy when they are attacked by a third person with whom they share a long-standing relationship outside of work. The Record in the instant case shows no such relationship between Charla Louis and her attacker. In fact, it indicates that the two never knew each other before the incident. Thus,

Charla Louis' Estate's suit does not fall within this narrow exception, and Workmen's Compensation is to be the Estate's sole remedy.

The next issue is whether the hospital was negligent in providing security for its employees. To maintain its cause of action, the Estate must prove that the hospital breached its duty to provide a safe workplace and that this breach was the proximate cause of the incident.

An employer is not an insurer of its employees' safety; however, the employer may be required to take reasonable precautions to protect its employees when the place or character of its business or its past experience allows the employer to reasonably anticipate harm. A hospital necessarily must allow many people access to its buildings. Mindful of this, the hospital employs a staff of security guards. There is no history of criminal conduct on the hospital premises which would have put the guards on a heightened alert. The guards' care and discretion in the conduct of their duties was commensurate with that which their past experience led them to anticipate. The guards provided competent protection within the reasonable expectations of the security program.

The guards' conduct was not a substantial factor in causing the incident. There is no evidence as to how the intruder managed to re-enter the hospital. At most, the guards' conduct created a harmless and passive condition that was but a remote circumstance in the events of the morning. The cause of the incident was the superseding criminal act of Michael Bronstein.

The Estate has failed to prove that the hospital breached its duty to use reasonable care or to take precautions. The facts in the record do not permit an inference of negligence or support a finding of proximate cause. Therefore, the lower court's finding of negligence should be reversed.

ARGUMENT

I. WORKMEN'S COMPENSATION SHOULD BE THE EXCLUSIVE REMEDY FOR THE INJURIES SUSTAINED BY CHARLA LOUIS IN THE COURSE OF HER EMPLOYMENT FROM AN ATTACK BY A THIRD PERSON WHEN NO RELATIONSHIP EXISTED BETWEEN CHARLA LOUIS AND THE THIRD PERSON PRIOR TO THE ATTACK.

A. *Workmen's Compensation Is Intended to Be the Sole Remedy for Injuries Sustained in the Course of One's Employment.*

The negligence suit filed by the Administrators of the Estate of Charla Louis (hereinafter referred to as the Estate) is barred by Workmen's Compensation. Section 303 of the Workmen's Compensation Act states the exclusive nature of the liability of an employer to an employee under

Workmen's Compensation. *Wagner v. National Indem. Co.*, 492 Pa. 154, 162, 422 A.2d 1061, 1065 (1980). The Act was amended by the Pennsylvania legislature in 1974, emphasizing the exclusivity of Workmen's Compensation. The 1974 amendment reads, in part:

> (a) The liability of an employer under this act shall be exclusive and in place of any and all other liability to such employees, his legal representative, husband or wife, parents, dependents, next of kin or anyone otherwise entitled to damages in any action at law or on account of any injury or death as defined in section 301(c)(1) and (2). . . .

Pa. Stat. Ann. tit. 77 section 481(a) (1986).

The Supreme and Superior Courts of Pennsylvania interpret this amendment as evidence of the legislature's intent in making Workmen's Compensation the employee's sole remedy for work-related injuries and as barring common law tort actions by an employee against his employer. The Superior Court in *Hefferin v. Stempkowski*, 247 Pa. Super. 366, 369, 372 A.2d 869, 871 (1977), stated that "by this amendment the Legislature made the Pennsylvania Workmen's Compensation Act a complete substitute for, not a supplement to, common law tort actions."

In *Wagner v. National Indem. Co.*, 492 Pa. 154, 162, 422 A.2d 1061, 1065 (1980), the court discussed the advantages of Workmen's Compensation for employer and employee:

> [U]nder the Workmen's Compensation Act, both the employer and the employee relinquished certain rights to obtain other advantages. For the worker, he no longer had to prove negligence; in return, the employee had to accept a limited, though certain, recovery. The employer, on the other hand, guaranteed compensation to an injured employee in return for the exclusivity of the workmen's compensation liability of its employees.

Therefore, under the appellate courts' interpretation of the recent 1974 amendment to the Workmen's Compensation Act, the Estate's negligence suit should be barred. Louis was injured in the course of her employment. Thus, her Estate's sole remedy for her injury should be through Workmen's Compensation. To allow the Estate to pursue a common law tort action would defeat the legislative intent of the Workmen's Compensation Act—to provide a quick legal remedy for injuries sustained in the course of employment without the need for lengthy and costly legal battles at the expense of employee and employer alike.

> B. *The Attack Upon Charla Louis Was Not for Reasons Personal Within the Meaning of the Workmen's Compensation Act and Is Only Compensable Through Workmen's Compensation.*

The attack on Charla Louis is covered by Workmen's Compensation and does not fall within the narrow exception expressed in the Workmen's

Compensation Act which allows the plaintiff to pursue a common law tort action. This exception is expressed in section 301 of the Act:

> The term "injury arising in the course of his employment," as used in this article shall not include an *injury caused by an act of a third person intended to injure the employee because of reasons personal to him,* and not directed against him as an employee or because of his employment. . . .

Pa. Stat. Ann. tit. 77 section 411(1) (1986). In light of the legislature's intent that all work-related injuries should be covered by Workmen's Compensation, this exception is to be construed narrowly. *Rodgers v. Broadbents Spray Rentals,* 22 D. & C.3d 617, 623 (Del. 1981).

For this exception to apply, Pennsylvania courts have held that the employee and attacker must have known each other before the attack took place and the attack must have arisen out of personal animosity which developed during the time the employee and assailant knew each other. Thus the courts have held that some form of pre-existing animosity between a third party assailant and his victim must exist in order for the plaintiff to be allowed to sue outside of Workmen's Compensation. *O'Rourke v. O'Rourke,* 278 Pa. 52, 122 A. 172 (1923), *Workmen's Comp. App. Bd. v. Borough of Plum,* 20 Pa. Commw. 35, 340 A.2d 637 (1975), *D'Agata Nat'l Inc. v. Workmen's Comp. App. Bd.,* 84 Pa. Commw. 527, 479 A.2d 98 (1974), *Haas v. Brotherhood of Transportation Workers,* 158 Pa. Super. 291, 44 A.2d 776 (1945), *Rathburn v. Sussman Brothers,* 127 Pa. Super. 104, 193 A. 488 (1937).

In the instant case, there is no evidence of any pre-existing animosity between the third party and the employee. Bronstein attempted to rape and did kill Charla Louis. He denied that he had known her before the day of the incident. A fellow prisoner testified that Bronstein admitted, ". . . I went into the hospital hoping I could find a nurse or somebody who would be alone or isolated, and I would have the opportunity to do it to her. . . ." (R. 73). To qualify as a personal attack there has to be a prior relationship between attacker and victim. The Record fails to show this, as two crucial points are noticeably absent: 1) that Bronstein knew Charla Louis before the day of the incident, and 2) that Charla Louis knew Bronstein before the incident. Since the Record fails to show these facts, summary judgment should be entered against the Estate as the attack on Louis does not fall within the exception to the Workmen's Compensation Act.

In Pennsylvania cases where an employee was attacked in the course of employment by a third party who was not a co-employee, and where there was no pre-existing animosity between the third party and the employee, Workmen's Compensation was held the sole remedy for the employee.

O'Rourke v. O'Rourke, 278 Pa. 52, 56, 122 A. 172, 173 (1923) (no personal animosity where employee in course of employment attacked by drunkard); *D'Agata Nat'l Inc. v. Workmen's Comp. App. Bd.*, 84 Pa. Commw. 527, 529, 530, 479 A.2d 98, 99-100 (1974) (employee in the course of employment shot by robber not known to employee); *Rathburn v. Sussman Brothers*, 127 Pa. Super. 104, 107, 193 A. 488, 489 (1937) (no personal reasons or personal enmity, where nightwatchman in course of employment shot by robbers not known to him). In *Haas v. Brotherhood of Transportation Workers*, 158 Pa. Super. 291, 44 A.2d 776 (1945), a janitor in the course of employment became involved in an argument with a visitor to the building. At the culmination of the quarrel, the janitor was shot by the visitor. The janitor and visitor had never known each other before the quarrel. *Id.* at 295, 44 A.2d at 778. Workmen's Compensation was awarded in this case. According to the court, the oral argument between the employee and the third party, who had never known each other before the argument, did not create the "personal reasons" necessary to take the case out of Workmen's Compensation. *Id.* at 295, 44 A.2d at 779.

Thus, the courts have held that an attack by a third person upon an employee where the employee and third person did not know each other prior to the attack was not an attack motivated by personal reasons and was compensable under Workmen's Compensation. In the instant case, the record indicates that Louis and Bronstein did not know each other before the attack. Following the weight of authority, the attack on Louis should be compensable through Workmen's Compensation only.

In some cases where the attacker and the victim did know each other before the attack, Workmen's Compensation has been granted. *Cleland Simpson Co. v. Workmen's Comp. App. Bd.*, 16 Pa. Commw. 566, 567, 332 A.2d 862, 863 (1974) (victim worked at the same place of employment as assailant for approximately five weeks), *U.S. Steel Corp. v. Workmen's Comp. App. Bd.*, 10 Pa. Commw. 247, 249, 309 A.2d 842, 843 (1973) (striking plaintiff with clenched fist was culmination of five days of intermittent arguments), *Meucci v. Gallatin Coal Co.*, 279 Pa. 184, 185, 123 A. 766, 767 (1924) (victim and assailant were boss and miner at work). In *U.S. Steel*, the assailant and victim were co-employees who had not known each other prior to the day when the victim was ordered by his boss to place some trash bins near the assailant's work place. Five days of argument ensued between the co-employees about the garbage pails until the assailant struck the victim in the face with his clenched fist. The assailant testified he did not know his victim prior to the garbage pail incident. 10 Pa. Commw. at 249, 309 A.2d at 843. These five days of argument between victim and assailant did not create enough personal animosity to take the incident outside of Workmen's Compensation. *Id.* at 249, 309 A.2d at 843.

Cleland Simpson is another case involving co-employees where the court held the attack did not fall under the personal reasons exception to Workmen's Compensation. In *Cleland Simpson*, a sales clerk was stabbed to death by a psychotic co-employee who believed that the sales clerk had broken a date with him. The clerk had worked at the store for five weeks. There was found to be no acrimonious relationship between the assailant and victim. 16 Pa. Commw. at 571, 332 A.2d at 865. The court held that for the injuries to be taken outside of Workmen's Compensation "there must be some intention on the part of the assailant to inflict the injury or the death for personal reasons." *Id.* at 571, 332 A.2d at 865. Here the attack was the result of the delusions of a paranoid schizophrenic. A psychiatrist testified that the attack could have been on anyone. *Id.* at 571, 332 A.2d at 865. The court held that the attack was not motivated by personal reasons directed toward the attack victim and was therefore covered by Workmen's Compensation exclusively. The requisite in this case was that the personal reasons be directed toward the specific victim. *Cleland Simpson*, 16 Pa. Commw. at 571, 332 A.2d at 865.

The facts in *Cleland Simpson* are similar to the instant case. Bronstein's fellow prisoner stated that Bronstein confessed " . . . I went into the hospital hoping I could find a nurse or somebody who would be alone or isolated, and I would have the opportunity to do it to her . . . " (R. 73). This evidence shows that the victim of Bronstein's attack could have been anyone and that the attack was not directed specifically toward Charla Louis. Under the *Cleland Simpson* holding, Bronstein's attack lacks personal reasons directed toward a specific victim and should therefore be compensable only through Workmen's Compensation.

The attacks intended to fall outside of Workmen's Compensation are limited to those involving longstanding animosity between the employee and attacker. This longstanding animosity can arise out of a lengthy relationship at work between two co-employees, as in *Gillespie v. Vecenie*, 292 Pa. Super. 11, 15, 436 A.2d 695, 697 (1981) (long running feud between two employees held "personal"), *Mike v. Borough of Aliquippa*, 279 Pa. Super. 382, 389, 421 A.2d 251, 254 (1980) (friction between victim and assailant who were co-employees lasted for several months prior to attack), *McBride v. Hershey Chocolate Corp.*, 200 Pa. Super. 342, 351-354, 188 A.2d 775, 776-778 (1963) (eight years of animosity between co-employees resulted in attack), and *Scott v. Acme Wire Products, Inc.*, 13 Pa. Commw. 546, 549, 319 A.2d 436, 438 (1974) (considerable animosity between victim and assailant who were co-employees existed before attack). In these cases Workmen's Compensation was denied: "[A] physical attack following a long running feud between two employees has been held to be 'personal'." *McBride, 279 Pa. Super. at 390, 421 A.2d at 255.*

The required animosity can also arise out of non-work-related matters. *Boone v. Workmen's Comp. App. Bd.*, 43 Pa. Commw. 452, 402 A.2d 569 (1979). In *Boone*, a co-employee shot another co-employee. In this case, the attack was held to be non-work-related and for personal reasons. *Id.* at 453, 402 A.2d at 569. The assailant and victim spent a considerable amount of time together outside of work and the motive for the attack was the supposed breakup of their relationship. Thus, the type of personal reasons required by the statute to take an attack out of Workmen's Compensation involves a long-standing relationship between the assailant and victim which culminated in an attack directed at the employee for reasons not related to their employment.

In applying this definition to the Estate's case, the court should hold Workmen's Compensation to be the sole remedy for the Estate. The record fails to show the long-standing relationship between attacker and assailant necessary to establish personal reasons for the attack.

In *Sklar v. Albert Einstein Medical Center*, 67 D. & C.2d 211 (Phila. 1974), an employee of the medical center was assaulted by an assailant who dragged her into the hospital bathroom and tried to rape her. The Medical Center filed preliminary objections claiming that a suit in negligence for failure to provide adequate security was barred by Workmen's Compensation. The court dismissed the Medical Center's preliminary objections, stating that it was "reasonably inferrible from the complaint of attempted rape; that the assailant's motive was personal to him . . . " *Id.* at 213.

There are two points which distinguish *Sklar* from the instant case. First, *Sklar* is a denial of the Medical Center's preliminary objections to the complaint because the court found an implicit allegation of personal reasons in the complaint. In the instant case, however, the court is working with more than just a complaint. The court has a substantial record in front of it to evaluate and make a decision regarding the validity of the personal reasons allegation.

Secondly, the *Sklar* court implies that the statute only requires "reasons for the attack [that] are purely personal to the assailant" to allow the plaintiff to pursue a common law remedy. 67 D. & C.2d at 212. This suggestion proposes that the test necessary to find personal reasons is a one-sided inquiry. The *Sklar* court states that courts need only look into the mind of the assailant and find a reason in his mind for the attack regardless of whether he ever shared any kind of relationship with his victim before the incident.

If this were the only requisite to establish personal reasons, the entire purpose of the Workmen's Compensation Act would be destroyed. By simply finding any motive in the mind of the attacker, the personal reasons requirement would be satisfied, and no attack on an employee by a third person would ever be compensable through Workmen's Compensation. To protect public policy and legislative intent, it is imperative that the courts maintain the interpretation of reasons personal as including the specific requirement of a long-standing relationship between victim and attacker based on animosity or enmity. Since the facts in the case before the court fail to indicate such a relationship between Charla Louis and Bronstein, the Estate's common law tort action should be barred and Workmen's Compensation should be the only recourse for the Estate of Charla Louis.

II.   ST. MARY'S HOSPITAL CANNOT BE HELD LIABLE UNDER A NEGLIGENCE THEORY FOR THE PROGRAM AND ATTACK ON CHARLA LOUIS BECAUSE THERE IS NO HISTORY OF CRIMINAL ACTS OCCURRING ON THE PREMISES WHICH WOULD HAVE ALERTED THE HOSPITAL TO THE LIKELI-HOOD OF SUCH HARM.

The Estate's action is premised on a negligence theory of liability. However, as the court emphasized in *Murphy v. Penn Fruit Co.*, 274 Pa. Super. 427, 418 A.2d 480 (1980), negligence is not established by the mere happening of an attack on the decedent. *Id.* at 432, 418 A.2d at 483. The Estate must plead and prove each element of the tort to establish liability. The necessary elements to maintain a negligence action are: a duty or obligation recognized by the law, requiring the actor to conform to the standard required; a failure to conform to the standard required; a causal connection between the conduct and the resulting injury; and actual loss or damage resulting to the interests of another. *Morena v. South Hills Health System*, 501 Pa. 634, 642, 462 A.2d 680, 684 (1983), quoting William Prosser, *Law of Torts*, § 30 at 143 (4th ed. 1971). Each of these elements will be examined in turn as they apply to the facts of this case.

A.   *The Hospital Has a Duty to Use Reasonable Care in Protecting Its Employees from Harm that Can Be Reasonably Anticipated.*

The hospital acknowledges the duty it owes to its employees. Only the nature of the duty need be considered. The Pennsylvania courts have not addressed the question of an employer's duty to its employee under a negligence theory; however, because duty, in any situation, is predicated on the relationship between the parties, the standard of care adopted by the courts in the context of other relationships provides a helpful guide.

Specifically, the Pennsylvania courts have adopted § 344 of the Restatement (Second) of Torts (1965) which sets forth the duty a business owes to its patron to protect him from acts of third persons. *Moran v. Valley Forge Drive-In Theater, Inc.*, 431 Pa. 432, 246 A.2d 875 (1968). Where a possessor of land who holds it open to the public for business purposes knows or has reason to know, either from past experience or from the place or character of its business, that there is a likelihood of conduct on the part of third parties which may endanger the patron's safety, the possessor may be under a duty to take reasonable precautions to protect against such conduct or to warn the patron of the possibility of such tortious acts. *Id.* at 436-37, 246 A.2d at 878.

The Pennsylvania Supreme Court has observed that a possessor of business premises is not the insurer of the safety of its patron. *Moran*, 431 Pa. at 436, 246 A.2d at 878. Therefore, liability only occurs where the possessor fails in its duty either to take reasonable care to discover whether dangerous conduct of third persons is occurring or is likely to occur or to take reasonable care to provide appropriate precautions against harm that can be reasonably anticipated. *Carswell v. SEPTA*, 259 Pa. Super. 167, 172, 393 A.2d 770, 773 (1978).

The hospital is a possessor of land which it operates for the business purpose of providing health services. Miss Louis was on the hospital premises to promote the hospital's business purpose as well as to receive the benefit of employment. The hospital, because of the control it has over the premises, is in the best position to provide for the employees' safety. Its duty is to use reasonable care in taking precautions to protect its employees from harm that can be reasonably anticipated.

B. *The Hospital Took All Reasonable Precautions to Guard Its Employees.*

Once a duty has been found, the issue then becomes whether the hospital has breached its duty. To sustain its burden of proof, the Estate must show either that the hospital did not take reasonable precautions to protect its employees or that the hospital did not exercise reasonable care in implementing those precautions.

1. The hospital provided security guards who conducted a systematic security program.

In *Lillie v. Thompson*, 332 U.S. 459 (1947), the Supreme Court held that the employer had a duty to take reasonable precautions to protect employees when working conditions created a possibility of harm by intruders. In *Lillie*, a female telegraph operator was required to work a night shift alone in an isolated railroad yard. She was assaulted when an intruder forced his way into the office when she opened the door. The Court suggested that reasonable precautions might have included lighting the premises and providing a patrol or guard. *Id.* at 461.

Two aspects of the Court's holding are significant. First, the Court required the employer only to take reasonable precautions against attack. The Court did not indicate that the employer had to insure the employee's absolute protection from all harm. Second, the Court required the employer only to take precautions against harm that was likely given the employee's working conditions, *i.e.*, an isolated railyard known to be frequented by dangerous characters. The Court did not extend the employer's responsibility to all possibilities of harm.

In *Lillie*, however, the employer took no precautions whatsoever to provide the female employee with a protected workplace. St. Mary's Hospital is aware that the character of its business requires it to allow relatively free access to a large segment of the public. Emergency patients arrive at all hours of the day. Visitors come and go. Deliveries are made. Staff report for duty around the clock. Given the character of its business, the hospital acknowledges the need for security and has taken precautions accordingly.

St. Mary's Hospital follows the very precautions outlined by the Court in *Lillie*. It employs a force of security guards and conducts a systematic security program. (R. 91, 93). Guards are stationed at the information desk to assist visitors. (R. 96). Guards also patrol the exterior of the building and the corridors, secure various entrances, and check on employees to see that they are safe. (R. 124, 130).

George Knapp was on patrol duty the morning of July 25, 1982. He testified that he had often spoken to Miss Louis in the course of checking on her while making his rounds. (R. 120). In fact, Knapp testified to having done just that the morning of the attack. He had checked on Miss Louis little more than half an hour before the incident. (R. 119, 120). The hospital, through its security force and procedures, takes all reasonable measures within its power to mitigate the risk of harm to its employees.

    2.   The security guards used care and discretion in guarding and patrolling to protect employees from harm that reasonably could be anticipated.

It would be unreasonable to expect an employer to take precautions against that which it cannot anticipate. Consequently, in the employer-employee context and similar relationships (business-patron, hospital-patient, carrier-passenger) no liability is normally imposed upon the party having the duty to protect if the incident is sudden and unexpected. *Kline v. 1500 Mass. Ave. Apartment Corp.*, 439 F.2d 477, 483 (D.C. Cir. 1977). A person must be able to anticipate at least the general form that potential harm might take before he can be expected to protect against it. *Morgan v. Bucks Assoc.*, 428 F. Supp. 546, 549-50 (E.D. Pa. 1977).

What can reasonably be anticipated is often best indicated by past experience. In *Sklar v. Albert Einstein Medical Center*, 67 D. & C.2d 211 (Phila. 1974), a female employee was pulled into a bathroom in the Medical Center by an attacker attempting to rape her. The court held that because of evidence of previous similar incidents, the hospital should have been on notice that other assaults were likely to occur in the absence of remedial security.

In the present case there is no record of any prior violent incidents occurring at the hospital attributable to lack of security. However, evidence of non-violent criminal acts may be sufficient to put security on notice to anticipate violent criminal acts. *Morgan*, 428 F. Supp. at 551. In *Morgan*, a shopping mall employee was assaulted in the parking lot while she was walking to her automobile after leaving work. Mall security knew of the occurrence of numerous auto thefts, but there was no history of criminal assaults. The court concluded that knowledge of the auto thefts was sufficient to put security on notice to reasonably anticipate the likelihood of danger to visitors. *Id.*

In the present case, not only were there no similar incidents that would have put the hospital on notice, but in addition there was no evidence of any general criminal activity. Given what the security guards could reasonably anticipate, they acted with reasonable care in discharging their duties. Although the hospital had notice that Mr. Bronstein had entered the building two days prior to the assault, it had no notice of his inclination toward violence, but only of his propensity to get coffee from the hospital vending machines. When Mr. Bronstein entered the hospital for the first time the morning of the attack, security guard Knapp observed him as he was entering the building and questioned Bronstein's purpose in entering the hospital. (R. 94, 96). Knapp followed Bronstein, scanning him from head to toe looking for anything that might indicate that he posed a threat. (R. 102). Finding nothing, Knapp immediately escorted Bronstein out of the hospital, warning him that the hospital was off-limits. (R. 113). With Bronstein safely outside, Knapp locked the doors behind him, giving them a firm push to be certain that they were secure. (R. 116). He then went to check on Miss Louis, and finding her at work as usual, resumed his security patrol. (R. 119, 120).

"Nothing is so easy as to be wise after the event." Branwell, B., in *Cornman v. Eastern Counties R. Co.*, 4 H. & N. 781, 786, 157 Eng. Rep. 1050 (1859). The guards' conduct can only be judged by what they knew the morning of the incident and not by what they might know now. The hospital is not to be judged by the consequences but rather by its conduct.

The guards used reasonable care in handling Mr. Bronstein's presence. They provided protection within the reasonable expectations of the security program. These security precautions are reasonable absent some showing of a history of criminal acts on the premises that would have put the hospital on notice of a need for greater security.

Even if the hospital had maintained security personnel that would constitute a veritable police force, there can be no guarantee of omnipresent, constant protection. Bolted doors and locked windows rarely stop criminals bent on crime. The employer cannot be expected to defeat all the designs of felony.

The risk of harm from criminal conduct is with us everywhere. Everyone faces this risk every day in society at large. Any attempt, no matter how steadfast, by an employer to insulate its employee from this risk may fail. The mere fact that an employee may be exposed to risk cannot be the basis for imposing liability. *Cf. Feld v. Merriam*, 506 Pa. 383, 402-03, 485 A.2d 742, 751 (1984) (analogous logic applied to landlord-tenant).

    C.   *The Evidence Does Not Show a Causal Connection Between the Security Guards' Conduct and the Attack Upon Ms. Louis.*

The Pennsylvania Supreme Court has adopted the analysis of "legal" or proximate cause in section 433 of the Restatement (Second) of Torts (1965). *Ford v. Jeffries*, 474 Pa. 588, 594, 379 A.2d 111, 114 (1977). Under this analysis the question is whether the defendant's conduct was a "substantial factor" in producing injury. *See* Restatement (Second) of Torts § 431 (1965) (outlining considerations important in determining whether conduct is substantial factor in producing harm). Ordinarily, the determination of whether defendant's conduct was a substantial cause of plaintiff's injury should not be taken from the jury if reasonable minds may differ as to whether the defendant's conduct was a substantial factor in causing the injury. *Vattimo v. Lower Bucks Hosp., Inc.*, 502 Pa. 241, 247, 465 A.2d 1231, 1234 (1983). *See also* Restatement (Second) of Torts § 434 (1965) (describing functions of court and jury in determining legal cause). Where there is no issue of material fact, however, and the remoteness of the causal connection between the defendant's conduct and plaintiff's loss is clear, the question becomes one of law for the court. *Reed v. Paris Neckwear Co.*, 34 Leh. L.J. 464, 469 (1972). *See also* Restatement (Second) of Torts § 434(a)(c) (1965) (court determines causation in any case in which jury may not reasonably differ on issue).

In *Reed*, two boys entered a building through an unlocked door and lit a torch to light their path. Sometime later the building was destroyed by fire. The court held that even if the occupier of the building knew that children entered the building, the act of defendant in leaving the door unlocked was not the proximate cause of plaintiff's loss of his building. The court reasoned that to have notice that children entered the building to play basketball was a far cry from having notice that the building would be burglarized and burned. The superseding criminal act of third persons was the proximate cause of the loss. *Reed*, 34 Leh. L.J. at 469. Generally, an intervening criminal act breaks the chain of causation and negates liability based on negligence. *Abdallah v. Caribbean Sec. Agency*, 557 F.2d 61, 63 (3d Cir. 1977).

Similarly, for the hospital to have had notice that Bronstein was in the building buying coffee from the vending machines was a far cry from being charged with notice that he would re-enter the building and harm someone. The hospital's negligence, if any, created a harmless and passive condition that was but a remote circumstance of the events of the morning. The cause of the attack was the superseding criminal act of Michael Bronstein.

There is nothing in the record to indicate how Bronstein got back into the hospital. The record does state that Bronstein was in the hospital two days before the incident. (R. 94). It also states that on the night of the incident, Bronstein walked past one guard before being stopped and escorted out by another. (R. 98). Finally, a door was found open an hour after the incident. (R. 63). The record does not reveal by whose act or in what manner the door came to be open. We do not know how Bronstein got in the second time. A conclusion of negligence can only be reached through a long chain of compounded inferences. Without knowing more it is impossible to conclude that the guards' conduct was the proximate cause of the injury.

Yet, the trial court held that the hospital had breached its duty and that this was the legal cause of the injury. There is not enough information to give reasonable minds a basis on which to differ, much less to conclude that the hospital was responsible for the incident. Therefore, it is appropriate that the lower court's ruling be reversed and summary judgment be granted in favor of the hospital.

In the alternative, if there is some basis for a divergence of views on this issue, the case should be remanded and the question put to the jury. At trial, additional facts relevant to Bronstein's re-entry into the hospital can be considered along with the question of legal cause. Then the jury may properly determine whether the guards' conduct was a substantial factor in causing the incident.

CONCLUSION

For the reasons set forth above, Appellants respectfully request that the judgment of the Court of Common Pleas of Berks County, Pennsylvania be reversed, and that summary judgment be entered against the Appellees.

Respectfully submitted,

_____

Robert M. Maxwell, Jr.

Lorijean Golichowski Oei

Attorneys for Appellant

IN THE
SUPERIOR COURT OF THE COMMONWEALTH
OF PENNSYLVANIA

_____

March Term, 1987

_____

No. 19

_____

ST. MARY'S HOSPITAL,

Appellant

v.

ADMINISTRATORS OF THE ESTATE OF CHARLA LOUIS,

Appellees

_____

**On Appeal from
The Court of Common Pleas
Berks County, Pennsylvania**

_____

BRIEF FOR APPELLEES

_____

Mark E. Steiner

Attorney for Appellees

(Matthew Bender & Co., Inc.) (Pub.676)

TABLE OF CONTENTS

[Illustrative page references are to original document.]

TABLE OF CITATIONS

STATEMENT OF JURISDICTION

This is an interlocutory appeal from the Court of Common Pleas, Berks County, Pennsylvania. Jurisdiction is conferred under 42 Pennsylvania Consolidated Statutes Annotated § 702(b) (Purdon 1981).

QUESTION PRESENTED

I. Whether the estate of a hospital employee who was attacked and murdered while working, by an assailant with personal motivation to commit sexual assault, is limited by the remedies of the Workmen's Compensation Act.

STATUTORY PROVISIONS

Pa. Stat. Ann. tit. 77, § 411(1) (1986)

The terms "injury" and "personal injury" in the act shall be construed to mean an injury to an employee . . . arising in the course of his employment and related thereto. . . . The term "injury arising in the course of employment" as used in this article, shall not include an injury caused by an act of a third person intended to injure the employee because of reasons personal to him, and not directed against him as an employee or because of his employment.

Pa. Stat. Ann. tit. 77, § 481(a) (1986)

The liability of an employer under this act shall be exclusive and in place of any and all other liability to such employees, his legal representative, husband or wife, parents, dependents, next of kin or anyone otherwise entitled to damages in any action at law or otherwise on account of any injury or death as defined in section 301(c)(1) and (2).

STATEMENT OF THE CASE

Charla Louis, the decedent, was employed by Saint Mary's Hospital ("the Hospital") and worked on the night shift in the Medical Records Office (R. 2). At approximately two a.m. on July 25, 1982, George Knapp, a security guard at the Hospital, saw Michael Bronstein enter the Hospital through the emergency room door and walk toward the vending machine area (R. 2, 76, 103). George Knapp confronted Michael Bronstein as he exited the vending machine room (R. 2, 77, 103). Michael Bronstein stated he had entered the Hospital to purchase a cup of coffee (R. 76). Michael Bronstein testified at his criminal trial that he often entered the Hospital just to purchase a cup of coffee (R. 76).

George Knapp asked Michael Bronstein to leave through the emergency room door; however, Michael Bronstein insisted on leaving through an exit in another part of the Hospital (R. 103, 104). George Knapp permitted Michael Bronstein to use this other exit, but escorted him out (R. 77, 104-15). Both men proceeded through a corridor located in an isolated part of the Hospital and passed by the Medical Records Office, where Miss Louis worked (R. 77, 104-15). After Michael Bronstein left, George Knapp did not check the doors of the Medical Records Office or warn Miss Louis of Michael Bronstein's recent presence (R. 117-21).

Approximately one hour after this incident, Michael Bronstein reentered the Hospital and abducted Miss Louis from her office at knife point (R. 72-74). Michael Bronstein forced Miss Louis to exit the building and go toward his car so he could rape her (R. 72-74). When Miss Louis refused to stop screaming, Michael Bronstein murdered her by stabbing her to death just outside the Hospital (R. 72-74). Michael Bronstein has been convicted of attempted rape, first degree murder and burglary (R.1).

Michael Bronstein was not employed by the Hospital, but testimony from the transcript of Michael Bronstein's criminal trial and the depositions of Linda Bach and John Feldman indicate that Miss Louis and Michael Bronstein may have known each other in some capacity prior to the assault (R. 3, 4, 57).

Almost one hour after Michael Bronstein murdered Miss Louis, Mr. Ross, a utility mechanic for the Hospital, found a side door of the hospital laundry room tied open with a clothes hanger (R. 63-64). Security guard George Knapp did not recall checking this door prior to the fatal attack on Miss Louis (R. 123, 124).

The Administrators of the Estate of Miss Louis brought this civil action, asserting a wrongful death and survival claim based on the negligence of the Hospital (R. 5). The Hospital moved for summary judgment, asserting that the Estate may only recover under the Workmen's Compensation Act (R. 5, 14). The Court of Common Pleas of Berks County, Pennsylvania denied this motion. The Hospital then moved to amend that court's order to contain a statement that the case warrants immediate appellate attention under 42 Pennsylvania Consolidated Statutes Annotated § 702(b) (Purdon 1981) (R.14).

SUMMARY OF THE ARGUMENT

The Estate's negligence suit is not barred by the provisions of the Workmen's Compensation Act. The Act covers all injuries that arise because of a work-related circumstance, but specifically excludes personally motivated assaults by third parties. Michael Bronstein should be considered a third party because he was never employed by the Hospital. Michael Bronstein was personally motivated in that he entered the Hospital with the specific intent to rape Miss Louis. His motivation could not have been work-related because Miss Louis was not required to have any personal contact with the public and therefore did not risk or provoke sexual assault while performing her job. Thus, the assault did not arise from Miss Louis's employment and a negligence action based on the Hospital's failure to provide a safe place to work is not barred by the Act.

ARGUMENT

I. THE ESTATE OF CHARLA LOUIS, A HOSPITAL EMPLOYEE, IS NOT LIMITED TO THE REMEDIES OF THE WORKMEN'S COMPENSATION ACT WHEN, WHILE WORKING, SHE WAS ATTACKED AND MURDERED BY AN ASSAILANT WITH PER-SONAL MOTIVATION TO COMMIT SEXUAL ASSAULT.

A. *The Estate Cannot Be Limited by the Act Because the Act Disallows Compensation for All Personally Motivated Assaults by Third Parties.*

The Appellant, Saint Mary's Hospital ("the Hospital"), contends that the administrators of the Estate of Charla Louis ("the Estate") are barred by the Workmen's Compensation Act, Pennsylvania Statutes Annotated, title 77, § 411(1) (1986) ("the Act") from bringing a wrongful death and survival action based on the Hospital's negligence (R.7). The circumstances surrounding Miss Louis' death indicate this is not so. The Estate is not limited by nor is the Hospital insulated by the Act.

Section 481(a) of the Act states that "liability of an employer under this act is exclusive and in place of any and all other liability to . . . anyone otherwise entitled to damages in any action of law on account of any injury or death" covered by the Act. Pa. Stat. Ann. tit. 77, § 481(a) (1986). The covered injuries and the one exception are defined in Section 301 as:

> The terms "injury" and "personal injury" in the act shall be construed to mean an injury to an employee . . . arising in the course of his employ-ment and related thereto. . . . *The term "injury arising in the course of employment" as used in this article shall not include an injury caused by an act of a third person intended to injure the employee because of reasons personal to him and not directed against him as an employee or because of his employment.*

Pa. Stat. Ann. tit. 77, § 411(1) (1986) (emphasis added).

The facts do not indicate in any way that the assailant Michael Bronstein attacked Miss Louis for reasons arising from or related to her employment other than the fact that Miss Louis was on the Hospital's premises at the time she was assaulted. However, there is strong evidence that Bronstein attempted a personally motivated sexual assault. Applying the language of section 411(1), the Estate's action against the Hospital is not barred by the Act.

B. *Even Though Charla Louis Was Present on the Hospital's Premises as Required by Her Job, Her Estate Is Not Limited to Recovery Under the Act, Because the Third Party Attack Was Personally Motivated.*

The Hospital alleged that Michael Bronstein attacked Charla Louis simply because she was present in the Medical Records Office as required by the duties of her employment (R. 26). Even if true, this alone does not limit the Estate's remedies to those of the Act.

In the leading case of *Dolan v. Linton's Lunch,* 397 Pa. 114, 152 A.2d 887 (1959) the Pennsylvania Supreme Court construed the statutory exclusion of personally motivated attacks by third parties. In that case, the plaintiff, while properly performing his duties on the employer's premises, was beaten without provocation by a fellow employee. *Id.* at 116, 152 A.2d at 889. The court held that the plaintiff's action was not barred by the Act if the assailant was personally motivated. *Id.* at 117, 152 A.2d at 889.

In interpreting the statutory language, the Pennsylvania Supreme Court rejected the argument that the injuries were compensable just because the victim was properly performing his job on the premises of his employer at the time of the attack. The court stated:

[I]f the attack is directed against the employee for personal reasons not connected with his employment, even though the assaulted employee is at that time pursuing the business of his employer, the legislature has stated in specific terms that the resulting injury is not an "injury . . . in the course of his employment" as that term is used throughout the act.

Id. at 119, 152 A.2d at 890.

The court concluded:

The present plaintiff is not affected by either the coverage or surrender provisions of the act. *The act excludes from its coverage attacks upon an employee whether or not they are caused by the condition of the employer's premises or by the operation of his business affairs thereon so long as the reasons for the attack are purely personal to the assailant.* In such a case the plaintiff is permitted to pursue his common law remedy.

Id. at 125, 152 A.2d at 893 (emphasis added). *Accord Mike v. Borough of Aliquippa,* 279 Pa. Super. 382, 421 A.2d 251 (1980); *Workmen's Compensation App. Bd. v. Borough of Plum,* 20 Pa. Commw. 35, 340 A.2d 637

(1975); *McBride v. Hershey Chocolate Corp.*, 200 Pa. Super. 347, 188 A.2d 775 (1963).

1. Preexisting personal animosity is not dispositive or even highly indicative of the assailant's motivation since his motivation at the time of attack is at issue.

During previous proceedings on this case, the Hospital maintained that the lack of any personal animosity between Miss Louis and Michael Bronstein prior to the attack is dispositive or at least highly indicative that the attempted rape was impersonal (R. 39-40, 45). This is not so. Preexisting personal animosity has been highly indicative of personal motivation only in cases involving attacks by fellow employees. The reasoning is that "[n]ormally, when an employee is injured in an attack by a fellow employee, there is a rebuttable presumption that the claimant is covered by the Act and the one claiming otherwise bears the burden of showing an intention to injure owing to reasons personal to the assailant." *Mike*, 279 Pa. Super. at 388, 421 A.2d at 254; *See, e.g., O'Rourke v. O'Rourke*, 278 Pa. 52, 122 A. 172 (1923); *U.S. Steel Corp. v. Workmen's Compensation App. Bd.*, 10 Pa. Commw. 247, 309 A.2d 842 (1973). In *Mike*, the presumption that the assault was work-related was strengthened by the fact that the court found personal animosity because of prior work-related incidents. However, at the time of the assault, the court held that the assailant was personally motivated. Therefore, the Act did not bar a common law action. *Mike*, 279 Pa. Super. at 391-392, 421 A.2d at 255-256.

No such presumption exists in the present case. The record does not indicate that the Hospital employed Michael Bronstein at the time of the attack, or at any previous time. Thus, the lack of any preexisting personal animosity in this case does not mean the court should find that Michael Bronstein's attack was work-related. In *Sayre v. Textile Machine Works*, 129 Pa. Super. 520, 195 A. 786 (1937), the court states, "in the present, as in every other compensation case, we must deal with the concrete condition presented by the evidence . . . Prior decisions are controlling only when the facts substantially arose in a similar way." *Id.* at 524, 195 A. at 88. The facts of the Estate's case are substantially different from cases involving personal assaults by fellow employees.

The Estate does not here admit that no animosity existed between Michael Bronstein and Charla Louis prior to the attack. In fact, the record indicates otherwise. The strongest evidence of preexisting animosity in the record is found in the deposition of Miss Linda Bach (R. 3-4). Miss Bach indicates she had a hurried conversation with Miss Louis prior to the attack and during that conversation Miss Louis indicated that somebody had been bothering her (R. 3-4).

Unfortunately, this evidence is not conclusive of the existence of preexisting animosity between Miss Louis and Michael Bronstein. Only Miss Louis or Michael Bronstein could conclusively answer the question as to the existence of personal animosity prior to the assault. As she is dead and he is in prison and hostile to our present action, any finding of preexisting animosity would have to be inferred (R. 1, 30-31). In light of this and the fact that we are not here bound by the analysis of prior cases involving attacks by fellow employees, the Estate urges the court to consider concrete facts presented by the record which indicate that Michael Bronstein's attack on Miss Louis was personally motivated.

2.   The nature of sexual assault indicates personal motivation in the form of anticipated sexual gratification; rape is not usually motivated by work-related activity.

Fights or murders may occur because of sudden uncontrolled anger. In the work place this anger may arise because of events either related or unrelated to the work of an employee. In each case, the particular facts that surround an assault on an employee will determine whether recovery is limited to and/or covered by the Act. *Sayre*, 129 Pa. Super. at 524, 195 A. at 788. However, it is hard to conceive of an attempted rape occurring because of a sudden uncontrolled fit of anger arising from a work-related dispute. Fights and murders may occur spontaneously and often occur in the presence of witnesses. A sexual assault, however, is not as spontaneous and is harder to complete unless the victim is isolated. Also, attempted rape indicates the presence of a very personal motivation in the form of anticipated sexual gratification. This motivation is usually not present when a person commits an assault which is not sexually related. Thus, cases involving sexual assault on the job are categorically different from those involving other types of assault. They should be viewed as personally motivated unless there are facts indicating otherwise.

The Estate's action presents a situation almost identical to that presented in *Sklar v. Albert Einstein Medical Center*, 67 D. & C.2d 211 (Phila. 1974). In *Sklar*, the assailant entered a hospital, pulled an employee into a restroom, and attempted to rape her. *Id.* at 211. At the time of the attack, the employee was properly performing her duties. *Id.* In finding that the assault fell within the exception to compensation provided by the Act, the court stated, "defendant's contention that the averments state an occurrence of an injury compensable by Workmen's Compensation and hence not actionable at common law is without merit." *Id.* at 212.

The court in *Sklar* placed considerable weight on the act of rape itself. The court states:

The complaint alleges that the assailant threw plaintiff "to the floor and attempted to rape her." While that pleading does not declare in *ipsis verbis* that assault was for "personal reasons," it is somewhat of a strain on imagination to conclude that the omission of such a conclusionary statement renders the alleged action "impersonal" so as to return the cause of action to the Workmen's Compensation Act remedy.

Id. at 213.

Enoch v. Penn-Harris Hotel Co., 71 D. & C.2d 463 (Dauphin 1976), presents a similar situation. A hotel elevator operator, properly performing her job, was raped by a former employee of the hotel. At the time of the attack, the victim was unaware that the assailant was a former employee. *Id.* at 465. In upholding the denial of the defendant's motion for summary judgment, the court emphasized the personal nature of rape. The court stated that " . . . the act of rape by its very nature is a personal one, motivated by lust, wantonness, . . . or some equally obnoxious motive totally unrelated to the victim's employment status." *Id.* at 465.

The present case is almost identical to the situations presented in *Sklar* and *Enoch*. Thus, the Estate's negligence suit is consistent with precedent.

C. *Because Charla Louis's Job Did Not Require Her to Have Personal Contact with the Public, She Did Not Assume the Risk of Personal Assault, and, Therefore, the Assault Is Not Covered by the Act*

While performing her job, Miss Louis was not required to have personal contact with the public and so she did not assume a risk of personal assault by a member of that class. Her normal duties required that she work in the Medical Records Office during the early morning hours (R.1). Miss Louis was isolated from the public while working and had reason to believe that she would be protected by the Hospital's security personnel (R. 50-60, 88-100).

Rape cases have occurred in other jurisdictions where the court has ruled that the victim assumed the risk of personal assault because the victim's job required extensive contact with the public. In these cases, the courts ruled that Workmen's Compensation was applicable because the injury arose from a risk inherent in the job. *Enoch*, 71 D. & C.2d at 470.

In *Giracelli v. Franklin Cleaners & Dryers*, 42 A.2d 3 (N.J. 1945), a girl working in a cleaning establishment was raped by a customer who followed her into a back room. *Id.* at 590-591, 42 A.2d at 3. The court held that the victim was exposed to the attack as an employee required to deal with the public, and as such, the crime was a risk attached to employment. *Id.* In *Employers Insurance of Atlanta v. Wright*, 133 S.E. 2d 39 (Ga. 1963), the court was presented with a situation similar to that described in *Giracelli*. The court held that the employee could recover under Workmen's Compensation because the time, place, and risk for such an attack arose from her employment. Also, in *Commercial Standard Insurance Co. v. Marin*, 488 S.W.2d 861 (Tex. 1972), a woman was raped and murdered as she opened a gas station just before daylight. The court concluded that her employment " . . . did not merely provide the time and place for the assault, . . . [b]ut, conditions of her employment increased the risk of such attack, and subjected her to a danger incidental to such employment." *Id.* at 869. It should be noted that these three cases were procedurally different in that the employees wanted to secure Workmen's Compensation benefits and not evade them as the Estate does in the present case.

If Miss Louis's job required her to have substantial contact with the public, she may have assumed a risk of some personal assault. For instance, if Miss Louis had been a security guard at the time of her attack, she would have assumed some risk of personal assault committed by the public at large. A security guard is covered by the Act when he is shot by robbers. *Rathburn v. Sussman Bros. & Co.*, 127 Pa. Super. 104, 193 A. 488 (1937). The risk of such injury being inflicted by a third party is part of the risk involved in the job of a security guard. However, the Estate would argue that if the intruders entered with the specific intent to commit sexual assault on a security guard, then any injury should not be covered because it would have been inflicted by a personally motivated attack which did not arise due to a work-related circumstance. In other words, a security guard does not assume the risk of sexual assault during the proper performance of his job.

There may be certain jobs which, when properly performed, motivate or provoke sexual assault. If an employee performing one of these jobs is raped, then the provisions of the Act might properly apply. It is not difficult to imagine sexual assault being provoked by a stripper, go-go dancer, centerfold or prostitute. *Enoch*, 71 D. & C.2d at 470. However, Miss Louis's position in the Medical Records Office was not such a job. She did not provoke Michael Bronstein's attack, nor did she perform a job which has an inherent risk of sexual assault. Thus, the Estate's action should not be barred by the Act.

CONCLUSION

For the reasons set forth, the Estate of Charla Louis respectfully requests that the court affirm the decision of the trial court denying the Motion for Summary Judgment and allowing the Estate to pursue its common law remedy.

Respectfully Submitted,

_____

Mark E. Steiner
Attorney for Appellees

This brief was written for a federal appellate court.

**IN THE
UNITED STATES COURT OF APPEALS
THIRD CIRCUIT**

February Term 1991

No. 89-39

BOYD BOSWELL AND WANNA TAPPA KEG FRATERNITY,

Appellants

v.

**REGENTS OF THE UNIVERSITY OF HYSTERIA AND PETER
LEIKMANN,**

Appellees

On Appeal from

The United States District Court

Eastern District of Pennsylvania

BRIEF FOR APPELLANTS

Neil Rosen

Attorney for Appellants

TABLE OF CONTENTS

TABLE OF AUTHORITIES

454 U.S. 263 (1981)

OTHER AUTHORITIES

STATEMENT OF JURISDICTION

The United States Court of Appeals for the Third Circuit has jurisdiction over this matter pursuant to 28 U.S.C. sec. 1291 (1982).

QUESTIONS PRESENTED

I. Does the responsibility for protecting the rights of students to obtain an education and preventing disruptions on campus give the administrators of Hysteria University the authority to adopt a code of conduct aimed at preventing the use of insulting and provocative language or symbols directed at individuals or small groups with the purpose of insulting or stigmatizing those individuals on the basis of their personal identity, and did the University properly apply this code to students who posted a sign reading "NO FAGGOTS!!!" at the entrance to a university function which was open to the entire university community?

II. Is the use of insulting and provocative language or symbols directed at individuals or small groups with the purpose of insulting or stigmatizing those individuals on the basis of their personal identity protected by the First Amendment?

CONSTITUTIONAL PROVISIONS

United States Constitution, Amendment I:

"Congress shall make no law . . . abridging the freedom of speech."

STATEMENT OF THE CASE

On January 1, 1980, the Board of Regents of Hysteria University responded to the increase in prejudiced and potentially discriminatory activities spreading across the nation's campuses by adopting a code of conduct aimed at assaultive speech. (R. 2-3). Applied when students direct insulting or provocative words at individuals or small groups with the purpose of insulting or stigmatizing the targeted individuals on the basis of their personal identity, the "Anti-Hate Speech" Code is designed to prevent discriminatory harassment or intimidation. (R. 2-3). The Annual Hysteria University Fall Blow-out is a traditional campus event open to all members of the university community. (R. 3). Each year different student groups compete to sponsor the Blow-out, and the sponsoring organization is responsible for all activities at the Blow-out. (R. 3-4).

Wanna Tappa Keg fraternity won the competition, and its president, Boyd Boswell, was ultimately responsible for all the activities at the 1980 Blow-out, which took place in Hysteria University Student Activities Building. (R. 4).

A few weeks prior to the Blow-out, Boswell saw Dean Leikmann, the Dean of Students for Hysteria University, and a male companion on the street. (R. 5). Boswell was intrigued by the pair and decided to follow them. (R. 5). He tailed Dean Leikmann for eight blocks and observed his actions. (R. 5). Upon entering a restaurant frequented by gay couples, Dean Leikmann saw Boswell behind him. (R. 5). Dean Leikmann was startled and upset by this encounter. (R. 5). There was no further contact between Boswell and Dean Leikmann. (R. 6).

The Fall Blow-out occurred on September 20, 1989. (R. 3). At the beginning of the event Boswell assigned members of Wanna Tappa Keg to man the only entrance. (R. 4). Early on in the festivities, a sign was placed on the entrance. (R. 4). The sign read as follows:

NO WIMPS!!!

NO WEIRDOS!!!

NO FAGGOTS!!!

(R. 4). The words on the sign were written in black magic marker with 10 inch high letters. (R. 4). Next to the words "NO FAGGOTS!!!" was placed a picture of Dean Leikmann. (R. 4). The evidence at trial showed that Boswell and other members of Wanna Tappa Keg made the sign. (R. 5).

For fear of the personal and professional ramifications that could have resulted if the University community were to discover his sexual preference, Dean Leikmann had chosen not to disclose his homosexuality. (R. 5). As a result of the appellants' announcement, this fact became known to the public. (R. 6). After the Blow-out, word of the incident quickly spread through the university community. (R. 6). Dean Leikmann became the target of insults and vandalism on the campus. (R. 6). The number of students seeking counseling from Dean Leikmann dropped markedly following the Blow-out. (R. 6).

Subsequently, Dean Leikmann instituted university proceedings against Wanna Tappa Keg and Boswell for violating the Code of Conduct. (R. 6). They were disciplined in accordance with required university procedures. (R. 6). Afterwards, Boswell and the Fraternity filed suit in the United States District Court for the Eastern District of Pennsylvania, alleging, under 42 U.S.C. sec. 1983, that Dean Leikmann and the University violated their First Amendment rights. (R. 1). The court concluded that the sign was not speech, but conduct outside the scope of First Amendment protection and that any expressive elements constituted unprotected speech. (R. 6-7).

SUMMARY OF ARGUMENT

It is the duty of the administration of Hysteria University to prevent disruptions of the school environment and to protect the rights of students to obtain an education. The University can expect its students to conform to reasonable standards of conduct. When student activities cause these harms or violate reasonable standards of conduct, the University has the authority to discipline the offending students. Students who direct insulting or provocative language or symbols at individuals or small groups of individuals on the basis of their personal identity with the purpose of insulting or stigmatizing their targets may be disciplined, because their expressive activities cause the harms the University has the authority to prevent. The sign posted at the entrance to the Fall Blow-out, which referred to gay men as "faggots," was such an expression, and Mr. Boswell and Wanna Tappa Keg were appropriately disciplined under the Code of Conduct regulating such activities. The expressive elements of this act were not protected by the First Amendment, because they were "fighting" words that created harms the University was authorized to prevent.

ARGUMENT

I. STUDENTS MAY BE DISCIPLINED WHEN THEIR EXPRES-
    SIVE ACTIVITIES INTERFERE WITH THE RIGHTS OF OTHERS
    TO OBTAIN AN EDUCATION, DISRUPT THE ACADEMIC EN-
    VIRONMENT, OR DEMONSTRATE AN UNWILLINGNESS TO
    CONFORM TO REASONABLE STANDARDS OF CONDUCT.

A. The Appellants' First Amendment Rights Must Be Interpreted on
    the Context of the Academic Environment.

In Tinker v. Des Moines Independent School District, 393 U.S. 503
(1969), the Court held that students could not be suspended for wearing black
armbands as a protest against the Vietnam War unless the school officials
could reasonably anticipate "that the wearing of armbands would substantially interfere with the work of the school or impinge on the rights of other
students." Id. at 509. Since otherwise free speech might adversely affect
school operations or the rights of other students, the Tinker Court determined
that the First Amendment rights of students must be applied "in light of the
special circumstances of the school environment." Id. at 506. The Tinker
decision has been incorporated by the Court in cases involving the expressive
activities of college students. See Widmar v. Vincent, 454 U.S. 263, 267-68
n.5 (1981); Healy v. James, 408 U.S. 169, 180 (1972).

In Healy, the Court considered the First Amendment right of college
students to form associations and ruled that a university could withhold
recognition of a student group if it could show that the group would interrupt
classes or interfere with the opportunity of others to obtain an education. Id.
at 189. Recognition can also be withheld if student groups are unwilling to
"adhere to reasonable campus law." Id. at 193. The Court implied that
"reasonable campus law" was equivalent to "reasonable standards respecting
conduct." See id. at 192-93. Thus, a university may regulate student
expression that demonstrates an unwillingness to follow reasonable standards of conduct. See also Esteban v. Central Mo. State College, 415 F.2d
1077, 1089-90 (8th Cir. 1969) (Blackmun, J.) (upholding the suspension of
students whose expression violated reasonable rules of conduct), cert.
denied, 398 U.S. 965 (1970).

Recognizing the critical nature of this decision, Chief Justice Burger
emphasized that students and administrators are responsible for "maintaining
an atmosphere in which divergent views can be asserted vigorously, but
civilly, to the end that those who seek to be heard accord the same right to
all others." Healy, 408 U.S. at 196 (Burger, C.J., concurring). Civil discourse
is particularly important in the university environment because that environment is the quintessential marketplace of ideas. Absent rules of civil
discourse, there "is no marketplace for ideas, but a bullring." A. Bickel, The

Morality of Consent 77 (1975). This forms the basis of the University's position. The administration is responsible for maintaining an environment that facilitates the exchange of ideas between all members of the academic community. By adopting the Anti-Hate Speech Code, the administration protects the rights of minority students to participate fully in the exchange of ideas and warns all members of the community that speech which intentionally insults or stigmatizes students on the basis of their minority status will not be tolerated. (R. 2-3).

B.   The Anti-Hate Speech Code Is a Legitimate Exercise of the Administration's Rulemaking Power.

The appellants contend that the regulation violates their First Amendment rights. (R. 1). This contention fails because it overlooks "the College administration's broad rulemaking power to assure that the traditional academic atmosphere is safeguarded." Healy, 408 U.S. at 194, n.24. Students who use slurs and epithets declare their hostility toward others and cast doubt on their right to participate in the life of the university. In so doing, they poison the academic atmosphere. See Sweezy v. New Hampshire, 354 U.S. 234, 250 (1957) ("Scholarship cannot flourish in an atmosphere of suspicion and distrust.").

The Anti-Hate Speech Code is a proper response to this harm. Even the court that struck down an analogous regulation at the University of Michigan stated that "[u]nder certain circumstances, racial and ethnic epithets, slurs, and insults . . . could be constitutionally prohibited." Doe v. University of Michigan, 721 F. Supp. 852, 862 (E.D. Mich. 1989). The circumstances in which these expressions could be prohibited do not include speech in the classroom. Id. at 864-67. Hysteria University's regulation applies only when students insult others "on the basis of their sex, race, color, handicap, religion, sexual preference, or national and ethic origin." (R. 3). Moreover, that the Code applies only if student groups targeted for exclusion cannot easily be defined does not mean that there was no attempt to exclude the third group. Such a reading ignores the impact upon gay members of the community: it warns them that the environment is hostile and encourages them to stay away. Boswell and the Fraternity were properly punished under the code because the sign purposely insulted gay men, referring to them as "faggots"; and because it discriminated against gay men. This combination of evils is the harm that the Code was designed to prevent. Cf. Brandenburg v. Ohio, 395 U.S. 444 (1969) (holding that speech can only be restricted when it is directed toward creating and is likely to create harms which the state may prevent).

Nonetheless, the appellants may contend that they took no affirmative steps to exclude gay men from the Blow-out. This defense ignores the fact that they had already taken a step toward excluding gay men by making and posting the sign or by failing to take it down. That they took no additional steps is not a defense.

Even if the evidence is viewed most favorably to the appellants, there is a firm basis for upholding the application of the Code to their conduct. As sponsors of the Blow-out, Boswell and the Fraternity were responsible for all activities at the Blow-out. This includes a duty to keep the Blow-out open to the entire community. At a minimum, it was their duty to remove the sign. By breaching this duty, they violated the university policy of non-discrimination.

C. The University's Mandate to Safeguard the Academic Environment Is a Sufficiently Compelling Reason to Justify a Content-based Regulation of Speech.

In Widmar v. Vincent, 454 U.S. 263 (1981), the Court protected the First Amendment right of college students to form religious associations. However, the Court noted that a university "differs in significant respects from public forums such as streets or parks or even municipal theaters." Widmar, 454 U.S. at 267-68 n.5. Unlike other public forums that must be held open to all members of the community for expressive activities, the mission of the university is the education of its students. Therefore, it may regulate activities on campus that are incompatible with that mission. See id. Activities that disrupt the academic climate of fear are inimical to the academic environment. Lastly, students were discouraged from seeking Dean Leikmann's advice and, consequently, their right to obtain an education, including consultations with the Dean of Students, was unjustly limited.

Boswell and the Fraternity will argue that "faggot" is only a word, and that the injuries inflicted are not the result of words, but rather of actions. This distinction obscures the harm that the Code seeks to prevent. "There is such a thing as verbal violence, a kind of cursing, assaultive speech that amounts to almost physical aggression, bullying that is no less punishing because it is simulated." A. Bickel The Morality of Consent 72 (1975). It is precisely this "verbal violence" that the Anti-Hate Speech Code properly restricts. It is "bullying" because it seeks to intimidate its targets and interferes with the right of students to obtain an education. If the court draws the distinction the appellants urge, it will prevent the university from protecting the rights of students who are subjected to these verbal assaults and will force the university to postpone discipline until the verbal assaults result in physical violence.

That members of the University community may have to tolerate gratuitous and personal attacks off-campus should not mean that they have to tolerate the same attacks on campus. The Supreme Court has stated that a university is a forum unlike public sidewalks or parks. Widmar, 454 U.S.

at 267-68 n.5. It exists so that its members can participate in vigorous debate and even heated discussions. But if it cannot stop its members from using insulting and "fighting" words, then "the discussion degenerates into a name-calling contest without social value and, human nature being what it is, to a fight or perhaps a riot." Kunz v. New York 340 U.S. 290, 312 (1951) (Jackson J., dissenting). What the state was unable to prohibit in the streets of New York City, it need not tolerate on its campuses. As then Justice Rehnquist observed in Healy,

> [t]he government as . . . school administrator may impose upon . . . students reasonable regulations that would be impermissible if imposed by the government upon all its citizens. And there can be a constitutional distinction between the infliction of criminal punishment, on the one hand, and the imposition of milder administrative or disciplinary sanctions, on the other, even though the same First Amendment interest is implicated by each.

Healy, 408 U.S. 169, 203 (Rehnquist, J., concurring).

II. THE ANTI-HATE SPEECH CODE OF HYSTERIA UNIVERSITY REACHES ONLY UNPROTECTED SPEECH.

Whether the court applies the "fighting" words doctrine from Chaplinsky v. New Hampshire, 315 U.S. 568, 572 (1942), or the distinction between advocacy and action articulated in Brandenburg v. Ohio, 395 U.S. 444, 447-49 (1969), it should reach the same result: the expressive activities regulated by the Anti-Hate Speech Code are unprotected.

Under Chaplinsky, speech which is used to inflict injury or incite a breach of the peace has so little value that its restriction does not raise a constitutional issue; the Anti-Hate Code is restricted to such "fighting" words. Chaplinsky, 315 U.S. at 372. Under Brandenburg, speech can only be restricted when it is directed towards creating and is likely to create a harm that can legitimately be prevented; because the speech restricted by the Anti-Hate Speech Code interferes with the right of other students to obtain an education, it meets this test. Brandenburg, 395 U.S. at 447. Cf. Norton v. Discipline Comm. of East Tenn. State Univ., 419 F.2d 195 (6th Cir. 1969), cert. denied, 399 U.S. 906 (1970) (upholding the suspension of students whose pamphleteering led the university to conclude that they intended to cause disturbances).

The Anti-Hate Speech Code does not "prescribe what shall be orthodox in politics, nationalism, religion or other matters of opinion" and should not be attacked as an attempt by the state to do so. See West Virginia State Bd. of Educ. v. Barnette, 319 U.S. 624, 642 (1943) (holding that the state could not require students to pledge allegiance to the flag). The University embraces the view that "[t]olerance of unwelcome, unorthodox ideas or information is a constitutionally protected policy not to be defeated" by the efforts of intolerant individuals. Kunz v. New York, 340 U.S. 290, 301 (Jackson, J., dissenting). However, there is a vast difference between expressing ideas or communicating information and calling gay men "faggots." Such epithets "are always, and in every context, insults which do not spring from reason and can be answered by one. Their historical associations with violence are well understood, both by those who hurl and those who are struck by these missiles." Id. at 299. (Jackson, J., dissenting).

The violence which lurks below the surface of such speech is amply demonstrated by the facts of this case and illustrates the difference between the exchange of ideas and the hurling of epithets. This is the distinction that the University has drawn. The University must tolerate the former, no matter now abhorrent it finds the view expressed, but the latter need not be tolerated because the University has a duty to protect the rights of all its students to obtain an education. In Beauharnais v. Illinois, 343 U.S. 250 (1952), the Court considered a statute similar in purpose to the Anti-Hate Speech Code. The law then at issue prohibited public expressions which "expose[ ] the citizens of any race, color, creed, or religion to contempt and derision." Beauharnais, 343 U.S. at 251. Speaking for the Court, Justice Frankfurter stated that it was "a law specifically directed at a defined evil" and held that this legislative attempt to address the "tension and violence between the groups defined in the statute" was not proscribed by the Constitution. Id. at 253, 261-63, 266.

Although Beauharnais has been questioned, the doubts arise from the problems of group libel law. Nowak, Rotunda & Young, Constitutional Law, sec. 16.32 (3d ed. 1986). But the problems of group libel law need not concern us; what concerns us and concerned Justice Frankfurter were the harms created by "hate-speech" and the corrosive influence it has on our communities, particularly college campuses.

> [A] university is not merely an arena for the discussion of ideas by students and faculty; it is also an institution where individuals learn to express themselves in acceptable, civil terms. We provide that environment to the end that students may learn the self restraint necessary to the functioning of a civilized society and understand the need for those external restraints to which we must all submit if group existence is to be tolerable.

Papish v. University of Mo. Curators, 410 U.S. 667, 672 (1972) (Burger, C.J., dissenting). The "Anti-Hate Speech" Code was intended to be a "positive first step in curbing the violence that seems to be overtaking our youth at a time when they should be learning the proper values that will guide them in the future." (R. 3). If the decision below were reversed, it would be telling the University that it must abandon this time-honored role.

CONCLUSION

For the reasons set forth, Appellees respectfully request that the judgment of the United States District Court for the Eastern District of Pennsylvania be affirmed.

Respectfully submitted,

_____

Neil Rosen
Attorney for Appellees

The next brief won the award for "Best Brief" at the regional level in the 1991 National Moot Court Competition. It conforms to the rules governing briefs submitted to the Supreme Court of the United States, and the format is therefore slightly different from that of other briefs in this Appendix.

No. 91-829

IN THE

Supreme Court of the United States

OCTOBER TERM, 1991

MARVEL CHEMICAL CORP.,

Petitioner,

–against–

WEBB SCIENTIFIC PRESS, INC.,

Respondent

ON WRIT OF CERTIORARI
TO THE UNITED STATES COURT OF APPEALS
FOR THE FOURTEENTH CIRCUIT

BRIEF FOR PETITIONER

Maria T. Browne
Susan T. Sakura
John C. Yang
The George Washington
University
716 20th Street, N.W.
Washington, D.C. 20052

(Matthew Bender & Co., Inc.)

(Pub.676)

QUESTIONS PRESENTED

I.   Whether photocopying of portions of scientific journals for ease of reference during medical research falls within the fair use exception to copyright law.

II. Whether the Seventh Amendment of the United States Constitution preserves Marvel's right to a jury trial for determination of statutory damages under copyright law.

TABLE OF CONTENTS

[Illustrative page references are to original document.]

TABLE OF AUTHORITIES

[Illustrative page references are to original document.]

Page

UNITED STATES SUPREME COURT CASES:

UNITED STATES COURT OF APPEALS CASES:

UNITED STATES DISTRICT COURT CASES:

UNITED STATES STATUTES:

OPINIONS BELOW

The opinions and orders of the United States District Court for the Southern District of Gotham are unreported and are contained in the Transcript of Record (R. 1-13). The opinion of the United States Court of Appeals for the Fourteenth Circuit is unreported and appears in the Transcript of Record (R. 14-18).

CONSTITUTIONAL AND STATUTORY PROVISIONS

The text of the following provisions relevant to the determination of the present case are set forth in the appendices: U.S. Const. art. I, § 8, cl.

13; U.S. Const. amend. VII; 17 U.S.C. § 107 (1988); 17 U.S.C. § 504 (1988).

STATEMENT OF THE CASE

In 1989, while conducting important research on the medical application of radioactive isotopes, David Banner, Ph.D., photocopied portions of issues of the Journal of Experimental Radiotherapy (R. 8). Dr. Banner copied three journal articles that were directly related to his research: "Climbing to New Heights in the Utilization of Selenium" by Dr. Peter Parker; "Transmogrification Theory of Isotopic Activity" by Dr. Diana Prince; and "Shedding Light on Radiotherapeutic Values" by Professor Hal Hordan (R. 8). The articles contained facts and formulas necessary and relevant to his continuing scientific endeavors (R. 8). Dr. Banner placed the copies in his personal files and occasionally brought them into the laboratory for ease of reference during experiments (R. 9).

Dr. Banner holds a doctorate degree in nuclear medicine (R. 8). Through his research, he has contributed to scientific progress, including the development of the revolutionary anti-baldness drug "benzoyl" in the 1980s (R. 9). He has worked for Marvel Chemical Corporation ("Marvel" or "Petitioner") at its Central City facility for the past three years (R. 9). While working for Marvel, Dr. Banner studied the many effects of exposure to radioactive elements (R. 9). As part of his experiments concerning radioactive isotopes and their effects on cancer, Dr. Banner discovered Fadium, a new isotope and possible cancer cure (R. 9). Dr. Banner's research further revealed that adverse side effects outweigh the curative aspects of the drug (R. 9).

Webb Scientific Press ("Webb" or "Respondent"), a for-profit corporation, had 1989 revenues of $14.25 million (R. 6). One of the largest corporations of its kind, Respondent distributes eighty-eight journals relating to science and medicine (R. 6). Respondent sells annual journal subscriptions worldwide for prices ranging from $80 to $625 per journal (R. 6). Research scientists provide the material for Webb's journals in exchange for a fee and distribution of the works (R. 6). The scientists allegedly assign their copyright interests in the material to Respondent, though the validity of these assignments was never addressed by the courts below (R. 6 n.1). Respondent in turn includes the articles in its journals and places a copyright symbol at the bottom of the first page of each article (R. 6).

Marvel develops and markets many products, including several that have proven instrumental in the treatment or cure of minor diseases and illnesses (R. 7). Marvel employs scientists and engineers dedicated to the research and development of its products and spends nearly $18 million per year on its research efforts (R. 7). Of that sum, Marvel spent $261,991 on journal subscriptions in 1989 (R. 7). Marvel subscribes to fifty-three journals for the benefit of its Central City scientists and has multiple subscriptions to many journals (R. 7). The journals are routed sequentially to scientists who sign the appropriate distribution lists (R. 7).

Respondent instituted this case in the United States District Court for the Southern District of Gotham alleging copyright infringements by Marvel (R. 5). Respondents sought statutory damages for these violations, foregoing any claim for injunctive relief. Subsequently, Petitioner demanded a jury trial for the damages action (R. 1). Respondent's motion to strike Marvel's demand for a jury trial was granted by the district court on September 4, 1990 (R. 4). After a bench trial, the court issued its decision and order on November 25, 1990, finding Marvel not liable for copyright infringement (R. 13).

The United States Court of Appeals for the Fourteenth Circuit affirmed the district court's opinion with respect to the denial of a jury trial, but reversed, by a divided court, on the finding of fair use on the copyright issue. This Court granted certiorari on August 22, 1991, to consider all of the questions raised by the record (R. 19).

SUMMARY OF THE ARGUMENT

Dr. Banner's photocopying of Respondent's scientific journals easily falls within the fair use exception to copyright law. Congress codified the fair use exception to copyright law to ensure dissemination of knowledge and ideas by enabling people other than the copyright holder to use copyrighted material in a reasonable manner without the copyright holder's consent. The court of appeals erred in its conclusion that Dr. Banner's photocopying did not constitute fair use.

The copyright laws enumerate four non-exclusive factors to be considered in determining whether a use is fair. They are: purpose of the use; nature of the work; amount of work copied; and effect on the work's potential market. The photocopying in this case demonstrates the precise activity the fair use exception was designed to protect.

Dr. Banner copied the articles in good faith for the purpose of advancing his research on the medical application of radioactive isotopes. The journals from which Dr. Banner made copies were scientific and factual in nature. Precedent clearly mandates that scientific and fact-based works favor a finding of fair use. The amount and substantiality of the copy compared to the entire work must be considered. The comparison in the present case should be made between the three articles Petitioner copied and the journals themselves, which are about 300 pages in length. Dr. Banner's use of the journal is insubstantial and should not be considered an infringement.

Finally, Marvel's use does not impair the marketability of Respondent's journal. There has been no showing of either actual or future economic harm. Respondent has a thriving business that has not suffered from Marvel's use. Photocopying articles for private files is widespread in the research community and there is no evidence it has hindered the economic success of Respondent's journal. Sustaining Marvel's actions will not create a subversive impact on Respondent's business.

The lower courts also erred in striking Marvel's demand for a jury trial. Two lines of analysis support Marvel's Seventh Amendment right to a jury trial. First, Marvel's right to a jury trial exists because copyright law traditionally provides for the right, and that right was not altered by subsequent revisions to the law. Second, Marvel's right exists because the three-part balancing test developed by this Court weighs in favor of a jury trial.

Marvel's Seventh Amendment right to a jury trial is supported by the original copyright actions that were triable to a jury in 1790. The statute does not explicitly deny this right, and case law clearly indicates that the legislature intended cases under the original law to be tried to a jury. Subsequent revisions to this law never altered the right. Consequently, Marvel's right to a jury trial is the same as the one existing in 1790. Absent clear legislative mandate, this right cannot be revoked.

Even if the statute is ambiguous as to the right to a jury trial, this Court's jurisprudence dictates that Marvel's right exists under the remedies provision of the current copyright laws. Marvel's demand for a jury satisfies all three factors considered by this Court's balancing test. Copyright violations traditionally have been determined by juries; the remedy sought is legal and analogous to other actions triable by jury; and the practical abilities of jurors are suited perfectly to the determination of the issues in this case. Thus, this balancing test mandates allowing Marvel's demand for a jury trial.

ARGUMENT

I. DR. BANNER'S PHOTOCOPYING OF RESPONDENT'S JOURNAL ARTICLES FALLS WITHIN THE FAIR USE EXCEPTION TO COPYRIGHT LAW.

The Copyright Act balances the fundamental interest in the dissemination of knowledge and ideas with the copyright holder's economic privilege to control dissemination. A copyright does not grant an absolute monopoly to its holder; the scope of the privilege is limited by explicit provisions of the Copyright Act. 17 U.S.C. §§ 107-118 (1988). Congress codified a fair use exception in section 107 to enable people other than the copyright holder to use copyrighted material in a reasonable manner without the holder's consent. Publ. L. No. 94-553, § 101, 90 Stat. 2541, 2546 (1976) (codified at 17 U.S.C. § 107 (1988)). The fair use provision manifests Congress' understanding that dissemination of knowledge is the best method to fulfill its constitutional mandate to "promote the Progress of Science and useful Arts." U.S. Const. art. I, § 8, cl. 13.

Section 107 establishes that a "fair use . . . is not an infringement of copyright," and provides the following examples of fair use: "criticism, comment, news reporting, teaching . . . , scholarship or research." 17 U.S.C. § 107 (1988). The section defines four non-exclusive factors to be considered in determining whether a use is fair. The factors enumerated in section 107 are: (1) purpose of the use; (2) nature of the copyrighted work; (3) amount of work copied; and (4) effect on the work's potential market.[1]

Dr. Banner's use of the three articles from different issues of Respondent's <u>Journal of Experimental Radiotherapy</u> demonstrates the precise activity the fair use exception was designed to protect. Dr. Banner copied the articles in good faith for the purpose of advancing his research of radioactive isotopes. The published articles were factual in nature and constituted only a small portion of each journal issue. Banner's isolated photocopying for his own personal use had no effect on the current or future market for Respondent's scientific journals.

Fair use is a mixed question of law and fact, and where the trial court's findings of fact are sufficient, the appellate court may resolve the issue of fair use as a matter of law. <u>Harper & Row, Publishers, Inc. v. Nation Enters.</u>, 471 U.S. 539, 549 (1985). Accordingly, the court of appeal's conclusion on this point is open to de novo review on appeal. The court of appeals erred in its decision that Dr. Banner's use does not fall within the parameters of fair use. Petitioners respectfully request that this Court reverse the court of appeals and reinstate the decision of the district court on the issue of copyright infringement. In the alternative, if the Court agrees with the legal reasoning of the court of appeals, Petitioners request the Court to remand this case to the district court for more complete factual findings on the issue of fair use.

A. DR. BANNER'S RESEARCH-RELATED PURPOSE FOR PHOTOCOPYING RESPONDENT'S JOURNAL ARTICLES CLEARLY FAVORS FAIR USE.

Dr. Banner copied three articles from Respondent's scientific journals to advance his untrodden research on radioactive isotopes. Section 107 of the Copyright Act expressly provides that "the fair use of a copyrighted work, including . . . research, is not an infringement of copyright." 17 U.S.C. § 107 (1988). The district court correctly concluded that once a use

---

[1] For the full text of section 107, see Appendix C.

is categorized as research, assessment of the first fair use factor should end, and the factor be weighed in favor of a finding of fair use. Furthermore, the public's intense interest in the dissemination of scientific knowledge requires that Dr. Banner's use be protected. Finally, the court of appeals erred in its cursory conclusion that Dr. Banner's sole purpose for photocopying the articles was to increase Marvel's profits.

1. Dr. Banner's research-related purpose for photocopying the articles automatically satisfies the purpose prong of the statutory analysis.

Section 107 delineates research as one category that constitutes a fair use of copyrighted material. Id., See supra p. 7. Accordingly, if an alleged infringer can establish that the purpose of a use is for research, analysis of the first factor should end, New Era Publications, Int'l v. Carol Publishing Group, 904 F.2d 152, 156 (2d Cir.), cert. denied, 111 S. Ct. 297 (1990), and that factor should be weighed in favor of fair use, Williams & Wilkins Co. v. United States, 487 F.2d 1345 (Ct. Cl. 1973), aff'd by an equally divided Court, 420 U.S. 376 (1975). It is well settled that the law gives copying for scientific purposes a broad scope in the fair use determination. See, e.g., id. (finding that copying of medical journals by government agency constituted fair use); Loew's, Inc. v. Columbia Broadcasting Sys., 131 F. Supp. 165, 175 (S.D. Cal. 1955) (giving broader scope to doctrine of fair use in field of learning), aff'd sub nom. Benny v. Loew's, Inc., 239 F.2d 532 (9th Cir. 1956), aff'd by an equally divided Court, 356 U.S. 43 (1958).

Dr. Banner copied three journal articles, "Climbing to New Heights in the Utilization of Selenium" by Doctor Peter Parker, "Transmogrification Theory of Isotopic Activity" by Doctor Diana Prince, and "Shedding Light on Radiotherapeutic Values" by Professor Hal Jordan, to gain easier access to the material for study and research in his related field of study (R. 8). While at Marvel, Dr. Banner studied the medical application of radioactive isotopes, including possible cures for cancer (R. 8). He copied the articles at the premises of the Central City research laboratory, which is devoted to the development of products with medical applications (R. 7). With a Ph.D. in nuclear medicine, Dr. Banner has contributed enormously to the field of medical research (R. 8). Clearly, Dr. Banner's sole purpose in copying the articles was for research and therefore the first factor should be weighed in favor of fair use.

2. The public's interest in advancing medical science mandates protection of Dr. Banner's valid research purpose for copying the articles.

To promote science and useful arts, courts have subordinated the copyright holder's interest in maximum financial return to the greater public interest in the development of art, science, and industry. See, e.g., Williams & /Wilkins, 487 F.2d at 1352; Rosemond Enters., Inc. v. Random House, Inc., 366 F.2d 303, 307 (2d Cir. 1966), cert. denied, 385 U.S. 1009 (1967). When distribution would serve the public interest in the free dissemination of information, and preparation of new material would require some use of prior materials dealing with the same subject matter, courts have favored a finding of fair use. Association of Am. Medical Colleges v. Cuomo, 928 F.2d 519 (2d Cir.), cert. denied, 60 U.S.L.W. 3262 (U.S. Oct. 7, 1991). The public's interest in dissemination of information is founded in the First Amendment. Triangle Publications, Inc. v. Knight-Ridder Newspapers, Inc., 626 F.2d 1171, 1179 (5th Cir. 1980).

In Mazer v. Stein, the Supreme Court stated that "the copyright law, like the patent statutes, makes reward to the owner a secondary consideration." 347 U.S. 201, 219 (1954). Society advances because researchers build upon the work of their predecessors. Scientists often rely upon established principles to promote the discovery of new theories and solutions. After all, "[a] dwarf standing on the shoulders of a giant can see farther than the giant himself." Zechariah Chafee, Reflections on the Law of Copyright, 45 Colum. L. Rev. 503, 511 (1945).

Furthermore, public interest in dissemination becomes progressively stronger as the material moves along the spectrum from fancy to fact. National Business Lists, Inc. v. Dun & Bradstreet, Inc., 552 F. Supp. 89 (N.D. Ill. 1982). To find otherwise would frustrate the very objective of publishing scientific works: communication of useful knowledge to the world. See Feist Publications, Inc. v. Rural Tel. Serv. Co., 111 S. Ct. 1281, 1290 (1991).

Dr. Banner's use serves to promote revolutionary scientific research and is the epitome of a "purpose" that serves the public interest. Banner copied the articles to facilitate his research concerning radioactive isotopes. As demonstrated by his outstanding record, Dr. Banner's research may produce facts concerning possible cures for cancer and other diseases. Whether Dr. Banner produces a new medicine or treatment, or discounts a potential solution, he contributes to scientific progress. In the public's best interest, this Court should find that Dr. Banner's purpose in copying the articles favors fair use.

3. Dr. Banner's purpose for photocopying the articles does not constitute a commercial use.

The court of appeals erred in its conclusion that, notwithstanding the "development . . . of revolutionary—and perhaps life-saving—medical drugs and treatments," Dr. Banner photocopied portions of Respondent's journal solely to increase Marvel's profits (R. 16). First, courts have characterized uses as noncommercial, notwithstanding the fact that the user stands to make a profit from the copying. See New Era, 904 F.2d at 156 (finding fair use despite anticipated profit from book containing use); Maxtone-Graham v. Burtchaell, 803 F.2d 1253 (2d Cir. 1986) (finding that educational elements far outweighed commercial aspects of a work), cert. denied, 481 U.S. 1059 (1987).

Second, section 107 delineates explicit examples of fair use, including teaching, news reporting and research, which generally are conducted for profit. Congress undoubtedly knew, upon drafting section 107, that the majority of today's revolutionary research is attributable to huge-profit making corporations, such as Marvel. See Harper & Row, 471 U.S. at 593 (1985) (Brennan, J., dissenting). Accordingly, to negate a fair use argument because the research was conducted for profit is to render meaningless the congressional imprimatur placed on such issues.

Further evidence of congressional intent on this matter exists in the House Report to section 108 of the Copyright Act. Pub. L. No. 94-553, § 101, 90 Stat. at 2546 (1976) (codified at 17 U.S.C. § 108 (1988)). In the report, Congress explicitly labels as non-infringing, "[i]solated, spontaneous making of single photocopies by a library in a for-profit organization [such as the research and development departments of chemical corporations] . . . even though the copies are furnished to the employees for the organization for use in their work." H.R. 1476, 94th Cong., 2d Sess. 75 (1976), reprinted in 1976 U.S. Code Cong. & Admin. News 5659, 5691. Although it is unclear from the record whether Dr. Banner photocopied the articles on machines located in Marvel's on-site library, it is clear that such a library existed and that Banner copied the articles at the research facility. Banner's use is sufficiently similar to the use set out in the House Report to warrant application of Congress' intent that such photocopying constitutes fair use.

The court of appeals referred to a test set out in Harper & Row in support of its conclusion on this issue. 471 U.S. at 562. The Harper & Row Court stated the test for commercial nature to be "whether the user stands to profit from exploitation of the copyrighted material." Id. The present case is distinguishable from Harper & Row. First, in Harper & Row, the user published President Ford's unpublished written memoirs with knowledge of the copyright and with "the intended purpose of supplanting the copyright holder's commercially valuable right of first publication." Id. The Court found that such intent supersedes the ordinary presumption of good faith in the fair use analysis. Id. at 564. Dr. Banner copied the materials in good faith, as a true scholar, with only incidental commercial effects.

Second, Dr. Banner's use allies more closely with the personal use for time-shifting[2] found to be a noncommercial, nonprofit activity. Sony Corp. of Am. v. Universal City Studios, Inc., 464 U.S. 417, 443 (1984). Dr. Banner copied the works for the sole purpose of viewing the articles at a later date when they would be more useful to him. He did not retransmit the work, he simply put the copies in his file for personal use and occasionally used them for ease of reference during experiments.

Finally, the user in Harper & Row was a direct competitor of the copyright holder, a traditional characteristic of the user in cases finding commercial use. See, e.g., Supermarket of Homes, Inc. v. San Fernando Valley Bd. of Realtors, 786 F.2d 1400 (9th Cir. 1986); Bellsouth Advertising & Publishing Corp. v. Donnelley Information Publishing, 719 F. Supp. 1551 (S.D. Fla. 1988), aff'd, 933 F.2d 952 (11th Cir. 1991). Neither Dr. Banner nor Marvel compete with Webb Press in the journal publication market. To the extent that Respondent and Marvel share common subject matter, the work is complementary, not supplementary.

The research purpose of Dr. Banner's good faith photocopying clearly outweighs any attenuated, potential profit-making motive attributable to Marvel. Accordingly, the court of appeals should be reversed, and the use should be characterized as for research and weighed in favor of fair use.

B. THE SCIENTIFIC AND FACTUAL NATURE OF RESPONDENT'S PUBLISHED WORK WEIGHS IN FAVOR OF FAIR USE.

Courts continually have distinguished between works that are factual in nature and those that are creative in nature. Respondent's scientific journals easily fall within the broad scope of fact-based works that favor a finding of fair use. Even if the Court finds that Respondent's works contain some elements of creativity, the doctrine of merger, which states that some works combine facts and creative elements in such a way that they cannot be separated, precludes applying that characterization to the work in its entirety. Finally, the published nature of Respondent's work also favors a finding of fair use.

1. The subject matter of Webb's copyrighted journal is factual and informational in nature.

This Court long has recognized that the fact/expression dichotomy severely limits the scope of protection in fact-based works. Feist, 111 S. Ct. at 1290 (citing numerous cases). The fact/expression dichotomy is premised on the fundamental principle that "no author may copyright facts or ideas,"

---

[2] The Sony Court defined time-shifting as copying for the purpose of viewing something at a later date. 464 U.S. at 443.

id. (quoting Harper & Row, 471 U.S. at 547-48), because facts and ideas constitute materials in the public domain. This dichotomy serves to accommodate the competing interests of copyright and the First Amendment. Triangle Publications, 626 F.2d at 1179.

The court of appeals conceded that the copyrighted journal was "factual in nature" and agreed with the district court that this factor favored a finding of fair use (R. 16). Furthermore, courts traditionally have classified scientific and medical materials as factual and informational in nature. See, e.g., Williams & Wilkins, 487 F.2d at 1354.

Webb, one of the largest publishers of scientific and medical journals, solicits articles directly from research scientists. It is undisputed that Webb's eighty-eight journals are all scientific in nature, including the particular journal at issue in this case, the Journal of Experimental Radiotherapy. Scientists customarily rely on such journals to begin their experimental research where the prior author stopped, and therefore these journals serve an informational purpose. Melville Nimmer, Nimmer on Copyright, § 13.05[A], at 13-59 n.23 (1983). The factual and informational nature of Webb's scientific journals gives broader scope to the fair use of the work. See, e.g., Feist, 111 S. Ct. at 1290; Consumers Union of United States, Inc. v. General Signal Corp., 724 F.2d 1044 (2d Cir. 1983), cert. denied, 469 U.S. 823 (1984). The object of communication inherent in scientific works would be frustrated "if the knowledge could not be used without incurring the guilt of piracy of the book." Baker v. Selden, 101 U.S. 99, 103 (1880). Scientists should not be discouraged from relying upon the work of their predecessors. Accordingly, precedent dictates that Webb's copyrighted material be classified as factual.

   2. **The presence of creative elements in the journals does not alter the fact-based nature of the work.**

The doctrine of merger governs works in which facts are not easily separable from expression. Kern River Gas Transmission Co. v. Coastal Corp., 899 F.2d 1458 (5th Cir.), cert. denied, 111 S. Ct. 374 (1990). When an idea and its expression are inseparable, "copying the expression will not be barred, because protecting the expression in such circumstances would confer a monopoly of the idea upon the copyright owner free of the conditions and limitations imposed by" intellectual property law. Herbert Rosenthal Jewelry Corp. v. Kalpakian, 446 F.2d 738, 742 (9th Cir. 1971) (citing Baker v. Selden, 101 U.S. 99 (1880)).

The facts used in the scientific formulas and theories contained in Respondent's journal cannot be separated from any expression therein. To the extent that the journal materials contain expressive material, the facts and expression merge and the doctrine dictates that the material be classified as factual.

3. The published nature of Respondent's journal favors a finding of fair use.

The published nature of Respondent's work is critical to the analysis under factor two of section 107 because "the scope of fair use is narrower with respect to unpublished works." New Era, 904 F.2d at 157 (quoting Harper & Row, 471 U.S. at 564). In Harper & Row, the Court acknowledged that even substantial quotations might qualify as fair use in the case of a published work. New Era, 904 F.2d at 157. The "traditional published/ unpublished dichotomy" weighs published material in favor of fair use. American Medical Colleges, 928 F.2d at 524.

Respondent's journals constitute previously published works. Mr. Banner was not attempting to misappropriate Respondent's work or the authors' right of first publication. The conclusions of both lower courts, that the journals were factual in nature and favored a finding of fair use, should be upheld.

C. PETITIONER ONLY COPIED A PORTION OF THE WORK AND NOT THE ENTIRE JOURNAL.

The third non-exclusive factor enumerated by Congress regarding fair use assesses the amount and substantiality of the copy compared to the work as a whole. Respondent is in the business of publishing, so the journal as a whole should be considered the work of the Respondent and not the individual articles found in the journal, which were created by non-staff researchers. The amount and substantiality of the work copied is just one factor this Court should consider and is not dispositive of the fair use issue. Dr. Banner only reproduced for his own personal use an insubstantial portion of the work of Respondent. Thus, this factor militates in favor of fair use.

1. The entire journal, not the individual articles, constitutes the work of the Respondent.

Respondent is one of the largest publishers of scientific and medical journals, enjoying a worldwide distribution chain (R. 6). Respondent currently publishes eighty-eight journals, earning revenues in 1989 of $14.25 million (R. 6). Although Respondent has been a publisher for sixty-four years, it has never employed one author to create the articles it publishes (R. 6). Only after they have completed the articles do these authors submit their work to the Respondent. The Respondent's business is compiling articles rather than writing the articles and thus the journal as a whole is the work of the Respondent.

That Respondent holds that the copyrights to the individual articles do not necessitate a finding that each article is the work of the Respondent. In Triangle Publications, the court allowed a newspaper to reproduce the covers of past issues of TV Guide, even though the covers themselves were individually copyrighted. 626 F.2d at 1178. "We find unpersuasive Triangle's argument that the cover of TV Guide is separately copyrighted and that therefore Knight-Ridder has reproduced an entire work." Id. at 1177 n.15 (emphasis in original).

Similarly, in the present case, even though each article in Respondent's journal is copyrighted individually, this Court should treat the entire journal as the work of the Respondent. The discoveries and ideas found in the journals of the Respondent are the product of independent scientists and researchers who assigned their rights to Respondent for a fee (R. 6). Upholding Marvel's actions would not discourage the original authors from vigorously pursuing further scientific research, because they themselves do not gain an economic advantage from the copyrights.

Case law also has sustained the practice of copying an entire article if done for a reasonable purpose. For example, governmental medical research organizations validly may make one copy of an entire article from medical journals. Williams & Wilkins, 487 F.2d at 1345. The Williams & Wilkins court gave many examples of when copying the entire work would be considered fair use: single copies to attorneys or courts for use in litigation, photocopies of recent decisions to the court from the publisher, a judge giving a colleague a copy of a law review article, newspaper clippings sent to a friend and so on. 487 F.2d at 1353. In Williams & Wilkins, the court criticized the proposition that copying the entire work can never be considered fair use as "an overbroad generalization, unsupported by the decisions and rejected by years of accepted practice." Id. at 1353; see also Whitol v. Crow, 309 F.2d 777 (8th Cir. 1962); Leon v. Pacific Tel. & Tel. Co., 91 F.2d 484 (9th Cir. 1937).

Furthermore, this Court has held that video-recording an entire copyrighted television program was not violative of the copyright law, because of the large amount of programming that was not copied. Sony, 464 U.S. at 417. In Sony, even though defendant's video-recording machines allow an individual to copy an entire television program, the Court found it significant that the huge volume of programming still available for viewing was not affected. Id. at 443. Here, Dr. Banner's personal use of three articles should be considered fair because of the many articles that he did not reproduce. The majority of Respondent's works are still available for sale and consumption by the public. Thus, Marvel has not infringed upon the rights granted to the Respondent by the copyright laws.

Dr. Banner copied three articles that were 18, 42, and 21 pages in length. Each journal issue was at least 300 pages in length, which means that Dr. Banner cumulatively only copied about 11% of the Respondent's journals. Dr. Banner's reproduction of one copy of the journal articles for his own private files was as innocuous a use as any of the above-mentioned examples.

2. Each factor enumerated in section 107 is not dispositive of the question of fair use.

Even if this Court finds that Dr. Banner copied the entire work, his use is still justified by the overwhelming interest in this country to advance cancer research. It is not dispositive of the case if a singular article is considered the work of the journal publisher. See Williams & Wilkins, 487 F.2d at 1353 ("There is, in short, no inflexible rule excluding an entire copyrighted work from the area of 'fair use.' ").

D. PETITIONER'S USE DOES NOT AFFECT SUBSTANTIALLY THE POTENTIAL MARKET FOR OR THE VALUE OF THE JOURNAL.

Respondents did not meet their burden of showing either actual harm or future harm to the marketability of their journal. Rather, Dr. Banner's private use of three articles can be sustained as a valid time-shifting device. Dr. Banner's educational and research-oriented use should be exempt from Respondent's licensing demands because it neither hampers the incentives for creativity nor significantly lessens the financial gain for Respondents.

1. Dr. Banner's photocopying was a valid time-shifting device used to assist in his research and was not a commercial exploitation of the journal.

Time-shifting is a method of using the same article, but at a time and place more convenient for the consumer. In Sony, the Court held that time-shifting is valid because: (1) it does not lessen the consumer market; (2) individuals do not resell the tapes; (3) it may actually enlarge the market by allowing persons to view the programming at a convenient time; and (4) some owners of copyrighted materials allow time-shifting. 464 U.S. at 443, 456. Here, Dr. Banner copied each of the articles only once. He placed the copies in his personal file for use in the laboratory. He did not resell the articles; rather, he merely studied them at his convenience in a separate room. This practice is customary and widespread among scientific researchers, as attested to by Dr. Steve Rogers in the bench trial below (R. 11). Even so, the discrete photocopying of one article for personal convenience does not destroy Respondent's financial gain from publishing its journal.

2. Direct resale or retransmission of a copyrighted work is prohibited under the statute; educational and scientific uses are valid.

The monopolistic right granted to copyright holders is premised on the right not to have one's work retransmitted without approval. United Video v. FCC, 890 F.2d 1173 (D.C. Cir. 1989). Free dissemination of information becomes impossible, however, when practices such as those engaged in by Marvel are prohibited. Thus, Marvel's status as a for-profit organization is irrelevant to this inquiry. National Business Lists, 552 F. Supp. at 96. Marvel does not directly earn profits from the resale of Respondent's articles; it engages in medical and scientific research by using the journal articles to learn about advances in the field. That Marvel may someday make a profit from the learning gleaned from Respondent's journal creates a causal link too attenuated for any court to assess.

By analogy, the law allows students to make copies of educational materials so that they can enrich their minds and expand their knowledge. See Marcus v. Rowley, 695 F.2d 1171 (9th Cir. 1983). Society allows this practice in the hope that someday the students will become economically independent and can use their knowledge to secure employment. It matters not that they are making profits from their knowledge base; their success is any society's goal. As the law encourages education by allowing materials to be reproduced without the author's consent, so should society allow Dr. Banner the right to reproduce these articles as a fair use of the works. Again, it should not matter that Dr. Banner is a successful "student" and learns well from his readings. The goal of free dissemination of information is to encourage further advances in society. If the government impinges upon this free exchange of information, key technological advances would be thwarted.

3. Respondent's income derived from licensing fees is not a factor to be considered under section 107.

Section 106 grants to the copyright holder the right to control the reproduction of his or her work. 17 U.S.C. § 106 (1988). Respondent in the present case argues that its monopolistic rights are affected by a showing of loss of income from royalty checks (R. 17). Webb currently charges an authorization fee of $4 per copy of an article or a blanket fee of $10,000 for unlimited photocopying of articles from any journal Respondent publishes (R. 7).

Although the legislative scheme assumes a right to license one's work, Congress also intended that any reproduction that falls into the fair use exception would be (1) unauthorized, (2) free of charge, and (3) equally valid as a copy paid for by money. Thus, Respondent's argument is tautological. If this Court finds that Marvel's reproduction was a fair use, then the fact that Respondent charges other customers a licensing fee is irrelevant to the question of economic harm to the Respondent.

4. Copyright protection creates incentives for creativity, a goal that will be furthered by Dr. Banner's scientific use.

Photocopying articles for private use is common in the scientific community (R. 11 n.5). The nature of research in radioactive isotopes is such that scientists build upon the knowledge and experience of past projects. Any strides made by Dr. Banner in his research will spur on further efforts by other researchers in the field. Furthermore, any notoriety that Dr. Banner's research brings to this area of research will increase the interest on the part of investors and provide greater sums for research in general, which in turn helps other scientists in the field. Hence, far from impinging on the creative incentives for further research, Dr. Banner's work may even improve the chances of more research in this field in the future.

E. IN THE ALTERNATIVE, THE COURT OF APPEALS IN-CORRECTLY DETERMINED THE LEGAL ISSUES IN FAIR USE WITHOUT ADEQUATE FACTUAL FINDINGS BELOW.

Fair use is a mixed question of law and fact. Harper & Row, 471 U.S. at 449. Where, as here, the reported facts are insufficient, the appellate court must remand to the trier of fact for further factual findings. See id. at 549. The district court record omits substantive facts, such that the court of appeals could not have correctly reached its legal conclusions.

For example, the record does not state the number of journal issues from which Dr. Banner photocopied articles, which is crucial to determining the amount of the work copied. See supra pp. 18-21. Second, the district court never addressed the validity of the assignments of the copyrights from the authors to Respondent, a fundamental factor in determining Respondent's standing to sue.[3] Finally, the record fails to establish the exact location of the photocopying machine where Banner copied the articles, which would allow Petitioners an added statutory defense codified in section 108 of the Act. 17 U.S.C. § 108 (1988); see supra p. 13. This Court should reverse the court of appeals on the issue of copyright or, at least, remand to the district court for further factual findings.

II. MARVEL HAS A RIGHT TO A JURY TRIAL TO DETER-MINE LIABILITY FOR STATUTORY DAMAGES CAUSED BY THE ALLEGEDLY WILLFUL VIOLATION OF THE COPYRIGHT LAWS.

The Seventh Amendment to the United States Constitution states that "[i]n Suits at common law, where the value in controversy shall exceed twenty dollars, the right to trial by jury shall be preserved." U.S. Const. amend. VII. The right to a jury trial has been described by Alexis de Tocqueville as "one form of sovereignty of the people." Democracy in America 273 (John Mayer trans. 1969) (13th ed. 1850).

---

[3] Standing requires that Respondents prove an economic harm through a valid assignment either in the Journal of Experimental Radiotherapy or in the articles. See Association of Data Processing Serv. Orgs. v. Camp., 397 U.S. 150, 154 (1970).

Marvel has a right to a jury trial under two independent approaches. First, the current statutory damages provision,[4] when analyzed in conjunction with the legislative history, demonstrates congressional intent to preserve Marvel's right to a jury trial. Second, even if the statute and the legislative history fail to provide an answer, the balancing test developed by this Court to determine whether a right to a jury trial should be denied weighs in favor of allowing a jury trial.[5] This analysis satisfies the constitutional mandate to "preserve" the right to a jury trial. See Curtis v. Loether, 415 U.S. 189, 195-98 (1974); Ross v. Bernhard, 396 U.S. 531, 538 n.10 (1970).

This Court need not defer to any ruling made by a lower court in interpreting the nature and extent of the right to a jury trial; rather, a de novo standard of review is applicable. See, e.g., Peel v. Attorney Registration and Disciplinary Comm'n, 110 S. Ct. 2281, 2291-92 (1990) (noting that the Court must undertake de novo review of a First Amendment issue because it is a question of law); New York Times Co. v. Sullivan, 376 U.S. 254, 284-86 (1964) (stating that the Court will review the record independently on issues of constitutional significance). Under de novo view, this Court should scrutinize the entire record.

A. MARVEL'S HISTORICAL RIGHT TO A JURY TRIAL UNDER PREVIOUS COPYRIGHT ACTS WAS NOT ALTERED BY SUBSEQUENT AMENDMENTS TO THE STATUTE.

Marvel's right to a jury trial is embodied in the current copyright legislation. This right has not been altered since the first copyright legislation in 1790. Under the original Act, the issue of copyright infringement and damages was a question of law determined by the jury. See, e.g., Backus v. Gould, 48 U.S. (7 How.) 798, 810-11 (1849) (noting that in an action of debt for a copyright violation, the jury determines the extent of the violation even though damages are already established by statute); Wheaton v. Peters, 33 U.S. (8 Pet.) 591, 667-68 (1834) (remanding a suit brought under the 1790 Copyright Act to a jury to determine certain facts). Although the Copyright Act of 1909 included statutory damages as a subsection of the damages provision, Congress did not intend this addition as a substantial change to the nature of the remedy. Because Congress has not revised this statute substantially since 1909, the statutory damages provision of the current copyright statutes does not affect Marvel's historical right to a jury trial.

---

[4] For the complete text of section 504, see Appendix D.

[5] Even if this Court finds that only certain issues necessitate a jury trial, the "clean-up" doctrine mandates that in mixed actions of law and equity, the legal claims must be tried first to preserve the parties' rights. See Beacon Theatres, Inc. v. Westover, 359 U.S. 500, 508 (1959). Thus, this Court must remand this case if any issue presented is triable by jury.

1. Marvel had a right to a jury trial under the original copyright statute and subsequent amendments retained this right.

Under historical copyright actions, Marvel would have had an unequivocal right to a trial by jury. The first federal copyright statute, enacted in 1790, provided for fixed damages of fifty cents for each infringing sheet "to be recovered by action of debt." Act of May 31, 1790, § 2, 1 Stat. 124 (1790), reprinted in William Patry, The Right to Jury Trial in Copyright Cases, 29 J. Copyright Soc'y 139, 155-56 (1981).[6] At this time, no equity jurisdiction existed in many states. The Federalist No. 81, at 490 (Alexander Hamilton) (Charles Rossiter ed. 1961). Consequently, all citations for copyright violations were tried to the jury. See, e.g., Wheaton, 11 U.S. (8 Pet.) at 667-68.

The Copyright Act of 1909 was the basis for the current remedies provisions. For the first time, the Act included several different remedies, including sections on injunctions and damages. Ch. 320, 35 Stat. 1075 (1909), reprinted in 1 Legislative History of the 1909 Copyright Act 41 (E. Fulton Brylawski & Abe Goldman eds. 1976) [hereinafter 1909 Legislative History].[7] The Act provided two types of damages: actual damages contingent upon proof by the plaintiff and statutory damages[8] between $250 and $5000 to be awarded "as the court shall appear just." Id. The legislative history of the Act does not provide any rationale for the amendments to the former remedies. Specifically, nothing in the legislative history supports removing the determination of damages from the jury and vesting the decision with the judges.

Although the most recent revision of the remedies provisions for copyright violations amended some of the language of section 504, it did not alter the parties' right to a jury trial. Copyright Act of 1976, Pub. L. No. 94-553, § 101, 90 Stat. 2541, 2585 (1976) (codified as amended at 17 U.S.C. § 504 (1988))[9] In the absence of clear congressional intent to the contrary, a statute must be interpreted as maintaining the existing statutory scheme and balance of legal rights. See, e.g., Edmonds v. Compagnie Generale Transatlantique, 443 U.S. 256, 266-67 (1979) (stating that if Congress intended to change a preexisting right, some indicia of congressional intent would exist in the legislative history); Fourco Glass Co. v. Tranmira Prods.

---

[6] For the complete text of the 1790 Act, see Appendix E.

[7] For the complete text of the 1909 Copyright Act, see Appendix F.

[8] Also referred to as "in lieu of" damages, as specified in the 1909 Copyright Act. Id.

[9] The only modification to the statute since 1976 is an increase in the statutory minimum and maximum penalties. For the full text of the current statute, see Appendix D.

Corp., 353 U.S. 222, 227-28 (1957) (stating that Congress intends no substantive change to the law unless clearly expressed). The minor amendments made by the Copyright Act of 1976 can only be interpreted as congressional intent to maintain the parties' right to a jury trial. Thus, Marvel's right is preserved.

2. The text of the statute is unclear and does not preclude Marvel's right to a jury trial.

The lower courts fundamentally misinterpreted the statutory language to preclude the use of juries. The text of the statute is remarkably similar to the text passed in the Copyright Act of 1976, with revisions made to the monetary limits on awards to adjust for inflation. Pub. L. No. 100-568, § 10(b), 1023 Stat. 2853, 2860 (1988) (codified at 17 U.S.C. § 504(c) (1988)). Nevertheless, the lower courts denied Marvel's request for a jury trial, in part because the language of the statute indicated that the amount of the award must be "as the court considers just" (R. 2) (quoting 17 U.S.C. § 504(c)(1) (1988)). The courts' reliance on this language is completely misplaced.

The term "court" always has been used interchangeably to refer to the judge, jury, or both. See, e.g., Curtis v. Loether, 415 U.S. 189 (1974) (requiring a jury for an alleged Fair Housing Act violation despite the statute's use of the words "if the court finds"). Even the Constitution uses the word "court" despite its clear intent to include both judge and jury. See 2 The Debates in the Several State Conventions on the Adoption of the Federal Constitution 113 (Jonathan Elliott ed. 1891) (noting that during one state's ratification debate, one delegate clarified the intent of the Constitution by stating that "[t]he word court does not, either by a popular or technical construction, exclude the use of a jury to try the facts"); The Federalist No. 81, supra p. 28, at 490 (dispelling "all doubt that the supposed abolition of the trial by jury, by the operation of [the Seventh Amendment], is fallacious and untrue" (emphasis in original)).

The legislative history for the Copyright Act of 1976 reflected the multiple definitions attributable to the word "court." The House Report stated that the plaintiff may elect to recover statutory damages "at any time during the trial before the court has rendered its final judgment. H.R. 1476, supra p. 13, at 162, reprinted in 1976 U.S. Code Cong. & Admin. News at 5578. In this case, "court" must refer to both the judge and the jury because in an action for actual damages, a jury right clearly exists. See Broadcast Music, Inc. v. Club 30, Inc., 567 F. Supp. 36, 38 (N.D. Ind. 1983) (noting that "[w]ere the plaintiff seeking actual damages, the right to jury would be inviolate"); Glazier v. First Media Corp., 532 F. Supp. 63, 65 (D. Del. 1982) (stating that no controversy existed as to the plaintiff's right to a jury trial). Even the lower court in this case agreed that "[i]t is beyond peradventure that the right to a jury trial is extant where a copyright owner seeks to prove and recover the <u>actual</u> damages caused by an infringement" (R. 2-3) (citing <u>Arnstein v. Porter</u>, 154 F.2d 464, 468 (2d Cir. 1946)). Thus, Congress must have intended the word "court" to be used in place of judge and jury in this context.

Furthermore, Congress used the word "court" repeatedly when addressing the actual damages provision of section 504. <u>See</u> H.R. 1476, <u>supra</u> p. 13, at 161 (noting that the amendment gives the "court specific unambiguous directions concerning monetary awards" and also stating that because "only those profits "attributable to the infringement' are recoverable . . . , it will be necessary for the court to make an apportionment"), <u>reprinted in</u> 1976 U.S. Code Cong. & Admin. News at 5777. Standing alone, the word "court" is insufficient to preclude the use of jury trials for the determination of statutory damages. Thus, the lower court erred in summarily determining that "the repeated references to the "court' in [section 504] would seem to indicate" no right to a jury trial (R. 3).

Because neither the text nor the legislative history of the revisions alters the rights of the parties to a jury trial, the legislature retained the historical use of juries for determining damages caused by a copyright violation. The judge would sit alone in a copyright infringement if the only remedy sought by Marvel had been injunctive relief. Introducing statutory damages as an alternative remedy did not alter Marvel's rights to a jury trial.

3. <u>Case law favors Marvel's right to a jury trial for damages exceeding the statutory minimum and requiring a showing of willfulness.</u>

Precedent strongly supports Marvel's right to a jury trial in this case. Lower courts consistently have held that when the plaintiff asserts claims for damages exceeding the statutory minimum and increased damages for a finding of willfulness, a right to a jury trial must exist. <u>See, e.g.</u>, <u>Video Views, Inc. v. Studio 21, Ltd.</u>, 925 F.2d 1010, 1014-16 (7th Cir.), <u>cert. denied</u>, 60 U.S.L.W. 3262 (U.S. Oct. 7, 1991); <u>Gnossos Music v. Mitken, Inc.</u>, 653 F.2d 117, 119-21 (4th Cir. 1981); <u>Educational Testing Servs. v. Katzman</u>, 670 F. Supp. 1237, 1242-43 (D.N.J. 1987). These cases reach this conclusion by recognizing both the historical role of the jury in determining copyright violations and congressional silence in altering this right.

In contrast, courts have denied jury trials under section 504 only when the plaintiff sought solely statutory minimum damages. <u>See, e.g.</u>, <u>Cable/Home Communication Corp. v. Network Prods., Inc.</u>, 902 F.2d 829, 852-53 (11th Cir. 1990); <u>Twentieth Century Music Corp. v. Frith</u>, 645 F.2d 6, 7 (5th Cir. Unit B 1981); <u>Chappell & Co. v. Palermo Cafe Co.</u>, 249 F.2d 77, 82 (1st Cir. 1957). These courts have summarily dismissed demands for juries, relying on cursory distinctions between law and equity. See Cable/Home Communication, 902 F.2d at 852 ("We quickly dispense with this contention."); Frith, 645 F.2d at 7 ("This appeal seems to present very simple questions."). Marvel's right to a jury is unaffected by these cases because the Respondent has claimed both damages over the statutory minimum and increased damages based on a finding of willfulness.

B. BECAUSE STATUTORY DAMAGES ARE LEGAL REMEDIES RATHER THAN EQUITABLE ONES, CASES DECIDED AFTER THE MERGER OF LAW AND EQUITY SUPPORT MARVEL'S RIGHT TO A JURY TRIAL.

Even if this Court finds that the statute is unclear as to whether Marvel has a right to a jury trial, the modern principles of civil procedure dictate that Marvel has a right to a jury trial under a three-part test. This test requires: (1) that the cause of action, or the cause of action most analogous to a cause of action not existing at the time of the Bill of Rights, is one traditionally determined by juries; (2) that the remedy for the cause of action is legal in nature rather than equitable; and (3) that the factual determination is one that is within the practical abilities and limitations of the jury. Ross, 396 U.S. at 538 n.10. In an action for statutory damages under section 504, all three elements strongly favor Marvel's right to a jury trial for determining both whether an infringement occurred and what damages are due as a result of the alleged violation.

1. Marvel has a historical right to a jury trial for all actions arising under the copyright laws.

Marvel retains the right to a jury trial that traditionally existed for all copyright infringement cases. Section 504(c) preserves the cause of action existing under copyright laws enacted in 1790. Under these laws, juries adjudicated all aspects of copyright infringement except for injunctive relief.

Prior to the merger of law and equity, the custom for determining copyright violations and damages based on this action strongly favored using juries. Actions for copyright protection existed at common law since the development of the printing process. Under the common law, authors had the right to sue for an injunction, for damages, or for both, upon discovery of an unprivileged publication of their work. See Patry, supra p. 29 at 146. The first recognized statute protecting the rights of publishers was the Act for the Encouragement of Learning, passed in England in 1710. See William Symons, Law of Copyright, in Modern American Law 451, 453 (1915). Known as the Statute of Anne, this statute punished violators through forfeiture of all infringing copies, with damages assessed at one penny per infringing sheet. Patry, supra p. 29, at 146.

When the United States ratified the Constitution, most states already had copyright laws in effect; similar to the Statute of Anne, these were all actionable at law. See Patry, supra p. 29, at 150. They provided for fixed statutory awards upon proof of infringement rather than awarding damages based solely on proof of damages. In these cases, jury trials were allowed. Id. at 15051; see supra pp. 28-29. Consequently, no question exists as to Marvel's historical right to a jury trial in a copyright case prior to the merger of law and equity.

2. Statutory damages for copyright infringements are legal, rather than equitable, remedies that confer a right to jury trial.

In determining whether a newly created statutory remedy is legal or equitable, the Court should find the remedy that is most analogous to the remedy at issue and determine whether a right to a jury trial exists under that remedy. Marvel has a right to a jury trial under the statutory damages provision of the copyright laws because all analogous remedies provide jury trials.

A survey of analogous statutory remedies and their treatment by this Court leads to the inescapable conclusion that section 504(c) preserves the right to a jury trial. The most analogous statutory remedy is the damages provision for trademark infringements. 15 U.S.C. § 1117 (1988) (providing that the "court shall assess such profits and damages," even though "the court may in its discretion enter judgment for such sum as the court shall find to be just," including treble damages for an intentional violation). This Court found that a right to a jury exists under trademark laws. See Dairy Queen, Inc. v. Wood, 369 U.S. 469, 477-79 (1962). Specifically, Dairy Queen cited a copyright case in concluding that an action for damages based on trademark infringement was cognizable in a court of law. Id. at 477 & n.15 (citing Arnstein v. Porter, 154 F.2d 464 (2d Cir. 1946)). Justice John Harlan, in concurrence, further emphasized the legal nature of copyright actions, stating that "[a] jury, under proper instructions from the court, could readily calculate the damages flowing from this alleged trademark infringement, just as courts of law often do in copyright and trademark cases." Id. at 480-81 (Harlan, J., concurring). Thus, Marvel's right to a jury trial has been endorsed by this Court in Dairy Queen.

The Fair Housing Act also provides remedies similar to section 504(c). 42 U.S.C. § 3613(c) (1988). Under the Act, juries determine actual and punitive damages while courts determine the propriety of injunctive relief. See Curtis, 415 U.S. at 196-97. Likewise, the remedies provisions for federal copyright violations provide several remedies; section 504 provides legal remedies whereas sections 502 and 503 provide equitable ones. Like Curtis, this separation is clear from the face of the statutory structure. The placement of statutory relief within the damages section of the remedies provisions also indicates the legal nature of the remedy. The statutory scheme provides several different remedies for copyright infringement. Not only can plaintiffs claim damages, but they can sue for injunctive relief and for forfeiture of the infringing items. 17 U.S.C. §§ 502-503 (1988). The availability of purely equitable forms of relief indicates the legal nature of statutory damages.

One final example demonstrates the legal nature of statutory damages for copyright violations. Under the federal wire tapping laws, Congress allowed the recovery of statutory civil damages for illegal wiretaps. 18 U.S.C. §§ 2510-2521 (1988). Under this provision, "the court shall assess . . . statutory damages of not less than $50 and not more than $500" for a first-time offender. Id. at § 2520(c). Courts have interpreted this language to mean that juries must decide whether to award damages and the amount of damages. See, e.g., Rodgers v. Wood, 910 F.2d 444 (7th Cir. 1990); Scutieri v. Paige, 808 F.2d 785 (11th Cir. 1987).

These statutes differ significantly from Title VII of the Civil Rights Act, which does not allow jury determinations of back pay. See, e.g., Slack v. Havens, 522 F.2d 1091 (9th Cir. 1975); Robinson v. Lorillard Corp., 44 F.2d 791, 802 (4th Cir.), cert. dismissed, 404 U.S. 1006 (1971). The remedies provision of Title VII clearly indicates that back pay is an equitable remedy that is incident to an injunction. Compare 42 U.S.C. § 3613(c)(1) (1988) (Title VIII Fair Housing Act) (stating that "the court may award to the plaintiff actual and punitive damages, . . . and . . . may grant as relief, as the court deems appropriate, any permanent or temporary injunction, temporary restraining order, or other order") with 42 U.S.C. § 2000e-5(g) (1988) (Title VII) (stating that "the court may enjoin the respondent from engaging in such unlawful employment practice, and order such affirmative action as may be appropriate, which may include . . . reinstatement . . . with or without back pay . . . or any other equitable relief as the court deems appropriate"). Whereas the Fair Housing Act provides actual damages as well as equitable relief, Title VII explicitly limits back pay to situations where the court has issued an injunction.

Lastly, section 504 provides increased damages for willful copyright violations. The scienter of "willfulness" is not an equitable consideration; rather, this element is punitive in nature. Similar to other statutes that provide for increased damages on a showing of willfulness, this statute's use of increased damages provides further legal remedies.

By analogy, antitrust laws provide for treble damages upon a showing of willfulness. 15 U.S.C. § 77k(e) (1988). Courts consistently have ruled that this section requires a jury. See, e.g., Beacon Theatres, Inc. v. Westover, 359 U.S. at 504; Standard Oil Co. v. Arizona, 738 F.2d 1021 (9th Cir. 1984), cert. denied, 469 U.S. 1132 (1985). Specifically, courts have found that the determination of "willfulness" is a question uniquely fit for jury determination. See Hohmann v. Packard Instrument Co., 471 F.2d 815 (7th Cir. 1973).

Thus, Respondent's claim for increased damages as provided by section 504 is most analogous to actions allowing treble or punitive damages for a finding of willfulness, legal remedies that were tried to juries.

3.   The factual determination of the appropriate statutory damages to be awarded is within the special expertise of the jury.

The third prong of the Ross test focuses on the practical abilities and limitations on the jury. Ross, 396 U.S. at 538 n.10. Unlike an antitrust case, this case is not so complex that juries would misunderstand the issues and misapply the facts to the case. See, e.g., In re Japanese Elecs. Prods. Antitrust Litig., 631 F.2d 1069 (3d Cir. 1980) (denying a jury trial because the complexity of the case, when tried to a jury, would deny the parties' Fifth Amendment right to due process), rev'd on other grounds, 723 F.2d 238 (3d Cir. 1983) (en banc), rev'd on other grounds, 475 U.S. 574 (1986). A copyright case presents the simple issue of whether a user has copied unfairly a work that is protected by copyright. Although the jury must determine the extent of the violation and whether a fair use defense may apply, these issues are highly fact-specific. See supra pp. 25-26. Juries determine the facts; judges determine the law. See Harry Kalven & Hans Zeisel, The American Jury 149 (1966) (studying the jury process empirically and concluding that "contrary to an often voiced suspicion, the jury does by and large understand the facts [and] that the jury's decision by and large moves with the weight and direction of the evidence"). This case evokes the core of the jury's factfinding function. Juries must decide any factual questions that arise in copyright infringement cases.

The remedial statutes demonstrates a proper concern for limiting jury discretion. By establishing maximum and minimum penalties, Congress avoids unjust results based on inappropriate biases. See, e.g., Davis v. Omitowoju, 883 F.2d 1155 (3d Cir. 1989); Boyd v. Bulala, 877 F.2d 1191 (4th Cir. 1989). Limiting awards does not remove cases from the jury, it merely limits jury discretion. Thus, the jury's role is preserved while recognizing the competing social goal of moderating damage awards.

The American jury acts as the final public check on state actions. As Chief Justice (then Justice) William Rehnquist has stated, "the right to trial by jury in civil cases [is] an important bulwark against tyranny and corruption, a safeguard too precious to be left to the whim of the sovereign or, it might be added, to the judiciary." Parklane Hosiery Co. v. Shore, 439 U.S. 322, 343 (1978) (Rehnquist, J., dissenting). Accordingly, the policy supporting the right to a jury also should be weighed under this factor. The right is pivotal as a core value ensuring the balance of power in the American system, providing the public imprimatur of approval on both legislative and executive actions as well as a check on the judiciary in interpreting the law.

The jury system developed in direct response to judicial tyranny. Although judges purported to interpret and apply the law in a just manner, judges often were puppets of the sovereign. See Shannen Stimson, The American Revolution in the Law 49-50 (1990) (noting the political and economical stranglehold held by the sovereign against the judge). In response, juries were created to check the power of the sovereign, providing justice through deliberation and adjudication by peers. It was, therefore, both a privilege and a duty to serve as a juror during these times.

Although some of these historical perils no longer exist in the American judicial system, the same duty and honor renders the juror, and the use of juries, vital to the current system. See Harry Kalven, The Dignity of the Civil Jury, 50 Va. L. Rev. 1055, 1062 (1964). The jury is still the best arbiter of facts. Legislatures expect juries to weigh facts, balance interests, and mitigate circumstances when rendering the final verdict and awards. Finally, the jury system gives citizens an opportunity to participate in the democratic process. See Donald Michael, The Right to Trial by Jury: How Important?, 27 Trial 16, 18, (1991) (recounting personal experience as a federal district court judge when impanelling a jury). Because most citizens serve as a juror at some time in their lives, this process gives them a rare opportunity to affect the American system directly.

CONCLUSION

For the reasons set forth above, Petitioner respectfully requests this Court to reverse the judgment of the United States Court of Appeals for the Fourteenth Circuit. Accordingly, Petitioner requests this Court to dismiss the claim against Marvel Corporation. In the alternative, Petitioner requests this Court to remand the case for a jury trial on facts not discovered or determined by the lower courts.

APPENDIX **VI**

ORAL ARGUMENTS

We have chosen three sample oral arguments from well-known United States Supreme Court cases. One of the cases, *Miranda v. Arizona*, 384 U.S. 436 (1966), is a landmark case that you may have either read or heard about. *New Jersey v. T.L.O.*, 469 U.S. 325 (1985), is an interesting case concerning the search of a high school student's purse by school officials. Chapter 14 of this book includes detailed facts from this case. *Hishon v. King & Spalding*, 467 U.S. 69 (1984), involves a woman lawyer claiming sex discrimination by a law firm.

We chose these arguments as a good sampling of how arguments proceed, which is often unpredictable. In *Brown*, the attorney had the opportunity to present a lengthy prepared statement, which is not always the case. On the other hand, *New Jersey v. T.L.O.* had many questions and answers from the very beginning. Some of the arguments have more detailed discussions of the law than others, some more detailed discussions of the facts.

A summary of the final decision in each case precedes the argument. Where it may be helpful for your understanding of the argument, summaries of major precedents appear in footnotes.

MIRANDA v. ARIZONA

384 U.S. 436 (1966)

Here is the oral argument on behalf of the petitioner, Ernesto A. Miranda, the defendant in a criminal prosecution for rape and kidnapping. In this case and two companion cases, the prosecution introduced statements obtained during incommunicado interrogation in a police-dominated atmosphere without full warning of constitutional rights. The Supreme Court held that the statements were inadmissible, because the police obtained them in violation of the fifth amendment privilege against self-incrimination. This landmark decision established the necessity for police to give complete "Miranda warnings" to in-custody suspects in criminal cases.

PROCEEDING

THE CHIEF JUSTICE: No 759, Ernesto A. Miranda, Petitioner, versus Arizona. Mr. Flynn, you may proceed.

MR. JOHN J. FLYNN

ON BEHALF OF THE PETITIONER

MR. FLYNN: Chief Justice, may it please the Court, this case concerns itself with the conviction of a defendant of two crimes of rape and kidnapping. The sentences on each count of 20 to 30 years are to run concurrently.

I should point out to the Court in an effort to avoid possible confusion that the defendant was convicted in a companion case of the crime of robbery in a completely separate and independent act; however, the Supreme Court of the State of Arizona treated that conviction as a companion case and a companion decision, and portion of that record have been appended to the record in this case, as it bears on the issue before the Court.

The issue before the Court is the admission into evidence of the defendant's confession under the facts and circumstances of this case, over the specific objections of the Trial Counsel that it had been given in the absence of counsel.

The Trial Court in June of 1963, prior to this Court's decision in Escobedo,[1] allowed the confession into evidence. The Supreme Court of the State of Arizona in April of 1965, after this Court's decision in Escobedo,

---

[1] In Escobedo v. State of Illinois, 378 U.S. 478 (1964), the Supreme Court reviewed a case in which a police investigation was no longer a general inquiry into an unsolved crime but had begun to focus on a particular suspect in police custody. The police refused him the opportunity to consult with counsel and did not warn him of the constitutional right to remain silent. The Court held that the police had denied the accused the right to counsel in violation of the sixth and fourteenth amendments, and his statements therefore were inadmissible.

affirmed the conviction and the admission of the confession into evidence. This Court has granted us review.

The facts in the case indicate the defendant in the case a 23-year-old, Spanish-American extract, that on the morning of March 13, 1963, he was arrested at his home, taken down to the police station by two officers named Young and Cooley, that at the police station he was immediately placed in a line-up.

He was there identified by the prosecutrix in this case and later identified by the prosecutrix in the robbery case. Immediately after the interrogation, he was taken into the police confessional at, approximately, 11:30 a.m.; by 1:30, they had obtained from him an oral confession.

MR. JUSTICE BRENNAN: What is the police confessional?

MR. FLYNN: The interrogation described in the transcript is interrogation No. 2, if Your Honor please.

He denied his guilt, according to the officers, at the commencement of the interrogation, and by 1:30 confessed. I believe the record indicates that at no time during the interrogation and prior to his oral confession, was he advised either of his rights to remain silent, his right to counsel or his right to consult with counsel, or, indeed, such was the practice in Arizona at that time admitted by the officers in their testimony.

The defendant was then asked to sign a confession to which he agreed. The form handed to him to write on contained a typed statement, as follows, which precedes his handwritten confession:

> "I, Ernesto A. Miranda, do hereby swear that I make this statement voluntarily and of my own free will, with no threats, coercion or promises of immunity and with full knowledge of my own free will, with no threats, coercion or promises of immunity with full knowledge of my legal rights, understanding any statement I make may be used against me."

This statement was read in to him by the officers, and he confessed in his own handwriting. Throughout the interrogation the defendant did not request counsel at any time. In due course the Trial court appointed counsel to defend him in both cases, and defense counsel requested a psychiatric examination, which has been made—and the medical report—has been made a portion of the transcript of the record in this, as it enlightens us to the portion or some of the factual information surrounding the defendant.

MR. JUSTICE FORTAS: I am sorry to interrupt you, Mr. Flynn. You said that Miranda was not told that he might remain silent. Did you say that?

MR. FLYNN: That is correct.

MR. JUSTICE FORTAS: Is there a dispute as to that?

MR. FLYNN: Yes, there is, Your Honor. I believe it arises as a result of the appendix to the robbery conviction. To this respect, I would answer Your Honor's question by referring to page 52 of the petitioner's brief and to the appendix at the top, at which the question was asked by Mr. Moore, the Trial Counsel, "Did you say to the defendant at any time before he made the statement you are about to answer to, that anything he said would be held against him?"

The answer: "No Sir."

Question: "You didn't warn him of that?"

Answer: "No, Sir."

Question: "Did you warn him of his rights to an attorney?"

Answer: "No, Sir."

"Mr. Moore: We object, not voluntarily given."

"Mr. Turoff: I don't believe that is necessary."

"The Court: Overruled."

On page 53, the succeeding page, a portion of the same record indicates further examination concerning this conversation, starting, approximately, one-third down the page:

Question: "Had you offered the defendant any immunity?"

Answer: "No, Sir."

Question: "In your presence, had Officer Cooley done any of these acts?"

Answer: "No, Sir."

Question: "About what time did this conversation take place, Officer?"

Answer: "Approximately, 1:30."

Question: "Shortly after Miss McDaniels made her first statement, is that correct?"

Answer: "Yes, sir."

Question: "Can you tell us now, Officer, regarding the charge of robbery, what was said to the defendant and what the defendant answered in your presence?"

Answer: "I asked Mr. Miranda if he recognized . . ."

and there the questioning terminates.

MR. JUSTICE FORTAS: I was referring to page four of your brief in which you say that Officer Young believes that Miranda was told that he need not answer their questions.

MR. FLYNN: I was about to continue, if Your Honor please, to page 54 in which we find the question:

"You never warned him he was entitled to an attorney nor anything he said would be held against him, did you?"

Answer: "We told him anything he said would be used against him, he wasn't required by law to tell us anything."

Consequently, this would answer Your Honor's question, except bearing in mind that the record clearly reveals that from the line-up and the identification to the interrogation room, the officers established the time as 11:30, and that the confession was completed and signed at 1:30.

Reading the testimony of the robbery conviction, it is apparent to me that the officers, when they recite or when they answered on page 54 of the transcript that he had been advised of his rights, were again relating to this formal typed heading, which would be at 1:30, the time he signed a confession; that, hence, there really is no conflict in the record as to when he was advised of his rights.

The further history relating to this defendant found in the psychiatric examination would indicate that he had an 8th-grade education and was found by the Supreme Court that he had a prior criminal record and was mentally abnormal. He was found, however, to be competent to stand trial and legally sane at the time of the commission of the alleged acts.

Now, the critical aspect of the defendant's confession, I think, is eminently demonstrated when during the trial the prosecutrix was asked the question concerning penetration, in which she first responded that she thought it was by finger, under questioning by the prosecuting attorney.

Immediately thereafter, she expressed uncertainty as to the manner or method of penetration, and, after some prompting, responded to the prosecuting attorney that it had been, in fact, by the male organ.

On cross examination, she again expressed the uncertainty in relation to this penetration, which, of course, is the essential element of the crime of first-degree rape in the State of Arizona. She responded to his question that she simply was unsure whether it had been by finger or by penis. Of course, the defendant's confession neatly corrects this account, which otherwise would have been engendered.

In precise terminology, the defendant wrote, "Asked her to lie down, and she did. Could not get penis into vagina. Got about one-half—parenthesis and then one-half inch written—in."

The only thing missing, or the only thing that the officers failed to supply in words to this defendant at the time he wrote this confession was in violation of Section 13-611 Arizona Revised Statutes. Then, of course, they would have had the classic confession of conviction, because they could have argued that the man knew the statutory provision relating to rape.

The State, as I read their response, take no issue with the facts outlined to this Court, except to say we offer to State his mental condition and minimized his educational background, and, also, the concern that is expressed by Mr. Justice Fortas concerning at what state of proceeding he may have been advised of his right to remain silent.

The Petitioner's position on the issue is simply this: The Arizona Supreme Court, we feel, has imprisoned this Court's decision in Escobedo on its facts and by its decision is refusing to apply the principals of that case and for all practical purposes has emasculated it. Certainly, every court desiring to admit a confession can find distinguishing factors in Escobedo from the fact situation before it.

I would like to, very briefly, quote from the transcript of the record which contains the Arizona decision at page 87. It will be noted that the court in Escobedo Case set forth the circumstances under which a statement would be held as admissible, namely, one, the general inquiry into an unsolved crime must have begun to focus on a particular suspect.

Two, a suspect must have been taken into the police custody; three, the police in its interrogation must have elicited an incriminating statement; four, the suspect must have requested and been denied an opportunity to consult with his lawyer.

Five, the police must not have effectively warned the suspect of his Constitutional rights to remain silent.

When all of these five factors occurred, then the Escobedo Case is a controlling precedent. The Arizona Supreme Court, having indicated its clear intention to imprison the Escobedo decision, set about to do precisely that.

First, as to the focusing question, it indicated that this crime had occurred at night. Consequently, despite the positive identification by the defendant by two witnesses, which the State urged were entirely fair line-ups, the Supreme Court of Arizona indicated that even then perhaps under those facts, the attention had not focused upon this defendant.

I think this is sheer sophistry and would indicate the obvious intent of the Arizona Supreme Court to confine Escobedo and distinguish it whenever possible.

Next, the Court found the defendant was advised of his rights from the reading of the typed portion immediately preceding the transcript. It permitted that document to lift itself by its own bootstraps, so to speak, and indicate here was a man who was knowledgeable concerning his legal rights, despite the facts and circumstances of his background and education.

They further found that he was knowledgeable, because he had a prior criminal record, though in the decision he indicated this would be knowledge of his rights in court and certainly not his rights at the time of the interrogation.

(Matthew Bender & Co., Inc.)

I think the numerous briefs filed in this case indicating the substantial split in the decisions throughout the various states, the circuits and the Federal District Courts, indicate the interpretation that has been placed upon Escobedo.

On the one hand, we have the California decision in Dorado. We have the Third Circuit decision in Russo, which would indicate the principal and logic are being applied to the decision, and in the words of Mr. Justice Goldberg, that, "when the process shifts from the investigation to one of accusation, and when the purpose is to elicit a confession from the defendant, then the adversary process comes into being."

On the other hand, the other cases that would distinguish this have found and give rise to what I submit is not really confusion by merely straining against the principle and logic in this decision.

MR. JUSTICE STEWART: What do you think is the result of the adversary process coming into being when this focusing takes place? What follows from that? Is there then a right to a lawyer?

MR. FLYNN: I think the man at that time has the right to exercise, if he knows, and under the present state of the law in Arizona, if he is rich enough and educated enough to assert his 5th Amendment right, and if he recognizes that he has a 5th Amendment right, to request counsel, I simply say that stage of the proceeding, under the facts and circumstances in Miranda of a man of limited education, of a man who certainly is mentally abnormal, who is, certainly, an indigent, that when that adversary process came into being, that the police at the very least had an obligation to extend to this man, not only his clear 5th Amendment right, but to accord him the right of counsel.

MR. JUSTICE STEWART: I suppose if you really mean what you say, or from what you gather from what the Escobedo decision says, the adversary process starts at that point and every single protection of the Constitution comes into being, does it not, and I suppose you would have to bring a jury in there?

MR. FLYNN: No, Your Honor, I wouldn't bring a jury in. I simply would extend to that man those Constitutional rights that the police took away from him.

MR. JUSTICE STEWART: That isn't the question. My question is what are those rights when the focusing begins? Are these all the canopy of rights guaranteed to the defendant in a trial?

MR. FLYNN: I think the first right is the 5th Amendment right, the right not to incriminate oneself, the right to know you have that right and the right to consult with counsel, at the very least, in order that you can exercise the right, Your Honor.

MR. JUSTICE STEWART: I don't fully understand the answer, because, if the adversary process then begins, then what you have is the equivalent of a trial, is it not, and then, I suppose, you have a right to judge and a jury and everything else that goes with a trial right then and there. If you have something less than that, then this is not an adversary proceeding, and you don't mean what you are saying.

MR. FLYNN: I think what I say, when I am interpreting adversary proceeding, is that it means that at times a person who is poorly-educated, who in essence is mentally abnormal, who is an indigent, at an adversary proceeding, he is at the very least entitled at that stage of the proceeding to be represented by counsel and to be advised by counsel of his rights under 5th Amendment of the Constitution, or he has no such right.

MR. JUSTICE STEWART: Again, I don't mean to quibble and I apologize, but I think it is first important to define what his rights under the Constitution are at that point, that he can't be advised of his rights, unless somebody knows what those rights are.

MR. FLYNN: That is precisely my point, and the only person that can adequately advise a person like Ernesto Miranda is a lawyer.

MR. JUSTICE STEWART: What would a lawyer advise him that his rights then were?

MR. FLYNN: That he had a right not to incriminate himself, that he had a right to be free from further questioning by the police department, that he had the right at the ultimate time to be represented adequately by counsel, and that if he was too indigent or too poor to employ counsel, the state would furnish him counsel.

MR. JUSTICE STEWART: What is it that confers the right to a lawyer's advice at that point and not an earlier point? Would it be the 6th Amendment?

MR. FLYNN: No. The attempt to erode or take away from him the 5th Amendment right that already existed, and that was the right not to convict himself.

MR. JUSTICE STEWART: Didn't he have that right earlier?

MR. FLYNN: If he knew about it.

MR. JUSTICE STEWART: Before this became an adversary proceeding.

MR. FLYNN: Yes, Your Honor, if he knew about it, and if he was aware — if he was knowledgeable.

MR. JUSTICE STEWART: Did he have the right to a lawyer's advice earlier?

MR. FLYNN: If he could afford it, yes, and if he was intelligent and strong enough to stand up against police interrogation and request it, yes.

MR. JUSTICE STEWART: I don't understand the magic of this phrase of focusing that all of a sudden it becomes an adversary proceeding, and I suppose you, literally, mean that if it becomes an adversary proceeding, the defendant is entitled to all the rights under the Constitution that would be given in a criminal trial. If you mean less than that, then you do not mean it is the equivalent of a trial.

MR. FLYNN: I simply mean that when it becomes an adversary proceeding, a person in Ernesto Miranda's position needs the advice of counsel, and if he is barred from his rights, then there is no due process of law being afforded a man in Ernesto Miranda's position.

MR. JUSTICE FORTAS: Is it possible that prior to this so-called focusing or say prior to arrest, and I know to you fellows it does not always mean the same thing, that a citizen has an obligation to cooperate with the state, give the state information that he might have relevant to a crime; that upon arrest or this focusing, the state or the individual then assumes the role of adversary, and there is at least a change in that relationship between the individual and the state, and, therefore, in their mutual rights and responsibilities. I don't know whether that is what my Brother Stewart is getting at, and perhaps it is unfair to discuss this through you.

(Laughter)

MR. FLYNN: I think the only comment that I can make is that, without getting ourselves into the area of where precisely focusing begins, that I must in this instance limit the facts and situations in the Ernesto Miranda Case, because for every practical purpose, after the two-hour interrogation, the mere formality of supplying counsel to Ernesto Miranda at the time of trial in what I would submit would be nothing more than a mockery of his 6th Amendment right to be represented in court or formality at the time the trying takes place.

This simply is not a matter of record. It is in the robbery trial, and I think it so illustrates the position of what occurred in the case of persons who have confessed, as Ernest Miranda.

The question was asked in the robbery trial, which preceded the rape trial by one day:

"The Court: Mr. Moore, are you ready to go to trial?"

Mr. Moore: "I have been ready. I haven't anything to do but, for my man, but sit down and listen."

MR. JUSTICE BLACK: May I ask you one question? In reference to this 5th Amendment, let's forget it. The amendment advised that no defendant should be compelled to be a witness against himself. **(Inaudible)**

He said several times in determining whether or not the witness in question would be compelled to be a witness against himself, that in this his lack of wealth, his standing or his lack of standing — what does that have anything to do with it? Does the amendment not protect the rich and the poor or anyone?

MR. FLYNN: I would say that it certainly and most assuredly does protect, that the state of law today, as announced by the Arizona Supreme Court under those guiding principals certainly does protect the rich, the educated and the strong, those rich enough to hire counsel, those who are educated enough to know what the rights are, those strong enough to withstand police interrogation and assert those rights.

MR. JUSTICE BLACK: I am asking you only about the 5th Amendment provision that no person will be compelled to be a witness against himself. Does that protect every person, or just some persons? I am not talking about in practical effect. I am talking about what the amendment is supposed to do.

MR. FLYNN: It protects all persons.

MR. JUSTICE BLACK: Can the police compel him to testify? Does that have anything to do with it?

MR. FLYNN: At the interrogation stage, if he is too ignorant to know that he has the 5th Amendment right, then certainly that has something to do with it, Your Honor. If the man at the time of the interrogation knows nothing about the 5th Amendment, knows nothing of its concept or nothing of his rights, then, certainly, his literacy—.

MR. JUSTICE BLACK: (Interrupting) He would have more rights than an intelligent man, more than just the 5th Amendment right alone, not to be compelled to be a witness against himself?

MR. FLYNN: Perhaps I have not expressed myself clearly.

MR. JUSTICE BLACK: Who does that cover?

MR. FLYNN: It covers everybody, Your Honor. Clearly in practical application, in view of the interrogation and the facts and circumstances of Miranda, it simply had no application because of the facts and circumstances in that particular case and that is what I am attempting to express to the Court.

Now, the Arizona Supreme Court went on, in essence, we submit, and turned in its decision primarily on the failure of the defendant in this case to request counsel, which is the only really distinguishing factor that they could find.

MR. JUSTICE STEWART: Is there any claim in this case that this confession was compelled or was involuntarily taken?

MR. FLYNN: None at all, Your Honor.

MR. JUSTICE WHITE: Do you mean that there is no question he was not compelled to give evidence against himself?

MR. FLYNN: We have raised no question that he was compelled to give this statement in the sense that anyone forced him to do it by coercion, by threats, by promises or compulsion of that kind.

MR. JUSTICE WHITE: Of that kind. Was it voluntary or wasn't it?

MR. FLYNN: Voluntary in the sense that the man at a time without knowledge of his rights —.

MR. JUSTICE WHITE: (Interrupting) You claim his 5th Amendment rights were violated?

MR. FLYNN: I would say his 5th Amendment rights were violated.

MR. JUSTICE WHITE: Because he was compelled to do it?

MR. FLYNN: Because he was compelled to do it.

MR. JUSTICE WHITE: That is what the Amendment says.

MR. FLYNN: No. 1, because he was compelled; two, he was mentally incompetent to exercise his judgement and mentally—.

MR. JUSTICE WHITE: (Interrupting) You say he was compelled?

MR. FLYNN: I say it was taken from him at a point in time when he should have been afforded the 6th—.

MR. JUSTICE WHITE: (Interrupting) I am not arguing the amendment. To violate the amendment, you have to be compelled to do it.

MR. FLYNN: In the sense that Your Honor is using the word compelled, Your Honor is correct.

MR. JUSTICE WHITE: I was talking about the Constitution and if he was compelled to do it.

MR. JUSTICE BLACK: That doesn't mean that he has to have a gun pointed at his head.

MR. JUSTICE WHITE: Of course, he doesn't. He was compelled to do it. Isn't that right, according to your complaint?

MR. FLYNN: Not by gunpoint, as Mr. Justice Black has indicated. He was called upon to surrender a right that he didn't really appreciate that he had.

MR. JUSTICE WHITE: I understand the circumstances. I just want to find out if you claim that his 5th Amendment rights were being violated. If they were, it must be because he was compelled to do it under all circumstances.

MR. FLYNN: I would say that it was because of lack of knowledge, or, for lack of a better term, failure to advise, denial of the right to counsel, failure in the proceeding when he most certainly needed it.

MR. JUSTICE BLACK: Control and custody—why would that not tend to show some kind of coercion?

MR. FLYNN: The whole process of someone being raised and told to tell the truth and respect authority.

MR. JUSTICE BLACK: Was he allowed to get away after that, at will?

MR. FLYNN: No, Your Honor. He was confined under arrest.

MR. JUSTICE BLACK: The state moved against him by taking him into custody, did it not?

MR. FLYNN: That is correct.

THE CHIEF JUSTICE: I suppose you would say, Mr. Flynn, if the police had said to this young man, "Now, you are a nice young man, and we don't want to hurt you, and so on and so forth. We are your friends, and if you will just tell us how you committed this crime, we will let you go home, and we won't prosecute you," that would be a violation of the 5th Amendment and that, technically speaking, would not be compelling him to do it. It would be an inducement, would it not?

MR. FLYNN: That is right.

THE CHIEF JUSTICE: I suppose you would argue that is still within the 5th Amendment, wouldn't you?

MR. FLYNN: It is an abdication of the 5th Amendment, right.

THE CHIEF JUSTICE: That is what I mean.

MR. FLYNN: Because of the total circumstances existing at the time, the arrest, the custody, the lack of knowledge, the statutes—.

THE CHIEF JUSTICE: (Interrupting) The indication of that kind of a confession, where it would be better for you and so forth?

MR. FLYNN: That, of course, is an implied promise of some help or immunity.

THE CHIEF JUSTICE: That is not compulsion in the sense of the word as Mr. Justice White has implied it.

MR. JUSTICE BLACK: As I recall, in those cases there were, or those cases that were on the 5th Amendment—(Inaudible).

In the words of the 5th Amendment conferred in the early case by Justice White the fact that inducement is a compulsion and must be thought of in that category, therefore, violated the amendment of not being compelled to give evidence against yourself.

(Matthew Bender & Co., Inc.)

MR. FLYNN: I am sure Mr. Justice Black is far better than I—.

MR. JUSTICE BLACK: (Interrupting) But it does not begin, I suppose on the wealth, the standing or the status of the person so far as the right.

MR. FLYNN: I think that perhaps I used a bad choice of words, if Your Honor please, in the context. It is my mistake.

I would like to state in conclusion that the Constitution of the State of Arizona, for example, has in statehood provided to the citizens of our state in language precisely the same as the 4th Amendment to the Federal Constitution as it pertains to searches and seizures, yet, from 1914 until this court's decision in Mapp v. Ohio, we simply did not enjoy the 4th Amendment right or the scope of the 4th Amendment rights that were enjoyed by most of the other citizens of the other states of this union, and those persons were under Federal control.

In response to the Amicus from New York and the Amicus from the National Association of Defense Attorneys that would ask this Court to go slowly and to give the opportunity to the states, to the legislature, to the courts and to the Bar Association to undertake to solve this problem, I simply say that whatever the solutions may be, it would be another 46 years before the 5th Amendment right in the scope that it was intended, I submit, by this Court in Escobedo, will reach the State of Arizona.

We are one of the most modern states in relation to the adoption of the American Law Institute rules. We have a comparable rule to Rule 5. To my knowledge, there has never been a criminal prosecution for failure to arraign a man, and there is no decision in Arizona that would even come close to the McNabb or Mallory Rule in Arizona.

In fact, the same term that Miranda was decided, the Arizona Supreme Court indicated that, despite the necessity and requirement of the immediate arraignment before the nearest and most successful magistrate, that Mallory v. McNabb did not apply in Arizona.

NEW JERSEY v. T.L.O.

469 U.S. 325 (1985)

Here are the oral arguments of both the petitioner, New Jersey, and the respondent, a juvenile. Chapter 14 of this book also includes the facts of this case. A New Jersey assistant vice principal of a high school searched a student's purse and found cigarettes, marijuana, and marijuana paraphernalia. The state later brought delinquency charges against the respondent before the juvenile court, which held that the Fourth Amendment applied to searches by school officials but that the search in question was reasonable.

Ultimately, the United States Supreme Court held that the Fourth Amendment's prohibition on unreasonable searches and seizures applies to searches by public school officials and that school officials act as representatives of the state, not merely as surrogates for parents of students. In addition, school children have legitimate expectations of privacy and do not waive them by bringing items onto school property. School officials, however, need not obtain a warrant before searching a student, and the legality of a search depends on the reasonableness of the search. The Court held that the search in this case was reasonable.

PROCEEDINGS

CHIEF JUSTICE BURGER: We will hear arguments first this morning in New Jersey against T.I.O.

Mr. Nodes, you may proceed whenever you are ready.

ORAL ARGUMENT OF ALLAN J. NODES, ESQ.,

ON BEHALF OF THE PETITIONER

MR. NODES: Mr. Chief Justice, and may it please the Court, last term the State of New Jersey argued before this Court that the Fourth Amendment exclusionary rule should be held inapplicable to school searches conducted by school teachers and school administrators.

Following argument, this Court requested additional briefing and argument on the issue of whether under the facts and circumstances of this particular case the vice principal's search of the student's purse violated the Fourth Amendment at all.

We suggest that there was no constitutional violation in this case. We argue firstly that the Fourth Amendment should be held inapplicable to school searches. That amendment was intended as a deterrent to law enforcement officers and police officers, and was not intended to be used against private citizens or against those who act in loco parentis.

We believe that school teachers do act in loco parentis. I will address the in loco parentis functions of school teachers later in my argument, and I would refer to my brief for the remainder of the argument concerning the applicability of the Fourth Amendment.

We would also urge that —

QUESTION: You mean of the exclusionary rule, don't you?

MR. NODES: I beg your pardon?

QUESTION: You mean of the exclusionary rule?

MR. NODES: Of the exclusionary rule or the Fourth Amendment. We would rely on the briefs for the exclusionary rule and for the application of the Fourth Amendment. I would like to argue the standard to be applied assuming that the Fourth Amendment is held to be applicable to school searches.

And we believe that the standard which should be applied to school searches should be lower than probable cause, and in fact should be a standard of reasonable suspicion.

QUESTION: Mr. Nodes, assuming the applicability of the Fourth Amendment, do you think that on this record there was probable cause for the search?

MR. NODES: Yes, I do, Your Honor. I believe that what we had in this case was an instance where a person who was very, very reputable witnessed an action which was a violation of a school regulation. He reported this violation to another person, who is also reputable.

Now, what he said was, he saw a cigarette in a person's hand, and I believe that it is pure common sense to believe that when one sees a cigarette in a person's hand, that that person will also be carrying cigarettes in a pack somewhere on their person. So, I —

QUESTION: Or, that the person is holding it in the hand because they intend to smoke it or are smoking it? Because they are going to some it?

MR. NODES: Yes. The fact that they have the cigarette indicates firstly that they are smoking it, secondly, that they have cigarettes, and I believe that that is all the vice principal actually needed in this case.

QUESTION: Well, Mr. Nodes, assuming again the applicability of the Fourth Amendment, if you are right that there was probable cause shown here, why should we address the question whether something less would satisfy?

MR. NODES: Well, I believe for two reasons. Firstly, I don't believe that it is settled that probable cause should be the standard to which school teachers should be held. In this case, of course, the New Jersey Supreme Court found that there wasn't probable cause and there wasn't even reasonable suspicion, even though we argued all along that probable cause was present.

The mere fact that we have met the highest possible standard, or that we argue that we have met the highest possible standard which could be enunciated does not mean that this Court could not set forth the appropriate standard for lower courts to follow in future cases.

I believe that —

QUESTION: Or that this Court could disagree with you that there was probable cause in this particular case.

MR. NODES: Very clearly this Court could disagree with that, and then it would be necessary to determine what lower standard would apply and whether or not we had met that lower standard.

QUESTION: What was the rule of the school? It was no smoking, right?

MR. NODES: There were school rules that there was no smoking in certain areas. T.L.O. —

QUESTION: And she was smoking in that area?

MR. NODES: Yes, that is correct.

QUESTION: Isn't that the end of the case? Why do you have to go and search?

MR. NODES: Well, I think that, Your Honor, the reason why we did go and search, and it may very well be that we did not have to go and search, but the reason that we did go and search was that the principal was trying to be fair to the student. Rather than merely accepting the word of the teacher who said, I saw two students smoking, he had a —

QUESTION: Well, suppose that the teacher reported that the child had cursed. Would that be enough? You wouldn't have to get additional proof for it, would you?

MR. NODES: No, I don't believe that it would be necessary to get additional proof.

QUESTION: Why do you need extra proof here?

MR. NODES: I don't believe that we had —

QUESTION: Well, didn't she deny it?

MR. NODES: I do not believe we had to have additional proof here. That does not mean that it is wrong for us to obtain additional proof.

QUESTION: Well, I am just raising the question. Is it necessary to violate somebody's rights in order to add on to the necessary ingredients for conviction?

MR. NODES: No, we would not advocate violating somebody's rights in order to add additional evidence.

QUESTION: I can understand — you didn't need to search to get the — I don't mean conviction, the action of the school board. You didn't need the search.

MR. NODES: We could have — the vice principal could have disciplined T.L.O. without the search. I do not agree that we had to violate somebody's rights in order to get additional evidence. I believe that the vice principal was able to get the additional evidence with absolutely no violation of the person's rights.

What the vice principal ended up doing was listening to what the student had to say. The student presented a defense. The vice principal talked to the student, and asked the student what the student had to say for herself. Under Goss v. Lopez, this was the proper standard.

I believe that it is appropriate, not mandatory, but appropriate then —

QUESTION: What is the defense to — because she wasn't smoking?

MR. NODES: The defense was a total denial of smoking, and the additional element —

QUESTION: Did she say that?

MR. NODES: — that she couldn't have been smoking then because she never smoked at all. And I believe that by demonstrating whether or not this person smoked, the vice principal had a much better idea of whether or not she was smoking on that particular occasion.

Yes, the vice principal could have said to T.L.O., "T.L.O., I am going to believe the teacher, who is totally credible, and I am going to assume without checking anything that you are lying to me." I think the vice principal tried to act more reasonably than that.

I think the vice principal tried to ensure that the school regulations were followed, but at the same time was also trying to ensure that a possibly innocent person wasn't punished. And I think that an action of that type should be condoned rather than criticized.

QUESTION: All I can say is, schools are different from when — when I went to school, if a teacher said something, the vice principal believed the teacher and not the student.

(General laughter.)

QUESTION: That was when I went to school.

MR. NODES: That could very well be the case. (General laughter.)

MR. NODES: Your Honor, I would suggest also when I went to school searches were allowed much more easily.

QUESTION: I never got one hearing the whole time I was in school.

MR. NODES: But this Court has now decreed that in certain circumstances there will be at least limited hearings, and I think that this is what the vice principal followed. He did give a limited hearing before imposing discipline, and he didn't just give a pro forma hearing and at the end of the hearing say, okay, now I am going to ignore what you said.

He checked what the juvenile had said, and he checked what the juvenile said, in an extremely reasonable manner, because we believe that at the very least he had a reasonable suspicion that an infraction had occurred, and that evidence of the infraction —

QUESTION: May I ask you, in the prior argument you seemed to accept the standard that the New Jersey Supreme Court laid down. I am not sure whether you still do or not.

MR. NODES: The standard reasonable suspicion, the name reasonable suspicion is —

QUESTION: That is not my question.

MR. NODES: Yes, we —

QUESTION: My question can be answered yes or no.

MR. NODES: Do I accept the standard —

QUESTION: That they laid down.

MR. NODES: No, I do not.

QUESTION: I didn't think — you have changed your position, haven't you?

MR. NODES: I think that that is a proper interpretation. I believe that the name reasonable interpretation is an appropriate name for a standard.

QUESTION: But the question, I suppose, is reasonable suspicion of what, and in your view I gather it is a suspicion of any violation of any school regulation would justify a search, whereas they say it has to be suspicion of a crime or of something, a major disorder. Is that right?

MR. NODES: No. I believe that they said crime or violation of school disciplinary regulations.

QUESTION: Would seriously interfere with school discipline or order.

MR. NODES: Yes, I don't think that first of all it would have to be a serious infringement, and I don't think —

QUESTION: So you disagree with that part.

MR. NODES: So I disagree with that part, but more than that, I disagree with their application of the announced standard to this case.

QUESTION: I understand, but you also do disagree with their standard. You would take the view, I take it, that if there was reasonable suspicion that the purse contained, say, a note or a diary or something that would disclose a violation of any rule, the rule requiring students to be on time for athletic games or something like that, they could still search?

MR. NODES: I think that you have to evaluate the need for the evidence and whether or not —

QUESTION: Well, the purpose is exactly the same, to find out if there is evidence of infraction of a school regulation that does not involve harm, physical harm or anything like that, just the child may have been late to school. Could they search to determine that?

MR. NODES: Yes, I believe that they could, provided that student is carrying that diary and that information with them. I believe that that would be constitutionally permissible.

QUESTION: Mr. Nodes, would you believe that if a reasonable suspicion standard is applied, that it would have justified a strip search of the pupil in this case?

MR. NODES: I believe that when we are dealing with what we are classifying generally as school searches, we are talking about searches which would normally be made for violations of school regulations and school disciplines rather than law enforcement searches.

QUESTION: What standard do we apply to determine the validity of the search, assuming one is authorized? How far can you go in the search?

MR. NODES: I believe that a search of, for instance, lockers, items which a person carries into school, or searches of clothing or pockets would be within the normal area which a teacher under the normal functions of a teacher could search. I believe —

QUESTION: Do you think then that a male teacher could conduct a pat-down search of a young woman student at age 16 to find the cigarettes?

MR. NODES: I believe that that would be constitutionally permissible. I would note that as in the area with airplane searches and with most police searches, if it can be avoided, that simply is not done. I don't expect that that is something which would occur.

Now, if that does occur, if there is a pat-down of a female by a male teacher or administrator, or if there is a strip search, and that search is for anything except a constitutionally permissible purpose, if there is any evidence of harassment or anything of that type, of course, other actions can be brought, the same as they could against —

QUESTION: Well, do you concede that there would be a further requirement in any event that the extent of the search itself would have to be reasonable under the circumstances considering the age and sex of the child and the circumstances?

MR. NODES: Yes, I would agree with that. I would agree that we are not advocating strip searches of students to find out whether or not they have been smoking cigarettes, and I don't think that that is what is normally held to be a school search, and in fact I believe that there are the laws, the regulations, and possibly other parts of the Constitution —

QUESTION: Well, I am more concerned with your view of what the Constitution requires rather than your view of what is normally done in the school scene.

MR. NODES: I believe that the extent of the search could become part of the standard, and while it might be reasonable to search a person's pockets, search a person's jacket, the person's locker, or person's purse for a certain item, it would not in may instances, possibly the same circumstances, be permissible to strip search the student.

I think it would almost never be permissible.

QUESTION: If the school official suspected the commission of a crime and called a policeman to the scene, would the policeman conducting a search at the school have a higher standard in any event, in your view?

MR. NODES: I believe when it becomes a police search —

QUESTION: Probable cause?

MR. NODES: — yes, a higher standard, possibly probable cause, depending on the circumstances, would apply.

QUESTION: Is there any regulation against the possession of cigarettes?

MR. NODES: In this particular case, there was no regulation in this school against the possession of cigarettes. It was permissible for the student to possess cigarettes. The search which —

QUESTION: Are you going to get to the question of whether there is a difference between people on the street and students in the school?

MR. NODES: I am not sure I fully understand Your Honor's question.

QUESTION: The difference between a man or a woman walking on the street, downtown Washington, and a student, a minor, in a school.

MR. NODES: Well, I believe that there are many differences between a person on the street — I believe that first of all there may be a difference between a minor on a street carrying a purse —

QUESTION: Well, we don't have to worry about a minor on the street. We are worrying about a minor in the school here, and the comparison I am surprised you haven't made in your analysis is that there is a difference between a student who has been sent to school by the parents and is required by law to go to school in the school quarters and a person walking on the street, an adult.

MR. NODES: Well, I believe that when a student is sent to school, of course, the school and the state takes on a responsibility for ensuring not only that that student is educated, but also that that student is safe and secure while in school, and that discipline is maintained while in school.

QUESTION: Well, Mr. Nodes, you think there is such a difference that the Fourth Amendment shouldn't apply at all?

MR. NODES: I believe —

QUESTION: That was your first submission.

MR. NODES: Yes, I believe that there is such a significant difference in the function performed by the school teacher during the school day that the Fourth Amendment shouldn't apply. However, the same arguments would also be applicable concerning a reduced standard.

QUESTION: Right.

MR. NODES: The teacher does act in an in loco parentis manner during the school day. Now, it is possible that since the advent of mandatory compulsory education up until a certain age, that the traditional Blackstonian views and reasons for imposing the in loco parentis doctrine would no longer apply.

However, when we look at what is happening in fact, it is clear that as far as the supervision of juveniles, the teacher acts in loco parentis. Firstly, the student spends as much as a third of his or her day attending a public school. During that period, the teachers and administrators provide the only supervision which that juvenile, that student has, and in many ways they take the place of and perform the functions of parents.

QUESTION: That's correct.

QUESTION: And does that mean that their authority then to make searches, if the Fourth Amendment is completely inapplicable, extends to any kind of search, strip search or otherwise?

MR. NODES: I believe that if the Fourth Amendment is inapplicable, of course, the Fourth Amendment would not itself forbid strip searches. However, I think that strip searches are such an egregious example, and the courts, the Circuit Courts have continuously held this, that there could quite possibly be another constitutional violation.

QUESTION: What one?

MR. NODES: It is possible that under <u>Roshen</u>, for instance, this would be considered such an invasion of the person's privacy, and such an unwarranted invasion that it would be constitutionally impermissible. However, I think that even that, it would not be necessary to use that.

I believe that strip searches can be stopped very easily without the Constitution, and I might note that in many of the strip search cases there has been either a finding of no constitutional violation or there has been no punishment of the violators. I believe primarily the cases say no punishment of the violators because of the circumstances.

But for two reasons, those searches will be stopped. First of all, I believe that in all states people are becoming more sensitive to strip searches whether they are conducted by law enforcement authorities or by other persons, and there are laws now which limit even the authority of a police officer to conduct a strip search.

However, maybe even more importantly, the factors which were noted in <u>Ingraham v. Wright</u> by this Court —

QUESTION: Well, if I understand your argument, though, Mr. Nodes, it is that because the Fourth Amendment is inapplicable, nothing in the Fourth Amendment can restrain a strip search of a student by a teacher?

MR. NODES: I believe that that would be correct, yes.

QUESTION: What is the basis for that argument? You are saying they are not unreasonable searches? Is that what it is? In terms of the text of the Fourth Amendment.

MR. NODES: As far as the text of the Fourth Amendment, I believe that the Fourth Amendment was directed at the state acting as the state. Now, in certain circumstances I believe that the state can take on a role which is traditionally held by private persons.

QUESTION: So what you are saying is, it is not unreasonable.

MR. NODES: It is not unreasonable —

QUESTION: Even a strip search is not unreasonable.

MR. NODES: Yes. That is not unreasonable. It would not be unreasonable for a private person, and in this instance it is not unreasonable for the state.

QUESTION: Are you saying that the school and the teachers and the authorities stand in the shoes of the parent?

MR. NODES: Yes, at least as far as the supervision and welfare of the student is concerned. The school teachers and administrators ensure that the students arrive at school properly. They ensure that they behave while they are in school. They maintain discipline.

If there is an injury or sickness, the school teacher or school administrator is the first person responsible for taking care of that. In many instances, a parent can't be contacted. The school makes the decision as to whether or not a doctor or a hospital will be called in.

QUESTION: Well, Mr. Nodes, we are dealing here with a public school, are we not?

MR. NODES: Yes, we are.

QUESTION: And there are laws requiring children to attend that school, whether they want to or whether their parents want them to or not. Isn't that so?

MR. NODES: That's correct.

QUESTION: And you contend that this isn't state action then, when the state acting in the school setting conducts a search? Is that your position?

MR. NODES: No, I would not say that there is no statute action involved in this case. What I would say ——

QUESTION: Now, we found state action, I suppose, for occupational and health safety inspections, and for welfare workers, and in other administrative agency searches, have we not?

MR. NODES: Yes, the Court has.

QUESTION: But you think somehow schools are different, even though the law requires the student to be there?

MR. NODES: Yes, I do, and maybe it isn't even though the law requires the student to be there, quite possibly. I believe it is because the law requires the students to be there. The state has intentionally taken on a function which the parent normally exercises. The state does have, obviously, the ultimate parens patriae function, to ensure the welfare of all students.

However, that function is normally taken over by the parent. When the state takes that function back and says for a period of time, and for as much as a third of the student's day, we will take custody of the student, and we will ensure that during this period the student's wellbeing is maintained, in addition to educating the student, then I believe it becomes reasonable for the person who has not only these functions but also these responsibilities to act under different standards than the state would normally act under.

QUESTION: Would that go to a reform school?

MR. NODES: I believe that a reform school —

QUESTION: Are you saying that the Fourth Amendment doesn't apply in the reform school?

MR. NODES: I believe that either my argument that the Fourth Amendment doesn't apply or that a lower standard is required would apply to a reform school, yes.

QUESTION: Why don't you take the position it is not involved in this case?

MR. NODES: I beg your pardon?

QUESTION: Why don't you take the position that the question is not involved in this case? Isn't it that you want the broadest rule you can get?

MR. NODES: No, I am not —

QUESTION: Isn't that what you are up to?

MR. NODES: No, no, I am not asking for the broadest rule I can get. I was attempting to answer —only answer Your Honor's question. I don't believe that that is necessary for this case.

However, I do believe that it is an example of the function which the state takes over. Your Honor used the term reform school. Very often the state takes custody of a juvenile even though the juvenile has done nothing wrong.

In New Jersey we have shelters for juveniles who are in need of supervision, and juveniles placed in these facilities can be there simply because their parents haven't taken care of them, and I believe that that would be similar to the school situation, where the state has taken over part of the function of the parent.

QUESTION: You are arguing the Fourth Amendment issue because the Court directed you to argue it. Is that not so?

MR. NODES: That's correct. We do believe, again, that if the Fourth Amendment does apply, that a standard lower than probable cause is warranted, and I think that although the in loco parentis arguments would also have application here, and although I think it is apparent that students have a lesser expectation of privacy while attending a public school than they would have on the street, I believe that very simply the educational system cannot properly operate if teachers are required to abide by a probable cause standard.

We must have discipline in the schools, and this discipline cannot be maintained by teachers who are encumbered by the same rules and regulations as police officers are.

QUESTION: Mr. Nodes, assume for a moment that the New Jersey court is correct in saying that the Fourth Amendment applied, that a reasonable suspicion standard was the appropriate standard for review.

Do you think that that means individualized suspicion under the New Jersey rule, or would that mean, for example, that if the school authorities suspected there were drugs being used in the restrooms, they could install two way mirrors or listening devices based on a generalized suspicion?

MR. NODES: Your Honor, I think that that probably would be determined by the type of investigation which they were attempting to conduct. I am not sure exactly how far they could go with minor school violations.

QUESTION: Well, I was curious to know what you thought the New Jersey rule was, whether it required individualized suspicion or something else.

MR. NODES: I believe that the New Jersey court was, because of the contours of this case, talking about individualized suspicion, and they simply weren't faced with a standard where a school had to take care of a situation, for instance, where knives were being brought to school every day, and they might have to search students coming into the school to make sure there were no knives being brought in.

That could raise a whole new set of problems, but the New Jersey court didn't have to deal with those questions in this case.

QUESTION: Mr. Nodes, you are not adopting the New Jersey court standard, and I would be interested to know your answer to Justice O'Connor's question. Supposing the school had reasonable suspicion that the restroom was being used to smoke in, as was the case here. Could they put in two-way mirrors?

That you can answer yes or no.

MR. NODES: I believe that they could put in two-way mirrors. I believe other things —

QUESTION: Under your standard, they clearly could.

MR. NODES: Yes, they could. I believe even if the Fourth Amendment applied under the reasonable suspicion standard they could, or they could search students on their way into the restroom.

QUESTION: Why would you need reasonable suspicion of anything under the Fourth Amendment to put two-way mirrors in a restroom? That is — you know, why is that a violation of the Fourth Amendment at all, to do that?

MR. NODES: I am not sure that it would be.

QUESTION: No, I am not either.

QUESTION: You don't think there is any expectation of privacy in a restroom?

(General laughter.)

MR. NODES: There are many —

QUESTION: That is a serious question.

MR. NODES: I understand.

QUESTION: Apparently you don't.

MR. NODES: I understand that, but I would assume that the two-way mirrors would replace the mirrors which would already be up in the men's room, and I assume that that would be the mirrors in front of which you normally stand to comb your hair or make sure that your clothing is appropriate, and things like that.

I don't believe that the more private areas of a men's room are going to have mirrors, two-way or otherwise. So that was the assumption that I was making in my question — I mean, in my answer.

In this case, we believe that the problem with the standard as enunciated by the New Jersey Supreme Court, again, assuming the Fourth Amendment applies, is that the court acted as if it were actually operating under a probable cause standard, and as if it were actually evaluating the actions of a police officer.

The Court first drew a line between a good hunch and a reasonable suspicion. They admitted that there was probably a good hunch, but said that there wasn't a reasonable suspicion.

I believe it is very hard to draw a line of this type, and as I said before, I believe that at the very least there was a reasonable suspicion in this case. However, I think more importantly what the Court should be looking to is a common sense approach to the problems that school teachers face each day while trying to maintain order and discipline in schools.

And I don't believe that if the courts are going to evaluate situations like this with the strictness that they evaluate police officer searches, that it is going to be possible for teachers, first of all, to know what they can and cannot do, and secondly, for them to be able to maintain any order and discipline.

I think that a much more common sense approach is needed in judicial review of the standard, assuming that a reasonable suspicion standard is adopted. I believe that the vice principal in this case did take a very reasonable and did take a very common sense approach to ensuring that both school regulations were followed and that a student wasn't punished unnecessarily, and that the New Jersey Supreme Court rather should have condoned this action, and viewed in this light the actions of the school vice principal were totally appropriate and should have been affirmed by the New Jersey Supreme Court.

I would reserve the rest of my time for rebuttal.

CHIEF JUSTICE BURGER: Very well.

ORAL ARGUMENT OF ICIS DE JULIO, ESQ.,

ON BEHALF OF THE RESPONDENT

MS. DE JULIO: Mr. Chief Justice, and may it please the Court, throughout the course of this litigation, the juvenile respondent has maintained that the search of her purse by the vice principal of her high school violated her Fourth Amendment rights, and that as a result the evidence which was seized from her could not be admitted against her in a criminal proceeding.

The State of New Jersey suggests that no constitutional violation occurred because the Fourth Amendment does not apply to searches conducted by school personnel.

The great majority of state and lower federal courts that have considered this question have agreed with the Supreme Court of New Jersey that searches conducted by school personnel do come within the ambit of the Fourth Amendment, and we would submit that this conclusion is constitutionally required.

As a matter of historical fact, it is true that the framers of the Constitution adopted the Fourth Amendment in response to the repression that they had experienced at the hands of the King's colonial revenue agents. The compulsory government-sponsored system of education which we now have simply did not exist at the time, so it is unlikely that the framers considered either including or excluding school personnel from the ambit of the Amendment.

QUESTION: What would be your view, Ms. De Julio, about the same factual situation in a private school, not a public school?

MS. DE JULIO: Your Honor, I would submit that that would be outside the scope of the Fourth Amendment, since the Fourth Amendment has never been applied to purely private action.

QUESTION: In other words, there is no state action then?

MS. DE JULIO: No, Your Honor.

QUESTION: Then you are going to have two different rules on searches.

MS. DE JULIO: Yes, Your Honor, you would. You would have —

QUESTION: All parochial and private schools will have one rule, and the public schools another.

MS. DE JULIO: That would be correct, Your Honor. The Fourth Amendment has never been applied to purely private action, even though in certain cases, for example, the case of a search by an employer of an employee, there might certainly be significant —

QUESTION: I suppose it isn't relevant to this case, but is it possible that that might lead parents who want their children to be in schools where cigarettes aren't floating around and drugs aren't being used to take their children out of public schools and put them in private schools?

MS. DE JULIO: Your Honor, I think that that is somewhat oversimplifying the situation for two reasons. One is that the standard promulgated by the court below does not prevent public school officials from conducting searches when they are reasonably necessary for the pursuit of their educational responsibilities, and when there are some reasonable grounds to believe that the student is either engaging in criminal conduct or has violated some school rule that would disturb or disrupt safety and order in the school.

We would submit that that is a very workable, flexible standard, and is —

QUESTION: Ms. De Julio, do you think there is any school rule not related to safety that would justify a search of a child's pockets or purse or lunch bag or whatever?

MS. DE JULIO: I would have to concede that there might be. It is difficult to know the many circumstances which might arise. I would certainly submit that the offense of smoking in the restroom would not be the type of infraction which would in itself justify the search of a student.

The threat to safety and school order is simply not at the level that would warrant such an extreme intrusion into the area of personal privacy.

QUESTION: What about smoking marijuana in a restroom?

MS. DE JULIO: Certainly smoking marijuana or use of drugs, because of the dangers to the student, might very well justify a search under proper circumstances.

QUESTION: You would distinguish marijuana from tobacco then on the basis that marijuana is more harmful, or on the basis that probably smoking marijuana might be a crime?

MS. DE JULIO: I would suggest that both factors would be taken into consideration. Obviously, many dangerous activities also violate the law. So there are times when both of those considerations would converge.

QUESTION: Well, suppose there was the same report as occurred in this case, except the report was that the student was smoking marijuana in the restroom, and that that is contrary to not only school rules but to the law.

Now, would that furnish whatever cause might be required to search the purse?

MS. DE JULIO: Well, Your Honor, it would certainly be the type of infraction that might justify a search. The question —

QUESTION: Of the purse.

MS. DE JULIO: Well, that would be a second question.

QUESTION: The inference would be, if you are smoking marijuana, maybe you have got it in your purse. Is that it?

MS. DE JULIO: Well, I think the information would have to be evaluated, as we do with the police.

QUESTION: Well, let's evaluate it on the facts of this case. They call a student in. She denies that she was smoking marijuana at all. She never smokes marijuana. And the official says, well, I would like to — the teacher says you were smoking. Now, I want to look in your purse. And she says, no. And so he searches it anyway.

Now, would that be reasonable suspicion? If the reasonable suspicion standard is the proper one, would it be satisfied in that situation?

MS. DE JULIO: I think not, simply because the information did not implicate that the marijuana was being possessed by her either in her clothing, her purse, or anywhere else. Even with regard to the police, the police may observe a criminal violation taking place. That does not necessarily lead immediately to the conclusion that a search can be conducted.

QUESTION: Ms. De Julio, at most we are talking about probable cause, not mathematical certainty. What about Mr. Nodes' argument that if you see someone puffing on a cigarette, it is a reasonable inference that he has got more on his person where that came from, whether it is marijuana or tobacco?

MS. DE JULIO: Well, Your Honor, I think in the facts of this case that isn't necessarily the proper inference to be drawn. There were a number of students in the girls' restroom, one of whom did candidly acknowledge that she was smoking.

I think that the inference that all of them possessed tobacco cigarettes, or in the alternative hypothetical that they all possessed marijuana in their purse would not be reasonable. It may well have been, and may have been the case, that perhaps they were all passing one cigarette around, and no one possessed anything.

QUESTION: Don't you recognize the difference that marijuana is contraband and cigarettes are not?

MS. DE JULIO: Certainly that is a very important difference in this case, and the problem with the search conducted here is that even if the information had been that the student was seen tucking a package of cigarettes into her purse, there was no reason for the principal to locate and seize that package.

QUESTION: Well, is it customary in New Jersey schools for students to pass one tobacco cigarette around to several different people?

MS. DE JULIO: Your Honor, I believe that occurs with a fair amount of frequency, or so I am told. But I think that the problem here is simply that the search was for something which was not against school rules to possess, was not illegal or contraband per se, and also had —

QUESTION: Well, it was a violation of the rule to smoke in the location of the restroom, was it not?

MS. DE JULIO: Yes, certainly it was.

QUESTION: What if the school official just said, hand over any cigarettes that you have, and the student handed them over, and the school official confiscated them? Is that a violation of the Fourth Amendment?

MS. DE JULIO: Well, I guess it would be there the question of whether the student's consent to relinquish the materials was knowing and a voluntary one. Assuming that it were, then I suppose it would be —

QUESTION: Well, suppose it is not. Is that a violation then of the Fourth Amendment?

MS. DE JULIO: I believe that it would be, since the —

QUESTION: And if a third grader is chewing gum in school, in violation of the teacher's established rule of preventing that, would it be a violation of the Fourth Amendment if the teacher confiscated the child's gum?

MS. DE JULIO: Well, I think in that circumstance the rule may be that the student is not permitted to possess bubble gum in school. The problem here in this particular school, and I certainly think —

QUESTION: Well, let's assume that's the rule. May the teacher then search the child's pocket, or confiscate the gum?

MS. DE JULIO: Well, again, I would certainly break down a bubble gum situation in that it may not be a serious enough threat to school order to warrant a search, but if it were a situation where the item was —for example, the case involving firecrackers. The item was certainly one that could jeopardize safety and order in the school.

QUESTION: What about a crib sheet, evidence of cheating on a test?

MS. DE JULIO: That might under proper circumstances, yes, support a reasonable search. Again, the contours of the search under the New Jersey court standard, the search has to be reasonable in light of the purpose.

QUESTION: Incidentally, Ms. De Julio, I gather you don't agree with your colleague that even a probable cause standard would be satisfied here, assuming the applicability of the Fourth Amendment.

MS. DE JULIO: No, we do not believe that the information which the principal had satisfies even the lesser standard of reasonable grounds, and certainly the extent of the search went far beyond any scope that would be constitutionally permitted, even if he had arguably had reasonable grounds to open the purse.

QUESTION: Incidentally, am I correct that as a matter of state law consent is no justification unless those consenting have been told they didn't have to?

MS. DE JULIO: There is a component in the New Jersey standard for consent search that the individual be aware that he has a right to refuse. With regard to a student, I am —

QUESTION: That is a matter of state law, is it?

MS. DE JULIO: Yes, Your Honor. The student in New Jersey is required by state law to submit to the authority of teachers, so it would be doubtful that a student could realize that he could refuse, because under a state statute, I am not sure that he could, and that fact, the fact that students are by law required to submit to the authority of a teacher we submit is one of the most important reasons why school officials must be considered governmental action for Fourth Amendment purposes.

A private citizen could stop a child on the street, ask to see what he had in his pockets, and the child could say no, and walk away. But in the school context, the lawful authority, the teacher, the school administrator, can compel the student to submit to the intrusion of a search, and the student has no recourse but to submit.

This is exactly the type of governmental harassment which we submit the framers of the Fourth Amendment designed the Amendment to protect against.

QUESTION: May we come back to the standard for just a moment? You used the term reasonable grounds. Do you distinguish that from reasonable suspicion?

MS. DE JULIO: Your Honor, I don't believe that the New Jersey Supreme Court intended to distinguish from reasonable suspicion or reasonable cause. The school case literature, of which there is now a large number of reported decisions, about equally use the term reasonable cause, reasonable grounds, or reasonable suspicion.

All of those terms have been used and have a body of case law.

QUESTION: You would accept reasonable suspicion, would you?

MS. DE JULIO: I don't believe that there is any meaningful difference, or that there was intended to be any meaningful difference. The New Jersey Supreme Court, I believe, adopted reasonable grounds because that standard had been used by several prominent cases in the area, and was one that was recognized and understood by persons involved with the school search issue.

QUESTION: Would you ever require probable cause?

MS. DE JULIO: Yes, Your Honor. I think that the New Jersey Supreme Court very clearly stated that as the intensity of the intrusion increases, the standard of reasonable grounds may very well approach or become that of probable cause. Certainly in the area of strip searches, I would submit that the search cannot be reasonable unless there is probable cause at a minimum, and even then, of course, there may be problems with the proper scope of the search.

But I think the New Jersey Supreme Court recognized that the term school search could encompass a broad spectrum of intrusions, some, as is with the case with the police, are rather minimal, stopping a student in the hallway and asking a question, but at the opposite end, of course, there could be much more intrusive searches into purse, pockets, clothing, and of course perhaps the ultimate indignity of a strip search.

So, we would submit that as formulated, the reasonable grounds test covers a certain portion of the intrusions, but that as the intrusion becomes more severe, we are talking about probable cause at the ultimate end.

QUESTION: Having in mind the facts of this case, what more would have been required in your view to satisfy the requirement to make the search of the purse?

MS. DE JULIO: In this case, I don't believe that a search could be properly made, since it had no relationship to the offense.

QUESTION: Well, suppose three teachers observed the girl smoking, actually smoking, and brought her into the principal's office and said, as soon as we called her attention to her smoking in violation of the rules, she put the cigarette out and put it in her purse.

What then? Would they be permitted to search the purse?

MS. DE JULIO: Well, Your Honor, certainly the information would implicate the purse, but again, I think that we are talking about a situation where the fact of a search may just have been completely inappropriate under the circumstances.

QUESTION: Well, would it be appropriate in these circumstances? Or are you telling us that they must go down and get a policeman and go to a magistrate and get a warrant?

MS. DE JULIO: No, Your Honor. Certainly I am not saying that. In this particular case, we are talking about an infraction which was complete in itself. To borrow Justice Marshall's example, if the student had been cursing in the hallway, the infraction is complete in itself. There would be no basis to conduct a search because there is nothing that a search could contribute to the —

QUESTION: But here the girl denied that she has cigarettes.

MS. DE JULIO: She denied that she smoked. And certainly the question of whether she smoked or not would not have been determined by the discovery or the failure to discover cigarettes in her purse. To take the opposite approach, if the principal had opened her purse and had not found a package of cigarettes, if he had found nothing in her purse, that would not have acquitted her of the infraction.

QUESTION: That may be so, but what if he had found them, like he did? Do you mean that doesn't support the inference that she was smoking?

MS. DE JULIO: No, Your Honor, simply because under school rules it was proper to smoke in certain areas of the school, and —

QUESTION: Well, I know. I am not suggesting that possession would infringe a school rule, but if the young lady denies that she was smoking, and that she never smoked, and then it turns out she has got cigarettes in her purse, you don't think that supports the inference that she had been smoking?

MS. DE JULIO: It may support it somewhat, but I don't believe that it is determinative, simply because she could have been carrying someone else's cigarettes, and I think we are talking about a chain of inferences.

Certainly there are any number of things which might in some way contribute to proof, but when we are talking about a chain of inferences, we have already gone three steps away from the infraction at hand.

It is not permitted for the police to go searching or to obtain a warrant when they have some amorphous idea that there might be something that would be evidential. They cannot go into the house of a suspect and take away everything in the house on the theory that some of it might at some point prove evidential.

QUESTION: May I ask this question? We are talking about standards a good deal. Ordinarily police officers or otherwise trained state personnel make the judgments as to whether there are reasonable grounds, reasonable suspicion, probable cause.

Is it your view that teachers should be held to the same standard of good judgment as police officers?

MS. DE JULIO: I think so, Your Honor.

QUESTION: Whatever the standard?

MS. DE JULIO: Whatever the standard, because I think first of all that the educators operate in a much more — an easier environment than the police do. The police are frequently on the street dealing with strangers and circumstances that are changing from minute to minute.

The educator deals with a group of students whom he probably knows very well, whom he will continue to see on a daily basis, and in many instances has a far better basis to make an informed judgment. Also in many instances if he suspects, has a hunch that something is going on that he feels might be a violation of the law or school rules, the student will be back in the classroom on a regular basis. The teacher can simply continue to make observations and see if that hunch —

QUESTION: Does knowing the student well enable one to make a judgment as to what is reasonable cause or what is probable cause, reasonable suspicion, do you think?

MS. DE JULIO: One of the factors which the New Jersey court pointed to in assessing whether reasonable grounds exist is the age, school record, and past history of the student, and I think that those are tools which sometimes the police are able to utilize in their determinations of probable cause, but I think it would be, of course, appropriate to evaluate those criteria in determining whether reasonable grounds existed.

QUESTION: Does New Jersey provide any special training for teachers with respect to making these judgments?

MS. DE JULIO: Well, I believe that New Jersey provides a great deal of ongoing training for teachers in myriad of fields, both academic and professional.

QUESTION: Of course.

MS. DE JULIO: This would perhaps become part of it. But I would like to call Your Honor's attention to a recent recommendation of the National School Board Association. They recommended that law-related education as a program be adopted by schools because they have found that it is very effective in preventing delinquency and contributing to a safer school environment.

QUESTION: How many teachers are there in New Jersey, roughly?

MS. DE JULIO: I don't know, Your Honor. Quite a large number.

QUESTION: But in this case it was the vice principal. It wasn't a teacher.

MS. DE JULIO: It was a vice principal. Yes.

QUESTION: Suppose the teacher reports to the vice principal that a particular young man, student, a male student has been threatening other students with a knife, and perhaps brings that student into the office. Would you say the same thing, they could not ask him to produce the knife or conduct a pat-down search, not a strip search, a pat-down search?

MS. DE JULIO: I think that under those circumstances a pat-down search might be appropriate, yes. Certainly when weapons are involved, the immediate threat — we recognize that with regard to the police, and permit frisks when the circumstances suggest that there is a weapon and that there is a danger of harm.

But again, I think we have to make a distinction —

QUESTION: Well, what makes the — the fact that somebody saw the person threatening someone with a knife, how does that support the inference that it might be in his pocket?

MS. DE JULIO: Well, again, the nature of the information would have to be — would have to suggest that conclusion.

QUESTION: I know, but does it or doesn't it?

MS. DE JULIO: I think if the information were fresh that, you know, this was seen right away, the inference —

QUESTION: What was wrong with the inference about the cigarettes?

MS. DE JULIO: Well, again —

QUESTION: The information was very fresh.

MS. DE JULIO: The fact of the students being in, first of all, being together in the restroom, that the cigarettes were not being seen being taken out or removed, they were being consumed, and also the fact that possession of cigarettes, again, was not prohibited by school rules. There was no reason to seize them. Whereas a knife I would assume would be prohibited by rules in every school, and a teacher would be well within his or her rights to seize a knife, even if it was seen just being displayed, and not being used in a threatening manner toward another student.

QUESTION: Getting back to this case, is there anything in the record where the principal said, if we don't find cigarettes in your purse, we will drop the charges?

MS. DE JULIO: Absolutely not, Your Honor, and I would submit that in the face of the eyewitness testimony of the teacher, the principal could not have ignored the infraction based upon the failure to find cigarettes in the purse.

I would also suggest that the principal, if he cared to investigate further, could have very simply questioned the other girls in the restroom. One of those girls was present in his office, and had candidly admitted that she was smoking.

QUESTION: Of course, Ms. De Julio, a lot of Fourth Amendment law is based on second guessing of what people right on the spot did. This would have been more reasonable. This would have been a little better. But really the test is whether this particular reaction was reasonable. It was not whether it was the best, or whether something could have been proved or not.

MS. DE JULIO: That is certainly true, and I am only suggesting that in response to the concern that what else could the principal have done to be fair. Certainly it is quite correct that hindsight is better than foresight, but once again I think that we have to recognize that we are not dealing here with an exigent situation.

Smoking in the restroom is certainly an infraction of school rules, and is certainly a problem that the school had to deal with, but it just simply does not rise to the level of a student possessing a weapon and threatening other students, or selling drugs in the restroom.

There was no immediate harm. It was not a situation, as the police frequently have to contend with, where a split second decision had to be made.

QUESTION: Well, I suppose you do agree in general, though, that a school needs to respond quickly and informally to violations of its rules by the students, do you not?

MS. DE JULIO: Certainly, but I —

QUESTION: How do you think it would impact then on that interest of the school to require the assistant principal to drop everything and go down to the police station and get somebody to authorize a search?

MS. DE JULIO: I am not suggesting that that should be a requirement. We have not at any point during this appeal here argued that a teacher should be required to get a warrant.

In this particular circumstance, I think what I am trying to — the distinction that I am trying to draw is between infractions of school rules which have to be dealt with in some way but which do not implicate a search, and which simply are not serious enough.

In day to day life there are many adults who smoke cigarettes in places where it is not legal to do so, but it would be difficult for a police officer to justify seizing an adult that he sees coming out of an elevator smoking a cigarette illegally and conducting a search.

The level of the infraction, the level of harm, the level of jeopardy is just simply not such that we would authorize that type of conduct.

Certainly if the — another New Jersey case, State in the Interest of G.C., where the principal was told by a student that another student was selling drugs in the restroom, the court found that the principal acted perfectly reasonably in apprehending that student and searching her and seizing those drugs.

That is the kind of threat where a search may be immediately required, and where a school administrator would be found to have acted perfectly reasonably.

QUESTION: Suppose the vice principal had been apprehensive about the Fourth Amendment problem and said to the girl, sit down, picked up the phone, called the mother, said, come over to the school, the mother said, I can't get there for 15 minutes. The girl was required to sit there. Is she under arrest?

MS. DE JULIO: No, Your Honor, I don't believe that she is under arrest.

QUESTION: Can he require her to stay there?

MS. DE JULIO: Yes, I believe under New Jersey law certainly he can.

QUESTION: If when the mother got there she took the purse and opened it, would the mother be violating the Fourth Amendment?

MS. DE JULIO: No.

QUESTION: What is the difference between the mother and the teacher in your view?

MS. DE JULIO: Well, the difference is, I think, the difference between private action and governmental action. There have been cases which have recognized that private citizens —

QUESTION: Only the state action factor is different. Is that it, in your view?

MS. DE JULIO: Yes, Your Honor, I think — with regard to the Fourth Amendment.

QUESTION: In other words, the parent has an inherent right to open the purse of the girl, but there is no inherent right on the part of the teacher?

MS. DE JULIO: Certainly the Fourth Amendment would not be violated by the parent conducting a search herself or himself.

QUESTION: Haven't you got a little bit of state action mixed in with the mother's action when the mother is there at the command or request of the state, and the mother is responding to the state's inquiry?

MS. DE JULIO: Well, certainly, if it were found that there had been any coercion or attempt to mislead or in some way implicate the parent as a tool of law enforcement, there might be, and the New Jersey Supreme Court recognized that in certain school searches if police instigation were found, or some attempt to circumvent the Fourth Amendment, that might be dealt with as a Fourth Amendment problem.

But in a purely parental situation, where a parent, acting as a parent, searches a student, searches their child, that evidence would not be proscribed by the Fourth Amendment, even if it had been seized under circumstances that we would not perhaps find to be proper, such as the employer breaking into the desk of an employee. That might violate certain criminal statutes, but it would not prevent the state from utilizing that evidence in some —-

QUESTION: Would you have any problem with metal detectors such as those we have outside the Court being at the schoolhouse door?

MS. DE JULIO: Well, certainly that is well outside the facts of this case, but assuming that hypothetically the cases allowing the use of a metal detector on a general basis, such as the airport, or that line of cases, are based upon the idea that the individual is voluntarily seeking the service that makes it necessary for him to go through the gate.

Here, with students, they are compelled to attend school, so by forcing them to walk through a metal detector, which is a more minimal intrusion into privacy, certainly, but the element of choice is simply not there.

An adult can choose to take a plane or not, knowing that a metal detector is one of those things he will have to submit to, but a child is required to go to school, and cannot refrain.

QUESTION: Even if you had an epidemic of use of knives in a particular school, no metal detector?

MS. DE JULIO: Well, certainly there would have to be some showing that this particular tool was necessary, but apart from that, again, I think that the distinguishing factor, the factor which makes that type of search possible and constitutionally permissible in an airport and not in a school is the element of voluntariness.

QUESTION: What about searching purses, as takes place in this building?

MS. DE JULIO: Well, once again, the individuals who enter this building do so —

QUESTION: Is that the only difference, that they enter the building voluntarily?

MS. DE JULIO: I think that that is certainly a significant difference.

QUESTION: What about a prison? Would you say you can't have metal detectors at a prison because the people going to prison aren't going there voluntarily?

MS. DE JULIO: Well, Your Honor, certainly the difference between a prison and a school is a critical factor in the analysis. This Court last term found that inmates have no expectation of privacy in their cells based upon the nature, goals, and operations of a penal institution.

I don't believe that any of the factors which were utilized in the Court's analysis of a prison have application in a school. First of all, we are not talking about confining people who have committed crimes and have shown that they are dangerous.

QUESTION: But it at least suggests that your voluntariness analysis is not good for all cases.

MS. DE JULIO: Well, I think it is a factor that has to be taken into consideration. Prison —

QUESTION: You are a respondent here. How voluntarily have you come?

MS. DE JULIO: I personally have come voluntarily, although certainly someone would have had to appear on behalf of the respondent. That I think is a voluntary assumption on my part.

But I think that the prison analogy fails also because the lack of rights is part of the punitive feature of prison, whereas certainly in an educational context respecting the constitutional rights of students is considered part of the educational purpose of schools.

Thank you.

CHIEF JUSTICE BURGER: Very well.

ORAL ARGUMENT OF ALLAN J. NODES, ESQ.,

ON BEHALF OF THE PETITIONER — REBUTTAL

MR. NODES: Mr. Chief Justice, and may it please the Court, I believe that the analysis which was just given concerning the distinction between a student in a public school and a student in a private school has some importance in evaluating the difference between a juvenile and an adult.

Last term in <u>Shaw v. Martin</u> this Court noted that juveniles are continuously under some form of custody or another, and this does not mean custody with total liberty, and it doesn't mean custody except when a student attends a public school.

What it really means is that they are under that form of custody and the amount of custody which will ensure their safety and their wellbeing, and that is why society insists on adult supervision of juveniles, and that is why society insists that the juveniles do be under continual custody.

QUESTION: Mr. Nodes, may I ask you a question on that? Supposing a juvenile, a young lady in this case, was riding in an elevator with a law enforcement officer, and she smoked in his presence. Would he be free to search her purse in this elevator?

MR. NODES: I don't know if a search of the purse would be at all — I don't know if there is any kind of a violation that has occurred under your hypothetical.

QUESTION: There is a no smoking sign in the elevator. There is a city ordinance against smoking. I should have made that clear.

MR. NODES: I think the violation would be smoking a cigarette, and in that case there would be really no relevance at all to whether or not she had additional cigarettes.

QUESTION: What if she denied she smoked? Just like this girl did.

MR. NODES: It would be very difficult. If he was the same person who observed her, there is no question of his credibility. He doesn't have to do this to check his own credibility.

QUESTION: Then in this case the vice principal could search the purse but not the teacher who saw her in the restroom. Is that what you are saying?

MR. NODES: I think that the vice principal could search the purse. I think there would probably be less need for the teacher to search the purse, or if the vice principal had directly seen it, there would be less reason for him to do it. And I think that is something that —-

QUESTION: What if the officer in my example took her to the station, and then the person at the station says, I would like to search your purse. Could he have done it?

MR. NODES: I believe the further you become removed from individual direct observation, the more need for proof of credibility there is, and the more need for credibility proof you have, the more necessary the search.

QUESTION: Is there anything in this record to show that the vice principal didn't trust the teacher's veracity?

MR. NODES: No, there isn't anything to show that he didn't trust the teacher's veracity. What there is is, there is evidence to show that he was willing to give the student the benefit of every doubt, and we feel that that is something which is appropriate, and which he should not be criticized for, at the very least.

But whether the Fourth Amendment is held inapplicable or whether a lower standard is applied, we feel that what is necessary is that teachers be given an immediate and effective means of conducting searches and performing other disciplinary factors, and we believe that either by ruling the Fourth Amendment inapplicable or by holding a much lower standard than probable cause to be appropriate, that this can be accomplished.

Thank you.

CHIEF JUSTICE BURGER: Thank You, counsel.

The case is submitted

(Whereupon, at 11:03 a.m., the case in the above-entitled matter was submitted.)

HISHON v. KING & SPALDING

467 U.S. 69 (1984)

Here are the arguments for petitioner and respondent in *Hishon v. King & Spalding*. Petitioner, a woman lawyer, began employment in 1972 as an associate with respondent law firm, a general partnership. The firm terminated her employment in 1979 after deciding not to invite her to become a partner. She filed suit and stated that the firm used the possibility of ultimate partnership as a recruiting device to induce her and other young lawyers to join the firm.

The Supreme Court held that the petitioner had stated a claim cognizable under Title VII of the Civil Rights Act of 1964 and that she was entitled to prove her allegations of sex discrimination. According to the Court, once parties establish a contractual relationship, the provisions of Title VII apply and forbid unlawful discrimination.

IN THE SUPREME COURT OF THE UNITED STATES

ELIZABETH ANDERSON HISHON   )

)

Petitioner   )

)   No. 82-940

v.   )

)

KING AND SPALDING   )

Washington, D.C.

Monday, October 31, 1983

The above-entitled matter came on for oral argument before the Supreme Court of the United States at 1:02 p.m.

APPEARANCES:

EMMIT J. BONDURANT, II, ESQ., Atlanta, Georgia; on behalf of the Petitioner.

PAUL M. BATOR, ESQ., office of the Solicitor General, Department of Justice, Washington, D.C.; as amicus curiae.

CHARLES MORGAN, JR., ESQ., Washington, D.C.; on behalf of the Respondent.

CONTENTS

PROCEEDINGS

CHIEF JUSTICE BURGER: We will hear arguments next in Hishon against King and Spalding.

Mr. Bondurant, you may proceed whenever you are ready.

ORAL ARGUMENT OF EMMIT J. BONDURANT, II, ESQ.

ON BEHALF OF THE PETITIONER

MR. BONDURANT: Mr. Chief Justice, and may it please the Court:

Next summer we will observe the 20th anniversary of the 1964 Civil Rights Act. It is ironic that after almost 19 years of the existence of that Act we are before this Court to discuss the question of whether or not that Act applies to sex discrimination in the private practice of law in the most highly compensated, and outside the judiciary, the most prestigious positions of the legal profession.

QUESTION: Highly compensated as compared to the judiciary?

(Laughter)

MR. BONDURANT: Yes. I think I said most highly compensated, and outside of the judiciary, most prestigious, Your Honor.

QUESTION: I see.

QUESTION: A slight question as to where you put the comma, isn't it?

(Laughter)

MR. BONDURANT: I don't think the Court was misinformed as to the intent.

The lower courts in this case held that because the Respondent was organized as a commonlaw partnership, acts of discrimination, which the complaint alleges, were practiced by that firm in the selection of partners were outside the coverage of the Act.

Thus, even though the complaint specifically alleged, and the lower courts accepted it as true, as, of course, they must for purposes of ruling upon a motion to dismiss, that the firm engaged, pursuant to a 100-year pattern and practice, of discrimination against women in the selection of partners. The lower courts nevertheless ruled that that discrimination was outside the coverage of Title VII and that Title VII afforded the Petitioner no remedy for that discrimination.

An analysis of this case must begin, of course, with the statutory language of the Act. There is no question in this case that King & Spalding is not an employer or a person covered by the Act. That is undisputed. It is plainly a firm engaged in the practice of law in the course of interstate commerce with 15 or more employees and with offices in two cities.

Nor is there a question in this case as to whether or not Ms. Hishon, an associate for almost eight years with the firm, was an employee of the firm. She plainly was employed as an associate.

The question in this case rather is whether or not the particular acts of sex discrimination which the complaint alleges were practiced by King & Spalding, admittedly an employer, against Ms. Hishon, admittedly an employee covered by the Act, were themselves unlawful employment practices covered by Section 703 of the Act.

We believe that the answers to these questions are in the affirmative.

First, let me point out by stating that the Petitioner agrees with the position taken by the Solicitor General that it is really not essential in this case to reach of the broader question of whether or not the partnership relationship; that is the relationship between an individual partner and the institution itself is an employment relationship.

For reasons that we have set forth in the brief, we think an affirmative answer to that question is indicated in this and other cases. However, this case can be decided on the narrower ground, that in her particular position as an associate of the law firm, the opportunity to be considered for partnership on a fair, equal, and non-discriminatory basis was both a term, condition, and privilege of her employment and employment opportunity, both of which were explicitly within the protection of Section 703 of the Act and were, when the firm practiced sexual discrimination in making those decisions, were unlawful employment practices within the meaning of the Act.

The complaint clearly and specifically alleged that the firm held out and represented to the Petitioner and to all other associates whom it sought to recruit, the opportunity for fair, non-discriminatory consideration for partnership after completion of five or six years' employment with the firm and hard and satisfactory work during that period.

QUESTION: Did they all become partners?

MR. BONDURANT: No, Your Honor, they all did not become partners. But, the firm held out to the Petitioner and to other associates the opportunity to be so considered and by holding out that opportunity the terms, conditions, and privileges of her employment included the opportunity for fair, non-discriminatory consideration for partnership.

When that was denied her, and that is what the complaint alleges, that she was not given fair, non-discriminatory consideration for partnership, the firm committed an unlawful employment practice covered by Section 703, which is —

QUESTION: But, you would still be here if the ultimate decision was that based on sex or race?

MR. BONDURANT: That is correct, Your Honor.

QUESTION: So, consideration isn't what you are really talking about I don't suppose. You can consider all you want to, but if the bottom line is you don't get into this partnership because of your sex, you would still be here making the argument, but you would have to say that the selection of a partner may not be based on that.

MR. BONDURANT: That is correct. And, the process of selection —

QUESTION: You are using too many words then. You may not select partners based on sex or race.

MR. BONDURANT: Certainly from among associates, that is true. We also believe that that is true if one were considering partners from the outside, but that is not this case.

This case is strengthened by the fact that the express representations of non-discriminatory consideration were made and it is the opportunity for advancement which every associate possesses in his or her capacity as an employee of the firm which is and becomes both an employment opportunity and a term, condition, or privilege of employment.

It does not make a difference that the position of partnership is or is not itself within the coverage of the Act, for in the labor cases, this Court has recognized, as have the lower courts, that where a federal statute applies, as in the labor cases, and is violated, it does not make a difference that the opportunity for promotion is being withheld for an unlawful reason under one of those statutes, even though the position to which the employee would have been promoted was entirely outside the coverage of the Act.

Thus, in this case, the complaint specifically alleged that she possessed in her position as an employee the opportunity to be considered and be promoted to a partner, that it was an opportunity for advancement, that it was withheld on the basis of sex, and, therefore, is plainly within the literal language of Section 703 of the Act

QUESTION: So, if you win on that basis, if, in hiring associates, the law firm says that we will make our selection of partners unrestricted by the terms and conditions of Title VII, would that get them off the hook?

MR. BONDURANT: No, Your Honor, it would not. If the firm —

QUESTION: Well then, it isn't a term and condition of employment.

MR. BONDURANT: I disagree with Your Honor. I think the firm will be covered by Section 703.

QUESTION: So, it is a legal term.

MR. BONDURANT: I am not sure what Your Honor means by that.

QUESTION: Well, I mean it is imposed by the operation of law, not by contract.

MR. BONDURANT: It is imposed by the operation of law, it is reinforced, whereas in this instance, the complaint alleges that the firm explicitly held out as an inducement fair, non-discriminatory consideration for partnership after five or six years of employment.

In our view, it would not make a difference if the firm had been silent; that is if the firm's business practices are such that the firm regularly reviews its associates and evaluates them for promotion to partnership and does so on a basis that is prohibited by Title VII, that would have violated Title VII even if the firm were silent in terms of representations it makes to an associate.

QUESTION: Mr. Bondurant, what part does the representation by the firm play over and above what the law otherwise requires?

MR. BONDURANT: Your Honor, it plays no part other than reinforcing the notion.

QUESTION: Well, if it plays no part, how can it reinforce?

MR. BONDURANT: Well, let me put it in this sense. We believe that if the firm were silent that it would nevertheless be covered under Section 703. That is that the opportunity for advancement which one possesses as an associate adheres in the relationship and that where a firm regularly promotes associates to partnership from that relationship, that that is an opportunity of the employment and an implicit term, condition, privilege of employment that could not be withheld on the basis of sex.

That case, we believe, becomes even stronger, where to induce one to enter into the relationship in the first instance, the firm holds out the opportunity for nondiscriminatory consideration for employment after five or six years.

If you were employed by a law firm and the law firm said to you, we make no representations to you whatsoever as to non-discriminatory employment, but nevertheless, the practice is to review and evaluate associates as they progress and to select from among those associates those who will be allowed to advance in the partnership and the remainder to be terminated by the firm, we believe that is a term, condition, and privilege of employment.

QUESTION: Supposing — Do they still have that 15-employee limit in Title VII where people employing less than 15 aren't covered by it?

MR. BONDURANT: The 15 or fewer employee limit excludes business establishments with fewer than that number of employees.

QUESTION: Supposing a firm with 15 fewer employees made a representation that we are an equal opportunity employer and we follow all the guidelines of the EEOC, would that be actionable under Title VII even though they had less than 15 employees?

MR. BONDURANT: No, Your Honor, it would be actionable, if at all, under state law, because Title VII explicitly excludes coverage from employers with fewer than 15 employees.

QUESTION: Mr. Bondurant, let's assume that the Petitioner had been admitted to partnership in King & Spalding and two or three years after young partners of the same rough age and experience were up for promotion within the firm, be entitled to a greater percentage of participation, would your position be the same?

MR. BONDURANT: Your Honor, let me answer it in two ways. First, that is not our case.

QUESTION: I know that.

MR. BONDURANT: This question is a denial of the admission to partnership itself and whether it is actionable under Title VII.

Secondly, under the broader theory which we advocate, it is our view that that would be covered by Title VII.

The question under Title VII is whether or not the relationship between a lawyer practicing with a firm and the firm itself is an entity, is an employment relationship; that is does it have the principal attributes of employment as a matter of economic reality, it is not a formalistic relationship, and, therefore, if, for the sake of a hypothetical, after three years as a member of the partnership the firm should simply vote to reduce a female or black partner's earnings to zero as a method of excluding them from the partnership, having being compelled to admit them in the first instance under an order of the court. It is our view that that would be independently actionable under Title VII.

QUESTION: You have touched on two or three factual situations. Your answer is, with respect to any change in status within a partnership down through the years, any partner may claim discrimination on the basis of sex or race?

MR. BONDURANT: Well, not quite any partner. The partner must first be within the protective group.

QUESTION: Don't go quite so fast. What is the answer to my question?

MR. BONDURANT: Pardon me. If the partner were in the protective group of persons covered by Title VII, if the partner believed that there was a causal connection between the decision made by the institution itself affecting compensation, terms, or other conditions of employment, it would be actionable under Title VII in our view.

QUESTION: You are saying that a partner is an employee of the firm always?

MR. BONDURANT: We are saying that for purposes of Title VII the relationship between a partner and a law firm has sufficient attributes of —

QUESTION: Can't you just answer that question? We are dealing with the issue of whether or not Title VII applies. It only applies if an individual is an employee. Now, is it your position that a partner, once a partner, always is a employee for purposes of Title VII?

MR. BONDURANT: For purposes of Title VII, the answer is yes.

QUESTION: Yes.

QUESTION: And, every year when participation is reconsidered the firm would be confronted with this sort of a litigation?

MR. BONDURANT: The only consequences, Justice Powell, of applying Title VII to either the admission decisions of partnership or the compensation decisions of partnership are to outlaw prohibited forms of discrimination. It is our view that that is not going to create a great disruption within partnerships, it is not going to diminish the quality of the legal profession, nor is it going to diminish in any way —

QUESTION: What has that got to do with this case?

MR. BONDURANT: The question of compensation at some later point. In our view, Mr. Chief Justice, it is not this case. This case is whether or not Ms. Hishon claiming — that is an associate in the first instance —

QUESTION: Well, is it relevant whether your view of the case or your friend's view of the case would enhance or do otherwise to a particular law firm or to law firms generally? Is that relevant?

MR. BONDURANT: Your honor, it is not relevant other than it is a broad policy consideration to reinforce the applicability of Title VII to law firms. Lawyers, after all, as our adversaries point out, occupy a rather unique position within the community, but it is that position, we suggest, which advocates for and not against coverage of Title VII. It is more important that excluded minorities progress within the legal profession than in any other capacity, because lawyers are in a unique position to influence the course of events in ways that businessmen, bankers, corporate vice presidents, and other people, all of whom are covered by Title VII, do not have the same capacity.

QUESTION: Mr. Bondurant, would you concede that judgments are made with respect to a variety of qualifications when the partnership decision is made?

MR. BONDURANT: Absolutely.

QUESTION: And, many of those judgments are subjective.

MR. BONDURANT: I would also concede they are subjective just as they are in the question of whom an ordinary business enterprise would employ for a particular position, particularly one of higher than a menial capacity.

QUESTION: So, it is possible a firm may need somebody to do damage suit litigation and if an individual in competition with that associate was very good at corporate law, would those factors be considered?

MR. BONDURANT: As long as none of the prohibitive factors covered by Title VII were factors in the decision, the firm is free to provide and apply subjective criteria in determining who to admit to partnership and how to award those who it has admitted to partnership.

But, it is our view that sex is not one of those factors which affects that decision-making process and that Congress has specifically proscribed that as a factor.

QUESTION: And, one more question. Suppose a law firm needed a new tax partner and the word got around and half a dozen people, established tax lawyers applied. I am talking now not of an associateship, but a partnership, would Title VII apply?

MR. BONDURANT: Your Honor, under the broader argument which we make, we would take the position that it does apply, but the Court need not go far as to decide that question in this case.

QUESTION: Well, I asked you whether it would apply and you answered yes.

MR. BONDURANT: The answer is yes. The considerations may be subjective. The proof problems for the lawyer claiming that because he was Jewish he was turned down as tax partner in a large firm may be difficult, but they are not insurmountable and they do not take claim outside the coverage of Title VII.

I will reserve the remainder of my time for rebuttal unless there are further questions from the Court.

CHIEF JUSTICE BURGER: Mr. Bator?

ORAL ARGUMENT OF PAUL M. BATOR, ESQ.

AS AMICUS CURIAE

MR. BATOR: Mr. Chief Justice, and may it please the Court:

The government's submission in this case is quite straightforward and we ask the Court in this case not to decide the difficult questions as to whether and what extent partners may ever themselves be regarded as employees of a partnership. On that question the government has not taken a position.

We feel that whatever view one takes on that question, Ms. Hishon's complaint in this case stated a good cause of action under Title VII, because Title VII clearly and sharply provides that women employees may not be treated worse than male employees, the statutory language that there may not be discrimination with respect to the terms, conditions, or privileges of employment.

Now, as an associate, Ms. Hishon and the other associates of the firm were concededly employees and her complaint alleges that she was treated worse than the male employees with respect to a central element of the employment relationship, one that is absolutely critical to every young lawyer at a large firm like King & Spalding.

QUESTION: Mr. Bator, I hate to interrupt you so early, but it would help me if you could tell me —-Perhaps this is not a fair question — Does Title VII apply to the faculty of a law school?

MR. BATOR: Yes, sir.

QUESTION: And, what about the tenure decision? Does it apply to that?

MR. BATOR: The lower courts have unanimously held and the government's position has been that the tenure decision is covered by Title VII.

QUESTION: Are there cases so holding?

MR. BATOR: There are cases.

QUESTION: Are they cited in your brief? I just haven't —

MR. BATOR: They are cited and in the Second and Third Circuit. There are cases so holding or at least so assuming. There are questions that, of course, go into the question whether on the particular facts —

QUESTION: Does this apply all the way up the line to associate professor, to full professor, to chair professor?

MR. BATOR: Yes, sir.

QUESTION: To the dean?

MR. BATOR: Yes. If a law firm excluded women for consideration for dean of a law school, I believe that Title VII would be violated.

QUESTION: What about the very bottom of a law firm? How about hiring?

MR. BATOR: I believe that it is universally conceded that in hiring associates a law firm may not exclude. In fact, one of the peculiarities in the position that Mr. Morgan has before this Court is that he says at the hiring level, where you are bringing in associates, you cannot exclude women, but, in effect, he says, you can hire them for a different and discrimination-against, slot; that is for a lesser consideration when you get to the partnership turn.

As I understand the position of Mr. Morgan and the Respondent in this case, it is that the law firm is wholly free to adopt an explicit role. For instance, that women will be considered for partnership after ten years, but men will be considered after six years. He says that —

QUESTION: What about lateral entry to partnerships?

MR. BATOR: Directly into the partnership? That is the question, Your Honor, that the government —

QUESTION: It is withholding a position?

MR. BATOR: It has not taken a position.

QUESTION: Mr. Bator, is there anything in the legislative history of Title VII to indicate that Congress intended to insulate decisions regarding the selection of partners from Title VII's provision?

MR. BATOR: Selection of partners from the outside.

QUESTION: Right. Or —

QUESTION: From the inside.

QUESTION: — from the inside, either way.

MR. BATOR: There is nothing directly related to law firms. The legislative history is very clear since 1972 that a central concern of Congress was access of groups, women, and blacks in particular, to the higher professional, managerial, and elite positions of society. That issue was very centrally camped when an amendment was proposed that would have excluded from Title VII the choice of doctors to practice on the staff of hospitals. And, Congress rejected that amendment precisely on the ground that it is that kind of highly sensitive position as to which Congress was especially keen that discrimination should end.

Now, in that respect, to us it seems quite irrelevant whether partners themselves are associates. We are quite willing for the Court to assume for purposes of this case that partners themselves are not employees, that they are owners, like stockholders. It is clear that if a corporation with ten stockholders wanted to find new stockholders and went out and sold stock to new stockholders that Title VII would not have anything to do with the case.

But, if that same corporation makes the ownership of stock part of a stock plan for employees, then it cannot ration that on sexual or racial grounds. It cannot say we will only admit men to the stock options plans.

In other words, ownership is not employment, but if ownership is distributed to the employees as a regular practice as one of the elements of employment, then Title VII cuts in and says you cannot do it on a racial or sexual ground.

QUESTION: Could you have — I take it then the government would say the law firm couldn't take sex into consideration at all even for affirmative action purposes or for quota purposes.

MR. BATOR: In promoting or —

QUESTION: No, entry into the partnership.

MR. BATOR: Our argument is restricted to the proposition, Justice White, that insofar as admission to the partnership is a term, condition, and privilege of an employment relationship. So, if there were no employment relationship theretofore —

QUESTION: No, I know, but I am talking about this case where there was an employment relationship and the law firm says, well, I think we ought to have six or eight lady partners but no more or we should have 20 to 30 but no more.

MR. BATOR: Your Honor, that, I guess would become then subject to the more general and obviously very sensitive question of whether rectifying previous discrimination, to what extent affirmative action or other plans would be a problem.

But, that, we think, would cut into the general background Title VII law as it applies to ordinary situations; that is there would be no special rule with respect to —--

QUESTION: Would Title VII apply to a situation where a woman or any other person claiming the protection of the Act has pointed out that for the ten years that she had been in the firm she had never been assigned a case to argue in the courts of appeals or the Supreme Court and that was an area reserved for men — that would be the claim — and, in fact, the record would show that only men had been assigned those assignments. Would that be cognizable under the Act?

MR. BATOR: Yes. If she is an employee of the firm —

QUESTION: Wait a minute, a partner now.

MR. BATOR: She is not a partner.

QUESTION: We have gotten over the hump.

MR. BATOR: She is now a partner.

QUESTION: She is now a partner.

MR. BATOR: That is a question which I am unable to answer, Your Honor, because it would depend on this additional question, whether the partners themselves are employees.

I should put this qualification on that.

QUESTION: Your friend said the partners aren't employees.

MR. BATOR: We have not joined the Petitioner on that submission. The government is arguing this case on a narrower issue which relates entirely to the way in which King & Spalding treats its associates and we are saying for that purpose it is irrelevant whether the partners are themselves employees or owners or whether you pierce the partnership veil as it were.

Now, with respect to our submission —

QUESTION: May I just ask you another question?

MR. BATOR: Yes.

QUESTION: In the year 1983, with women being a third of the students in the law schools of the United States, is this really a problem? And, I ask one supplemental question. If you are a partner in a law firm, you are very careful about selecting new partners because it affects your profits. In other words, you want the strongest possible person regardless of sex, color, or race. That may not have been true 20 or 30 years ago when people had lots of prejudices they don't have now, but I can't imagine a law firm deliberately discriminating against somebody if the firm made a judgment that the individual would increase the profits of the law firm.

MR. BATOR: Your Honor, this may be a decreasing problem, but when Congress acted, first in 1964, and in 1972, it was a very active problem, it was really a virulent problem. And, that is the time as of which that statute speaks.

So, the fact — and to some extent that it is no longer a problem is itself maybe a product of Title VII in the background; that is to say that since everybody concedes that at the intake stage, when young associates are first hired, Title VII does apply. Of course, law firms have had to accustom themselves to overcoming these ancient prejudices and they have learned, we have all learned, as we have learned on faculty, that, in fact, the prejudice was simply inexcusable.

And, that really, I think, pushes me into what is my last point with respect to Mr. Morgan's submission.

CHIEF JUSTICE BURGER: You are now using your friend's time.

MR. BATOR: I think I will back off and leave my friend his time.

CHIEF JUSTICE BURGER: Very well.

MR. BATOR: Thank you.

CHIEF JUSTICE BURGER: Mr. Morgan?

ORAL ARGUMENT OF CHARLES MORGAN, JR., ESQ.

ON BEHALF OF THE RESPONDENT

MR. MORGAN: Mr. Chief Justice, and may it please the Court:

The Petitioner in brief particularly and here, discussing 20 years as of next year on the Civil Rights Act of 1964, has made a point of whether or not King & Spalding and lawyers are above the law and whether or not the case of Respondent would place them there. I submit that it wouldn't.

Of all the professions in the United States and probably of all of the sundry people who perform services in our society, lawyers are the most regulated.

However, from time to time there are certain kinds of activities that lawyers find necessary for their work. For instance, the privileges that are granted with respect to the attorney/client privilege, the fact that lawyers can state things in courts that are at least qualifiedly privileged and often have absolute immunity from liable.

QUESTION: I am not sure I grasp what you meant by the statement that they are the most regulated. Regulated — Which regulation are you speaking of —

MR. MORGAN: Well, sir —

QUESTION: The structure of the bar or the potential of a particular court?

MR. MORGAN: The structure of the bar as well as the structure of sundry courts, that lawyers are a member of the bar over a period.

Bar associations, first of all, do regulate lawyers. Lawyers are regulated on entry into the profession, all the way through it, and all the way out of it, often not as much as they should be, but certainly more than other professions it seems to me. And, as such, it is not a question of are lawyers above the law, but it is a question of whether or not the Congress intended to cover them as to this law, and it is secondly a question as to what protections lawyers are granted by the society and by the law and by the Constitution in order to perform their necessary function in the society.

We submit to you that lawyers are entitled to the highest degree of First Amendment associational freedom. We submit that and we think Congress understood that at the time it enacted the Civil Rights Act of 1964.

You will note in our briefs that we have discussed the existence of lawyers in Congress, the large number of them and the people involved in the passage of the Civil Rights Act of 1964, and the number of law partners in Congress, who didn't talk about lawyers and law partners, but did talk about doctors when they made their points that are made in briefs about professional coverage, and, the fact that the lawyers in Congress certainly had in their minds that they were lawyers.

Now, they wanted to eliminate, I believe, based on only one statement in the record, the 1963 statement by Congressman McCulloch. They wanted to eliminate discrimination in the employment of professionals.

Senator Javits and others discussed questions with respect to hospitals and the elimination of discrimination with respect to people being able to practice medicine in hospitals.

Congressman McCulloch mentioned law along with other professions in 1963 in a preliminary report.

When you turn to the year 1964, there is only one statement involving partnerships in the record of the debates which the New York Times termed so voluminous —I mean the weight of them was so gigantic. And, that one statement was made by Norris Cotton, Senator Cotton, and he was commenting on the fact — He was speaking against the provision to lower the coverage of employees, who at that time, as I recall it, was 25.

When Senator Cotton was speaking, he said this would be so absurd. When you have that small an operation, it is almost like a partnership.

Now, that is it as far as the record is concerned. There is nothing in the Solicitor General's brief. There is nothing in the Petitioner's brief. There is no other intention of Congress to cover law partnerships.

QUESTION: What sort of a partnership do you suppose Senator Cotton was thinking of, coming, as he did, from New Hampshire?

MR. MORGAN: Well, he came from New Hampshire, but he was also, as I recall it, the senior partner in a law firm in New Hampshire, Cotton, Tesreau — I have forgotten the names. It is spelled out in the brief. I think he was thinking of that partnership to start with, his own, because he was, after all, a partner in a law firm at that time.

QUESTION: But, a lot of the partnership problems that you refer to in your brief, seems to me are covered by the 15 employee requirement, you know, if you are talking about a small partnership.

QUESTION: Are there any 15 member law firms in New Hampshire?

(Laughter)

QUESTION: You know there are not, don't you?

MR. MORGAN: I thought there might be one, maybe two, but I certainly don't know. I haven't spent a lot of time in New Hampshire.

QUESTION: Mr. Morgan, you concede though, I guess, that the law partnership of over 15 associates is an employer of the associates within the meaning of Title VII, don't you?

MR. MORGAN: We have not taken a position to the contrary. We have not taken any position —

QUESTION: Well, I am asking you now. You surely agree that it is an employer under Title VII of the associates.

MR. MORGAN: It is an employer of associates under Title VII which poses certain problems for a portion of my case, for example.

QUESTION: All right.

MR. MORGAN: If King & Spalding, or any other law firm employs lawyers who then sue King & Spalding, there may be an invasion of the attorney/client privilege.

According to Petitioner, law partners and associates do the same thing, there is no difference between them. Therefore, why shouldn't a promotion system take place as though the law firm were a corporation? And, if that took place, it would be just kind of a stair-step progression from a GS-8 to a GS-15 to a GS-18 which must be a partner.

Now, their contention then is based upon the fact that the employees of the partnership — Partnerships are clearly spelled out in the statute. There is hardly a way to take another position than the one I just took. It says partnerships are employers. It doesn't say they are employees. Certainly, if a partnership is an employer, it is very difficult to figure how partners would be employees.

QUESTION: Well, we don't have to decide that, do we?

MR. MORGAN: Well, I think when looking at congressional intention, you have to see at what Congress had in mind and Congress —

QUESTION: Well — But, the Petitioner in this case says you don't have to decide that. All you have to do to decide this case is to decide whether the associate is an employee and, therefore, is fair consideration without regard to sex a term or a condition of that employment?

MR. MORGAN: Well, in response to Justice White's question, he stated, of course, she would be here anyway going right into the firm.

Now, their position, both Petitioner — One of Petitioner's three positions and the position of the Solicitor General — Their position is that terms, conditions, and privileges of employment, that that covers a promise to fairly consider an employee or a prospective employee at the time of hire and then six years later you are supposed to enforce it.

Now, let's see if that is what Congress had in mind, because, first of all, the rules of construction say that no words in the statute have surfaced, you have to consider the entire statute.

First, it is the Equal Employment Opportunities Act that creates an Equal Employment Opportunities Commission.

The Solicitor General states if there is either a pension plan or he was talking about a stock option plan with a corporation, that it would have to be treated equally for everybody and I agree with that.

But, in this particular instance, where you have terms, conditions, privileges of employment and you get into those words, you run squarely into the rest of the congressional intention which is clearly stated in the following way: It says — And, it defines people. When it gets to members, it is talking about labor organizations, not partnerships. When it gets to "it shall be an unlawful employment practice for an employer to discriminate," it then goes on "with respect to terms, conditions, or privileges of employment."

Now, remember, these outsiders they were talking about bringing into the firm and King & Spalding has many of those. That is in the record.

There is no set way here as for that Swaine and Moore had of the <u>Lucido</u> case coming straight up where they took in nobody.

Now, with respect to this particular case, Petitioner would say you need go no further with respect to the ramifications of your decision. You need not even think about remedy because we do not want to be in the partnership, therefore, just consider it my way within this structure. It strikes me that is not the way the Court should do business. I think you have to think about the ramifications of it and what the true intention is.

Another phrase: "It shall be an unlawful employment practice." It says that a person can't limit or segregate or classify his employees or applicants for employment in any way which would deprive any individual of employment opportunities or otherwise adversely affect his status as an employee.

Now, that is what Petitioner didn't like, was a status as employee.

QUESTION: May I ask you about the hypothetical question the Solicitor General gave? Supposing the firm had a rule that male associates are eligible for partnerships after six years and female associates are eligible for partnerships after ten years. Would that comply with the Act? What is your view of that?

MR. MORGAN: The Act is not applicable to partnerships, so consequently they could do that.

QUESTION: That would be a permissible disparate treatment on the basis of sex?

MR. MORGAN: It would be permissible as a — It would be permissible as a disparate treatment if they just did that. Let me give you — Let me strike an example.

QUESTION: If they write it out, that is the rule. When they come here they tell the women you will be eligible in ten years and they tell the male employees you will be eligible in six years.

MR. MORGAN: Put it in the employment booklet, just like is happening all over the country now as these job-right cases are developing under state law. Employers, some of them, except for those who are frightened of doing it, are putting on the face of it, you should understand that you acquire no rights when you come here.

QUESTION: No. My hypothesis is that you acquire — If you are a male, you acquire the right to be considered for a partnership after six years, if you are a female, you acquire that right after ten years. Now, why doesn't that fall right squarely within the language of the Act?

MR. MORGAN: If I lay it out when the associate is hired —

QUESTION: Right.

MR. MORGAN: — and I tell the associate at the time of hire that later the associate will have to work here for ten years before the associate could become partner. Well, I think we are assuming something that not even, of course, the complaint says, but as far as the —

QUESTION: No, but your legal position, I think, has to say that in the eighth year the male and females are not being discriminated against — are not being treated differently on account of sex.

MR. MORGAN: I am saying two things. One, if I say that outright as a partnership, I just tell folks, whether I tell them in writing or tell them orally and I just say, look, it takes eight years for women to be good lawyers and six years for men to get to be good lawyers and then we are going to consider them.

The answer is did Congress desire to cover the partnership decision? My answer is no, not under Title VII. Might there be an actional square, sure. Could the action be brought, sure, but not under Title VII and the second answer.

If you take Justice Powell's statement about why in the world would a partner want to keep out someone who is going to make them a profit, which happens to be the theme of Petitioner's case — Petitioner says, good heavens, law firms are businesses and we are making all of this money all over the world and that is the central theme of law practice. If that is the case, then any law firm who would make such an averment of six and eight year differentials to employees at law school in the United States from which they hire, would be laughed off the campus and would promptly go out of business.

QUESTION: Mr. Morgan, on this — on carving out this exemption for law firms, with the number of law firm representatives in Congress, why didn't they spell it out if they intended to do it? One, they knew how to spell it out, and, two, they were lawyers.

Am I not correct that every member of the Judiciary Committee in the House is a lawyer?

MR. MORGAN: Yes.

QUESTION: They drafted this bill. How can you say they didn't mean to cover lawyers?

MR. MORGAN: Well, sir —

QUESTION: That is your position, isn't it?

MR. MORGAN: That is my position. It was so obvious and so apparent that three decisions of this Court surely would apply.

One of them is, of course, Catholic Bishop. Secondly — A second decision that would apply would be Yeshiva, because they identify, and the third decision would be Bell Aerospace.

You know, Congress can sit over there and they can't think of every crazy thing somebody is going to bring up and if they did, then they would write an exception in for that. But, in this particular instance, Congressman McCulloch, Chairman, himself a partner in a law firm, Congressman Seller who had been with a law firm previously and may have been at the time, but he was previously, and partners in law firms sitting there, some of them, could never even conceive that anyone was going to come and say, well, we are going to make partners under Title VII.

QUESTION: You mean out of all the partnerships that you can imagine, law partnerships were alone exempt or are you suggesting that all kinds of partnerships were exempt?

MR. MORGAN: Well, I am suggesting that as far as Congress was concerned all of them were. There is higher protection to law firms than accountants and there were more lawyers — I was talking about lawyers because lawyers are in Congress —

QUESTION: So, your submission really is that no partnerships are covered by this insofar as entry is concerned into the partnership?

MR. MORGAN: Sure. There is no question about that in my mind. That is what Justice Goldberg wrote there within two or three days of the passage of the Act in his concurring opinion.

QUESTION: So, we should judge this case as though this were a partnership of engineers or —

MR. MORGAN: No, no.

QUESTION: Rather than lawyers. Can't we just forget it is lawyers?

MR. MORGAN: No, no, no.

(Laughter)

MR. MORGAN: If we forgot it was lawyers, we would be like Congress forgetting to write an exception.

QUESTION: I understood Justice White's question and your response has confused me. Are real estate partnerships, banking partnerships, medical partnerships all in the same category under Title VII, whatever that category is?

MR. MORGAN: No, sir, but in most of those you do not — Are they all in the same category, yes, sir.

QUESTION: I thought you answered me that no partnership was subject to Title VII in terms of entry.

MR. MORGAN: Yes, that is what — Let me complete that. No partnership in terms of entry, however, that question is not before the Court. The question that is before the Court, because no constitutional question is implied with —

QUESTION: Your submission, as I understand it, would cover any partnership.

MR. MORGAN: I beg your pardon?

QUESTION: Your submission would cover any partnership for rationale for your position.

MR. MORGAN: Oh, no. I think — In the first place, assuming that all business partnerships have a right of commercial association, then they would be covered and they would have a lower standard of constitutional rights with respect to what is done to them by the government through the

EEOC, which would assume jurisdiction, than is a law firm which is an advocacy organization if there has ever been one. That is why law partnerships are different from other partnerships and that is what is before the Court.

QUESTION: What cases from this Court support you in suggesting that lawyers have this very high claim to resist government regulations because they are advocates.

MR. MORGAN: No, no, that is not — What we say is that law firms are advocacy organizations which handle litigation as was pointed out in NAACP in Button. In the Button case, we talked particularly, the Court did, about use of litigation to political ends. Law firms certainly are constantly petitioning Congress, petitioning for a redress of grievance in court or out of court, and doing those things that are clearly protected by the First Amendment. That is what we say about the advocacy rights of law firms.

As far as whether or not that gives them a higher standard of protection, surely it does when a question is asked in an interrogatory such as here by the Plaintiff, which could be asked in the EEOC, just in the case preceding.

QUESTION: Well, supposing that Congress is not trying to deter advocacy expressly, it is saying that law firms are going to be subject to minimum wage laws, maybe they have to bargain collectively with representatives of their employees, they are subject to the Civil Rights Act. Now, I wouldn't think that any of those things raised any constitutional question whatsoever.

MR. MORGAN: Your Honor, as I recall, on the minimum wage, they would come off as a professional exemption, but —

QUESTION: Let's assume Congress decided to repeal a professional exemption.

MR. MORGAN: All right. As far as the purely business and economic aspects of law firms, to wit, Fair Labor Standards Act and the minimum wage laws, I think you are right.

QUESTION: But, we are not dealing with purely business — You apparently feel there is some higher, loftier goal of a law firm than making money. And, even, let's put in that higher, loftier goal. Why can't Congress do just what it wants to with respect to law firms with minimum wages, civil rights, collective bargaining?

MR. MORGAN: Because what it does is it takes in this particular instance and places an advocacy agency of the federal government overseeing the law firms.

The case you just heard before this case involving EEO-1 reports, in that particular case — Law firms file them too. They don't file partners, you know, numbers of partners as employees, they just file associates.

Now, the EEOC decides to go against a law firm. It has a subpoena power and it can subpoena the law firm's documents. In this particular case, King & Spalding's responses, as are contained in the record and the District Court, say she didn't get along with our clients in effect amongst other things and those are the reasons we didn't admit her.

Now, at that point, they asked an interrogatory question and the interrogatory question goes directly to the questions of what matters did you handle for clients, what matters did she have problems with, who do you represent?

QUESTION: That assumes that lawyers in their dealings would need confidentiality in a way that lots of other organizations don't. I dare say that Shell Oil, which was the party to the prior case, probably has a lot of papers they would like to keep from the government about hiring decisions in their top echelon, but I don't think they have had the affrontery or perhaps ambitious visions of their business yet to say that the Constitution prevents the government from doing it.

MR. MORGAN: I certainly hope not, but lawyers are different. Lawyers are essential to the enforcement of the Constitution.

Let me give you some examples.

QUESTION: Mr. Morgan, now Congress knew full well how to write exemptions from Title VII and it put in three. And, you are asking us to just produce another one out of some abstract concept about lawyers. If Congress had intended to have this exemption, wouldn't it have said so?

MR. MORGAN: No, no. Congress did not exempt lawyers from their hiring policies. Congress —

QUESTION: That is precisely what we are talking about.

MR. MORGAN: Congress exempted partnerships as employees and partners as employees.

We raised the question of the First Amendment to come under Catholic Bishop and other cases to demonstrate a rule of construction with respect to the statute which says that the statute should not be interpreted in such a manner as would require a restriction of the constitutional liberties that do attach the law firms with respect to their duties and it doesn't matter whether it is a lease case with respect to Mr. Justice Stevens and Mr. Justice Brennan talking in terms of going across the country and lawyers almost having a due process property right and the right to practice and to hire lawyers being involved in the representation they do. Justice Brennan talking about the NAACP versus Button, that it was not the equal protection clause that mattered, it was this, like a firm of lawyers —

QUESTION: It is a little different. The NAACP was a non-profit corporation.

MR. MORGAN: But, you see —

QUESTION: And, your client is not a non-profit —

MR. MORGAN: I hope not.

(Laughter)

QUESTION: If it is, I was getting ready to say you are in bad shape.

(Laughter)

MR. MORGAN: If it is, nobody would want in.

Now, let me just mention to you from NAACP versus Button —

QUESTION: Excuse me. What difference does it make to your case and your arguments whether the proposition you are advancing applies to medical partnerships, real estate partnerships, and engineering partnerships? I thought your argument was that a partnership of any kind is a consensual arrangement and governmental power can't intrude into consensual relationships. And, I have understood that was about the theme of the Fourth Circuit, was it not?

MR. MORGAN: Yes, sir, the Eleventh Circuit. That is our argument. Our argument goes beyond that because law firms are involved as First Amendment protected entities. That is the only reason we have brought in the First Amendment. We don't say the statute is unconstitutional in its application. You don't get to that under what we interpret.

QUESTION: You haven't mentioned the right of association which we have said is guaranteed by the First Amendment.

MR. MORGAN: We go into it in depth in brief. We do talk about it and when I go to that associational right, I go to the Button case and I go to Justice Brennan's words in there. And, it says the protections in Button would apply as fully to those who would arouse our society against the objectives of the Petitioner. Expression —- the Constitution protects expression and association without regard to race, creed, political affiliations, truth, popularity or even social utility of the ideas and beliefs.

QUESTION: Does that apply to stockbrokerage partnership firms in New York?

MR. MORGAN: As far as partnership coverage of Title VII, yes, the same rule would apply to them. As far as the rules that apply to lawyers, no.

QUESTION: So, they can exclude all women and all minorities?

MR. MORGAN: In their partnerships, yes.

QUESTION: In —

MR. MORGAN: In partnerships, yes, sir. If they are a partnership, they can do so.

QUESTION: What you want us to do is to write an exemption that Congress didn't write and then there would be people — I won't say you — but there will be some people who will say we are legislating. Is that what you want?

MR. MORGAN: Well, sir —

QUESTION: Do you want us to legislate?

MR. MORGAN: I think what we are talking about here is not you legislating it, but since there is not a word in the record of Congress that they desired to cover partnerships as anything other than employers —

QUESTION: Is there a word that says they didn't intend —

MR. MORGAN: Only one sentence that would indicate it and that is Senator Norris Cotton, and he comes close to saying, this is crazy folks, this would be as bad as —

QUESTION: You are not really saying there is only one question. The Act itself doesn't exclude lawyers, law firms, and these associates are employees and you concede the law firm is an employer. So, that —We do need to go to legislative history, do we?

MR. MORGAN: It excludes partners as employees by including them as employers.

QUESTION: That may be so, but neither — The government's position doesn't go to whether a partner is an employee. It is a much narrower ground that the associate is an employee and part of his terms of employment is fair consideration.

MR. MORGAN: I understand the government's argument.

APPENDIX **VII**

GRAMMAR AND PUNCTUATION

Some people enjoy the great fortune of having learned the rules of grammar and punctuation in eighth grade, high school, or college. Others have learned a few rules here or there or by osmosis. If you fall into the latter group, it is time to make sure that you know at least the basics. If you are very deficient, you need to consult one of the many books on writing composition and grammar. If you do not already have one of these grammar books from college or high school, you should get one. You also should consult with a writing specialist at either your law school or college.

This Appendix is not designed to be a comprehensive remedial handbook. Instead, it reviews the rules of grammar and punctuation most likely to create difficulties for the law student. Part A explains six rules of grammar and offers exercises to help you test your learning. Part B reviews the main rules for using commas, semicolons, colons, and dashes. It also discusses quotations.

Part A: Grammar

Part A discusses six rules:

1. Make Sure Each Modifier Unambiguously Refers to the Word that You Want It to Modify

2. Make Sure Each Pronoun Clearly Refers to the Word for Which It Is a Substitute

3. If You are Referring to a Singular Noun, Use a Singular Pronoun. If You are Referring to a Plural Noun, Use a Plural Pronoun

4. Make the Subject Agree with the Verb

5. Use "Its" to Denote the Possessive and "It's" to Abbreviate "It is"

6. Use "Which" to Introduce a Nonrestrictive Clause. Use "That" to Introduce a Restrictive Clause

Rule 1. Make Sure Each Modifier Unambiguously Refers to the Word that You Want It to Modify

A modifier is a word, phrase, or clause that describes, alters, or clarifies another word in the sentence. For example:

The statute gives manufacturers a second incentive to comply with the regulations.

"Second" tells us more about "incentive." It modifies "incentive." "To comply" also is a modifier. It tells us more about "incentive" the incentive is designed to encourage manufacturers to comply with the regulations.

Watch out for misplaced modifiers. A sentence has a misplaced modifier when the reader might think that the modifier applies to a word different than the one the writer intended. The problem arises when the modifier is in the wrong location. Here is an example:

The court discussed the need for a written contract in a brief paragraph.

"In a brief paragraph" might modify "discussed" and tell us how much space the court's opinion devotes to this topic. Alternatively, it might modify "written contract" and tell us how long the written contract should be. Because of the location of the modifying phrase, the reader may not know which message you intended to communicate. Presumably the phrase modifies "discussed." If so, the sentence has a misplaced modifier. You can clear up the ambiguity by relocating the phrase. Here are some acceptable alternatives:

In a brief paragraph, the court discussed the need for a written contract.

The court discussed, in a brief paragraph, the need for a written contract.

The court, in a brief paragraph, discussed the need for a written contract.

Sometimes, a poorly written sentence contains the modifier, but not the word to which the modifier applies. Here is an example:

Faced with a statutory deadline, it is important to proceed quickly.

Who is faced with a statutory deadline? The sentence fails to tell us. The initial phrase is a dangling modifier, because the sentence does not contain the word it modifies. The problem is easy to fix:

Faced with a statutory deadline, counsel must proceed quickly.

The next example illustrates a related problem:

Faced with a statutory deadline, quick action by counsel becomes necessary.

As written, the initial phrase seems to modify "quick action." However, the phrase must modify the actor, "counsel." To solve the problem, place the modifier next to the word it modifies:

Faced with a statutory deadline, counsel must act quickly.

Exercise

Please rewrite so that the modifiers unambiguously refer to the words you want to modify.

1. To prevail before an appellate court, a sound record must be developed before the trial court.

2. Once considered a major part of the Civil Procedure course, only modest attention is paid to the forms of action in today's law school curriculum.

3. The commission encouraged the companies immediately to go into production.

4. They only praised the decision, but not the rationale.

5. After examining the complaint, it is necessary to consider possible pretrial motions.

Rule 2. Make Sure Each Pronoun Clearly Refers to the Word for Which It is a Substitute.

The professor questioned the student about the issue that he was exploring.

Does "he" refer to the professor or the student? Was the professor exploring the issue or was the student exploring it? The sentence does not tell us in an unambiguous fashion.

Here are three ways to rewrite the sentence, assuming "he" refers to the professor :

1. The professor questioned the student about the issue that the professor was exploring.

2. In exploring the issue, the professor questioned the student about it.

3. The professor explored the issue and questioned the student about it.

Be particularly careful when you use "this," "that," or "those." Make sure the pronoun clearly refers to an antecedent. For example:

The court encountered criticism for making a de novo review of the evidence. This is not the function of an appellate court.

To what does "this" refer? We can solve the problem with a simple revision:

The court encountered criticism for making a de novo review of the evidence. Making such a review is not the function of an appellate court.

Exercise

Please revise these sentences so that the pronouns clearly refer to the words for which they are a substitute.

1. A friend of the decedent testified that she had been harassed at work in the weeks before the assault.

2. The plaintiff granted a single interview to a reporter. This would be inconsistent with the court's definition of media access.

3. The evidence was quite scanty. That made the prosecutor nervous.

4. Although taking exams dominates the month of December, it rarely is as taxing as students expect it to be.

5. The distinction between public and private figures is that they have media access to refute any defamation.

Rule 3. If You are Referring to a Singular Noun, Use a Singular Pronoun. If you are Referring to a Plural Noun, Use a Plural Pronoun.

Study this sentence:

If the corporation files for bankruptcy, they must notify their creditors.

"Corporation" is singular. The proper pronouns are "it" and "its". "They" and "their" are incorrect.

If the corporation files for bankruptcy, it must notify its creditors.

Here is another example:

Although the insurance company's representatives accepted the premiums, they now refuse to honor the policy.

The subject of the second clause is the insurance company, not the insurance company's representatives. Therefore, the correct pronoun is "it."

Although the insurance company's representatives accepted the premiums, it now refuses to honor the policy.

Exercise

Please revise these sentences so that single pronouns refer to single nouns and plural pronouns refer to plural nouns.

1. The Third Circuit was correct in determining that the statements were capable of defamatory meaning. Their decision should be upheld.

2. This practice creates a monopoly-like situation for the third party in which they are free to do whatever they wish.

3. The appellant's punitive damage claim should be dismissed because their fraud claim has been dismissed.

4. Every person in the neighborhood was asked to sign their name to the zoning petition.

Rule 4. Make the Subject Agree with the Verb.

If the subject of the sentence or clause is singular, the verb must be singular. If the subject is plural, the verb must be plural. Although we know this rule, we sometimes break it by being careless.

In each of these examples, the subject and verb do not agree:

1. A variety of rhetorical devices appear in the appellate brief.

2. A lay dictionary, as well as a legal dictionary, are essential to an office library.

3. Either of the appellant's rationales require the court to accept a highly innovative argument. ("Either" means "either rationale.")

Exercise

Please revise these sentences so that subjects and verbs agree.

1. Everyone of them say they met the deadline.

2. None of the memoranda recommend pursuing the matter.

3. The newspaper coverage in the surrounding counties were extensive.

4. Neither of the cotenants wish to partition the acreage.

5. The best part of the brief are the last five pages.

Rule 5. Use "Its" to Denote the Possessive and "It's" to Abbreviate "It is."

"It's" is the contraction of "it is." "Its" is the possessive of "it." Just as the possessive pronouns "her" and "his" have no apostrophe, the possessive pronoun "its" has no apostrophe.

> Although the argument appears innovative, its roots extend well into the last century.

"Its roots" means the roots of the argument. The pronoun refers to the argument. Because "its" is a substitute for "the argument's," it is in the possessive and has no apostrophe.

Because legal writing is formal, contractions should be used only rarely. Therefore, rarely, if ever, will you use "it's." If you tend to confuse "it's" and "its," remember that in legal writing, the correct word almost always is "its."

Here are two correct examples.

1. Although both parties claimed the privilege of using the easement, neither was willing to pay for its maintenance.

2. According to the first witness, the defendant shouted, "It's time for a couple more beers."

Rule 6. Use "Which" to Introduce a Nonrestrictive Clause. Use "That" to Introduce a Restrictive Clause.

Here is a simple way to decide when to use "which" and when to use "that." If you can or should place a comma before the clause, use "which." Otherwise use "that."

> The memo that I wrote under considerable time pressure is surprisingly good.

Suppose I wrote only one memo. The clause gives the reader additional information: I wrote it under time pressure. The information in the clause is not essential to identify the memo that is discussed in the sentence. We call this clause a nonrestrictive clause, because it adds information, but is not essential to identifying the word or clause that it modifies. In a sense, it is parenthetical. We should place a comma before the clause and begin the clause with "which."

However, suppose I wrote several memos and wrote one of them under time pressure. In this case, the clause does more than give the reader additional information; it identifies the memo that I am discussing. We call this clause a restrictive clause, because it is essential to identifying the word or clause that it modifies. We do not place a comma before the clause, and we begin it with "that."

Exercise

Please rewrite the sentences that use "which" and "that" improperly.

1. Every business that qualifies can seek a tax exemption.

2. The building, which overlooked the river, attracted many tenants. (Assume several other buildings also overlooked the river.)

3. The building which overlooked the river attracted many tenants. (Assume that only this building overlooked the river.)

4. The comma that precedes the clause is unnecessary. (Assume that the sentence contains two commas.)

Part B: Punctuation

Part B explains how to use the comma, colon, semicolon, and dash correctly. It also discusses how to punctuate quotations.

1. The Comma

The rules concerning commas are in flux. The conventional rules require commas in specified situations. In many of these situations, however, the trend is to omit the comma when it does not help the reader to understand the sentence.

Here are six rules for using commas:

a. When using a conjunction to separate the independent clauses in a compound sentence, place a comma before the conjunction

b. Use a comma after an introductory phrase or clause.

c. Use commas to set off words, phrases, and clauses in a sentence.

d. Use commas to separate words, phrases, and clauses in a series.

e. Use a comma between two adjectives that modify a verb.

f. Use commas in dates.

a. When using a conjunction to separate the independent clauses in a compound sentence, place a comma before the conjunction.

An independent clause is a clause that could stand alone as a sentence. A compound sentence has two or more independent clauses joined by a semicolon, colon, or a conjunction, such as "or", "but", or "and". Place a comma before the conjunction. Here are two correct examples:

An independent clause must have a subject and a verb, but a phrase need not have them.

An independent clause must have a subject and verb, and it must be able to stand alone as a sentence.

When the subject of both clauses is only in the first clause, place a comma before the conjunction, unless the conjunction is "and." Here are two correct examples:

An independent clause must have a subject and verb and must be able to stand alone as a sentence.

An independent clause must have a subject and verb, but need not include a preposition.

Pitfall: Do not separate two independent clauses with a comma. This construction is called a comma splice. Here is a bad example:

An independent clause can stand on its own as a sentence, a dependent clause cannot.

If you wish to place two independent clauses in the same sentence, separate them with a semicolon or with a comma and a conjunction. We can correct the bad example this way:

An independent clause can stand on its own as a sentence, but a dependent clause cannot.

Pitfall: Do not confuse a conjunction with a transitional word that functions like an adverb. Such transitional words include however, therefore, thus, and moreover. Do not treat these words as conjunctions. Consider this bad example:

The word "and" is a conjunction, however, the word "however" is not.

This sentence is a compound sentence consisting of two independent clauses. Because "however" is not a conjunction, no conjunction separates them. In the absence of a conjunction, you must separate them with a semicolon:

The word "and" is a conjunction; however, the word "however" is not.

b. Use a comma after an introductory phrase or clause. The rule is self explanatory. Here are two good examples:

1. After an introductory phrase, use a comma.

2. In the absence of a conjunction separating independent clauses, you may decide to use a semicolon.

c. Use commas to set off words, phrases, and clauses in a sentence.

Use commas when the word, phrase, or clause is really parenthetical or otherwise interrupts the sentence. Here are three good examples:

1. A comma, one type of punctuation mark, is overused more than other punctuation marks.

2. A comma, however, has many uses.

3. A grammarian would agree that, as a general rule, a writer should use commas to set off a parenthetical.

Instead of using a comma, you also can use parentheses or dashes. See the discussion of dashes later on in this appendix.

d. Use commas to separate words, phrases, and clauses in a series.

Here is an example:

> Punctuation marks include the comma, the period, the colon, the apostrophe, the question mark, and the semicolon.

Sometimes writers find the last comma unnecessary—here, the comma after "question mark"— and omit it. However, sometimes the last comma is necessary to avoid ambiguity:

> The curriculum includes courses in Property, Contracts, Trusts and Estates, and Legal Writing.

Here, the last comma makes it clear that Trusts and Estates is a separate course from Legal Writing.

e. Use a comma between two adjectives that modify a noun.

Here is an example:

> An obtrusive, well-placed comma helps the reader out. If the clause does not seem necessary, you may omit it: A comma helps the reader to understand a long, complex sentence.

f. Use commas in dates.

Place a comma between the day of the month and the year:

> September 22, 1945.

Under the traditional rule, you should use a comma between the month and the year when you are not specifying the day:

> March, 1952.

However, most writers omit the comma.

2. The Colon

A colon indicates that the words before the colon lead the reader to expect what comes after the colon. For example:

> There are three ways to punctuate the end of a sentence: a period, a question mark, and an exclamation point.

The words before the colon lead us to expect the writer to tell us what three punctuation marks can end a sentence. The words after the colon fulfill the expectation. Sometimes a comma will serve the same purpose:

In legal writing, there is one punctuation mark that we almost never use, the exclamation point.

Here we could have used a colon instead of the second comma. Because a colon is more dramatic and legal writing tends to prefer understatement, most legal writers use a comma instead of a colon when they can.

You also can use a colon to introduce a quotation:

The judge frequently quoted Justice Holmes: "The life of the law has not been logic; it has been experience."

2. The Semicolon

Use the semicolon in three situations:

a. When you want to combine two sentences into one sentence, separate them with a semicolon. The semicolon indicates that the two sentences—now independent clauses—have a close connection, but not close enough to use a conjunction. For example:

A semicolon can separate two independent clauses in a sentence; its use indicates a close connection between the clauses.

b. When the second independent clause in a sentence begins with a transition acting as an adverb—such as however, therefore, or moreover, separate the clauses with a semicolon. For example:

You can join independent clauses with a conjunction; however, sometimes a semicolon seems more appropriate.

c. Use a semicolon to separate items in a series when there are commas within some of the items. For example:

Use a semicolon to show the close connection between independent clauses; to precede a transitional adverb such as however, therefore, or thus; and to separate items in a series when there are commas within some of the items.

3. The Dash

Use dashes to set off words that interrupt the continuity of a sentence. For example:

Use dashes—make one by typing two hyphens next to one another—to set off words that interrupt the continuity of a sentence.

Use dashes when the interruption is a major one. Otherwise, use commas or parentheses, whichever seems appropriate. Usually parentheses draw the least attention to the interruption. For example:

A dash (not a parenthesis) signals a major interruption in a sentence.

4. Quotations

The Bluebook, Rule 5, prescribes the rules for punctuating quotations. See Lesson Three in Appendix I. Here is a summary of important rules:

a. Do not enclose block quotes with quotation marks.

b. When you omit words from the middle of a quoted sentence, insert three periods separated by spaces and put a space before the first period and after the last one (. . .). For example:

> James Madison recognized a limitation on the danger of factions: "The influence of factious leaders may kindle a flame within their . . . states, but will be unable to spread a . . . conflagration through the other states."

c. When you are using the quotation as a full sentence and are omitting words at the beginning of the quoted sentence, do not use the three periods. If the first word you are quoting is not capitalized, capitalize the first letter and put it in brackets. For example:

> James Madison recognized a limitation on the danger of factions: "[F]actious leaders may kindle a flame within their particular states, but will be unable to spread a . . . conflagration throughout the other states."

d. When you are using the quotation as a full sentence and are omitting words at the end of the quoted sentence, use four periods. Separate the periods with spaces and put a space before the first period. The last period is the period that ends the sentence. For example:

> James Madison recognized that factions could disrupt the political process in an individual state: "The influence of factious leaders may kindle a flame within their particular states. . . ."

e. When you are quoting two consecutive sentences and omitting words at the end of the first sentence and at the beginning of the second sentence, use four periods. Separate the periods with spaces and put a space before the first period and after the fourth period. If the first word of the second sentence, as quoted, is not capitalized, capitalize the first letter and put it in brackets. For example:

> For James Madison, the cure for factions lay in the great size of the republic: "In the extended republic of the United States . . . a coalition of the majority of the whole society could seldom take place on any other principles than those of justice and the general good. . . . [T]he larger the society . . . the more duly capable it will be of self-government."

f. Place a period or comma inside the quotation marks. Place a semicolon or colon outside the quotation marks. Place a question mark inside the quotation marks if it is part of the quoted material. Place a question mark outside the quotation marks if it is not part of the quoted material.

APPENDIX **VIII**

SETTLEMENT AGREEMENTS

SETTLEMENT AGREEMENT

Regarding the Employment of Pastor Smith
of the Salvation Baptist Church of Mission Viejo

Parties:

Reverend Tommy Smith (Pastor)

Committee to Vacate the Pulpit, Salvation Baptist Church of Mission Viejo (Church)

Recitals:

1. The Pastor was hired by the Congregation and Board of Trustees of Salvation Baptist Church in June of 1995 at a salary of $80,000 per year. The Pastor was hired to increase the membership of the Church and to oversee those church functions consistent with pastoral duties established by the By-laws of the Salvation Baptist Church of Mission Viejo.

2. At the hiring interview of Pastor Smith, Pastor Smith stated that he never committed an act of adultery.

3. Between June 1995 and April 1996 the Board of Trustees of the Salvation Baptist Church of Mission Viejo received a phone call from lawyers representing congregation members in Northern California who have brought suit against the Pastor for sexual misconduct. Reverend Smith was deposed and admitted to the sexual misconduct.

4. Consistent with the Church's By-laws, the Board of Trustees called a congregational meeting to determine an appropriate course of action. The result was a 101 to 7 vote in favor of terminating Reverend Smith's employment. Reverend Smith refused to acknowledge his termination and also rejected an offer by the Board of Trustees to leave for $80,000. Pastor Smith then filed suit and the Church counterclaimed.

5. After the June 21, 1996 vote, which terminated the Pastor's employment with the Church, the Pastor restricted access to the church by changing the locks and security codes. Reverend Smith then attempted to fire the Board of Trustees, withdraw church funds and close the church account. The bank initiated a freeze on all funds until the disagreements within the church were settled. Reverend Smith then opened another bank account, listed himself as the sole signer, and began depositing church funds into the new account.

6. The "Committee to Vacate the Pulpit", composed of members of the Board and congregation, was formed to effect the removal of Reverend Smith.

7. The church obtained an injunction to enforce the June 21, 1996 vote and restrict Pastor Smith's access to Church facilities and financial matters.

8. On July 10, 1996 Reverend Smith rallied another congregational meeting and secured a vote allegedly reinstating him as Pastor.

Agreement:

The Parties agree that:

1. The Church shall pay Pastor the sum of $35,000. This sum represents a final payment for any services, expenses, damages and demands made by the Pastor in conjunction with his employment at the Salvation Baptist Church of Mission Viejo.

2. If the Church fails to pay the Pastor, within thirty (30) days of this agreement, the sum in paragraph one (1) of this agreement, the Church shall pay the Pastor an additional amount equal to five percent (5%) interest compounded daily on the sum of $35,000.

3. The Pastor's employment will be terminated effective October 27, 1996 at 5:00 p.m.

4. The Church and Pastor shall sign a confidentiality agreement that neither party will disclose in any manner, either prior to or after the date of this agreement, any incidents, circumstances, and other communications regarding the hiring, firing, or general employment of Pastor Smith, the Salvation Baptist Church of Mission Viejo, the Church's Board of Trustees and its congregation. This confidentiality agreement shall be referred to as a "gag order" and shall be effective October 25, 1996 at 5:00 p.m. except as provided under paragraph five (5) and six (6) of this agreement.

5. The Church shall make a statement to the congregation at the Salvation Baptist Church on Sunday, October 27, 1996 at the 10:30 a.m. worship service. This statement shall have two components.

  (1) It will "neither confirm nor deny the circumstances associated with the termination of Pastor Smith and his departure from the Church."

  (2) It will notify attending congregational members of the posting of Pastor Smith's telephone number, for two consecutive Sundays beginning October 27, 1996 and ending November 3, 1996, between the hours of 7:00 a.m. and 8:00 p.m. The telephone number, (714) 555-HELL, will be displayed on the Church bulletin board on these dates and times so that members who wish to communicate with the Pastor may do so.

6. The Pastor shall make one statement to the congregation at the Salvation Baptist Church of Mission Viejo on Sunday, October 27, 1996 at the 10:30 a.m. worship service. This statement shall consist of an "apology to the congregation for any problems that may be attributable to his (Smith's) conduct during his (Smith's) term as Pastor."

7. The Pastor shall remove his (Smith's) personal effects on October 27, 1996 after the 10:30 a.m. worship service and before October 28, 1996 at 12:00 a.m. The Pastor shall be accompanied by the Treasurer of the Salvation Baptist Church of Mission Viejo. Any disputes arising from the removal of Pastor Smith's personal effects shall be arbitrated within thirty (30) days of October 27, 1996 by a registered arbitrator for the County of Orange. Any decisions made as the result of that arbitration shall be binding upon all parties to this settlement agreement, the Salvation Baptist Church of Mission Viejo, its Board of Trustees and congregation.

8. Effective October 28, 1996 at 12:00 a.m., the Pastor shall cease all communications with the Church and its congregational members, except as provided under Paragraph 5(2) of this agreement. The Pastor agrees not to solicit, overtly or surreptitiously, any members of the Salvation Baptist Church of Mission Viejo, except as provided under Paragraph 5(2) of this agreement. Pastor further agrees not to enter upon the premises or property, real or personal, of the Salvation Baptist Church of Mission Viejo, except as provided under Paragraph 5(2) of this agreement.

9. The Church agrees that Fred Williams shall vacate his position as Chairman of the Board for the Salvation Baptist Church of Mission Viejo. Fred Williams shall retain his position as a congregational member of the Salvation Baptist Church of Mission Viejo and cannot seek re-election to its Board of Trustees any sooner than the December/ January 1997 election term.

10. If any terms of this settlement agreement are not complied with in any manner, both the Pastor and Church shall appear before an arbitration board registered with the courts in the County of Orange. The prevailing party shall be reimbursed for all attorneys' fees incurred in conjunction with the mediation of a settlement term dispute. Both the prevailing and losing party shall be bound by the decision or decisions of the arbitration board, including any provisions for penalty sanctions and fees.

11. This agreement serves as a release of all past and future claims by either party for any incidents, circumstances, and other communications regarding the hiring, firing, or general employment of Pastor Smith with the Salvation Baptist Church of Mission Viejo.

Signed and effective October 25, 1996, in the city of Anaheim, State of California, County of Orange.

AMY GODFREY
Attorney for Pastor

LARRY GERMANO
Attorney for Pastor

NICOLE FULLER
Attorney for Church

WENDI EDELMAN
Attorney for Church

SETTLEMENT AGREEMENT BETWEEN JAMES KELK, MARISA KELK AND MARY LOUISE SOLOMON

PREPARED BY

Ms. Toula Arvanitis,

Counsel for James and Marisa Kelk

and

Richard G. Adams,

Counsel for Mary Louise Solomon

SETTLEMENT AGREEMENT

This settlement agreement is made between James Kelk and Marisa Kelk (the Kelks) and Mary Louise Solomon (Solomon). THE PARTIES AGREE AS FOLLOWS:

1 BACKGROUND

1.1   On June 1, 1996, James Kelk (Kelk) and Solomon entered into an agreement in which Solomon agreed to be artificially inseminated with Kelk's semen, and to conceive and deliver a child.

1.2   Solomon was inseminated with Kelk's semen, conceived, and is pregnant with the child.

1.3   Kelk promised to pay all of the medical expenses connected with the insemination, pregnancy and delivery not covered by Solomon's medical insurance, transportation expenses, and maternity clothing up to a total of $4,000.00.

1.4   Kelk agreed to place $15,000.00 in an escrow account upon notification of Solomon's conception. These monies were to be distributed to Solomon after she had surrendered custody of the child to Kelk.

1.5 Upon learning that Solomon's father was an alcoholic and that her mother was addicted to pain killers, Kelk told Solomon that he did not intend to take custody of the child, although amniocentesis revealed no defects in the fetus.

1.6 Kelk alleges that when asked about her family history, Solomon purposefully withheld this information, and that this failure to disclose fraudulently induced him to enter into the contract, when he would not have assented to the contract if he had known of the facts omitted.

1.7 Solomon alleges that her conduct did not constitute fraud; that Kelk never asked about her parents; and that such specific information was not part of the agreement. She further alleges that Kelk has committed an anticipatory breach of the contract entitling her to damages equal to the payments promised in the original agreement.

1.8 Neither Kelk nor Solomon wishes to maintain custody of the child after its birth.

1.9 Both parties desire to enter into an accord to avoid the uncertainties and the burden and expense of litigation and to provide for a timely adoption of the child by another party.

2   DEFINITIONS

2.1 "Child" refers to the as yet unborn child, carried by Solomon, who is the result of the artificial insemination of Solomon with the semen of James Kelk.

2.2 "Surrogacy Contract" refers to the June 1, 1996 agreement between the Kelks and Solomon.

2.3 "Claims" refer to all claims, demands, obligations, damages, actions and causes of action of any kind, for any relief, on any basis, arising from the Surrogacy Parenting Contract.

3   TERMS AND CONDITIONS

3.1 The terms that follow are predicated on the confirmation, through both blood and DNA tests, that James Kelk is the natural father of the Child.

3.1.1 Unless the condition of the Child prohibits the drawing of blood, these tests are to be conducted immediately upon the birth of the Child.

3.1.2 If, in the opinion of the attending physicians, the health of the Child would be compromised by the taking of blood immediately upon birth, the parties agreeto proceed as though James Kelk is the natural father until the tests may be conducted.

3.2 If the blood and DNA tests establish that James Kelk is not the natural father of the Child, then:

3.2.1 This Settlement Agreement and the Surrogacy Contract shall be considered void and all provisions of these agreements retracted.

3.2.2 Any monies paid to Solomon by the Kelks under either agreement shall be repaid by Solomon within a reasonable time.

3.3 The Kelks agree to release the $15,000.00 held in escrow upon verification that James Kelk is the natural father (see. § 3. 1).

3.4 Time is of the essence in this agreement, and both parties agree to act expeditiously in signing papers, attending meetings, providing information, or any other activity related to the adoption of the Child by a third party or the placement of the Child with the appropriate California authorities.

3.5 The Kelks agree to bear the costs of securing a third party to adopt the Child and will exercise good faith in expeditiously attempting to find such a person.

3.6 If a third party willing to adopt the Child cannot be found within 90 days after the birth of the Child, both parties agree to relinquish all parental rights and to place the Child with the appropriate California authorities.

3.7 In the event a third party is found who is willing to compensate the Kelks for the relinquishing their rights under the Surrogacy Contract, Solomon shall not be entitled to any of that compensation.

3.7.1 The Kelks shall not make compensation by third parties to the contract the primary criteria for determining the adoption of the Child. The best interests of the Child are of paramount importance.

3.8 The Kelks agree to pay four hundred dollars ($400.00) on the first of each month following the birth of the Child, until the Child is either adopted or placed with the appropriate California authorities.

3.9 Once the Child is adopted or placed with the appropriate California authorities, both parties agree to release each other from any obligations under the Surrogacy Contract.

3.10 Each party shall bear its own attomey's fees and other legal costs arising from the disputed Surrogacy Contract.

3.11 Either party may elect to maintain custody of the Child.

3.11.1 If the Kelks elect to maintain custody of the Child, they will follow the terms of the Surrogacy Contract, and the Kelks will bear Solomon's legal expenses.

3.11.2 If Solomon elects to maintain custody of the Child, then she will repay the $15,000.00 to the Kelks within a reasonable period of time and will release the Kelks from any future legal obligations to the Child.

4 DECLARATIONS

4.1 Each party agrees that if the facts, with respect to which they execute this agreement, should be found to be different from those now believed, this agreement will remain in effect. Each party expressly accepts and assumes the risk of such possible differences in facts. Neither party is relying on any representation not expressly set forth within this agreement.

4.2 This agreement shall not be considered an admission by either party of the correctness of any claims or allegations advanced by either party.

4.3 The invalidity, in whole or in part, of any term of this agreement does not affect the validity of the remainder of the agreement.

4.4 This agreement signed by both parties constitutes a final written expression of all the terms of this agreement and is a complete and exclusive statement of those terms.

4.5 This agreement supersedes all previous agreements between the parties and may be modified or rescinded only by a writing signed by both of the parties.

4.6 This agreement is governed by the laws of the State of California.

4.7 Any dispute between the parties arising out of this agreement or any of its terms. shall be submitted to binding arbitration governed by the rules of the American Arbitration Association.

4.7.1 Each party will select an arbitrator of its choice and the two arbitrators chosen will then select a neutral arbitrator to hear the dispute.

4.7.2 The prevailing party shall be entitled to recover costs, expenses, reasonable attomey's fees, costs of arbitration, and other compensation or relief as the arbitrator shall decide.

4.8 Both parties warrant that they have had advice from counsel throughout the negotiations leading to the preparation and execution of this agreement, and that they have read it carefully and understand its terms and consequences.

The parties whose signatures appear below agree to everything contained in this agreement.

Dated:_____ by:_____

James Kelk

Dated:_____ by:_____

Marisa Kelk

Dated:_____ by:_____

Mary Louise Solomon

This Plea Agreement was filed in The United States District Court for the Central District of California. It is the actual text of the Plea Agreement prepared and negotiated by the Department of Justice.

NORA M. MANELLA
United States Attorney
DAVID C. SHEPER
Assistant United States Attorney
Chief, Criminal Division
MICHAEL J. GENNACO
Assistant United States Attorney

1300 United States Courthouse
312 N. Spring Street
Los Angeles, California 90012

Telephone: (213) 894-5872

Attorneys for Plaintiff
United States of America

UNITED STATES DISTRICT COURT
FOR THE CENTRAL DISTRICT OF CALIFORNIA

UNITED STATES OF AMERICA,
 	
      Plaintiff,
 	
      v.
 	
DANNY E. WILLIAMS,
 	
      Defendant.
	No. CR 96-715(A)-TJH
	
	PLEA AGREEMENT FOR
	DANNY E. WILLIAMS

Plaintiff United States of America, through its attorney of record, hereby files this plea agreement with defendant Danny E. Williams in the above-captioned matter.

DATED: This 27th day of October, 1997.

Respectfully submitted,
NORA M. MANELLA
United States Attorney

DAVID C. SHEPER
Assistant United States Attorney
Chief, Criminal Division

MICHAEL J. GENNACO
Assistant United States Attorney
Attorneys for Plaintiff
United States of America

(Matthew Bender & Co., Inc.)

PLEA AGREEMENT

<u>United States v. Danny Edward Williams</u>, CR 96-715(A)-TJH

INTRODUCTORY PARAGPAPH

1. This constitutes the plea agreement between you, Danny Edward Williams, and the United States Attorney's Office for the Central District of California ("this Office") in <u>United States v. Danny Edward Williams</u>, CR 96-715(A)-TJH. The terms of the agreement are as follows:

PLEA

2. You agree to plead guilty to Counts Two and Three of the First Superseding Indictment in <u>United States v. Danny Edward Williams</u>, CR 96-715(A)-TJH, Counts Two and Three charge you with interference with a federally protected activity, in violation of 18 U.S.C. § 245(b)(2)(B) and 18 U.S.C. § 2.

NATURE OF THE OFFENSE

3. In order to be guilty of violating 18 U.S.C. §§ 245(b)(2)(B) and 2 as charged in the First Superseding Indictment, the following must have occurred: (1) you willfully used force or threat of force; (2) to injure, intimidate, or interfere with, or attempt to injure, intimidate, or interfere with a person; (3) because of that person's race and because that person was participating in or enjoying, or in order to intimidate that person from participating in or enjoying, a facility provided or administered by a subdivision of a state, in this case, the public streets of Lancaster, California; and (4) your conduct or the conduct of a co-participant in the offense resulted in bodily injury to that person. By signing this agreement, you admit that you are, in fact, guilty of committing these offenses.

PENALTIES AND RESTITUTION

4. The statutory maximum sentences that the Court can impose for <u>each</u> conviction of 18 U.S.C. § 245(b)(2)(B) as charged in the First Superseding Indictment are as follows: a 10-year period of incarceration; a 3-year period of supervised release; a fine of $250,000; and a mandatory special assessment of $100.

Accordingly, the total maximum sentence for all of the offenses to which you are pleading guilty is a 20-year period of incarceration; a 3-year period of supervised release; a fine of $500,000; and a special assessment of $200.

5. You may be required to pay restitution for the full amount of the loss caused by your activities. You further agree that any restitution imposed

by the Court may not be discharged, in whole or in part, in any present or future bankruptcy proceeding.

6. If you are placed on supervised release following imprisonment and you violate one or more of the conditions of supervised release, you may be returned to prison for all or part of the term of supervised release, which could result in your serving a total term of imprisonment greater than the statutory maximum stated above.

7. You further recognize that if you are presently on probation, parole or supervised release in another case, your conviction in this case may result in revocation of such probation, parole, or supervised release.

FACTUAL BASIS

8. You and this Office agree and stipulate to the following statement of facts:

On April 28, 1996, you and a juvenile assaulted Eric Miller, an African-American man, as Miller exited a Blockbuster Video store, located at 2701 West Avenue L in Lancaster, California. As Miller was about to enter his car and leave the Blockbuster parking lot, you approached him and shouted racial slurs. You then swung a baseball bat at Miller several times, attempting to strike him with the bat. Miller succeeded in dodging your swings. The juvenile then struck Miller in the head and neck with his fists. Miller was able to run to safety inside the Blockbuster store but sustained injury as a result of the blow to his head and neck. You and the juvenile drove away armed with the bat in search of other African-Americans on the streets of Lancaster to assault or intimidate.

On July 8, 1996, you and two juveniles were driving along a public street in Lancaster, California, when you saw Marcus Cotton and Angela McKinzie, two African-Americans, walking down the street. One of the juveniles told you to stop the car because he wanted to assault Cotton. You stopped the car behind Cotton and McKinzie so that the juvenile could exit the car. The juvenile yelled "white power" and racial slurs as he charged towards Cotton and punched Cotton in the face. As the juvenile continued to assault Cotton, you and the second juvenile yelled "white power" and words to the effect of "get him." You then exited the car and joined in beating Cotton, who had been knocked to the ground. As Cotton lay curled up in a fetal position on the ground, you repeatedly hit and kicked him. The second juvenile approached with a knife and stabbed Cotton in the back several times, while punching Cotton with his other hand. During the assault, you and the juveniles yelled racial slurs. The juvenile who had initiated the attack continued hitting and kicking Cotton after you and the second juvenile had returned to your car. He then walked over to McKinzie, spit in her face, and yelled a racial slur at her. He returned to the car and the three of you drove away, leaving Cotton lying bleeding on the sidewalk. Cotton sustained four stab wounds and other injuries as a result of the assault.

At the time you committed these assaults, you belonged to the Nazi Low Riders, a skinhead group in Lancaster, California, which advocated separation of the races and the use of violence and intimidation to rid the streets of Lancaster of African-Americans. You assaulted Marcus Cotton and Eric Miller because they are African-American and you did not want African-Americans on the public streets of Lancaster.

SENTENCING FACTORS

9. You and this Office agree and stipulate to the following applicable sentencing guideline factors:

Base Offense Level for Underlying Offense of Aggravated Assault	: 15	[U.S.S.G. § 2H1,l(a)(1), § 2A2,2(a)]
Specific Offense Characteristics		
Dangerous Weapon Used	: +4	[U.S.S.G. § 2A2,2(b)(2)]
Serious Bodily Injury	: +4	[U.S.S.G. § 2A2,2(b)(3)]
Multiple Offense Adjustment	: +2	[U.S.S.G. § 3D1,4]

In addition, you understand that this Office's position is that your offense level should be increased an additional 2 levels for obstruction of justice, pursuant to U.S.S.G. § 3Cl.ll for your escape from Impact House on January 18, 1997.

The parties agree that no additional specific offense characteristics or adjustments are appropriate.

10. You understand that there is no agreement as to your criminal history or criminal history category, and that your criminal history could alter your offense level if you are a career offender. In the event you are a career offender and your offense level is so altered, the parties are not bound by the sentencing factors stipulation set forth in paragraph 9 above.

11. You understand and agree that neither the United States Probation Office nor the Court is bound by the stipulations referenced in this agreement and that the Court will, with the aid of the presentence report, determine the facts and calculations relevant to sentencing. You further understand that both you and this Office are free to supplement these stipulated facts by supplying relevant information to the United States Probation Office and the Court, and this Office specifically reserves its right to correct any and all factual misstatements relating to the calculation of your sentence. You

understand that the Court cannot rely exclusively upon the parties' stipulations in ascertaining the factors relevant to the determination of your sentence. Rather, in determining the factual basis for the sentence, the Court will consider the stipulations, together with the results of the presentence investigation, and any other relevant information. You understand that if the Court ascertains factors different from those contained in the stipulations, you cannot, for that reason alone, withdraw your guilty plea. You further agree that in the event the Court's sentencing calculations are different than those set forth in paragraph 9 above, the parties agree to maintain their view on appeal or collateral review that the calculations of paragraph 9 are consistent with the instant facts, but maintain the right to argue on appeal and collateral review that the Court's calculations are not reversible error.

CONSIDERATION BY OFFICE

12. In exchange for your guilty plea and your complete fulfillment of all of your obligations under this agreement, this Office agrees:

a. To recommend a two-level reduction in the applicable sentencing guideline offense level, pursuant to sentencing guideline 3E1.1(a), provided that you demonstrate an acceptance of responsibility for this offense by virtue of your conduct up to and including the time of sentencing.

b. This Office further agrees to recommend an additional one-level reduction in the applicable sentencing guideline offense level, pursuant to sentencing guideline 3E1.1(b), if you demonstrate an acceptance of responsibility for this offense by virtue of your conduct up to and including the time of sentencing and the adjusted offense level as calculated by the Court is 16 or higher.

c. At the time of sentencing this Office will move to dismiss Count One of the First Superseding Indictment against you. You agree, however, that at the time of sentencing the Court may consider the dismissed count and any uncharged conduct in determining your sentence, including but not limited to the propriety of any departure from the applicable guideline range.

d. This Office agrees it will not bring criminal charges against you for your escape from Impact House on January 18, 1997,

WAIVER OF CONSTITUTIONAL RIGHTS

13. You understand that by pleading guilty, you will be giving up the following Constitutional rights: You have the right to plead not guilty and the right to be tried by a jury. At a trial, you would have the right to the assistance of counsel and if you could not afford an attorney, the Court would

appoint one to represent you. During the trial, you would be presumed innocent and a jury would be instructed that the burden of proof is on the government to prove you guilty beyond a reasonable doubt. You would have the right to confront and cross-examine witnesses against you. If you wish, you could testify on your own behalf and present evidence in your defense. On the other hand, if you did not wish to testify or present evidence, that fact could not be used against you and a jury would be so instructed. You would also have the right to call witnesses on your behalf and to subpoena those witnesses. By pleading guilty, you will be giving up all of these rights. By pleading guilty, you further understand that you will be waiving any and all rights to pursue any applicable affirmative defenses, any Fourth Amendment or Fifth Amendment claims, and any other actual or potential pretrial motions previously filed or to be filed. Finally, by pleading guilty, you understand that you may have to answer questions posed to you by the Court, both about the rights that you will be giving up and about the facts of this case. Any statements made by you during such a hearing could be used against you in a criminal prosecution for perjury or false statements.

PARTIES TO AGREEMENT

14. You understand that the Court is not a party to this agreement and the Court is under no obligation to accept this Office's recommendation regarding the sentence to be imposed. Further, even if the Court disregards this Office's recommendation and/or imposes any sentence up to the maximum established by statute, you cannot, for that reason, withdraw your guilty plea, and will remain bound to fulfill all of your obligations under this agreement. You understand that neither the prosecutor, your attorney, nor the Court can make a binding prediction or promise regarding the sentence you will receive.

15. This agreement is limited to this Office and cannot bind any other federal, state or local prosecuting, administrative or regulatory authorities. This agreement applies only to criminal violations relating to you.

NO ADDITIONAL AGREEMENTS

16. Except as expressly set forth herein, there are no additional promises, understandings or agreements between the government and you or your counsel concerning any other criminal prosecution, civil litigation or administrative proceeding relating to any other federal, state or local charges that may now be pending or hereafter be brought against you, or the sentence that might be imposed as a result of your guilty plea pursuant to this Agreement. Nor may any additional agreement, understanding or condition be entered into unless in writing and signed by all parties or made on the record in court.

If a fully executed copy of this agreement is not returned to me by 5:00 p.m. on Monday, October 27, 1997, it will be automatically withdrawn and thereafter of no legal effect or force.

This agreement shall be effective upon execution by you and this Office.

AGREED AND ACCEPTED

UNITED STATES ATTORNEY'S OFFICE

FOR THE CENTRAL DISTRICT OF CALIFORNIA

_____

NORA M. MANELLA
United States Attorney

_____

CAROLINE C. WITTCOFF
Assistant United States Attorney

_____

MICHAEL J. GENNACO
Assistant United States Attorney

I have read this agreement and have carefully reviewed every part of it with my attorney. I understand the terms of this agreement, and I voluntarily agree to each of the terms. Before signing this agreement, I consulted with my attorney. My attorney fully advised me of my rights, of possible defenses, of the Sentencing Guideline provisions, and of the consequences of entering into this agreement. No other promises or inducements have been made to me, other than those contained in this agreement. Furthermore, no one has threatened or forced me in any way to enter into this agreement. Finally, I am satisfied with the representation of my attorney in this matter.

_____   _____
Date   DANNY EDWARD WILLIAMS
                                              Defendant

I am Danny Edward Williams' attorney. I have carefully reviewed every part of this agreement with my client. Further, I have fully advised my client of his rights, of possible defenses, of the Sentencing Guideline provisions, and of the consequences of entering into this agreement. To my knowledge, my client's decision to enter into this agreement is an informed and voluntary one.

_____   _____

Date   W. MICHAEL MAYOCK
Counsel for Defendant

CERTIFICATE OF SERVICE BY MAIL

I, JUDITH MC FANN, declare:

That I am a citizen of the United States and resident or employed in Los Angeles County, California; that my business address is Office of United States Attorney, United States Courthouse, 312 North Spring Street, Los Angeles, California 90012; that I am over the age of eighteen years, and am not a party to the above-entitled action;

That I am employed by the United States Attorney for the Central District of California who is a member of the Bar of the United States District Court for the Central District of California, at whose direction the service by mail described in this Certificate was made; that on October 27, 1997, I deposited in the United States mails in the United States Courthouse at 312 North Spring Street, Los Angeles, California, in the above-entitled action, in an envelope bearing the requisite postage, a copy of: PLEA AGREE-MENT FOR DANNY E. WILLIAMS

Addressed To: MICHAEL MAYOCK, ESQ.
35 South Raymond – SUITE 400
PASADENA, CA 91105

at his last known address, at which place there is a delivery service by United States mail.

This Certificate is executed on October 27, 1997, at Los Angeles, California.

I certify under penalty of perjury that the foregoing is true and correct.

_____

Judith MC FANN

INDEX

[References are to text and appendix pages. Pages start at '1' for each new appendix, e.g., App-III 23-24.]

A

I–1

[References are to text and appendix pages. Pages start at '1' for each new appendix, e.g., App-III 23-24.]

[References are to text and appendix pages. Pages start at '1' for each new appendix, e.g., App-III 23-24.]

[References are to text and appendix pages. Pages start at '1' for each new appendix, e.g., App-III 23-24.]

[References are to text and appendix pages. Pages start at '1' for each new appendix, e.g., App-III 23-24.]

[References are to text and appendix pages. Pages start at '1' for each new appendix, e.g., App-III 23-24.]

CONTENT (See WORDS)

CONTEXT
Generally . . . 102
Checklist . . . 109-110

CONTINGENT FEES
Attorney's fees . . . 150-151

CONTRA
Use of . . . 312

CONTRACTIONS
Avoiding . . . 138

CORPUS JURIS SECUNDUM
Research . . . 74; 79-84

COUNTERCLAIMS
Generally . . . 236
Additional defendant, against . . . 229
Sample . . . App-II 13

COURTS OF APPEALS, UNITED STATES
Generally . . . 12
Citing to cases of . . . App-I 14

COURT SYSTEM
Generally . . . 9-10
Appellate courts
    State . . . 10
    United States Courts of Appeals
        Generally . . . 12
        Citing to cases of . . . App-I 14
California court system, diagram of . . . 11
Circuit courts (See subhead: Courts of Appeals, United States)
Courts of Appeals, United States
    Generally . . . 12
    Citing to cases of . . . App-I 14
Diagram of federal court system . . . 13
District courts
    Generally . . . 12
    Citing to cases of . . . App-I 14
Federal courts
    Generally . . . 12
    Circuit courts (See subhead: Courts of Appeals, United States)
    Courts of Appeals, United States
        Generally . . . 12
        Citing to cases of . . . App-I 14
    Diagram of . . . 13
    District courts
        Generally . . . 12
        Citing to cases of . . . App-I 14

COURT SYSTEM—Cont.
Federal courts—Cont.
    Supreme Court
        Generally . . . 12
        Citing to cases of . . . App-I 13-14
Rules of
    Generally . . . 102; 230
    Appellate briefs, affecting . . . 306
State courts
    Generally . . . 10
    Appellate courts . . . 10
    California court system, diagram of . . . 11
    Citing to cases of . . . App-I 6-10
    Trial courts . . . 10
Supreme Court
    Generally . . . 12
    Citing to cases of . . . App-I 13-14
Trial courts . . . 10

CREATIVITY
Memoranda, using legal creativity in writing . . . .
  170

CROSS-CLAIMS
Pleadings . . . 229

CROSS-REFERENCES
Citation form for . . . App-I 19-20

CURRENT LAW INDEX
Research . . . 92; 94

D

DASH
Using . . . App-VII 9

DEDUCTIVE REASONING
Legal logic . . . 39-41

DEFENSES
Affirmative . . . 236
Inconsistent . . . 236

DEMURRERS
Answer, in . . . 236
Motion to dismiss, compared to . . . 255

DENIALS
Answer, in . . . 236

DE NOVO **REVIEW**
Appeals . . . 279-280

DICTA
Authority, persuasive . . . 38

DICTA—Cont.
Case briefs, treatment in . . . 30
Definition . . . 127
Misuse of term . . . 127

DICTION (See WORDS)

DIGESTS
Research . . . 85-89

DISCOVERY
Generally . . . 3; 239
Admission, requests for (See REQUESTS FOR AD-
    MISSION)
Document production (See DOCUMENT PRODUC-
    TION)
Interrogatories (See INTERROGATORIES)
Motion to compel
    Generally . . . 256-257
    Confer with opposition prior to court action,
        requirement to . . . 257
    Evasive answer . . . 257
    Failure to respond, sanctions for . . . 257
    Incomplete answer . . . 257
    Sanctions for failure to respond . . . 257
Requests for . . . 240-241

DISSENTING OPINIONS
Case briefs, treatment in . . . 30

DISTRICT COURTS
Generally . . . 12
Citing to cases of . . . App-I 14

DOCUMENT PRODUCTION
Generally . . . 239-240; 242-243
Exercise . . . 243
Objections to requests for . . . 243

DRAFTING
Generally . . . 219
Form books, use of (See FORM BOOKS)
Jury instructions (See JURY INSTRUCTIONS, sub-
    head: Drafting)
Settlement agreements (See SETTLEMENT AGREE-
    MENTS, subhead: Drafting)

DRAFTS
Multiple, need for . . . 113

E

EDITING
Appellate briefs . . . 313

ELECTRONIC DATABASES (See COMPUTER
    RESEARCH SERVICES)

ELLIPSES
Citations, in . . . 312

ENCYCLOPEDIAS, LEGAL
Generally . . . 73-84
American Jurisprudence . . . 74-79
Corpus Juris Secundum . . . 74; 79-84

EQUITY ARGUMENTS
Generally . . . 251
Appellate arguments, in . . . 336
Placement of . . . 109
Policy arguments, compared to . . . 251

ETHICS
Motion practice, in . . . 258-259
Negotiations, in . . . 216-217

EUPHEMISMS
Oral argument, in . . . 331

EYE CONTACT
Oral argument, during . . . 332

F

FACTS
Affidavit stating that facts are true and correct; sample
    . . . App-II 14
Case briefs, in . . . 27-28
Client opinion letter; inclusion of facts provided by
    client . . . 158
Interrogatories, questions about facts in . . . 241
Law to fact, applying . . . 41-42
Memoranda, section in (See MEMORANDA, sub-
    head: Facts)
Persuasively stating . . . 250-251
Requests for admission; specific facts, request for
    . . . 243
Statement of . . . STATEMENT OF FACTS

FEDERAL COURTS (See COURT SYSTEM)

FEES (See ATTORNEY'S FEES)

FILING
Appellate briefs . . . 274
Memoranda . . . 166

FINAL JUDGMENT
Appeal from . . . 277

FOOTNOTES
Case briefs, treatment in . . . 30

[References are to text and appendix pages. Pages start at '1' for each new appendix, e.g., App-III 23-24.]

[References are to text and appendix pages. Pages start at '1' for each new appendix, e.g., App-III 23-24.]

[References are to text and appendix pages. Pages start at '1' for each new appendix, e.g., App-III 23-24.]

[References are to text and appendix pages. Pages start at '1' for each new appendix, e.g., App-III 23-24.]

[References are to text and appendix pages. Pages start at '1' for each new appendix, e.g., App-III 23-24.]

[References are to text and appendix pages. Pages start at '1' for each new appendix, e.g., App-III 23-24.]

[References are to text and appendix pages. Pages start at '1' for each new appendix, e.g., App-III 23-24.]

[References are to text and appendix pages. Pages start at '1' for each new appendix, e.g., App-III 23-24.]

[References are to text and appendix pages. Pages start at '1' for each new appendix, e.g., App-III 23-24.]

[References are to text and appendix pages. Pages start at '1' for each new appendix, e.g., App-III 23-24.]